Brian L Foster

SECOND EDITION

Strategies
of
Social Research
The Methodological Imagination

H. W. Smith
University of Missouri

PRENTICE-HALL, INC.   Englewood Cliffs, New Jersey 07632

Library of Congress Cataloging in Publication Data

SMITH, HERMAN W. (date)
  Strategies of social research.

  (Prentice-Hall methods of social science series)
  Bibliography: p.
  Includes index.
  1. Sociological research. 2. Sociology—
Methodology. I. Title.
HM48.S55   1981   300'.7'2   80-14565
ISBN   0-13-851154-3

*Editorial/production supervision and interior
design by Linda Schuman
Cover design by 20/20 Services Inc.
Manufacturing buyer: John B. Hall*

Prentice-Hall Methods of Social Science Series
Editors: Herbert L. Costner and Neil Smelser

Printed in the United States of America

10 9 8 7 6 5 4 3 2 1

PRENTICE-HALL INTERNATIONAL, INC., *London*
PRENTICE-HALL OF AUSTRALIA PTY. LIMITED *Sydney*
PRENTICE HALL OF CANADA, LTD., *Toronto*
PRENTICE-HALL OF INDIA PRIVATE LIMITED, *New Delhi*
PRENTICE-HALL OF JAPAN, INC., *Tokyo*
PRENTICE-HALL OF SOUTHEAST ASIA PTE. LTD., *Singapore*
WHITEHALL BOOKS LIMITED, *Wellington, New Zealand*

To **MARY**

who constantly teaches me
what a best friend is

and **ERIK** *and* **CRAIG**

Each of you in your own way makes it all worthwhile.

Contents

Tables

Illustrations

BOXES

Preface

Those of you who are familiar with the first edition of this text will find this edition heavily revised and reorganized. Hardly a page escaped the hindsight of five years of classroom use. At the same time, continuity with the first edition can be found through the inclusion of materials in this edition which students and professors alike have found useful. Much of this original material, however, has been revised with an eye to readability.

The chapters have been reorganized to make methods more presentable to the student. I thank my colleague Judith Handel for this suggested reorganization. Our experience has been that students have virtually no idea of what "data," "science," or "methods" are at the start of their research methods course. Hence, Judith experimented with the present reordering of chapters. Charles Sprague, another esteemed colleague, continued this experiment in his classes. These experiments appeared to help students grapple with and grasp complex concepts better without the need for extensive watering down of materials—which would have risked oversimplification of important concepts.

Part One contains three chapters intended to introduce students to what sociology as a science is all about. Chapter 1 has always been, in my mind, much more than an introduction to ethics. The examples in that chapter introduce the student to a variety of types of sociological and behavioral research. Nevertheless, this chapter has been broadened beyond the original one which conceived of ethics almost entirely in terms of research participants. Now the ethics chapter is more balanced in terms of discussions of professional issues such as honesty and accuracy of data, the social impact of social science, and the effects of type of research design on ethical issues.

Chapter 2 is, for all practical purposes, a new chapter. The intention was to give students a better grasp of some rules for understanding how scientists go about deciding what is worthwhile data and what are researchable questions. These improvements were made in order to prepare students for Chapter 3's introduction to generating researchable hypotheses. One of the most difficult concepts for students to grasp is that of operationalization. Hence, I gave considerable revision attention to that concept in both Chapters 2 and 3.

Part Two, The Production of Data, was reorganized with two things in mind. First, the four most utilized methods were placed at the beginning, with less utilized methods following those chapters. Second, chapters on direct observation (Chapters 4 and 5) were positioned first as they set the standards or ideals by which most scientists would like science to operate, with all other methods viewed as deviations (however necessary) from this ideal. The field research chapter (4) was heavily revised with an emphasis on its qualitative and processual nature. Structured Observation (Chapter 5) covers such varied types of tools (content analysis, observational instruments, and so on) that I have tried to reorganize it with simplification in mind. It also includes a new (optional) section on special problems of analysis of observational data. Surveys (Chapter 6) covers much the same material as in the original version. There is much more emphasis, however, on telephone, self-administered, and randomized response survey methods than was true of the earlier edition. This reflects changes in the field. New materials on survey quality control have also been added. Chapter 7, Experimental Principles, Variations, and Approximations, has been overhauled. This material is usually quite abstract for the beginning student. Hence, more concrete examples were added to aid the student's understanding. Simulation and Gaming (Chapter 8) has not been significantly altered because the research technique developments in that area have not changed radically and because students have generally found the material enjoyable and understandable. The last chapter in Part Two, Chapter 9 (Evaluation Research) has been somewhat rewritten to introduce the student to the potential job market for evaluation researchers, as well as the exciting changes taking place in its methodology.

Part Three, Improving Data Quality, now consists of four chapters. Chapter 10 (Sampling) has gone through revisions with the objective of simplifying materials which are traditional stumbling blocks for students. Chapter 11 (Scaling and Measurement) has been simplified through the dropping of statistically based materials and through better examples of multidimensional scaling logic. Chapter 12 (Reliability, Validity, and Operationalization) is much helped by later placement in the text. Experience has shown that students grasp it much more readily after having read Part Two chapters. New materials in this chapter emphasize statistical conclusion validity. Chapter 13 (Triangulation) still stands as a summary of earlier chapters to a large extent.

Part Four, The Analysis and Presentation of Data, consists of one old chapter with revisions (Chapter 14 on Strategies and Logic of Data Analysis) and one completely new chapter (15 on Research Reporting).

Several other important additions should be emphasized to the instructor. First there are over twice as many suggested research projects as in the original edition. These projects are generally ordered from easiest to hardest. They have all been successfully pretested in the classroom. They have been found to make the learning of how to do methods much easier. Second, because most of our students will never actually be engaged in doing professional research, much of the new material in the text emphasizes *evaluating* research rather than *doing* it.

It could be said that behind every successful writer is an understanding manuscript typist. Thanks are due to Barbara Harrington for providing me with that understanding. She also kept seemingly unrealistic writing deadlines on target. My thanks also to Profs. Herb Costner (University of Washington), Theodore C. Wagenaar (Miami University), and James R. Marshall (State University of New York, Buffalo) for their critical and useful suggestions for improvements in writing style and readability. And last but not least to my production editor, Linda Schuman, who helped expose, expunge, and expurgate my writing sins. Whatever writing sins are left are of my own doing but fewer and better hidden because of the efforts of fine colleagues and friends such as these.

PART ONE

Introduction to Research

If I have seen farther, it is by standing on the shoulders of giants.

attributed to Sir Isaac Newton

. . . (I)n the natural sciences, (we are told) each succeeding generation stands on the shoulders of those that have gone before, while in the social sciences, each generation steps in the face of its predecessors.

E. Galenter, ed., *Automatic Teaching: The State of the Art.* New York: John Wiley, 1959, p. 167.

Ethical Commitments
in Social
and Behavioral Research

> *Knowledge* of *man is not neutral in its import; it grants power* over *man as well.* [1]

In the relatively short time that the social and behavioral sciences have claimed to be part of the scientific tradition, it is surprising how little concern has been given to ethics. Indeed, much has been made of the idea that social science is "value-free" or "value-neutral." The value-free and value-neutral myths are founded in the dilemma that science describes an *is* world, while ethics prescribes an *ought* world. In other words, the social scientist, as scientist, is supposed to be objective. Hence, things should *not* be described as he or she *wishes* they were, rather *as* they are. Somehow, according to this myth, the sociologist, while doing research, protects the outside world from personal values.

If science were just about the description of reality there would be no dilemma. The dilemma, however, rests in a paraphrase of the quotation at the beginning of this chapter: Knowledge of humankind grants

[1]Robert Friedrichs, *A Sociology of Sociology*, 1970, p. 164.

power *over* humankind. Scientific knowledge is not ultimately divorceable from its use by humankind because scientists are not interested in simply describing present reality but wish ultimately to predict future events. Science as a *descriptive* enterprise implies science as *prediction.* Prediction may lead to greater *control,* and control of other humans is not only a scientific decision. Control of other humans is also a moral or ethical decision.

Some social scientists would object that the social and behavioral sciences have thus far limited themselves to data *about* humans—that they have little concern with the *manipulations* of humans. Recent events support the contention that sociological investigation shows increasing concern with manipulation of humans. But even in research where manipulation of humans is not evident, such talk only disguises ethical problems. As noted by Ernest Nagel (1961:452),

> ... every branch of inquiry aiming at reliable general laws concerning empirical subject matter must employ a procedure that, if it is not strictly controlled experimentation, has the essential logical functions of experimental inquiry.

In other words, just because a researcher has never depended on research through experimentation does not mean that he or she can be absolved of producing knowledge that is without the *logic* of experimentation. Sociologists who depend heavily on survey research (and most still do) increasingly use techniques in their analysis that *approximate* experimental controls. Hence, experimental control is a relative matter.

A general maxim of science is that the more control the scientist has over participants in a study, the more valid are the findings. Paradoxically, the more experimental control there is over participants, the greater the ethical problems created. As Friedrichs (1970:167–196) has incisively observed, all scientific research has an implicit or explicit commitment toward change. Thus, unless one is willing to take the sociologist as some sort of priestly overlord of the social order, the researcher is forced, knowingly or not, into value stances. Suppose you are trying out some new educational technique on an experimental basis. By what authority can you justify better educating one group (the experimental group) than another (the control group)? Or let us suppose you are studying some type of illegal behavior such as organized teen-age shoplifting. Should you report this activity to the authorities? As a third example, what about the administration of a measure of self-esteem used to assess students at an elementary school? Should you report low self-esteemed participants to teachers? On the one hand, the teacher might use this information beneficially by singling the student out as needing more confidence bolstering through positive reinforcement of classroom efforts. On the other hand, you risk initiating a self-fulfilling prophecy by reporting this because the teacher may then knowingly or unconsciously treat the participant in psychologically damaging ways. The researcher cannot really cop out by "doing nothing." No choice *is* a choice. The researcher, implicitly or explicitly, has responsibility for inducing or denying change to study participants.

While social and behavioral scientists are far from complete consensus on a universal set of ethical rules to be followed in research involving human participants, they are in general agreement that the researcher must be prepared to ask: Are the scientific objectives of the study proportionate to the risks to the study participants (World Medical Association 1964; U.S. Department of Health, Education and Welfare 1971)? That is: Do the potential scientific benefits outweigh any possible risks to participants? While a vocal minority of researchers still argue for a uniform, absolute code of ethics for application to all research situations, and still another vocal faction claims all ethical decisions should be dictated solely by the researcher's conscience, this question makes the academic distinction between behavioral scientists who are ethically *absolute* or *relative* virtually meaningless. The now generally accepted scientific–objectives–versus–participant risks proposal argues neither for an impossible, *uniform* set of ethics (ethical absolutism) nor for *ethically relative* standards dictated by the individual researcher's conscience (Becker 1964:280; Dalton 1964:71). Recognition is given to the fact that the researcher's ethical obligation must *match* the study risks. While the vast majority of researchers observe this rule, we shall see in the next section that those few researchers who ignore this ethical maxim create an undesirable climate for future research.

We turn now to some contemporary examples of ethical dilemmas resulting from research control over humans and to a discussion of some ethical problems posed by these examples. This discussion will be followed by a consideration of steps being taken by social scientists and behavioral science oriented agencies to set up specific ethical regulatory mechanisms within the spirit of what we termed the scientific–objectives–versus–participant risks maxim.

CONTEMPORARY ILLUSTRATIONS OF ETHICAL "FALLOUT"

Each of the following cases illustrates moral problems inherent in the research process. These case histories are intended to suggest needs for procedural safeguards in regulating social and behavioral research. It should be noted that these cases are far from typical of socio-behavioral research. Nevertheless, most laypersons can hardly distinguish between the transgressions of the few and the overwhelming majority of ethical scientists.

The Goldzieher Contraception Case

In the fall of 1969 a San Antonio physician, Joseph Goldzieher, set up a study to test the side effects of birth control pills (*Behavior Today* 1971). The 398 women, mostly Mexican-Americans, were divided into four experimental groups and a control group. Three groups were administered commercially marketed birth control pills, one group was given an experimental birth control pill, and the fifth group received placebos (sugar pills). All of the women apparently thought they were taking oral contraceptives. Approximately a year and a half later the Federal Drug Administration found the experimental birth control pill unsafe and, hence, cut short Goldzieher's study. But by this time seven subjects had become pregnant—six in the placebo group, the seventh in the experimental pill group.

Several investigative teams, one from the San Antonio Medical Society, another from the FDA, reported Goldzieher's methodology valid and ethical. Apparently, the study participants had signed informed consent forms that cautioned them to use prescribed, backup contraceptives. Yet seven women now have seven babies they did not want. Goldzieher attributes the pregnancies to the women's carelessness in using the prescribed backup contraceptives and would rather focus on the study conclusions that side effects of contraceptive pills are often psychosomatic rather than directly physiological.

The ethics evaluation teams also seem to have concluded that the benefits of this kind of study outweigh individual participant risks and to have ignored the question of who is concerned with the participant's welfare. This case suggests that current ethical codes for human research (U.S. Department of Health, Education and Welfare guidelines 1971) which emphasize informed consent and confidentiality may not sufficiently safeguard the ethical regulation of research.

Project Camelot

While the previous case was not a sociological study, it did raise important issues for the ethical conduct of social research. By contrast, Project Camelot was not only conceived by a primarily social science oriented agency but also had dramatic effects on the conduct of American social science research outside of the United States. Project Camelot was to have had a $6,000,000 budget, financed by the U.S. Department of Defense—an amount clearly mammoth by comparison to any previous social science funding. The ostensible focus of the study was to collect data on the nature and causes of revolutions in underdeveloped countries. More interesting yet, from the point of ethical commitments, was the aim to *prevent* revolutions.

Camelot was conceived in late 1963. The project never got off the ground. Ironically, a country not involved in the study provided the impetus for stopping Camelot. In 1965 the Chilean Senate and press released a statement by John Galtung, an eminent Norwegian sociologist, denouncing the project.

This Chilean political pressure caused immediate halting of the project by concerned members of Congress and State Department officials and eventual termination of the project directly by then President Lyndon Johnson. A major consequence of the affair was a new policy set down by President Johnson stating that governmental sponsorship of foreign-area research could not be undertaken if the Secretary of State judged it to affect adversely United States foreign relations (Horowitz 1965:47–48).

There were several value biases running through the entire project history. First, the primary question asked was: How can revolutions be prevented? No apparent concern was given to revolution as a beneficial or productive force. Second, the project social scientists let the Department of Defense assume virtually complete responsibility for defining what problems would be of researchable interest to the project. Thus the nagging questions: Did the Defense Department, with the implicit help of project social scientists, actually determine project outcomes, or did it determine project goals?

Several unfortunate ethical precedents were established with the demise of Project Camelot. One was that of social scientists refusing not to be dealt with honestly as professional authorities of science. The social science client was allowed to use project social scientists as "hired help" so that the client came to determine project outcomes tailored to the client's needs without regard to the professional's scientific needs. As summarized by Irving Horowitz (1965:47),

> Project Camelot was intellectually, and from my own perspective, ideologically unsound. However, and more significantly, Camelot was not cancelled because of faulty intellectual approaches. Instead its cancellation came as an act of Government censorship, and an expression of the contempt for social science so prevalent among those who need it most. . . . We must be

careful not to allow social science projects with which we may vociferously disagree on political and ideological grounds to be decimated or dismantled by Government fiat.

It is worthwhile stressing that Horowitz is not crying for the funding of intellectually, ideologically, or ethically unsound research. Rather, he is pointing to an important consequence of the Camelot debacle: Namely, because Camelot was cut short due to its politically threatening nature rather than its lack of scientific merit, research of much greater scientific and ethical merit may likewise suffer the same fate as Camelot.

Sociologists have been slow to realize that their observations have impact on the participants as well as on others (as shown in Camelot). The next illustration will reveal some of the interactive impact and the contingent ethical dilemmas faced by contemporary social scientists when their scientific and nonscientific roles touch and even overlap.

The "Springdale" Case

During the early 1950s, Arthur Vidich spent a two-and-one-half-year period as a Cornell University project field director and participant observer living in "Springdale." Sometime after he had moved away from the area, he completed a book, *Small Town in Mass Society,* which was to create a furor in the community he had studied and in the university he had then been associated with. The points of controversy were essentially (*Science News,* 102 [no. 2]: 17–32)

1. Should individuals be identified in the book?
2. If individuals were identified, what—if anything—should be done to avoid damage to them?
3. Did Vidich have a right to use—or should he be allowed to use—project data which he did not gather himself? Who "owns" project data?

One of the jointly ethical and methodological problems faced by Vidich was the small number of village officials. Because of this small number, it was impossible to disguise completely references to each individual. Furthermore, community dynamics were impossible to discuss without identifying individuals.

A second issue joined by the controversy is one not previously encountered in this chapter—the issue of who "owns" project data. This issue is a common one in science. The difficulty is most controversial in scholarly conversations between scientists and in professor-student relations. At times, it is extremely difficult in such discourse to tell where one's own thinking leaves off and another person's begins.

This problem becomes further accentuated in bureaucratized research where subordinates may collect and even analyze data without even formal acknowledgment by the project supervisor. (In some governmental agencies the subordinate may *write* the final report with the director listed as head or sole author.) As noted by Howard S. Becker (1968:415), many of these problems could be cleared up if there were a common written agreement on junior staff–project director obligations and rights at the hiring. The same can be said of professional relations with participants. The social scientist has an obligation to be explicit about the rights and obligation bargains made with participants and should stick to any such bargains made. Becker makes it clear that no appeal to "scientific objectivity" should release the researcher from those obligations.

One lawsuit raised questions as to how scientific credit is apportioned and who does the apportioning (*Science News* 1972:102–103). Oreste Piccioni, a physicist and professor at the University of California at San Diego, filed suit against two physicists at the Berkeley campus, Emilio Segré and Owen Chamberlain. He claimed that he designed an experiment that led to the discovery of the antiproton, which he revealed to Segré and Chamberlain under an oral agreement that the three would jointly carry it out. Piccioni claimed they cut him out of participation in the experiment and never gave him credit for his idea. (The experiment led to the 1959 Nobel prize for both Segré and Chamberlain.) Unwritten scientific custom dictates that the scientists settle these matters among themselves informally. However, this litigation throws open the ethical Pandora's box of which scientist did what part of the work and who didn't really do very much. These questions raise important points since more and more scientific work involves from two to even twenty or thirty scientists.

The next case indicates the need for clearly specified rights and obligations in the researcher–participant relationship. Just as informed consent needs to be spelled out in researcher–researcher contacts, researcher–participant relations need explication before the research begins. Otherwise, participants may easily be subjugated to the level of nonhuman objects.

The Tuskegee Study

In 1932 the U.S. Public Health Service started conducting an experiment, recently come to light, on the effect of syphilis. Several hundred Tuskegee, Alabama, black men known to have syphilis were medically examined at regular intervals by Public Health Service officials. From the moment the study began government officials apparently withheld treatment of the disease in order to determine what effects syphilis has on the body. Further, the suspicion has been raised that the study would not have been undertaken with white persons as the guinea pigs. (It should be noted that medical experiments on "the pill" also were conducted on nonwhite populations, that is, Puerto Ricans, before the birth control pill was released to the general public.) In fact, the National Medical Association has gone so far as to charge the study officials with genocide of poor and uneducated blacks, many of whom died or were severely incapacitated as a result of their syphilis. Both the Springdale and Tuskegee studies showed unnecessary political repercussions because of a lack of informed consent from participants. The next example reveals this same deficiency.

Unobtrusive Measurement Problems

One of the gravest questions of ethics has been raised by the growing popularity of so-called "unobtrusive measurements" (measures on participants who are not aware they are being measured—to be discussed in Chapter 5). It is becoming increasingly as possible and probable to use "hidden" hardware in social science research as it is in sleuthing. One of the first cases of the use of such methods, with resulting ethical repercussions, came out of a University of Chicago study of the jury deliberation process through hidden microphones placed with the approval of the court and counsel for both sides (Strodtbeck, James, and Hawkins 1955). Unfavorable public response ended the study. Present protocol has been to *simulate* jury deliberations in the small groups laboratory. Perhaps one of the best cases can be made for ingenious experimental and simulation studies in situations like those in which extremely sensitive institutional structures might otherwise appear to be tampered with.

Altered States of Consciousness
and Stress Settings

In addition to problems caused by uninformed consent, a number of studies conducted in recent years attempt to alter a person's state of consciousness or induce great personal stress. Imagine a person in an experiment pulling on a lever which ostensibly induces electric shock in another person seen through a one-way mirror. As one person pulls the lever further down, the shock to the other supposedly increases to dangerous proportions. Such types of experiments have occurred (Milgram 1963) in a few social psychological laboratories in recent years. Or imagine a person being hypnotized so that his or her attitudinal *affect* towards cigarette smoking may be changed to see what happens to attitudinal cognitions (beliefs) (Rosenberg 1960). Again, imagine a setting in which one person is induced into a situation where four others (actually experimenter confederates) perceive physical reality in a fashion the opposite of what the one person perceives (Asch 1956). In each of these situations the persons have undergone experimental manipulation that is explicitly deceptive or potentially psychologically or physically harmful. Increasingly, behavioral scientists have concerned themselves with how to discourage research that unnecessarily harms participants, does so against their will, and harms them out of proportion to the scientific and practical benefits due from the project. In some instances where persons are unnecessarily harmed or experimented upon without their consent, some medical journals now refuse to publish the experimental report, so as to penalize the researcher for unethical conduct (Pappworth 1968). Indeed, many, if not most, social psychologists would not even consider conducting the Asch confederate or electric-shock type experiments today because of the known needless psychological damage incurred in similar experiments. This type of research has given much impetus to growing informal and formal collegial control over what may ethically be done by the researcher.

Most of the cases presented to this juncture have dealt with experimental manipulations of participants. While these types of studies are more typical of social psychological research, the vast majority of sociologists do not use experimental methods. Most sociologists utilize nonmanipulative methods such as questionnaires. Even here, as the following case shows, the researcher must be aware of possible unethical exploitation of participants (although normally participants can be protected from exploitation by inquisitors who should not have access to the data files).

The Proposed National Data Bank and Longitudinal Studies

Some social scientists have been increasingly pressing for a National Data Center that would facilitate statistical analysis for social research and end part of the duplication of effort by private survey organizations. While such a repository might provide a valuable information resource for social science, it also poses special threats to individual privacy. Sawyer and Schechter (1968) have recommended a number of safeguards for such data repositories that could be, and probably should be, adopted by existing behavioral science agencies in the conduct of their research. For example, they recommend that the computer should be programmed to require positive identification such as a fingerprint or voice record of all authorized users. Second, the computer should record each user and specify the data used. Third, the computer should reject requests for data on specific individuals.

A special problem arises in assuring confidentiality of longitudinal data (data collected over time). If data is collected over time on given subjects, it has to be matched up to given persons, thus allowing for the potential breakup of anonymity obligations. Astin and Baruch (1970) have devised a "link file" system for insuring data security and respondent anonymity for some types of data. They recommend that data collected during each time period be kept on two physically separate data files—one file containing the person's research data and an arbitrary identification code, the second file containing the person's name, address, and the same identification code. At a later date when the second time period data is being collected, a third file will be created—the "link file"— which contains only the identification codes for each time period. (See Campbell and others 1977 for recent improvements.)

One of the major legal problems faced by the researcher is that— unlike doctors and clergy—a pledge of confidentiality has little legal support. Subpoenas currently have legal priority over researcher pledges of confidentiality. Until such time as the judicial and congressional system gives a privileged information status to social science researchers, it may be necessary in some cases for the scientist to deposit a link file at a computer or other research-type facility located in a foreign country.

The problem of confidentiality is joined to the constitutional amendments protecting freedom of speech and freedom of the press. Currently, the American Civil Liberties Union (ACLU) reports over 200 trial cases involving governmental attempts to gain rights to reporters' information sources. The mass media's contention is that freedom of the press requires the protection of confidential sources of information. They contend such sources will dry up if the sources feel they cannot give information with the confidence that they will be protected from governmental repression. Correspondingly, the academic community has become increasingly alarmed over governmental attempts to gain rights to their scholarly research sources. The American Anthropological Association, the American Political Science Association, and the American Sociological Association recently presented an amicus brief to the Supreme Court in a case involving Professor Samuel L. Popkin of Harvard. The associations asked for a decision that the First Amendment to the Constitution protect the confidentiality essential in scholarly and scientific research. Until such time as a favorable Supreme Court decision is reached, or a federal law is passed, protecting scholarly and scientific data source confidentiality, researchers will find it difficult to gain confidential access to many kinds of data, particularly data concerning deviant or criminal behavior. Furthermore, where they are intrusted with such confidential data, they may be increasingly subpoenaed for governmental access to such data sources. In the event the subpoenaed researcher has promised confidentially to informants, this will mean unnecessary jailings of researchers for failure to divulge information sources and the avoidance of "sensitive" research areas to avoid legal hassles—a bleak picture indeed for scientific advancement. Problems associated with such protections of confidentiality are shown in the following example.

The "Moonies" and the "Doomsday Cult"

During the mid-1960s John Lofland (1966) chronicled a small, deviant religious sect. In publishing his study as the *Doomsday Cult* he attempted to disguise names and places for ethical reasons. This cover was apparently "blown" in 1977 with the publication of an article by Frederick Lynch that pointed out striking similiarities between "Doomsday Cult" and mass media accounts of Reverend Sun Yun Moon's Unification Church movement. Because of implications of strong ties of the Unification Church to the South Korean government and of the strongly authoritarian milieu of this cult, a number of serious ethical questions can be entertained. First *if* Lofland's research notes contain information showing that the Unification Church's ties to the South Korean government are threatening to the United States national security, should he withhold such data? How should one weigh the civil liberties of members of such groups or of scientific investigation versus governmental challenges to confidential sources of information? Is a *potential* threat to the well-being of a nation more important than risks of exposure of the privacy of individuals or of research files?

Second, does the totalitarian nature of such a cult's grasp over its adherents excuse exposing research files for the sake of "freeing" cult members from tyrannical rule? The Jonestown massacre raised a public furor over the alleged illegal activities of other religious cults. Does the researcher have an obligation to reveal confidential information if there is evidence of a group's threat to its members' civil liberties?

Lofland and Lynch have chosen the side of confidentiality of information. To date, Lofland has kept silent on the question of whether or not the Doomsday Cult and the Unification Church are the same. Lynch (1977:85) believes that the researcher's professional status in the eyes of laypersons would be better served through protecting the sanctity of confidential information in research files. By contrast, Porter (1977), in response to Lynch's article, has stated that "human life is worth more than research money or having an article or book published" (p. 203). As such, he would not find it acceptable to shield murder, rape, or terrorism in the face of lost research opportunities, but he would see no need to be alarmed by the Unification Church's involvement in bribery or other Korean government–connected scandals. Clearly, one's ethical choices hinge on one's own role concepts as citizen and as professional sociologist. But the roles may create moral and ethical dilemmas for the researcher because each may invite actions that may be logically in conflict.

Several Recent Cases of Fraud

In contrast to the ethics of protecting truthful information, what should scientists do when they uncover scientific hoaxes or frauds? Several such hoaxes have come to light and give us reason to ponder the ethics of knowingly publishing false data as if it were the truth.

In 1961 the eminent British psychologist Cyril Burt published a paper "Intelligence and Social Mobility" in which he attempted to give proof that intelligence is the genetic inheritance of the social upper crust of society. The paper came to be regarded as a classic and led to his becoming the first psychologist ever to be knighted. This title was frequently cited by white supremacists as "proof" that whites inherently are more intelligent than blacks. In 1976 Professor Leon Kamin publicly stated that this paper contained several "extremely improbable statistics." Then in 1978, *Science* published evidence by D. D. Dorfman proving that the IQ figures that Burt claimed established the intellectual superiority of upper classes were concocted.

Second, during the last several years Carlos Castaneda has written five books that have been enormously popular. Ostensibly these books (1971, 1973, 1974a, 1974b, 1978) were based on extensive field research Castaneda did for his Ph.D. dissertation. This cycle of "Don Juan" narratives has attracted a large group of Castaneda aficionados despite negative reviews by authorities on the Yaqui culture of Mexico—the subject of the five books. Murray (1979) has summarized the body of evidence attesting to the fradulent basis of the books and has analyzed the books' scientific reception. His study recounted persuasive evidence that Castaneda did not do fieldwork among the Yaqui but conducted library research in the UCLA library. The authenticity of Castaneda's data was also found wanting because of illogical sequencing of events in several of the books, failure to specify Spanish and Indian translations of key concepts, and the lack of cultural or ethnographic documentation.

Why did not eminent anthropologists—who believed this work to be a hoax—publish their judgments? S. D. Barnes (1972) points out that scientific communities usually use informal communication channels to notify each other of suspect work. This means that such informal communication channels are invisible to scholars in other disciplines and to the general public. A sociologist, Marcello Truzzi (1977), has called upon UCLA to consider revoking Castaneda's doctorate and on the American Anthropological Association to investigate the case. Murray (1978) points out that fraud of this type is particularly serious because it is almost impossible to replicate fieldwork—unlike laboratory experiments. Hence social scientists must take on trust the research findings presented in their colleagues' works.

The proportion of scientists who create such hoaxes is probably quite small. But these cases show how vulnerable science has become. They emphasize the need for scientists to protect scientific knowledge in a better way from the costs of worthless data accumulations and public distrust of science.

ETHICAL SUGGESTIONS AND GUIDELINES

Up to this point we have given a number of specific examples of ethical problems and possible ways to prevent or circumvent sociopolitical repercussions while still doing professional research. These cases show clearly, however small a sample of research they represent, that the researcher does not operate in a vacuum. All scientists are affected when a single unethical research act becomes public. Project Camelot is not typical of cross-cultural studies. Tuskegee is not representative of medical research. Nevertheless, the American government and public reacted sharply to cross-cultural research because of Camelot and just as sharply to sociobehavioral and medical research because of the Tuskegee study.

Treatment of Research Participants

There are two mainstream approaches to the protection of human participants. The first, more legalistic, is to secure strictly construed informed consent at any cost to research because the rights of the present individual outweigh the interests of a future group. The second, more medical and scientific, emphasizes individual and peer responsibility on the part of researchers as the participants' best protection. In practice, social scientists have used a combination of the two approaches.

Informed Consent. In the eyes of many persons the most important function of research regulation is to ensure that informed consent has

been secured. The doctrine was first developed in law from two principles: the duty of disclosure in a fiduciary relationship (that is, attorney or
other professional and client) and the right of a person of sound mind
to decide what will happen to his or her body. Its application to experimentation was defined in the Nuremburg Code of 1947.

> The voluntary consent of the human subject is absolutely essential. This
> means that the person involved should have legal capacity to give consent,
> should be so situated as to be able to exercise free power of choice without
> the intervention of any element of force, fraud, deceit, duress, over-reach-
> ing, or other ulterior form of constraint or coercion; and should have
> sufficient knowledge and comprehension of the elements of the subject
> matter involved as to enable him to make an understanding and enlight-
> ened decision. This latter element requires that before the acceptance of
> an affirmative decision by the experimental subject there should be made
> known to him the nature, duration, and purpose of the experiment; the
> method and means by which it is to be conducted; all inconveniences and
> hazards reasonably to be expected; and the effects upon his health or
> person which may possibly come from his participation in the experiment.

Informed consent is the major issue for research participant advocates because researchers must juxtapose protection of participants
against (1) serving their profession by obtaining the best possible information, (2) serving science by increasing knowledge, and (3) possibly
serving future generations by taking part in evolving better social policies. Hence, the researcher is far from impartial and—many people argue
—should be monitored by independent groups.

Practically speaking, the researcher is obligated to insure that any
participant understands what participation in the study will involve and
that consent to participate is obtained without coercion. Where the research involves manipulation of persons, as is true of experimentation,
more stringent rules apply than in studies involving participation without
manipulation, such as most interviews. In the latter, more elaborate procedural explanations and warnings are appropriate in order to assure
participants of dignity of treatment and the right to privacy.

Informed consent assumes procedures involving persuasion, cooperation, tact, and consensus. Nevertheless, it is generally recognized that
deception or concealment is often necessary for research to be done
validly. In experiments, informed participants may act as they *think* the
researcher wishes them to act. In observational research, persons who
know they are being observed may act abnormally in order to cover up
their true feelings or behavior. Hence, the researcher occasionally feels
the need to make decisions to hide or withhold information about the
nature of the study during data collection. Where the researcher manipu-
lates persons experimentally without informed consent, it is normally

expected that he or she will, upon completion of the study, give an explanation of the research procedures in language the participant will understand. At the completion of the study the investigator is obligated to detect or to remove or correct any misunderstandings or undesirable consequences of participant manipulations. This obligation to correct undesirable consequences is more necessary the more serious the undesirable consequences.

Even though participants give informed consent, it is generally agreed that they are free to withdraw consent or to discontinue participation at any time.

Although this generally accepted code of ethics is designed under the assumption that all humans require protection from possible harm, Galliher (1973) has persuasively argued that not all individuals or groups require the same degree of protection. He points out that the poorly educated and economic and racial minorities are most vulnerable to exploitation. He feels they need more elaborate warnings and explanations than more educated, wealthier persons. Many researchers would include children, prisoners, and the mentally infirm as needing stronger than average safeguards from potential exploitation.

Consent should be obtained, whenever practicable, from the participants themselves. But when the subject group will include individuals who are not legally or physically capable of giving informed consent, because of age, mental incapacity, or inability to communicate, the researcher should consider the validity of consent by next of kin, legal guardians, or by other qualified third parties representing the participants' interests. In such instances, careful consideration should be given not only to whether these third parties can be presumed to have the necessary depth of interest and concern with the participants' rights and welfare, but also to whether these third parties will be legally authorized to expose the participants to the risks involved.

Galliher, on the other hand, believes that no right to privacy should be applied to research on persons involved in roles *accountable to the public*. He makes a cogent argument for protection of *private* roles (father, lover) but *not* publicly accountable roles (business executive, governmental head) on the grounds that a democratic society has a moral duty to hold individuals accountable in their organizational and occupational roles. Hence, he feels subterfuge may be an acceptable and ethical researcher tactic in studies of public roles where the individual(s) studied would not knowingly permit the data to be collected.

Confidentiality. A second generally agreed upon norm is that the investigator should keep in confidence all information obtained about research participants. The general idea, again, is the protection of the individual's privacy. As we noted earlier in Becker's comments on the Springdale case, prior agreements, defining responsibilites of the researcher and participants must be made clear and must be honored by the investigator. Simply from a practical point of view, this maxim is necessary, if only because—as newspaper reporters will testify—the investigator's sources of information will quickly dry up if his or her trust is breeched.

Again, Galliher (1973:98) notes an important potential exception to this rule: "The revelation of wrongdoing in positions of public trust shall not be deemed to be confidential information within the meaning of this rule." Otherwise, unless release of confidentiality is formally granted to the researcher by the individual or organization under study, all promises should be honored.

In a recent precedent-setting case, a California court has ruled that academic researchers have the right to protect confidential sources of information. The court noted the importance of the free flow of informed communications and the need for preserving confidentiality of information in denying a motion by Pacific Gas and Electric Company to force Prof. Marc Roberts, a professor of political economics at Harvard University, to turn over notes from confidential interviews. Happily for social scientists, the court decided the social costs of forcing disclosure were greater than the value of the evidence to the party that was seeking it.

Participant's Rights and Welfare. There should be awareness that investigators may, quite unintentionally, introduce unnecessary or unacceptable hazards, or fail to provide adequate safeguards. This is particularly the case when the project crosses disciplinary boundaries, involves new or untried procedures, or involves established and accepted procedures which are new to the personnel applying them.

Data-gathering procedures should be limited to information that is essential to the research project. Additional safeguards include the securing of identifying information in locked spaces. Coded identification should always be kept in secure places, distinctly separate from the data.

Participant's Risk/Potential Benefits Ratio. Known or foreseeable risks to persons must be outweighed by the probable benefits that may accrue to them and/or humanity by their project participation. This risk/potential benefit ratio is particularly important the more manipulative control the researcher exercises over persons. For instance, a true experimental situation would demand that more attention be paid to the ratio than would an interview study where participant demands (*risks*) typically are more minimal. Further, this ratio should be judged in light of the relative significance of the research. The more important the research question and the more likely the research design will shed light on that question, the more participant risk may be tolerated in comparison to participant benefits. Contrariwise, the more trivial the research program, the less acceptable will be risk, deception, and involuntary participation.

In particular, deception has increasingly been called into question. Kidder and Campbell (1970) talk of the "deceptive-deprecatory-exploitive attitude" that many researchers hold toward participants. Kelman (1967), in the same vein, argued that deception not only violates norms of respect for participants, but it also may have the unintended consequence of creating suspicion and hostility, thereby influencing research outcomes. Kelman therefore proposed that researchers should (1) stop the use of unnecessary deception, (2) minimize (or counteract) the negative consequences of deception where it is felt deception is necessary, and (3) explore the use of new methods such as simulation (see Chapter 8) and role-playing as alternatives to subject deception.

Researchers appear to be coming to a consensus on how much stress and deception are allowable. For instance, psychologists reacted very strongly against a study by Berkum and associates (1962) where participants were deceived into believing death was imminent. The general feeling was that there are less damaging ways to study reactions to psychological stress. In the previously mentioned deceptive administration of harmful shock experiment (Milgram 1963), follow-up studies (Ring, Wallston, and Corey 1970) revealed that about 84 percent of the persons expressed positive reactions with respect to their participation and by contrast only 1.3 percent expressed negative reactions. Of course, Milgram took extraordinary postexperimental procedures to insure that participants did not suffer long-term psychological damage.

An example of an informed consent statement may be found in Box 1-1 (p. 20). Generally speaking, an informed consent statement should include

1. A fair explanation of the procedures to be followed, including an identification of those that are experimental
2. A description of any attendant discomforts and risks
3. A description of any benefits to be expected
4. A disclosure of any appropriate alternative research procedures that would be advantageous for the subject
5. An offer to answer any inquiries concerning the research procedures
6. A statement that the participant is free to withdraw consent and to discontinue participation in the project or activity at any time
7. Research procedures explained in language that the participant understands

8. Written agreement including no exculpatory language through which the subject is made to waive or to appear to waive any legal rights or liability for negligence
9. Documented informed consent.

While these types of statements can be valuable, the editor of the *New England Journal of Medicine,* Ingelfinger (1975), has pointed out that even under the best of circumstances, the participant cannot really understand what he or she is consenting to in the sense that the experimenter can. More complete information has been shown to be more confusing than helpful. Hence, he believes that the investigator/participant relationship inherently contains some elements of coercion. If so, the ideal becomes to minimize coercion while attempting to balance this with valid methods. In a recent study, Singer (1978) has shown the crosspressures at work in attempting to juggle these two concerns. Asking for an informed consent signature in a social survey reduced responding by about

---

BOX 1-1   Sample Informed Consent Statement

The research I am participating in involves research subjects viewing filmed discussions of several people and answering questions about how accurately they remembered what these people said, what they did, and how they looked. My role in the research is as a "stimulus person." I will be one of the people that research subjects will answer questions about.

As a participant I understand that
1. My participation is completely voluntary.
2. I do not have to participate in any part of the discussion that I do not want to.
3. I am free to stop the discussion at any time.
4. I am free to ask that my film (or parts of it) not be used as part of the research.
5. My film will be edited and a ten minute segment will be selected for part of the research.
6. My name will never appear on any part of the film or any related research materials.
7. It is possible (but unlikely) that a research subject might know me and therefore recognize me in the film.

As part of the informed consent I have viewed a sample of the type of test that the research subjects will take.

Signature   Date

7 percent. Furthermore, higher quality data were obtained by asking the respondents to sign a consent form afterwards, rather than before the interviews as one would expect in fully informed consent.

Peer Responsibility

Earlier we pointed out that there are two major ways in which participants' rights are currently protected. The second, peer review, has slowly evolved a codified policy. Because of the conflict over whose peers —the researcher's or the participant's—can best protect research participants, some organizations, such as HEW, have made provisions to insure that all parties have some say in the proceedings. HEW requires that at least one nonemployee be included in the review boards and that community attitudes be taken into account. Indeed, the National Commission for the Protection of Human Subjects is by law composed largely of non-researchers. Most universities now have human participant review boards patterned after HEW regulations to review research procedures ahead of time. Generally speaking these review boards require informed consent forms (see Box 1–1 for an example), clear statements of research procedures, and statements of the potential risks and benefits to research participants. These types of reviews by colleagues and other concerned individuals are often extremely helpful in minimizing risks to participants. Often these review boards recognize dangers not foreseen by the investigator and make recommendations for safeguards that did not occur to the investigator.

Some Professional Issues

Honesty. Earlier we mentioned several cases of outright falsification of data. Scientists generally have strong commitments to honesty; at least one scientist, Paul Kammerer, committed suicide because of disgrace over falsification of his data (Koestler 1971). More subtle forms of cheating include concealing negative evidence, incorrect analysis of results, and "covering up" data results. The costs to scientists of such falsifications is a loss of faith in the enterprise of science. Most scientists resist such temptations because they run the risk of professional ostracism. Furthermore, they realize that dishonest results will mislead other scientists. But it only takes one celebrated case of faking to increase doubt about all honest findings.

Accuracy. Sloppy or inaccurate researching and reporting is perhaps as devastating to scientific progress as falsification. It is comparable to malpractice, for any scientist is obliged to meet the highest research standards. Carelessness and ignorance of good methodology are just as detrimental to scientific progress as deliberate falsification. Many of the following chapters will deal with means to gather and interpret data more carefully. If knowledge of such procedures is limited, the researcher has an obligation to consult experts who have better information. In writing up the data, biases that are impossible to control should be presented so that others may evaluate the data's limitations and attempt to control for these biases in later work.

Type of Research Design

The type of research design may call for more or less stringent ethical concern. Survey research is generally more innocuous than experiments. While surveys may invade personal privacy, the Survey Research Center at the University of Michigan has collected data on Americans that indicate Americans do not feel they have been oversurveyed. The study also shows that they generally enjoy participating in surveys. Such findings augur well for sociologists since the largest body of sociological data is still collected from surveys.

At the other extreme are experiments. Increasingly sociologists have become connected with large-scale research in evaluating community change, educational innovation, and governmental policy alterations. For example, large-scale negative income tax experiments conducted in Seattle and Denver indicate that the negative income taxes contributed to increased divorce rates and lower work production. Do researchers have the right to conduct experiments that have unknown, possibly harmful, effects? If good reason exists for believing the innovation will have highly beneficial effects, is it right to withhold some groups from better conditions (more substantial learning, higher salaries, increased job security) or to give harmful or inferior treatments to other groups (to deprive randomly selected poor children of the benefits of "Head Start" programs)? Does the researcher have the right to impose his or her values and attitudes on those he or she is attempting to change? Perhaps informed consent is more important in these large-scale social experiments than in smaller laboratory ones because their impact is likely to be stronger and to affect larger populations.

The fact that the investigator believes something needs to be changed implies what he or she thinks is ideal. Ideals reflect values and goals. What the researcher thinks of as ideal or a problem may not be the same as what the group or those individuals in the social experiment think. Recently there has been a cry of outrage over an experiment in which juvenile delinquents were briefly placed in prisons with hardened adult criminals. The experimenters claim the experience of being totally frightened substantially reduces further delinquent behavior (*Behavior Today* 1979:1). This type of experiment emphasizes the inadequacies of individuals rather than the societal structure that may cause delinquency. Those most directly affected by the goals of such projects may have quite different values concerning the worth of extreme fright or "problem" behavior.

Field research is another type of methodology that tends to explore private or sensitive areas of social life. There is little excuse for disguising one's observations of others in the name of science. One's identity as a sociologist implies that participants be informed about what information the investigator will collect and how it will be used in order to give group members the right to conceal what they consider private. Such honesty with field study participants does not seriously bias data collection. For example, some of our department's students decided to study a witches' coven. They were more than surprised at the group's willingness to give them permission. Their participation in group activities and behaviors quickly helped them gain the group's confidence.

The protection of participants' right to privacy requires that anonymity of individuals, groups, and locations be protected. Sometimes the field researcher uses fictitious names to protect anonymity. Where this is not practicable the researcher must consider how the published study may affect the lives of those studied and take precautions to gain consent from the study participants for the use of sensitive information. If social scientists do not adhere to high standards, they will be regarded —particularly by participant groups—with mistrust and suspicion. It is unethical for a social scientist to "deliberately misrepresent his identity for the purpose of entering a private domain to which he is not otherwise eligible; and . . . to deliberately misrepresent the character of the research in which he is engaged" (Erickson 1967).

Social Impact of Social Science

We said earlier that knowledge is not neutral. It can be used and misused. Attitude-change research can be used to decrease prejudice or to convince people to buy things they do not need. Data on management-employee relations might be used to control employees or to substantiate a union's demands. Accordingly, some sociologists have assumed responsibility for speaking out on important issues. Charles Moskos, an expert on military sociology, has appeared before congressional committees to communicate social science research findings about the military draft. James Coleman has testified before congressional committees on school desegregation policy.

Diener and Crandall (1978:212) point out two ethical questions in the application of social science findings: Will they be used to limit people's freedom in an unjustified and dangerous way? Will only the powerful or elite profit from the application of the research? Responsible social scientists have been careful to be vigilant on both dangers.

It is impossible to give detailed ethical guidelines for every situation. The American Sociological Association, like other professional groups, has affirmed a code of ethics that should guide the sociologist in any area of research. This code of ethics is presented in Box 1–2.

DISCUSSION

> *Ethically neutral, value free*
> *tweedle dum, tweedle dee.*
> *Nazi S.S., Schweitzer human—*
> *value free, all the same.*
>
> (Gray 1968, *Sociological Quarterly* 9:76)

We started this chapter by pointing out that the social scientist is not value-free or value-neutral in his or her research. The least that can be asked of a researcher is, first, that he or she has an awareness of values biases and how they influence research efforts, and second, that an attempt is made to minimize value positions in research.

We have stated that researchers have an implicit, if not explicit, commitment either to change or to the status quo. These commitments have ethical implications which must be dealt with by the researcher. Although there are many different ethical positions on the scale from ethical relativism to ethical absolutism, in practice social scientists have been moving strongly in the past decade toward common agreement on basic ethical guidelines for the conduct of research involving human subjects.

It is true that crosspressures provided by various societal pressure groups will work against the establishing of one uniform ethical code for scientific inquiry. Increasing numbers of sociologists are becoming aware that this fact does not absolve the researcher of ethical responsibility. As is true of any other role, the role of researcher involves obligations as well as rights, and some of these obligations are ethical in nature.

BOX 1-2 Code of Ethics of the American Sociological Association

1. *Objectivity in Research.* In his research the sociologist must maintain scientific objectivity.

2. *Integrity in Research.* The sociologist should recognize his own limitations and, when appropriate, seek more expert assistance or decline to undertake research beyond his competence. . . .

3. *Respect of the Research Subject's Rights to Privacy and Dignity.* Every person is entitled to the right of privacy and dignity of treatment. The sociologist must respect these rights.

4. *Protection of Subjects from Personal Harm.* All research should avoid causing personal harm to subjects used in research.

5. *Preservation of Confidentiality of Research Data.* Confidential information provided by a research subject must be treated as such by the sociologist. . . . Even though research information is not a privileged communication under the law, the sociologist must, as far as possible, protect subjects and informants. . . . The obligation of the sociologist includes the use and storage of original data to which a subject's name is attached. When requested, the identity of an organization or subject must be adequately disguised in publication.

6. *Presentation of Research Findings.* The sociologist must present his findings honestly and without distortion. There should be no omission of data from a research report which might significantly modify the interpretation of findings.

7. *Misuse of Research Role.* The sociologist must not use his role as a cover to obtain information for other than professional purposes.

8. *Acknowledgement of Research Collaboration and Assistance.* The sociologist must acknowledge the professional contributions or assistance of all persons who collaborated in the research.

9. *Disclosure of the Sources of Financial Support.* The sociologist must report fully all sources of financial support in his research publications and any special relations to the sponsor that might affect the interpretation of the findings.

10. *Distortion of Findings by Sponsor.* The sociologist is obliged to clarify publicly any distortion by a sponsor or client of the findings of a research project in which he has participated.

11. *Disassociation from Unethical Research Arrangements.* The sociologist must not accept such grants, contracts, or research assignments as appear likely to require violation of the principles above, and must publicly terminate the work or formally disassociate himself from the research if he discovers such a violation and is unable to achieve its correction.

12. *Interpretation of Ethical Principles.* When the meaning and application of these principles are unclear, the sociologist should seek the judgment of the relevant agency or committee designated by the American Sociological Association. Such consultation, however, does not free the sociologist from his individual responsibility for decisions or from his accountability to the profession.

13. *Applicability of Principles.* In the conduct of research the principles enunciated above should apply to research in any area either within or outside the United States of America.

SOURCE: Code of Ethics of the American Sociological Association, Washington, D.C.

This is not to deny that ethical obligations change. Indeed they do. What is considered ethical in research today may not be considered so tomorrow. But the researcher has obligations to keep on top of such changes, not only for moral reasons but also for the practical one of research politics. Obviously, if he or she does not act in ethically accepted ways it can damage the reputation of the discipline, as we saw in Project Camelot; and, hence, it will become much more difficult for social scientists to do research of any kind, no matter how ethical.

Analytically, we have dealt mostly with the rights and obligations of the researcher and study participants. Project Camelot showed, by contrast, the need to define the rights and obligations of the scientific *client* or *consumer*. Even less attention has been paid to the ethical rights and obligations of the public or society-at-large, in large part because of its heterogeneity and, thus, its inherent crosspressures which sometimes create impossible demands for the researcher. While problems of ethics in the researcher–subject relationship revolve around the obligations and rights of researcher–subject *interaction,* problems of ethics in the researcher–client and researcher–society-at-large relations most concern research *outcomes* or *goals.* Obviously these distinctions intermingle in some instances. In the Tuskegee study the researchers formulated a dishonest relationship with the study subjects since they withheld both known treatments and information of such treatments from the subjects. On the other hand, the researchers' goals were just as barren ethically given the fact that they were more interested in studying the bodily ravages of a particular disease than in collecting information which might better benefit society's treatment and understanding of syphilis. Indeed, rather than benefit society, Tuskegee-type studies can only serve to help widen the current racial split. Condoning attitudes towards research which accept the usage of human lives from certain segments of society to help improve the status of other segments can only serve to widen the gulf of distrust which already exists. Thus, regardless of the amorphous quality of such societal crosspressures, scientists who continue to condone such research will probably find their scientific rights via society increasingly called into question. On the other hand, society must come to recognize the need for protection of the legitimate researcher's rights to data confidentiality and scholarly research. Researchers must come to recognize that a variety of research techniques such as the use of deception, the invasion of privacy, the induction of mental or physical stress, and the administration of drugs may pose threats to the welfare and dignity of participants. In later chapters we shall return again and again to problems of ethics posed by particular methods, and we shall suggest some specific principles by which these ethical dilemmas may either be eliminated or at least minimized.

READINGS FOR ADVANCED STUDENTS

American Psychological Association, "A Guideline for Nonsexist Language in APA Journals," 1977. A useful pamphlet for nonsexist considerations in the writing of research.

American Sociologist, 13 (August 1978). Contains several useful exchanges of importance to this chapter, including one on covert CIA funding of research, a second on risks and benefits to subjects of fieldwork, and a final one on recent developments in confidentiality and the protection of human subjects.

BERMAN, G., H. C. KELMAN, AND D. P. WARWICK (eds.) *The Ethics of Social Intervention,* 1978. With the rise of large scale social experimentation (see Chap. 9), this becomes an important source of knowledge.

E. DIENER AND R. CRANDALL, *Ethics and Social and Behavioral Research,* 1979. Highly recommended for breadth, sensitivity, and detail of coverage.

A. M. RIVLIN AND P. M. TIMPANE, *Ethical and Legal Issues of Social Experimentation,* 1975. Sensitive treatment of the ethics of social programs and social experiments by members of the Brookings Institution.

M. A. RYNKIEWICK AND J. P. SPRADLEY, *Ethics and Anthropology: Dilemmas in Field Work,* 1976. Useful discussions of professionalized voyeurism, Machiavellian manipulation of participants, problems of dealing with damaging data, and possible uses to which published materials could be put.

F. A. S. *Public Interest Report.* Monthly newsletter that often covers issues on ethics in addition to being the organ for an important science lobby on Capitol Hill. Many distinguished scientists belong to the Federation of American Scientists, giving this newsletter a powerful voice in our government and abroad.

Office of Federal Statistical Policy and Standards, Department of Commerce. "Statistical Policy Working Paper 2: Report on Statistical Disclosure and Disclosure-Avoidance Techniques." Covers disclosure-avoidance techniques in tabulations and data releases and the protection of individuals versus public needs for information.

SUGGESTED RESEARCH PROJECTS

1. Discuss the adequacy of the ethical guidelines presented in this chapter for research involving some fairly sensitive area such as group pressure dynamics or the social effects of marijuana.

2. Hold a role-playing ethics discussion in class in which one side takes the ethical absolutist position and the other side takes an ethical relativist position. Reverse roles at the class period halfway mark.

3. Formalize your own guidelines for some specific research involving human subjects (for example, observation of hospital staff conflicts, interviewing on attitudes towards abortion). Discuss how these guidelines might affect the rights and obligations of the researcher, subjects, clients (if any), and the public-at-large.

4. The following set of questions are posed for you as a guideline for examining your own ethical position:

   a. What types of research would you be willing to do for money?

   b. Under what circumstances would you lie to a research participant?

   c. When would you divulge confidential information? (To save a life?)

d. To what extent would you practice things for which you are not qualified or lack competency?

e. To what extent will you obey professional codes of ethics, society's laws, or institutional policies if they are incompatible with your own?

f. When would you divulge test or record information?

g. How tolerant are you of peers' unethical practices? When would you turn someone in?

h. How would you remedy a situation if you found out you made a mistake?

i. To what extent would you accept responsibility for negligence or errors?

j. What would you need to know before you experimented with a new method?

k. To what extent do you impose your own morality on others?

l. How much of yourself do you commit to your work?

m. To what extent do you evaluate your effectiveness?

2

The Start
of Scientific Investigation

*Method is precisely the choice of facts: it
is needful then to be occupied first with
creating a method, and many have been
imagined, since none imposes itself . . .*

Henri Poincaré
Science and Method (1921)

We cannot know everything. Every second thousands of things occur
around us. There are an infinite number of things that might sustain our
interest. If our time was limitless perhaps we could have the luxury to
"look and notice well." But there isn't time to see everything. We are
forced to make choices. We are forced to be selective. Try to account for
everything that has occurred around you in the last five minutes. Who
said what? Who did what? What smells, tastes, tactile sensations, or other
sensory stimuli did you observe? If you carried this exercise to its logical
conclusion you would find out, as several other authors have (Pittenger,
Hockett, and Danehy 1960), that you could write an entire book on
describing the facts you had observed in those five minutes and still not
have described everything.

Why did you notice only some things and not others? Perhaps you recalled some things more readily than others. Hall (1966, 1959) has observed that Americans have learned *not* to pay attention to certain facts such as how others smell or feel. We stand relatively long distances apart from each other, we do not breathe on each other in our conversations, and we look away from each other while we talk. Some cultures use such facts to determine if the other person is angry, happy, or sad. Our culture emphasizes that what you say is more important than what you do. *Which* facts are you going to observe?

The problem of the burden of an infinite number of facts to be observed may be solved in a number of ways. First of all, we could allow the pure caprice of our curiosity to determine our choice. But to do so would imply that all facts are equally important. Surely that is not the case. If you are interested in determining whether your brother is angry with you, you probably select out certain types of facts as more important than others. His tone of voice, for instance, is probably a better determinant than the color of the shirt he's wearing. In the same way, the scientist has to have rules for deciding which facts are most important. Poincaré (1921) has summarized a useful set of rules for collecting scientific facts.

Rule 1: The more general a fact, the more precious it is.

In Poincaré's words, "The most interesting facts are those which may serve many times; these are the facts which have a chance of coming up again" (p. 17). Let us examine social interaction as an example. If everything you did or said was done randomly, then knowledge of what you have done or said would be worthless to us in predicting what you will do or say in the future or how others will respond to you.

What if we could establish that there are a limited number of elemental types of interaction? Although communications experts believe there are at least 270,000 discrete human gestures, we are coming to recognize elemental *groups* of gestures which greatly simplify our gathering of facts about interaction. Using methods for grouping large numbers of facts into much smaller units, Berman, Kelman, and others (1976) have analyzed eleven basic types of human emotions. After analyzing numerous small groups, Wish and Kaplan (1977) identified five basic types of communication content (cooperation, intensity, dominance, formality, and task orientation).

What facts are likely to reappear? Poincaré gives us the second rule of the scientific method.

Rule 2: Choose those facts that *seem* simple.

His reasoning was that if this simplicity is real we are likely to meet this simple fact again and again. If it only *seems* simple, then the fact's actual complexity makes its elements indistinguishable. Hence, in the truly simple case we will meet this single fact again many times while in the apparently simple but actually complex case, the apparent simplicity is probably due to *non*random occurrence of facts together.

As illustration, suppose we want to study some large social movement such as the storming of the Bastille, the march on Selma, or some other collective action. Wohlstein and McPhail (1979) point out that an elemental form of collective behavior is collective locomotion—such as marching. The apparent complexity of collective behavior is simplified by what people are doing in common (marching, chanting) or in relation to one another (pushing against other persons). While viewing films of collective locomotion, they observed: How many persons commenced movement at the same time? How many persons' footfalls were in step? How many persons were moving in the same direction at the same time? Comparisons of videotapes of pedestrian behavior with marching band behaviors and simulated marching demonstrators showed clear relationships between these simple elemental features and the types of social situation analyzed. These measures were not random but predictable and occurred over and over again regardless of the collective behavior analyzed.

Where are these simple facts? How does the scientist locate them? Poincaré's answer was:

Rule 3: Seek it in the infinitely small and the infinitely great—that is, in the two extremes.

In the collective behavior example above, the answer was found in the infinitely small. At the other extreme, sociologists will often refer to a more macroscopic concept or characteristic such as a whole culture. In explaining differences in nonverbal communications, Edward Hall (1976) proposed that large-scale cultural differences are responsible for explaining why some people stand close together, why others are inhibited in their touching behavior, or why some cultures use smell and others do not in social interaction.

To paraphrase the quotation heading for this chapter, the primary task of method is to choose among facts—to choose the interesting facts. Once one has established the interesting facts—those that occur over and over again in their simplicity—Poincaré stated that the scientist loses interest in them because they no longer teach us anything new. What does the scientist do once a fact is apparently beyond doubt and a rule is well established?

Rule 4: Once one has established regularities, turn to the most accentuated exceptions from the rule.

This rule helps us to recognize likenesses hidden under apparent divergences. Hence these exceptions tend to be the most instructive. Why do these exceptions overturn our established rule? What is it about these cases that gives our rule the greatest possibility of failing? By understanding these more blatant exceptions to our simple fact, we often discover that the characteristics that seemed discordant at first actually share simple resemblances.

Rosenberg and Pearlin (1978) give a classic example of this. They were interested in the apparent contradictions in the relationship between social class and self-esteem. Results indicated almost no association between these two variables for younger children, a modest association for adolescents, and a moderate association for adults. Rather than assume that the relationships were too unlike, too variable, too capricious, or too complex, they searched for general principles governing self-esteem among children and adults. They point out that all humans regardless of age "learn their worth by observing their behavior and its outcomes" (p. 72). But one's feeling of self-worth "depends on the awareness and importance of that element" (p. 72) to oneself. Adults tend to have more awareness than children of their true location in the stratification system and hence should be able to attach more importance to their knowledge, explaining the differences in association through one simple rule.

All of the above examples should show that the scientist does not randomly choose the facts he or she observes. To do so would be exceedingly cumbersome, wasteful, and useless. One must choose among these countless random facts to eliminate the useless ones. The rules Poincaré laid down help to guide our choices. But he said that it is almost impossible to state these rules precisely; in practice, he hypothesized that these facts must be felt rather than formulated because science is interested in the harmonious ordering of parts (facts).

Rule 5: Choose the facts which contribute the most to this harmony.

It is not the facts but the *relationships* between facts that result in this universal harmony. The scientist comes to recognize scientific facts *because of* their harmony. Simplicity is beautiful. Hence we prefer to seek simple facts. The choosing of facts most fitting to contribute to this harmony is similar to the artist choosing from among the features of his or her topic those that perfect the picture and give it character and life. It is this that gives value to certain facts.

It is the harmony of what appeared on the surface to be a complex, perhaps random, association between social class and self-esteem that is appealing in Rosenberg and Pearlin's study. Its beauty is in its condensation of much human experience into a slender volume. The constant tendency in science is to search for such economy of thought and economy of effort in explanation and description.

THE SCIENTIFIC PROCESS

We have said that the scientist wishes to choose the facts most fitting to the harmonious ordering of the parts of whatever he or she is studying. What types of methods are useful for accomplishing this goal? Figure 2–1 gives us some simplified notions of this process. So far we have talked mostly about observation of interesting facts. And we have noted that those facts that are most interesting are those that lead to empirical generalizations. Ultimately empirical generalizations are only interesting to the scientist when they can be used to formulate theories and hypotheses. Figure 2–1 indicates that two methods are important in this regard: logical induction and logical deduction.

Logical induction starts with specific observations in order to establish general principles. Earlier we gave the example of observing your brother for signs of anger. Returning to that example, we have observed that his mother says she dislikes red garments and an untidy room. We have

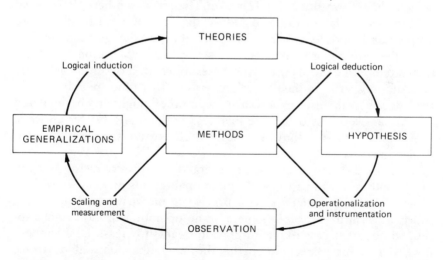

FIGURE 2–1 *Principal components and their idealized relationships in the scientific process.*

Adapted from Walter Wallace (ed.), *Sociological Theory* (Chicago, Ill.: Aldine Publishing Company, 1969), p. ix.

observed that for the most part your brother does not wear red and his room is generally tidy. However, after an argument with his mother, we observe your brother wearing a red shirt and notice that his room is quite messy. We might conclude (induce) that these are subtle ways in which he is venting his displeasure with his mother. Having formed a general principle that your brother shows his displeasure towards your mother by doing things he knows displease her, we might now deduce specific expectations of his behavior that can be tested through further observation.

Logical deduction is the process of using general principles to derive specific expectations. For example, we might deduce that your brother feels it is safer to scapegoat his hostility towards his mother on other people or objects. If we notice things that fit this deduction, such as his kicking the wastebasket or abusing his little sister after an argument with his mother, then we might conclude that our deduction is correct. If we do not find such observations that fit our principle, then we know that we need to refine our principle.

Social science has a goal of generalized understanding based on these two types of logic. Ultimately the scientific process is oriented towards deriving *specific* predictions based on these general principles. We might start out by asking what kinds of cues people give off when they attempt to deceive others. We might make observations of people when they were deceiving others and when they were not. Then we might compare these two situations. Harrison, Hwalek, and others (1978) used procedures similar to these to induce that people tend to give more hesitant and more lengthy answers when they are being deceptive than when they are being honest. Having set up a generalization, we might then attempt to deduce other hypotheses to test it. If deceivers are more hesitant and verbose, then we might assume that other people, having been deceivers themselves at some time or other, might find hesitant and verbose answers less believable than less hesitant and briefer answers. Indeed, the Harrison study indicates that observations confirm this generalization.

Figure 2–1 also focuses upon several other types of methods. First, our hypotheses lead us to need operationalizations of what we wish to observe. An *operationalization* is the precise means we use to measure that which we wish to measure. Sometimes an operationalization would appear to be rather easy to measure. If one wants to measure lefthandedness, why not just ask people whether they are lefthanded, ambidextrous, or righthanded? Although that may appear to be a good operationalization, studies (Hardyck and Petrinovich 1977) show that if one gives people simple tests of manual dexterity such as opening up umbrellas, this operationalization measures only the hand normally used for writing rather than true handedness. Similarly, in the operationalization of age, asking how old a person is tends to elicit answers that are rounded off at 20, 25, 30, 35, and so on. A somewhat better operationalization is to ask a person's month and year of birth. Most of the remaining chapters in this book will center around better means of making observations. The point to note here is that it is important for a scientist to detail as explicitly as possible the ways in which he or she operationalized a study so that other scientists may judge how accurately and adequately those operationalizations test the study hypotheses. Most of the rest of this text will focus on the bottom half of the research process as outlined in Figure 2–1. The rest of this chapter will discuss the top half of that figure.

DISTINGUISHING FEATURES
AND QUALITIES OF THEORIES

Theories differ in terms of several important qualities. Wallace (1971) distinguishes among theoretical (1) structure, (2) explanatory-predictive strategy, (3) scope, (4) level of abstraction, (5) parsimony, and (6) language. Several of these qualities interact with research methods in important ways.

Scope and Abstraction

Theoretical *scope* has to do with the range or inclusiveness of the theory. An ultimate goal of science is to have theories of the widest possible scope. It would be more satisfying to have explanations for an entire social system's operation rather than for specific components of that system, such as bureaucracy or urbanization. Similarly, it would be more satisfying to have explanations of bureaucracy or urbanization rather than just of *small* bureaucracies or *Western* urbanization or *twentieth-century* urbanization.

In general, the relationship between theoretical scope and methods is fairly direct. The wider the theoretical scope of the theory to be tested, the more varied the data needed to test the theory. Wallace (1971:107) notes that "theories of great scope . . . are more apt to be induced from prior theories of lesser scope than to spring full-blown from abstract speculation." Wider theoretical scope satisfied Poincaré's first rule.

Theoretical *level of abstraction* deals with how grounded in concreteness one's theories are. The more concretely grounded in actual observations, the less abstract the theory. Because more abstract theories are more distant from concrete observations, they cannot be tested as directly as less abstract theories: Thus, the more abstract the theory, the greater the reliance on theoretical assumptions. For this reason Blalock (1969:152) proposes that

> The higher the level of abstraction ... the more difficult it will be to link measured indicators to these abstract concepts. Also, the wider the variety of situations to which the theory applies, the greater one's choice of indicators and, perhaps, the greater the reliance that should be placed on the use of multiple indicators.

While scope and level of abstraction are related dimensions, Wallace (1971:110) emphasizes that they are not synonymous: "Although an increase in level of abstraction implies an increase in scope, an increase in scope does not necessarily imply an increase in level of abstraction." For example, if we increase the level of abstraction from that of friendship networks to status networks, we will have to increase the level of scope since status implies a wider variety of situations than friendship. However, if we were studying status among factory workers and decide to expand our scope to status among blue-collar workers, no increase in abstraction would be necessary.

We ultimately desire theories of greater abstractness just as we want theories of greater scope. The reason for this, as Zetterberg (1963:21) has illustrated, is that the greater the variety of events which our theories can account for, the greater the *information value* of our propositions. It would be more scientifically informative to have propositions dealing with "bureaucratic hierarchy" or "familial role bargains" than with "political party jobs" or "husbands."

Scope and abstraction have been the subjects of much debate and controversy in sociology. Robert Merton (1967:45) has challenged the beliefs of those sociologists who wish for an all-encompassing theory of social life. Merton (1967:51) would advise us that

> To concentrate entirely on special theories is to risk emerging with specific hypotheses that account for limited aspects of social behavior, organization, and change but that remain virtually inconsistent.
> To concentrate entirely on a master conceptual scheme for deriving all subsidiary theories is to risk producing twentieth-century equivalents of the large philosophical systems of the past, with all their varied suggestiveness, their architectonic splendor, and their scientific sterility.

Merton urges us to seek "theories of the middle-range"—that is, to build upon our special theories in all their lack of splendor. We should, he claims, *consolidate* these special unabstract, uninclusive theories into more general formulations (logical induction), rather than working from general to more specific theories (logical deduction). Glazer and Strauss (1967) reiterate Merton in calling for empirically "grounded" theory obtained from social research.

Interestingly, Diana Crane (1972) suggests that at least one of the Mertonian extremes of theory distortion, special theories, are typical of the early stages of scientific disciplines, while middle-range studies involving hypotheses-testing are typical of more mature stages.

Theoretical Structure

Another important quality of theories involves the use of rules of logic or of causality. Zetterberg (1963:26–34) lists six ways of structuring scientific propositions.

First, one may systematically list an *inventory of determinants* in which one lists the various independent variables which may influence a particular dependent variable. Kingsley Davis and Judith Blake (1956:217) list over a dozen causes of fertility rates such as: "the greater proportion of women in permanent celibacy, the lower the fertility rate."

Second, one may systematically list an *inventory of results.* In contrast to an inventory of determinants, this list of propositions shows the dependent variables which are a *consequence* of a particular independent variable. Morris Janowitz (1956:193) lists a number of consequences of mobility such as: "the greater the social mobility of a family, the greater the instability of a family."

Third, *chain patterns of propositions* take the form: $A \rightarrow B \rightarrow C$. Terence Hopkins (1964:23) has listed the following flow of determinants, among others: "persons of higher authority tend to receive more prestige; persons with more prestige become more sought after interaction partners."

Fourth, *matrixes of propositions* have the characteristics of all variables, being both an independent and dependent variable (that is, $A \rightarrow B$ and $B \rightarrow A; A \rightarrow B \rightarrow C \rightarrow A$). George Homans in *The Human Group* (1950:18) states, "If the frequency of interactions between two or more persons increases, the degree of their liking for one another will increase, and *vice versa.*"

The fifth and sixth types of theoretical structure differ from the previous four in that the first four types deal with causal structures while the last two deal with manipulating rules of logic to reduce the number of propositions to a simpler level or to generate new hypotheses. The student interested in such important axiomatizing processes will find the Zetterberg monograph (1963:61) a particularly valuable source to begin with.

Explanatory-Predictive Strategies

Theories in social science have two functions: (1) *to explain* how things *have* worked in the past and (2) *to predict* how those things *will* work in the future. Wallace (1971:90) argues cogently that we should be interested, as scientists, in empirical generalization which *combines* explanation and prediction: "We want to know how things must work." It would be much more scientifically satisfying if we could say we have a theory of bureaucratic organization that goes beyond describing twentieth-century bureaucracy by predicting twenty-first–century bureaucracy.

In early stages of research the researcher may simply be interested in describing what has been observed. Careful and precise descriptions may be very useful for determining how much poverty exists, how many people are unemployed, what people think will happen to the U.S. economy, or for whom they would vote for President. Ultimately such description is not satisfying to the scientist in and of itself. In the final analysis, to describe is unsatisfying because we wish to know why poverty exists and how to predict what causes poverty. Chapter 3 will give a number of rules for improving theoretical statements in order to improve their explanatory-predictive value.

Parsimony

Parsimony refers to the simplicity of a theory. This rule does *not* argue for simplicity for simplicity's sake. Rather, it states that, *relative* to other theoretical explanations of the same phenomenon, the one with more economy of thought is best. In Karl Popper's words (1961:142): "Simple statements . . . are to be prized more highly than less simple ones *because they tell us more; because their empirical content is greater; because they are better testable.*"

A word of warning: Simple is used here in the sense of having one or a few parts, *not* of being easy to understand. Einstein's general theory of relativity is admired for its parsimony, but few people would say it is an easy theory to understand. Likewise, social scientists search for explanations that explain a phenomenon using the minimum number of needed statements. Why should we use an explanation of ten causes of some phenomenon if one with nine causes works as well? Duncan (1979) and Goodman (1979) have analyzed models of intergenerational (father to son) occupational mobility. The most parsimonious model—one of perfect independence of father's and son's occupations—has been repeatedly found to be too simplistic for describing the observed data. One could add other variables to explain the data, such as occupational inheritance, occupational mobility barriers, social origins, or achieved status effects. Duncan's article tested five different models and found that it was possible, among other conclusions, to disregard explanations based on status disinheritance *without losing descriptive accuracy in two of the models.* Hence, these more parsimonious models are favored as explanations.

Turner (1978) has reformulated Blau's (1977) "primitive" theory of social structure from thirty-four theorems to thirteen theorems and six more abstract axioms through logical deduction, without losing analytic accuracy.

Many of the methods used by sociologists to help choose the most parsimonious explanation are beyond the scope of this chapter. Students with advanced statistical knowledge who are interested in such tools might wish to refer to works by Goodman (1978) or Cooley and Lohnes (1971) for some means of statistically testing for parsimony.

Theoretical Language

Scientific language differs from ordinary everyday language. Everyday English is more often than not quite ambiguous. The words of everyday language are always susceptible to more than one meaning. For example, does the word "American" refer to North Americans, South Americans, middle-class Americans, or American Indians?

Everyday language also may be *culture-bound,* as in the case of the Austrian occupation, grazier, which has no directly comparable American counterpart (Broom and Jones 1969:657); or it may not be free of *ideological bias,* as in many lay uses of the term *deviant.*

Hubert Blalock (1969:27) states,

> The careful reworking of verbal theories is undoubtedly one of the most challenging tasks confronting us. The major portion of this enterprise will undoubtedly consist of classifying concepts, eliminating or consolidating variables, translating existing verbal theories into common languages, searching the literature for propositions, and looking for implicit assumptions connecting the major propositions in important theoretical works.

In Chapter 3 we shall consider a number of practical rules that should be followed in formulating theory for research application.

Falsification and Verification

The final quality of a theory should be its falsifiability or verifiability. Science is ultimately concerned with the truth of theories. A good part of scientific effort is concerned with formulating research problems that are testable. If one cannot adequately test a theory for falsehoods or truths, scientists will either lose interest in the problem or attempt to reformulate it so that it is testable. A classic case in point is the continuing debate over how much heredity and environment control human life. Over the past one hundred years scientists have alternated between periods of intense interest in properly formulating the problem, despair over how ill-formulated their problem was, and renewed interest in reformulating the problem. We joke about the medieval attempts to prove how many angels could be found on the head of a pin, but historical analysis of scientific progress shows many examples of similar, untestable problems. Mathematicians have a saying that solutions cannot be found until problems are stated correctly. Chapter 3 will in large part be concerned with helping you learn how to state research problems correctly.

THE INESCAPABILITY OF THEORY IN RESEARCH

Cumulative knowledge does not operate outside the confines of theory. To quote Jay Forrester (1971:53),

> Each of us uses models constantly. Every person in his private life and in his business life instinctively uses models for decision-making. The mental image of the world around you which you carry in your head is a model. One does not have a city or a government or a country in his head. He has only selected concepts and relationships which he uses to represent the real system. A mental image is a model. All of our decisions are taken on the basis of models. The question is not to use or ignore models. The question is only a choice among alternatives.

We cannot, as Forrester points out, ignore theory—we can only choose among alternative theories.

As one of my earlier mentors, John Scott, used to say in his lectures: The facts do *not* speak for themselves. It is a fact that American blacks save less money than whites. One might therefore reason (theorize) that blacks are less thrifty than whites. However, if one allows for the fact that blacks earn less money than whites, it turns out that blacks save proportionately *more* of their income than whites. These descriptive statements give conflicting interpretations. Which one are we to believe? Obviously, one's methods of analysis in this case are important.

Theory is always implicated in the research process. Unfortunately, that theory is often implicit—hidden from view. One of the first lessons the student of methodology must learn is that he or she brings implicit theoretical biases into the research situation: the problems selected for study, the manner chosen to study those problems, and the idiosyncratic observations made. No matter how ex post facto (after the fact) the conclusions drawn from the data, the methodological procedures followed will have a great effect on the theoretical or practical conclusions drawn from the data. Consequently one major purpose of later chapters will be to orient the student to the theoretical limitations and advantages of various research methods.

Dionysians and Apollonians

There are several currently accepted approaches to doing scientific research. Albert Szent-Gyorgyi, the famous biologist, has differentiated (1972:966) between scientific Apollonians and Dionysians. He states that Apollonians tend to develop established lines of research while Dionysians rely more on intuition and are more open to new, unexpected alleys for research. The Apollonian clearly sees the future lines of his or her research while the Dionysian knows only the direction in which he or she wants to go out into the unknown. Szent-Gyorgyi makes it very clear, however, that Dionysians are *not* unsystematic in their observations. Indeed, the Dionysian use of "intuition" probably involves both conscious and subconscious reasoning, only the end product of which becomes fully conscious. The Dionysian researcher, hence, usually needs to make theory and methods more *explicitly* systematic.

An interesting distinction paralleling Szent-Gyorgyi's Apollonian-Dionysian dichotomy is Borgatta's (1961) distinction between saltshaker and shotgun approaches to research. The saltshaker methodology is Apollonian in nature. It attempts to develop established lines of research systematically. By contrast, the shotgun approach denotes a much more intuitive attitude which revolves around new, unexpected alleys of research. This chapter section might well be designated "In Defense of the Saltshaker as Opposed to the Shotgun Approach to Research." In other words, it argues for the researcher, particularly the neophyte, to be relatively choosey about what kinds of facts he or she will look at or for.

Exceptions to this rule do exist. Borgatta (1961:433) eloquently argues that when one is looking for new sources of explanation, one should explicitly throw in "the kitchen sink, the garbage pail, or whatever else is available that has not been looked at yet."

Nevertheless, let us consider for a moment the extreme of throwing in everything including the kitchen sink. Suppose we are designing an inquiry into the factors making for good leadership. Dunnette (1958:363), in a review of one study that used the "shotgun" approach, estimated that the researcher had collected data testing at least 3,963 hypotheses. Dunnette reasoned that, logically, one could expect 160 of those hypotheses to be judged *statistically* significant *by chance alone.* Hence, there would be little means for judging whether the author's conclusions were *supported* because they were theoretically sound (*sociologically* significant) or merely quirks of fate resulting from the use of a shotgun approach.

Perhaps, then, the most telling criticism of the "shotgun" approach is its fundamental lack of purpose or reason for being. One might well ask of "shotgun"-produced data: data for what? In line with this reasoning Ray Mack tells a story (1969:54) of a conversation he once had with a doctoral candidate at a professional convention. The candidate said he had just started to work on his dissertation. Mack asked him what he planned to study. The fellow said that he did not know but he was going to use a sophisticated technique called analysis of covariance. To quote Mack: "Such enthusiasm for tools as opposed to products reminds one of a little boy hard at work with hammer, nails and wood, uncertain of what he is building." Once again we have an example of tendencies to put the cart before the horse.

The basic principle to be learned from these tales is this: To speak of doing research without a theoretical basis is naive. There is always theory *implicit,* if not explicit, in all research (Wallace 1969:xi). The one-time use of a questionnaire implicitly means the phenomenon it measures will be measured in a static way. One-time questionnaires are an extremely poor means of measuring phenomena undergoing change. If the researcher has theoretical reason for believing the phenomena he or she is studying is undergoing some change of importance to the study, then a corresponding methodological decision should be made to use some more appropriate technique than a one-time questionnaire. Thomas Kuhn put it more generally (1970:59): "The decision to employ a particular piece of apparatus and to use it in a particular way carries an assumption that only certain sorts of circumstances will arise." Another way of stating Kuhn's thesis is that the selection and use of a particular measurement technique implicitly expresses the researcher's assumptions about the nature of the phenomenon investigated.

Paradigms and Science

There is an old saying that a discovery is an accident finding a prepared mind. "Prepared mind" is the key phrase. As was stated earlier, there is always theory implicit, if not explicit, in the research process. But, unfortunately for many scientists, not all theory is as successful as other theory for explaining a particular phenomenon. Kuhn once again has aptly described this process.

An investigator who hoped to learn something about what scientists took the atomic theory to be asked a distinguished physicist and an eminent chemist whether a single atom of helium was or was not a molecule. Both answered without hesitation, but their answers were not the same. For the chemist the atom of helium was a molecule because it behaved like one with respect to the kinetic theory of gases. For the physicist, on the other hand, the helium atom was not a molecule because it displayed no molecular spectrum. Presumably both men were talking about the same particle, but they were viewing it through their own research training and practice.[1]

Kuhn would say that each scientist was in possession of a different *paradigm*. A paradigm, in this sense, stands for the entire constellation of beliefs, values, techniques, and so on shared by the members of a given community. And it should be noted in the above example that each paradigm acted as a filter for what each scientist "saw."

Paradigms are the assumptions or conceptualizations—either explicit or implicit—underlying any data, theory, or method. Paradigms act, therefore, as "world views" suggestive of research questions or problems. Kuhn observes that scientific paradigms tend to (1) represent radically new conceptualizations of a phenomenon, (2) suggest new research strategies or methodological procedures for gathering empirical evidence to support the paradigm, (3) offer new problems for solution, and (4) explain phenomena that previous paradigms are unable to explain. Or, as Tart (1972:1203) puts it, paradigms are a kind of "super theory."

Paradoxically, while paradigms provide sets of assumptions by which the person interprets experience, they operate so automatically that their proponents do not seriously question or challenge their inadequacies. Hence, Kuhn spoke of the "blinding function" of paradigms. This blinding mechanism is useful to the extent that it prevents the scientist from wasting time on "trivia" while centering attention on "sensible problem areas." Unfortunately, when data does not fit the existing paradigm, rather than the paradigm being reevaluated, Kuhn has shown that the conflicting data is typically rejected or misperceived.

Because of the potential pitfalls of any paradigm, science has developed four basic criteria to minimize faulty accumulations of knowledge (Tart 1972:1205–1206).

1. Commitment to search constantly for better means of making observations
2. Observations which are public in the sense that any properly trained observer could replicate them
3. Theory which consistently and logically accounts for what has been observed

[1] T. S. Kuhn, *The Structure of Scientific Revolutions* (Chicago: University of Chicago Press, 1970), p. 50. Reprinted by permission of The University of Chicago Press, © 1970 by The University of Chicago.

4. Theory which has observable consequences from which it must be possible to make predictions that can be verified by observation.

The same paradigmatic process operates in the social science community. We cannot, in other words, look upon any scientific product as simply the systematic analysis of raw sensations. Thus, no matter how intuitive a scientist may claim his or her research to be, the very scientific paradigms or conceptualizations he or she has

1. Act as a screen through which only those aspects of experience that are consistent with the paradigm are filtered
2. Set limits to the scientific questions he or she might ask.

Yet it would be a mistake to react negatively to paradigms. Paradigm commitments, as pointed out earlier, are necessary to the formulation and expression of scientific problems. And, in fact, as will shortly be seen, these two "limitations" may actually be used to the scientist's advantage in scientific discovery.

Some Simplified Behavioral Paradigms

We have noted that scientific paradigms act as filters for our experiences and limitations to the scientific questions we can ask. Ritzer (1975) has argued that there are currently three different paradigms in sociology and that each of these paradigms is tied to a particular methodology. At the risk of oversimplification, this section delineates, through an example provided in more detail by Erickson (1972a), how particular paradigms may affect the researcher's scientific endeavors.

An old social truism would have us believe that "you can choose your friends but not your family." Indeed, in societies where there was, or still is, strong parental involvement in mate selection, this truism reflects family culture. As family cultures changed in industrializing countries, this truism became "you can choose your friends and mate but not your family." More recently yet, some observers of highly industrialized countries (Winch, Greer, and Blumberg 1967) would probably agree that this truism could be further modified to "you can't choose your family but you can choose your friends and some of them (your friends) come from your family."

So far the modest changes in the original paradigm have been due in large part to actual shifts in familial structure in industrialized countries. But Erickson has recently been exploring the implication of a more radical model reflected in the truism "you can choose your friends to be your family." If one considers this last truism with serious intent, as

Erickson has, it becomes apparent that certain social phenomena that have in the past been labeled (measured) as nonfamilial can now be viewed not only as quasi-familial in nature but also as giving clarification to the nature of familial organization. Erickson has been able to reconceptualize *certain* homosexual relationships as having familiallike exchanges and activities. Then, he has indicated how these quasi-familial structures can be seen as determinants of familial change. The serious student of the family will recognize how revolutionary this paradigm is by comparison to traditional familial research. In the first place, it ignores the sociologically dominant "social systems" approach (Friedrichs 1970) in favor of organizational and interactional analysis conceptualized by Farber (1968). Second, it treats both familial factors *and* urbanization as determinants of familial change, rather than *just* urbanization, which has been the dominant sociological concern. In other words, by modifying and reconceptualizing current familial paradigms, Erickson has been able to explore more profitably familial change in his ongoing research.

A second example comes from research into socialization. For decades most research into child socialization explicitly and implicitly treated the child as a passive recipient of socialization through its parents, despite the theory (Mead 1934) that humans are active participants in their environment. Earlier research used interviews with parents as its source of facts, but by doing so it neglected the significance of interaction between mother and infant and the active contributions that each makes to the other in shaping their ongoing dyadic behavior. Recent research stemming from a paradigm stressing the impact of the infant as a source of formation, regulation, and even distortion of the mother's behavior (Jones 1972; Lewis and Rosenblum 1974) has used observational methods that have lent clear support to Mead's notions of children as active participants in, rather than passive recipients of, their own socialization.

It would be a mistake to assume that there are "good" and "bad" or "right" and "wrong" paradigms. There are, rather, more or less profitable paradigms. No paradigm is ever a completely accurate representation of social reality. Some paradigms, however, give more insights into a particular phenomenon than do other paradigms. The utility of any paradigm (or theory, for that matter) is a function of its efficacy of (1) prediction, (2) explanatory power, and (3) productivity in generating new theory.

Few theories or paradigms measure up in terms of each of these three criteria. Behavioral sociologists who have based their work on the paradigmatic premises of Skinnerian operant conditioning have proved the efficacy of prediction and the explanation of their theories. Hamblin, Buckholdt, and others (1971) have used token economy systems to alter the behavior of inner-city children who had been labeled culturally deprived, disturbed, and unteachable. Students were awarded tokens for meeting previously defined behavioral objectives. These tokens could be exchanged for a variety of goods and opportunities. Bizarre and disruptive behaviors were treated by terminating reinforcement for the behaviors and simultaneously reinforcing other, more accepted social behaviors. But such behavioral theories have not been very productive in generating new theory.

By contrast, Marxian theory has proven to be poor at prediction but has good explanatory power of class conflicts and stratification and has stimulated the generation of much new theory on stratification and power (Whitt 1979).

Make no mistake: We always use paradigms, even if they are simply common-sense truisms of which we are unconscious. Many of the early students of family organization had difficulty in conceptualizing kinship networks of relatively exotic cultures simply because they were implicitly structuring their conceptualizations of those cultures in terms of their experiences with Western nuclear family types.

Likewise, Moore (1973:953) has pointed out the extent to which scientific paradigms influence common-sense explanation.

> The question of human origins is a concern for all human groups who have consequently produced answers (theories, hypotheses, myths) describing man's origins according to their respective cultural traditions. A class confrontation [has developed between] parties who believe they have the Truth. . . . They should both recognize that the two versions of creation presented in Genesis and the version of human origins espoused by the evolutionists are merely different paradigms based upon different bodies of culturally biased data. They should then realize that what was once an appropriate explanation of the origin of man for pastoral nomads may not be adequate for the city dwellers of the 20th century. Scientific explanations may not be ultimate, but they have provided our culture's accepted answers for several hundred years.

Levels of Social and Behavioral Analysis

It may be of some help to you in understanding the differences between sociological paradigms and other behavioral paradigms if we classify the *types* of social and behavioral variables that exist and briefly study their relationships. A number of types of such variables exist.

First, *background variables* refer to variables that *place* the individual into the social structure via relatively *ascribed* positions. Examples of such commonly used variables would include age and social status. Second, *personality variables* refer to relatively permanent psychological characteristics such as "authoritarian personality." Third, we speak of *behavioral or attitudinal variables* as more microanalytic descriptions of a person than an umbrella term such as "personality." For example, we often talk of "discriminatory behavior," "minority-group prejudice," or "aggression" without the need for hypothesizing an "authoritarian personality." Finally, we speak of *social structural variables* as referring to characteristics of groups. Included under this type would be such things as "cohesion," "stratification," "social networks," or "bureaucratic structure."

While social scientists are interested in each of these types of variables, they usually limit their research to studies that involve background, behavioral-attitudinal, and social structural variables in *independent* (causal) variable roles. Hence, their interest in personality variables usually is in terms of them as *dependent* variables (effects). The social scientist is therefore generally more interested in hypotheses involving the effects of social economic status (background variable–independent variable) on authoritarianism (personality variable–dependent variable) rather than the reverse causal order (which is of legitimate research interest for psychologically oriented scientists). We can see once again how the scientist's paradigmatic stances affect individual research interests. Specifically, different disciplines emphasize different sets of variables. A sociologist might be interested in how a bureaucratic as opposed to entrepreneural social structure affects a person's authoritarianism or in how changing family structure affects the economic structure. The psychologist, by contrast, might have more interest in how authoritarian personality affects bureaucratic functioning.

Actually, as shown in Figure 2-2, the research paradigm may be more complex than a bivariate analysis. For example, two types of *interdisciplinary* models might stress one of the three-variable relationships shown in Figure 2-2, because the dependent variable (attitude) has both social and psychological causal antecedents.

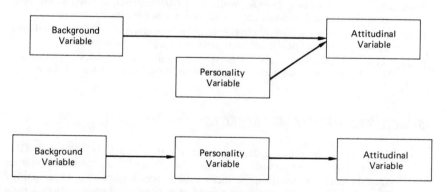

FIGURE 2–2 *Types of three-variable relationships.*

SUMMARY

We started out by examining five general rules for selecting facts. Because there is an infinity of facts and because not all facts are equal in importance, it was suggested that we focus on facts that (1) are more recurrent, (2) seem simpler, and (3) are found in the two extremities of the infinitely great and the infinitely small. Once we have located and established such regularities of facts, we (4) turn to the most pronounced exceptions from our rules. Finally, (5) we choose those facts that contribute the most to a harmonious relationship among the facts.

We then discussed two important methods—logical induction and logical deduction—for attempting to choose facts most fitting to this harmonious ordering of information. The theories that order these facts have important qualities of (1) structuredness, (2) explanatory-predictive strategy, (3) scope, (4) abstractness, (5) parsimony, (6) language, and (7) falsifiability.

A theme throughout the chapter has been that paradigms, theory, and method are inextricably related. Some ways in which these interrelationships affect the research process were examined. The testability of theory was noted as being critical to the stages of research that we are to consider in later chapters. If the theory is not testable, then the researcher cannot confirm or reject it on empirical grounds. Hence, Chapter 3 will consider criteria for constructing testable theory.

READINGS FOR ADVANCED STUDENTS

PETER ACHINSTEIN, *The Concepts of Science,* 1971. Addresses the formal issues of philosophy of science and its development.

THOMAS KUHN, *The Structure of Scientific Revolutions,* 1970. Discusses, in a still controversial but meticulous and well-written fashion, how science is actually done.

HENRI POINCARÉ, *Science and Method,* 1964. Poincaré is concerned with the basic methodology and psychology of scientific discovery, especially in mathematics.

JAMES WATSON, *The Double Helix,* 1968. A personal account of the DNA-RNA revolution by the Nobel-Prize-winning biologist in a manner complimenting Kuhn's thesis.

SUGGESTED RESEARCH PROJECTS

1. Consider a friend's or relative's behavior that you have observed. Give several possible explanations for this behavior. What "facts" appear to support each explanation? Which tend to contradict that explanation? What types of additional facts would you need to decide between each explanation?

2. Find a word that is more abstract yet is encompassed by the word:
   a. Business
   b. College
   c. Father
   d. Male
   e. Marijuana.
3. Find a word that is less abstract yet is encompassed by the word:
   a. Caregiver
   b. Riot
   c. Sociology
   d. Vehicle
   e. Personality.
4. Turner (1974:80) has summarized a set of *assumptions* underlying Marx's theory of economic determinism.
   a. While social relationships display systemic features, these relationships are rife with conflicting interests.
   b. This fact reveals that social systems systematically generate conflict.
   c. Conflict is therefore an inevitable and pervasive feature of social systems.
   d. Such conflict tends to be manifested in the bipolar opposition of interests.
   e. Conflict most frequently occurs over the distribution of scarce resources, most notably power.
   f. Conflict is the major source of change in social systems.

   Turner's summary also includes these key *propositions* (1974:82).

 I. The more unequal the distribution of scarce resources in a system, the more conflict of interest between dominant and subordinate segments in a system.
 II. The more subordinate segments become aware of their true collective interests, the more likely they are to question the legitimacy of the existing pattern of distribution of scarce resources.
   A. The more social changes wrought by dominant segments disrupt existing relations among subordinates, the more likely are the latter to become aware of their true interests.
   B. The more practices of dominant segments create alienative dispositions among subordinates, the more likely are the latter to become aware of their true collective interests.
   C. The more members of subordinate segments can communicate their grievances to each other, the more likely they are to become aware of their true collective interests.
      1. The more ecological concentration of members of subordinate groups, the more likely communication of grievances.
      2. The more the educational opportunities of subordinate group members, the more diverse the means of their communication, and the more likely they are to communicate their grievances.

D. The more subordinate segments can develop unifying ideologies, the more likely they are to become aware of their true collective interests.

    1. The greater the capacity to recruit or generate ideological spokesmen, the more likely ideological unification.

    2. The less the ability of dominant groups to regulate the socialization processes and communication networks in a system, the more likely ideological unification.

III. The more subordinate segments of a system are aware of their collective interests and the greater their questioning of the legitimacy of the distribution of scarce resources, the more likely they are to join overt conflict against dominant segments of a system.

A. The less the ability of dominant groups to make manifest their collective interests, the more likely subordinate groups are to join in conflict.

B. The more the deprivations of subordinates move from an absolute to relative basis, the more likely they are to join in conflict.

C. The greater the ability of subordinate groups to develop a political leadership structure, the more likely they are to join in conflict.

IV. The greater the ideological unification of members of subordinate segments of a system and the more developed their political leadership structure, the more polarized the dominant and subjugated segments of a system.

V. The more polarized the dominant and subjugated, the more violent the conflict will be.

VI. The more violent the conflict, the more structural change of the system and the greater the redistribution of scarce resources.

Use logical inductive procedures for arriving at the more general assumptions from the key propositions. Show, in other words, how some key propositions might be induced from the assumptions.

5. Use the assumptions in Project 4 to deduce some observations necessary to test these assumptions. Explain why some types of observations would be inappropriate because of their level for testing these assumptions.

6. In this project use Poincaré's rules for deciding what types of facts should be observed to test the assumptions and propositions in Project 4. For example, what types of social facts might help us delimit "conflicting interests," "social systems," "distribution of scarce resources," "subordinate groups," or "more violent conflicts"?

7. Compare Marx's assumptions section with his key propositions section as defined by Turner in Project 4 by using the concepts of theoretical (1) structure, (2) abstractness, (3) explanatory-predictive strategies, (4) scope, (5) levels of abstraction, (6) parsimony, (7) language, and (8) falsifiability. Justify your conclusions.

8. Classify the theoretical assumptions and propositions in Project 5 by the level(s) of analysis of their independent and dependent variables.

Generating
Testable Theory

3

> . . . theories ought not to be invented in the
> abstract by conceptual specialists; they
> should be adequate to the tasks of explana-
> tion posed by the data. [1]

Chapter 2 was relatively abstract in conceptualization. Although this chapter is oriented more towards less abstract, practical principles for formulating theoretical problems and testable hypotheses, we should not lose sight of the abstractions presented in Chapter 2 because we will find that we need to reintroduce them in this and later chapters. Here we first consider the formulation of theoretical problems. Then we shall turn to nine rules for generating researchable hypotheses from our theoretical problems.

FORMULATION OF THE THEORETICAL PROBLEM

Perhaps the best way to start research is for you to examine some phenomenon you wish to understand, or understand better. The next step is to start maintaining a file in which you will record "ideas, personal

[1] A. Stinchcombe, *Constructing Social Theories*, 1968, p. 3.

51

notes, excerpts from books, bibliographical items and outlines of projects" (Mills 1959:198). For instance, a concept with which I am fascinated is "ambivalence"—polar feelings of love and hate. For some time I have kept a file for the purpose of systematic reflection on ambivalence. As the researcher accumulates file material, he or she usually will find a need to subdivide it into a number of topical areas. In my ambivalence file, I found it useful to subdivide the material according to various types of ambivalence.

C. Wright Mills (1959:196–206) recommends using files as a sort of research journal that includes both the most undeveloped and most finished of one's ideas. He included such diverse resources in his files as: snatches of conversations overheard, dreams, ideas produced through systematic review of his research problems and plans, notes taken to group the structure of an author's arguments, particular themes or topics sketched from books, ideas on people among (and in close contact with) those he wished to study, types of professions in which he was interested, hunches and possible research designs to test these hunches, restatements of various authors' arguments, reasons and arguments for accepting or refuting particular arguments, and definitions of key concepts and logical relations between these key concepts.

In addition to these types of materials I like to add systematic library research. This involves primarily library *topical* catalogue searches and searches of journal abstracts such as *Sociological Abstracts.* By using a list of possible synonyms for (and other sources of potential research on) ambivalence, such as "mixed feelings" and "emotional conflicts," the researcher systematically checks the topical index and journal abstracts for leads to research on the subject of interest. Any leads that pan out are checked for other references to the subject, which in turn are checked for useful references, and so on until all possible leads to further references appear to be exhausted.

At this point the researcher's routine will shift from library research to structuring the growing file into testable research questions. Mills (1959:201, 211–212) points out that one of the best ways to start this process is to rearrange the filing system. Indeed, he goes so far as to suggest seriously that the researcher dump all the file contents haphazardly on the floor and then start from scratch in resorting the contents. The reason for this is that it is a (drastic) means of discovering *chance* combinations of various ideas and notes. In terms we have used in a previous chapter, this process helps loosen paradigmatic stances through shifting the researcher's perspective to hitherto unrelated phenomena.

Another method of achieving potentially valuable paradigmatic shifts is to work with the opposite of the phenomenon being studied: pure emotions in the case of ambivalence, normalcy in the case of deviance.

Intellectual reasoning of the types mentioned above will at some point have to give way to (1) formulation of testable hypotheses and (2) formulation of means of testing these hypotheses.

Hence, as a check on faulty accumulation of knowledge, we have spoken of a need for theory that (1) has observable consequences, (2) is verifiable through observations, and (3) is internally consistent and logical. The next several sections will focus on further specifications of theory construction in relation to these three criteria. Chapters to follow will give strategies for testing hypotheses.

PRINCIPLES OF THEORY CONSTRUCTION

Current definitions of theory range from "a set of statements or sentences," "symbolic constructions," and "a summary of known facts" to the "employment of concepts" (Shaw and Costanzo 1972:7–8). By these definitions scientific knowledge could consist of entirely descriptive statements like "all social systems have identifiable status hierarchies," "the instincts or needs of the id are satisfied by real or imaginary sense impressions," or "the probability that a male in the United States will enter the same occupation as his father is 0.10 if his father is (or was) a laborer." While such descriptive statements are of interest to scientists, ultimately the scientist wishes to go beyond mere descriptive statements in order to construct hypotheses or propositions that attempt to *explain* empirical relationships. Strictly speaking, a scientific *theory* is a "set of *interrelated hypotheses* or propositions concerning a phenomenon or set of phenomena" (Shaw and Costanzo 1972:7).

A *scientific hypothesis* consists of *two or more* variables linked by some relationship(s). For instance: "If the rate of succession (changes in membership) in an organization is constant, then an increase in organizational size will be followed by an increase in formalization of the organizational structure and procedures." Or: "The lower the rate of job turnover in a work group, the higher the work productivity." Notice that the quantitative variables "rate of succession" and "rate of job turnover" differ from qualitative variables like "id," "status hierarchies," and so on.

A *concept* is a classification by definition of some phenomenon, which may or may not be variable. A *quantitative variable* is a particular type of concept, namely, a classification into *two or more* mutually exclusive and totally inclusive categories that explicitly vary *in degree*. Although "Protestant," "Catholic," "Jew," and "other religions" provide mutually exclusive and totally inclusive classifications of the concept "religion," they *cannot* be ordered by degree of "religiousness." By contrast, we can order, by degree, population density into mutually exclusive and totally inclusive classifications (less than 2 people per square mile, 2 to 10, 11 to 100, or 101 or more people per square mile). The scientist is more interested in quantitative variables like "population *density*" than qualitative variables like "population" because he or she can more easily formulate hypotheses of wider scope using quantitative variables. The classifications of a concept must be *ordered by degree* in order to be a quantitative variable. Qualitative variables like "family," while classifiable into mutually exclusive and totally inclusive categories (like matrifocal, patrifocal), lack the criteria of degree of order. As a general rule, then, concepts classifiable into *types* are qualitative variables. Table 3–1 gives some examples of qualitative variable concepts and some quantitative variables generally associated with each.

The basic thesis of this section is that the researcher should work at learning to translate from qualitative variables into quantitative variables and quantitative variable *relationships* (scientific hypotheses). A qualitative variable is a nominal classification of types of things which can *only* be differentiated as alike or unalike. On the other hand, a quantitative variable can be differentiated by *degrees* or *levels* of continuous connections. A variable may have one of several scale properties. Quantitative variables are represented by a *continuum* of values along some *dimension*. Qualitative variables are based on nominal scales. *Nominal scales* refer to

Table 3–1

Examples of Quantitative Variables Generally Associated with Particular Qualitative Variable Concepts

Qualitative Variables	*Some Associated Quantitative Variables*
Family	amount of familial conflict degree of family cohesion
Bureaucracy	degree of stratification degree of centralization degree of rationalization
Religion	amount of religious attendance degree of religious fervor amount of religious ritual
Urban	density of population proportion of farm to nonfarm workers
Organization	amount of coordination degree of absenteeism
Young	years in age

qualitative observables that are *only* arbitrarily classifiable in terms of same or different, (male-female), equivalent or nonequivalent (family, nonfamily), or either-or terms (similar or nonsimilar attitudes). Nominal scales use, in other words, what some researchers term the "virginity principle"—that is, a mere check to see whether or not something is there. Codes for qualitative variables such as sex (male, female), race (Caucasian, Negroid, other), or interaction categories (question, answer, positive reaction, negative reaction) are of this nature. For instance, "1" = female, "2" = male is an arbitrary coding system. One could just as well reverse these codes to read "2" = female and "1" = male.

Qualitative variables, being based on nominal scales, are relatively uninteresting in science since by definition "they do not permit a wide variety of scores," and hence they "deny the many shades of grey that exist" (Hage 1972:12). In fact, as Hage (1972:13–15, 36–39) illustrates, little progress has been made in any scientific discipline until the field switched from qualitative (nominal) variables to quantitative variables. In large part this is because quantitative variable relationships are more precise. Two statements that on the surface appear equivalent are: (1) When persons A and B have similar attitudes, they will like each other and (2) the more similar the attitudes of A and B, the more they will like each other. But Figure 3–1 (p. 56) shows this is a false conclusion.

Figure 3–1 shows either-or (nominal) connections to lack the precision of continuous connections since the continuous statement contains more information (linear versus nonlinear) as well as more *complex* (wider scope of) information for a *whole range* of values on the continuums for variables x and y. Hence, scientists prefer to work with quantitative scale properties where possible.

It is not always possible to transform concepts into quantitative variables immediately. In research situations where empirical evidence is lacking it may only be possible to use "sensitizing concepts"—that is, to use qualitative variables that refer only to *what* will be observed as opposed to the more quantitative variables that refer to *how* it will be observed. But science cannot depend on sensitizing concepts for long without the growth of cumulative knowledge being retarded.

If one can observe greater-than or less-than aspects of a variable in addition to same-as or different-than aspects, then the concept has the minimal criteria for being classified a quantitative variable; it is a variable that we define as having *ordinal scaling* properties. Many measures of social stratification ("upper," "middle," "working," and "lower" class) and most attitude scales ("strongly approve," "approve," "disapprove," "strongly disapprove") are ordinal. While numeric assignment to ordinal variables is less arbitrary than with nominal variables, one must be cautious in interpreting the meaning of the numbers: Person A "very strongly approves" of an attitude statement, while person B "strongly

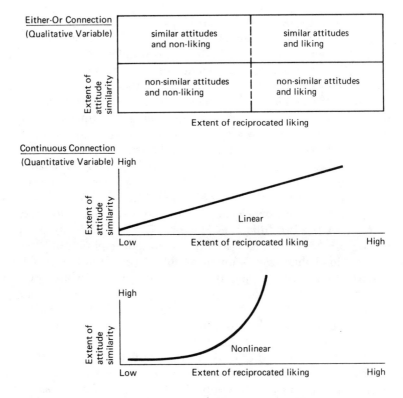

FIGURE 3–1 *Qualitative variable versus quantitative variable statement connections.*

approves" and person *C* just "approves." Rank ordering these approvals in strength—3, 2, 1—does *not necessarily* mean that the difference between rankings 3 and 2 *equals* the difference between rankings 2 and 1.

If, on the other hand, we can *determine* the exact numeric intervals between such ranks but do not have a natural zero point, the variable has *interval* scale properties. There are few sociological or behavioral variables that have this characteristic. IQ is an example since it has no natural zero point, and the distance between scores of 80 and 90 is equivalent to the difference between IQs of 110 and 120. (However, collapsing such quantities often changes the scale type. "IQ" would be ordinal if 1 = IQs less than 60, 2 = 60 to 100, 3 = 101 to 135, and 4 = 136 or more, since the differences between interval midpoints are not equal.)

Finally, in addition to the qualities of the other three types of scales, *ratio scales* employ an absolute (fixed, nonarbitrary) zero point. With an absolute zero point one may determine and employ various ratio or fractional transformations. Examples of such variables would include birth and death rates, age, population density, family size, and family income. (Again, by grouping such data the scale may lose its features of ratio scaling.)

Table 3–2 summarizes the information provided by each type of scale. Notice that as the researcher proceeds from nominal to ratio scales the number of properties held by the scale increases; for example, while nominal scales have only *one* of the four scalar properties, ordinal scales have *two*.

Generally speaking, the first rule of constructing good hypotheses should be

Rule 1: Search for variable measurements with the most quantitative characteristics available.

The history of any science shows a gradual paradigmatic shift towards variable concepts with more quantitative characteristics. The reasons for this are quite simple: The *precision* and scope of any theory are much greater with more quantitatively measured variables. Sociology has participated in this scientific trend; compare early *ordinal* measures of social class (North and Hatt 1947) with more recent *interval* measures Blau and Duncan 1967). During the early preparadigmatic stages of any science most measures are probably qualitative (nominal concepts) as in the early physical theories of color that were measured nominally by their names (such as green); but with the development of paradigmatic stages in physics more quantitative measures were developed as witnessed by the current measurement of colors by their wavelength. There is an important point to be made from this: Precise quantitative measurement

Table 3–2
Typology of Scalar Properties

	Scalar Properties			
Scale Type	Different-Same Equal-Unequal	Greater-Than or Less-Than	Measurable Interval	Absolute Zero Point
Nominal (qualitative)	yes	no	no	no
Ordinal (quantitative)	yes	yes	no	no
Interval (quantitative)	yes	yes	yes	no
Ratio (quantitative)	yes	yes	yes	yes

is more critical in testing theory than any *allegedly* intrinsic qualitative (nominal) characteristic of whatever is observed.

Hage (1972:16–28) gives five techniques of searching for and creating quantitative variables out of qualitative concepts. First, the researcher can search for *implied dimensions underlying* qualitative concepts, particularly ideal types or typologies. In Durkheim's (1951) discussion of the causes of suicide, he uses nominal categories (Protestant, Catholic, Jew); yet a careful reading shows that the main variable underlying this conception is the degree, or amount, of religious dogma in each religion. Sometimes the nominal concept has a number of implied dimensions.

Campbell (1958a) provides a good example of this method in studying the qualitative concept "social group" where he notes four underlying dimensions: *degrees* of proximity, similarity, perceived common fate, and perceived spatial pattern.

Second, one can often create new variables by comparing conceptual *synonyms or analogies* in a search for *more abstract* synonyms or analogies. Price (1972) used the synonym technique in his study of organizational measurement. He noted that implicit in some studies using concepts like "participation in decision making," "organization control," "power," or "influence" is the degree of organizational centralization. Similarly, Hage (1972:22) points out that Simmel's analogies conceptually linking socialism, children's games, and price competition implicitly depend on two variables: intensity of subjective conflict (hate) and intensity of objective conflict (physical damage or loss to the other party).

Third, one can search the literature for *discrepancies* to a hypothesis or *rarely occurring associations* between phenomena. Cognitive dissonance theory got its start in this manner. A number of social psychologists were interested in the exceptions to situations of cognitive balance. Out of this interest grew a literature showing degrees of cognitive imbalance which were dependent on such variables as the amount of external force applied to the individual.

The preceding three techniques of variable construction are useful in situations where the researcher has an already existing literature of cumulative knowledge to analyze. The remaining two techniques can be applied when there is no such existing literature. Glazer and Strauss (1967) provide an example of the fourth technique: the comparison of diverse conceptual contents to discover new variables.

Glazer and Strauss were interested in the concept of status passages. The first step of their method is, hence, to specify a clear definition of the concept to be analyzed. Thus, they relate their interest in studying the effects of a person's movement through a series of differentiated positions or roles (birth, marriage, job promotion, job demotion). The second step is to provide as much diversity as possible to the concept. For instance, studies of status passage should include such conditions as polio recovery, army induction, failure at work, and bureaucratic promotion. The third and final step is to *compare* the *different combinations* of dimensions that might account for differences in reactions to each status-passage type. Status passage into the army is more regulated than passage into marriage, which is more regulated than passage into the role of dying cancer patient. By contrast, passage into the cancer patient role is less desirable than army induction, which is typically viewed as less desirable than passage into matrimony. In such ways, variable combinations (that is, *degrees* of regulation and desirability in the above example) may be formulated to study the conditions under which status passage is managed. This technique requires some firsthand knowledge of the diverse contents to be compared if the researcher is to speculate successfully which are the potentially important dimensions causing the diversity of conditions studied.

Fifth, Hage suggests that we can often profit in generating new variables through *ordering many* concepts from more to less abstract. Hage (1972:27) came upon the idea of *degree of normative equality* by identifying components of social structure with their underlying basic dimensions.

Dimension	Social Structure (distribution of)
Knowledges	Complexity
Powers	Centralization
Rewards	Stratification
Rights	?

He noted that "social structure defined as distribution and the concept of rights" lacked a variable conception and, hence, had to be invented.

Just as the history of science has come to show the superiority of more quantitative variables, it has also shown the superiority of variables of wider scope (Willer and Webster 1970). Willer and Webster note that variables of lesser scope are more specific to particular situations and more directly observable. Therefore, they are more easily testable than variables with greater scope, but those with lesser scope have less generality. The explanatory power of variables of lesser scope is more restricted to the particular situations in which they were observed. Variables of greater scope provide explanations for a greater diversity of situations; and variables of greater scope provide more parsimonious explanations. Obviously, it is more parsimonious to explain suicide rates through the general concept of anomie (normlessness) than through specific indicators like religious affiliation, marital status, or urbanization. Variables of lesser scope find their primary use as observable indicators of variables of greater scope.

Willer and Webster give a three-stage means of formulating variables of wider scope reminiscent of Hage's first, second, and fifth techniques for creating variables. First, the researcher compiles a list of low-scope assertions that he or she has good reason to believe are related. Durkheim's (1951) classic study of suicide starts with a large number of assertions of low scope: Married persons are less likely to commit suicide than unmarried persons, and Protestants are more likely to commit suicide than Catholics.

Second, taking those low-level assertions that receive empirical verification, the researcher asks what, if anything, these assertions have in common. What, for example, might Protestants and unmarried persons have in common? Durkheim felt that each of these categories of people were more likely to be *anomic* (normless) than Catholics or marrieds.

Third, having isolated a potential variable as a candidate for an explanation of wider scope, the researcher attempts to set up a variety of situations with which to test hypotheses. Durkheim asked himself: If it is true that anomie is a more parsimonious explanation of suicide, what other variables of low scope could be used to test this hypothesis? He reasoned that since urbanization was associated with anomie, data should show that more urbanized countries like France have higher suicide rates than low urbanized countries like Ireland. Willer and Webster call this three-stage process "abduction." Our second rule of theory construction is

> Rule 2: The researcher should progressively develop and refine variables through abduction. That is, he or she begins with low-scope assertions but wishes to end with wide-scope assertions that are logically based on assertions of low scope.

A third rule proposed by Davis (1970:17) is

> Rule 3: Make the variable's scale properties explicit by stating all of the variable's mutually exclusive and totally inclusive categories by degree.

With some variables, like income expressed in dollars, it is relatively easy to list all categories. Unfortunately, social scientists often use conceptualizations such as "role conflict," "social change," or "bureaucratic structure" without necessarily explicating the categories. A good habit would be to state the *intensities* of role conflict, *amounts* of social change, or number of *levels* of bureaucratic structure, or whatever else has been named as a variable.

Rule 4 brings us back to the topic of operationalization.

> Rule 4: Describe the means used to sort observations into variable catego-
> ries in sufficient detail so that the methods may be evaluated and
> replicated by others.

"Personality disintegration" and "schizophrenia" provide good examples of poorly operationalized variables (Szasz 1961) that are, unfortunately, currently still in much use by social scientists. Variables of this type have highly unreliable measures. If others cannot replicate the measures (poor reliability), it follows, as will be discussed in greater detail in Chapter 11, that validity must also be low. For that matter, consider the case of *high* reliability of a variable; again this does *not* insure the validity of the measure. For instance, eyeblink rates are high in intercoder reliability. Some researchers (Ponder and Kennedy 1927) have found high eyeblink rates to provide a fairly good nonverbal measure of anxiety. Nevertheless, a high eyeblink rate can be an indicator of nonanxious personality at some times and in some persons.

As an extended example of good specification of one's research operations, consider Lever's (1978) desire to study the complexity of children's play and games. She wanted to measure six dimensions of complexity in both: number of roles, interdependence of players, size of play group, explicitness of goals, number of rules, and team formation. In a footnote she commented that she had to operationalize the distinction between "play" and "nonplay" through disregarding activities like attending church services or doing household chores and eliminating activities like reading books, going to the movies, talking on the phone as pastimes and solitary play rather than as interpersonal play. Table 3–3 specifies in enough detail the operations Lever made so that other researchers can critically evaluate her operationalizations or replicate her research. Notice in Table 3–3 how each complexity score is composed of the sum of attributes (presence = 1, absence = 0) of five concepts.

A second illustration of good specification of research operationalization comes from a study by Burstein and Freudenburg (1978) on the impact of public opinion, antiwar demonstrations, and war costs on Senate voting on ending U.S. involvement in Vietnam. Senate voting results were taken from the *Congressional Quarterly Almanac* (1964–1973), and each vote was treated as if it took place on the first day of the month in which it was taken. Battle deaths were taken from U.S. Senate Committee on Foreign Relations and U.S. Department of Defense statistics summed to the beginning of the roll-call month or estimated where only quarterly or

Table 3-3
Coding and Complexity Scores of the Most Frequently Listed Diary Activities

Type I.	*Complexity Score = 0*
	One role (0); low interdependence (0); play (0); no rules (0); no teams (0)
	Examples: listen to records, drawing, work with clay, ice skating, exploring woods, taking a walk, jumping roofs, kite flying
Type II.	*Complexity Score = 1*
A.	One role (0); high interdependence (1); play (0); no rules (0); no teams (0)
	Examples: cheerleading practice, dancing, singing, catch
B.	One role (0); low interdependence (0); game (1); few rules (0); no teams (0)
	Examples: bowling, skittle bowl, pool, race electric cars
Type III.	*Complexity Score = 2*
A.	Two or more roles (1); high interdependence (1); play (0); no rules (0); no teams (0)
	Examples: dolls, jumprope
B.	Two roles (1); low interdependence (0); game (1); few rules (0); no teams (0)
	Examples: tag, hide-and-seek, kick the can
C.	One role (0); high interdependence (1); game (1); few rules (0); no teams (0)
	Examples: simple card games, 2-square; 4-square
Type IV.	*Complexity Score = 3*
	One role (0); high interdependence (1); game (1); many rules (1); no teams (0)
	Examples: chess, checkers, Monopoly
Type V.	*Complexity Score = 4*
	One role (0); high interdependence (1); game (1); many rules (1); team formation (1)
	Examples: Newcombe, Capture the Flag
Type VI.	*Complexity Score = 5*
	Two or more roles (1); high interdependence (1); game (1); many rules (1); team formation (1)
	Examples: football, soccer, ice hockey, punch ball, kickball

SOURCE: Table adapted from Lever (1979:475).

annual data were available. Public opinion was measured using Gallup poll results for the month of the roll call. The point is that the researcher is obliged to specify his or her operations *in sufficient detail* for others to evaluate the validity of the variables. This raises a fifth rule (Davis 1970:17).

> Rule 5: Always consider the alternative variable names which might be more appropriate for a given set of operations and the alternative operations which might be more appropriate for a given variable name.

You may recall having heard at some time of a scale purporting to measure "authoritarianism." The original scale used to measure "authoritarianism" (Adorno and others 1950) actually measures other personality dimensions besides authoritarianism, and it only measured *one type* of authoritarianism (right-wing). In order to avoid the fallacies of improper measurement, the researcher must be highly critical of the research methods which he or she claims measure particular variables. The more abstract (the higher the scope of) the variable, the more cautious the researcher should be in assuming it is measuring what he or she purports to measure. For example, age is of such low-level abstraction that it would be *less* necessary to consider the question, "What is your age?" as tapping other variable dimensions than "age" by contrast to a highly abstract variable tapped by an attitude scale such as "political extremism" or a measure of "community structure." (Parenthetically, the age question does *not* measure *pure* "age" as evidenced by survey research. Many people forgetfully tend to round off their ages to the nearest 0 or 5, such as 25, 30, or 45. It is useful to remember that *no* measure is ever perfect. Some means of measuring, however, are better than other means of measuring any particular phenomenon. The idea, then, is to get the best means of measuring any particular variable.)

The more abstract the variable, the more consideration that should be given to alternative ways of measuring that variable. Chapter 13 will be partially concerned with the question of alternatives to single measurements of variables.

The sixth rule is one of the most often misunderstood rules.

> Rule 6: Variables without a ratio scale base should be treated as basically arbitrary and relatively meaningless.

The major problem with nonratio variables is that they lack a natural zero point. Thus, nonratio, one-variable distributions are arbitrary since they have *no intrinsic lower boundary*. Although they may be *descriptive* on a low information level: "Group A had a low rate of productivity," the problem is that usually such one-variable statements are used to imply two-variable assertions—logically false assertions of an *explanatory-predictive* nature. Yet statements of that form are virtually meaningless without a *comparison* with some other group or time, unless they are based on a natural ratio scale.

Ironically, most of social science's more sophisticated variables have nonratio bases: IQ, anomie, personality integration, social stratification, and racial heterogeneity. Although the distributions of *single* variables like racial heterogeneity may be meaningless *in and of themselves,* when one measures *relationships* of such variables ("the more racially heterogeneous a city, the more likely minority groups will be integrated into their communities"), the variables can be made meaningful even though they may lack ratio scale qualities. Thus

> Rule 7: Form habits of formally analyzing variables through their relationships.

As James Davis (1970:2) succinctly puts it,

> Since assertions about relationships between variables are the heart of research, when reading you should learn to pounce on the words and phrases which claim relationships. It is often the case that pages of introductory discussion and definitions of variables yield only a sentence or two where the author "actually says something"—where he asserts a relationship between variables.

The remaining rules are attempts to describe the use of and construction techniques for variable *relationships.* We have discussed how poor everyday English is for describing variables; it is even more disastrous in expressing variable *relationships.*

Formal (continuous) theoretical statements can be connected by a *multitude* of "If so . . . then so" solutions. Rapoport (1968:xiii–xiv) writes,

> . . .The propagation of heat. . .can be read as an infinite number of causality statements, such as "*If* the temperature on the boundary of the sphere at time zero was T_1 and at every point within the sphere T_2 *then* the temperature of a point at such and such a distance from the center of the sphere will be such and such at time such and such.
>
>   The formal language of mathematical physics is literally infinitely richer than the "vulgate language" of causality, because the equation which embodies physical law contains within it literally an infinity of "If so . . . then so" statements, one for each choice of values substituted for the variables in the equation.

The most simple-minded theoretical statements are the "either-or" type (which usually contain some form of the verb "to be"), such as: "If person A likes person B and B dislikes person C, person A will tend to dislike person C" or "All societies are stratified." Such statements are limited to only *one* "If so . . . then so" statement. Continuous theoretical statements of the form "the greater the dislike person A has for person B and the greater liking person B has for person C, then the greater the tendency for person A to dislike person C" present a somewhat more intricate web of "If so . . . then so" statements, but they are still more simple minded than a mathematically formalized statement that can deal with situations where not only several "causes" converge on a single "effect" but also where the "causes" and "effects" all *interact* with each other (Rapoport 1968:xiv), such as the equation for the "ideal gas" that reads

$$PV = RT$$

where P is the pressure, V the volume, T the temperature, and R is a constant for all gases. We prefer theoretical statements that have the greater degree of continuousness and preciseness in specifying "If so . . . then so" solutions. Obviously, however, such preferred theoretical statements require interval or ratio scale based variables.

Sociologists are only now starting to discover such formalized relationships. Jasso (1978) has recently used empirical work on perceived judgments about the fairness or unfairness of income earnings to derive a Law of Justice Evaluation. He points out that earlier research into this question suggested that "judging oneself overpaid produces guilt and judging oneself underpaid produces anger" (p. 1399), but because we have lacked precise measures of how much injustice people feel, we have been unable to test adequately the responses of persons to each kind of injustice. His work has indicated that our justice evaluations are a logarithmic function of the ratio of actual amounts to just amounts of socially distributed goods:

$$\text{justice evaluation} = \ln \frac{\text{actual amount of goods}}{\text{just amount of goods}}$$

Ultimately, we prefer such formalized statements because they give us unambiguous claims, which makes them more easily subject to falsification-verification due to their more elegant preciseness of statement.

Davis (1970:19) points out that "the sentence-verb-object structure makes it difficult to describe *mutual* relationships." Likewise, Hage

(1972:35) illustrates how verbal theoretical statements containing some form of the verb "to be" also cannot connect variables with constants, powers, and coefficients. How does one, in a single clause, easily express Homans's (1950) propositions that "liking tends to lead to more interaction" and "more interaction tends to lead to more liking"? Also, as we have pointed out, the *strength* of variable relationships is usually extremely inexact as in the use of "tends to" above; what precisely does a "strong," "mild," or "weak" relationship denote?

It is helpful to learn not only how to analyze variable relationships formally but also how to summarize such relationships through relational diagrams. Rule 7 can be strongly implemented by the use of the conventions (Davis 1970:23) listed below and illustrated in Figure 3–2. (Do not be disturbed by the unfamiliar terminology; terms like "controlled," "conditional," and "indirect" are explained in detail in Chapter 14.

> Rule 8: Link variables using the following conventions:
>   a. *Solid* lines for unqualified assertions that two variables are related (A→B)
>   b. *Broken* lines for *plausible* (not unqualified) assertions that two variables are related
>   c. *Hatched* lines ++→ when it is claimed that
>   1. The relationship disappears or changes appreciably when some other variable is "controlled." (*A* ++→ *B*)
>   2. The relationship is "because of," "due to," or "explained by" some other variable. (*A* ++→ *B*)
>   3. The variables are related "indirectly" or "through" some other variable. (*A* ++→ *C* ++→ *B*)
>   d. Multiple diagrams for "conditional" variables (where the relationship depends on the *level* of some other variable)
>   e. Where no assertion of relationship is made, connect the variables by a question mark (X ++→ (?) ++→ Y)
>   f. Where causal direction is asserted draw arrows from the independent to the dependent variable.

In Figure 3–2 you may observe a number of these Rule 8 conventions in operation. Socioeconomic status (SES) and mental ability are viewed as potentially on the same footing from a causal standpoint—that is, either may affect or be affected by the other. SES has a plausible direct effect on academic performance since it has precedence in temporal order. The influence of significant others is directly affected by SES and academic performance. The influence of significant others also intervenes between these three other variables in influencing a person's level of occupational aspiration.

It should be emphasized that not all scientific models will be this easily transferred into formal variable relationship form. In many cases,

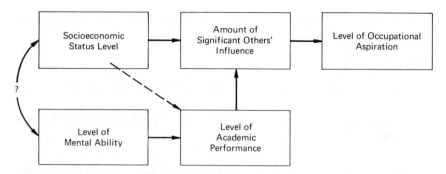

FIGURE 3–2 *Simplified model of the antecedents of occupational aspiration.*

Adapted from Sewell, Haller, and Portes 1969:85.

an author will be quite sloppy in explicating variable relationships, and this results in considerable ambiguity as to how the variables can potentially be defined and related. Herein lies much of the necessity for restating in terms of formalized variable relationships prior ambiguous scientific work since through such analysis it is possible to expose flaws or gaps in the work's theory and methods. This is particularly true when we combine *two or more related* variable relationships into a *formal theory*. In such formal theories we can test for *logical consistency* of variable relationships through the several deductive axiomatizing methods mentioned earlier as employed by Zetterberg (1963).

One formal hypothesis of the type we have mentioned is not enough to make a true theory. A theory must be composed of *at least two* related propositions; the dependent *or* independent variable must be *shared* by at least two hypotheses. Thus the final rule is

> Rule 9: Link two or more formal propositions through a shared independent or dependent variable where possible.

A classic example of such practice is seen in Durkheim's *Suicide* (1951). The dependent variable in the following *special* theory is shared by each of the following operational, formal hypotheses:

1. Catholics are less likely than Protestants to commit suicide.
2. Married persons are less likely than unmarried persons to commit suicide.
3. Married persons with children are less likely than married persons without children to commit suicide.

From these types of concrete relational operational observations, Durkheim inductively produced a number of more abstract formal hypotheses that make up a theory closer to what we termed earlier *middle-range* theory, such as,

1. Suicide rates vary directly with the degree of individualism.
2. Suicide rates vary indirectly with the degree of group cohesion.

From such a theory it is then possible to deduce a number of testable statements.

1. Suicide rates in countries like Spain should be lower than in countries like Germany since:
   a. Incidence of Protestantism is lower in Spain, and
   b. Protestantism has higher degrees of individualism than Catholicism, the dominant religion of Spain.

Note that a theory is defined in terms of formal hypotheses *rather than* taxonomies, categorizations, or ad hoc classification. Taxonomical works, such as the Parsons (1966:5–29) "General Conceptual Scheme of Action," may be an important *conceptualization* exercise for a science, but as we have seen already, concepts are not necessarily variables. Variable relationships are of more interest scientifically than conceptual pigeonholes for categorizing things.

While testability is a primary criteria for starting research, other factors are also important. Chapter 11 will consider three other important criteria—reliability, validity, and operationalization—as further means of evaluating and developing research.

Once the researcher has formulated a theoretical problem and generated researchable hypotheses, the task of producing data to test these problems or hypotheses normally follows. Part 2 will explain the major methods of producing social data used by social and behavioral scientists.

READINGS FOR ADVANCED STUDENTS

HUBERT BLALOCK, *Theory Construction,* 1969. An introduction to formal and mathematical theory construction in sociology.

JANET SALTZMAN CHAFETZ, *A Primer on the Construction and Testing of Theories in Sociology,* 1978. Written expressly for the undergraduate with little knowledge of the philosophy of social science with exercises to help develop precision of thought and analytic skills.

PAUL DIESING, *Patterns of Discovery in the Social Sciences,* Part 1, 1971. Gives in-depth coverage of formalization of theory as a method.

GERALD HAGE, *Techniques and Problems of Theory Construction in Sociology,* 1972. The first good how-to-do-it book in theory construction, in this author's opinion.

C. Wright Mills, "On Intellectual Craftmanship," in his *The Sociological Imagination,* 1959. A classic statement on how one of our most brilliant sociologists did (and suggests others do) research.

Hans Zetterberg, *On Theory and Verification in Sociology,* 1963. A guide to inductive and deductive methods of logic.

SUGGESTED RESEARCH PROJECTS

1. Operationalize the variable "age" as (a) nominal, (b) ordinal, (c) interval, and (d) ratio in scale, if possible.

2. Choose some concept of interest to you (such as family cohesiveness, delinquency, conflict resolution) and start doing systematic library searches for research. Use Mills's filing system to develop this file for use in the datagathering chapters that follow.

3. Write down some variables associated with each of the following concepts:

    a. Fascism

    b. Culture

    c. Socialization

    d. Community

    e. Immigration

    f. Geographical mobility

    g. Family cohesion.

4. For each of the associated variables in Project 3 write out two explicit operationalizations of different scale properties (one nominally scaled, the other interval scaled).

5. Write a clear and complete formal hypothesis for each of the following pairs of concepts. Specify dependent and independent variables in each case. Specify the nature of the relationship in each proposition.

    a. Popularity; interest in school

    b. Ethnocentrism; formal education

    c. Course grade; degree of conformity to professor's ideals; creativity; peer popularity; course assignment time.

6. In Project 5c above, diagram these hypotheses as shown in Rule 8 conventions. Justify the logic of the order of your variables. Is your theoretical model complete enough? Are there other variables that you might add to explain your dependent variable better? Explain and justify your answer. Is the theory parsimonious? Why or why not?

7. Specify at least two different possible operationalizations for each of the variables in your Project 5 or 6. Compare advantages and disadvantages of each operationalization.

8. Using the nine rules of constructing a formal theory, (1) criticize the following four "hypotheses" (Brown and Gilmartin 1969) and (2) formalize them, if possible, into continuous theoretical statements:

a. ... to assess the importance of talent and achievement relative to that of academic environment [in determining scientific productivity] (Crane 1965:700, in Brown and Gilmartin 1969).

b. ... to assess roughly the proportion of managers with upward and downward career orientations and to explain variations in terms of other variables (Tausky and Dubin 1965:726, in Brown and Gilmartin 1969).

c. Occupational and municipal government characteristics influence the occurrence of riots; demographic and housing characteristics do not (Lieberson and Silverman 1965:887, in Brown and Gilmartin 1969).

d. ... we wished to investigate the extent to which varying self-concepts are a function of the consistency of self-definitions given to the boys by significant others, as those definitions are perceived by the boys themselves, and to determine, as far as possible, who the significant others really are (Schwartz and Tangri 1965:924, in Brown and Gilmartin 1969).

9. Critically review the following three forms of sociological exchange theory in terms of how each measures up to this chapter's nine rules for constructing a formal theory. Attempt to improve these theories using these nine rules.

a.

(1) In any given situation, organisms will emit those behaviors that yield the greatest reward and the least punishment.

(2) Organisms will repeat those behaviors that have proved rewarding in the past.

(3) Organisms will repeat behaviors in situations that are similar to those in the past in which behaviors were rewarded.

(4) Present stimuli that on past occasions have been associated with rewards will evoke behaviors similar to those emitted in the past.

(5) Repetition of behaviors will occur only as long as they continue to yield rewards.

(6) An organism will display emotion if a behavior that has previously been rewarded in the same, or similar, situation suddenly goes unrewarded.

(7) The more an organism receives rewards from a particular behavior, the less rewarding that behavior becomes (due to satiation) and the more likely the organism to emit alternative behaviors in search of other rewards. (Adapted from Turner 1974:222)

b.

(1) If the frequency of interaction between two or more persons increases, the degree of their liking for one another will increase, and vice versa.

(2) Persons whose sentiments of liking for one another increase will express these sentiments in increased activity, and vice versa.

(3) The more frequently persons interact with one another, the more alike their activities and their sentiments tend to become, and vice versa.

(4) The higher the rank of a person within a group, the more nearly his or her acitivites conform to the norms of the group, and vice versa.

(5) The higher the person's social rank, the wider will be the range of his or her interactions. (Homans 1950:112, 118, 120, 141, 145)

c.

(1) If in the past a particular stimulus situation has been the occasion on which an individual's activity was rewarded, then the more similar the present stimulus situation is to the past one, the more likely he or she is to emit the activity, or similar activity, now.

(2) The more often within a given period of time an individual's activity rewards that of another, the more often the other will emit the activity.

(3) The more valuable to an individual a unit of the activity another gives, the more often he or she will emit activity rewarded by that of the other.

(4) The more often an individual has in the recent past received a rewarding activity from another, the less valuable any further unit of that activity becomes to him or her.

(5) The more to an individual's disadvantage the rule of distributive justice fails of realization, the more likely he or she is to display the emotional behavior we call anger. (Homans 1961:53, 54, 55, 75)

10. In his important article, "A theory of social structure: an assessment of Blau's strategy" (published in the November 1978 *Contemporary Sociology*), Jonathan H. Turner attempts to reformulate and make more coherent a major theory proposed by Peter M. Blau. Using the principles of theory construction in this chapter, (a) would you come up with the same or a similar reformulation as Turner's? Why or why not? (b) Use the principles of theory construction in this chapter to further reformulate the axioms and theorems in Turner's Table 3 or 4.

PART TWO

The Production of Data

The first step is to measure whatever can be easily measured. This is okay as far as it goes. The second step is to disregard that which can't be measured or give it an arbitrary quantitative value. This is artificial and misleading. The third step is to presume that what can't be measured easily isn't very important. This is blindness. The fourth step is to say what can't be easily measured really doesn't exist. This is suicide.

attributed to
Daniel Yankelovich

Strategies
of Field Research

If a choice were possible, I would naturally prefer simple, rapid, and infallible methods. If I could find such methods, I would avoid the time-consuming, difficult and suspect variants of "participant observation" with which I have become associated. [1]

In Chapter 2, we stated that science is committed to making good, direct observations. All methods are concerned with attempting to minimize faulty knowledge based on observation. In the chapters in this section we shall see that some methods are better than others at different times for approximating this criterion.

Field research refers to a number of techniques aimed at producing direct observations of people's own written or spoken words and behavior. One of the key techniques of this methodology that separates it from other methods is participant observation. Participant observation is char-

[1]Melvin Dalton, "Preconceptions and methods in *Men Who Manage,*" *Sociologists at Work,* ed. Phillip Hammond (Garden City, N.Y.: Doubleday/Anchor, 1964), p. 60.

acterized by the researcher's intense immersion in some social setting. Total participation allows the researcher to experience a social setting from the occupant's point of view; it can create an understanding of groups and experiences about which we may know little or nothing.

This ability to gain insight into the subjective features of social behavior is the key objective of field studies. We live in a "taken-for-granted" world. The field researcher attempts to understand this "taken-for-granted" world. Eliot Liebow's study of the black men in a Washington, D.C. ghetto proves the unique observational contribution of field research. In one scenario, Liebow (1967:29–34) discusses the assumptions of middle-class whites that blacks are irresponsible men who would turn down an honest day's work. Liebow details a typical scene in which a truck driver attempts to enlist laborers from the men standing around a street corner; the driver recruits only two or three men out of the twenty to fifty he contacts. From the truck driver's point of view, Liebow speculates, "these men wouldn't take a job if it were handed to them on a platter" (p. 30). But Liebow's field observations from the men's overall point of view reveals a very different representation of the man-job relationship. First of all, Liebow describes observations showing that a large percentage of these apparently "jobless" corner men actually do have jobs. There is one who works nights, another who is a trashman—with today being his day off, another who works at a liquor store which has not yet opened for business, and others who have jobs but are temporarily laid off due to the weather. Some of the employed men are off today for personal reasons. One, for example, has a funeral to attend this morning while another has to appear as a witness at a trial. In fact, out of all the men on the corner, Liebow's field notes accounted for all but a handful. Liebow concludes that "it is not enough to explain (these street corner men) away as being lazy or irresponsible or both because an able-bodied man with responsibilities who refuses work is, by the truck driver's definition, lazy and irresponsible" (p. 34).

Field research, then, is oriented towards allowing us to see people in the context of their lives, to study the meanings of and consequences of their social reality. This chapter will address the general nature of field studies, data collection and recording, data quality control and hypothesis generation and evaluation, and observer training. Richardson (1953) has listed recurrent problems and procedures in field work relations that we wish to touch upon in this chapter.

1. Types of general and specific knowledge about an organization or community obtained before entering the field
2. Sources from which information about an organization or community may be obtained

3. Preparation for entry into the field
4. Initial field research activities
5. The structuring of the field worker's role
6. The sequence and timing of field activities
7. Incentives the field worker offers informants
8. The selection of sponsors and informants in the research area
9. Ways of dealing with rumors encountered while in the field concerning field workers and the research project
10. Reporting research progress and findings to persons in the organization or community being studied
11. The ethical problems involved in field research
12. Human relations within the research team and the emotional costs of doing field work.

Schatzman and Strauss (1973) and Bogdan and Taylor (1975) offer many suggestions for each of these points that go beyond those offered in this chapter.

THE GENERAL NATURE OF FIELD STUDIES

Zelditch (1962:567–568) describes three broad classes of information that the field worker is interested in collecting: (1) incidents and history, (2) distributions and frequencies, and (3) generally known rules and statuses.

Incidents and histories are single events or cases (such as a baptism, a sports contest, or a conversation) or a series of such events in a specified period of time; they may include what the participants state the importance of the event to be. *Distributions and frequencies* are the number of members or the number of times members have or do things, such as the number of members who are married, the number of times a mother spanks her child, or the number of members who wear a certain ornament. *Generally known rules and statuses* are the informants' accounts of what statuses exist and who occupies them, what constitutes such things as adultery or illegitimacy, how political power is supposed to be passed from one person to another (inheritance, election), and so on.

Zelditch (1962:571–572) also distinguishes among three broad types of field strategies: (1) participant observation, (2) informant interviewing, and (3) enumerations and samples.

Participant observation includes observing and participating in the events, interviewing participants during the events, and maintaining stable relationships in the group. Using a restricted definition of "informant," *informant interviewing* is interviewing an informant only about other people (not him- or herself) or only about events that are not currently happening. *Enumerations and samples* include surveys and observations involving little participation that can be repeated and easily counted.

Table 4–1 shows the general adequacy and efficiency of each method for collecting each type of information.

Both Strauss and others (1964) and Dean, Eichhorn, and Dean (1967) have emphasized the relative nonstandardization, unstructuredness, and process-oriented nature of field work as perhaps its most distinctive features. Chapter 2 emphasized the need for theoretically directed research, yet the aim of field methods is "to make a virtue of non-standardization by frequently redirecting the inquiry on the basis of data coming in from the field to ever more fruitful areas of investigation" (Dean, Eichhorn, and Dean 1967:275). This is not to say that field methods are atheoretical. Indeed, good field methods usage is as grounded in theory as any method. But field methods tend to be more flexible and adaptable to the exploration or reformulation of emerging theoretical concerns.

Of course, this flexibility has its drawbacks. The unstructuredness of field methods makes it more conducive to hypothesis *generation* than hypothesis *testing*. Second, unstructured data are less conducive to statistical analysis than are more structured data.

Table 4–1
Types of Information by Methods of Obtaining Information

Information Types	Methods of Obtaining Information		
	Enumerations and Samples	Participant Observation	Interviewing Informants
Frequency distributions	Prototype and best form	Usually inadequate and inefficient	Often, but not always, inadequate; if adequate it is efficient
Incidents, histories	Not adequate by itself; not efficient	Prototype and best form	Adequate with precautions, and efficient
Institutionalized norms and statuses	Adequate but inefficient	Adequate, but inefficient, except for universal norms	Most efficient and hence best form

SOURCE: Reprinted from "Some methodological problems of field studies" by M. Zelditch, Jr., *American Journal of Sociology* 67:566–576 by permission of The University of Chicago Press © 1962 by The University of Chicago.

Another distinctive quality of most field work has to do with field relations; the more the researcher finds it necessary to participate in the field setting, the more the research role will depend on the ability to establish successful trust relationships with participants. Both the difficulty in establishing appropriate trust relationships and the flexibility of field methods contribute to a need for guarding against these becoming major sources of study bias. The field worker will find it easier to form informant contacts with some persons rather than with others; this raises the question: How will these relations bias data collection toward certain points of view as opposed to other potential, but untapped, field relations? In the same vein, how might the emerging hypotheses attract the field worker toward an unrepresentative picture of the field setting? These are the types of questions that the field worker must constantly ask throughout the observational period.

Even though field work has a number of such potentially crippling disadvantages, it also has a number of advantages over more structured methods. Dean and his associates (1967:276–279) have listed a number of such advantages.

1. The researcher can reformulate the problem as he goes along. Thus, the field worker is less committed to perspectives which may have been misconceptualized at the onset of the project.
2. Because of closer contact with the field situation, the researcher is better able to avoid misleading questions.
3. The impressions of a field worker are often more reliable for classifying respondents than a rigid index drawing upon one or two questions in a questionnaire.
4. The field worker usually is in direct contact with the data in the field.
5. He may ease himself into the field at an appropriate pace.
6. Categories may be constantly modified for more suitable analysis of the problem at hand.
7. If he starts out on the wrong track, the field worker has less reason to jinx his study because of relatively little commitment to standardized collection methods.
8. Difficult-to-quantify variables are probably less distorted by unstructured observation and interviewing.
9. The field researcher has a big advantage . . . in delicate situations where covert research is essential.
10. Surveys are generally more expensive than field observations and interviewing. [On the other hand, Becker (1970:52–53) points out that participant observation is typically much more time consuming—with field work often consuming 12 to 18 hours a day for over a year's time.]

Participant observation, thus, may produce data that are extremely "rich" in detail and specificity. Unfortunately, like a good sauce, it can be "too much of a good thing, more than anyone needs or can put to good use" (Becker 1970:52). In later sections we shall see how this richness can be utilized.

THE DYNAMICS OF FIELD WORK

We have characterized field research by its subjection of the field worker to intense periods of social interaction. To understand better the dynamics of this social interaction, we will employ a conceptualization of six interrelated social processes found in all social relationships—recruitment, socialization, interaction, innovation, social controlling, and logistical allocating—which will help to determine how the field worker goes about doing research (McCall and others 1970).

Recruitment

All organizations from the smallest two-person group to the largest bureaucracy have interests in obtaining and avoiding new members. Typically, the major problem for a field researcher involves entry into the field setting, getting a foot in the door of the group he or she wishes to study. It is difficult to give hard and fast rules for this process since "the impact of recruitment on an organization is largely determined by the number, abilities, and interests of its members" (McCall and others 1970:22). The field worker must use the following general tactics: (1) agreeing to meet the rules of the group, (2) actively "selling" oneself to influential sponsors, or (3) offering inducements to the group or its members. Students in our anthropology department found that by submitting to the norms of a witches' coven—which entailed nudism at group meetings—they were easily accepted as potential recruits even though coven members knew full well they were there as observers. Humphreys (1970) found that the easiest way to study homosexual tearooms was through accepting the role of "watchqueen" or voyeur-lookout. Liebow's classic study of street-corner blacks was made possible through his adoption of the clothing, mannerisms, and speech patterns of the men he was observing.

By contrast, studies of formal organizations often require more precise approaches. Moskos's (1976) study of U.N. peace-keeping forces was made possible by his status as an accredited correspondent from the Canadian Defense Ministry. In formal organizations it often becomes necessary to assure the host that you will not be a threat to the organization and to convey a sense of serious purpose and sincerity concerning your project. Usually it is wise to consent that there will be no journalism, no exposure of hosts, no names, and no publications of results unless agreed upon by both the researcher and the host. Empathy for the host, and respect for the host's point of view is necessary to establish trust and to neutralize any sense of threat. A general explanation such as "the purpose of the research is to understand the host's organization for scientific reasons of explanation" will suffice.

It is important to remember that recruitment is an ongoing process. Just because one has a foot in the door does not mean the host cannot slam the door shut at a later time. The field researcher is a guest; violations of the organization's code of rules, role reversals, or stepping out of the role of field worker may threaten the life of the project.

It should be apparent that establishing and maintaining model field relations is *not* simply a matter of strategies for entering the research setting. Rather, the field researcher must *constantly* work at *negotiating* his or her role. Following Schatzman and Strauss's (1973:18–33) lead, the model field worker would continuously renegotiate the field relation phases in roughly the following order:

1. Casing the proposed research site to determine (a) its substantive (theoretical) suitability, (b) the feasibility of project carry-through in terms of the researcher's resources, and (c) suitable tactics for negotiating entry.
2. Preparation of a brief written document with which to present him- or herself and his or her study to the organization he or she proposes to research. This document "identifies the researcher, the sponsor or organization affiliation, study objectives, and methods of work" (1973:23–24). This document

   should assure all hosts of confidentiality and very explicitly separate the researcher from any given source of power within or outside the group. . . . It clearly shows the researcher's respect for integrity of the members and their work. . . . [It] should indicate approximately how long, with their permission, the study will go on and how much or how little work will be demanded of them . . . [the researcher] will wisely indicate in the statement that in due time he will have some interesting and useful "observations" to offer. (1973:24–25)

   (A useful example of such a letter is presented on pages 25–26 in Schatzman and Strauss.) Of course, this document may be forgone in informal movements, although it will be necessary in those situations to have a consistent "storyline" by which to present oneself.
3. The researcher not only *promises* "confidentiality, respect, objectivity," and the behavior of a "guest" in "the house of a host" but *acts* in such a manner from site entry through exit.
4. Negotiation of the researcher's *entry* will take the form of attempting "to bargain around mutual interests." This may take different forms. It may mean appealing to the researcher's perspective and tools as means of focus-

ing on problems of interest to both the hosts and researcher. It may mean incorporating some of the hosts' suggestions into the project. Either way, "the investigator is a guest and will leave a gift in the form of abstracted information that is of value to the host" (1973:31). Further, the experienced field researcher will realize that the negotiation for his or her entry and access is *always* open to renegotiation. Thus, after a trial period of time, the hosts may feel enough trust to grant more freedom of access. Entry should not be viewed as an all-or-none component in field relations. Rather, entry is best seen as a continuum from least to most "secret and sacred of rites and of thoughts" with the researcher continually working at entry through building trust and renegotiation in *each* research relationship.

A neglected problem in field research involves the issue of derecruitment. At some point the researcher must wrestle with leaving the particular field because the study is coming to an end. We take it for granted that all parties in a relationship will benefit in some manner. Stephans (1978:100) points out the problems involved in this issue in her journal.

> "Aristotle" asked me today in the bar what I was going to do when the study was completed. He wanted to know if I planned to "abandon" them. I found myself fumbling for adequate assurances that I hoped to maintain ties with a number of people in the hotel.

The derecruitment process, then, may cause much ethical discomfort for the researcher because of obligations and responsibilities built up during the course of the study.

Socialization

This process requires the learning of beliefs, habits, skills, goals, values, and norms of a group. Any organization has a vested interest in making members part of its unique culture. Socialization is a two-way process. The organization under study will wish to discipline and coordinate the field worker's behavior in order to protect the continuity of its culture. The field researcher who wishes to understand the organization must cooperate to the extent of learning what is unique about the group.

At the same time, the researcher who is resocialized into the host's group risks the danger of "going native." Hence, the field worker finds it necessary to resist the host group's attempts to change beliefs, skills, or values that would damage the observational process. The more extensive the group's efforts to strip or supplant the researcher's beliefs or skills, the more important it is that the researcher "leave the field" from time to time to regain perspective and keep a low profile within the organization.

As an active participant in one's own socialization, the field re-searcher should continually monitor his or her own behavior to "keep in role" and appear as nonthreatening as possible. Most researchers who use this method recommend waiting until one has left the field setting before taking notes. The researcher attempts to remain *relatively* passive during actual time in the field and not challenge the behavior or verbal-izations of the hosts. If he or she acts too obtrusively, the events observed may differ significantly from those that occur when the researcher is absent. The field researcher is in the field primarily to collect data. If he or she participates too actively in the host group, that can interfere with the ability to observe and record the group behavior of interest.

On the other hand, the field worker who does not participate enough finds that group members will be reluctant to interact in his or her presence or to share information. Treading the fine line between too much and too little participation causes all new field researchers discom-fort. A rule of thumb is to participate when it is essential for group acceptance but not to participate when it would cause competition for status or withdrawal by the host or group members.

McCall and Simmons (1969:25) point out that there are a variety of roles that can be assumed by the researcher and that each can be useful for gaining some type of information, getting in and out of certain places, and talking to certain people. But each role also has its disadvantages, places that can't be visited, and people who can't be talked to. The researcher should be careful to play the role that will gain him or her the most valid information.

Perhaps the most crucial decision concerns the degree of openness allotted to the researcher's role. (Another crucial question concerns *access* to the research setting. Habenstein [1970] has collected many useful ideas on how to gain access to which the reader may wish to refer.) Gold (1958) distinguishes between four ideal-typical field roles: complete par-ticipant, participant-as-observer, observer-as-participant, and complete observer.

The *complete participant* conceals his or her observer role from those observed and remains a covert observer "in disguise." Two major prob-lems are inherent in this role (Gold 1958:220). One is that the researcher may become handicapped by being too self-conscious about performing in an assumed role. The other is that he or she may play the role so convincingly that he or she may actually "go native." In order to avoid this, the researcher should take breaks during participation to reflect back and analyze field behavior. Beyond these limitations, it also should be noted that the complete observer role has been heavily criticized for its ethical implications. Thus, for both ethical and practical reasons most situations are more appropriately analyzed through one of the explicitly defined observer roles.

The *participant-as-observer* spends more time participating than observing, but those observed are aware of his or her role. Again, the dangers of "going native" are present. Also present is the danger of informants overidentifying with the field worker and his or her role.

When contact with subjects is relatively brief, formal, and openly classified as observation, we speak of the *observer-as-participant.* Here the major sources of bias are likely to be misperceptions caused by the brief and formal nature of the field worker's contact. In Schatzman and Strauss's (1973) view the danger is that the field worker will see "motion" rather than "action" because the observer-as-participant role makes it difficult to get at *meaning.* In part this limitation is due to the fact that the observer-as-participant engages in telling him- or herself what he or she is seeing as opposed to understanding action from the point of view of the study. However, this limitation is also a function of the fact that the observer-as-participant role is not as conducive to the establishment of trust relationships as a strictly participatory role.

Finally, the *complete observer* role is illustrated by systematic and detached eavesdropping and reconnaissance. Gold (1958:221) points out that this is rarely a dominant field worker role; usually it is used only to "case" the setting to be observed prior to committing oneself to the study setting. The major problem with this role is ethnocentrism (Gold 1958:221): "reject[ing] the informant's views without ever getting to the point of understanding them."

Kahn and Mann (1952) have pointed out that field relations often call for somewhat more complex operations than Gold's article suggests. They point out that where "cliques, factions or multiple authority structures characterize the organizations to be studied, or where the organization to be studied has a close interdependent relationship with some other organizational structure" (1952:5), it will be necessary for the field worker to gain access to the research site by more than one path simultaneously. If the researcher does not do this he or she risks (1) being identified with particular groups and (2) the appearance of slighting or bypassing particular leadership factions.

Multiple entry is useful in studying overlapping authority structures. However, organizations tend to be hierarchically organized. Kahn and Mann (1952:7) point out that "since the researcher requires spontaneity and cooperation rather than docility and obedience, it is not enough for him to use the ready-made authority structure." Rather, they (1952:8) suggest that the researcher "ask the head of the organization only that he himself agree to the project and that he agree to have the question put before the next level in the organization" and go on down the hierarchy. This procedure, so-called "contingent acceptance" by various levels of the organization, has risks of rejection by particular echelons, but it provides better cooperation and information if followed through successfully.

Janes (1961) has emphasized that the field-worker role undergoes five separate phases: newcomer, provisional acceptance, categorical acceptance, personal acceptance, and imminent migrant. Rapport is specific to the fourth phase, personal acceptance. Erickson (1971:192) indicated this life cycle of field relations personally.

> At first—obviously identified as a stranger—I was "that sociologist who is doing a study of our group." As I and my family—wife, three year old son and six year old daughter—increased our participation, the labelling changed. Eventually, when introduced to visitors, I found myself referred to by some members as a friend with no attention paid to sociologist or researcher.

The last phase, imminent migrant, is an often ignored yet extremely crucial period for field studies. As the researcher starts "cooling out" of the field in preparation for ending the study, field relations take on a particularly new character: Rarely will new information be informally volunteered by subjects and anxiety increases among the study population over the researcher's impressions and findings. The researcher often finds it useful during this stage to spend most of the time interpreting and reviewing the study findings with the study group.

An important point is that as the researcher proceeds through the field-worker–role life cycle, the quality and quantity of the data collection will be affected by his or her position in the life cycle. A later section will discuss methods of checking on and controlling for data reliability and validity in relation to the researcher's role.

Of course, the researcher's role definitions will not be completely self-defined—they will also be partly defined by those within the group studied and partly by the social situation. In order to control for reactivity of the observer and to guard against "going native," many researchers have cautioned that the field worker should not become "too active" in the group being studied. However, "practical circumstances of the research setting may not allow the observer much choice" (Cicourel 1964:41–42).

Interaction

A good definition of interaction is "WHO come together for WHAT activities WHEN and WHERE" (McCall and others 1970:24). The type of interaction necessary in the field researcher's role is circumscribed by the desire to collect good data. Two types of interaction are important for our analysis: first, the type of interaction appropriate for the field worker and, second, the most appropriate ways to observe and record interactional occurrences on the part of the host group.

Field roles.   The field worker interacts in a role of participant-observer that gives rise to intrinsic tensions because he or she is at the same time both an insider and an outsider to the social setting being observed. One's interaction in the social world under study tends to generate a syndrome in which the outsider is absorbed into the group and its ideologies. This makes it difficult for the participant-observer to leave the group setting. It also makes it difficult to view objectively and to examine critically the group's definition of reality. Early in the recruitment process, the researcher uses tactics like courting, charming, or cajoling to be allowed into the host's world. Now, to understand this subjective world, the researcher allows him- or herself to be seduced by it and its occupants. From this may evolve a dangerous process: The researcher may forget his or her place on the outside. In interaction with our hosts we play at being one of them; this may lead to our being mistaken for one of them. The host's offers to legitimize the researcher's presence through insider roles is quite common (resident sociologist, visiting friend, honorary member, affectionate mascot) and may be well meaning, but it is disruptive to the researcher's role. To be an insider means that one is guided by the experiential world of the participants of a particular social setting. An outsider to that system is not guided by the rules and prescriptions of this experiential world. As such, he or she is a potentially threatening figure and may find it too easy to adopt an insider's perspective to reduce the tension. This may result in uncritically accepting the host's perspectives.

Observing and recording observations.   One of the recurring problems with field methods is the simultaneous, recurring, and often conflicting roles that the field worker must fulfill. At the same time that rapport is being established with a particular organizational faction, he or she may be attempting to deal with rumors that threaten already established relations with other factions, directly participating in ongoing events, rummaging through organizational archives for important historical documents, and keeping track of and sorting through large masses of observations.

While it is difficult to lay down specific procedural rules for collecting and recording field observations, several researchers (for example, McCall and Simmons 1969:76; Erickson 1971) have followed procedures that could profitably be used in most field settings.

According to this viewpoint the field worker, while in the field, must become quite conscious of the roles he or she is playing and must be detached from the situation being studied. The researcher must be able psychologically to stand off to the side as he or she gathers data and view the situation with introspective skepticism ("Is that really what is happening?"), cynicism ("Can I believe that?"), and marginality to the group being studied.

The complexity and difficulty of the field worker role is made more obvious when we consider the fact that as the observer utilizes the above backstage "objective self" for analytic perspective, he or she must also present frontstage behavior that creates an acceptable rapport with the study group. This frontstage behavior implies that one avoids actually asking the host: "Is that really what is happening?" or "Can I believe that?" Rather, one asks questions that help the hosts express true opinions and concerns. The trick is to avoid questions that might intimidate the hosts or lead them to tell the researcher only what they think he or she wants to hear. One of the most important components of the field worker's role is *not* to take anything for granted. Howard Becker, one of our foremost participant observers, counsels his students to play dumb by using phrases like "I don't understand what you're saying," "What do you mean?," or other ways of pressing the host for clarification.

The field worker is asked to walk a tightrope between *active participation* in the group, which may help to gain acceptance within the group but tends to interfere with introspection and *passive observation,* which cuts down on the possibilities of "going native" while helping his or her analytic perspective but can lead to ethnocentrism and loss of rapport. A further dilemma is that while a worker's marginality to the group is necessary for introspective purposes, "certain types of information will not be available to researchers who remain too marginal" (Cicourel 1964:45).

In addition to the above-mentioned field-work attitudes and roles toward the observational period, the field researcher needs occasions for literally and figuratively "leaving the field" for periodic reviews of what has happened and where the research is going. It is usually more practical to separate *recording* of the observations from the actual observations themselves. Note taking during observation is usually extremely reactive; notes that are taken down in the field often are kept to a minimum and, where possible, unobtrusively made.

One of the gravest problems with this time separation of recording from observation is the fallibility of recall processes. Nevertheless, the following procedures often make the retrospective observation process more reliable and valid: The first days in the field are normally spent in simple selection of problems, concepts, indices, and their definitions (Becker 1958). The first stages of recording usually will entail simple self-debriefing recall processes on a low level of abstraction; who did what, who said what to whom, the context of what happened, and notations of potential field researcher reactivity and biases due to changing field relations and *interpretations* of what subjects "think" or "mean" clearly differentiated from pure descriptive materials. Put somewhat differently, it is necessary to distinguish between the most *inferential* (what one "means") data and the least inferential (what one said or did) data. This last point is extremely important. One wants to describe, not evaluate, when recording notes. The good researcher does not evaluate a person in field notes as "repulsive." Instead, one notes Person X "had a pock marked face," "repeatedly cut off his colleague's conversations," or whatever else one *interprets* as repulsive. Rather than generalize observations and events such as "Children were acting out," the researcher uses specific descriptions ("two six-year-olds threw pencils at the teacher"). Verbal interaction is often modified by nonverbal communication that highlights the meaning of the words; compare the information provided by "Carol said 'no,' " with that given by the note, "Carol played with her shirt collar, stuttered, gulped, and then said 'no.' "

Richness of detail is important to field work, as well as distinctive of it, because—unlike most other methods—it is difficult to replicate field research. Hence, the richness of information allows other researchers to derive their own conclusions if they do not agree with the analysis.

Once one has been in the field for a short length of time it is good to leave the field setting to (1) gain the perspective of an outsider and (2) write down as much detail as possible before memory decay sets in. The field researcher finds it necessary to organize and sift through this collected mass of rich information. Several suggestions for recording data are wise to keep in mind.

First, make use of the previously mentioned self-debriefing exercises. Second, reread, and "free associate" from, raw data to reconstruct the field events and thereby uncover observations not noted earlier. Third, note changes in field relations for similar reasons: Changes in roles, as is true of changes in any inferential perspective, create dangers of falsely attributing changes in oneself to changes in the group being studied. Thus, the researcher starts out by keeping a field diary that is distinguishable from an ordinary personal diary in the above-noted important ways. (See Appendix A for sample field notes.)

Retrospective observation also entails more abstract processes. This involves the painstakingly reiterative process of running through the considerable number of field notes collected in order to redirect and reconceptualize the observation.

Sometimes new lines of pursuit are noted during observation. However, Erickson (1971:194) and McCall and Simmons (1969:76) believe that more frequently hypotheses emerge, are redesigned, and are generated through data filing and processing. For example, it should be noted in Appendix A how field notes are processed according to abstract concepts such as "leadership," and "peace movement."

In order to give easy access to data based on such indexing and to avoid the time-consuming process of thumbing through a chronologically ordered field diary to search for particularly indexed materials, McCall and Simmons (1969:76) suggest the following system. Folders are made for each variable, category, and hypothesis. Field notes are typed daily on mimeograph stencils and several copies are run off. (One copy is placed in a cumulative file in chronological order, acting as a regular field diary.) Different subjects are circled in red on each copy and the copies are then filed in folders. The stencils are also filed chronologically so that when new categories arise during the study, the previous pages of field notes can be duplicated, circled, and filed appropriately.

Each subject folder is reviewed periodically and interpreted. A position paper is written, documenting statements with dates and page numbers. After the paper has been written, the material used is put in a dead file unless and until it is needed later for clarification.

This filing system makes data on each subject readily accessible; one does not have to go through the entire diary. The position papers help with the analysis of the incoming data and may suggest new categories to be indexed. Erickson (1971:194–195) further explains the utility of this system.

> Numerous files were generated along gross topical lines. Fieldnotes were then proposed so all data bits relevant to a particular file were noted. This file was then processed as a separate corpus which in turn usually generated numerous sub-files. In a fashion analogous to card sorting on a particular variable or characteristic, these files frequently brought new light to the data and thus generated propositions that did not suggest themselves in raw fieldnote form. . . .
>
> This file [Appendix A] was repeatedly processed on various dimensions. For example, indicators of the six analytic structures were noted. When a reference was marked for a particular structure, such as leadership or authority, that bit was then also filed under the relevant topic in a separate folder. Virtually every marginal reference indicates a distinct sub-file. In some cases after these sub-files were generated, still more sub-files were forthcoming as was the case with the bits marked "Rural Move."

Similar to the notetaking distinction McCall and Simmons and Erickson make is Schatzman and Strauss's (1973:99–105) recommendation that the field researcher *label* notes according to whether they are observational (ON), theoretical (TN), or methodological (MN). An *observational note* is a statement of who said or did what, when, where, and how. *Theoretical notes* are inferential declarations; they are the field researcher's interpretations, inferences, hypotheses, and conjectures of observational *meaning. Methodological notes* are "observational notes on the researcher himself and upon the methodological process itself." In addition, Schatzman and Strauss recommend the use of *analytic memos* that elaborate on or tie together theoretical notes. Analytic memos "develop and put closure to some idea."

As the field worker's findings increase, the study will turn further away from discovery of hypotheses and more toward testing hypotheses. The first stages of this change in study orientation will normally be a search for the *typicality* of observations (observational frequencies and importance). Thus, the observations now may become more systematic, as in Erickson's (1971:193) statistical tabulations of communal member religious perspectives: "We isolated all key personages and coded them in terms of their being sectarian or non-sectarian, their being affirmed or not and in terms of which fellowship member played what character." Notice how the labeling of notes by type (ON, TN, MN) and titles and subtitles (vocation, rural move) requires large margins on the left. Good final notes provide sufficient detail for (1) storage and retrieval of the observed times, places, and circumstances and for (2) control over the analysis process in terms of facilitating the need for more observations for "negative, conflicting or supporting evidence."

So far our discussion of the field worker's role has emphasized participant-observer activities. Other field data often are used in conjunction with field notes in order to gain a greater understanding of the setting; historical records of the organization, newspaper morgues, correspondence, official documents, and diaries are often used for context. Since these methods are covered in other parts of this text, they will not be covered in duplicate here. (See Chapter 6 on interviewing for suggestions on open-ended and more formal interviewing skills and Chapter 5 for dealing with already available data sources for suggestions on historical records or archival data.)

Innovation

Any change in the social setting's division of labor, norms, or goals that might result from the field worker's presence may threaten the validity of the study. The larger the group under study, the less probability that the researcher will have any undesirable effects. The types of roles discussed earlier in this chapter have different innovating effects. The covert observer's low "spy" profile may mean that his or her role as a *researcher* will not cause any innovations per se. But the covert observer who comes in as a *complete participant* may have innovating effects—particularly in small groups. At the other extreme, the field worker who takes on the complete observer role has potential innovating problems through high profile as an observer but not as a participant.

It should be pointed out that most people in natural situations find it difficult to act unnaturally for any length of time. Documentary files such as those done by Wiseman clearly show that the innovating presence of participant observers and their equipment (tape recorders and movie cameras) may be quite minimal over a long period of field work, particularly in large groups or formal organizations.

The field worker's role usually changes over time. Any change in this role may have innovative effects to which the field worker must be constantly alert; the researcher must be able to differentiate between natural internal changes in the host group and changes introduced by the field worker's presence.

Social Controlling

The field worker who takes on the role of participant observer does well to remember that someone is observing *his* or *her* activities. Social controlling is an ever continuing process. We tend to think of rewards for conformity, or punishments for deviancy, as ways of reinforcing a group's culture. But there are more subtle ways of social controlling that may affect the field worker. Role definition is one of the more important yet subtle ways of controlling a field worker. As a field worker, the researcher may be defined into having access to some places, times, or people but not to others. (It is partly for this reason that field workers try to cultivate informants. *Informants* are people who can do things for the researcher or who have access to places from which the researcher is barred.)

Social controlling through the field worker's role as defined by the hosts is a particular problem in organizations with a complex or highly hierarchically defined division of labor. If the field worker is authorized by management to study assembly line workers, the workers may define the field worker as "one of them rather than one of us." Hence, the field worker must always be aware of how his or her role is or might be defined by various members of the host group, the potential social controlling effects of those role definitions on the goal of obtaining data, and potential ways to circumvent these constraints to data collection without threatening the project's continued existence.

Logistics

The researcher as a field worker has numerous demands placed on his or her time and energy. Likewise, the social group under study may feel threatened by the additional demands placed upon it by the field researcher. The researcher entering into the field has the problem of how research roles and other resources (time, energy, money) will be distributed.

The researcher has multiple identities that may lead to a necessary segregation of roles and audiences. The researcher may find there are problems of scheduling his or her roles so that both the researcher and the host group minimize inconsistent demands of competing roles or unrealistic pressures of too many role demands. In highly stratified organizations, in particular, the field worker is often placed in highly unrealistic multiple identities. Managers may expect the field worker to report any irregular activities of the rank and file, while the rank and file may see the field worker as a threat to their privacy or even as a means of improving job conditions.

Even in small groups the field worker finds it impossible to study everything. In Liebow's study of black street-corner men, he got to know about twenty of the men on a relatively personal level over an intensive year and a half study. Decisions on how to collect information best inevitably end up weighed against the realistic needs for budgeting one's roles. Stephens (1978:99–100) graphically writes,

> In this type of study the researcher flirts with exhaustion. You can't really be yourself. You're always public. Even when you're in your room, you're busy planning the next day's work. Leaving the site doesn't really remove one psychologically from a preoccupation with the study. It's difficult, this stricture against being my "real" self. I always have to control my reactions and frequently find myself sacrificing spontaneity for strategy.

Organizing field operations.   In the earliest stages of gaining formal entry to the research setting we saw that it was important for the investigator to case the site. Once entry has been achieved it becomes necessary to *extend* this casing in order to gain a picture of the parameters and complexity of the universe to be observed and its components. This is the only means by which the researcher can attempt to be systematic in organizing field operations. Schatzman and Strauss (1973:36) suggest that the researcher organize operations through three maps: social, spatial, and temporal.

The "social map" notes frequencies (the *how much*) and types (the *what*) of persons, roles, channels of communication, status hierarchies, and so on. The "spatial map" locates the *where* of persons, events, power, organizational segments, and channels by which persons and resources pass from one location to another. The "temporal map" deals with the *when* of people and events.

These mapping routines have several important functions. First, they help the researcher know what the *boundaries* and *substance* of data gathering will be. Second, from these mappings, the field researcher may form strategies of *sampling* since he or she cannot possibly look at everything. Third, the maps help to *organize times* and *locations* in the field. Fourth, the maps help to anticipate potential problems (demanding time schedules, problems of hierarchical communication) and unanticipated research foci. Fifth, the maps help him or her judge the magnitude of the research task. Sixth, the mapping tour acts as a means of introduction to the people he or she will later study more intensively.

The final step in organizing research is to *start* observations with the higher echelons and *quickly move on* to lower echelons. Schatzman and Strauss (1973:47–48) explain that this move has two rationales. First, the researcher wishes to establish *independence* from the leadership. Hence, he or she "must not appear to be reporting findings." Second, the "view from the top" is typically a rather special one where the researcher will be able to get a good working start on organizational overview, operations, functions, present and future rationale, and history from which to branch out in observing at lower echelon subsites.

Light (1975) has proposed that the field worker construct a sociological calendar as a device for condensing and analyzing data about social processes. He points out that humans measure their activities and developments through time. In constructing a sociological calendar, the field worker attempts to work out the *latent* units of time in a social organization by contrast to *manifest* units such as days, weeks, and months. In Becker and others' (1961) study of medical students at the University of Kansas Medical School, Light has reanalyzed the socialization process of the medical student through the natural pacing of social events (Figure 4–2). His calendar suggests that the medical school years show clear changes in student perspectives from broad, idealistic concerns with the sick, through pragmatic "getting through" concerns, to a more tempered idealism. Each of these phases is associated with particular social demands placed on the student's time and energy. Hence, the sociological calendar helps the field worker think more rigorously about his or her data and brings out structural relationships between data that might not have been noticed otherwise.

Summary

We have used McCall's six fundamental organizational processes— recruitment, socialization, interaction, innovation, social control, and lo-

Table 4-2
Calendar 1 Changing Perspectives on Idealism, Based on "Boys in White"

Structure	Premed.	High pressure, highly structured lectures, reading, exams		A variety of clinical experiences		Anticipating graduation
Time (Semesters)	Point of entry	1st	2nd–4th	5th	6th–7th	8th
Perspectives (Mid–1950s)	General idealism	From idealism to getting through	Getting through (GT)	From GT to maximizing experience	Maximizing experience (ME)	From ME to tempered idealism
			Suspended idealism			

SOURCE: Light (1975). Reprinted from "The sociological calendar: An analytic tool for fieldwork applied to medical and psychiatric training" by D. Light, Jr. *American Journal of Sociology* 80:1145–1164. By permission of The University of Chicago Press, © 1975 by The University of Chicago.

gistics—to highlight the process of doing field work. Their order is arbitrary because all six processes occur simultaneously and because they influence each other. The following section of this chapter will discuss the problem of quality of field data.

DATA QUALITY CONTROLS

We will see in later chapters that various methods have unique vulnerabilities to invalidation and unreliability. For instance, laboratory experiments are particularly susceptible to effects of the test situation (Rosenthal 1966), and interviews are susceptible to interviewer bias effects (Cannell and Kahn 1968). Field research also is subject to particular invalidating and contaminating factors. Some of these are listed below with some appropriate quality control checks (McCall 1960a:132–135):

Observational Data

Field worker

1. *Reactive Effects*—Where available, the field worker should compare informant interview accounts of similar events where the field worker was not present; if the above is not possible, then he or she should ask informants if the observer's presence seems to affect the events observed.
2. *Ethnocentrism*—Comparison of field worker interpretations with relevant respondent and informant interviews for incomplete or inaccurate interpretations.
3. *Going Native*—Comparison of field notes on comparable observational settings at different points in the research for changes in viewpoint. Reflection on researcher's sympathies and antipathies toward the subjects as sources of bias.

Interview Data

4. *Knowledgeability*—Reflection should be given to whether interviewee gave direct, firsthand data; confidence in his or her objectivity, introspectiveness, interpersonal sensitivity.
5. *Reportorial Ability*—Knowledgeability and ability to report one's knowledge may be independent of one another; therefore, the researcher must consider the reliability of the interviewee's memory, the interviewee's ability to express him- or herself well in detail and on issues that may seem obvious to him- or herself.
6. *Reactive Effects of Interview Situation*—Did the interviewee seem to be straining to give the researcher the kinds of information he or she thinks the researcher wants, or did he or she appear to withhold information?
7. *Ulterior Motives*—Was the interviewee trying to rationalize, muckrake, slant results, expose something, and so on, casting doubt on the account's accuracy?

8. *Bars to Spontaneity*—Did the interviewee seem overanxious about possibilities of being overheard?

9. *Idiosyncratic Factors*—These are mostly what Campbell and Stanley (1963) call maturational or historical effects: the subjects' immediately past mood, fatigue, or drinking. Did such immediately prior factors affect the testimony uncharacteristically? Was there notable discontinuity with previously expressed reports?

Table 4–3 gives a hypothetical example of how the researcher may use the above checks in crudely assessing data quality. For instance, in Table 4–3 reactive effects (category A) were noted four times by the field researcher in observing a single observational event and were absent in nine other notes on the same event. Hence, the data quality for that event is rather good (9/13 or .69).

As McCall points out, these data-quality indexes serve two major purposes (1969a:137). The first is to serve as a quality-control check for the particular factors that may contaminate the data with the intent of reducing their influence on future data. The other is to note in the write-up of the research to what extent the contaminating factors have been avoided.

Table 4–3

Sample Work Table for Determining Data Quality Profile and Data Quality Index on a Single Substantive Point

1 Category of Potential Contamination	2 Influence Present (No. of Items)	3 Influence Absent (No. of Items)	4 Data Quality Value
A	4	9	.69
B	3	10	.77
C	4	9	.69
Observational quality index			.72
D	7	18	.72
E	10	15	.60
F	15	10	.40
G	12	13	.52
H	14	11	.44
I	4	21	.84
Interview quality index			.59
Overall data quality index			.63

SOURCE: McCall (1969a:137). McCall/Simmons, *Issues in Participant Observation*, ©1969, Addison-Wesley Publishing Company, Inc., Table 1 on p. 137. Reprinted with permission.

We stated near the beginning of this chapter that reliability and validity checks are usually built into field research as it proceeds or after it is completed. Confidence in field research would be greater if researchers would get in the habit of using McCall's techniques during the beginning and middle stages of field work as a means of providing direction to the types of data that need to be collected if quality of data is to be improved to the point where it has sufficient reliability and validity. Of course, McCall's techniques only work if the researcher is at least marginally self-aware to begin with. There is no one blinder than one who either will not or cannot see oneself. Thus, ironically, McCall's technique helps but is affected by the same biasing effects it is designed to counter.

The nine quality-control checks also explain why the researcher must maintain *backstage* attitudes of skepticism, cynicism, and introspection. This is not to say that the researcher has to be cynical about human nature. Rather these attitudes are necessary components of the scientific process. One can be no less cynical toward oneself than one is toward one's subjects if one is to be able to properly evaluate the data. In other words, by taking on the role of cynical introspectionist, one tries to give the data the most rigorous data-quality evaluation possible, given the qualitative nature of field data. Such evaluation must include cynical or skeptical role-playing toward all instruments of data collection, including oneself.

Implicit in these introspective role-playings is the awareness that there is reciprocity in any role relationship or transaction. As Schwartz and Schwartz (1955:348) have noted,

> The participant observer is an integral part of the situation he is observing. He is linked with the observed in a reciprocal process of mutual modification. Together the observer and the observed constitute a context which would be different if either participant were different or were eliminated. In the course of an investigation the observer and observed become important to each other, and it is the background of their past experiences together, merging with and reflecting itself in a present situation, which determines the nature of the reciprocity. Continuing observed-observer transactions influence in many ways both the kinds of data that emerge (for the observer creates them to some degree) and the registering, interpreting, and recording of them.

Becker and his associates (1961) take a somewhat different approach to hypotheses evaluation. They analyze field data in a framework like that suggested by Table 4–4. Becker and his associates (1961:43) do not have a strict formula, but only some ground rules for interpreting data in this type of table. First, there should be more volunteered state-

Table 4-4

Becker's Tabular Model for Hypotheses Evaluation

		Volunteered	Directed by the observer	Total
Statements	To observer alone			
	To others in everyday conversation			
Activities	Individual			
	Group			
Total				

SOURCE: Becker, H. S., Geer, B., Hughes, E. C., and Strauss, A. L. *Boys in White: Student Culture in Medical School.* Chicago: University of Chicago Press, 1961, p. 43. Reprinted by permission of the University of Chicago Press, © 1961 by the University of Chicago.

ments than directed ones. Second, there should be a similar or greater number of statements made to others than to the observer alone. If the number of statements made to the observer alone is over 50 percent, then the proposition should be questioned. Third, the activities should make up 20 to 25 percent of the total data collected.

HYPOTHESIS GENERATION

Simple submersion in and observation of data are insufficient, albeit necessary, components of field methods. These data are made important through various techniques of hypothesis generation. This section will explain a few of the more important analytic means used by field researchers in generating and evaluating hypotheses from qualitative data.

Case Analysis: Serendipity and the Single Datum

The serendipitous datum—the surprising, anomalous, and unexplained observation—has long proved to be of interest to sociologists (Merton 1967; Barton and Lazarsfeld 1955) because of the way it redirects theoretical attention. Barton and Lazarsfeld (1955:322) point out that such case observations have two different uses. The first is that they create problems such as trying to explain what they are and what they do.

The second is that some variables may be found in the qualitative observations that cannot be measured directly.

"Observations which raise problems" go against our theoretical or
common-sense expectations. Hence, they provide challenges to scientific
inquiry. Selltiz, Jahoda, Deutsch, and Cook (1959:42) have pointed out
that the field worker, because of his or her role as a stranger or newcomer
to an organization, is in a good position to pick out problematic facts that
are taken for granted by those accustomed to the locale. Hence, probably,
most serendipitous data are noticed in the beginning stages of field work,
before the observer has grown accustomed to the research setting. The
strategy of "leaving the field" at periodic intervals also contributes to
fresher perspectives. Upon reentrance into the field setting the researcher will have regained some of his or her ethnocentrism that, however short-lived, may give much leverage in terms of observing things
that otherwise might have been unnoticed or taken for granted. Informants who hold particular types of marginal or deviant roles may be
helpful in generating unexpected data. Dean and others (1967:284) have
listed the following kinds of informants as useful sources of such information:

1. Informants who are especially sensitive to the area of concern.

    The *outsider,* who sees things from the vantage point of another culture,
    social class, or community.

    The *rookie,* who is surprised by what goes on and notes the taken-for-
    granted things that the acclimated miss. And, as yet, he or she may have
    no stake in the system to protect.

    The *nouveau statused,* who is in transition from one position to another
    where the tensions of new experience are vivid.

    The naturally *reflective and objective person* in the field. He or she can
    sometimes be pointed out by others of his or her kind.

2. The *more-willing-to-reveal informants.* Because of their background or status,
   some informants are just more willing to talk than others.

    The *naive informant,* who knows not whereof he or she speaks. He or she
    may be either naive as to what the field worker represents or naive about
    his or her own group.

    The *frustrated person,* who may be a rebel or malcontent, especially the one
    who is consciously aware of blocked drives and impulses.

    The *"outs,"* who have lost power but are "in-the-know." Some of the
    "ins" may be eager to reveal negative facts about their colleagues.

    The *habitue* or *"old hand,"* or *"fixture,"* who no longer has a stake in the
    venture or is so secure that he or she is not jeopardized by exposing what
    others say or do.

    The *needy person,* who fastens onto the interviewer because he or she
    craves attention and support. As long as the interviewer satisfies this need,
    he or she will talk.

The *subordinate,* who must adapt to superiors. He or she generally develops insights to cushion the impact of authority and may be hostile and willing to "blow up."

Of course, not only does each of these types of informants give useful and unique types of information; they each also present unique sources of bias. Hence, the researcher must always be aware of the dangers of reliance on each as sources of data.

Some single observations, while not surprising in and of themselves, may have usefulness as indirect measures of qualitative social and behavioral variables. Barton and Lazarsfeld (1955:329) give a good example of indirect measurement of social contact between two neighboring towns.

> During the heyday of Crystal her people and those of Mineville were not so well acquainted as might be supposed. . . . Hotly contested baseball games and the communities having celebrated together on the main day of festivities for each—Miner's Union Day—were not indications of far-reaching person relations. This is shown by the measure of social distance evidenced by the fact that a young man whose reputation was such in one town that its "respectable" girls refused to associate with him could go to the other and fraternize with its "best" young women.

Qualitative Typologies and Analytic Induction

Qualitative typologies have proven to be one of the best means by which one takes large amounts of raw data and attempts to summarize them. For instance, Ball (1972) created an ordinal classification system of games.

	Value
No game of any type	0
Chance only	1
Strategy only	2
Skill only	3
Strategy and chance	4
Chance and skill	5
Skill and strategy	6
Strategy and skill and chance	7

At one end of a continuum may be placed typologies that are a simple, crude list of types such as Clark and Trow's (1960) typology of college student roles: "Joe College," "Don's," "Vocational," and "Nonconformist." Each of these types is defined individually without clear logical relationship to the others. At the other extreme are typologies like

Ball's in which each type is a systematic and logical compound of a small number of attributes. In either case, the researcher may artfully provide a classification that includes basic elements or dimensions summarizing the raw data.

Sometimes one finds it useful to take two or more such qualitative typologies and cross-classify them to obtain a set of logical typological combinations. An example is Becker's (1963) typology for the study of deviance.

	Obedient Behavior	*Rule-Breaking Behavior*
Individual perceived as deviant	Falsely accused deviancy	Pure deviant
Individual not perceived as deviant	Conforming	Secret deviant

One of the more prevalent qualitative typology techniques is the *analytic induction method* (Robinson 1951). Analytic induction studies the conditions, C, under which some phenomenon, P, occurs, as shown in Table 4–5.

Quite simply, one takes cases where the phenomenon (P) occurs or does not occur ($\bar{P}$) and tabulates for each whether the conditions under which that phenomenon (or lack of it) are present (C) or not ($\bar{C}$). Strictly speaking, the researcher hopes that the upper-right and lower-left cells are void of cases for the condition C to be both a necessary and sufficient explanation of P. However, if the upper-right-hand cell has cases and the lower-left cell is void, then he or she still may say that C is a necessary albeit insufficient condition for P to occur. If the lower-left cell has cases and the upper right cell is void, he or she may say that C is a sufficient but not necessary condition for P to occur. If only a small portion of cases are found in either the lower-left or upper-right cells then one has only

Table 4–5
Fourfold Table for Analytic Induction Demonstration

	P	$\bar{P}$
C	X	?
$\bar{C}$	0	X

SOURCE: W. S. Robinson, "*The Logical Structure of Analytic Induction*," *ASR*, 16(1951), 816.

a weaker interpretation left—namely, that P and C tend to co-occur, or (if a causal hypothesis) that the occurrence of P is a partial condition, though not sufficient or necessary, for C's occurrence.

Rather than coding data into a scheme such as is suggested in Table 4-5 and *then* analyzing it, Glazer (1965) has suggested that coding and analyses be combined for discovery of theory; this is what he calls the *constant comparative method.* In this method one starts out by "coding each incident in the data in as many categories of analysis as possible" (Glazer 1965:440). After a few codings the researcher may find a conflict in how or why to code some instance theoretically that will call for logically reconciling recordings. Glazer (1965:441–442) points out that

> ... as the coding continues the constant comparative units change *from* comparison of incident with incident *to* incident with properties of the category which resulted from initial comparison of incidents. For example, in comparing incident with incident we discovered the property that nurses are constantly recalculating a patient's social loss as they learned more about him. From then on each incident on calculation was compared to accummulated knowledge on calculating, not to all other incidents of calculation.

Note that as has been pointed out by Becker (1958:653) participant observation has *sequential* operations: "Important parts of the analysis [are] being made while the researcher is still gathering his data." This provisional analysis not only gives direction to further data gathering, it also gives direction to reliability checks and to further hypotheses generation.

HYPOTHESIS EVALUATION

In Chapter 3 we considered a number of rules for formalizing and operationalizing our hypotheses. A distinction we did not make at that time which has some utility in evaluation or testing of hypotheses is the difference between *descriptive* and *causal* hypotheses. A descriptive proposition infers only simple association between two or more variables such as in the hypothesis "the greater the person's status inconsistency, the more politically liberal his or her beliefs." A causal hypothesis would infer the determination of one variable from the other in addition to simple association, as in "greater status inconsistencies cause greater liberalization of political belief." Since each type of proposition is based on different criteria, the evaluation of each type is best handled separately.

Descriptive Hypotheses

In order to assess a hypothesized association between variables, McCall and Simmons (1969b:229–230)[2] point out the need to determine

1. How accurately population members are classified in terms of the variables
2. How accurate the sampling was from the population in respect to such variable classifications
3. The pattern of the results of such classification as compared to that asserted in the proposition.

The approach taken in evaluating the hypothesis will depend on when the hypothesis emerged (McCall 1969b:237).

1. The *interpretation of incidents* approach is used when a hypothesis emerges (when the researcher is analyzing the data) either after data collection is completed or too late in the collection to follow that particular lead. These hypotheses usually have little effect on the researcher's major conclusions.
2. *Pinpointing operations* are used when "hypotheses emerge during data collection and there is enough time left to collect data on that hypothesis, but it is not important enough to warrant in-depth study."
3. The *measurement approach* is used for central propositions that usually emerge early in data collection and warrant in-depth study.

In the "interpretation of incidents" approach the researcher sifts through the data sorting according to similarity of account content; he or she then attempts to make sense theoretically out of these sortings. "Pinpointing operations" refers to the formulation of uniform and specific combinations of theoretical indicators that are applied to all cases relevant to evidence for or against a proposition. "Measurement" refers to logical deductions as to a number of operationalizations which could indicate a theoretical construct (McCall 1969b).

Causal Hypotheses

Two criteria which must be evaluated in causal hypothesis evaluation in addition to the association factor already mentioned for descriptive hypotheses are (1) proper time sequencing of the variables and (2) rival causal explanations. While field research rarely discredits most of the rival causal hypotheses, the more rival explanations discounted, the

[2]McCall/Simmons, eds., *Issues in Participant Observation: A Text and Reader* (Reading, Mass.: Addison-Wesley, 1969).

greater the credibility of the field work data conclusion. The time sequencing of the variables implies that the independent variables must be shown to have either preceded, or occurred simultaneously with, the dependent variable. Thus, as long as the dependent variable can be shown not to have preceded the independent variable causal explanation, it is rendered plausible. Notice, however, that the field researcher can never prove that just because two variables are associated and time-ordered and other rival explanations are discounted that therefore one variable causally determines the other—he or she can only add substantial weight to the argument of causality.

FIELD TRAINING, RELIABILITY, AND VALIDITY

While reliability and validity are matters that can be handled to some extent while in the field, as shown in the last two sections, concern with reliability and validity should be built into training sessions before field work begins. Unfortunately, little thought has been given to field training techniques in the past. Training techniques discussed in Chapters 6 (Survey Methods) and 5 (Structured Observation) may profitably be of use in field worker training. On the other hand, Bennett (1960) points out that field work is more than a set of techniques for the collection of data. Bennett, accordingly, has designed a course contrived to train field workers. The first part of his course has standard formal instruction in specific field-work techniques such as rapport, informant interviewing, and the like.

The second part of the course is designed to make students aware of individual perspectives as a significant element in observation and interpretation. Ethnographic documentary films unfamiliar to the students are shown to the classes for the students to practice observational note taking. Finally, students actually put these techniques to use in some social setting. During the second and third phases of the course students and professor analyze each other's notes.

Some conclusions of general interest to field work have been noted concerning individual perceptual approaches to observation and interpretation. Three general observation patterns have been found (Bennett 1960:436–438): (1) The "empirical ethnographer" records events in chronological order. Descriptions are detailed and no interpretations are made. For example, a group of children is described as being absorbed in learning manual skills, each playing alone in spite of physical proximity to other children. (2) The "holistic ethnographer" makes gestalts, emphasizing the "emotional-aesthetic" whole and interpreting to some extent. A holistic ethnographer would describe the same group of children by emphasizing how slow their movements were and the periods when the children simply sat still. (3) The "social anthropologist," being mostly in social structure and system, summarizes details and emphasizes interpersonal relations. For example, the children are described as being easily distracted, and the speed of their movements is described as being affected by their mood.

In addition, some students showed highly idiosyncratic variations in observation and interpretation (Bennett 1960:436).

1. Subjective introjection of sensual feeling tone—identification of textures, guesses as to odors and tastes, inferences or observations as to emotional states of characters
2. Use of adjectives in description—some avoided this completely, others used them more or less carefully
3. Use of personal experiences and cultural comparisons—"this society resembles my own. . . ."
4. Use of ready-made frames of reference—"feudal, authoritarian system," "rigid sex mores," "the woman's role is subordinate to the man's."

If significant progress in higher reliability and validity is to be made in field work, thought will have to be given (1) to making field workers more aware of these types of biases in their own work and (2) to techniques for training field workers into or out of these perceptual patterns as dictated by the nature of particular field research needs. We noted earlier in this chapter that the model field worker starts out by noting the "what, when, where, and how much" of any field setting. This is comparable to Bennett's "empirical ethnographer" pattern. Toward the middle portions of the field project more time is spent on the "how and why" of the setting. The researcher becomes more interested in interpretive reconstruction of the data. Finally, the "analytic memo" scheme of note taking proposed by Schatzman and Strauss (1973) comes into play during later stages of model field work and is comparable to the "social anthropologist" pattern.

Field method reliability and validity depend in large part on *what* is being observed *when.* Poggie (1972) has shown that field data quality is in large part a function of its *reliability.* That is, he found that key informants were "most precise in the domains of reporting in which they are reliable." By comparing social survey data to his key informants' reports, Poggie found his informants to give the most valid information in response to directly observable public phenomena, concrete referents, and noncontroversial responses requiring little evaluation or inference (What percentage of the houses here are made of adobe?). The least valid responses were those to questions concerning information about non-directly observable matters (What percentage of the people sleep in beds?).

Erickson (1973) has extended Poggie's arguments in the time dimension. He presents evidence indicating that reliability and validity vary in predictable manners over the course of a field study (see Figure 4–1).

Figure 4–1 shows that the dangers of the two greatest sources of poor data quality are inversely related. At the start and finish of field work, there is minimal danger of going native and great danger of ethnocentrism. In the middle of field work the situation reverses itself with the greatest danger from going native and the least danger from ethnocentrism. Data collected at times 2 and 4 are viewed, by Erickson, as being the least contaminated by going native and ethnocentrism. Therefore, he believes that data collected at those times should be weighted more (by contrast to data collected at other times) in hypotheses testing.

Erickson also suggests that field training include sessions devoted solely to recording self-observations while in the field. Such sessions could be helpful as exercises in data-quality diagnosis. Further, self-observation diagnostics may suggest needed revision of the study design.

In the past, field studies have given little attention to means of evaluating and increasing reliability and validity. This chapter has focused on such means in large part because of the unique contributions to knowledge field studies can impact when carried out in a manner consistent with standards of scientific rigor. It is hoped that this chapter has shown that quality field data may be collected with good validity and reliability. Many researchers, trained since World War II, have looked down upon field studies as somehow unreliable and imprecise measurement devices. We know now, however, in large part due to the persistent

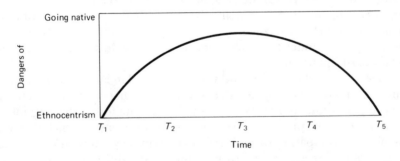

FIGURE 4–1 *Hypothesized relation of going native and ethnocentrism to data quality over time.*

Source: Erickson (1973).

experimentation of field workers such as Schatzman and Strauss, McCall, and Bennett, that field workers can be trained in ways that meet high standards of reliability and validity.

> [Participant observation] refers to a characteristic blend or combination of methods and techniques. . . . [it] involves some amount of genuinely social interaction in the field with the subjects of the study, some direct observation of relevant events, some formal and a great deal of informal interviewing, some systematic counting, some collection of documents and artifacts, and open-endedness in the direction the study takes. (McCall and Simmons 1969:1)

As evidenced by the above quote, field research techniques in general, and that part of field research known as participant observation in particular, are eclectic. Field research involves a little of the topics to be described in later chapters on sampling, measurement and scaling, interviewing, and unobtrusive methods. However, field study involves a distinctive attitude toward research and combination of methods.

Several words may help further an understanding of what field research is and how it is differentiated from other methods. First, participant observation *need not* be less systematic than other methods. Social situations that have a relatively high degree of known organization may be more profitably served through more structured methods, while less structured social situations or those where the structure or organization is not known to the researcher beforehand may be more usefully studied through participant observation—particularly in the early stages of research. We will note in Chapter 13 that all data collection is subject to certain sorts of bias and that sometimes the biases can be systematized and dealt with. Thus, an important difference between unstructured participant observation and the more structured techniques described in Chapter 5 is typically our *awareness* of bias. For example, structured observational biases tend to be more explicit, while participant observational biases, though perhaps just as systematic, tend to be more hidden from view. More important, they are different types of biases. The source of participant observation biases tends to come from the interactional nature of the observer's role, while structured observational biases tend to arise from biases built into the coding system.

Second, while the *implicit* nature of participant observation biases is often viewed as a basic weakness of the method's reliability and validity, field methods often incorporate a number of internal checks on reliability and validity. Stated somewhat differently, other techniques normally have reliability and validity built into the observational instrument *prior* to their use; participant observation normally builds in reliability and validity checks *prior to, during, and after* observation.

Third, participant observation data, while usually much more open-ended in nature than data based on other methodologies, generally can be systematically coded after the fact. An extended example of these reliability and validity checks and systematic coding procedures has been given in an earlier section of this chapter. The open-endedness of field research may be considered one of field research's strong points in the study of social situations where little is known beforehand about organization, structure, and other key factors.

Fourth, another key advantage of field research is its ability to shed light on *processes* or *dynamics* of social situations. Field research data can be gathered over long periods of time for many variables. Other methods rarely approach this adaptability to the study of social dynamics. For instance, structured observations may be gathered over long time periods but usually for only one or a few variables. Surveys, on the other hand, can be used to collect data on a large number of variables but are generally impractical for reuse on the same populations more than a few times.

Fifth, "sampling in participant observation is not completely or finally designed and executed in advance of data collection but is continually carried on through the study" (McCall and Simmons 1969:64). While some type of sampling method is generally used in field studies, unlike most other methods it will not be fully prescribed in advance but is likely to be dictated by the emerging field situation and theory.

READINGS FOR ADVANCED STUDENTS

R. Bogdan and S. J. Taylor, *Introduction to Qualitative Research Methods,* 1975. Many practical "how to do it" suggestions make this an excellent text for the beginner to field research.

F. Gearing and W. Hughes, *On Observing Well: Self-Instruction in Ethnographic Observation for Teachers, Principals and Supervisors,* 1975. Available for $3.00 payable by check to SUNY at Buffalo, to the Center for Studies of Cultural Transmission. Excellent introduction on how to do ethnography and put it to practical use.

B. Glazer and A. L. Strauss, *The Discovery of Grounded Theory,* 1967. Shows how one may use analytic induction procedures in generating theory from qualitative data.

R. W. Habenstein (ed.), *Pathways to Data,* 1970. Excellent suggestions for one of the biggest problems in field work: getting access to the research setting.

L. Schatzman and A. L. Strauss, *Field Research,* 1973. Compact but informative account of strategies for entering, organizing, watching, listening, recording, analyzing, and communicating in field research.

H. Schwartz and J. Jacobs, *Qualitative Sociology: A Method to the Madness,* 1979. Excellent account of specialized field research topics and qualitative methodologies such as formal sociology, ethnomethodology, and phenomenology that are beyond the scope of an introductory text.

SUGGESTED RESEARCH PROJECTS

1. Take as detailed field notes as possible while viewing an ethnographic documentary film *without sound.* (If your university has none in stock both the University of Texas and Indiana University, among other sources, have a wide film selection at nominal cost.) Compare your notes with other observers' in terms of the particular perceptual schemes noted in the chapter.

2. The same as Project 1 above, but the film is shown with sound this time and you are to take notes on assigned subjects (male-female roles, physical setting) and write up notes after class at home. Notes should be analyzed in class for the abundance of detail recorded, feel for aesthetic description and interpretation, nature of inference made, questions or hypotheses raised for further exploration, discernible biases.

3. Find one person who is representative of a "culture," group, or organization (president of a college fraternity, "old settler" in house-trailer camp, and so on). Give an exploratory, nondirective interview with the objective of getting a "feel" for the person and his or her culture. From this interview construct a more focused list of questions worthy of theoretical follow-up. In writing up your field experience include: (a) the final observational notes, (b) methodological notes including self-observations, and (c) some theoretical notes that lead into your (d) follow-up question list.

4. In the following exercises you are to provide a brief field report in the style of Appendix X and incorporating earlier suggestions on taking field notes:

   a. Observe *new* members of some group and report on socialization techniques used.

   b. Conduct an analysis of some job area open to the public (emergency room, train depot, store, restaurant) and compare and contrast your findings with those of another student in terms of the social consequences of the settings' social and physical characteristics.

   c. Describe the interaction in a primary group to which you belong. Focus on negotiations between persons. After data collection, attempt to organize the raw data, using Appendix A as a model and following this framework: (1) the *extent,* or range and temporal duration of the negotiations; (2) the *stages* of negotiation, such as goal communication; (3) *strategies,* ranging from payoffs to bargains, group pressure, or to stalemates, and (4) *outcomes* such as win-lose, no compromise, and evolved beliefs.

5. An exercise for community field-work acclimation is to choose a neighborhood that is unfamiliar to you. To "get to know" the community, map and enumerate residences in the area. Walk through all parts of the neighborhood; look at each structure. Note abandoned buildings and differential residential densities. For each block draw a map with every building on the block, labelling the building by street address, making an estimate of the number of housing units in the building, indicating whether the building is occupied or vacant. After estimating the number of persons living in each building, attempt to gain entry to the building to query residents on the number of people in each building or unit. Make a note of actual versus estimated numbers of units and persons.

5

Structured Observation

The emphasis on public observations in science has had a misleading quality insofar as it implies that any intelligent man can replicate a scientist's observations. This might have been true early in the history of science, but nowadays only the trained observer can replicate many observations. [1]

Any scientific theory must have observable consequences. It also must be possible to make predictions from that theory that can be verified by observations. One area of observation involves self-reported observations in the nature of attitudinal and survey-type data. However, this type of data is of a private nature in the sense that it can be verified only by the individual reporting the behavior. Unfortunately, even though many people are able to communicate their experiences to themselves and others, many others are unable to conceptualize certain of their own

---

[1]Charles Tart, "States of Consciousness and State-Specific Sciences," *Science* 176 (1972), 1205.

experiences for themselves, much less adequately communicate them to others.

Comparisons of direct observations of mother-child interaction with the mothers' self-reports show large discrepancies. Mothers tend to report that they spend about four hours daily interacting with their children age six or less. Trained observers with stop watches have come up with contrasting estimates of approximately one half hour, of which a good portion of the interaction is of a negative sort ("Go out and play in the sandbox, Johnny"; "Keep yourself busy fingerpainting while Mommy does the dishes" [Yarrow, Campbell, and Burton 1964]). Similarly, most persons believe they spend large amounts of time talking, yet experts in the area of nonverbal communication estimate that less than 15 percent of our daily waking hours are devoted to verbal behavior (Birdwhistell 1970).

Self-reported data are simply inadequate for recording the complexities of many kinds of interactions. No parent could possibly remember how many times he or she smiled at an infant during a feeding, nor what stimuli evoked his or her smiles. This points to another, more basic problem discussed in the Tart quotation above: the fact that even intelligent humans may not be able to observe in the same manner as trained observers. Brazelton and others (1974) have analyzed films of mother-child interaction in terms of what and how stimuli evoke responses. They found quite subtle interactional periods in which a mother subconsciously *followed* the baby's *lead* by decreasing her behaviors in response to the baby's decrease in his or her own behaviors. *Who* is *actually* socializing whom versus *who thinks* she is socializing whom?

Much of the difference between the ways in which the scientist and layperson observe hinges on paradigms. The scientists trained in structured observational techniques may well use quite different assumptions, rules of logic, and means of communication (both to themselves and to others). Tart (1972:1208) suspects that

> . . . there are enormous differences between the states of consciousness of some normal people. Because societies train people to behave and communicate along socially approved lines, these differences are covered up.
>
> For example, some people think in images, others in words. Some can voluntarily anesthetize parts of their body, most can not. Some recall past events by imagining the scene and looking at the relevant details; others use complex verbal processes with no images.

Scientific communities also intensively train their graduate students over relatively long periods of time. This training includes techniques of systematically observing various phenomena of professional interest. For instance, ecologists are trained to make quick, yet accurate, estimations of the size of animal herds. Ethologists often come to know *individual* members of beehives, bird flocks, and baboon colonies at sight. As the social and behavioral sciences have matured, they too have come to recognize the need for reorganizing and structuring their direct observations of individuals and groups. In large part the recognition of this need has hinged on the scientific dictum of *consensual validation:* There must be reliability of observations between trained observers.

WHY USE STRUCTURED OBSERVATION METHODS? SOME PROS AND CONS

One reason for structuring observations has already been alluded to: the more structured the measurements, the more clarity that may be given to a particular theory. Second, the fact that the *form* of observation schemes reconceptualizes a given phenomenon may lead to reformulated and serendipitous theory. Willard and Strodtbeck's (1972) systematic observation of latency of verbal response (average time taken to begin speaking when asked to complete sentence stubs) has recently been shown to be a more effective predictor of individual participation in groups than past, alternative predictors.

Third, as we will see in Chapter 6, recall of past behavior and events through questionnaires and interviews is often highly unreliable. Thus, a preferable alternative may be to observe directly behavior or events. Direct observation often has higher quality than recalled information. A good example of this again comes from studies of mother-child interaction. Survey evidence indicates that most American mothers appear to be convinced that their male babies are (or were) more active and aggressive than their female babies. Careful observations by Will, Self, and Datan of babies—whose gender was unknown to the observers—less than six months old have failed to replicate "common sense" experiences of gender differences in motor behavior, exploratory behavior, and so on (*Behavior Today,* October 7, 1974).

Fourth, structured observational measures are adaptable to many different research settings. On the one hand, one can apply structured observations within experimental settings. On the other hand, many naturalistic behaviors and social events have sufficient formality, habituation, regularity, or stability that they are sufficiently open to structured observation (Weick 1968; Reiss 1971). Indeed, as Reiss (1971:8) points out,

It is no easy matter to conclude that an event is not amenable to systematic observation. . . . One can easily become convinced that a theoretically observable event is not amenable because the design precludes observation. Nowhere is this more apparent than when questions are raised about past behavior in relation to present behavior. Clearly one can not observe the past.

Fifth, participants often are in no position to introspect. Children may not be able to respond verbally or in writing; adults may not be detached enough about their children's behavior to recall various events or behaviors. Or they may be too inarticulate, as in Riesman and Watson's (1964:313) study of cocktail party behavior where "people had no language for discussing sociable encounters."

GENERIC FACETS
OF STRUCTURED OBSERVATION

Structured observation has several facets that distinguish it from most everyday observation. First, structured observation is relatively precise in specification of what is to be observed, ignored, and recorded. Second, structured observation, as already pointed out, may entail the use of measuring techniques and instruments that are foreign to common everyday observations.

There are a number of features that most structured observational techniques are consciously designed to measure: form, duration, frequency, antecedents, and consequences of particular behaviors and social structures, and relationships between behaviors, attitudes, and social structures. Of these features, observational *form* is generally the most abstract from common everyday observations. While some observational forms may have a common-sensical meaning (Bales's [1970] distinction between questions, attempted answers, positive and negative reactions), many of the observational techniques that will be discussed in the next section of this chapter are not intuitively obvious social and behavioral measurement instruments—their observational *form* is based more in scientific validation rather than everyday validation. For instance, eye-blink rates (which have been used by some scientists as a measure of anxiety) have typically been thought of by the layperson as invariant and nonsocially determined. However, in this particular case, predictive validation studies (Ponder and Kennedy 1927) have established the usefulness of eye-blink rates as measures of social anxiety.

Duration of an observational form refers simply to the length of time the form lasts. Duration can be a particularly important, albeit a simple measure of social and behavioral patterns. Harrison and others' (1978) study of cues to deception showed that deceptive answers were longer in length and were preceded by greater hesitations than nondeceptive answers.

Frequency of observed social or behavioral units refers to the number of times any event recurs in a given period. Frequency may either be calibrated in terms of *absolute* number of recurrences or *relative* (percentage) number of occurrences. Gerbner (1978) and his associates have been interested in monitoring changes in the frequency of violent television-character portrayals during prime time viewing hours, including gender of the perpetrator and victim of the violence. He has found associations between occurrences of violent portrayals on television and children's actual use of violent behavior by children who viewed these programs.

Antecedent and *consequent* behavior-pattern studies direct attention towards the types of behaviors (or social structures) that precede or follow other behaviors (or social structures) in time. That is, each facet deals with complementary aspects of social and behavioral developmental patterns. At relatively microlevels of data collection, for instance, Brazelton and others' (1974) study of mother-infant interaction found clear antecedent-consequent patterns as shown in Figure 5–1. Time is measured in seconds on the horizontal axis and the number of behaviors on the vertical axis. A line above the horizontal axis indicates that the person was looking *at* his or her partner; below the horizontal axis it indicates the person was looking *away* from his or her partner. Clear antecedent-consequent patterns of attention-nonattention sensitivities are shown in Figure 5–1. To quote from Brazelton and others (1974:63),

> ... the mother and baby are looking at each other, smiling and vocalizing together. The baby begins to cycle and reach out to her. At *a* he begins to turn away from her. She responds by looking down at her hands, and she stops her activity briefly. This brings him back to look at her at *c*. Her smiling, vocalizing, and leaning toward him bring a smiling response from him. In addition, his arms and legs cycle and he coos contentedly as he watches her. As he turns away she first adds another behavior and gestures. He, however, adds to his activities extraneous to her reminders and turns away from her. She gradually cuts out all her activity and by *e* she looks away from him. Immediately afterward he begins to look back to her, and the cycle of looking at each other begins again at *f.*

At more macroscopic levels, Wohnstein and McPhail (1979) have attempted to identify the antecedent forms of collective behavior such as

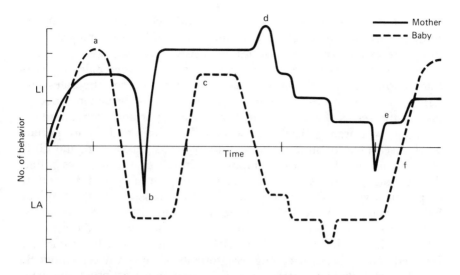

FIGURE 5–1 *Number of behaviors added in a five-second interaction.*

Source: Brazelton, T. V., B. Koslowski, and M. Main. "The origins of reciprocity: The early mother-infant interaction," in *The Effect of the Infant on Its Caregiver,* M. Lewis and L. A. Rosenblum, eds. Copyright 1974 by John Wiley & Sons, Inc. Reprinted by permission of John Wiley & Sons, Inc.

the size, shape, and locomotive patterns of small clusters of persons during formative stages of large crowd gatherings through measures of size, direction, and velocity of movement of collective locomotion.

OBSERVATIONAL PARADIGMS

Following the lead of Weick (1968:381), we shall distinguish among and discuss four general classes of observational paradigms: linguistic, extralinguistic, nonverbal (body movement), and spatial. However, we shall see that there is considerable overlap (blurring) of these distinctions in some observational systems.

Linguistic Measures

Social and behavioral scientists have paid more attention to the development and use of structured verbal observations than to other types of behavioral observations. This is somewhat unfortunate. Research on the importance of verbal versus nonverbal communication (Birdwhistell 1970) indicates that verbalizations make up only about one-half of the communication compared to nonverbalizations in various studies. Further, studies of *what* is communicated by either means often show interesting redundancies and inconsistencies.

The most generally known and used system has been Bales's (1970) Interaction Process Analysis Schema. Ironically, however, the Bales system has not yet contributed much to sociological or behavioral theory. Part of the reason for its lack of theoretical importance may hinge on criticisms by Borgatta (1962) that (1) the Bales system does not permit much discrimination in terms of *intensity* of verbal interaction, and (2) it obscures some theoretically important interaction categories while differentiating between others that have never proven to be of theoretical or practical value. Thus, Borgatta (1962:279) has revised the original Bales formulation. Borgatta's revision, Interaction Process Scores (IPS), is shown in Table 5–1. The numbers in parentheses show the major relationships of the original Bales IPA with the revised Borgatta IPS. Detailed instructions for coding assignments are given in Appendix B.

IPA and IPS have been more widely used than most other linguistic observational schemes because of their general adaptiveness to a large variety of situations. IPA has been used to study differences between normal and psychotherapeutic groups, leadership and follower roles,

Table 5–1
Interaction Process Scores Categories

01	Common social acknowledgments (1a)
02	Shows solidarity through raising the status of others (1b)
03	Shows tension release, laughs (2)
04	Acknowledges, understands, recognizes (3a)
05	Shows agreement, concurrence, compliance (3b)
06	Gives a procedural suggestion (4a)
07	Suggests a solution (4b)
08	Gives opinion, evaluation, analysis, expresses feelings or wish (5a)
09	Self-analysis and self-questioning behavior (5b)
10	Reference to the external situations as redirected aggression (5c)
11	Gives orientation, information, passes communication (6a)
12	Draws attention, repeats, clarifies (6b)
13	Asks for opinion, evaluation, analysis, expression of feelings (8)
14	Disagrees, maintains a contrary position (10)
15	Shows tension, asks for help by virtue of personal inadequacy (11a)
16	Shows tension increase (11b)
17	Shows antagonism, hostility, is demanding (12a)
18	Ego defensiveness (12b)

SOURCE: Borgatta (1962:220).

group performance characteristics, effects of group size on performance, and developmental trends in small group discussions, among other things. In addition to the above areas, IPS has been adapted to research concerned with peer ratings, role-playing, and child socialization into adult interaction patterns.

A quite different observational tactic has been developed for the study of encounter groups by Marks (1972). Her Encounter Group Observation Method (E. GOM.; see Table 5–2) focuses on three types of group processes: transitions, episodes, and interludes. Marks provides intercoder reliability rates ranging from 0.75 to 1.00. This system has proved theoretically interesting in discriminating between high- and low-change encounter groups.

There are a number of other systems for systematically uncovering more specific aspects of interaction. Simon and Boyer (1974) have edited an exhaustive anthology of observational instruments with data on quality which is worthwhile checking before attempting to formulate a new system. Their anthology includes instruments for the gamut of interactional situations that could be observed.

Any currently available scheme for structuring and observing social interaction has certain disadvantages. First, the word "interaction" in IPA, IPS, and other such schemes is misleading in the sense that interdependent *inter*actions are *not* observed—rather, what one person says or does to another person is coded. Smith (1972*a*) has discussed this problem at length in terms of how one "knows" whether several people are simply coacting in each other's presence or actually interacting. Regardless of the methods used, it is apparent that IPS, IPA, and similar schemes are based in large part on an *inferential* process.

Perhaps the best way of attacking the observation of social interaction is to use a number of different structured methods. Smith (1970) has used traditional IPS along with action-reaction tables (Raush 1965), as well as measures of the amount of, types of, and concurrent (simultaneously occurring) verbal actions in groups. This methodology points to two more weaknesses of the traditional interaction process systems. That is, second, they usually grossly ignore the *complexity* of interaction; and, third, they have traditionally been concerned only with *sequentially* occurring interaction while ignoring *simultaneously* occurring interaction. More attention will have to be given to multiple interactional indicators and to simultaneous interaction analysis. Fourth, linguistic observational paradigms have consistently shown biases of central tendency, coding relativism, and contamination from associated cues (Campbell 1958).

Central tendency biases were first noted by Bales (1950). He noted that observers tended to choose less affectual coding categories. Thus, he

Table 5–2

Encounter Group Observation Methods

Group Process Categories

Transitions: Transitions are defined as: a brief series of interactions or events in a group which suggest a change in direction or process.

Episodes: Episodes are packages of group interaction. An episode is defined as a period of group interaction (minimally 3 or 4 minutes but often longer) which
1. occurs between two transitions and
2. has a unitary surface content.

Interludes: Interludes are periods of interaction of any duration in which there is no sense of direction for the group.

Transition Categories

Primary Types

A shift in focus or content: A shift from one or more speakers to another or others and/or a shift from one topic to another.

A shift in the level of feeling: A shift in the intensity of expression (verbal or nonverbal) or feelings present in the group as a whole.

A shift in specificity: A shift from specific-to-general or general-to-specific in content focus, target person(s), or feeling level.

Subsidiary Types

Silence: Any whole group silence 10 seconds or longer.

Structured leader intervention: Any leader intervention with structured suggestions that the group then carries out.

Unstructured leader intervention: Any leader statement that redirects the group interaction but which is not structured or agendized.

Episode Categories

Introduction-Warm Up: An episode in which members are clearly introducing themselves to each other, getting acquainted or reacquainted and/or are clearly "introducing" (warming-up for) the group meeting.

Play: An episode in which the group is having fun together with a clearly positive feeling in the group as a whole and without noticeable tension.

External Discussion: An episode in which the group is talking about things related to the group (the "here-and-now") but on a discussion level with little or no feeling

Table 5-2
Continued

	Episode Categories (continued)
	involved or personal importance attached to the discussion.
Meaning Exploration/ Expression:	An episode in which one or more members express and/or explore personally important and meaningful statements, where the major focus is on the meaningful content and not on the direct, raw, or unmediated expression of feeling.
Feeling Exploration/ Expression:	An episode in which one or more members are directly expressing and/or exploring feeling statements for themselves or with each other.
Problem Work/ Confrontation:	An episode in which an individual's, dyad's, or group problem or conflict is being directly confronted and worked at on a feeling level and/or an episode in which members are enacting basic feelings towards or with each other.

SOURCE: Marks (1972).

suggested (arbitrarily) that when a choice could be made between a more affective and less affective code, that the more affective one should be chosen.

Coding relativism means simply that one is coding more recent behaviors relative to past behaviors. While this may not produce much bias within a particular observational setting, it is possible that bias may be much greater *between* quite "foreign" settings (child versus adult, "deviant" versus "normal"), since behaviors are more likely to be judged by the current setting. That is, coding may well be more influenced by *contamination from associated cues* (Campbell 1958:356).

Extralinguistic Measures

Mahl (1957) has classified extralinguistic behaviors by their vocal, temporal, interactional, and verbal-stylistic dimensions. The *vocal dimension* includes pitch, loudness, and timbre among its characteristics. An instrument known as a voice spectrometer (Hargreaves and Starkweather 1963) records such variation in verbal behavior with good accuracy. Soskin and Kauffman (1961) have shown that judges can with reasonable accuracy infer emotional states of speakers from voice spectrometer readings alone.

The *temporal dimension* refers to such things as rates of speaking, duration of utterances, and rhythm. One of the few sociologists to concern himself with time patterns, Chapple (1949) developed an interaction chronograph to assess temporal aspects of interaction. More recent innovations such as Automatic Vocal Transaction Analyzers (Cassota, Jaffee, Feldstein, and Moses 1964) are less inferential in that they do not require an observer's presence to record sound-silence and intensity fluctuation sequences of subjects. Another temporal indicator that has proven useful recently in the study of small group interaction is the previously mentioned latency of verbal response (Willard and Strodtbeck 1972).

Continuity of speech is an extralinguistic dimension that includes patterns of hesitation, interruptions, and errors. Smith (1970) has shown interruption patterns indicative of socialization from child into adult interpersonal relations.

A final example of continuity of speech measures of potential relevance to sociologists is Mahl's (1959) Speech Disturbance ratio. Sentence changes, repetitions, stutters, omissions, incomplete sentences, tongue slips, and incoherent sounds are summed and divided by the number of words spoken by the subject. This indicator has been shown to differentiate among social, situational, and personality anxiety.

The *verbal-stylistic dimension* has been of some interest to sociologists. It involves peculiarities of vocabulary, pronunciation, dialect, and characteristic expressions. Osgood (1960) found that suicide notes, when compared to ordinary letters, had less diversity of vocabulary, greater repetition, less discriminative use of words, higher redundancy, more distress words, a larger number of all or none words, and more qualifications of verbs ("I might have loved you" as opposed to "I loved you"). Labov (1964) studied speech patterns in New York's Lower East Side. Not only did Labov find phonetical difference between socioeconomic classes, but he also found different styles of speech under different social situations for each class.

A word of caution in the use of extralinguistic measures is offered by Weick (1968:391).

> Extra-linguistic behavior varies in subtle ways and generally requires sensitive apparatus or a well-trained observer if it is to be recorded accurately. In some naturalistic settings it will probably be impossible to secure some extra-linguistic measures because of noise, simultaneous speech, whispering, etc. Despite these limitations . . . most of these measures seem to be of sufficient promise that effort devoted to field adaptation will not be wasted. Furthermore, many of these measures can be scored from tape recordings which observers can often obtain readily.

Body Movement Measures

Birdwhistell (1970) has pointed out that, contrary to many researchers' beliefs, (1) nonverbal communication is often not redundant of simultaneous verbal communication, and (2) humans spend very small amounts of interactional time vocalizing. Ekman (1965:441) reinforces Birdwhistell's observations.

> . . . the classes of information provided by nonverbal behavior can serve to repeat, contradict, or substitute for a verbal message, as well as accent certain words, maintain the communication flow, reflect changes in the relationship in association with particular verbal messages and indicate a person's feelings about his verbal statement.

Weick (1968:383) has summarized evidence showing that "the upper half of the face provides reliable cues for discriminating negative emotions, whereas the lower half of the face provides more cues for discriminating positive emotions." Ekman (1965) suggests that head and facial cues communicate information about *types of* affect experienced while body position may give information about *level of intensity* of affect. Exline (1963) has suggested that exchanged glances, or eye contacts, are normatively bound by such features as sex composition in interaction or group size. Most interesting, perhaps, is the work of Scheflen (1964) that shows postural congruence between persons who like each other and postural incongruence in dislike and status-differentiation situations. Leventhal and Sharp's (1956) notation system for facial expressions is reproduced in Table 5–3, p. 122.

A study discussed in *Behavior Today* (November 11, 1978) reported that the left side of the face, whose functioning reflects activity in the right hemisphere of the brain, tends to be the more emotional side. Hence, indications of extreme disparity between expressions on the left and right sides of the face may be important for the researcher's focus of attention.

Both Birdwhistell (1970) and Ekman (1965) have used motion picture films of facial, hand, and body movements to study "kinetic" (micromomentary expressions literally quicker than the eye) human movements. When the motion picture frames are slowed to one-sixth of their normal speed, up to two-and-one-half times more expressions are detected than at normal speeds.

Bennett (*Behavior Today*, November 10, 1977) has reported research showing that when a falsehood is uttered, a one-sixtieth of a second facial expression of rapid eye movements takes place. By way of contrast, the blinking of an eye takes about one-fifth of a second. Such micromomentary movements are promising for studies of honesty and lying.

Hall (1963) has provided a number of nonverbal (he calls them "proxemic") notation systems, as shown in Figure 5–2 (p. 123). The observer has the option of using either a pictographic symbol, mnemonic symbol, or number code in each case.

An illustration of how the system is used is given by Hall (1963: 1021).

Table 5–3
Symbols Used to Score Facial Expressions

Symbol	Meaning

Forehead

Comfort

——— 1. Smooth (permanent thin wrinkles may or may not be present)

≋ 2. Horizontal creases or folds (wrinkled) extend across forehead

Discomfort

— ≋ — 3. Horizontal creases or folds in middle, smooth on either side

○ ⊞ 0 4. Horizontal depression, grated effect, or vertical depression

Brow

Comfort

— — 1. Brows horizontal, no ridge or depression between or over either brow

— ⌒ 2. One brow raised

ᵥᵥ ᵥᵥ 3. Slight fluttering (up and down) of one or both brows

⌒ ⌒ 4. Both brows raised

Minor Discomfort

⌣ ⌣ 5. Depressions over one or both eyebrows

⋰⋅⋰⋅ 6. Fluttering of brows leading to occasional V formation

Major Discomfort

\ / 7. Medial approximation of brows with clear V formation

\ₛ /ₛ 8. V formation between brows and depression over one or both brows

Eyelids

Comfort (normal state)

≡ ≡ 1. Lids motionless except for normal blinks, no creases in upper lid if eye closed

Discomfort

≈ ≈ 2. Fluttering (up and down movement) of upper lids

₹ ₹ 3. Creases in upper lids occur without movement

₹₹ ₹ ≈≈ 4. Both (2) and (3) occur simultaneously

= = 5. Eyes closed with exaggerated creases of upper lids and creases surrounding eye

≂ ≂ 6. Opening and closing occurs at high rates

SOURCE: From H. Leventhal and E. Sharp, "Facial expression as indicators of distress." In S. S. Tomkins and C. E. Izard (eds.), *Affect, Cognition, and Personality: Empirical Studies.* Copyright © 1965 by Springer Publishing Company, Inc., New York. Used by permission.

1. Postural sex identifier

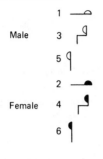

Male 1
3
5
2
Female 4
6

2. Orientation of bodies (SFP axis)

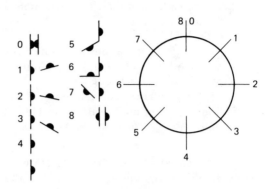

3. Kinesthetic factors

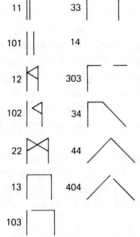

11		33	
101		14	
12		303	
102		34	
22		44	
13		404	
103			

4. Touch code

caressing and holding	0
feeling or caressing	1
prolonged holding	2
holding or pressing against	3
spot touching	4
accidental brushing	5
no contact	6

6. Thermal code

contact heat	the	1
radiant heat	thr	2
probable heat	th	3
no heat	t͟h	8

5. Retinal combinations (Visual code)

foveal	f	1
macular (clear)	m	2
peripheral	p	3
no contact	nc	8

7. Olfaction code

differentiated body odors detectable	do	1
undifferentiated body odors detectable	ubo	2
breath detectable	br	3
olfaction probably present	oo	4
olfaction not present	o	8

8. Voice loudness scale

silence	si	0
very soft	vs	1
soft	s	2
normal	n	3
normal+	n+	4
loud	l	5
very loud	vl	6

FIGURE 5–2 *Notation system for proxemic behavior.*

Source: Hall (1963). Reproduced by permission of American Anthropological Association from the *American Anthropologist* 65 (5):1963.

1. Two men standing (postural code 55)
2. Facing each other directly (orientation code 0)
3. Close enough that hands can reach almost any part of the trunk (kinesthetic code 101)
4. Touch does not play any part (touch code 6)
5. Man speaking looking at, but not in the eye, partner only viewing speaker peripherally (visual code 23)
6. Close enough that radiant heat would have been detected (thermal code 2)
7. Body odor but not breath detectable (olfaction code 2)
8. Voice very soft (loudness code 1)

As Hall's extensive research has shown (1976, 1966, 1959), there is considerable proxemic variation culturally and subculturally.

At a more microlevel of analysis, Clynes (1973) has devised an indirect way of measuring "shapes" of emotions through fingertip movements and pressures. In Figure 5–3, fingertip pressure is measured vertically and horizontally and averaged by computer. Clynes used subjects in the U.S., Japan, and Bali. He discovered that the shapes followed the same pattern; the shape for love looks essentially the same no matter what the subject's cultural background. His findings have stimulated work by professionals in disciplines such as anthropology, music, and psychotherapy.

Mehrabian (1972) has distinguished between four different dimensions to body movement: (1) immediacy (proxemic), (2) relaxation, (3) body appendage movements, and (4) facial expressions. The first and fourth dimensions have already been discussed. The relaxation dimen-

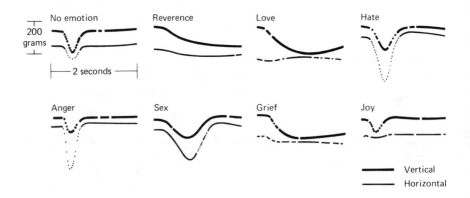

FIGURE 5–3 *The measure of emotions.*

Source: M. Clynes, "Sentics: Biocybernetics of emotion communication," *Annals of the New York Academy of Science,* Vol. 220, Article 3, 1973.

sion involves such indicators as degree of arm-position asymmetry, leg-position asymmetry, sideways lean, and hand or neck relaxation. Body-appendage movement has to do with measures of trunk swivel, rocking movements, head nodding or shaking, gesticulation, self-manipulation, object manipulation, and leg and foot movement measures. Mehrabian cites an impressive array of studies in which these measures have proved to have high reliability and validity.

Weick (1968:382) again warns that "although nonverbal behavior holds promise for observational research because of its visibility, naturalness, and discriminability, it can also be too subtle to record unless the observer has been trained to be sensitive to it." There is technical apparatus for recording and describing many bodily movements (see Weick [1968:381] or Mehrabian [1972] for suggestive bibliographies) but much of it is designed more for laboratory use rather than for naturalistic field studies.

Spatial Measures

Hall (1963:422) has defined proxemics as the study of "man's need to lay claim to and organize territory, as well as to maintain a pattern of discrete distances from one's fellows." How humans use and perceive space is coming to be seen as extremely important. Human use of space is not random. The study of the nonrandom regulation of human space is one of the more interesting methodological developments in sociology and related disciplines in recent years. For instance, population densities have been associated with social class, mental hospital admissions, fertility rates, and juvenile delinquency rates.

The mapping of human-space usage can be quite enlightening. In a touring exhibition of Shinjuku, the central district of Tokyo and one of the most densely inhabited areas in the world, a New York City architect, Peter Gluck, mapped out the inhabitants' subjective experiences of living. Figure 5–4 illustrates the volcaniclike pedestrian flows in the Shinjuku subway station and throughout the entire area. Darker shades show areas of greater human flow; lighter and greyer shades represent more inactive or dormant areas. Human traffic flows along various arteries and can be easily visualized and traced. Other experiential maps in this exhibit showed Shinjuku inhabitants' perceptions of "fronts" (public, formal areas) and "backs" (private, informal areas) similar to Goffman's (1971) use of frontstage- and backstage-behavior concepts, perceptions of individual "turf" (familiar places) by males versus females, and daily rhythms of territorial activity through graphs of lighted versus darkened areas of the city by time periods of several hours.

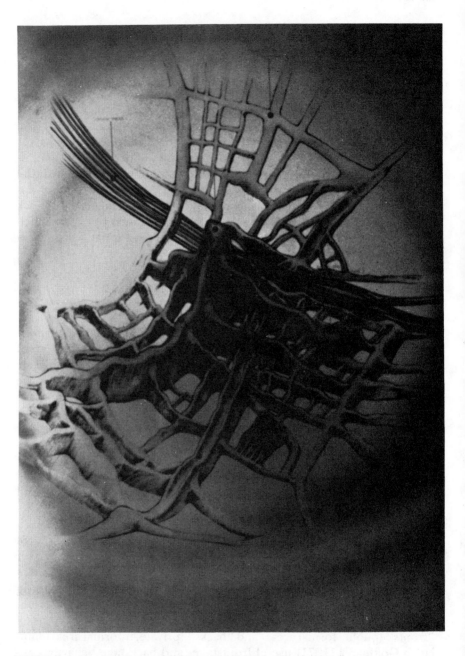

FIGURE 5–4 *Experiental map of Shinjuku (Central Tokyo) pedestrian flows.*

Photo credit: H. W. Smith.

For other creative examples of social mapping, the student might turn to the journal *Ekistics*, which tends to specialize in macrostudies of human territorial use. For more microexamples, there is the journal *Environmental Psychology and Nonverbal Behavior*. Sociologists have long had an interest in studying territorial- and spatial-behavior patterns. Such studies do not have to involve complex mappings. Taeuber and Taeuber (1965) studied the nonrandom distributions of white and nonwhite residences in major U.S. cities from 1940 to 1970. They found that residential segregation was greater in Northeastern industrial cities than in Southern cities. Little change in segregation was found over the thirty-year period for most of the cities studied. Another example is provided by aerial photographic studies of traffic on Los Angeles freeways that showed the average car gets on at one exit ramp and off at the *next*, contrary to the popular opinion that L.A. drivers spend most of their time traveling long distances on their freeways. Often when observations are structured, one finds many such surprising facts.

OBSERVATIONAL RECORDING DEVICES

The observational schemata discussed to this point, with a few exceptions, have been presented in a format that is adaptable to simple note taking. However, there are a number of mechanical means of recording observations that we shall discuss in some detail in the present section. Most of these devices will preserve, to greater or lesser degrees, a permanent record of the events one is studying. While some researchers (Bales 1950) caution against the use of such devices for retrospective coding of data, we agree with Weick (1968:411) that the use of mechanical recording devices usually gives us greater flexibility than observations done by hand.

Observer Self-Interview Schedules

Reiss (1971:11) has proposed a sort of observer self-interview schedule format for structured observations. The following observer self-interview is asked in the past tense since it was filled out by the observer following each observational transaction:

32.   Was a personal and/or property *search* attempted or conducted by the Police? (1) yes (go to 32a); (2) no (go to 33).

32a.   What kind of search was attempted or conducted? (1) personal ("frisk") (go to 32b); (2) property (e.g., auto or house) (go to 32c); (3) both personal and property (continue with 32b *and* 32c).

32b.   If "personal":

32b-1. Would observer say this "frisk" was necessary for the protection of the officer(s)? (1) yes; (2) no; (9) don't know.

32b-2. Did the police ask the possible offenders permission before this "frisk" was conducted? (1) yes; (2) no; (9) don't know.

32b-3. Did the possible offender(s) *object* to being "frisked"? (1) yes (go to 32b-3a); (2) no (go to 32b-4).
32b-3a. What was said by each of the offender(s)?
32b-3b. What was said by each of the officers?
32b-3c. Was the "frisk" conducted after objection? (1) yes; (2) no.

32b-4. Was a weapon or other possible evidence found? (Check all that apply.) (1) gun; (2) knife; (3) other weapon (Specify); (4) narcotics evidence (Specify); (5) stolen property (Specify); (6) other evidence (Specify); (7) none found; (9) don't know.

32c. If property:

32c-1. Was this search attempted or made prior to an arrest? (1) yes; (2) no; (9) don't know.

32c-2. How did the police attempt or manage to gain entrance? (1) simply entered without asking permission; (2) asked and were granted permission; (3) asked permission and were refused, did not enter; (4) asked permission and were refused, entered anyway; (5) gained entrance with search warrant; (6) other (Specify); (9) don't know.

32c-3. Were there any objections to the attempt to gain entry? (1) yes; (2) no; (9) don't know.
32c-3a. What was said by the parties objecting? (Specify for each party.)
32c-3b. What was said by each officer?

32c-4. Were there any objections to the search? (1) yes; (2) no; (9) don't know.

32c-5. Was a weapon or other possible evidence found? (1) gun; (2) knife; (3) other weapon (Specify); (4) narcotics evidence (Specify); (5) stolen property (Specify); (6) other evidence (Specify); (7) none found; (9) don't know.

32c-6. Was a property search of a *vehicle* attempted or conducted? (1) yes (go to 32c-6a); (2) no; (9) don't know.
32c-6a. Was the vehicle search attempted or conducted at or near the scene of a possible crime? (1) yes; (2) no; (9) don't know
32c-6a1. Where was it conducted? (1) street or alley away from traffic or public view; (2) moved to parking area or yard away from public view; (3) moved to police station; (4) other moved (Specify).
32c-6b. Did the police look closely at the vehicle's interior without actually reaching or climbing into it? (1) yes; (2) no; (9) don't know.
32c-6c. Did the police enter the vehicle and search it at any time? (1) yes; (2) no; (9) don't know.
32c-6d. Was any weapon or other possible evidence found in the search? (1) gun; (2) knife; (3) other weapon (Specify); (4) narcotics evidence (Specify); (5) stolen property (Specify); (6) other evidence (Specify); (7) none found; (9) don't know.

One of the more interesting features of this observational technique is that it may introduce quality in recording as high or higher than that found in survey research since the instrument does not differ materially from interview schedules and questionnaires because it is filled out by a *trained* observer as opposed to an untrained participant or respondent.

Reiss (1971:18) also notes the danger of observer oversocialization ("going native") into the participant's way of life as a source of measurement error. Observers need to be tested before and after entry into the observational setting to assess the effects of oversocialization.

Portable Event Recording Systems

The increasing interest in observational research has led many researchers to search for means that allow the researcher the ability to record, score, and store behavioral data. Two of the more popular instruments in use are the Datamyte 900 and 901 marketed by Electro/General Corporation. These are hand-held, solid-state transistor instruments that can store up to 16,000 and 32,000 bits of information, respectively, collected over periods of up to 8 hours on rechargeable batteries. They are lightweight (4 lbs.) and portable (10 x 12 x 2 in.). The data are recorded in computer code, making it readily transferable to most computers for analysis. One can generate flexible coding systems with the 14 different character keys (0–9, C,F,H,*). It is possible to take samples of data using a built-in beeper every .5, 1, 1.5, 2, 3, 4, 5, 10, 16, or 32 minutes. Elapsed time to the nearest .10 second can also be entered on the record.

These features make for a recording system that is adaptable to a wide variety of uses. Scientists in fields as varied as sociology, zoology, and ethology have used Datamytes. The observer may record behaviors directly in natural settings, indirectly from original recording media such as videotapes, or even through remote entries from the participants themselves. Complex behavioral codes based on the participant's code, activity code, and location code may be entered as well as multiple interactive-behavior studies.

This versatility has contributed to sociologists using the Datamyte to study police-civilian interactions, U.S. Navy training units, child abusing families, and full-term and premature infants' responses to their mothers and strangers.

Two other portable recording systems have been described recently in a special October 1977 issue of *Behavior Research Methods and Instrumentation:* the DCR-II cassette system by International Instruments Incorporated (Canada) and the SSR System 7 developed by Semeiotic Systems Corporation. These systems are roughly comparable to the Datamyte system.

Anyone wishing to use such hardware should realize that they are quite expensive (in 1979 the prices were: $650 for the SSR-7; $2,490 for the Datamyte 900; and $4,068 for the DCR-II). Furthermore, researchers must be carefully trained in the use of each of these devices. Digital dexterity as well as an investment of time are two training requirements. In addition, beyond problems with simple recording of data, the difficulties encountered in the analysis of recorded data are formidable compared to other types of research in sociology. The Datamyte can store up to 32,000 bits of information, and that information is data collected over time; this means the researcher must have, or develop, competence in working with very large amounts of behavioral data in "streams" or sequences.

Sound Tape Recordings

Sound tape recordings have provided a principal source of permanent record making. These devices are often not adequate for the recording of even fairly simple events. For instance, a three-person group discussion, after recording with good microphones strategically placed, may prove to have many undecipherable points of verbal interaction due to simultaneously occurring verbal exchanges between two or three members. Further, it is not as easy as one might think to distinguish speakers by voice (including even the *sex* of the speaker).

Nevertheless, a sound recording may be very helpful in recall of past events. Smith (1970) found that even a year after a sound-recorded set (96) of experimental sessions, he could still visually recall much of the session detail by replaying the tapes.

Audiovisual Tape Recordings
and Motion Picture Films

The recent mass production of fairly inexpensive portable audiovisual tape recorders, with prospects of further future reductions in price, has introduced a record collection method with advantages and disadvantages similar to that of motion picture film.

Events may be filmed or taped from different angles to provide independent reliability checks. At the same time, the angle choice is subjective and may distort the event's nature. Both film and tape have permanency. Both, too, have no limits on the size or complexity of the event that can be recorded. Both permit time sampling, although the camera is more adaptable in this regard since it can be set up to time sample mechanically with no need for human overseeing.

However, both tapes and film have disadvantages. Perhaps one of the most crucial is that (Weick 1968:413) "lenses, especially telephoto lenses, also foreshorten perspective. This means that if an investigator filmed a group of persons who were standing quite far apart, on film they would appear to be packed closely together." Maccoby and others (1964) have shown that both film and tape are affected by type of lighting.

Films and tapes are subjective documents of what an observer thinks of as important. Bellman and Jules-Rosette (1977) ingeniously turned this disadvantage into an advantage by having naive filmmakers make films showing how they feel about themselves and their world. Thus, one could use this technique to indicate what is important or unimportant to particular groups of people. Only film can presently be shown in slow motion, however; tapes, unlike film, are immediately usable upon taping.

Some documentary filmmakers (notably Robert Wiseman) have claimed that there is little if any subject reactivity to openly placed cameras. Wiseman's technique is to go around "shooting" empty cameras for several weeks before he actually starts filming in order to acclimate his participants to the camera's presence. Edward Hall has stressed similar points in his university lecture and laboratory discussions on the field usage of the 35 mm camera. Birdwhistell (1970), as we saw in an earlier section, has used time-lapse photography as a method of studying gross bodily movements in spatial behavior studies.

Some researchers recommend the use of black and white film or tape in most settings to cut down on irrelevant, distracting stimuli that might affect the observer. Even so, audiovisual tape or film is sufficiently complex that it may have to be aided by magnification, repeat viewing, and slowed motion (Ekman and Friesen 1965). At one extreme I have spent an average of six hours simply transcribing an hour of taped small group discussions. At the other extreme, Wohlstein and McPhail (1979) state that the amount of time required for them to produce, code, and analyze their film records was 200 hours for each minute of film record.

Still-Picture Photography

Reiss points out (1971:14) that

The reader may test some of the problems that arise in the use of still and motion-picture photography by examining the highly interesting, if not always definitive, set of pictures assembled by the President's Commission on Campus Unrest to depict violence at Kent State University. . . . The absence of any study design, the sheer unpredictability of events, and the dangers inherent in the situation once violence erupted limited data collection and analyses. Yet, the Commission was able to assemble 58 photographs depicting the main sequence of events and cast of characters in the situation by utilizing the work of at least 15 different photographers who were in one observational role or another. Despite obvious difficulties in the use of the photographs, investigators were able to document more reliably the roles and events than was possible from separate observer accounts.

Edward Hall has recently been teaching the use of still photography techniques for the study of spatial relationships. He sends students out into the field with 35 mm cameras with instructions to take at least 150 black and white snapshots of particular situations. For example, one might take pictures of persons waiting at a "Don't Walk" light or going through revolving doors. The analysis of such data is particularly painstaking. One arranges the pictures by different potentially useful criteria such as sex or age of participants, size of group, sex or racial composition of group, and so on, while looking for distinguishing characteristics of each categorization. While the technique has led to some interesting observations (blacks and whites stand quite differently when talking to members of their own races), inferring what these patterns mean is not always obvious. Heshka and Nelson (1972) used photographs in conjunction with a known measurement standard to reliably calculate interpersonal speaking distance (nose-to-nose) as a function of age, sex, and relationship.

Goffman's latest work *Gender Advertisements* (1976) is a brilliant example of how much one can reveal through examining photographs or other still-motion media—in this case, advertisements. Goffman's technique is to focus on particular areas of the body (knees, hands, eyes) and particular forms (finger biting, sucking, head-eye contact). He groups these sets of ads in a series by gender. Then he will switch sexes for the last several ads as a technique for examining and documenting the symbolic forms of social life.

THE QUALITY OF STRUCTURED OBSERVATIONS

Quality of data is typically measured by two different concepts: reliability and validity.

Reliability and Validity

Reliability (conceptualized as "stability" and "precision") of observational data may be measured by several different means. The most common method is to correlate observations made by several observers of the same phenomenon. Interscorer correlations are subject to several errors (Byrne 1964:49): First, it is possible for scorers to have similar *total* scores but disagree on many *individual* scores; second, it it possible for scorers to score consistently in different directions (for one scorer to score lower than another). Unfortunately, correlations cannot always detect such differences. Gellert (1955:194) stated that data usually have higher reliability if (1) the observer uses fewer categories for coding the data, (2) there is greater precision in defining the observational categories, and (3) there is less inference in making classifications. In addition to these coding system qualities, the setting of the study and behavior of the subjects also affect reliability. Campbell (1961:340) has pointed out that poorer quality observations are associated with less direct accessibility to our basic senses of touch, smell, sight, taste, and hearing and conversely with more intangible, indirect, or abstract stimuli.

Observers may also be a source of unreliability and invalidity. Ironically, the nonparticipant observer role often makes the observer conspicuous since our society has no norms for relationships where a nonmember is present but nonparticipating (Goode and Hatt 1962:122). Weick (1968:370–373) summarized various instances of nonparticipant observer interference such as heightened paranoia, creation of hostility and uncertainty, and predictable changes in verbal and behavioral content of those observed. Obviously, while one could solve the interference problem through observer concealment, this creates additional problems of ethics. Barker and Wright (1955) have argued that concealments are never justified unless the behavior is open to public inspection anyway. Riesman and Watson (1964:267), by contrast, have justified observer concealment when the observer does not misrepresent the activities he or she joins in, even though he or she may have additional interests in those activities; "if the friendly interaction is entered in good faith, with no other objectives being *in addition to* and not *instead of,* we see no serious violation of ethical standards." Observer concealment is not an all-or-nothing thing. One can be partially concealed, as in Riesman and Watson's study, or one can conceal the fact that one is making observations while concealing who or what is being observed (Weick 1968: 374).

Reiss (1971:15) notes that one must often consider the social acceptability of recording observations within a situation; this may require pretests of the *modes* and *times* of observational recording. Reiss also points out that since observers must legitimate their positions as observers, the visible evidence that one is working (recording) is often an aid to legitimation of one's role. Further, he notes that often by *showing* participants what one is recording one may allay their suspicions (1968:15). Another solution to reactivity caused by nonconcealment of the observer is the "absorbing situation strategy" (Strauss and others 1964), where the situation being observed is sufficiently engrossing and demanding of the participant's attention that he or she at least temporarily forgets the observer's presence.

Reliability and validity are also affected by observation category classification requirements. Weick (1968:423) suggests that "category systems vary greatly in the amount of contextual information that the observer needs in order to assign a behavior to a category. The general rule is that context should be used as sparingly as possible, and the immediate situation should be the sole basis for categorization."

Since most observation involves inferences, most investigators make efforts to have their observers be explicit about the inferences they make. Barker and Wright (1955:217) require their observers to set apart their observational inferences in brackets or separate paragraphs.

It should be noted that satiation or boredom may also contribute to observer unreliability. Rather than ask observers to code constantly, it is often best to specify time-interval observation samples. For instance, Flanders (1960) scored the dominant interaction pattern in every three-second time interval. As Weick (1968:424) notes, specified time-interval observation will tend to lower error "because observers readily adopt a rhythm and habitually watch for the prescribed interval of time with surprisingly little variance."

The second important quality of good data is validity (conceptualized as the best approximation to the truth). Dunnette (1958) gives four different possible sources of poor validity in observational data.

1. Inadequate sampling of complex stimuli
2. Imprecisely defined or inadequately understood observational categories or definitions
3–4. Subtle changes in the environment and persons observed.

Bott (1934:184) has argued that observers should worry more about validity than reliability. As Weick (1968:406) has noted, "If demands for inference and judgment are reduced, . . . then the problems of reliability also tend to be reduced."

Observer Training

Observers need to be effectively trained. They must be familiar with the situations to be encountered and with the instrumentation used.

Reiss (1971:26) has suggested the use of audiovisual materials in training since they expose all observers to common situations. Already existing films and television materials which present natural situations for observations may be used. Practice in estimating crowd size could be made from films of animal herds or mass gatherings of humans shown for short time periods.

Observers should be instructed in training sessions as to formal rules that should be followed in their roles as nonparticipant observers. Often the setting in which the observers operate will have formal or informal modes of conduct which the observer should be aware of and trained to respond to in given ways necessary to maintain legitimation of the observer role and reliability of data collection.

Heyns and Zander (1953:404–407) suggest that observers watch and record observations before learning the researcher's system. The rationale is that this procedure teaches the observer the complexity of cues available for observation and the need for precise classification norms.

Bales (1950) suggested that observers proceed from coding written protocols to tape recordings to actual situations to provide a gradual progression from low amounts of potentially confusing impinging outside stimuli to higher amounts. "Consensus sessions," in which the researcher meets with observers to discuss problems and methods of coding of pilot study situations after the fact, have been used by Bales (1950) for increasing reliability of observations.

Heyns and Zander (1953) have used role-playing or "reality practice" techniques similar to those explained in interviewer training. The observers take turns playing the observed and observer roles in order to gain sensitization to key observation processes. An excellent technique that might be used in conjunction with role-playing is audiovisual recordings that can be played back for feedback opportunities.

Ironically, not much of a literature exists on reliability of observational data or on training of observers.

Speculatively, however, it would appear reasonable to suppose that structured observation reliability will differ according to the amount of inference required of the system. An inferential system such as Bales's IPA probably requires training in introspection and in the gestalt patterns of its categories. By contrast, relatively noninferential systems such as eye-blink frequencies should require much more particularistic training methods.

SPECIAL PROBLEMS IN THE ANALYSIS
OF OBSERVATIONAL DATA

Chapter 14 will deal with general problems in the analysis of social scientific data. However, observational data are particularly difficult to analyze because of the problems of (1) sheer quantity of data and (2) the fact that they are typically collected in a streamlike fashion.

Some facets of observational data are quite amenable to conventional data analysis. Observational form, frequency, and duration do not typically present special problems of analysis. The problems of observational analysis arise mostly because most of our data analysis techniques are not very adaptable to antecedent-consequent, dynamic, or simultaneously occurring events.

Another problem of analysis is that categories in observational coding schemes are rarely independent. A truism of behavior is that almost everything is associated with everything else and that behaviors that occur close together in time will be more similar than those occurring far apart. For instance, a person cannot be both active and inactive at the same time. And some behaviors such as sleep are characterized by other behaviors such as inactivity. These facts raise unique problems of how to code and analyze observationally-based data.

A final problem: Which measure is best for description and analysis? One of my crucial problems in investigating the development of social interaction across several ages (Smith 1977) was a decision as to which measures would best represent Piaget's concept of egocentrism. After much deliberation I decided to test three different measures. Two of these measures were *frequency* measures: (1) the mean number of verbal interruptions of another's verbal behavior and (2) the mean number of people talking at the same time whenever more than one person was talking. A third measure was a *duration* measure: the percent of time in which more than one person was talking. The second and third measures showed increases from age five to age ten and then dramatically decreased. The first measure decreased steadily over all ages. Which measure should I have used? Because both frequency and duration are independent pieces of information, they may lead to different conclusions. Hence, all three measures seemed appropriate.

Furthermore, as is usually the case, which measure is "best" depends on the research question being studied. Menzel (1979:294–295) suggests that the researcher first ask, "What are we trying to account for?" and second, focus upon two different classes of questions: (1) spatial or locational questions such as, "Where will this individual (subgroup or group) go next?" and (2) psychological questions such as,

"What do the above facts suggest about the group's perceptual, cognitive, or social-affectional organization?" Once the researcher is satisfied that these answers are adequately answered, analysis can begin.

This section will give you some hints on the means used to analyze observational data and to suggest further readings of a more sophisticated nature for those who wish to go beyond these more elementary presentations. The presentation focuses on unique problems of three types of analysis: nonsequential, sequential, and concurrent analytic techniques.

Nonsequential Analysis

There are several different basic measures available in nonsequential data analysis. (1) The researcher can score each observational category for its frequency of occurrence. (2) Probability (relative frequency) can be calculated by dividing each individual frequency by the total number of observations. (3) The total duration (that is, seconds) of a score event can be measured. (4) The relative duration of each category (percent total duration) can be measured by dividing each individual duration by the total session time. (5) One can calculate measures derived from these others such as average-duration-per-occurrence (duration/frequency) and rate of occurrence (frequency/total session time).

In Chapter 2 we spent considerable time discussing some principles of how to go about *doing science,* several of which we find particularly helpful at this point. One of those principles was to search for regularities. Another was to focus on exceptions to those regularities. Lamb (1979) was searching for measures of attachment and affiliation between parents and their eighteen-month-old infants. Lamb found that two behaviors occurred more regularly as affiliative cues: vocalizing and looking, and another occurred as an attachment cue: physical proximity. But there were some puzzling exceptions to these rules. He hypothesized that when both parents were present the fact that the infant could divide its attention between two persons might explain differences between one and two parent situations. He reorganized his data to see if one- and two-parent situations explained these exceptions. This analysis showed that frequencies of four or five different measures of affiliative behavior, and three of his five attachment measures, were significantly different for one- and two-parent situations.

Returning to my previously mentioned study of child egocentrism for a second example, there is considerable research indicating that girls mature socially earlier than boys. This suggested that girls' and boys' egocentrism patterns were different. I compared each gender's data and concluded that after puberty girls showed less egocentric behavior at an earlier age than boys did. Generally speaking, this level of analysis is quantitatively sound without being conceptually overwhelming. One simply notes the incidences of observational categories and compares these incident profiles between groups of people, between individuals, or even between different measurements on the same group or individual.

An alternative to these *category profiles* is to identify the relative proportions of a participant's or group's total activities that are directed towards each individual or group in its immediate social environment. This *partner profile* enables the investigator to see how persons spend time with each available social partner. This strategy often requires who-to-whom matrices such as:

	To:				
	1	2	3	4	5
1					
2					
From: 3					
4					
5					

in which the researcher notes who did (or said) what to whom. For example, in studying the development of social interaction I was interested in differences across ages in who speaks to whom (Smith 1973). For each age group under study I kept records of who spoke to whom and found less differences in who initiated interaction between younger subjects than older subjects.

Sequential Analysis

Just as one can form profiles of data of a nonsequential nature, one can form profiles of data of a sequential nature. The simplest case is dyadic with two time periods. As an example of this consider the problem Vietze and others (1978:127) had in observing effects of mother's vocalization on infant-vocal onset. They separated observations by the ages of children (2, 6, and 12 months old), cases where neither the mother nor the child was vocal (NV), and those where only the mother was vocal (MV). Then they looked at these cases to see *how often* each was followed by both mother and child vocalizing (BV) and only infants vocalizing (IV). These probabilities are shown in Figure 5–5. The probabilities that a child will be vocal following the mother's initiation of vocalization in-

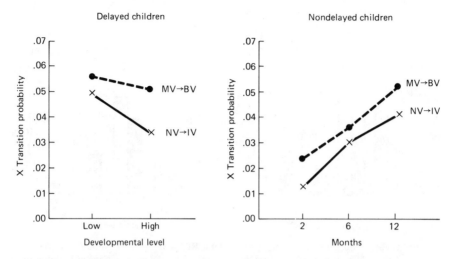

FIGURE 5-5 *Mean transition probabilities indicating the effect of maternal vocalization on contingent infant vocalization for nondevelopmentally delayed and delayed children.*

Source: Vietze, P. E., S. R. Abernathy, M. L. Ashe, and G. Fawlstich. 1978 *Observing Behavior,* Vol. 1, G. P. Sackett (ed). Copyright 1978 University Park Press.

crease from the second through the twelfth month of the study. How much of that is due to the mother's vocalization is interpretable by looking at the base probabilities (NV + IV) and subtracting that from the MV + BV probabilities.

Parke (1978) provides another relatively simple example of sequential analysis in Figure 5–6. He examined the changes in probability of a particular parental behavior in the ten-second interval following an infant behavior by asking what happens to the parent's behavior in the ten seconds after an infant emits some behavior. Powerful infant signals include behaviors such as coughing, spitting up, or sneezing. In Figure 5.6a we see that the conditional probability of a parent's behavior to stop feeding when this happens is 0.33. Compare this to the unconditional (baseline) probability in Figure 5.6b (that is, stop feeding when the baby does not emit one of these powerful signals) of 0.05. This is a much lower probability. The difference between baseline and conditional probabilities gives us the influence of one behavior on another.

The basic procedure in these examples is to (1) choose some behavior occurring in the data as a criterion of conditional behavior, (2) count the number of times this criterion follows each behavior as the very next

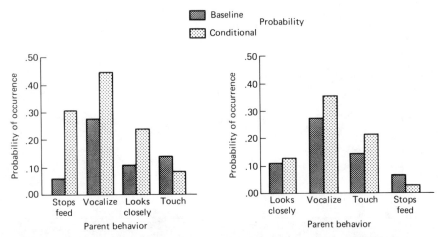

FIGURE 5–6a *Infant modifier (sneeze, spit up, cough) of parental behavior.*

FIGURE 5–6b *Infant modifier (positive vocalization) of parental behavior.*

Source: Parke, R. D. 1978 *Observing Behavior,* Vol. 1, G. P. Sackett (ed.). Copyright 1978 University Park Press.

behavior, and (3) compare these counts with the number of times these other behaviors occur over all conditions.

Increasingly, investigators are interested in looking at data over longer periods of time. Sackett (1974) has presented some simplified examples of this (see Figure 5–7). In the earlier two examples we were just interested in looking at the very next behavior that follows some criterion behavior. Here we look at the next behavior, the second intervening behavior, the third, and on. In this figure, peaks indicate higher probabilities that the behavior will occur and valleys lower probabilities of occurrence. If a behavior is sequentially independent, its conditional probabilities should be about the same as its simple, or unconditional, probabilities (indicated by dashed line in Figure 5–7). If you look at each of the graphs from left to right in turn you will note a rightward shift of the peaks suggesting probable sequences—even though actual sequences are not observed for more than two behaviors at a time. Figure 5–7 suggests the sequence of infant active, mother pat-stroke-jiggle, mother nurse, mother groom. An advantage of this method is that it can be used in the analysis of rhythmic or cyclic properties of interaction patterns.

A more rudimentary form of sequential analysis is simply to count instances in which particular behaviors occur within a given time. Patterson and Moore (1979) noted the number of fluctuations in a child's aversive responses for one-minute intervals. The roller-coasterlike fluctuations in aversive responses observed by this method did not make

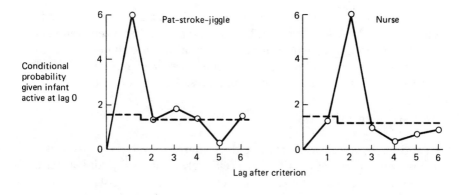

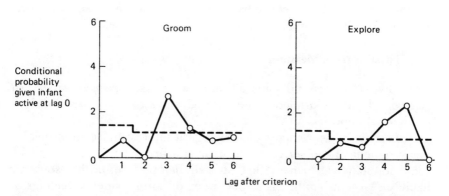

FIGURE 5–7 *Lagged conditional probabilities for four behaviors given previous infant activity. Dashed lines represent simple probabilities. Since with this type of data the criterion cannot follow itself, the number of behaviors that can occur at lag 1 is one less than for other lags; therefore simple probabilities at lag 1 are somewhat higher than elsewhere.*

Source: Sackett (1974:71).

much sense. This is a typical problem with simply making time-series counts of behavior. When Patterson and Moore then turned to analyzing mother-child *sequences* they found repetitive interactive patterns that explained the radical shift in complaint behavior on the part of the child.

Concurrent Data Analysis

One of the most difficult problems with observational data is that there are usually many things going on at the same time. Goffman (1971) is one of the more skillful describers of the simultaneous occurrence of many behaviors during social interaction. Unfortunately, there are no restrictions on how many behaviors can occur at once or for how long different combinations can last. Usually the researcher interested in concurrent or simultaneously occurring observations finds it necessary to use permanent records (film strips, videotapes) viewed numerous times in order to analyze the increased complexity of these situations.

ALREADY AVAILABLE DATA

In addition to directly observable data, there is a variety of primary and secondary sources of data open to relatively unobtrusive and structured observations that may be creatively utilized by sociologists. On the one hand there are primary data sources known as physical traces and signs; on the other hand are secondary sources that can be noted as archival records (Webb and others 1966).

Physical Trace Measures

Physical traces and signs fall into two classes: *erosion measures,* or signs of selective wearing of some material, and *accretion measures,* or signs of material deposits.

Erosion measurements of sociological interest most often involve measurement of the selectivity of wear and tear on various objects by some populations. Hayner (1964) studied theft patterns or the "souvenir habit" in large urban hotels as one index of hotel residents' feelings of estrangement. Wear on library book page corners and wear on museum tiles (Webb and others 1966:37) also have been used as evidence of use patterns.

Accretion measures, by contrast to erosion measures, are concerned with social depositings or accumulations. Mosteller (1955) measured frequency of dirt smudges, finger markings, and page underlinings in a study of differential usage of various sections in the *International Encyclopedia of the Social Sciences.* Siu's (1964) study of Chinese laundrymen analyzed the frequency with which calendars of nude female figures hung in their laundry shops; Sui found that such calendars reinforce the laundryman's belief in his association with prostitutes as legitimate. Sawyer (1961) estimated liquor consumption through counting the number of empty liquor bottles in trash cans. Conrad (1958) has observed that the bullfighter's beard is longer just before a bullfight than at the same time on any other day of the week; he hypothesized that this may serve as a measure of the bullfighter's anxiety or arousal. (Beards have likewise been noted to grow faster after sexual intercourse.)

The entire field of archaeology may be viewed as a science of inference from garbage and other residues. Broken pots, bones, and other fragmentary rubble accumulated over hundreds or thousands of years at a single site may be used to gain insights into the daily life of ancient peoples. Rathje (National Science Foundation 1979) has used these archaeological techniques as a means of gaining insights into American eating habits. Over a period of five years, his students have analyzed the daily refuse from more than thirty-five hundred households. His conclusions are that personal interviews, as opposed to actual examinations of garbage, are not likely to provide accurate information about eating and drinking habits. Tucson residents at all socioeconomic levels consistently understated the extent of beer they consumed and overstated the amount of milk they drank. They also overreported the number of cans and newspapers they recycled. Examination of actual refuse indicated that about 15 percent of all edible food purchased was thrown away as waste; the consumption of convenience and "junk" foods had been unaffected by talk about natural foods, recycling, and resource conservation; middle-class and lower-class diets were surprisingly similar; low-income households consistently wasted less food than households in middle-class areas; and inflation led to shifts in eating habits that promoted more waste as a result of unfamiliarity and appears to have had no effect on the consumption of baked goods, candy, jams, honeys, and other sweet products. Clearly, examination of actual refuse is an effective way of countering the tendency of persons to emphasize socially acceptable behavior in personal interviews.

Another interesting accretion study is one by Ley and Cybriwsky (1974). They studied the graffiti in Philadelphia neighborhoods and checked these observations with what local youth organizations and residents had to say about gang territories and areas of conflict. They found that the graffiti became thicker as you came closer to the center of the gang's territory. Where territorial control was uncertain, the graffiti was mostly aggressive, obscene, and violent in tone.

One may sometimes use accretion or erosion measures experimentally or quasi-experimentally. Schulman and Riesman (1959) indexed children's activity level through self-winding watches adapted to record the children's movements. One can easily imagine experimentally controlling the children's milieu in order to observe changes in their activity level.

Webb and his associates (1966:46) point out that

the examples provided suggest that physical evidence data are best suited for measures of incidence, frequency, attendance, and the like. There are exceptions. In a closely worked-out theory, for example, the presence or absence of a trace could provide a critical test or comparison. But such critical tests are rare compared to the times when the physical evidence— be it deposit or erosion—is one part of a series of tests.

Inconspicuousness, or unobtrusiveness, is the main virtue of erosion and accretion data. Another way of stating this point is that "the stuff of analysis is material which is generated without the producer's knowledge of its use by the investigators" (Webb and others 1966:50).

Archival Record Analysis

Sociologists have used archival records of various sorts more often in their research than physical trace measures. Webb and his associates distinguish between *public* archival records, normally prepared for examination by some audience and *private* archival records which generally speaking are not prepared for an audience.

Public archival records. Webb and others (1966) distinguish among four types of public records: actuarial records, political and judicial records, other governmental documents, and mass-media productions.

Actuarial records include formal records kept on birth, marriage, death, and disease. Christensen (1960) used birth and marriage records to estimate the incidence of premarital sex relations in different societies. Cherlin (1978) separated out census data on divorce and remarriage by presence of children to study the effects of familial structure on later divorce rates.

Actuarial records are produced not only by governments. Indeed, many organizations keep public actuarial records. Many professional associations keep member directories with potentially useful information such as that found in *American Men of Science* and *Who's Who in America.*

Political and judicial records have been among the most used records for sociological purposes. Critical role-call votes, aggregate voting records in relation to prointegrationist characteristics, and court decisions are among the vast storage of political and judicial records that have been and can be further utilized by social science investigators.

Other, more unorthodox records have been utilized creatively. Mindak, Neibergs, and Anderson (1963) showed decreased parking-meter collections to be associated with a Minneapolis newspaper strike. Webb and others (1966:73–74) refer anecdotally to city water pressure dropping with the end and beginning of television shows and commercials as measures of time usage. Likewise, Won and Yamamoto (1968) examined private security guard agency and supermarket shoplifting records in a study of deviant behavior.

The mass media also presents an enormous public archive that has been utilized in many studies. Obituaries and cartoons are among the vast possibilities presenting still virtually virgin territory for the social scientist.

Webb and others (1966:54) in their review of problems in the use of archival data point to what has been termed *"Croce's Problem"*—that is, "either one is uncertain of the data when only a limited body exists, or uncertain of the sample when so much exists that selection is necessary." The second part of Croce's Problem is solvable through modern sampling methods (see Chapter 10). The first problem presents the major obstacle since the missing data might well alter the evidence. Physical evidence data often survives and is deposited selectively. Government officials often edit or secretly classify information of great import to a balanced picture of their work (Baker and Fox 1972). Tombstones made of concrete or marble survive longer than wooden ones. Bookkeeping methods may subtly change, producing pseudochanges in time series data as in the Census Bureau's 1965 change of unemployment definitions. Thus, the physical evidence expert must become adept in selective survival and depositing of the evidence of interest to him or her.

Private archival analysis. While the main problem associated with public records is the normally large mass of such data that exists, the central concern with analysis of private records is their episodic nature and, thus, limited usage for analysis of lengthy time periods (Webb and others 1966:88). Webb distinguishes three classes of private archives: sales records, institutional records, and personal documents.

Sales data have been used to infer anxiety over air travel through sales of air-flight insurance (Webb and others 1966:90–91), popularity through sales diffusion of innovations through pharmacy records (Coleman, Katz, and Menzel 1957), and subliminal persuasion (Key 1974, 1976). Industrial and institutional records have been used to study such things as absenteeism and job turnover in relation to age, seniority, and worker's home-factory distance (Knox 1961). Stuart (1963) has used union grievance records to study racial conflict.

Personal documents may include autobiographies, diaries, letters, and life histories. *Autobiographies* must be treated with particular caution, as Denzin (1970:227) warns,

> ... the author of the autobiography may not always be fully aware of what has occurred in his life. Furthermore, he may dress up, beautify, or hide

what he is aware of. It is the job of the sociologist to probe and uncover such topics. . . . In the autobiography the sociologist must keep the record of experiences separate from the interpretation given them.

The *diary* is less susceptible to fallacious reinterpretation of past behavior by its author. The diary is a set of personal outpourings written discontinuously. Douglas (1967) and Jacobs (1967) have used intimate journals in their studies of suicide. *Memoirs* are more impersonal than intimate journals and normally are written in a relatively short period of time like autobiographies. While the memoir's impersonality reduces its psychological importance, its data may be of great interest as a history of organizational development, as in Horowitz's (1972) accounting of the first ten years of *Transaction* magazine.

Logs are accounts of meetings, events, visits, trips, and happenings. Barker (1968) has proven that the log, as a systematic time-budget record, provides an excellent picture of patterns of interaction in social settings.

Letters were used as the primary source of information in Thomas and Znaniecki's (1927) classic study of Polish immigration to America. Allport (1942:108–110) points out that the analyst of letters must consider who the letter's author is, its recipient, and the relationship between the author and recipient. Janowitz (1958) used letters and diaries captured from German soldiers in World War II to assess the impact of propaganda on German troops.

The *life history method* combines data gleaned from autobiographies, letters, and diaries where available and often supplements these sources with interviews and questionnaires for more systematic coverage of gaps in the life history. Denzin (1970:235) points out that

> Kimball Young . . . has presented perhaps the most elaborate guideline for the life history. He divides his proposal into the following areas: data on the family (including the subject, his father and mother); developmental history of the individual, including experiences confronted in childhood, pre-adolescence, adolescence, and adult life; the nature and meaning of the inner (subjective) life, including such topics as emotional stabilities, sense of the self, power devices, recreational and avocational activities, basic satisfactions, and work as value. This proposal completely covers the life-cycle. It has the advantage of being so complete that it could be used with a group, or members of an organization. It also contains recommendations concerning data on demographic and sociopersonal aspects.

Robertson's (1972) life-history study of the breakup of the Oneida Community used private papers, records, letters, and diaries.

Strategies of Analysis of Physical Trace and Archival Records

Physical trace and archival records present somewhat peculiar problems for observational analysis since, unlike previously mentioned observational measures, *structure* is *not* usually built into the measurement device. For instance, the Borgatta IPS builds in measures of form, frequency, and antecedents and consequences *prior* to the observation of particular behaviors. By contrast, physical trace and the archival data are already in existence, and, hence, the researcher must make observational decisions on data already in existence. These analytic decisions fall under the rubric of what is termed "content analysis." *Content analysis* refers to means of summarizing, standardizing, and comparing, or otherwise systematically transforming, already existing records.

One of the basic issues in content analysis is whether analysis should be qualitative or quantitative (Holsti 1969:5–12). Our own position implicitly has been that both types of content analysis are appropriate strategies because both types of analysis deal with *forms* and *antecedent-consequent* patterns of forms, while quantitative analysis deals with *duration* and *frequency* of forms and patterns. Another reason for using both quantitative and qualitative content analysis hinges on the fact that qualitative analysis may be equated with emphasis on problem *significance* while quantitative analysis emphasizes *precision* of measurement—both of which are necessary components of good operationalization. We need to ask right questions to which we then wish *exact answers*.

Holsti (1969:12–14) points out a second major controversy among content analysts: whether analysis should be limited solely to *manifest* content (those items which actually are physically present) or whether analysis may be extended to *latent* content (that is, an interpretive "reading between the lines" of symbolism underlying the physically present data). Holsti's conclusions for resolving this debate have much merit (1969:14).

> It is true that only the manifest attributes of text may be coded, but this limitation is already implied by the requirement of objectivity. Inferences about the latent meanings of messages are therefore permitted but . . . they require corroboration by independent evidence.

Because of dangers present in inferring latent symbolism, most content analysts wish "independent sources of corroborating evidence." This would mean the need to use some type of multi-method device mentioned in Chapter 13, such as independent coders, noncontent analytic data sources in addition to content analytic data, and so on. Espe-

cially when one is working with secondary sources of data, it becomes
important to have a great variety of potentially disconfirming or supporting evidence for hypothesis testing. Consistent support from varied
sources conveys validity strongly for an idea: There is more information to scan, more diverse tests to apply, and more chances to batter
the hypothesis with inconsistencies from the findings. Melbin's (1978)
study of nighttime social life in urban areas as resembling former fron-
tierlands is a good example of this. He combined analysis by historians,
census data, archival materials such as letters and autobiographies, newspaper reports, and unobtrusive measures such as reports of fights in
emergency calls to telephone operators to test his propositions more
adequately.

Good content analysis is disciplined by theoretical considerations
just as is any research method. Hence, content analysis should start with
a theoretical problem rather than with the already existing data. This
broader problem can then be translated into specific strategies for content analysis. For instance, assume we are interested in an often-cited
problem: Is editorial support of political candidates by particular newspapers reflected through biased news sections? This problem delimits the
data to be content analyzed to editorial and news sections of newspapers
during political election seasons.

The second strategy usually needed is to reduce the working universe of relevant data to manageable proportions through sampling design. The discussion in Chapter 10 of sampling strategies proves useful
at this stage. Assume the political election season runs from August 31
to November 7, and we have chosen a working universe of four papers
editorially "pro" and four editorially "con" towards some particular political candidate. That would leave us with approximately 552 newspapers
in our study. We could easily reduce that to more manageable analytic
proportions by taking a sample from pro and con newspapers without
loss of generality.

The third and final steps are to construct (3) analytic categories
tailored to our theoretical problem and (4) precise operational definitions of those categories. Since our theoretical interest in newspaper
coverage of the political campaigns involves some measure of *emphasis* or
stress on campaign coverage, several measures are suggested such as
number of stories and news inches given to the candidate by editorially
pro and con newspapers. Other possible measures might be size of head-
lines, number of stories on the front page, number of pictures of the
candidate, and position of stories on the front page. Measures of editorial
policy might include number of editorials for the candidate and number
of articles by national and local columnists for the candidate.

There are no easy means for describing specific tactics for setting
up content analytic categories and their operationalizations because the

types of research questions asked have such diversity that broad principles beyond those discussed are generally precluded. Several things,
however, are evident from the study of content analyses. First, different
content analytic operationalizations produce markedly different results,
particularly the more *latent* the analysis. Consequently, it is wise to use
more than one content analytic operationalization to avoid what we term
"irrelevant responsiveness of measures" in Chapter 11.

Second, "it is the *question* that counts, not the count itself" (Carney
1973:48), since trite questions can only produce trite answers. This implies that the content analyst must have a good background in and knowledge of the issues and documents under analysis. This also implies that
content analysis cannot be used as a "fishing" method. ". . . content
analysis cannot be used to probe round a mass of documents in the hope
that a bright idea will be suggested by such probing. Content analysis gets
the answers to the question to which it is supplied" (Carney 1973:284).

Third, special controls for researcher subjectivity are needed. Carney (1973:51) suggests several such procedures. For a start the researcher might have a panel of judges *independently* define the units of
analysis. Then the researcher could choose those units which were agreed
upon by most or all of the judges. Finally, the researcher could have a
panel of *independent* coders classify the subject matter into these selected
units.

Both physical traces and archival records may offer much observational material on "Who? What? Why? and How?" but used singularly
they often fail to answer "Why?" questions. Thus, it is generally more
useful to use physical traces or archival records *in conjunction with* other
methods. The main advantage of most physical trace and many archival
records is the general relief of reactive measurement effects found in
more traditional methods such as interview response set, observer
fatigue, and so on (Webb and others 1966:36).

However, *private* archival documents have the peculiarly major
problem of reactive effects. Gottschalk (1945:38) presents four probes for
assessing credibility of personal documents.

1. Was the ultimate source of detail (the primary witness) *able* to tell the truth?
2. Was the primary witness willing to tell the truth?
3. Is the primary witness *accurately reported* with regard to the detail under
   examination?
4. Is there any *external corroboration* of the detail under examination?

Of course, this assumes the documents to be authentic. Gottschalk (1945)
thus also identifies means by which the document's authenticity may be
assessed, including handwriting analysis, style of presentation, and possible anachronisms.

SUMMARY

Direct, structured observation is hardly new to sociologists. Recent Nobel prize winners such as Tinbergen and Lorenz are practitioners of this method. And in the last two decades social and behavioral scientists have been giving increased attention and prestige to the development of systematic and reliable observational methods. The scoring of observational data in the process has become highly complex, and objective standards of scientific acceptability have grown more strict. Striking advances have been made in ways to collect, store, and analyze observational data; anecdotal evidence and haphazard reports are no longer accepted as credible scientific evidence. There are now numerous accepted scoring systems, time sampling procedures, recording modes, and data analysis techniques available that have opened up new vistas and opportunities for use. The outcome is allowing researchers to ask a wider range of questions than was heretofore possible. The result is a paradigmatic shift (see Chapter 2) that is being recognized through such means as Nobel prize awards.

READINGS FOR ADVANCED STUDENTS

COLIN CHERRY, *On Human Communication,* 1978 (3rd ed.). Most discussions of content analysis are atheoretical. This classic is must reading for those who wish to inspire their work with theory.

ROBERT HARPER, A. N. WIENS, AND J. D. MATARAZZO, *Nonverbal Communication: The State of the Art,* 1978. An excellent account of the most recent important studies and methodological principles of paralanguage, facial expression, kinetics, the eye and visual behavior, and proxemics.

OLI HOLSTI, *Content Analysis for the Social Sciences and Humanities,* 1969. Still the classic text after a decade.

MICHAEL E. LAMB, S. J. SUOMI, AND R. G. STEPHENSON (eds.), *Social Interaction Analysis: Methodological Issues,* 1979. Sophisticated treatments of levels of analysis, computer programs, sequential analysis, and time-series analysis.

GENE P. SACKETT (ed.), *Observing Behavior.* Vol. 2: *Data Collection and Analysis Methods,* 1978. Excellent but advanced discussion of creating taxonomies, untangling streams of behavior, reliability, and other important topics. This text and the Lamb and others text make previous discussions of observational methods obsolete.

ANITA SIMON AND E. BOYER (eds.), *Mirrors for Behavior III,* 1974. An anthology of observational instruments for interactive situations with data on reliability and validity.

SUGGESTED RESEARCH PROJECTS

1. Decide upon a particular hypothesis with which to test these physical traces (a number of cars with CB antennas, garbage in trash cans). Describe how these indicators might be used to test your hypothesis. Discuss possible limitations to the use of these indicators for your hypothesis testing, and possible means, if any, of offsetting those limitations.

2. Consider some sources of ready-made data (physical trace or archival) not originally produced or collected for sociological purposes. Write a short essay on:

   a. The nature of the data

   b. Its reason for existence, who collected it, why it was collected

   c. How it might be used for sociological purposes

   d. Possible limitations to the data

   e. Possible means of offsetting those limitations.

3. Ask a college or high school basketball, baseball, or football coach for permission to observe practice sessions. Attempt to replicate Tharp and Gallimore's observational study of John Wooden (reported in *Psychology Today*, January 1976). Compare your findings with theirs, in terms of success of educational technique.

4. Do Project 3 but focus upon *duration* rather than frequency of Tharp and Gallimore's categories. Are the conclusions of this study different from those based on frequency? Why do you say that?

5. Do an observational study with another student using some already existing instrument such as those in Simon and Boyer's anthology (1974). After you both have independently collected information, share your data to write a paper analyzing this observational instrument from the following standpoints:

   a. Is it constructed in a simple, intelligible, and precisely defined way or not?

   b. Is it adequate to gain the information it was intended to gather or not?

   c. Is it practical to use or not?

   d. Is it objective and reliable in the sense that its procedures for obtaining information are accessible to other observers and readily replicated by them?

   e. Does it seem to distort the behavior under study?

   f. Does it summarize all the data desired succinctly and parsimoniously?

   g. Does it appear to violate any accepted legal or ethical standards?

6. Create and pretest an observational instrument that attempts to measure the form, duration, frequency, and/or antecedent-consequent pattern of some interactive situation. Use the questions in 5a–g above to analyze the adequacy of your measure.

7. Create an observational schedule to be used by an observer for retrospective structured observation of some formal interactional setting (professor-student classroom exchanges, marital bargaining, mother-child interaction) along the lines of Reiss's police-citizen observational schedule.

8. Conduct a content analysis of some aspect of collective behavior as described by the mass media (a comparative analysis of the types of news emphasized in two daily newspapers—one issue each from the present and from fifty years ago).

9. Observe a small group in a laboratory situation using one of the structured techniques discussed earlier and compare hand-recorded results with a videotape replay.

Surveys:
Use and Misuse
of the Interview
and Questionnaire

And were you beaten?
Was your mother? Sister? Dog?
(attach descriptive catalogue.)
Have you mystic inspiration?
Our thanks for your co-operation."

Distended now with new-got lore,
Our plump and pleasant men-of-war
Torture whimsey into fact,
And then, to sanctify the act,
Cast in gleaming, ponderous rows,
Ingots of insipid prose.
A classic paper! Soon to be,
Rammed down the throats of such as we.[1]

Survey methods include both interviews and questionnaires. The *questionnaire* is a self-administered interview. It requires particularly self-explanatory instructions and question design since there is often no interviewer or proctor present to interpret the questionnaire to the participant. An *interview* is a peculiar verbal interactional exchange "in which one person, the interviewer, attempts to elicit information or expressions of opinions or belief from another person or persons" (Maccoby and Maccoby 1954:499). In the extreme case an interview may be so highly standardized that the interviewer has a *schedule* of questions that are to be asked in exactly the same wording, question order, and even tone of voice. The reason for this high structuring is based on the desire to present all respondents with the same stimuli so that they are responding to the same research instrument. As we shall see in a later section, even a slight change in question wording or emphasis can cause differences in responses.

Richardson, Dohrenwend, and Klein (1965:40) have given the rationale for using highly structured interview schedules or questionnaires as based on the assumption that participants must have a common vocabulary if the stimuli (questions) are to elicit similar ranges of responses. Unfortunately, common vocabularies do not necessarily assure common definitions. The simple question, "Who is the head of this household?" will elicit appropriate responses virtually 100 percent of the time from white middle-class respondents, while English-speaking Puerto Rican immigrants often assume "head" to mean landlord. Unless the population to which the interview schedule or questionnaire is being administered is relatively homogeneous culturally, a less standardized form of inter-

[1]Submitted anonymously in lieu of an anonymous questionnaire in a study of student values and campus religion at the University of Wisconsin conducted by N. J. Demerath III and Kenneth G. Lutterman.

viewing may be more appropriate. In less standardized, or nondirective, interviews the interviewer plays a more passive and adaptive role, giving only enough direction to the questions so that the respondent will cover a topical area in depth while having more responsibility and freedom of expression.

QUESTIONNAIRE AND INTERVIEW
SCHEDULE DESIGN

Cannell and Kahn (1968:530) have defined the interview as a conversation with a purpose, specifically the purpose of information-getting. Of course, there are many ways to get information through conversations— some of them better than others. Many of the criticisms leveled against questionnaires and interview schedules hinge upon poorly designed questions. Often, then, we can drastically improve the efficiency and quality of data collection simply by asking questions that more appropriately measure whatever we wish to measure.

This subsection should be supplemented with the Chapter 11 subsection on "Informal Criteria for Attitude Statements." Those criteria are generally applicable to question formation as well as to attitude statement construction. The use of interview schedules and questionnaires is subject to the same standards of measurement with which we attempt to describe or represent any data.

The basic theme behind good questionnaire or interview schedule construction is based on the formulation of questions that give "maximum opportunity for complete and accurate communication of ideas between the researcher (or interviewer) and the respondent" (Cannell and Kahn 1968:553). They point out three components to this communication process: language, frame of reference, and conceptual level of questions.

Language typically involves a compromise between formulating the content of an information-getting question and searching for a shared researcher-respondent vocabulary with which to express that question. The researcher must always attempt to become aware of the participant's vocabulary breadth and limitations. Oversimplified or overdifficult questions will tend to lower respondent motivation to communicate.

Closely related to the problem of language is the problem of *conceptual level of difficulty.* Even if the respondent shares a certain common vocabulary with the researcher, they may not share the cognitive organization necessary for the respondent to answer the question. For example, both respondent and researcher might share the same vocabulary in the question, "Is your spouse basically tolerant or intolerant of ambiguity?" Nevertheless, the respondent's cognitive organization of observations and feelings about the spouse may not give him or her the ability to order his or her own experiences.

Frame of reference refers to the fact that most words may be interpreted from different points of view or perspectives. Even a simple word like "work" evokes different mental images in different persons. Bancroft and Welch (1946) found that when asked the question, "Did you do any work for pay or profit last week?," respondents reported in terms of what they considered their major activity. Many housewives who did part-time work answered "no" because they considered the work irrelevant to their major self-definition. Bancroft and Welch's solution was to revise the interview schedule by asking first what the person's major activity was. Then those who gave nonworker responses were asked whether in addition to their major activity they did any work for pay. It is necessary then to pretest questions adequately in order to see if the researcher's and respondent's frames of reference correspond. If they do not correspond, changes in question wording or order are necessary. Question wording has long been considered the number one problem in survey research. Hovde (1936) asked researchers what the major defects of survey research were and found that 74 percent named improperly worded questionnaires and 58 percent named faulty interpretations (frame of reference) the principal defects. Cannell and Kahn (1968) agreed with that conclusion thirty-two years later.

The Research Issue

Before you even think of writing questions you should have a clear idea of the information you wish to collect. If you do not have a good conception of the issue you are researching, how can you possibly make it meaningful to the respondents? Defining the issue involves stating it precisely through questions such as "What is being *assumed* about the issue?" Once you have fully recognized precisely what the issue is that you are researching you will be in a better position to evaluate any sacrifices in precision called for by your question wording.

In addition, the researcher should attempt to judge the meaningfulness of the issue to the respondents who will be answering questions. Often during pretesting, the researcher is surprised at how unmeaningful the questions are. Gallup polls show that less than half of the American adult population say they know what "socialized medicine" or "lobbyist in Washington" means. Ironically, however, if one were to ask a question such as, "Are you generally in favor of, or opposed to, socialized medicine?," most persons would prefer not to appear ignorant by giving some type of answer to this question other than a "don't know."

One of the most difficult tasks is to state exactly what the problem is. A clear understanding of objectives should include the following statements:

1. The population for which information is desired
2. The kinds of information desired from this population
3. The required precision of results.

Once these objectives are clear the researcher needs to translate these general concepts into specific definitions:

4. Each concept has to be operationally defined so as to depend as little as possible on subjective attitudes.
5. Each concept should be operationally feasible.
6. Definitions should be easily understood and comparable with common understandings of these concepts.

Open-Ended Versus Closed-Ended Question Design

The problem of meaningfulness of the issue to the researcher's respondents leads us into the problem of whether one should use open- or closed-ended questions. An *open-ended question* is a question that leaves the respondent free to respond in a relatively unrestricted manner. By contrast, *a closed-ended question* restricts choice of response by forcing the respondent to answer in terms of given categories or alternatives. Cannell and Kahn (1968:565) list five considerations in choosing between the open and closed question formats: (1) interview objectives, (2) respondent information level, (3) structure of respondent opinions, (4) respondent motivation to communicate, and (5) initial interviewer knowledge of the preceding respondent characteristics.

When the research objectives call for learning about the respondent's *level* of information, *frame of reference* in answering a question, or opinion *structure,* open-ended questions are most appropriate. If the objective is simply to *classify* an individual's attitude or behavior on some *clearly* understood dimension, then closed-ended questions are more appropriate. However, sometimes the researcher can use a battery of closed-ended questions that has more than one dimension as long as the dimensions are not too complex in number or structure in place of one open-ended question which may be more difficult to code.

The *level of respondent's information* calls for open-ended questions if the issue raised may be outside the experience of many respondents since, as we have seen, the respondent might otherwise choose blindly between closed-ended responses in order not to appear ignorant. Also, where levels of information among respondents may be extremely variable or unknown, the open-ended question may be especially useful.

The *respondent's thought structuring* also determines choice of open- or closed-ended questions. Closed questions require less "psychological effort" on the part of the respondent—that is, closed questions require less effort and ability to recall, order, and perhaps evaluate experience (Cannell and Kahn 1968:566). Closed questions generally involve the hazard of offering an easy choice that the respondent might not make if forced to recall, organize, and evaluate personal experience.

Open-ended questions demand more motivation on the part of the respondent since he or she does not have the aid of preset structured responses. Closed-ended questions, by contrast, demand little motivation and invite inappropriate responses where the respondent finds it hard to say "don't know."

Finally, as Cannell and Kahn (1968:567) state,

> The closed question appears to be best adapted to situations where (1) there are a limited number of known frames of reference from which the respondent can answer the question, (2) within these few possible frames of reference there is a known range of possible responses, and (3) within this range there are clearly defined choice points that approximate well the positions of respondents.

Actually, few good questionnaires or schedules use only open- or closed-ended question formats. Various combinations of each type will normally be present since the researcher is usually interested in a number of different variables or stimuli, each of which may call for varying question formats. Thus, the researcher must continually ask which type of question will best communicate the stimuli as well as best stimulate appropriate responses.

Open-Ended Question Design

Several different criteria are suggested in designing open-ended questions. First, the question should be relatively directive. It must provide the researcher's frame of reference; if it does not, the respondent may end up answering in any number of dimensions. Consider the following question, *"What are your thoughts concerning abortion laws?"* This question invites responses in any number of dimensions: opinions, attitudes, past, present, future, laws in particular states, and so on. While this variety of dimensions may well be what the researcher desires to tap, if he or she was interested in one dimension, such as current opinions about present abortion laws in Alaska, this question would need much more directiveness.

Second, it often is a good idea to indicate the number of thoughts expected from each respondent: for example, *"Other than members of your family, what three persons have provided the most important influences in your choice of occupations?"*

Third, it is often advisable to indicate a *probe* after a question so that the interviewer will try to obtain ideas which the respondent does not immediately think of: for instance, *"Anything else?" "What else?"* or *"Are there any others?"*

Fourth, it may often be possible to establish precoded answers for some open-ended questions such as, *"During the past year, with how many, if any, of your relatives did you have face-to-face contact?"* One might precode this question "0, 1–2, 3–5, 6–10, 11 or more." This type of precoding is particularly applicable to answers expressible in numbers. Such precoding makes later processing of the data for analysis much more efficient, both in cost and time.

One of the basic problems with using open-ended questions is that few people ever use the same words for expressing the same idea. This makes analysis difficult and often relatively unreliable. It is inexcusable to use a closed-ended questionnaire simply to avoid the content analysis problems of open-ended questions. Consideration should be given to converting open-ended questions to closed-ended questions through pretests. The researcher may find that a closed-ended question satisfies respondents' variety of responses, saving considerably on later codings of verbatim replies. There are two types of closed-ended questions: two-way and multiple-choice. Each will be discussed in turn.

Two-Way Questions

Payne (1951) has listed a number of criteria for forming two-way questions (where the respondent chooses between two choices). First, *avoid implied alternatives,* such as "or not." If the "or not" is spelled out in detail responses will generally be quite different than with the details of the "or not" alternative implied. It may not seem harmful to leave an alternative answer implied by "or not" in a question such as, *"Should doctors involved in giving illegal abortions receive stiff penalties, or not?"* However, experience shows that such implied alternatives usually decrease the alternative responses; therefore, an "or not" is usually not sufficient to represent fairly the negative alternative.

Second, it helps to state both the pro and con sides of an argument just as implied alternatives should be spelled out in fairness to all sides of an issue.

Some people think there should be no commercials of any kind in children's programs because they feel children can be too easily influenced. Other people while perhaps objecting to certain commercials, by and large see no harm in them and think children learn from some of them. How do you feel—that there should be no commercials on any children's programs or that it is all right to have them?

Notice, also, that while the *explanation* is more than twenty words long, the *question* itself is less than twenty words.

Third, except in rare instances (*"What is your sex?"*), two-way questions should have a "Don't know" or "No Opinion" answer provided. It is possible, for example, that many people in the above question on TV commercials have no real opinion.

Fourth, if a two-way question has a middle-ground position ("stayed the same"), it may be wise to state it, *"Do you think that race relations have improved, stayed the same, or deteriorated since the Watts riots?"*; this would be an improved version of the question, *"Do you think that race relations have improved or deteriorated since the Watts riots?"*

Fifth, alternatives should normally be *mutually exclusive* and *exhaustive*. However, where a compromise answer is possible, provision for answers such as "both alternatives" should be made. In the TV commercial study mentioned earlier some people might view TV commercials as sometimes a good thing, sometimes a bad thing. Unless it is realistic to force the respondent to chose between the alternatives, some form of "both alternatives" answer would be appropriate.

Sixth, it is often advisable to set up separate answer boxes for qualified answers. In the TV commercial question some respondents might be inclined to respond with "TV commercials might be unhealthy in some cases." You should decide whether it is realistic to be forced into a preset alternative or provided with a separate qualified-answer box.

Seventh, avoid the use of strongly polarized alternatives if you wish respondents to make choices between them. For instance, *"Should the U.S. end its Cold War commitments quickly by obliterating Russia with H-bombs, or should we immediately withdraw our troops completely from Europe?"* polarizes the choices too bluntly for most respondents.

Eighth, avoid unintended *double-choice questions* such as, *"Is your health better or worse now than it was a year ago?"* (Payne 1951:69), which has the double choice of better-worse and now-then. It might be better to remove ambiguity from the above question by rewording it to read, *"Is your health better now or was it better a year ago?"*

Multiple-Choice Questions

As was true of two-way questions, choices need to be mutually exclusive and complementarily balanced so that the number of alternatives on one side does not affect the distribution of replies. Second, all alternatives should be listed. If more than one choice is possible, explicit mention of this should be made. Thus, your decision as to whether you wish your respondents to express one choice or more than one should be clearly given.

Third, if you exclude certain choices in the question, this restriction should be explicitly kept in mind during analysis: An example occurs in the question, *"Aside from the expensiveness of abortions, which of these things would you say is the most important reason why most women would not obtain an abortion?"* In the analysis of answers to this question, the fact that *expense* has been excluded as a choice must be kept in mind so that readers are not misled by the data.

Fourth, a *card list* should always be given to the respondent if the question has more than three alternatives so that the respondent's answer is not based on just those responses he or she has not forgotten. For instance;

21. *Please tell me whether you think it should be possible for a pregnant woman to obtain a legal abortion* . . . (HAND CARD A—see accompanying example—TO RESPONDENT, READ EACH STATEMENT, AND CIRCLE ONE CODE FOR EACH.)

CARD A (goes with question 21)

A. If there is a strong chance of serious defect in the baby?

B. If she is married and does not want any more children?

C. If the woman's own health is seriously endangered by the pregnancy?

D. If the family has a very low income and cannot afford any more children?

E. If she became pregnant as a result of rape?

F. If she is not married and does not want to marry the man?

Fifth, "Don't know" or "No Opinion" answers should be provided for on the inverview schedule or questionnaire but need not appear on the card list.

Sixth, it is often wise to vary the order of *card list choices* so that the order of stimuli presentation is controlled. (There is a response bias for some persons of choosing the first or last choices.)

Other Types of Question Designs

George Gallup (1947) developed an approach to question design called the *quintamensional design* which has much proven merit in tapping opinions and attitudes. *Awareness* of the attitude object is first tapped through an open-ended knowledge question. Then *general attitudes* concerning the same object are ascertained with another open-ended question. Third, *specific attitudes* are then measured through a closed-ended question. Fourth, *reasons* for holding this attitude are tapped with an open-ended question. Finally, *intensity* of feeling is explored. The following sequence of questions on abortion follows this design.

1 *What, specifically, do "abortion laws" mean to you?*
2. *What, if anything, should your state legislature do about present abortion laws?*
3. *It has been suggested by some people that this state's present abortion laws are adequate. Other people feel the state's abortion laws are inadequate. Do you approve of abortion law change, or do you feel the abortion laws should remain unchanged?*
4. *Why do you feel this way?*
5. *How strongly do you feel about this—very strongly, fairly strongly, or not at all strongly?*

A second quintamensional example takes a slightly different tack.

1. *Have you heard or read about fluoridating public water supplies?* (Yes: ask Q. 2; No: skip to Q. 6.)
2. *As you understand it, what is the purpose of water fluoridation?*
3. *What is your opinion on fluoridating public water supplies? Do you feel it is very desirable, desirable, undesirable, or very undesirable?*
4. *Do you think the decision about whether or not to fluoridate the water supply should be made at the federal level, at the state level, or do you think it should be left to each local community?*
5. *Who should decide to fluoridate or not to fluoridate—elected officials, a health authority such as the health department, or do you think the people themselves should decide by special vote?*

Although there is not always a need for as many as five questions in exploring an issue, oftentimes the five components of the quintamensional design—awareness or familiarity with the issue, expression of individual attitudes, reactions to specific proposals, reasons for these opinions, and intensity of opinions—are useful in adequately covering the various dimensions of a research issue.

One of the most common serious errors made by neophyte survey researchers is the use of the *leading question*. For instance, *"Aside from murder, under what other circumstances do you feel the death penalty should be used?"* assumes that the respondent (1) believes in the use of the death penalty as justified (2) particularly in the case of murder. Neither assumption may be correct. Some respondents are likely to be either antagonized by the leading question or will acquiesce to the question even though they do not believe in the death penalty. A slightly more subtle leading question is, *"How do you feel sex discrimination should be combated?"* which assumes that the respondent feels it should be combated.

Implied alternative questions and questions with *only* a pro *or* con issue stated are even more subtle forms of the leading question. Survey researchers wish to avoid leading questions because they are interested in the *actual* opinions of respondents. Leading questions may give the respondent the idea that the researcher wishes a specific answer because of the built-in biases. Therefore, rather than give an actual opinion, many respondents may "comply" or acquiesce to the leading question. Hence, the neophyte question designer must be particularly careful to avoid leading questions. Experienced question designers occasionally break this rule with a specific purpose in mind, but inexperienced researchers would be better off not breaking this rule.

Perhaps the most common error in survey research is the use of *double-barreled* questions that ask a person to respond to more than one stimuli at a time by asking several questions at the same time. The problem is: Which stimuli is being responded to? The only correct solution is to break double-barreled questions into separate questions. An example of a double-barreled question is, *"Do you prefer to smoke pot in a small group or hash in a large group?"* The stimuli in this case are size of group and type of drug—with no way of knowing which is being used in the person's evaluation. A second example from a recent survey is, *"Do you feel that the increasing incidence of premarital and extramarital sex is basically good or bad?"* Many people are much more favorable towards premarital than extramarital sex. Hence, the question should be split into two questions.

Just because respondents are willing to answer such questions is no excuse for using double-barreled questions. Respondents often wish to please the researcher; willingness to respond offers no assurance that frame of reference problems are settled. Even otherwise quite sophisticated researchers unintentionally make double-barreled questions.

Thus, the survey designer should always be on the lookout for this problem.

Sleeper questions are sometimes used to measure how responsible a respondent is being in answering a questionnaire or schedule. Robert Winch of Northwestern University in still unpublished data used the sleeper question to weed out irresponsible subjects. He had a question asking students to rank order the prestige of campus fraternities and sororities with which they were *familiar.* Five of the thirty fraternities and sororities on the list were fictitious. If a respondent ranked any three or more of the five, the questionnaire was thrown out of the analysis.

Special care should be taken in the wording of questions designed to reconstruct the respondent's past actions or history. For example, the question *"How many times a month do you attend church?"* could better be phrased *"How many times during the last month did you attend church?"* The point is to avoid *averaging* questions since event participation (church attendance in this case) may vary so greatly that respondents cannot meaningfully figure an average event frequency in an accurate way. Thus, by revising the question to ask for *actual* event frequency over a *short* period of time, the interviewer may get more meaningful data. Also, care should be taken as to the *time* of year reconstructed history questions are asked because of possible cyclical variations. Church attendance figures would be higher than normal during the Christmas and Easter seasons, lower during the summer months.

The researcher also must consider how difficult it is for the respondent to answer accurately due to length of recall period. Consider these questions:

1. *During the last year, how many times did you visit a doctor for any reason?*
2. *During the last four weeks, how much money did you spend on restaurant meals?*

Sudman and Bradburn (1974) relate memory decay to (1) the importance of the event and (2) improper placement of events in time. The less important the event to the person, the more likely it will be underreported over lengthy time periods. By contrast, placement of events in time usually results in overreporting because respondents "telescope" time by including events outside the given reference period. A good rule of thumb is to keep recall periods no longer than one month.

Another serious problem is the use of *proxy respondents.* A standard procedure in some surveys is to allow an adult household member to report for any other household member. Comparisons of proxy reporting with self-reporting shows that proxy respondents may consistently and seriously underreport for other members of the same household for some types of information.

Question Wording and Readability

Attempt to keep sentence structure simple and to less than twenty words in length. Use the simplest wording possible that conveys the meaning intended. Words should always be keyed to the lowest educational level to be questioned. Thorndike and Lorge (1944) and Dale and Chall (1948) have listed the 1000 and 3000 most frequently used English words. For most purposes these words will express any thought you wish to convey in questions. Of course, you would want to use more technical jargon for some surveys—for instance, surveys of medical doctors about health practices.

Although the meaning of a particular word may seem obvious to you, it is often wise to consult a dictionary (and a dictionary of slang) for possible alternative meanings that might confuse the issue. While looking up definitions, look for possible alternative pronunciations which might better communicate the word. Often, good schedules have pronunciations of hard-to-pronounce words in parentheses following the word as an aid to the interviewer.

Abstract concept words such as "alienation," "anomie," "cohesion," and so forth should be avoided. If such complex issues are to be explored, use more indirect methods such as attitude scales.

If words you wish to emphasize are underlined or capitalized, misplaced emphasis can be reduced: *"What are your thoughts concerning LEGALIZED abortion?"*

Often respondents will jump the gun in anticipating a question. One way to reduce this problem is to state the conditions before the alternatives. Consider the following two questions:

1. *In the case of women who have had German measles during pregnancy, are you in favor of legalized abortion?*
2. *Are you in favor of legalized abortion in the case of women who have had German measles during pregnancy?*

The first question, by stating the conditions first, is likely to receive a more positive response since it forces the respondent to listen more carefully to the full question. The elimination of unnecessary punctuation helps the respondent realize the question is not complete because slight pauses by the interviewer are conducive to premature answers.

"How much?" questions are often too indefinite. *"How long on the average is your daily travel to work?"* can be answered in terms of miles or time. Spell out the system in which you wish the answer to be given.

There are also a number of ways in which a question may be loaded in favor of (or against) a particular issue. These should be avoided. Catch words, stereotypes, and prestige names alter response rates. *"Are you willing to have reasonable price increases with the hope that they will bring back prosperity?"* increased the affirmative response by 11 percent when the word "reasonable" was added. When a question was restated to include Eisenhower's name (*"General Eisenhower says the Army and Navy should be combined. . . . "*), 49 percent approved compared to 29 percent when his name was not included. On issues where respondents have weak opinions they are more likely to cling to key words and phrases. In other words, their responses to marginal issues tend to be distorted by more powerful question words such as "General Eisenhower" (Payne 1951:126).

Citation of the status quo also provides powerful influences. Any phrase that calls attention to existing conditions— *"As you know . . . ," "According to the law . . . ," "As it is now . . . "*—*gives a predisposition to higher approval for the question compared to the same question without one of these types of phrases.*

Personalized questions normally receive slightly different responses than similar nonpersonalized questions because some people treat "you" singularly (personally) and others plurally (their family, work associates).

1. *"Do you consider it desirable to balance the budget?"*
2. *"Is it desirable to balance the budget?"*

Payne (1951:158–175) and Parten (1950:206) give lists of other danger words that, like "you," tend to change response rates.

One of the most important points almost always overlooked by question designers is how the question will sound five to ten years from now. If one wants to collect data over a period of time, questions should remain constant. Even with a slight modification the wording change has to be considered as a possible source of change in response rates. Thus, good questions, in so far as possible, are designed to be relatively non-timebound. As an example, Otis Dudley Duncan (1972:2) has recently used good (relatively nontimebound) questions in a survey of changing work habits, life styles, and racial and social attitudes over the past twenty years.

Question Organization and Sequencing

The more complex, or less understood, the issue being measured, the more often a *battery* of questions should be used in preference to a single question. As we will see in Chapter 12, reliability increases with an increase in indicators. Quintamensional question designs are also often useful in this regard since they tend to lead the respondent through a meaningful exploration of the issue.

It is a good idea to facilitate smoother transition from question topic to topic within the survey with material written into the schedule or questionnaire. Nothing is more disconcerting for a respondent than jumping from topic to topic. At best, all that the researcher does when making abrupt transitions is to create so much stress that the respondent does not give much thought to any particular question; at worst, a lot of respondents will refuse to finish an anarchically-designed questionnaire, as is classically illustrated in the chapter-opening quotation. Examples of good transition statements include, *"Now in 1968, you may remember that . . . " "Just thinking about your family now, . . . " "Now another kind of question,"* or, *"Now, I should like to ask you some questions about . . . "*

Transitions to specific questions from specific answers should also be clearly marked for the interviewer since often particular questions are not applicable given previous responses. Thus instructions for a hypothetical question 12 might have instructions to "go to question 13" if "yes" or "skip to question 17" if "no."

Easy introductory questions (age, sex, number of children) are generally given at the beginning of the survey as a "warming up" exercise to engage respondents without taxing or threatening them. These are followed by the main, more complicated, and emotional questions. Riskier questions (such as income) often come late in the survey so that if the respondent refuses to continue, less information will be lost. Finally, a few easy questions are normally given at the end of the survey to provide some tension release, or "cooling off," for the respondent. If this is not done, the researcher risks the possibility of losing later interviews or creating an unpleasant interview-respondent situation in leave taking.

Sometimes, particularly in more unstructured interviews, question sequence should be varied as the following quotation from Kinsey and his associates (1948:48) shows:

> For unmarried college males, the sequence [should be] nocturnal emissions, masturbation, premarital petting, premarital intercourse with companions, intercourse with prostitutes, animal contacts, and the homosexual. For males who have never gone beyond the tenth grade in school, premarital intercourse can be discussed much earlier in the interview, because it is generally accepted at that social level; but masturbation needs to be approached more carefully if one is to get the truth from that group.

Any researcher who plans to have other persons do the interviewing generally provides a detailed interviewer's instructions guide. Instruction guides are important means of increasing the reliability and validity of one's data since they explicate problems that the interviewer can be expected to encounter and give standardized means of handling those problems. Appendix B gives an example of a well-thought-out interview guide. Appendix C gives an example of a well-thought-out interview schedule.

QUESTIONNAIRE TECHNIQUES

Just as the respondent's motivation to supply information is affected by the interviewer, a questionnaire also affects respondents. Parten (1950:158) points out that the attractiveness of a questionnaire can make all the difference in the recipient's motivation to fill it out and return it. Indeed, more care needs to be taken with questionnaire construction than with interview schedules because there will be no trained investigator present to explain question phraseology or instructions to the respondent. The questionnaire respondent will be more likely to misinterpret questions or omit essential items. Thus, the questionnaire must be simpler and more self-explanatory in form than the interview schedule.

The questionnaire also lacks the "personality" of an interview. Most people would prefer to talk about a subject than write out a detailed answer. Thus, a questionnaire must sell itself in order to gain and keep the interest of its recipient. (See Appendix D for an example of a good questionnaire.)

STRUCTURED INTERVIEWING TECHNIQUES

Before any interviewing is done, interviewers must be selected and trained. Even if the researcher is doing the interviewing and has done extensive interviewing in the past, he or she will find it necessary to pretest the schedule, preferably on respondents who will demand the most skill in interviewing. Not only does this pretest help in redesigning questions which turn out to communicate inappropriate frames of reference, but it also helps the researcher explicate problems that will have to be handled in standardized ways.

While there is little empirical evidence for characteristics that make for good or bad interviewing, Rogers (1942) has emphasized characteristics of counselors that appear relevant to good interviewers. Interviewers must have, or develop, a considerable degree of social sensitivity or "intraceptiveness": a tactful sensing of the reactions of respondents and appropriate interviewer responses in the interview situation. To some extent these traits may be learned.

Cannell (reported in ISR Newsletter 1977) has concluded that many respondents may not perform well because they do not know what is expected of them and because interviewers do not give them appropriate feedback on what is expected. In his study interviewers gave positive feedback indiscriminately for both good and poor respondent behavior. Refusal to answer a question, the worst possible respondent behavior, received proportionately the greatest positive feedback! Cannell concluded that the interviewer must learn (1) to clarify for the respondent what is expected to perform his or her role properly, (2) provide cues as to how to be most effective in answering particular questions accurately, and (3) motivate the respondent to work diligently to recall and organize information and to report even potentially embarrassing material. General instructions to the respondent that clearly define the goals of the interview would include:

> " . . . *In order for your answers to be most helpful to us, it is important that you try to be as accurate as you can.*"

In the case of a questionnaire it is necessary to provide specific cues or suggestions to clarify performance on a particular task, such as:

> *"For these next questions we'd like you to be as exact as you can about dates.* Please give me the date of . . . "

Feedback statements, both positive and negative, help depending on the probable answer to a particular question.

In order to obtain commitment to engage wholeheartedly in providing the information, Cannell found it best to have the interviewer explain the importance of complete information and then ask the respondent to sign a commitment agreement.

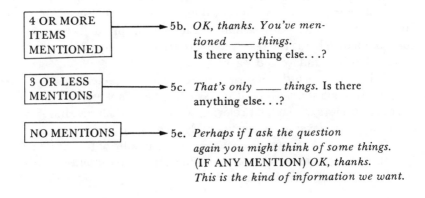

"I understand that the information from this interview must be very accurate in order to be useful. This means that I must do my best to give accurate and complete answers."

In exchange the interviewer then signs an agreement guaranteeing anonymity to the respondent. (A more detailed summary of these findings may be found in *Experiments in Interviewing Techniques* published by the National Center for Health Services Research [PHS HS Grant #00624]. Most large survey organizations spend considerable time and money in teaching interviewers the types of respondent responses they can expect to encounter and the types of standardized responses interviewers find most successful in dealing with them. Interviewer trainees are often put through both respondent and interviewer role-playing exercises, audio and visual tape-recorded sessions, and actual in-the-field training under the supervision of an experienced interviewer.

Most interviews require some type of introductory remarks in order to give the respondent some minimum level of understanding as to why he or she has been selected, who the interviewer is, and the nature of the research topic. For example,

"Good day. I'm from the Public Opinion Survey Unit of the University of Missouri. (shows official identification). *We're doing a survey at this time on how people feel about police-community relationships. This study is being done throughout the state, and the results will be used by local and state governments. The addresses at which we interview are chosen entirely by chance, and the interview only takes 45 minutes. All information is entirely confidential, of course."*

As Cannell and Kahn (1968:579) point out, respondents generally require early assurance on

. . . the interviewer's identity, the legitimacy of the research, the process by which they were chosen for interview, the protection which they may expect as respondents, the extent of the demands which are to be made upon them, and their own adequacy to meet those demands . . . the interviewer should also be prepared to become very explicit with respect to the uses of the data, the sponsoring agencies, and the kinds of reports to be issued.

Some type of identification (official letter or identification card) is usually helpful in establishing legitimate identity, as well as a phone number at the agency where the respondent may call for further proof. Often an advance letter is helpful. With the increasing number of salespeople and bill collectors who also ask questions, these measures are vital in establishing early rapport with respondents. In addition, the interviewer, consistent with earlier ethical statements in Chapter 1, should give enough information to the respondent so that he or she can give informed consent. However, there is no need to give complete details, which in many instances would not only be misunderstood but might in some instances bias the study results, as in a survey of homosexual behavior.

Occasionally the respondent puts up resistance. Typical resistance may take one of several basic forms. First, "Why was *I* chosen?" A good response to this might be, "In order to get an accurate picture of how people feel we pick some addresses simply by chance and then talk to somebody at those addresses." Second, "How confidential will what I say be?" One good response to this question would be, "When we get through, we put the interviews together and come out with a general picture of the country as a whole" or "We don't identify anybody; we want to get an idea of the general mood of the country." Third, "I'm sorry but I'm busy doing . . . " is a typical excuse. Good answers to this might run as follows; "It'll only take about _____ minutes. Perhaps I could come in and talk with you while you went on doing . . . I wouldn't hold you up any." Fourth, sometimes the respondent will say, "I don't actually know much about _____ anyway. You ought to interview somebody who knows more." Here, the interviewer might respond; "Well, you see, we're eager to get the opinions and ideas of many people. I guess there aren't any of us who know too much about the many complicated things in the world these days. Why don't we try a few questions and see how it goes?" Notice, here, how the interviewer has emphasized that expert knowledge is not necessary, merely opinions and feelings. Fifth, potential respondents often will ask, "What sorts of things will you ask me?" In these cases, typically, it is acceptable to say something corresponding to, "This is part of a study to find out what people are thinking about _____ and what their attitudes are towards _____ _____." Notice that even though this is vaguely stated, it normally satisfies respondents so that a detailed rundown of the interview schedule should be unnecessary.

Most survey organizations instruct their interviewers, once they have started the interview, not to stray beyond the question wording as printed on the schedule. However, occasionally nondirective probing is needed. Table 6–1 lists a number of such generally accepted probes.

Probably nine out of ten interviews will not tax the interviewer's skills. Most respondents will articulate responses and cooperate without much need for the interviewer to reinforce the "good respondent" role. However, every interviewer finds interview situations that call for particular reinforcement tactics.

At the one extreme are situations in which the respondent does *not* give complete, understandable, or unambiguous responses. The brief showing of understanding ("I see," "um-hm," "I understand") often is sufficient to encourage amplification or continuation of a response. How-

Table 6–1
Typical Nondirective Interview Probes

Brief expressions of understanding and interest

Examples: I see; um-hm; yes, I understand.

Research: Krasner (1958), Quay (1958), Richardson, Hastorf, and Dornbusch (1964), Salzinger (1956), Salzinger and Pisoni (1960), on the ineffectiveness of infrequent encouragement; Mandler and Kaplan (1956), on occasional respondent misinterpretation of "um-hm" encouragements; Hildum and Brown (1956), on the biasing effect of "Good" as an encouragement.

Brief expectant pauses

Research: Gorden (1954) and Saslow and others (1957), on the positive effects of short pauses (2–3 seconds) as compared to the negative effects of long pauses (in excess of 10–15 seconds).

Neutral requests for additional information

Examples: How do you mean? I'd like to know more of your thinking on that. What do you have in mind there? Is there anything else? Can you tell me more about that?

Research: Guest (1947), Shapiro and Eberhart (1947).

Echo or near repetition of the respondent's words

Example: *Respondent*—I've taken these treatments for almost six months, and I'm not getting any better. *Interviewer*—You're not getting better?

Research: No direct evidence, but agreement that sensitive use of the echo conveys close attention, sympathy, and encouragement to continue (Kahn and Cannell 1957; Richardson, Dohrenwend, and Klein 1965; Rogers 1951).

Summarizing or reflecting respondent expressions

Examples would follow respondent statements, stating the interviewer's understanding of a key feeling or meaning. Such summaries often begin with phrases like, "You feel that . . " or "You mean that. . . ."

Research: Rogers (1942, 1951), on effectiveness in counseling and psychotherapy; Campbell and others (1960), Couch and Keniston (1960), Lenski and Leggett (1960), on dangers of acquiescence bias; Beezer (1956), on limitation to acquiescence bias.

Requests for specific kinds of additional information

Examples: *Why* do you think that is so? *How* dis that become clear to you? *When* was that?

Requests for clarification

Examples: I'm not clear on that. Could you explain what you meant?

Repetition of a primary question

Examples: *Interviewer*—What kind of work do you do? *Respondent*—Work at the paper mill. *Interviewer*—I see. What kind of work do you do there?

SOURCE: Cannell-Kahn, "Interviewing," from Gardner Lindzey and Elliot Aronson, eds., *The Handbook of Social Psychology*, © 1954 Edition 2, pp. 581–582, Addison-Wesley Publishing Company, Inc. Reprinted with permission.

ever, the interviewer must be careful not to suggest favorable or unfavorable reactions to the respondent's responses since such reactions may cause serious reactive effects.

More neutral, and hence better tactics, often would be to repeat or summarize the respondent's words, neutrally ask for additional information, or simply repeat the question again. Sometimes *brief* periods of silence are an effective means of communicating that the interviewer expects a more complete response. Rapport, however, can be damaged by overuse of silence or lengthy (over 10 to 15 second) silences.

At the other extreme are situations in which the respondent may be too verbose, giving all sorts of irrelevant information while eating up valuable interviewing time. Here the interviewer must be careful to show interest while tactfully interrupting and leading the subject back into the interview. For instance, "That's an interesting point, Mr. Johnston, but . . . " or "I see. Now where were we? Oh yes, . . . " Generally speaking, such tactful negative reinforcement will quickly lead the respondent to structure responses more in line with the interviewer's intentions. Sometimes the interviewer may find it necessary to be more forceful by such phrases as, "Mr. Johnston, that's very interesting, but I have other interviews to finish today, and I would appreciate it if we could stick more to the questions." Or, "That's nice. Perhaps we could talk about that more after the interview is finished."

Also, respondents sometimes openly test interviewers for "right" answers. The most effective responses to such situations are the more neutral and vague appeals which show interest in the respondent such as, "There is no right answer. We're interested in your opinions." Or, "Your own ideas are what is most important to this survey."

Indications of interest in the respondent's answers may also be influenced by interviewer "presence" or nonverbal cues. It is often wise to train interviewers with audiovisual playbacks so they can view how their posture and vocal tone affect the interview process.

Although the various techniques outlined above are helpful in the interview process, they do not exhaust probing and directive needs of the interviewer. For example, the respondent may give inaccurate or inconsistent responses, irrelevant responses, nonresponses, or only partial reponses. Thus, the interviewer sometimes finds it necessary to summarize the respondent's answer, ask leading questions, provide more adequate frames of reference, interrupt respondents, or note inconsistencies.

The *summarizing technique* is a means of reflecting the ideas that the respondent is relating. It is used when the interviewer wishes the respondent to pursue ideas in greater depth. For instance,

Respondent: I don't seem to be getting well.
Interviewer: You don't see any improvement?

or

Respondent: Well, one thing, I don't get a chance to use my short-
hand. I don't take more than one letter a week. Most
of my work is just typing reports with hundreds of
tables and charts.
Interviewer: You feel that you can do higher level work?

or

Respondent: I thought maybe the U.N. was the answer to world
problems, but now I don't know.
Interviewer: You feel some doubts about it now?

Notice in these examples how the interviewer has summarized and reflected the respondent's feelings. When *accurate* summarizations are used
within a framework of *acceptance* of the respondent's feelings, they may
stimulate further conversation. However, if the interviewer inaccurately
summarizes or shows nonpermissiveness, the respondent may well
become defensive. Thus, the summarization technique demands atten-
tive listening, insight, ingenuity, and permissive attitudes on the part of
the interviewer.

Leading questions make it easier or more tempting for the respondent
to give an answer the interviewer suggests to the respondent. In effect,
an answer of "yes" to a loaded question merely indicates agreement with
the *language* of the question. Thus, leading questions encourage distorted
responses.

Occasionally this rule may be broken. In order to break the leading
question avoidance rule, one should have *strong reason* for believing the
respondent is reluctant to divulge information about him- or herself or
others. As Kinsey and others (1948:53–54) advocated,

The interviewer should not make it easy for the subject to deny his participation in any form of sexual activity. It is too easy to say no if he is simply
asked whether he has ever engaged in a particular activity . . . Consequently
we always begin by asking *when* they first engaged in such activity . . . and
since it becomes apparent from the form of our question that we would
not be surprised if he had had such experience, there seems to be less
reason for denying it. It might be thought that this approach would bias the
answer, but there is no indication that we get false admissions of participation in forms of sexual behavior in which the subject was not actually
involved.

Nevertheless, this technique is likely to backfire unless the interviewer is as sure of his or her reasons—that is, has correct premises—for leading the respondent as Kinsey was.

Language is always ambiguous. We saw earlier that each of us has idiosyncratic frames of reference which may confuse the communication process. We saw the need for incorporating specific frames of reference into some question designs; however, this may not be enough. Sometimes the interviewer will be required to supply a nonleading frame of reference for the subject. This is particularly true of questions that tap retrospective data. For instance,

> Interviewer: When was the last time you were hospitalized?
> Respondent: Hm. (long pause) Maybe six or seven years ago.
> Interviewer: Well, that would be 1974 or 1975. The Watergate scandal ended with Nixon resigning the presidency in the summer of 1974. Was your hospitalization before or after his resignation?

Notice how the interviewer has provided a "coathanger" or frame of reference by which the respondent may compare his or her past history.

Earlier we noted means by which to lengthen a response. Sometimes, by contrast, we wish to *shorten* a response—when a response becomes irrelevant, repetitive, or lengthy. Richardson, Dohrenwend, and Klein (1965:205) recommend *guggles* (short, staccato sounds like "ah" or the beginnings of words that are not completed) during the middle of the respondent's phrase or sentence. If this is ignored, increased guggling may show the respondent that the interviewer has something to say. *Interruptions* at the *end* of the respondent's phrase or sentence are less generally effective in shortening responses.

Often the interviewer may note inconsistencies between responses and wish to clarify them. Usually, a permissive attitude, summary of the alleged inconsistencies, and a request for clarification are all that are necessary. For example,

> Interviewer: Earlier you said that your husband worked for a research and development firm, but now you say that he is a teacher. Could you clarify this for me.

The interviewer might also have phrased the clarification request, "Could we go back over that for a moment?" Usually, repeating something the respondent said earlier in the interview will increase the respondent's motivation to respond since it shows that the interviewer feels what the respondent is saying is important and is listening attentively. However, the noting of inconsistencies must not appear to be a confrontation. Confrontation will normally jeopardize respondent participation because of its threatening nature. Whenever a question appears to threaten a respondent it may be wise to break off the subject, change to another topic, and return to the topic after respondent confidence has been regained.

Richardson and his associates (1965:218–222) point out that the *pace* or *tempo* of the interview can also be highly influential in motivating respondent communication. Many interviewers have difficulty in recognizing that their tempos are too fast or slow for particular subjects. If the interviewer tries to speed up the interview with respondents whose cultural or subcultural way of life is much slower than his or her own, he or she may well create confusion, impressions of harassment, or feelings of irritation or insecurity. By contrast, in interviews with busy corporation executives such respondents might be aggravated if the interviewer does not maintain a pace congenial with their busy schedules.

Finally, more flagrant probing errors by neophyte interviewers include such interviewer behaviors as the overuse of "Could you . . . ?" or "Can you . . . ?" type phrasings that *ask* for a "no" answer. Better phrasing would be of the form, "Please tell me. . . . " Particularly at the beginning of an interview it is useful to use this form over the former since the interviewer, by getting the respondent into appropriate role behavior early in the interview, will increase chances that the respondent will continue in that manner later in the interview. A second flagrant error is the phrasing of questions in the form "I suppose you would agree or feel that . . . "or "I guess that's all you want to tell me, hmm?" Such pseudo-clairvoyant language on the part of an interviewer is likely to be followed by acquiescent responses. A third error is the use of the word "just" which signifies lack of significance.

STRATEGIES OF DEPTH INTERVIEWING

Earlier in this chapter we noted that structured interviewing is most appropriate in classifying clearly understood attitudinal or behavioral dimensions. However, there are many situations in which the researcher poorly understands the respondent's frame of reference, information levels, and opinion structures. In these cases the researcher should resort to more unstructured, or depth, interviewing strategies. In a previous section we discussed some relatively unstructured techniques such as probing and summarizing, which even the structured interview has call for at times. Depth interviewing builds upon the use of such techniques.

However, because of the relative ambiguity of unstructured interview situations, it takes much more skill and practice to conduct depth interviews successfully.

Banaka (1971:21–30) discusses the need for trainees in depth interview tactics to reflect on (1) *inclusion*—how much they feel part of or excluded from the interview, (2) *control*—their perception of how much in control or out of control of the interview they are, and (3) *affection*—how they feel towards the interviewee. Of course, these are problems in structured interviewing as well, but because the depth interviewer has no "prepared script" (interview schedule) to fall back on, he or she has to develop special interpersonal skills that permit the interviewer rather than the respondent to structure the interview.

Inclusion problems must be tackled before control and affection problems because of the need to establish rapport with the respondent. For the interviewer, this often means coming to grips with the question, "Do I have the right to ask respondents about their private lives or personal opinions?"

Unless interviewers can deal with this problem they tend to give off nonverbal and verbal cues that reveal uneasiness. Any such signs of uneasiness on their part may easily dampen respondents' willingness to continue. Hence, interviewers must have a wide familiarity with their own emotional self. In an ongoing study I have been conducting concerning the social-psychological effects of rape, I have been using a female interviewer whom I selected in part because I felt she would not become anxious when asking quite obviously personal questions of the rape victims. From past experience with this interviewer I knew she had the necessary self-insight and emotional maturity to carry these interviews out without guilt or anxiety over entering into very private areas of the respondent's life. Experience shows that interviewers can ask almost anything of respondents and obtain answers if they can deal with their own moral-ethical qualms about delving into the respondent's life. By contrast, any displays of moral or ethical qualms on the part of the interviewer generally induce anxiety in the respondent.

The second issue is the problem of control. There is the danger that the respondent may take over control of the interview. The first means of dealing with control has been discussed under the topic of inclusion. If interviewers cannot handle their own emotions, they will easily be led by their respondents. Beyond this, a good tactic is to start with a *written general plan* of action. In the plan, interviewers outline a description of their research problem including a summary of data they feel will be needed to draw conclusions from the study. For instance, in my previously mentioned rape study, we decided on the following general plan:

I. Personal characteristics at the time of rape (age, income, education, religion, occupation, marital and parental statuses, number of brothers and sisters, and own birth order).

II. Personal knowledge of someone who had been raped or attempted rape.
   A. Their relationship to you at that time.
   B. The effect of this experience on them.
   C. The effect of this experience on you.
   D. Similarity–differences of own experience to theirs.

III. Conception of rape before own experience; differences from actual rape.

IV. Description of actual rape (or attempted rape).
   A. Where and when did it happen?
   B. Distinguishing features of the rapist—age, height, weight, ethnicity, estimated social class.
   C. Personal contact with rapist beforehand.
   D. Description of his behavior. Reaction to his behavior. His reaction to your reaction.

V. Who was told of the rape? Relatives, friends, authorities (police, psychologist, minister). Why were these particular people told or not told?
   A. Who told them? What was their reaction to the story? Your reaction to their reaction.
   B. If police told, describe their procedures in handling the case. Your reaction to these procedures.
   C. If police not told, why not?

VI. What happened to rapist? Was he caught, prosecuted, sentenced, incarcerated?
   A. How felt about rapist at time of rape?
   B. Afterwards?

VII. Noticeable effect(s) rape has had on life—changes in attitudes towards rape, men in general or particular, other women, sex, police, self.

VIII. What would you do if caught now in same or similar situation? Advice for other women facing same type of situation?

IX. Kind of sex education prior to rape.

X. Kinds of sex experience prior to rape.

XI. Motivations for participation in this study.

Unlike structured interviewing it is often unwise to hold rigidly to the general interview plan when doing depth interviewing. There have been a number of instances in this rape study when interviews would have been lost if the interviewer had stuck rigidly to the plan. Rather, the plan is most useful as a *checklist* of points to be covered but not necessarily in the order of the list no matter how logically laid out.

Control is often lost because the inexperienced interviewer may

1. Infer things not stated by the respondent
2. Fixate on the respondent's words by repeating exactly what was said

3. Ask questions that imply the researcher already knows the answer
4. Interrupt or anticipate the respondent's answers
5. Ask several questions before the respondent has a chance to respond to the first one.

By contrast, the respondent may diminish the interviewer's control by (Banaka 1971:17)

1. Being vague; answering "don't know"
2. Asking [the interviewer] a question about her- or himself
3. Resorting to long, rambling monologues
4. Interrupting [the interviewer] before he or she finishes a question
5. Asking [the interviewer] to clarify his or her questions
6. Talking in a very low voice so [the interviewer] can just barely hear.

The skillful depth interviewer learns to be on the lookout for signs that sufficient trust has not been established to control the interview situation.

There are a number of tactics that may prove useful to the interviewer in controlling the interview process. Banaka (1971:100) feels that good depth interviews can be analyzed in terms of the amount of factual and feeling questions asked. He feels that about 15 to 25 percent of the questions should ask for factual material; fewer factual questions make the interview suffer from lack of adequate foundation, and more than 25 percent indicates the interviewer may be too anxious to avoid asking for personal feelings. Likewise, the interviewer should be asking approximately 15 to 25 percent opinion and 15 to 25 percent feeling questions. Banaka points out that less skillful interviewers shy away from asking enough opinion and feeling questions. Furthermore, skillful interviewers ask a lot of *probing* questions—up to 50 percent of the questions (Banaka 1971:102)—in order to get closer to the specifics of the targeted topic.

Good depth interviewers usually use some nondirective feedback to the respondent on what they seem to be stating or feeling as a means of (1) showing their respondents that they have been listening and (2) encouraging the respondents to expose themselves more. Good interviewers totally avoid the use of advice giving, disagreements, agreements, and *inferences* to things not explicitly stated by a respondent. (While agreements—for example, "I think that's so"—are bad tactics because they verbally condition the respondent to alter responses, it is acceptable and desirable for the interviewer to show that he or she is listening through occasional encouragements such as "uh-huh" or "I see.") Of course, occasionally depth interviewers, no matter how skilled, may be faced with such complete lack of cooperation that they may have to explicitly raise the need to explore the relational tensions that block the interview.

Such tensions bring up the issue of affection, which tends to create the greatest problems in depth interviewing. American culture tends to support hiding the direct expression of feelings. Some of the means of avoiding such feelings are (Banaka 1971:17)

1. Objectifying the feeling by expressing an opinion about the other person or object involved
2. Denying feelings
3. Avoiding the use of the pronoun "I"; using "we" or "you" so that [the interviewer] can't tell who belongs to the feeling or opinion
4. Crying or acting embarrassed
5. Asking to be excused for a minute.

To the extent that interviewers let respondents avoid such feelings, they lose control of the interview. Often these avoidance cues are used to "test" interviewers. Once respondents find out that interviewers are (1) not made uncomfortable by self-disclosure *and* (2) wish them to explore rather than avoid such feelings, respondents will usually let down these defenses. Several of my rape respondents in response to extremely personal questions went through what they thought were "expected" crying spells. When, to their shock, they found the interviewer unwilling to be embarrassed by this affective behavior, they stopped these avoidance tactics and started openly discussing their feelings.

Depth interviewing obviously requires much more training in interpersonal skills than structured interviewing. The serious student of depth interviewing may profit by the role-play exercises outlined by Banaka (1971).

SURVEY METHOD VARIATIONS

Survey method variations include the telephone, face-to-face, self-administered, and randomized response. No one of these methods has been shown to have clear superiority over the others (Bradburn and others 1979). Each has its own advantages and disadvantages.

The telephone interview has appeal because it is convenient and produces a significant cost saving. About 99 percent of all U.S. households now have at least one phone—although only about 90 percent of all adults can be reached by phone due to incidence of transience, institutionalization, and so on. The rising cost of face-to-face interviewing has pushed some researchers in the direction of telephone surveys, as have social problems associated with urban areas where people are more nervous about opening doors to strangers and interviewers are more nervous about entering such areas. Other important positive features of good quality control in telephone surveys have been noted (*Behavior Today*, October 10, 1977): (1) Coders can quickly inform interviewers of interviewing techniques that create coding problems, (2) staff can meet with interviewers readily and on short notice—which has helped raise initially low response rates, and (3) a pool of potential interviewers who are fluent in a variety of languages can be on hand—which circumvents the expense of multilingual interviewers.

On the negative side, telephone interviews create a new kind of nonresponse, the broken-off interview that occurs in about 4 percent of the calls. Telephone interviews also produce less information; interviewers cannot describe housing or talk with neighbors, nor can they describe nonrespondents' characteristics.

Also, increasing numbers of persons have unlisted phone numbers. To overcome this problem, some survey organizations have been using random-digit telephone surveys. Response Analysis Corporation (1978a) analyzed the results of random-digit telephoning and discovered some interesting findings (*The Sampler from Response Analysis* [1978*b*], 12:1). First, one-fourth of their sample (in Delaware County, Pennsylvania) reported being called on an unlisted phone; this agrees with Bell Telephone of Pennsylvania data. Second, persons called on an unlisted phone were about as likely to participate in the survey as those called on a listed number. These are pulses for random-digit sampling. Third, on the minus side, slightly more than one-tenth of these households reported having two or more separate telephone lines or numbers—giving them double or more the possibility of being called by this method.

Another problem with telephone interviews has to do with converting "scale" questions so they can be used over the phone. Response Analysis (1975) also did a study comparing telephone with face-to-face interviews. It was impossible to give telephone respondents a personal interview safety scale such as:

Personal interview
safety scale

Very safe	10
Safe	{ 9 { 8
Kind of safe	{ 7 { 6
A little risky	{ 5 { 4
Risky	{ 3 { 2
Very risky	1

Nor could the interviewers ask the respondents to mentally "juggle" a tenpoint numerical scale with six verbal reference points. Instead, for each situation evaluated, the telephone interviewer first asked whether it was safe, risky, or somewhere in between. Then, if the respondent said safe (or risky), they went on to ask whether it was very safe or somewhat safe (or very risky or somewhat risky) under most conditions. However, Woltman and Bushery (reported in ISR Newsletter 1977) did a controlled experiment on data-gathering techniques in which they found significantly higher response rates by personal visit rather than by telephone. Hence, the researcher may find some types of issues (more personal or sensitive ones) better handled by personal visit.

QUALITY CONTROL IN SURVEYS

When things go wrong, interviewers are often blamed. Who are the interviewers? How are they supervised? How are they trained? What kind of quality control exists for their work? The Bureau of the Census has documented the contribution of interviewers to survey finding variability.

One way to reduce interviewer bias is through training programs. In a training program interviewers are taught why questions are being asked, how to ask the questions, what to do in special circumstances, how to fill out the questionnaires, how to react to potential refusals, and other essential information. Most reptuable survey organizations put considerable time and effort into training through week-long training sessions, manuals, and special training guides.

Another quality control check is to sample each interviewer's workload using a supervisor for verification. This has been found to be necessary by most reputable survey organizations in order to minimize interviews that are faked or sloppily done, to discover errors that call for correction and retraining on special problems, and to identify nonrespondent problems and characteristics.

Editing, coding, and nonresponse adjustments can also have substantial impact on the quality of data. Occupation, industry, place of work, and income are items that frequently require expert coding. One method of coding verification is to have a verifier recode a set of questionnaires with no knowledge of the codes originally assigned by a coder. A second is to have a verifier review the codes originally assigned Independent verification is more costly than the dependent type but has been found to giver higher quality control. Through these techniques it is possible to clarify difficult coding choices and questions and to weed out poor coders.

Editing is done to insure completeness of information and to resolve inconsistencies. Because missing data present severe problems for meaningful analysis, there has been much interest in how to analyze or handle missing data in a meaningful way (Kim and Curry 1977; Bailar 1978). Usually researchers delete missing cases from their analysis and then analyze the remaining data. Often it is possible, although expensive, to get estimates of nonrespondent groups or nonresponses to questions in order to estimate the bias introduced by missing data. A lack of attention to these problems usually signals a lack of quality.

A final quality control check is to insure that the sampling plan is executed faithfully. For example, persons selected may be out of town, at work, busy doing something else, or just not interested in participating. The evidence shows that people who are unavailable for interviews at the first attempt are normally different from those who are available. They are more likely to be working, to live in a smaller households, and to have higher incomes. As Lansing and Morgan (1971) showed in a follow-up of callbacks on respondents interviewed on the first call was $4188; on the second call it was $5880; on the third call it was $6010; and on the sixth or later callback it was $7443. Hawkins (1977) similarly showed in analyzing nonresponses that they tend to be overrepresented by males, Catholics and Jews, white-collar workers, high-income earners, married people, college graduates, and suburban residents. These differences are far from trivial. They clearly show the need for follow-up attempts to execute the sampling plan and to estimate the bias introduced by units unsuccessfully included in the sampling plan.

DISADVANTAGES OF SURVEY METHODS

In previous sections we have attempted to outline strategies of good interviewing. Nevertheless, surveys have a number of scientific disadvantages. First they are open to memory and viewpoint biases. Table 6–2 shows various known inaccuracies found in particular surveys.

Memory decay is greater with (1) more elapsed time since the event, (2) lesser occurrence of the event, (3) relative unimportance of the event, (4) stronger connection of the question to a person's self-esteem, and (5) less accessibility to relevant data. Thus, many data are inaccessible to the researcher since respondents often cannot recall events or misrecall various events. Green (1969:9), using interview data and clinical records in a study of contraceptive use in East Pakistan, found that people underreported both their use and knowledge of contraceptives. Approximately

Table 6–2
Inaccuracy of Report in Relation to Subject Matter

Subject	Respondents Giving Inaccurate Reports
Contributions to Community Chest	40%
Voting and registration	25%
Age	17%
Ownership of library card	10%
Ownership of driver's license	10%
Home ownership	4%
Auto ownership	3%
Possession of telephone	2%

SOURCE: Cannell-Kahn, "Interviewing," from Gardner Lindzey and Elliot Aronson, eds., *The Handbook of Social Psychology*, © 1954 Edition 2, p. 546, Addison-Wesley Publishing Company, Inc. Reprinted with permission.

20 percent of all males and 25 percent of all females who knew about contraceptives denied any use of them. Of all couples who had used contraceptives about 20 percent of husbands and 33 percent of wives denied ever having used them.

The implications of the use of interviews in reconstructing past events should be evident. The more reason we have to assume respondent memory decay, the less reason we should have to depend on the interview as a research technique.

Second, interviewer and questionnaire proctor biases present distorting influences. Even though good interviewer training emphasizes that structured questions should always be asked in exactly the same way regardless of situation or interviews, training never erases all the effects of extra-interview bias. The Bureau of the Census rigorously trains neophyte interviewers, yet they still find that unemployment rates are slightly lower in estimation when data collected by neophytes are compared to that collected by more experienced interviewers. Just the fact that an interviewer may become bored, tired, or hungry may affect presentation of interview stimuli. Further, even if one could control for such interviewer variations by making them robotlike, nonrational considerations such as their physical attractiveness, sex, age, and social statuses would still introduce bias into interviewing and questionnaire proctoring. Blacks will often answer a questionnaire differently if the proctor is black rather than white, even if responses are completely anonymous. Respondents will often be responding not only to questions as stimuli but also to interviewer/proctor characteristics.

Third, surveys depend heavily on the subject's motivation and ability to respond. Although motivation to respond is dependent on question design, interviewer characteristics and interviewer techniques are more important than question design. As Cannell and Kahn have emphasized (1968:574), "it is the interviewer who must make the interviewing experience and task sufficiently meaningful, sufficiently rewarding, and sufficiently enjoyable to attain and maintain the necessary respondent motivation." Many neophyte researchers naively assume that once a well-constructed questionnaire has been completed any person can provide the proper interview atmosphere. As we have made evident in former sections, nothing is further from the truth. Figures 6–1 and 6–2 show some simplified features of the basic social motivational influences on interview quality. Notice that factors like the participant's and interviewer's personality, attitudes, and behavior may affect the interview product. More specifically, factors like the respondent's dislike for interview content work against complete and accurate information reports, while interview elements such as the research agency's prestige provide motivation to provide complete and accurate information.

Respondents may not be able to answer questions even if they have the motivation to respond. Even if simple questions referring to ages of close relatives are asked, it is extremely likely that many respondents will be unable to tell you the age of their spouse or children. The Bureau of the Census has found that most wives have little idea of the kind of work their husbands' occupations involves.

Fourth, the most telling weakness of survey research is that it is "inappropriate for the study of many, if not most, social phenomena of interest to social scientists" (Phillips 1971:99). That is, the data collected are generally from individuals and only indirectly (if that) apply to interindividual phenomena such as interaction, social organization, and dynamic processes.

The scientific model is one of direct observation. Unfortunately, the survey method is only a poor approximation of direct observation. Chapters 4 (Field Research) and 5 (Structured Observation) come much closer to approximating our ideal models of direct observation. In those chapters we reviewed evidence that show the weaknesses of the survey method. The reader should keep those weaknesses clearly in mind in using or interpreting survey results.

THE STRENGTHS OF SURVEY METHODS

Given the above weaknesses it may seem surprising that social science methodology has become virtually synonymous with survey research.

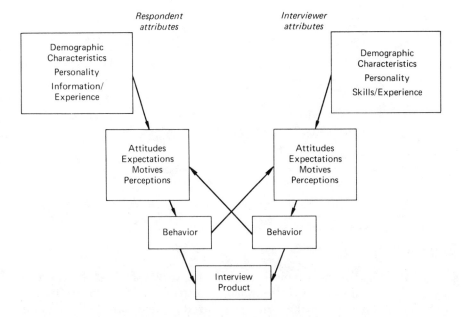

FIGURE 6-1 *Motivational model of the interview as a social process.*

Source: Cannell-Kahn, "Interviewing," from Gardner Lindzey and Elliot Aronson, ed., *The Handbook of Social Psychology,* © 1954 Edition 2, pp. 581–582, Addison-Wesley Publishing Company, Inc. Reprinted with permission.

The following reasons may be given in support of survey methods, although not necessarily in support of their widespread use in the social and behavioral sciences.

First, survey methods are often the sole way of retrieving information about a respondent's past history—for instance, sexual behavior, childhood experiences, and recreational activities. This is particularly true with behavior that occurs very irregularly, privately, or rarely (Kahn and Cannell 1968).

Second, as Richardson and his associates (1965) have indicated, surveys provide one of the few techniques available for the study of attitudes, values, beliefs, and motives. Indeed, many experimental researchers supplement their experimental designs with questionnaires or interviews in order to learn whether an intended variable actually had any effects.

Third, as pointed out by Selltiz and her colleagues (1959), survey methods may be adapted to collect generalizable information from almost any known human population. Except in the cases of extremely young children and persons with extreme physical or mental incapacities, survey methods have wide applicability.

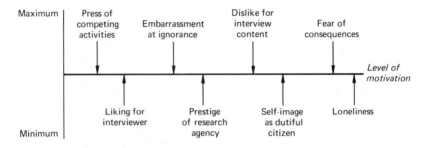

FIGURE 6–2 *Factors affecting the respondent's motivation to provide complete and accurate information to the interviewer.*

Source: Cannell-Kahn, "Interviewing," from Gardner Lindzey and Elliot Aronson, ed., *The Handbook of Social Psychology,* © 1954 Edition 2, pp. 581–582, Addison-Wesley Publishing Company, Inc. Reprinted with permission.

Perhaps the most typical rationale for survey analysis, however, is seen in the following two strengths: data structuredness and collection efficiency. That is, fourth, highly structured surveys have high amounts of data standardization. Hence, structured interviews are particularly amenable to statistical analysis (Galtung 1967). Fifth, they are extremely efficient in terms of providing large amounts of data at relatively low cost in a short period of time. (Cost is obviously a relative matter. Total costs for interviewing range up to $50 per interview in survey organizations.)

Ironically, these last two reasons may be the wrong reasons for using survey methods. The fact that large amounts of quantifiable data are collectable in a short period of time and with relatively low cost does not insure that the data will have direct bearing on the researcher's theory. Indeed survey data often seem to treat society as a simple aggregate of individuals. Thus, efficiency in data collection may often provide us with information that is of no relevance to the theoretical task at hand. It is doubtful whether Albert Reiss (1971) could have collected meaningful data on police-community interaction through a simple one-shot survey. Rather, he found it necessary to systematize naturalistic observation procedures. In fact, his findings on police brutality (1968) would have been unobtainable from traditional survey methods (Reiss 1971:8) since only 60 percent of the observations of police brutality were consistent with interview self-reports of victimization three months later. Also, Yarrow, Campbell, and Burton (1964), by comparing observations of mother-child interaction with recall of it in a questionnaire, showed consistency as low as 50 percent—low enough to disregard the mother's questionnaire reports.

SUMMARY

Survey methodology has come to be virtually synonymous with social scientific methodology. Brown and Gilmartin (1969) and Phillips (1971) found that approximately 90 percent of recently published research articles in the *American Sociological Review* and the *American Journal of Sociology* used interviewing or questionnaires as a primary source of data collection. In another content analysis, Cannell and Kahn (1968:529) found that approximately two-thirds of research reported in two basic social psychology texts utilized interview or questionnaire data. In each of these cases it is clear that data-collection procedures in the social sciences are heavily dependent on survey methods. This dependence on survey methods is in large part unfortunate because of methodological parochialism. Choice of methods should, as earlier argued, depend on the theoretical problem under investigation.

Interestingly, little controlled research has been done on the interview process, interviewer, and setting characteristics as influences on interview quality and question format. While there are signs that this situation is changing (Cosper 1972; Skipper and McCaghy 1972), much work needs to be done on the effects the interviewing milieu has on research results. Nevertheless, our main conclusion still stands that survey methods have been overutilized and should be both supplemented and replaced methodologically by other methods if sociologists wish to gain a more complex theoretical picture of the processes they study.

READINGS FOR ADVANCED STUDENTS

BARBARA S. BAILER, "The Evaluation of Sample Survey Data," 1979. A wide-ranging discussion of the evaluation of sampling plans, concepts and objectives, questionnaires, data collection, and data processing in survey research.

WILLIAM BANAKA, *Training in Depth Interviewing*, 1971. Particularly good for advice and training on unstructured interviewing techniques.

NORMAN M. BRADBURN, Seymour Sudman and Associates, *Improving Interview Method and Questionnaire Design*, 1979. Excellent presentation of the researcher's problems with people who answer untruthfully or refuse to cooperate when asked about threatening topics.

CHARLES F. CANNELL, *Experiments in Interviewing Techniques*, 1977. Details recent experiments with interviewer instruction, feedback, and commitment techniques to improve the quality of respondent information.

DON DILLMAN, *Mail and Telephone Surveys*, 1978. Guide to solving the practical problems of mail surveys.

STANLEY PAYNE, *The Art of Asking Questions*, 1951. Gives a detailed overview of the question-writing process at a highly readable level.

DEREK PHILLIPS, *Knowledge from What? Theories and Methods in Social Research,* 1971. Important critique of survey methods as a source for sociological theory.

Survey Research Center, Field Office, *Interviewer's Manual* 1974. A good reference source for practical tips and advice on interviewer techniques.

SUGGESTED RESEARCH PROJECTS

1. Design an interview schedule with the following minimum requirements:

   a. Five open-choice items

   b. Five two-way items

   c. Five miltiple-choice items

   d. Two quintamensional designs

   e. Appropriate transitional statements, card lists, and interviewer instructions should be included. (See Appendices B and C for model formats.)

   f. Attach a statement indicating the population for which the schedule is intended, since good question design is *relative* to particular populations.

2. Design an intentionally *poorly* designed questionnaire. Refer specifically, in parentheses, to what is wrong with each item.

3. Pretest an interview schedule in an actual role-playing situation. If your university or college has audiovisual equipment, perhaps the whole interview from introduction at the respondent's door to interview completion can be taped and rerun for didactic purposes.

4. The following statements have been selected from various sources. Evaluate each statement in terms of the criteria suggested for writing good survey items.

   a. How far must you travel to your present place of employment, if employed?

   b. About how many full days a week do you spend in your city?

   c. In what types of recreational activities, if any, do you engage?

   d. Would you prefer an increase in business establishments in your city?

   e. Are you married?

   f. Do you feel that marijuana smoking is a criminal act?

   g. What, if anything, would be your biggest fear of legalizing marijuana?

   h. Do you feel that a person found in possession of cocaine should be let go with no charges or do you think he or she should be imprisoned for 20 years or more?

   i. When President Carter cut grain shipments to the Soviet Union in retaliation for Soviet intervention in Afghanistan, did you feel the President was doing a good job on behalf of world peace?

   j. Do you favor the regulation of nuclear power plants and environmental protection legislation?

   k. Should those caught in possession of marijuana be convicted, or not?

    l. Do you feel the drug problem has improved or gotten worse during the past two years?

   m. Should industrial polluters be let go without charges or should they be imprisoned for five years or more?

   n. Do you feel there is a correlation between cigarette smoking and cancer or do you feel there is no correlation?

5. While observing an ongoing interview (such as in Project 3 above) use the following checklist to rate the interview on needed improvements:

   a. Did the respondent take control through

     (1) asking personal questions

     (2) resorting to long, rambling monologues

     (3) asking the interviewer to clarify questions

     (4) hostility or aggressiveness

   b. Did the interviewer make sufficient use of

     (1) eye contact

     (2) pauses

     (3) probes

   c. Did the interviewer

     (1) talk too fast

     (2) mumble

     (3) appear to be submissive

     (4) let the respondent take control by asking questions

     (5) give opinions

     (6) criticize questions

     (7) fake data

     (8) not pursue a more precise answer

     (9) force the respondent into certain answers

    (10) have enough knowledge

    (11) give own interpretation of questions

    (12) apologize for the interview

    (13) answer for the respondent

    (14) skip part of the interview

    (15) use words like "just" or "only"

    (16) give the impression of knowing what he or she was doing

    (17) appear to have sufficient knowledge of the interview schedule

7

Experimental Principles, Variations, and Approximations

All empirical proof is ultimately tied to the logic of the experiment, while the experiment focuses on the issue of control. . . . [Sociologists] try to introduce control at another level, in actually differentiating an experimental group from a control group. Here physical control is possible, although exceedingly difficult. Man is reluctant enough to be designated merely a statistical means to another's ends, whatever category he is assigned. . . . But again, the more thoroughly such control can be introduced, the closer one can approximate the canon of the logic of proof common to the community that is science. . . . Sociologists, then, are faced with decisions involving how much pressure to exert to bring individuals into their samples and the degree to which they should accept responsibility for changing or denying change to them. They must make this choice knowing that, other things being equal, increased control will enhance the validity of their conclusions. [1]

[1] Robert Friedrichs, *A Sociology of Sociology,* 1970, pp. 169–171.

As Robert Friedrichs notes, social and behavioral methodology *strives* to meet the ideals of the true experiment. We shall see in this chapter that for a number of practical and ethical reasons the true experiment cannot always be utilized. Nevertheless, researchers using nonexperimental methods have an increasingly wide variety of techniques available for approximating the control over variables found in experiments.

Why is there so much concern over the experimental ideal? Science is concerned with the *problem of causality*. We wish to discover hypotheses that both predict and describe the effects that certain variables (independent variables) have on other variables (dependent variables). The experimental method is the only method that *directly* concerns itself with questions of causality—notice I did *not* say *proves* causality. Science is *not* in the business of proving or accepting hypotheses; rather, its task is rejecting or disproving hypotheses. This is not a trite difference. It means that science can only *discard* hypotheses. Thus, by discarding one or more hypotheses we add slightly higher status to the multitude of undisproved hypotheses. There is a tale about Thomas Edison's thousands of unsuccessful attempts to make the first light bulb that may make this point clearer. The anecdote relates that he was asked whether all of his failures were discouraging. He supposedly replied to the effect that it was not discouraging since his experiments at least rejected some thousand implausible means of producing a light bulb, and hence he was that much closer to the truth.

As we shall shortly note, even strict experimental methods are open to rival or alternative explanations. The main advantage of the experimental method is that it *minimizes* the effects of extraneous (alternative or rival) variables that might confound the results. Wiggins (1968:390) has defined *internal validity* of a hypothesis as "the number of alternative hypotheses disproved." Thus, the more alternative hypotheses disproved by the method used, the higher or better the internal validity. True experimental methods, by this definition, have the highest internal validity of *any* method.

The main *scientific* problem with the experimental method, as with all methods, is the problem of *external validity:* the problem of how generalizable the results are. Are the findings that with college students conformity increases with lower self-esteem generalizable to any other populations? Even if these conformity findings are generalizable, the *extent* of generalizability may still be in question due to the nature of most experimental methods. That is, we find in science—social and behavioral science in particular—that various dependent variables usually have *multiple* causes. (Figure 3–2 in Chapter 3 shows a number of plausible social determinants of an individual's occupational aspirations.) One of the weaknesses of experimentation is that usually only one independent and one dependent variable are under study during the experiment, with all other variables logically excluded from the study. But in real life, single causes rarely can be found. Many experiments can be found lacking in external validity due to the fact that, while experimentally accounting for extraneous variables, they do not account for variation in terms of the way events occur in the real world.

Perhaps this point can be made clearer through pointing out an assumption found to underlie much experimental work: the assumption that *multiple* independent causes of some event are *additive*. In order to account for conformity, we might assume that if we ran *separate* experiments on variables known to influence conformity, such as "reward exchange, low self-esteem, democratic leadership and affiliation motivation" (Wiggins 1968:390), then we could add up the effects of each. Contrary to the additive assumption, we find that many variables, when considered in tandem, have much more complex interactive (nonadditive) effects. Since, in nature, dependent variables rarely can be assumed to be influenced simply by one independent variable, this means the validity of experiments with single independent variables will generally have less external validity than multiple independent variable experiments. Ironically, as will be shown in the next chapter section, multiple independent-variable experiments are relatively rarely performed in social and behavioral science due to the increasing experimental controls necessary for their conduct.

WHY EXPERIMENT?

The layperson often looks upon experiments, particularly laboratory experiments, with a great amount of skepticism and disdain over the relationship between "real life" and the experiment. Aren't experiments rather superficial and artificial creations of real-life scenarios? While a poorly designed laboratory experiment may not create realistic and relevant social situations, Drabek and Haas (1967), Aronson and Carlsmith (1968), and Wiggins (1968) have shown that high generalizability (external validity) of the laboratory experiment can be and often has been created.

A second objection to experimentation has to do with the experimental creation process: Experiments are often extremely difficult to design and (once designed) they are time-consuming to carry through to completion. As Aronson and Carlsmith (1968:3) point out,

> Typically, a single person must be seen for an hour or two by an experimenter and one or more assistants or confederates. Frequently the experimenter goes to elaborate lengths to set the stage, motivate the subject, and,

on occasion, to deceive him. After expending all of this time and effort, the investigator may obtain only a single datum, perhaps something as simple as a "yes" or a "no" response.

Given all the trouble an experiment normally takes, why not simply observe actual social behavior or survey attitudes and behaviors? The fundamental weakness of any nonexperimental study is its inability to specify cause and effect. One can find correlations galore between variables in nonexperimental science, but correlation alone never proves causation. The experiment is the only method where a change in one (the dependent) variable can be *unambiguously* assigned to a change in another (the treatment) variable. Furthermore, the true experiment provides "the opportunity to vary the treatment in a systematic manner, thus allowing for the isolation and precise specification of important differences" (Aronson and Carlsmith 1968:9).

TRUE EXPERIMENTAL DESIGNS

The goal of true experimentation is to vary the relevant independent variables while eliminating the effects of other variables. The basic designs treated in this section are the only research designs that currently satisfy this goal.

The Classic Experimental Design

The classic experimental design, often known as the pretest, posttest control group design, takes the following form:

Time 1	Time 2	Time 3	Time 4
Randomization of participants* into:			
Group 1	Pretest (O_1)	Experimental treatment (X)	Posttest (O_2)
Group 2	Pretest (O_3)	No treatment	Posttest (O_4)

*"Participants" may be individuals, groups, even nations. In actuality, there are many more than *one* participant randomly assigned to "group 1" and "group 2."

There are two randomized samples: an experimental treatment sample $(O_1 \, X \, O_2)$ and a control sample $(O_3 \, O_4)$. Both of the samples are as nearly alike as possible (due to randomization) at the time of pretesting. After pretesting (observing or measuring the alleged dependent variable) the presumed causal factor (independent or "treatment" variable) is introduced into the experimental sample but withheld from the control sample. At some later time, posttest measurements or observations of the dependent variable are taken. Any changes in the two groups are then compared according to differences in pretest minus posttest scores.

$$O_1 - O_2 = d_{E(xperimental)}$$
$$O_3 - O_4 = d_{C(ontrol)}$$

If d_E and d_C are significantly different, one *infers* that the experimental treatment is the cause. If the procedures outlined above have been rigorously followed, Campbell and Stanley (1963:13–16) have shown that each of eight threats to internal validity (see Chapter 11) may be ruled out as rival explanations of the experimental results. Assuming the experimental and control groups are pretested and posttested at the same times, history is controlled because historical events that might have affected d_E would also have had to affect d_C. (External validity is considered separately in another section of this chapter. Suffice it to state for the present that external validity, or the generalizability of experimental results, is not insured by the type of experimental design but rather by the "realism" of the experiment.)

A note on randomization as a procedure in experimental methods is crucial because of its widely misunderstood nature and functions in experimental control. Randomization is based on the employment of strategies using chance or probability procedures. Researchers randomize to eliminate as much systematic bias or error (threats to validity of their findings) as feasible. Another way of stating this principle more positively is to say they wish to achieve as much preexperimental equivalence (*not* equality) of groups as possible. Each participant should have an equal chance to be in any condition in the study. If the groups are preexperimentally equivalent, only the experimental treatment may logically explain any differences between the experimental and control groups because randomizing subjects into each group fairly insures that equivalent numbers of participants in each condition will be bored with the experiment, try to "psych it out," or be of the same age. Of course, there is a probability that any given randomization of units into experimental treatment or control groups may give inaccurate representations of each other. If you play any game of cards you know the chance of randomly drawing five cards from the same suit is possible but very small; the odds are also slim of drawing nonequivalent experimental and control groups in experiments. However, the only means of obtaining similar experimental and control groups is through randomization. Furthermore, the researcher will normally have some measure (pretest measures) of how accurately each group actually mirrors the other through observations or measurements taken *prior* to the introduction of the experimental variable.

A second issue in randomization has to do with *matching* procedures. Some researchers, due either to lack of the experimental control needed to randomize or simply to ignoring randomization, match individuals on the dependent variable (they might insure that the same number of lower-class participants were in each group if they wanted to study class status as a dependent variable). The researcher who matches individuals should at the very least randomly assign each pair of matched participants to the experimental and control conditions through the tossing of a coin or some equivalent procedure. Matching does *reduce* alternative explanations through *some* control (matching) over one (or more) dependent variables. Nevertheless, matching *cannot* control for *all* of the relevant factors that may influence the experimental results in the way that randomization would. Although matching procedures may often have to be substituted for randomization, it should be kept in mind that the research design will no longer be a true experiment.

How does the researcher go about randomizing participants into groups? Let us say you wish to study two groups (a control group and an experimental group). One of the best ways would be to assign each participant an arbitrary number $(1, 2, 3, \ldots n)$ using a list of random numbers (see Appendix F). Starting at an arbitrarily chosen point on that list you would proceed across rows and down columns picking numbers to be assigned to the participants until each had an assigned random number. Then, you might place all of the odd-numbered participants into one group and even-numbered participants into the other.

A few years ago McCall and his colleagues (1974) were interested in observational accuracy. They randomized students in introduction to sociology sections into experimental and control groups. As a pretest, participants viewed a videotape and then were given a written test to determine how accurately they had observed what people said, what people did, and how people looked on the videotape. The following week, experimental participants were given special instruction in making more accurate observations—which was not given to control participants. During the third week the observational accuracy test used as a pretest was used as a posttest. The results showed the treatment had a small positive effect in that experimental participants did slightly better on posttesting than did control participants.

The Posttest-Only Control Group Design

While the classic experimental design is normally utilized in most true experiments, some researchers *forgo the pretesting* of control and experimental groups.

Even though the posttest-only control group design controls for similarity of the experimental and control groups through randomization, it cannot give evidence supporting equality of each group *prior* to introduction of the experimental treatment. Ironically, while social and behavioral scientists have found it psychologically troublesome to wean themselves of preexperimental treatment of group "equality," most physical and biological experimentation forgoes pretesting.

There is general agreement that there is no substitute for the information supplied by pretest measurements, even though the posttest-only control group design removes the same internal validity factors as the classic experiment (Campbell and Stanley 1963).

Time 1	Time 2	Time 3
Randomization of participants into:		
Group 1	Experimental treatment (X)	Posttest (O_1)
Group 2	No treatment	Posttest (O_2)

However, this general agreement may well be ill advised because in many cases pretests often *change* participants in unwanted ways (*reactive effects*). In McCall and others' (1974) study it was observed that pretested participants did better than nonpretested ones on posttesting. Pretesting apparently makes participants more sophisticated on later tests. Hence, McCall and his associates no longer give pretests in this type of research.

A creative use of the posttest-only design is shown in a study by Isen and Simmonds (1978) on how good mood can facilitate everyday helping behavior. In order to induce good mood, a dime (the treatment) was *randomly* "planted" in the coin returns of public telephones. After leaving the phone booth, a person was approached by the experimenter, who requested help in filling out a questionnaire on the participant's mood. Comparisons of participants who had found a dime versus those who had not showed significant differences in willingness to help the experimenter and in the participants' self-reported moods, as predicted.

The Solomon Four-Group Design

This design combines the classical and posttest-only designs to determine (and thus control for) any reactive effects of testing (pretest measurements or observation).

Time 1	Time 2	Time 3	Time 4
Randomization of participants into:			
Group 1	Pretest (O_1)	Experimental treatment (X)	Posttest (O_2)
Group 2	Pretest (O_3)	No treatment	Posttest (O_4)
Group 3	No pretest	Experimental treatment (X)	Posttest (O_5)
Group 4	No pretest	No treatment	Posttest (O_6)

Second, as Campbell and Stanley (1963:25) note,

> . . . not only is generalizability increased, but in addition, the effect of X is replicated in four different fashions:
>
> $$O_2-O_1, O_2-O_4, \ O_5-O_6, \text{ and } O_5-O_3$$
>
> The actual instabilities of experimentation are such that if these comparisons are in agreement, the strength of the inference is greatly increased.

By comparing O_5 with O_6 or O_1-O_2 with O_3-O_4, we obtain two estimates of the effects of the *treatment* variable. By comparing O_6-O_3 with O_4-O_3, we obtain the effects of the *pretest* effects (if any). Control of pretest effects is the *only* advantage the Solomon design has over the classical and posttest-only designs. In fact, this is the design used by McCall and others (1974) to test for reactive effects of observational accuracy tests. Because of the fact that the researcher needs twice as many participants and groups as in the other two types of experimental designs, this design is normally used only when reactive effects of pretesting are suspected.

Factorial Designs

In each of the experimental designs illustrated so far, note that there are two essential requirements: (1) control over assignment of the independent variable and (2) randomization of the effects of extraneous variables that might otherwise confound the results. The many varieties of factorial designs *elaborate on the number of* experimental and control samples. For, as Fisher (1935:101) states, "we are usually ignorant which, out of innumerable possible factors, may prove ultimately to be the most important . . . [also] we have usually no knowledge that any one factor will exert its effects independently of all others." Thus, factorial designs set up *each* possible combination of the independent variables in classical or posttest-only form. For example, for two independent variables (X_1, X_2), the factorial design, using classical design form, would look like this:

Time 1	Time 2	Time 3	Time 4
Randomization into:			
Group 1	Pretest (O_1)	X_1, X_2 treatment	Posttest (O_2)
Group 2	Pretest (O_3)	X_1 treatment	Posttest (O_4)
Group 3	Pretest (O_5)	X_2 treatment	Posttest (O_6)
Group 4	Pretest (O_7)	No treatment	Posttest (O_8)

Obviously, if the factorial design used classic experimental pretests, we might find it convenient to "nest" a Solomon four-group design into the factorial design to account for testing effects. There is nothing really mysterious about factorial designs and their analysis. They may simply be viewed as a *group* of classical (or posttest-only) experimental designs that take into account the effects of *all combinations* of the independent variables. Their analysis can be visually understood through Figure 7–1.

Suppose, as tested in Figure 7–1, that we have tested the effects on IQ of two different classroom teaching methods (X_1 and X_2) which we have experimented with using a factorial design. If we look at the *differences* in each cell of row *and* column raw scores we often find rather complicated effects of each variable singly and in combination. For example, teaching method X_2 singly has the unwanted effect of slightly lowering (–5) the mean IQ, while method X_1 slightly raises (+5) IQ. However, the most interesting observation is the teaching of X_1 and X_2 methods *in combination,* which raises mean IQ a total 20 points. That is, there is a definite statistical "interaction" between X_1 and X_2 since the effect of each method should add to 0 [(+ 5) + (–5) = 0] in this example if the

	Treatment X_1	No treatment X_1	"Effect" of X_1 d_{X_1}
Treatment X_2	140 (O_2)	115 (O_6)	
No treatment X_2	125 (O_4)	120 (O_8)	+5
"Effect" of X_2 d_{X_2}		–5	20

FIGURE 7–1 *Hypothetical analysis of joint effects of two experimental treatments.*

Cell figures are mean scores in each sample of IQ posttest scores.

effects were additive, whereas the joint effects are actually 20. If two or more independent variables are additive, then their effects are *independent* of one another. Interactive effects, by contrast, imply that the variables act *jointly* or in concert. The factorial design has the advantage of testing whether the effects of two or more treatment variables are additive or interactive.

PROBLEMS OF EXTERNAL VALIDITY

The goal of science is to be able to generalize findings to diverse populations and times. For example, if an experiment on initiation rites (Aronson and Mills 1959) were to have high external validity, we should be able to generalize from it to initiation rites into college fraternities, De Molay, and even manhood in primitive tribes.

Unfortunately, most experiments have well-known disadvantages or limitations to such complete generalizability that we discuss in this section, following Wiggin's (1968) treatment of experimenter, participant, treatment, and measurement characteristics.

Experimenter Characteristics

There are a number of studies showing that the experimenter's personality (Sapolsky 1960), behavior (Sarason and Minard 1963), and statuses such as sex or age (Binder, McConnell, and Sjoholm 1957) affect experimental participants. The participant's perceptions of the experimenter's statuses, behavior, or attitudes may cause an experimenter-modeling effect consistent with the researcher's expectations or hypotheses. On the other hand, Rosenthal (1966) and Friedman (1967) have presented evidence that the experimenter's hypotheses may cause him or her to *perceive* the behavior of participants as consistent with the experimenter's hypotheses or even cause actual change in participants. In one of the more interesting cases of this phenomenon Rosenthal (1966) has had participants perform experimenter roles with Norway rats. These "experimenters" were told that specified rats were "smarter" than other rats, even though the rats actually had been randomly designated as "smart" or "dumb." Experimental results support the notion that the "experimenters'" preconceptions affected the rats' behavior in a way consistent with the "experimenters'" expectations.

There are several ways to minimize experimenter effects, although it is nearly impossible to eliminate them. One can minimize the involvement of the experimenter (Wiggins 1968:401) through: (1) the use of instructions to participants explaining that the experimenter prefers that they behave "normally"; (2) use of a naive substitute experimenter; (3) observer "blindness" as to which group (experimental or control) is being measured; and (4) populations of experimenters from which one may randomly sample for each experimental condition.

Participant Characteristics

There are two problems in terms of participants: participant *selection* and *mortality*. Selection problems concern motivations for volunteering and cooperating in an experiment and participants' beliefs concerning laboratory experimentation. Many experiments rely on "volunteers" from college classrooms. Participation on such a basis may be motivated by the experimenter as a grade or money giver. Whatever the source of participation motivation, it is clear that some motivations may affect the participant's experimental involvement (Diener and Crandall 1978:173–180).

Second, the participant's beliefs concerning the experimental procedures and hypotheses are particularly plausible sources of experimental invalidity. While there are many different types of participant beliefs that can act as sources of experimental invalidity, one of the more critical types concerns beliefs about what the experiment is attempting to test. "Psyching out" the experimenter may be motivated by several factors: a desire to be a "good" participant by acting as one thinks the experimenter wants one to act, or an attempt by the participant to throw off the study results by acting *contrariwise* to the manner in which the participant believes the experimenter wants.

One fairly straightforward way of controlling for such variations between participants is to have a control group simulate (role play) the experimental group through *pretending* to be confronted with the independent variable. The between-group variation may then be assumed to be due to the real independent variable (Wiggins 1968:409). Wiggins further suggests that several educational techniques might have to be used on participants to make them into "good" participants; these techniques would include things such as socializing participants into the value of the scientific approach and the value of behaving naturally. On the other hand, it might be necessary, in cases of participants who the researcher suspects might use experimental deception, or who have too much trust in the experimenter, to point out one-way mirrors, observers, and other ostensibly deceptive devices or artificial procedures (such as a practice shock).

Perhaps one of the best ways to control for participant characteristics is to design experiments where the participant is *not aware* of being in an experiment. If he or she is not aware of it, and the experiment setting seems natural, he or she will act normally as a matter of course. Christie and Geis (1970) have designed several such experiments in which they asked participants to be "experimenters," when in actuality they were still experimenting on the participants. Similarly, one could easily design nonlaboratory experiments in which participants assumed the experimenters to be newspeople from a fictitious local radio station. This problem of participant characteristics is referred to by Aronson and Carlsmith (1968:22) as the problem of *experimental realism*—that is, the extent to which the experiment is realistic to participants, involves them, and forces them to take it seriously.

Treatment Characteristics

In contrast to experimental realism is *mundane realism,* or the "extent to which events occurring in a laboratory setting are likely to occur in the real world" (Aronson and Carlsmith 1968:22). Just because a participant finds an experiment personally engaging does not do much, if anything, for the experiment's external validity. Stanley Millgram (1963) suggests that participants who administered what they thought to be severe electric shocks to other participants did so, in part, because they perceived that the victim had voluntarily submitted to being shocked. Thus, while severely shocking another person in real life might be thought of as antisocial behavior by the participants, their perceptions of voluntary participation may have liberalized their interpersonal behavior in the experiment. Wiggins (1968:412–413) suggests that, in order to achieve situational equivalence, or mundane realism, experiments would have to be set up such that: (1) participants do not perceive that all other participants have volunteered; (2) they are not aware that they are participating in an experiment; (3) they perceive the experimental task as related to some activity with which they have familiarity; (4) they meet with consequences similar to those they experience in real life; and (5) experimental ecological arrangements (seating arrangements, communication networks) are similar to real-life ecological arrangements. Often, in order to fulfill these requirements, only particular population settings and tasks would qualify for experimental manipulation. For instance, family decision-making experiments might well be best conducted using participants drawn from populations of persons with appropriate familial statuses, with the experiments conducted in living-room type settings while the participants are engaged in "normal" decisional processes such as buying a set of encyclopedias.

Measurement Characteristics

Observations, questionnaires, and interviews are commonly used in experimentation as measuring instruments. Observers and interviewers are particularly subject to changes in instrumentation—they learn, in the process of observing or interviewing, how to make different measurements, and their temporary motivational states (hunger, fatigue) may change the measurements. To the extent that they unwittingly make measurement changes during pretests and posttests, they contribute to instrumental invalidity.

Measuring instruments, even if they are reliable, may be *reactive;* their use may cause changes in the participant's behavior. For instance, one-way mirrors, cameras, and observers may all cause the participant to act atypically. Second, exposure to the instrument in a pretest may affect later exposure during posttest since the participant's awareness of the pretest measurement process may make him or her more sophisticated or mature in similar, later situations.

Statistical regression is a particularly noteworthy problem of measurement. (See Chapter 12 for a more extensive discussion.) The problem occurs in experiments when participants are assigned to particular treatments because of *extreme* scores on measurements (high IQ, low Machiavellian scores). Measuring instruments, in general, are better predictors of the *average* score: the further distant the observed score from the average score, the more unstable that particular score. Thus, a commonly observed phenomenon is to note that extremely high or low scorers on any test will score closer to the mean score on a retest. If the researcher is not aware of the confounding effects of statistical regression, he or she is likely to draw false conclusions. For instance, after administering an IQ test to participants at time 1, he or she will probably find in administering an IQ test at time 2 that the effect of the treatment variable appears to make students with high IQs "dumber" or those with low IQs "smarter," when actually this effect is due to scores "regressing" towards the mean. (See Chapter 12 for more details.)

The *time* of measurement (Campbell and Stanley 1963:31–32) is also a potentially misleading variable. One may measure for effects of treatment before they have time to "take," or after they have already waned, thus hiding the actual effect.

We previously mentioned the criteria of "blindness" to experimental conditions for participants. It is always wise to have experimental observers and interviewers "blind" as to the participant's experimental treatment status for similar reasons. We wish the measurer to be unaware of the type of (or lack of) treatment administered since such knowledge might influence the measurement process. Experiments in which both participant and measurer are unaware of the participant's treatment status are termed *double-blind.* Occasionally experimenters are also "blinded" to participant treatment condition through the use of an outside party administering treatment, in which case the experiment is termed *triple-blind.* The more blind conditions, the less the possibility of extraneous human factors confounding experimental results.

The ideal social experiment would involve the administration of *convincing placebos* to control groups, just as medical experimentation often requires administration of "sugar pills" that, to the participant, appear to be the experimental drug received in the experimental condition. On the one hand, convincing placebos restrict variations in participant responses; on the other hand, they help better insure "blindness" of the experimental conditions.

PLANNING AND CONDUCTING EXPERIMENTS

This chapter, to this point, has been fairly abstract in its treatment of experimental principles. This section will try to present the conception of concrete experiments, from operationalization of the original hypothesis in experimental form through postexperimental procedures. As Aronson and Carlsmith (1968:37) point out, "ideas—even interesting ones—are cheap in social psychology. The important and difficult feat involves translating a conceptual notion into a tight, workable, credible, meaningful set of experimental operations."

Operationalizing the Independent Variable

The researcher, in the conceptualization of the independent variable, must first ask what specific dimension(s) exists for independent variable (experimental treatment). Part of this question concerns the dimension of the *possible variation* inherent in the variable. If the researcher is interested in the effects of group cohesiveness, then he or she should determine operationally how to *manipulate* both low and high cohesiveness. Kurt Back (1950) created three experimental *high-cohesive* treatment conditions: one where participants were told they had been matched to almost exactly the person they had each personally described as ideal to work with; second, high cohesiveness based on motivation for task success through a five-dollar reward for the best story; third, high group prestige as a basis for high cohesiveness through telling treatment groups they were the best group the researchers had experimented with. Control groups were told none of these things.

It is important that the experimenter randomize which participants receive the treatment, as was true in the Back experiments. While this may sound parochial, one does not have to search far in the literature to find examples of "experiments that are not true experiments." Christie and Geis's (1970) book, *Studies in Machiavellianism,* has eleven "experiments," none of which randomizes the treatment or independent variable. (In fairness to Christie and Geis, it should be pointed out that they never intended to show causal, but rather only correlational, relationships through these eleven *studies.*) Nevertheless, many researchers make the mistake of assuming causality (as illustrated in Christie and Geis's book) through calling their studies experiments.

The pseudorandomization pitfalls (Aronson and Carlsmith 1968:40–42) are: (1) measuring the independent variable, for example Machiavellianism, and then looking at what happens to low and high Machiavellians under laboratory conditions; (2) allowing participants to assign themselves to the experimental conditions, as when Christie and Geis (1970:212) allowed participants to choose whose responses in an experimental group they wished to try to guess; and (3) the most subtle form of nonrandom assignment of participants which occurs in experiments where participants are assigned randomly to experimental treatments, yet the researcher finds his or her independent variable has not been powerful enough to discriminate dependent variable effects. Thus, he or she performs an "internal analysis" of the data by separating participants into two groups (those upon whom the manipulation seemed to work and those upon whom it did not) to check on the success of the treatment manipulation. Obviously this is not random assignment, although one often has to read the experimental procedures closely in order to find out that a particular researcher used internal analysis. The most proper use of internal analysis would be in pilot-testing stages where the researcher is trying to find the variable operationalization that sufficiently discriminates the behavior desired of participants in each experimental treatment.

The second question the researcher should ask of any operationalization concerns how he or she can *present* the experimental treatment(s) so that it has the best maximum impact on subjects. Most experimenters would probably agree that tasks that have a high amount of experimental realism and are motivationally engaging are preferred in terms of their impact on participants, as compared to having only a simple set of instructions read to the participant (a mistake often made by neophyte experimenters).

A third question concerns how "to prevent subjects from realizing the effect this variable is supposed to have on [their] behavior" (Aronson and Carlsmith 1968:42). Participants, you may recall from the previous chapter section, may act as "good" or "bad" subjects if they can guess "appropriate" behavior. Events participants cannot connect with the experiment are preferred: Christie's use of participants as "experimenters" when actually these persons were still being observed, or an "accident" such as in Darley and Batson's (1973) study of altruism. In this experiment Princeton Theological Seminarians who served as participants were asked to deliver an "important" message across campus. There were two treatment conditions: one in which the message should be delivered "immediately" and another in which time was not of great importance. On the way across campus, the participants' good Samaritanism was tested since they had to pass over the spot where a confederate was lying "badly hurt and bleeding."

In the presentation of the experimental treatment, the experimenter wants to be reasonably sure participants' understanding of instructions is standardized. Since participants may differ in their need for comprehensive instructions, Aronson and Carlsmith (1968:48) recommend that the experimenter keep a record of exactly what was said to each, in the interests of replicability. Note that this recommendation seemingly contradicts Wiggin's earlier stated belief in the need for standardized experimental treatments. Yet we can now see that there is often a conflict between standardizing experimental treatment and standardizing the participant's perception of that treatment. Obviously, the participant's *perception* is what we usually will wish to standardize in such cases of conflict. Pilot tests are critical in assessing the adequacy and convincingness of any such experimental treatment.

Operationalizing the Dependent Variable

Aronson and Carlsmith (1968:56) state that

> . . . it should be clear to the reader that the greater the degree of commitment demanded of the subject by the independent variable, the more confidence we can have in our experiment. For example, we would have a great deal of confidence that an experiment really involves antecedents of aggression if the experimenter reports that an experimental treatment induced more subjects to punch him in the nose (or even to volunteer to "meet him outside") than a control condition. We would have far less confidence if the experimental treatment resulted in a higher rating of perceived feelings of aggression as measured by a questionnaire.

Thus, the question of whether to measure the dependent variable by questionnaire, interview, or behavioral measures should hinge on the nature of the independent variable's strength. Due to the reactivity possible from the participant's knowledge of being tested, disguised or unsuspicious measures are an advantage. Rokeach and Cochrane (1972) have measured the attitude change of prejudice against blacks by having the NAACP send letters asking for contributions at periods ranging from several months to a year after the experiment.

Not only is it wise to try to eliminate participant awareness of treatment conditions and dependent variable measurements, but it is also useful to keep the experimenter unaware of the specific experimental treatments each participant is in and their hypothetical effects since, as we have already seen, the experimenter may unwittingly communicate his or her own biases.

The Postexperimental Interview

All too often in social and behavioral research the researcher is labeled, at worst, an "academic imperialist" and, at best, an "ingratiating person." We sometimes forget that the participants and respondents in our research have done us a large favor by submitting their valuable time and energy in our behalf. Often, we show a double standard towards, and ingratitude for, their services by our willingness to do almost anything to obtain their services, while once their services have been obtained we leave them without any benefits or explanations. Social science has enough problems with its image now as it is (Bode 1972). We should be building a more positive image of ourselves through postresearch explanations to our participants about how the data have benefited us (and hopefully our participants) in other ways than helping some college professor gain tenure through obscure publication. Simple practices such as sending a personal "thank you" note to respondents and participants help increase positive attitudes toward future research. Second, where potential benefits to participants (findings of "interest") are apparent, or asked for in return for the participant's services, a short summary of key findings in nonjargon language not only helps to build understanding about the value of social science among the lay public, but also helps gain more secure sources of future research populations. Indeed, by contrast, researchers have found it increasingly difficult to research certain populations because of lay perceptions of having been "milked" by researchers without any return for their own investment of time and energy.

In the case of the postexperimental interview, more will be needed than just a full explanation of the experiment. Diener and Crandall (1978:91) point out that the experimenter will want to determine, through the interview, the participant's reaction to the experiment and will probe to see if the experimental procedures worked, and if they did work how the participant perceived them. Any deception in the experiment should gradually be drawn out so that the participant has a complete understanding of what was done and why it was done. One of the most useful techniques is to ask the participant how the experiment could be made credible, pleasant, and so on. This procedure may actually help improve the experiment as well as give the researcher cues as to whether he or she must spend more time in undoing harm done by experimental procedures. Finally, in concluding the postexperimental debriefing the experimenter should attempt to convince the participant not to reveal experimental procedures to anyone.

QUASI-EXPERIMENTAL FIELD METHODS

The laboratory experiment may offer the most control in data collection, but nevertheless it has a number of inherent weaknesses like any method: Experimental participants are often viewed as passive objects to be manipulated; the manipulations are frequently distorted; fragmentary bits of behavior are torn from their natural context; reactivity from participant's knowledge of being experimented upon may be present; and larger social groups, organizations, and processes are often unadaptable to the confines of controlled laboratory conditions. Consequently, many social scientists (Bickman and Henachy 1972; Campbell 1969a; McGuire 1967; Ring 1967) have shunned the confines of the laboratory for field experiments that approximate experimental methods.

What is lost in control over variable manipulation and internal validity may often be gained in quasi-experimental field studies through loss of experimental artificiality, reactivity, and deception and gains in external validity from more naturally occurring variables and participant populations.

Quasi-experimental field studies differ in several important respects from true experiments. First of all, although true experiments may often introduce treatment conditions that are unfamiliar to participants, quasi-experiments often can (and should) make more subtle modifications or interventions not as disruptive (unfamiliar) to the participants. However, such studies may raise ethical considerations concerning the deception of large numbers of people who are not aware that they are part of an experiment. In more generic terms, the researcher using quasi-experimental methods can control the *when* and *to whom* of measurement and occasionally the *when of* experimental exposure. Unlike true experiments, however, there usually is little control over the *when* and *to whom* of exposure (randomized exposure) (Campbell and Stanley 1963:34). Occasionally the field experiment may have full experimental control, as was true in the already mentioned (Darley and Batson 1973) study of good Samaritanism among Seminarians. The best research designs should always be used, where feasible. Thus, if a naturalistic field study can be done with true experimental controls, the researcher will exercise more control over interpretation of findings, since he or she can reject more plausible rival hypotheses.

In the following discussion of types of quasi-experimental designs we shall start with weak designs and proceed to a discussion of relatively stronger designs.

The Interrupted Time-Series Design

Campbell and Stanley (1963:37) diagram the time-series experiment as follows:

$$O_1 \ O_2 \ O_3 \ O_4 \ X \ O_5 \ O_6 \ O_7 \ O_8$$

Thus in between the periodic measurement of some group or individual, (O_1 to O_8), an experimental treatment (X) is applied. Any discontinuity in recorded measurements is taken as an indicator of the effects of the treatment. History effects provide the most obvious weakness of the design (see Chapter 12).

Lewis-Beck (1979) tested the effects of the Cuban revolution by creatively conceiving of revolution as an experimental treatment in an interrupted time-series design. Campbell and Ross (1968) measured the effects of the 1955 Connecticut crackdown on speeding by comparing time-series data on traffic deaths before and after the crackdown. There are many problems pointed out by Campbell and Ross in interpreting Figure 7–2. For example, while the data seem supportive of the crackdown's effect, the pattern could have been caused by other interpretations, such as 1955 having been a particularly wet or snowy year and thus causing more dangerous driving conditions and more accidents, since there is not much difference between 1951–1954 and 1957–1959 data. Obviously, other measures such as randomly taken movies of highway traffic speeds would help in further clarifying the effects of the Connecticut reform.

Multiple Time-Series Designs

Where it is possible to provide a control group (though *without* randomization of treatment), the multiple time-series design should be used to give some indication of comparative, shared historical trends. For instance, Campbell (shown in Figure 7–2) provides comparative fatality figures for four states bordering on Connecticut that, therefore, provide *some* controls over weather conditions and other historical factors. As another example, Jennings (1978) compared the effects of a group called Samaritan (which offers counseling and help to potential suicides in British and Welsh towns) on suicide rates in England and Wales. He noted that between 1963 and 1973 the suicide rates in these two countries fell from 12 per 100,000 to 8 per 100,000, which was unique for all of Europe. However, comparison of towns that had a Samaritan branch with those that did not showed no appreciable difference in suicide rates between the two groups of towns throughout the period. Further analysis showed two likely reasons for the reduced suicide rate: (1) reduced carbon monoxide levels in the gas provided to homes and (2) improved medical and psychiatric services. This study shows quite clearly the reasons for the need for multiple time-series analysis as a means of reducing alternative rival explanations.

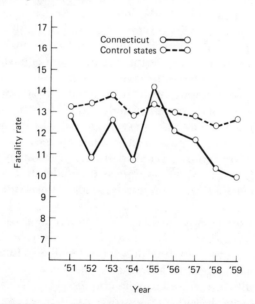

FIGURE 7–2 *Control series design comparing Connecticut fatalities with those of four comparable states.*

Source: D. Campbell, "Reforms as experiments," *American Psychologist,* 24:409–429. Copyright 1969 by the American Psychological Association. Reprinted by permission.

Nonequivalent Control Group Design

One of the most widespread field experiment designs that has equivalence to the classical design, except for the crucial factor of inability to randomize subjects into treatments, is the nonequivalent control group design.

		Time 1	Time 2	Time 3	Time 4
Nonrandomized	Group 1	Pretest	Experimental treatment	Posttest
Nonrandomized	Group 2	Pretest	No treatment	Posttest

Bryan and Test (1972) designed a creative measure of interpersonal helping behavior using this design in which the control condition involved a conspicuously placed woman with a flat automobile tire. In the model (treatment) condition, another car with a flat tire was placed one-fourth of a mile in back of the other one with a woman stationed watching a man change her flat tire. In the control condition, no model was present —thus, only the one flat-tired car and distressed woman were visible.

In a second such field experiment on helping behavior (Allen 1972) a subway passenger confederate gave wrong information to another passenger (second confederate) in front of a naive bystander. The dependent variable was whether the bystander corrected the misinformation. The independent variable was "deservingness" of the passenger's need for correct information as measured by total helplessness (tourist), model behavior (the second confederate had just given a woman, a third confederate, his seat), and total deservingness (confederate had just given his seat to the woman, a third confederate, loaded down with shoppingbags and boxes).

In a third such study Payne (1978) studied the cross-national diffusion effects of Canadian television on viewers' attitudes and cognitions. He attempted to overcome the problem of self-selection by isolating a small area of north central Minnesota that, because of its geographic location, was able to receive Canadian but not U.S. TV signals. Then he compared this sample with samples of areas that receive U.S. TV only, and those receiving both Canadian and U.S. TV signals (which showed significant national differences on such issues as taxes, energy, and peace). In these experiments the researcher has intervened in the *when* and *what* of treatment but has no control over randomizing participants into treatment. Campbell and Stanley (1963:448) point out that "the more similar the experimental and the control groups are in their recruitment, and the more this similarity is confined by the scores on the pretest," the more internal validity we can assume.

Separate-Sample Pretest-Posttest Designs

This design is obviously similar to both the nonequivalent control group design and the classical design:

Time 1	Time 2	Time 3	Time 4
Randomization into:			
Group 1	Pretest	*Probably* no experimental treatment	No posttest
Group 2	No pretest	Experimental treatment	Posttest

This design is especially useful in studying *large* social units. For instance, a quasi-experiment of this nature was introduced in Iceland to study the introduction of television. Since TV signals cannot travel long distances, it was possible to choose randomly which cities would get the experimental treatment (TV stations). The pretest was made on the control group, while the posttest was taken only on the treatment group, thus avoiding testing effects and reactivity of the experiment. The only major flaw in this design was the uncertainty as to whether certain members of the control group had exposure to the treatment variable (Payne and Peake 1977). For instance, it might be possible for certain persons to move between pretest and posttest from one city with a TV station to one without a station or vice versa. Or it is possible that subjects in a TV-stationless city might build a powerful enough receiver to receive signals from a distant city. Either way, the idea illustrated is that a control group may be "contaminated" fairly easily, confounding experimental results. Nevertheless, this design provides more assurance of high *external* validity than any other experimental or quasi-experimental method.

Campbell (1963:55) has suggested an expensive addition to the separate-sample pretest-posttest design which considerably strengthens control over internal and external validity. The addition may be represented as two control treatments.

Time 1	Time 2	Time 3	Time 4
Randomization into:			
Group 3	Pretest	No treatment	No posttest
Group 4	No pretest	No treatment	Posttest

The total four-group design is known as the separate-sample pretest-posttest *control group* design. The beauty of this addition is that randomization creates equivalence at two levels not achieved in the former design alone. That is, in addition to Groups 1 and 2 being equivalent at Time 1 due to randomization, Groups 1 and 3 are similar at Time 2 (pretest) and Groups 2 and 4 are similar at Time 4 (posttest), with the crucial exception of Group 2's exposure to the independent (treatment) variable. An important consequence of these similarities and differences is that this design is the only design discussed in this chapter that satisfies all internal validity factors as well as some external validity factors. By contrast, a design with Groups 1 and 2 alone does not deal with important invalidity threats (Campbell and Stanley 1963; Cook and Campbell 1979; see also Chapter 12).

NONEXPERIMENTAL DESIGNS

The majority of study designs used in the social and behavioral sciences are primitive by comparison to the true and quasi-experimental designs discussed earlier in this chapter.

The One-Shot Study

The most frequent design in the social sciences (one-time survey) is also the one with the *least* scientific value: the *one-shot* or *cross-sectional study*. The one-shot study may be represented by

Time 1	Time 2
Treatment variable introduced (X)	Posttest

At the worst extreme are one-shot case studies of single instances of some phenomenon. However, *without* other *explicit* instances of comparison, inference is always based on simple "expectations of what the data would have been had the X not occurred" (Campbell and Stanley 1963:6). Much of the "evidence" in favor of astrology and parapsychology has been of this type. Such studies usually give specific observations about particular events without comparable attention given to other, potentially nonconfirmable data. Figure 7–3 may shed some light on this logic. A case study of "seers" such as Jean Dixon usually focuses on category A. It gives details showing that the "seer" (X) has been able to make correct predictions about future events (Y). Implicit in such discussions is the (untested) assumption that a nonseer could *not* do as well as the seer (cell B) but would end up with mostly nonsuccessful predictions (cell D). Further, it is assumed that the seer would make fewer incorrect decisions (cell C compared to cell A) than by chance alone.

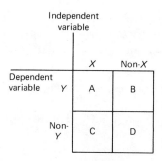

FIGURE 7–3 *A simplified two-variable, fourfold property space.*

Likewise, psychoanalytic methods typically focus on Cell *A* (for example, the effects of psychoanalysis on patient recovery rates) without proper attention to *comparative* recovery rates under nonpsychoanalytic means (cells *B* and *D*) or psychoanalytic recidivism rates (cell *C*). The point is that single-case studies (regardless of the fine detail collected) do not have adequate reference points or benchmarks for ruling out rival causal explanations. The minimum scientific requirement calls for at least one comparison with a case that did not receive the treatment variable.

Somewhat better than one-shot *case* studies are one-shot *correlational* studies. Most survey research falls under this heading. However, regardless of the sophistication of correlational analysis, correlation is only a necessary, *not* a sufficient, condition for causality. Indeed, correlational studies may be extremely misleading. One-shot correlational studies invariably show a direct relationship between age and prejudice. However, only when the researcher accounts for education (older generations have less education) does it become apparent that prejudice is not caused by aging processes. Hence, one-shot correlational studies (which make up over 60 percent of current research—see Chapter 13) too easily involve confounding of the independent and dependent variables. In studies of the economic growth of cities it is possible to see an association, in recent years, between startling economic growth of cities like Atlanta, Houston, and Dallas and aggressive, attention-demanding leadership in each city. However, there is no way of proving, using one-shot correlational studies, whether the leadership produced the growth, or simply rode its crest to acclaim.

Much of the recent advancement in statistical analysis in sociology has been directed towards improving causal analysis on one-shot correlational studies through the use of what is called ordinary least squares regression (see Cook and Campbell 1979: Chapter 7; also Chapter 14 in this text). Since many of our variables are difficult to manipulate in truly experimental ways, we often find it necessary to manipulate them statistically (as in the example of education and prejudice above). The goal is the same in any case: We try to control as many rival alternative explanations for our data as possible given the data that is practical to collect.

The One-Group Pretest-Posttest Design

Slightly better than the one-shot study is the following procedure:

Time 1	Time 2	Time 3
Pretest	Treatment variable	Posttest

This design is recommended only when *no better design is available* since it lacks a representative control group by which the researcher may make the necessary comparisons for eliminating rival alternative explanations.

Most *longitudinal studies* are of this type. Feldman and Hurn (1966) have been engaged in a longitudinal study of Puerto Rico (in which the "treatment variable" is *presumable* urbanization, industrialization, and/ or (!) modernization). Obviously, the confounding of variables may be as much of a problem in longitudinal studies as in correlational studies.

The Static-Group Comparison Design

This design can be visualized as:

Time 1	Time 2	Time 3
Group 1	Treatment variable (X)	Posttest
Group 2	No treatment	Posttest

Examples of this design would be studies comparing children who watch *Sesame Street* with those who have not watched *Sesame Street,* comparisons of marijuana smokers with nonmarijuana smokers, or victims of rape with nonrape victims.

The basic problem with this design has to do with lack of randomization procedures—that is, how participants were selected *into* comparison groups and how they selected themselves *out of* the study or a comparison group are grave cause for concern in interpreting differences found between the groups. Are these differences, or lack of them, due to actual differences or simply to the haphazard nature of each group's formation?

ETHICAL CONSIDERATIONS AND DECEPTION

The position expressed in Chapter 1 was that the scientist must be concerned with the physical health and mental well-being of his or her participants. Thus, this text's position is that deception or measures that cause discomfort to the participant should be avoided whenever possible. Experimenters have no special privilege to extract data under false pretenses or to expose people to physically or psychologically damaging situations.

Aronson and Carlsmith (1968:13) perceptively note that "the two goals of a social psychological experiment, impact and control, are in constant tension; as one becomes reasonably great, the other tends to be sacrificed." It therefore is usually necessary to compromise. In other words, one may have to give up some impact of experimental treatment (less anxiety-provoking initiation rites) and, thus, some control over participants rather than giving up the idea of experimentation (in this instance, the area of initiation rites). Extreme experimental treatments and devious cover stories can usually be discarded without seriously biasing experimental results. Of course, "blind" experimental treatments and placebo controls are also deceptive devices that may need to be forgone. Obviously, however, it is necessary at times to use both of these devices; in my (1978) study of the social effects of marijuana in which, due to the well-known nature of marijuana intoxication "experiences" to be heavily influenced by social setting (Becker 1953, 1967), triple-blind, placebo controls were a necessity. Participants were and should probably always be informed that deceptive conditions will be used in the experiment in such cases.

Fortunately, many experiments pose no such ethical questions. In many experiments the dignity, privacy, and safety of the participants is unquestionably preserved. Regardless of the ethical implications, the experimenter must always balance the extent to which new knowledge may be beneficial to all concerned parties against the ethical implications of the experiment.

SUMMARY

Experimental methods provide the models against which we measure the validity of causal relationships. Yet we have seen that for ethical and pragmatic reasons experimental methods must often be modified before adoption to use in social research. The issues of experimental *control* and *impact* provide crucial focal points in the design of research. An experiment is no better than the operationalization of its independent and dependent variables. Experiments often need behavioral as well as attitudinal or perceptual measurements.

Much of present-day social and behavioral science uses correlational and *ex post facto* (after the fact) types of designs; one instance is the one-shot survey in which the researcher correlates answers to one question (exposure to a pornographic film) with another (aggressive or sexual feelings afterwards). Participants in these instances are given the opportunity to classify themselves. While causation does imply that one variable must precede another in time in order to be the independent variable, ex post facto and one-shot survey correlational studies are subject to much higher distortion biases (memory attrition, reactivity) than experiments, whether true or quasi in nature. Indeed, even if the survey is conducted at several points in time with analysis based in terms of panel study methods of detecting causal priorities (Pelz and Andrews 1964), the data will still be extremely subject to regression effects (Campbell and Clayton 1961). Furthermore, there will always be ambiguity about what is the control group and what is the experimental group due to the ambiguity of participant self-classification (Campbell and Stanley 1963:67). Thus, naturalistic quasi-experimental studies will always, where feasible, be superior to correlational and ex post facto designs.

READINGS FOR ADVANCED STUDENTS

ELLIOT ARONSON AND J. MERRILL CARLSMITH, "Experimentation in Social Psychology," in G. Lindzey and E. Aronson (eds), *Handbook of Social Psychology*, vol. II, 1968. One reviewer appropriately stated that this chapter says everything the novice experimenter should know about experimentation that experienced researchers thought could not be written but had to be learned through trial-and-error experience.

LEONARD BICKMAN AND THOMAS HENACHY, *Beyond the Laboratory: Field Research in Social Psychology*, 1972. Examples of recent and ingenious quasi-experimental field studies.

DONALD CAMPBELL AND JULIAN STANLEY, *Experimental and Quasi-Experimental Designs for Research*, 1963. The classic introduction to the generic research designs, their weaknesses, and their strong points.

THOMAS COOK AND DONALD CAMPBELL, *Quasi-Experimentation: Design and Analysis Issues for Field Settings*, 1979. This is the latest sequel to the original classic Campbell and Stanley reference above. This is required reading for advanced students of methodology, but the use of sophisticated statistical techniques makes this book unintelligible to many laypersons.

The Social Animal. A film produced for the American Psychological Association, 1953. Visually presents several segments of actual social psychological experiments. Available through many university film centers.

SUGGESTED RESEARCH PROJECTS

1. During 1978 New York City experienced a prolonged newspaper strike. This strike eliminated the normally heavy flow of daily advertising by the commercial community in the city. Nevertheless, sales figures did not appear to be affected by the strike. The president of a major advertising agency was reported to have nervously observed that it made him wonder about the effects of advertising. What type of implicit research design underlies these observations? What alternative explanations might have accounted for the sales figures? What types of design might you propose to rule out these alternative explanations more clearly? Why?

2. Recently released figures show that blacks make up 27 percent of all Army personnel but 51 percent of all those now in Army penal facilities. These figures have caused a mild uproar from persons claiming that this is nothing unusual; the proportion of blacks now in Army prisons is roughly equivalent to civilian figures (blacks make up 12 percent of the country's population but 38 percent of the federal prison system). Others claim that these figures simply reinforce the fact that America is a racist society. Note the several different implicit research designs and "hypotheses" present in this debate. What alternative explanations are left to the imagination by these figures? How could you more adequately design a study to rule out alternative explanations? Explain which alternative could be ruled out, and why, in your discussion.

3. Pick some analytic (social control, socialization) features of social relationships (a good list can be found on pp. 191–193 of G. M. McCall and others, *Social Relationships*, 1970) for use in a true experiment. Outline key features of the experiment such as operationalization of variables, treatments, hypothetical expected experimental outcomes, ethics, instructions, and internal and external validity.

4. Outline a naturalistic, field quasi-experiment designed to test the same analytic features of social relationships used in Project 1 above. How does this quasi-experiment differ from the true laboratory experiment in terms of operationalization of variables, and so on?

5. Write a two-variable causal hypothesis. Provide a rationale for the variable relations. Specify in detail how variables are to be measured. Recommend a research design in which

   a. Sample characteristics are identified

   b. Comparison groups or control groups are explicitly identified

   c. Conditions of measurements are explicated.

   Using Xs and Os diagram the research design. Defend your selection of research strategy. What sources of internal invalidity are controlled, and which are not controlled? (Note: It is more important to demonstrate that you know the strengths and weaknesses in your design than to attempt the perfect design.) What groups, settings, and situations would the results of the proposed study generalize to?

6. Use Xs and Os to diagram the type of research design employed in Mazur's article (Appendix G) or some other journal article. What sources of internal and external invalidity are controlled and which are not controlled using this research design?

217

7. Revise your experiment or quasi-experiment project in Project 3 or 4 to include several structured observational measures from Chapter 5. Defend your choice of measures in terms of potential theoretical use, reliability and validity assessment of the measure, operationalization, and observer training techniques to be used.

8. A researcher used a factorial posttest-only type of design to collect the following information: (a) Group 1 members, the control group, were observed aggressing five times during an hour's posttest period; (b) Group 2 received a treatment of watching a TV program with much violence and during the posttest observation period were observed aggressing fifteen times; (c) Group 3 received a treatment of working on a frustrating problem and were observed during the observational period following that aggressing ten times; and (d) Group 4 received both treatments given to Groups 2 and 3. They were observed in the posttest period aggressing fifty times. Each group had equal numbers of subjects.

a. Set up the data in the format shown in Figure 7–1.

b. Is the joint effect additive or interactive? Why?

c. If the Group 4 observations had shown fifteen aggressions, would this figure modify your answer in 8b? Why or why not? If it had shown five aggressions would this have modified your answer? Why or why not?

d. If the groups had not been randomized, how would this affect your conclusions in terms of potential alternative explanations? Why?

Simulation
and Gaming

A game—nearly any game, not merely those termed "simulation games" constitutes a kind of caricature of social life. It is a magnification of some aspect of social interaction, excluding all else, tearing this aspect of social interaction from its social context and giving it a special context of its own. . . . [games are] an introduction to the idea of playing under sets of rules, that is, the idea of different roles. . . . [1]

Imagine you are a member of SIMSOC (Simulated Society). Sixty of your classmates also represent citizens of SIMSOC. All members of SIMSOC live in one of four partitioned regions, widely separated from each other. Travel between each region is regulated by public and private transportation tickets. You have a job as broadcasting chief of MASMED (Mass Media) by which you earn pay in SIMBUCKS for your responsibilities in running the National Broadcasting System. Your classmates have jobs such as sales vice-president of BASIN (basic industry), regional represen-

[1] J. S. Coleman, "In Defense of Games," *American Behavioral Scientist* 10(1966):3–4.

tative for INNOVIN (innovative industry), fund-raising chairman of POP (party of the people), SOP (society party) membership chairman, chief organizer for EMPIN (employee interests), and appeals judge for JUDCO (judicial council).

During the last class period you fired one of your reporters who, unable to find another job, died because as an unemployed person she could not obtain the subsistence necessary to pay her room and board. Your best friend, the chief organizer of EMPIN, has been arrested by a regional police force. You are upset because you haven't enough SIM-BUCKS to buy a travel pass to his region of SIMSOC to counsel with him.

You have just published the latest SIMSOC TIMES edition showing that while the standard of living is rising, social cohesion is at an all-time low and the nation's food and energy supply is decreasing. A news item has just been delivered stating that an earthquake has just hit one of the nation's four regions, and all communications with that region are disrupted indefinitely. You decide to run an editorial blasting SOP's political philosophy of decentralization as the basic cause of SIMSOC's ills. As the editorial is going to press your class instructor halts the game to assess your society's and your own personal progress during the previous hour. (Table 8–1 will give you a basic notion of SIMSOC's principal structure.)

The use of games like SIMSOC (Gamson 1978), and other means of simulating social processes as a research technique, is rather new as a serious professional interest in the social and behavioral sciences. Wilbert McKeachie (1972:66) relates how ten years earlier, when he was the new department chairman of psychology at Michigan, he had doubts about the professional gamble involved. As recently as 1966 James Coleman, then chairman of the Social Relations department at Johns Hopkins, wrote (1966:3–4) about the few professional sociologists wagering their professional lives that the construction of games and other simulations might "provide . . . that degree of abstraction from life and simplification of life that allows [us] to understand better certain fundamentals of societal organization." In the relatively short period of time since scientists at Michigan, Johns Hopkins, and other universities added simulations to the researcher's repertory of research techniques, clear evidence has been amassed for their research utility. On the other hand, simulation has deep roots in history. Chess has often been considered a simulation of medieval warfare, and systematic simulation of war through "war games" goes back two centuries.

Abelson (1968:275) has defined simulation as "the exercise of a flexible imitation of processes and outcomes for the purpose of clarifying or explaining the underlying mechanisms involved." Paraphrasing another simulations expert (Raser 1969), a simulation is a symbolic abstraction, simplification, and substitution for some system. In other words, a simulation is a theoretical model of the elements, relationships, and processes that may reasonably be included (and excluded) in symbolizing some system. It is *not* an attempt to get a perfect replication of that system.

Bell (1975) suggests three purposes for simulations: heuristic, educational, and research. First, simulations may help the theorist make a theory more explicit. Many advocates of simulations see them as ways of testing whether one really understands some phenomenon as well as one thinks one does. Plattner's (1975) simulation of peasant bartering and

Table 8-1
Glossary of SIMSOC Terms

---

1. *SIMBUCKS:* The basic currency of SIMSOC.

2. *Region:* One of four home areas where members live and work. Travel between regions is regulated by public and private transportation ticket purchases.

3. *BASIN:* The basic industry of SIMSOC with objectives to expand assets and income through stocks, bonds, and other investment procedures.

4. *INNOVIN:* Like BASIN, investment in INNOVIN stimulates long-term national growth but is a more speculative business venture, thus creating conflicts within society.

5. *POP:* Political party preferring decentralized planning and coordination, and individual autonomy.

6. *SOP:* Political party emphasizing the need for centralized leadership and guidance.

7. *EMPIN:* Organization working in behalf of employee's rights to adequate subsistence and fair share of the wealth.

8. *MASMED:* The mass communications industry with objectives of keeping the society informed of its development.

9. *JUDCO:* The judiciary branch of SIMSOC with rights of deciding whether agreements or actions of any member or group of members violates the basic rules of SIMSOC.

10. *Subsistence:* Measured by a member's obtaining of a subsistence ticket, without which he or she may become unemployed and/or die.

11. *Personal Goals:* Each person is requested to follow *one* of three personal goals in playing SIMSOC: the attainment of (a) power, (b) wealth, or (c) popularity.

12. *Public Programs:* The promotion of the food and energy supply, standard of living, social cohesion, and public commitment may be strengthened through monetary investment in (a) research and conservation or (b) welfare services.

13. *Food and Energy Supply (FES):* Indicator of given natural resources versus population needs.

14. *Standard of Living (SL):* Indicator of the society's consumption level.

15. *Social Cohesion (SC):* Representation of intergroup conflict and cohesion.

16. *Public Commitment (PC):* Measure of alienation versus social commitment and values.

---

trading (PEDLAR) was initially such an intellectual honing exercise. Second, simulations can be used to teach students about the operations of complex social systems. SIMSOC (Gamson 1978) is an excellent example of this purpose. Third, they can be used to test theories. The Prisoner's Dilemma, a game we shall spend considerable time discussing in a later section of this chapter, has often been used to test theories of cooperation and trust.

THE DECISION TO SIMULATE

Two basic considerations underlie the decision to simulate social process (Inbar and Stoll 1972:27): First, how much is known about the process? Second, what does the researcher want to *do* with the simulation?

Information about the process to be simulated is crucial to simulation design. This may seem paradoxical considering our definition of the purpose of simulation as "clarifying or explaining" underlying processes. It is not really paradoxical given the nature of feedback in simulations. The simulation researchers will start out by utilizing whatever information they have concerning the process to be simulated; they will use the *components* of the process and the sets of *conditions* assumed to operate in and between the components. Simulationists working with relatively imprecise information find it useful to start out with human-made simulations. As their informational precision increases they will tend to use human-machine simulations, and only under conditions of extremely precise information will they normally use strictly machine simulations (although we shall note exceptions to this rule).

The second consideration has to do with how the simulation information is to be used. Bell (1975) points out that simulations can be used for teaching as well as research purposes. Teaching purposes normally will call for human or human-machine simulations, while research may use any of the three generic types.

A third factor in simulation as in any methodological consideration is the time factor. Simulation is a time-consuming method, with satisfactory simulations not uncommonly taking two to ten years to complete.

Physical facilities also present problems in deciding to simulate. Some games, like Gamson's (1972) Simulated Society (SIMSOC), are satisfactorily run with simple facilities such as private rooms for each interest group; others, like Sakada's (1971) simulation of elementary social interaction (CHEBO) require fairly sophisticated computer facilities that have large memory *capacity* and high *efficiency* (and hence, low financial cost).

Practical considerations also include such things as

[Human] simulation, especially those with gamelike structures, require an investment of tedious hours of work on trivial tasks (such as designing and coloring a game board so that interest in and playability of the game may be enhanced). Similarly, in writing a program one faces the issue of *absolute* accuracy without exerting extreme rigor in his work; the designer may spend hours or days in an exasperating search among thousands of symbols to locate an error which turns out to be an omitted comma. (Inbar and Stoll 1972:254–255)

SIMULATION VERSUS EXPERIMENTATION

Experimentation, as we saw from Chapter 7, has virtues of control and replication. Chapter 7 showed that when one moves out into the field one normally loses some control over one's research variables, particularly in more macrosociological studies. One of the major advantages of simulation is that the researchers can artificially manipulate variables in such macrosociological settings in ways that one could simply not do in real life, either for practical or ethical reasons. (This does not mean that simulations do away with ethical implications. Indeed, as we shall note, ethical implications of knowledge gleaned from simulations may be very pronounced.)

Furthermore, we also saw in Chapter 7 that experiments normally can extrapolate to at best a few variables. By contrast, simulations (particularly computer simulations) may often handle a multitude of variables including both intrapersonal and interpersonal processes at the same time.

Sometimes experimentation may be used in conjunction with simulation and gaming. Indeed, we shall see that some simulations utilize experiments within their context.

Both experiments and simulations are often criticized for their lack of validity (artificiality). Again, as in Chapter 7, it must be emphasized that methods per se give neither validity nor invalidity to scientific knowledge. Simulations, as well as experiments, have been designed that closely proximate social processes. Abelson (1968:276) has coined the term *simulation gap* for referring to the extent that a simulation does not imitate some system. Simulations, unlike experiments, are best justified in the study of systems. *System* refers to any set of interrelated and interdependent entities: families, courts, bureaucracies, and nations.

DIMENSIONS AND PROPERTIES OF SIMULATION

Monroe (1968) refers to three types of simulation properties: iconic, analogue, and homologue. An *iconic* property is one transformed in size or scale but otherwise the same as the property represented. For instance, in SIMSOC, a small number of individuals are used to represent a much larger society and its components.

An *analogue* is a property substituted for another that behaves in much the same way as the original property; hence, the researcher often uses analogies in simulations. Raser (1969:31) has used college students of different nationalities as analogues to *culture* in games of international politics.

A *homologue* is a substitute property that bears only surface similarity to the property it represents, although in a good simulation a homologue should be a faithful symbolization. The SIMSOC political parties—SOP and POP—are *homologues,* respectively, of the present-day Democratic and Republican Parties. They are *not* intended to be *replicas* of those parties. An essential point to remember is that "the properties of a simulation need not *look* like the properties they represent; what is required is that they obey the same laws" (Guetzkow and others 1963: 53).

While the simulationist chooses the types of property substitutes necessary and most practical for a study, the nature of the phenomenon under study in turn delimits research design. Harris (1968:367) has noted six such basic dimensional aspects of any phenomenon that must be incorporated into the simulation.

1. *Descriptive versus analytic (inductive versus deductive) models*—Whether analysis will be the precise formulation of relationships and covariations *versus* the testing of cause and effect statements.
2. *Holistic versus partial models*—Is one interested in examining the total phenomenon *or* in holding part of the phenomenon constant while examining its impact on some subsystem?
3. *Macro- versus microanalytic models*—Whether aggregate levels and flows are the fundamental units *versus* the more basic elemental units of analysis.
4. *Static versus dynamic models*—While most simulations deal with change and trend developments, some are done to explore equilibrium or static models.
5. *Deterministic versus probabilistic models*—Models are "deterministic" if the "solution" of the model gives a unique set of results. "Probabilistic" models, by contrast, have variation determined by chance or random outcomes.
6. *Simultaneous versus sequential models*—In sequential analysis variable processes are viewed in a time series, cause-and-effect manner while in simultaneous analysis all variables are studied as if determined at the same time.

In the next several sections some instances of several types of simulation—human, human-machine, and machine—will be discussed. Table 8–2 summarizes the information presented in each type of simulation.

Table 8–2
Types of Simulation and Gaming

Descriptive Term	Simulator	Simulated	Remarks
1. Machine simulation	Computer	Individual psychological processes, social groups or abstract systems such as roles, communication networks, or sets of decision makers representing nations	*All-computer* simulations of psychological or sociological processes. In general, variables more formally preprogrammed and analogous to some "referent" system than other simulation and gaming types.
2. Human-Machine simulation	Human participant linked to computer	Abstract systems as noted above for type 1	Simulation preprogramming more formal and tentative, in general, than machine simulations. Interface between individual and computer simulations often used to sharpen formality of simulation. *Gaming simulations.*
3. Gaming	Groups of individuals a. dyadic b. triadic c. *n*-person	Archetypal individuals or roles; decision makers representing nations, communities, or organizations; situations of conflict or interdependence between decision makers	Besides size of group, important dimensions often include information level (whether individuals have perfect information or not) and perceived goal motivation (whether game is "zero-sum," "non-zero-sum," or "*mixed motive*"). Relatively small numbers of variables and well-defined goals and decision situations characteristic. *All-human* simulations.

HUMAN SIMULATIONS

Human simulations break down in practice into two types: gaming and international simulation.

International, or inter-national, simulation (INS) has been concerned basically with research and teaching on international relations (Guetzkow and others 1963). Since INS proved to be one of the first simulation games, there has been plenty of time to evaluate the decision process which entered into its making. Sullivan has provided a critique of INS's evolution.

Sullivan (1972), in reflecting on the difficulties present in simulating international relations in 1957–1958, found the difficulties to be twofold: (1) the small number of historical cases to build a simulation from and (2) the difficulty of access to first-hand information on diplomatic relations. Hence, the representativeness of the INS substitute properties may be questioned.

Further, INS simulators decided that three criteria should underlie the game (Sullivan 1972:114):

> (1) national actors free to choose their own goals and subgoals, (2) an intra-national environment programmed to their decision-making efforts, (3) a domestic and inter-national economic system programmed to produce decision consequences.

Nations were given fictitious names such as UTRO so that the game would be free of player's *interpretations* of real national actions and goals. Nevertheless, external validity of INS simulations can be questioned, particularly in terms of their ability to simulate task pressures found in international relations (Sullivan 1972:116). At any rate INS has proven to be a useful research technique for isolating important components and processes of internation decision making and diplomacy.

In the rest of this section various generic game models will be presented. Zaltman (1972) has suggested the playability of any game is a function of

1. The number of roles in the game
2. The heterogeneity of the audience
3. The complexity of the model
4. The number of learning objectives (if any).

No gaming model can serve as a universal model for all games. The size of the group is an important component of games. Games generally can be classified as two-person (dyadic), three-person (triadic), or *n*-person (more than three) participants. Each of these sizes has special features not found in the other two sizes. The fewer the players, the simpler the game in general. The more complex the game, the more forces a player is faced with that he or she cannot control, the more difficult it becomes to define the game's decisional processes. Good sources of information on two-person games can be found in Davis (1970), on three-person games in Caplow (1968), and n-person games in Dresher, Shapley, and Tucker (1964).

Other important dimensions to games are whether the players have perfect (equal and total) information or not, and whether the game is "zero-sum" or "nonzero-sum."

Very rarely in real life can perfect information be assured. For instance, only in parlor games can one usually find perfect information, as in chess, although games like bridge and poker are games of nonperfect information. Theoretically, games of perfect information are strictly determined (Zermolo 1912). On the other hand, game theorists lose chess matches. Thus, the objection can be raised that determinism of games of perfect information depends on players acting rationally. However, as Abelson (1968:280) points out,

> Sometimes a mathematical solution specifying rationally optimal play of the game is available. Often it is found, however, that subjects do not play according to this normatively "best" procedure. The obvious question then arises: "Under what circumstances do subjects not behave 'rationally'?"

The matter of imperfect information seriously complicates game outcomes since there is no predetermined rational play with which to predict outcomes. The choice of either strategy in simulation will depend on the purposes of the game, although imperfect information is more probable in social life.

Zero-sum games depend on the *assumption* of fixed rewards or payoffs; if rewards are constant, then if one person increases his or her rewards, some other's rewards must decrease. (Whether rewards are actually fixed or not does not matter—games have been run where the participants only *think* rewards are fixed with results similar to actually fixed rewards.) Many real situations are zero-sum by nature: war, time spent in social relations, and so on. Thus, in zero-sum games, the players have no common interests, making them purely competitive by nature. Nonzero-sum games, by contrast, tend to have "mixed motives" (partly competitive, partly cooperative) and thus lead to more complex outcomes. By contrast, a nonzero-sum game has no fixed payoff structure so that theoretically all players might lose or all might win.

Two-person, zero-sum games are unlike most problems that arise in everyday life, since they enable one to find universally accepted solutions; most real-life situations have no simple strategy which is clearly preferable, nor any single, clear-cut, predictable outcome.

Two-person, nonzero-sum games, because they tend to imitate more fruitfully (and shed light on) many social processes, have been used a great deal in simulations of things ranging from taxicab rate wars to nuclear disarmament models. A classic example of this type of game is the "prisoner's dilemma."

In the "prisoner's dilemma" game, as originally formulated by Tucker, two people have been arrested by the police as suspected accomplices in a crime. Each person is isolated from the other in separate cells. Both suspects are informed of the consequences of their confessing or remaining silent which are: (1) If one suspect confesses and the other partner does not, the one who confesses gets prosecutor's immunity and goes free while the other goes to jail for twenty years. (2) If both suspects confess, they each go to jail for five years. (3) If both suspects remain silent, they both go to jail for a year on a lesser charge of carrying concealed weapons (see Table 8-3).

Under the assumptions that (1) there is "no honor among thieves" and (2) each suspect's sole concern is self-interest, what should the prisoners do?

Now, each suspect will be forced to make a decision without knowing what the other's decision is. Hence, each suspect must consider each of the other person's alternatives and anticipate the effect of each of them on her-or himself. Each realizes that if the other confesses, he or she must either remain silent and go to jail for twenty years or confess and go to jail for five. On the other hand, if the other person remains silent, he or she can serve a year by being silent also or win freedom by confessing. It appears then, in either case, that our suspect would be better off by *confessing!* However, prisoner's dilemma outcomes are often determined by less rational choices. For instance, two naive prisoners, ignorant of this compelling argument for confessing, would both remain silent and go to prison for only a year.

Paradoxically, two sophisticated prisoners, primed with our com-

Table 8-3
Prisoner's Dilemma Game Outcomes

		Suspect 2	
		Confess	Do not confess
Suspect 1	Confess	(5 yrs., 5 yrs.)	(go free, 20 yrs.)
	Do not confess	(20 yrs., go free)	(1 yr., 1 yr.)

pelling advice, would confess and spend five years in prison contemplating their cleverness. Consistent behavior patterns have been observed in "prisoner's dilemma" type games conducted over a number of simulation trials, which differ by conditions of perfect versus nonperfect information, number of trials, personality of players, communication networks, and payoff significance. Prisoner's dilemma games have proven to yield good research evidence on interpersonal processes such as cooperation, competition, and trust and individual processes such as rationality in decision making. Granberg and others (1975) have shown clear effects (or lack of effects) of communication on prisoner's dilemma outcomes illustrated in Figure 8–1. Notice, between the fifteenth and thirtieth trials of this game, for example, how mutually cooperative responses increase for persons under communication conditions by contrast to noncommunication conditions.

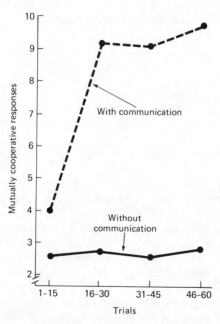

FIGURE 8–1 *Interaction of communication by blocks on mutually cooperative responses.*

Source: This figure, drawn from "Effect of communication on cooperation in expanded prisoner's dilemma and chicken games," by Donald Granberg, J. Scott Stevens, and Sandra Katz, is reprinted from *Simulation & Games,* 6:2(June 1975), 166–187 by permission of the publisher, Sage Publications, Inc.

Three-person games deserve special treatment because, in many respects, they are more simple in outcomes than two-person games. Caplow (1968) has shown coalition formation and payoff distribution to be clearly a function of player power. By contrast, n-person games often lead to rather obscure processes and outcome rationales. Still, the game theorist may focus on one aspect of the n-person game and disregard others. Aumann and Maschler (1964) chose to assume they were dealing with competitive players who could communicate freely and have simultaneous and instantaneous access to one another. They found that in situations where these assumptions are supported the range of payoffs for each coalition could be predicted. However, the price paid by this approach is a narrow set of conditions to which the game applies.

On the other hand, one can attempt to capture all the relevant features of a game in a single model, such as the Inter-Nation Simulation game, which will obscure the predictions of game outcomes but may offer solutions to the possible roles and norms that might arise under certain conditions.

The following steps summarize some criteria for designing human simulations:

1. Define the overall simulation objectives, attempting to give operational definitions of key components and processes.
2. Determine *scope* of the game in terms of time, place, and issues to be simulated.
3. Identify key actor's roles, social groups, or organizations making critical decisions.
4. Determine actors' objectives in specific contexts (power, wealth).
5. Determine actors' resources (physical, social, economic, information, political).
6. Determine the interaction sequence cycle or structure among actors.
7. Determine the decision rules or criteria on the basis of which actors decide what resources and information to transmit and what actions to take.
8. Identify potential constraints on actions of actors such as trust, legitimacy, and coalition formation.
9. Formulate scoring rules or win criteria. This should include *time* of winning, number and type of criteria (money earned, zero-sum), and, if there are more than one criteria for winning, the degree to which those criteria are interrelated. If more than one winner is possible, Inbar and Stoll (1972:275) suggest that the arrangements by which the winners are produced should be spelled out according to one of the following ways:

   a. hierarchical structure (players rank-ordered on winning criteria)

   b. group reference structure—that is, within each of the various competing or noncompeting groups in a game, a winner might be selected

   c. task structure—the difficulty of the task herein determines the number of winners and losers the game will yield.

10. Methods of allocation of resources should be determined.
11. Forms of game presentation, manipulation, and sequence of operations must be chosen. Some practical considerations include duration and available space, materials, and facilities.

A set of useful conventions for making and evaluating the objectives of good gaming simulations are summarized in Figure 8–2 (p. 232).

Orback (1979) has commented on the motivational aspects of learning caused by simulation games. He points out that researchers using simulation games have been somewhat baffled by the fact that participants normally find these techniques more interesting than traditional techniques. Orback's conclusions are that participants' responses to simulation games can be largely accounted for by the facts that they (1) allow persons greater freedom of thought, expression, and action, (2) have greater amounts of novelty involved, and (3) are not restricted by the judgmental or sanctioning inhibitions found in more traditional techniques.

MACHINE SIMULATIONS

Unlike human simulations where the decisions are made by human actors, machine-simulation decision making depends on extremely precise definitions. If racial equality and inequality processes are to be simulated, computer operationalization requires precision in defining "racial equality" to mean something such as equal proportions of all racial groups in each occupation and at each level of education and income.

Second, computer simulation requires that large amounts of data on the system to be analyzed be stored in the computer's memory. These data must be quantitative (ordinal, interval, or ratio) in nature. Generally speaking, these data must be reasonably accurate if the old computer wisdom "garbage in, garbage out" is not to prevail. Abelson (1968:283–308) gives a number of steps in the process of building computer simulations that are summarized below.

1. The problem should be too complex to be handled by traditional methods but not so global as to defy analysis.
2. The model must have identifiable *units* (individuals, groups, roles) with precisely defined *properties* (variables and constants). There must be some system *inputs* that put system properties into motion through specified *processes* and specified *phasing* or sequencing of processes through time, from which *consequences* may be drawn.
3. Organize the sequences of specified processes logically through flow charts as in Figure 8–3 (p. 233).

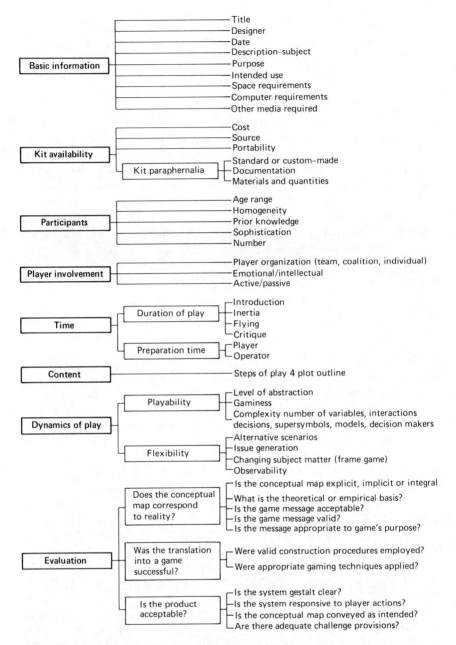

FIGURE 8–2 *Interpretive Criteria for Gaming Simulations.*

Source: This figure, drawn from "Toward a general theory of gaming," by Richard D. Duke, is reprinted from *Simulation & Games,* 5:2(June 1974), 131–146 by permission of the publisher, Sage Publications, Inc.

4. Investigate to determine a suitable computer since all computers do not have the same memory storage capacities for data and programs.
5. Choose a programming language that is efficient and can accommodate the various processes and sequences in the flow-charting.
6. Write the computer program.
7. "Hand simulation" of the program—run slowly through a simulation step by step to uncover unanticipated shortcomings in the program.
8. "Debug" the program.
9. Revise the model to improve it theoretically in terms of input specifications or programming options.
10. Utilize data to (a) explore a large set of reasonable assumptions during simulation runs to see which assumptions, if any, are critical in what degree; (b) gather data relevant to those propositions about which there is considerable quantitative ambiguity.

If you have a rudimentary knowledge of some computer language such as BASIC or FORTRAN, you might well profit from working with a good text on computer simulations such as Lehman's (1977).

An example of a large-scale simulation study has been going on at Northwestern University for several years now. Large amounts of data on all of the African countries have been stored in computer memory. The data include such things as each nation's population size, gross national product, newspapers per thousand population, illiteracy rate, and type of

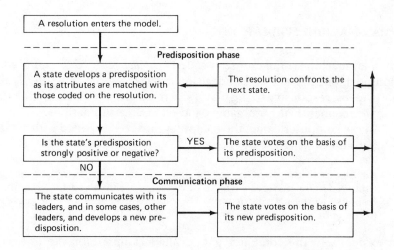

FIGURE 8–3 *United Nations simulation roll call model (revised).*

Source: This figure, drawn from "A computer model for prediction of voting in the United Nations," by Dorothy Dodge, is reprinted from *Simulation & Games,* 2:4(December 1971), 455–471 by permission of the publisher, Sage Publications, Inc.

legislature (bicameral, unicameral) for different time periods. Preliminary studies have used techniques such as discriminant function analysis for the study of African revolutions. Simply put, discriminant function analysis takes data based on several different sources (countries that have had recent revolutions versus those that have not had recent revolutions) and discriminates between those variables that appear to *predict* the criterion (revolution in this instance). While this study is still in its infancy, it points out potential ethical problems since computer simulation data, when accurate, may be seen to be useful for many nonneutral purposes (preventing or starting revolutions).

Another example of a computer simulation with more public recognition is the prediction of election outcomes. Election prediction programs typically make use of a large mathematical equation. The vote totals from a large number of key voting precincts are entered into the equation, along with information determined on the basis of past elections. The "model" in this simulation is the mathematical equation that simplifies and abstracts the results of many individual voters over the past several elections into one single mathematical expression. The success of these simulations can easily be testified to by the often small (less than 5 percent) election returns needed to make successful predictions and often counterintuitive results in which a candidate, with a minority of the votes in, is successfully predicted a final winner.

HUMAN-MACHINE SIMULATIONS

In human-machine simulations, so-called *computer games,* or gaming simulations, persons play the role of decision makers, but the computer is also a participant, responsive to the players' activities, and thus the simulation combines elements of both games and computer simulations.

In the computer game, the computer must be provided with a *script.* As Inbar and Stoll (1972:24) put it,

> Analogous to the dramatic use of the term, the script lists the messages conveyed to the player. Two kinds of messages are involved. One is a simple response to the player's actions. The other is instruction to the player as to the appropriate way [*he* or *she*] can respond to the computer.

For example, in the computer game called Hammurabi, the following computer-person "dialogue" could take place:

Computer: Hammurabi says: Welcome, New Village Manager. Your population is 1,000 people. You own 70 acres. You have 200 bushels of grain in store. Land is trading at 20 bushels per acre. How many acres of land do you wish to buy?

Player: 1.
Computer: You now have 71 acres and 180 bushels. How many acres do you wish to plant?
Player: No.
Computer: Error in format. That does not compute.
Player: 300.
Computer: But you only have 71 acres.
Player: 30.
Computer: The population is now 1071. How many bushels do you wish to use as food?
Player: 80.
Computer: There were 80 accidental deaths, 30 deaths from disease, and 120 deaths from starvation. The population is now 841. You have been replaced by a military junta.

Notice how the script structures the player's alternatives. If the player communicates outside of the computer-given alternatives, the computer types out something like "Error in format, that does not compute."

Computer games are more for teaching than research purposes because of their structured scripts. However, another type of human-machine simulation is productive in the area of research. This is a two-step gaming simulation. During the first step the human simulation takes place with probable characteristics such as described by Coleman (1964*b*: 1058–1059):

1. First a delineation of the principal roles in the system, and the structure of the system
2. A general model of purposive behavior of persons in roles, following the expanded notion of economic man set down in recent theoretical statements by Thibaut and Kelley (1959), Homans (1961), Blau (1960), Parsons (1963), and others
3. Detailed (though largely qualitative) observation of behavior of persons in each of the roles in the system to determine the principal costs and returns involved in each possible action by a person in the role
4. A synthesis of the above information into a simulated social system.

In the second step, the information gleaned from the human simulation is fed into a computer simulation as its data base. The value of this is apparent in reconsidering that computer simulation builds steps of selecting appropriate *processes* and *sequencing* of units. There may be many alternative processes and sequencings that seem plausible until one has human simulated, after which one may narrow down the choices to flowchart and program. Conceivably one may alternate human and computer simulations like this for some period of time before one hits upon the best modular fit.

Such a process is described in great detail by Plattner (1975). Originally he was interested in writing a program to interest students in the complexities and subtleties of the itinerant peddler as an exercise in economic decision making. Later, he attempted to assess agreement between findings (profit maximization, risk minimization) of his original fieldwork in rural Mexico and his computer simulation. This original work by Plattner is a good place to start reading for the student interested in pursuing how the simulationist goes about constructing a human-computer simulation.

VALIDATING SIMULATIONS

The basic principle for establishing the reliability of a simulation is that *successive runs should give similar results.* In the case of computers this principle rarely is a problem, but in games it may be. Thus reliability in games requires (Inbar and Stoll 1972:279–280) that

1. The physical equipment should not be cumbersome or impractical.
2. The rules should be as clearly and simply stated as possible.
3. The rules should be complete and self-contained.
4. The game should not overtax the player's span of attention.

Reliability, while important, never insures validity of any method. As with any method, there are several ways to assess validity of simulations. First, does the simulation appear reasonable or have face validity? For instance, did any unexpected event occur? Did players find the game realistic? Did expected events pan out? Second, one can compare simulation outcomes with some theoretically or empirically expected outcomes in the real world. Third, did unexpected processes, sequences, or structures emerge that violate the assumptions of the model? Fourth, do components of the simulation parallel those simulated? For example, "does the simulation reproduce historical outcomes or predict the future" (Raser 1969:144)? Finally, are the simulation's structure and processes isomorphic to those observed in the referent system?

Most of the criticism of simulations can be leveled in terms of how representative of, or generalizable to particular populations, settings, and independent and dependent variables the simulation is.

Lashutka (1977) has validated BAFA BAFA (Shirts 1974) as a simulated predictor of cultural adaptability in the selection of persons nominated to serve in the foreign service. Participants in BAFA BAFA are divided into two cultures—Alpha and Beta—which are assigned to separate rooms. Each group is provided with a booklet containing the rules of the culture, which must be learned and which will govern behavior of the group while members of the new culture. Alpha culture is a relaxed, English-speaking culture that values personal contact and intimacy within a sexist and patriarchal structure. Betas are aggressive money-oriented individuals. Beta communication is through Beta language (easily learned but seemingly complicated to outsiders). The simulation has been used to predict successfully both foreign service applicants' and Navy recruits' cross-cultural adaptability.

Unfortunately, none of the techniques mentioned can completely validate a simulation. In the words of Abelson (1968:343), "a simulation could be 'right for the wrong reasons.'" Kirk and Coleman (1963) have shown that one can simulate triad breakdowns with computers into "two against one" through *chance occurrence*. However, in real life there are other nonchance means of producing the same phenomenon. Thus, Abelson (1968:344) proposes that, where possible, the simulationist should show "that the fit was not so easy by changing the model in various ways and demonstrating consistent lack of fit, so as to render more plausible the simulated fit to reality."

An extreme, but common, problem of simulation validation is shown in what Dutton and Starbuck (1971:14) term "Bonini's Paradox."

> A model is built in order to achieve understanding of an observed causal process, and the model is stated as a simulation program in order that the assumptions and functional relations may be as complex and realistic as possible. The resulting program produces outputs resembling those observed in the real world, and inspires confidence that the real causal process has been accurately represented. However, because the assumptions incorporated in the model are complex and their mutual interdependencies are obscure, the simulation program is no easier to understand than the real process was.

SUMMARY

There are several rationales for attempting simulations. The most basic reason has to do with the complexity of human behavior. It is a fact of scientific life that research methods are in general most adaptable to rather simple and single processes. On the other hand, processes in the real world are complex and multiple. Hence, simulations recognize the fact that understanding social phenomena requires examining complex systems of interaction rather than isolated entities, multivariate (many variable) rather than univariate (single variable) analysis, and dynamic rather than static phenomena. Many research experts believe that simulations hold greater promise for imitating these more complex, multiple processes than more traditional research techniques.

A second reason for simulation occurs when analytic solutions to a scientific problem depend on sets of probabilities. As Inbar and Stoll (1972:8) point out, "typically such stochastic (probabalistic) models do not have an explicit simple solution. Instead it is necessary to make repeated trials of solutions of the model, to trace out the possible paths of the process."

Third, it is often more economical to simulate a given phenomenon than to study it in its natural setting. Computers may often be used to simulate in *seconds* what it might take decades or centuries to carry out in real life. Also, the simulation might help eliminate unnecessary waste or disaster as in computer simulations of traffic flow on highways.

Fourth, Lehman (1977:14) notes that simulations, through simplification, often make salient or visible a system's operating framework where the simulated system's natural complexity and detail are so great that they obscure the phenomenon.

Fifth, the researcher may be able to observe the effects of different kinds of variable manipulations through simulations. In SIMSOC, the instructor can manipulate or modify variables such as degree of economic scarcity or information flow to gain profitable insights into how the phenomenon works. Likewise, a game of a city might be played repeatedly with changes in key variables to see the possible effects of these changes on urban growth.

Sixth, the researcher may wish to simulate for ethical reasons. He or she may be able to simulate dangerous situations without actually creating them. For instance, we might want to simulate a race riot or revolution without the hazards of decreasing human safety.

READINGS FOR ADVANCED STUDENTS

M. D. Davis. *Game Theory*, 1970. Excellent and readable introduction to game theory and research.

Michael J. Fryer. *An Introduction to Linear Programming and Matrix Game Theory*, 1978. If you can solve simultaneous equations such as

$$3x + 2y = 7$$
$$-x + y = 1$$

then this is a delightful and creative introduction to the mathematics and logic of game theory.

Cathy S. Greenblat and Richard D. Duke. *Gaming-Simulation: Rationale, Design, and Applications*, 1975. One of the best and most comprehensive texts on gaming situations.

HENRY HAMBURGER, *Games as Models of Social Phenomena,* 1979. A semiprogrammed introduction to the language of game theory. Very relevant and interesting examples used on such topics as pollution problems, Chicken, and oil-field games.

RICHARD S. LEHMAN, *Computer Simulation and Modeling,* 1977. The most simplified and interesting "how to" presentation on creating a computer simulation that I have come across.

SUGGESTED RESEARCH PROJECTS

1. Using the eleven criteria for working up to a human simulation, design a game for testing some body of social or behavioral interest such as triadic breakdown, marriage counseling, or trust relations.

2. Design an experiment where simulation is used as a component.

3. Analyze an already existing game or simulation such as SIMSOC or INS in terms of Harris's dimensions of models (macro-versus microanalytic).

4. Run a classroom simulation of Bernhardt's FOUR WAY DECISION MAKING game (found in *Simulation and Games* 1978, pp. 227–231) to get the feel of problem-solving decision-making simulations. Rerun the simulation using some of the modifications suggested in that report. Write a short paper criticizing this simulation (using the eleven rules for human simulations); suggest alternative modifications based on your critique.

5. Check with a local computer center to see if they have a computer simulation game available for you to test out. (If not you can find one easily adaptable to your computer in Plattner, *Formal Methods of Economic Anthropology* [a special publication of the American Anthropological Association, 1975] written in BASIC.) Play the game a number of times. Use these sessions to work out (a) a flow chart of the program and (b) the decision rules that govern the computer's responses to your playings.

Evaluation Research

When people become so intelligent that they know how to choose as their representatives, persons of decided ability, who know something of human nature, who recognize that there are social forces, and that their duty is to devise ways and means for scientifically controlling those forces on exactly the same principles that an experimenter or an inventor controls the forces of physical nature, then we may look for scientific legislation.[1]

In the last few years, there has been a noticeable rise of interest in applying social science methodology to the evaluation and solution of large-scale social problems. This concern is shown in the increasing use of social science methods under the rubric of "evaluation research." Evaluation research is one of a diverse bundle of "applied research styles" (policy research, action research) that are often mistakenly lumped together although each has a different purpose and method.

[1]Lester Ward, *Applied Sociology,* 1906, p. 338.

Evaluation research is now commonly understood to mean the assessment of the effectiveness of social programs that were designed as tentative solutions to existing social problems.

This is quite different from most other types of applied research that attempt to search for solutions to social problems. Hence, the evaluation researcher is not like a consulting engineer searching for means to reach a given end. Rather, he or she is more like a quality-control inspector who tries to determine whether things are working as they were designed to work. Evaluation research seeks not to find solutions (as in applied research) but to assess programs designed as tentative solutions to social problems. The social sciences have had few people in the past whose roles corresponded to this evaluative role. Increasingly, however, organizations are demanding people trained to perform such evaluation functions. In assessing our department's M.A. program in evaluation research, we found an average of 1.6 jobs per graduate student. These jobs, many of which did not exist several years ago, had titles such as Evaluation Specialist (State Planning Agency), Internal Evaluator (Neighborhood Health Center), Planning Associate and Specialist (United Way), Research Analyst (Metropolitan Police Department), and Community-Staff Coordinator (University Department of Community Medicine).

Donald Campbell (1972) has envisioned a society of the future that has an explicit evolutionary evaluative mechanism built in; his future society uses social scientific methods for changing itself through evaluation of innovations and solutions to its problems. It then attempts further innovations and scientific evaluations as a feedback mechanism for resolving problems that arise. While Campbell's society is only visionary at the moment, the United States and several Northern European countries are beginning to take steps in its direction. As Weiss (1972:viii) notes,

> There are enormous demands today for skilled evaluators in all the new federal programs in education, vocational education, rehabilitation, crime and delinquency, mental health, antipoverty, health, community planning, model cities, family planning, addiction services, and so on. There is a need, too, for greater understanding of evaluation purposes and processes by practitioners and administrators in these fields who are expected (and often legally required) to cooperate with evaluation efforts and to put to use the findings that emerge from study.

Some examples of recent evaluation research studies reported in *Evaluation Quarterly* show the diversity of this demand.

1. Assessments of gun control laws on armed robbery, assaults, and homicide rates

2. Long-term impact of water conservation measures
3. Psychological effects of day care
4. Work release effects on criminal recidivism
5. Pathway design effects on reducing bicycle accidents
6. Compensatory treatment for disadvantaged college student assessment
7. The impact of increased enforcement of sanitation laws
8. The types of punishment most effective for drunken drivers.

BASIC VERSUS EVALUATION RESEARCH

Strictly speaking, there are no formal methodological differences between basic research and evaluation research. The methods, techniques, and research designs discussed in other chapters of this book may be used in either research realm. Suchman (1969:15) distinguishes evaluative methodology from basic research in three ways: (1) Evaluative research utilizes deliberately planned intervention of some independent variable; (2) the programs it assesses assume some objective or goal as desirable; and (3) it attempts to determine the extent to which this desired goal has been reached. As Suchman puts it, "evaluative research asks about the *kind* of change the program views as desirable, the *means* by which this change is to be brought about, and the signs according to which such change can be recognized." Hence the critical difference between evaluative and basic research is one of objectives rather than methodology. Both depend on the canons of scientific logic, but evaluative studies apply these canons to programs with social, political, and administrative objectives, while basic research is more likely to be concerned with more theoretical objectives. Rather than test a *theoretical* hypothesis of the form "a change in X will produce a change in Y," the evaluation researcher needs an *evaluative* hypothesis of the form "by a planned change in X, the probability of Y (judged desirable) increases." As an example, it is of little use to an educational decision maker to learn that high social status and high educational achievement are related (a theoretical hypothesis), *since he or she cannot change status.* What he or she needs is evidence showing how to raise the learning levels of children from lower-status minorities.

Weiss (1972:6–8) and Coleman (1972:3–4) list a number of specific criteria that distinguish evaluative research from other types of research. First, evaluation research is usually conducted for a client who intends to use the research as a basis for decision making. This is quite different from basic research that is interested mainly in the production of theoretical knowledge rather than dissemination or application of knowledge. Second, as we have already discussed, the basic researcher usually formulates his or her own research questions while the evaluation researcher deals with client questions as to whether the client's program is accomplishing what the client wishes it to accomplish. Third, the evaluation researcher wishes to measure whether the program goals are being reached. Other scientific investigators concern themselves only with "what is," rather than with comparisons of "what is" with "what ought to be" (the program objectives). Fourth, unlike basic research where the investigator normally has control over research procedures, the evaluation researcher works in a setting where priority goes to the program as opposed to the evaluation. This feature has several important consequences.

On the one hand, program priority means that the evaluation researcher's world, unlike the basic researcher's world, is constrained by real time. The evaluation researcher finds it necessary to deal within the time structure of the program being studied. Also, program priority over evaluation produces conflicts of interest and conflicts over control of resources since the interests of the program staff and the researcher are inherently competitive. The program staff are typically service oriented, and tend to see data-collection procedures as disruptive, potentially worthless (since they already believe in the worth of their program), and possibly threatening (since the evaluation may give negative results).

Fifth, other researcher–program staff conflicts are inherent in their different frames of reference. Each party has a different paradigmatic stance. The researcher's obligations lie in objectivity in evaluation and public dissemination and cumulation of project intervention results. Project staff usually feel that project data should be limited to in-house usage—particularly where negative results appear. This brings us to a sixth difference between evaluation and basic research. We have seen that scientific hypotheses strive for parsimony of explanation. Science wishes to generate a small number of predictions (laws and theories) that organize a great deal of diverse information. But the world of action often finds *redundancy* of information and results useful for policy decisions.

Given that there are definite differences between evaluation and basic research, there are still many similarities. Both types of investigation are subject to the same problems of reliability, validity, and operationalization, and each uses the same store of research methods, techniques, and principles discussed in other chapters. The evaluation researcher, then, must be competent in the use of the methodological principles and the tools presented in other chapters. Thus, while we shall emphasize differences between evaluation and basic research throughout later sections of this chapter, one must never lose sight of the need for a grounding in basic methodology.

Earlier it was pointed out that the sharpest distinction between evaluation research and basic research lies in the evaluation researcher's concern with program objectives and goals. These objectives and goals are normatively based in ways that the goals of basic science are not. Each type of research asks different types of questions. And as we discussed in Chapter 2, nothing is more important than the way the researcher defines his or her problems. All investigation is limited and oriented by the questions asked. The basic researcher asks questions concerning *what is, will be,* or *can be.* By contrast the evaluation researcher is interested in the program client's problems concerning the *gap* between what is and what "ought to be" or "should be." The basic researcher might ask her-or himself: what are (or can be or will be) the effects of a negative income tax on the stratification system? The evaluation researcher's *client* might ask how the stratification system (as is) can be changed to some ideal state (eliminated or reduced). The evaluation researcher then would be asked to assess the effectiveness of the client's proposed solution. Basic and evaluation researchers, then, define their problems differently. In the language of Chapter 2, each operates by quite divergent paradigms.

From a sociological frame of reference, the evaluation researcher's problems arise from a client's belief in the need for social change. The client's problem can be solved only through action or a change in some state of affairs. On the other hand, the basic researcher's problem is solved through increased knowledge that, ideally, yields an explanation that is tested by prediction and control. Hence, basic science is more conservative by nature than evaluation research.

Nevertheless, evaluation research is not ideologically radical. Groups interested in radical or rapid social change are unlikely consumers of evaluation research. Furthermore, evaluation research is sometimes used for conservative purposes because, typically, the evaluation researcher does not define the problem. Rather, some outside agency usually defines the problem or project goals. The evaluator is called in as an expert or as a person with specialized competence in understanding, predicting, and controlling the situation to be studied. The evaluator says, "Define the goal and I will see what means can be used to attain it, and what it will cost you." Hence, the contracting agency may predetermine (through its goals) costs and benefits of the status quo.

Since evaluation research concerns "social problems" as opposed to "theoretical problems," ideological issues are important to evaluation research. An important question arises: Who cares about the problem? Various interest groups may define the problem differently. The Caucasian-defined "black problem" becomes the "white problem" for many black groups. Hence, the crucial problems for evaluation research are political by nature. Representatives of various groups with vested interests in the program may have conflicting interests. Coleman (1972:15) perceptively notes that

> ... those interests likely to be *threatened* by a potential policy change are more likely to be activated than those interests likely *to be benefited*—simply because persons and corporate bodies experience a loss arising from change in the status quo as greater than an objectively equivalent gain arising from change in the status quo.

Hence, Coleman (1972:16) recommends that evaluation research design include the following five points:

1. An identification of interest groups with a *likely* vested interest in the policy outcomes
2. Determination of these interest groups' concerns
3. The types of information relevant to these concerns
4. A determination of optimum means to get this information
5. Decisions as how to report the results.

The first three of these five steps are particularly germane to the present discussion of for whom and for what purposes knowledge is sought. The dangers in not following Coleman's points are twofold. First, ignoring conflicting interest groups' concerns creates the danger of selecting criteria for evaluation that favor one interest group over the other. Second, selection of biased criteria creates the danger that measures of importance to accepting (or rejecting) conflicting interest groups' assessments of the program will be ignored.

The questions of "knowledge for what?" and "for whom?" are also complicated by paradigmatic differences between program administrators and researchers. Caro (1972:14) points out that program administrators tend to look for solutions of immediate problems while the investigator is usually more interested in measuring long-term problem solving. Second, administrators are disposed to "conceal inefficiency and resist disruptive change" while evaluators are more oriented to the measurement of social change. Third (Caro 1972:12), administrators (and, it might be added, many interest groups) are usually threatened by negative results since such results threaten the agency's public image and program continuation. As Campbell (1969) points out, most reforms are advocated by administrators as though they are certain to be successful. The researcher, lacking this ideological commitment, thus may appear as threatening to the program.

In large part, we have discussed the questions *"knowledge for what and whom?"* as if the purposes of evaluation functioned *ideally*. Brooks gives four such *ideal* functions of evaluation research.

1. The *accounting function*—to provide information to some agency on the benefits of some program relative to projected costs
2. The *feedback function*—to use evaluation results for the program being evaluated to draw upon
3. The *dissemination function*—to provide a basis of knowledge for other programs to draw upon
4. *Theory-building function*—"to clarify, validate, disprove, modify or otherwise affect the body of theory from which the hypotheses underlying the program were derived." (Brooks 1965:34)

More practically, however, the researcher finds the purposes of evaluation to include the following covert or overt rationales (Weiss 1972:11–17): postponement of decisions, ducking of administrative responsibility, public relations and prestige, or as a grant requirement imposed by outside funding authorities. To this list, Downs (1965) would add that many project administrators may wish to use scientific advice to (1) justify decisions already made or pet theories, (2) disprove the wisdom of rival theories, or (3) weaken the power of another administrator by subjecting his or her project to scrutiny.

Of course, many evaluation programs have much more honest and scientific grounds for existence. But the point is that the evaluator must be alert to other possible project rationales. The existence of such non-scientific rationales may affect the project evaluation process. Indeed, the very existence of such rationales points to potential conflicts of interest between the researcher and project staff that may have to be dealt with if the evaluation effort is not to be compromised.

SPECIFYING EVALUATION GOALS
AND SIDE EFFECTS

As may now be evident, there are a multitude of interest groups that may have vested interests in the evaluation process. The question then arises: *Whose* purposes shall be assessed? Shall the evaluator orient to the needs of his or her scholar peers, the project director, the project staff, the program's clients, the agency requesting the evaluation, or the funding agency? Each of these groups may assess the evaluation from different— possibly conflicting—perspectives. Some interest groups may wish to drop or add program goals. Others may wish to reallocate project resources among competing projects. Still others may be interested in simple rejection (or acceptance) of the program's approach. Some groups may not even see a problem worthy of evaluation.

Thus, the action researcher must find out who cares about the "problem" and why they care about it. This means he or she will have to explore the *values* of the groups with vested interests in (and opposed to) the project. Suchman (1967:158–159) shrewdly observes how values affect the objectives of the evaluator and program staff.

> In general, the evaluator will seek to measure achievement, while the program personnel will be more likely to emphasize effort or technique. The evaluator will be more concerned with higher level or ultimate objectives, while the practitioner will be more involved with lower level or immediate objectives. To the evaluator, the criteria of success will deal more directly with improvement in the status of the recipients of services, while for the staff, the tendency will be to seek criteria which reflect the smoothness and efficiency of the services themselves rather than their effect upon the people to whom the services are provided.

The types of questions the evaluator must ask of these interest groups at this stage are

1. What is the present state of the system? How does it work?
2. What is the desired state of the system? That is, what norm is desirable? How would that system work in its desired state?
3. How can the present system be moved toward this desired state? What would this cost with respect to other norms in the society; that is, what would be the side effects of such change?

Furthermore, since the need for the evaluation is *socially problematic* —that is, not all interest groups see a "problem"—it is necessary to ask,

4. Why have certain groups defined the situation as a social problem while others have not?

These types of questions are means of defining the interest groups' values in relation to the program objectives. Indeed, as Coleman (1972:7) points out, since "the research problem enters from outside any academic discipline, it must be carefully translated from the real world of policy or the conceptual world of a client without loss of meaning." Again, Downs (1965:31) states that "nearly half of the contributions made by an economic consultant in most cases is helping clients to clearly define problems." This rule may be easily applied to good evaluation research. Caro (1972:32) reiterates the importance of this point.

> . . . [the best advisors] do not approach giving advice as purely intellectual problem-solving, but as assisting specific people to make the decisions that will help them attain their personal and organizational objectives . . . it implies that they see each situation in its *full context* of social, organizational and personal implications.

Perhaps an analogy to theory testing in basic research will further clarify the need for clear definitions of program objectives. Our model basic researcher throughout preceding chapters undertook research only after formulating testable hypotheses. Likewise, the evaluator wishes to treat the evaluation project as the independent variable and the *desired* state of change as the dependent variable. As with basic research that is not tied to theory, it is not surprising that programs that fail to define their objectives prove unsuccessful at assessing those programs. Williams (1971:xiv) grimly observes that social science research has seldom been relevant to federal program evaluation simply because of *lack* of communication between researchers and federal agencies over the needs and goals of federal policy programs. Caro (1971:19) reaffirms Williams's position. He urges closer researcher–project staff collaboration in the identification of project goals and criteria in order to make evaluator's "work on variables more explicit, realistic, and perhaps more comprehensive than the objectives shown in official program documents." Wholey and associates (1970:28, 31) neatly sum up our argument.

> Most of the programs examined lacked adequately defined criteria of program effectiveness. This lack stems partially from the fact that the typical federal program has multiple objectives and partially from difficulties in defining objectives in measurable terms. . . . Most of the blame for the present state of affairs must be placed with program managers for failure to be explicit about their objectives and with evaluators for failure to insist on the guidance they need to define evaluation criteria.

Suchman (1967:39–41) provides a paradigm for probing deeper into program objectives than heretofore suggested.

1. *What* is the nature of content of the objectives?
2. *Who* is the target of the program?
3. *When* is the desired change to take place?
4. Are the objectives *unitary* or *multiple?*
5. What is the desired *magnitude* of effect?
6. *How* is the objective to be attained?

To this list we should add

7. What are the unintentional effects or side effects of the program objectives?

We shall now set up a hypothetical agency and follow through with a set of questions the evaluator might ask. Our agency is the United World Population Society. They claim to be concerned with the "population explosion crisis" and wish our evaluator to provide them with answers about the outcome of the current program to "control population growth." Our investigator will first want to know what they are trying to change—for instance, birth control attitudes, knowledge, behavior, or some combination of these? Then he or she will want to know *who* is the target of the program—men, women, adults, members of some social class? *When* do they expect the change to take place—immediately, in the short-, mid-, or long-range future? And how long is "long-range"—a year, five years, ten years? Are the program objectives unitary or multiple? Are they interested only in attitudes or attitudes and behavior? If the goals are multiple, what is their relative importance to the program? Are any of these goals incompatible (Weiss 1972:30–31)? What is the desired *magnitude* of effect of the program—zero population, a 5 percent decrease in births, or what? *How* are these objectives to be obtained—through literature distribution, formal classes, or tax incentives?

Another question concerns how the program objectives are to be attained. What are the program "inputs?" Inputs are the program activities that are designed to bring about the attainment of project goals. Project goals are often referred to by evaluators as "outputs" or "outcomes." (Greenberg summarizes essential input and output variables in Table 9–1, p. 250.) What are the negative side effects or unintended consequences of the program? Will it lower the GNP or cause a massively disproportionate cohort of youngsters relative to older people?

Cytrynbaum and others (1979) have described an enormously popular technique for individualized outcome measures called Goal Attainment Scaling (GAS). First, for each participant a goal selector or team decides on a realistic goal (or goals), and each goal is scaled, weighted, and described concretely in terms of a range of five favorable to unfavorable outcome points (+2, +1, 0, –1, –2) as shown in Table 9–2 (p. 251). Second, each participant is then *randomly* assigned to one of the treatments being evaluated. Finally, each participant is followed up after the project's termination for assessment of goal attainment by independent raters. There is even a journal devoted exclusively to GAS studies: *Goal Attainment Review.* Cytrynbaum and others (1979) warn that it is imperative not to deviate from the above three steps if meaningful data are to be collected.

We have noted in this section that evaluation is basically an appraisal of value. We have seen that the formulation of project objectives depends in large measure on *whose* values we consider and who the intended user of the results is thought to be. We have tried to give some

Table 9–1

A Listing of Input and Output Variables That Are Essential in a Program of Evaluation

	Output		
	Immediate Goals	Intermediate Goals	Long-Range Goals
Input	*Increase in knowledge, improved attitudes and practices*	*More positive health and improved status*	*Reduction in morbidity and mortality*
			ULTIMATE
1. Administrative pattern	Reduced dissatisfaction	Reduced disease	Reduction in death
a. Organizational chart			
b. Personnel staffing	Reduced disinterest	Reduced discomfort	Reduced disability
c. Funding plans			
d. Relationships with other agencies (horizontal and vertical)			
e. Built-in quality control measures			
2. Service statistics			
a. Operations analysis of services provided including cross-classifications by characteristics of services, recipients, and providers of service			
b. Feedback and feed forward operations including comparison with standards and quotas			

OTHER OUTPUT

1. Other favorable effects in community other than among recipients of service.
2. Untoward side effects

FINAL INDEX: Efficiency = $\dfrac{\text{Output (in terms of goal fulfillment)}}{\text{Input (in terms of dollars, services and/or personal time)}}$

SOURCE: Adapted from Greenberg 1972:161.

general guidelines for assessing values and the resulting objectives of evaluation programs. In the next section we return to problems of operationalization—how to make the evaluation researchable in valid and reliable ways.

Table 9-2
Sample Patient Goal Attainment Follow-Up Guide

Problem: Suicidal Behavior	Goal: 1　　　　Weight: 5
Most unfavorable treatment outcome thought likely (−2)	Makes serious suicidal gestures. Talking about suicidal gestures daily. Impulsive in other ward behavior. Refuses to attend groups and to participate in treatment program.
Less than expected success with treatment (−1)	No suicidal gestures, but still talks about killing self. Erratic participation in treatment program.
Expected level of treatment success (0)	Absence of suicidal gestures or talking about suicide for one week or less. Working and participating in treatment program.
More than expected success with treatment (+1)	Active participation in treatment program, especially family therapy groups.
Most favorable treatment outcome thought likely (+2)	Movement evident in family therapy, total elimination of suicidal concerns.

SOURCE: Reproduced from Jacobs and Cytrynbaum (1977).

DESIGN AND MEASUREMENT

The methods of evaluation research follow the same scientific principles as in basic research. Any differences between the two methods of research, therefore, are due only to differences in the conditions under which each type of research normally is conducted.

One of the basic differences in conditions between evaluation and basic research has to do with experimental control. That is, the evaluation researcher rarely has the control over research variables that is possible in basic research. In basic research we spoke of independent and dependent variables. But in evaluation research we typically speak of *project outcomes* or *outputs*. These output variables are not strictly equivalent to dependent variables because some of them may not be *intended* outcomes. Second, there are *project variables* that are the study's equivalent to independent variables—those variables under the researcher's control intended to bring about some social change. Then, there are what are termed *situational variables*.

Situational variables are any variables that are not subject to project control but are plausible candidates as independent variables. Coleman (1973:5) points out that evaluation research must control for the confounding or distorting effects of situational variables if the results are to have any meaning. Since the number of extraneous (situational) variables over which the researcher has control decreases as one moves from basic into evaluation research, the evaluation researcher has to learn how to control for the influence of them on study outcomes if this research is not to be subject to the criticism that the results are meaningless. Hence, he or she needs to give hard thought to selecting the strongest possible research design employable in the evaluation (see Chapter 7).

A second major difference between basic and evaluation research deals with the time framework of each. Evaluation research has built-in time scheduling that places unusually heavy demands on the researcher for timely research. Time pressures also affect the choice of research design and strategy. The researcher finds it necessary to fit his or her time schedule to the project's rather than the reverse, as is usually possible in basic research.

Third, evaluation research is not only more time bound than basic research, it also tends to be more space bound. Pressures typically exist to test immediate needs of a specific program. Little encouragement is given to generalizing from the results as in basic research. Thus, the researcher may find little encouragement to transcend the immediate phenomenon being evaluated in order to make sure project results that work in one situation will work in others.

A fourth major difference between evaluation and basic research concerns the researcher's role. The evaluation researcher's role is highly marginal. He or she is in the position of "being a doctor without patients or a professor without a class" (Rodman and Kolodny 1972:135). The evaluation researcher's marginality, nevertheless, must not be allowed to be exploited for political purposes. He or she must maintain his or her role by sticking by the canons of scientific verification and must *not* even *appear* to be partisan towards or manipulated by any group with vested interests in (or opposed to) the evaluation. To give such impressions can only serve to compromise the evaluation process.

A final difference between evaluation and basic research has to do with the ways variables are operationalized by each. While basic research operationalization is concerned with independent and dependent variables, evaluation research operationalization typically takes place using one or more of the following indicators (Suchman 1967:61): (1) effort or activity, (2) performance or accomplishment, (3) adequacy of performance or impact, (4) efficiency or input versus output, and (5) process or the *conditions of effectiveness.*

Strictly speaking, *effort* or activity variables are input variables since they measure what the program is doing or how it is doing it rather than program outcomes. Types of input variables that may need to be measured are characteristic of the program participants (race, sex, and relevant preprogram attitudes), length of program service, program staffing, and so on. Effort variables should not be used as measures of output even though program personnel like to be evaluated in terms of effort. As Suchman (1967:61) aptly states, "evaluation at this level has been compared to the measurement of the number of times a bird flaps its wings without any attempt to determine how far the bird has flown."

Performance measures program output in terms of policy objectives. There are countless examples of evaluations that have shown performance failure even though the program itself had excellent effort indicators. Thus, the researcher needs to be concerned with how the program outcomes measure up to the program's objectives. If the program is intended to reduce the social effects of surgery in children, does it actually do this? If it is designed to reduce the juvenile delinquency rate, does it reach this objective?

Adequacy of performance depends on *how high* the program's goals are set. Thus, rather than test for *total* program effectiveness or simple effectiveness versus no effectiveness, the researcher may be asked to research the *relative* effectiveness of program policy. "One fairly common index of adequacy consists of measuring the impact of one's program in terms of the rate of effectiveness multiplied by the number of people exposed to the program" (Suchman 1967:63).

Efficiency is a measure of program performance (output) in terms of effort (input). It asks whether the program outcomes can be justified in terms of project costs. In a later subsection we shall discuss several means of assessing project efficiency.

Process measures *why* a program is successful or unsuccessful. Usually evaluation research is concerned only with whether a program works or not. Process analysis goes into analysis with more depth by asking: What are the conditions that made the program successful or unsuccessful? Answers to this in-depth probing are then used to modify the program with the hope that the program will now be more successful (Suchman 1967:66). Berstein and Freeman (1975), after assessing the quality of 236 evaluation projects funded by the U.S. Department of Health, Education and Welfare, concluded that only about 60 percent of the projects had measures of both process and impact with an average reliability rate of only .69 for both. Hence, overall quality of these projects was appallingly low.

CONTROL OVER RESEARCH DESIGN

Administrative considerations have a way of coming into conflict with ideal research design. Program personnel will rarely let the evaluator have the freedom necessary to carry through the ideal evaluation. It is a rare program staff that will allow randomized control groups or treatment variations (Williams 1971:92). As Wolin puts it (in Rodman and Kolodny 1972:122), "In suggesting control groups, I am advocating denial of service, strongly opposed by every social work practitioner to whom I have mentioned it." Hence, the evaluator often has no choice but to select some nonequivalent comparison groups for quasi-control. Wholey and associates (1970:93) recommend the use of participants in different projects as comparison groups for one another so that the relative effectiveness of two or more program strategies can be compared since it is difficult to justify denying treatment to individuals.

Boruch and others (1978) nevertheless have cross-referenced over 300 randomized evaluation studies in such areas as health care and juvenile delinquency to show the feasibility of such field tests in spite of managerial, political, and other constraints that often exist. Connor's (1977) more detailed examination of twelve projects showed considerable researcher control over randomization regardless of whether the researcher was an insider or outsider to the program. Powers and Alderman (1979) and McKillip (1979) suggest creative ways to apply true experimental designs in field settings. Powers and Alderman point out, first, that where schools offer programs several times in an academic year the researcher can delay treatment to a randomly created control group that can obtain the treatment at a later date. Second, where there are multiple sections of a program, one can randomly assign sections to experimental and control groups. Third, scarce resources may preclude access to the program for all persons. In this case one can choose randomly from those participants desiring the program. As an alternative ethical and practical procedure, McKillip suggests randomizing participants who express no preference between control and experimental conditions.

A further problem of control concerns the sensitizing or reactive effects of evaluation measure (see Chapter 11). Rather than measure actual program effects, the evaluation researcher may be measuring placebo effects of people who know they are being evaluated and how they are being evaluated. In one of the largest social experiments ever run, the New Jersey Income Maintenance Experiments (Watts and Rees 1977), the treatment was so complex that the evaluators found that the more disadvantaged the participants, the less they understood and used the income maintenance benefits due them. Hence, this differential understanding created problems of experimental control over treatment allocations—a problem not uncommon to large social experiments.

While it is not a complete solution to the sensitizing problem, Caro (1972:23) recommends the use of behavioral rather than attitudinal measures to evaluate project outcomes. Scheirer (1978) points out that a common dilemma is that recipients' perceptions of benefits occurring tend to be positive despite signs to the contrary. For instance, recipients may report reduced anxiety or increased self-esteem but behavioral variables such as reduced unemployment or recidivism rates may not be found. The attitudinal measures are more suspect than the behavioral measures because of known reactive effects of perceptual distortion. Williams (1971:93–94) outlines four conditions necessary for sound evaluations.

> . . .(1) [A] clearly defined set of treatment variables specified in operational terms and implemented in the field to meet these specifications; (2) a design sufficiently general that the final results are likely to have broad application; (3) a data retrieval system likely to produce the statistically valid data required to measure significant interrelationships among critical variables and/or the project's effectiveness; and (4) either a design in a single project with sufficient diversity in treatments to allow meaningful comparisons with feasible alternatives or a broader experimental design presenting a set of treatment alternatives.

Types of Research Designs

An essential first condition for evaluating a program's impact is the ability to isolate what would have happened in the absence of the program. That is, we wish to distinguish between effects of the program and the effects of other forces. Given the best of all possible worlds the researcher would want to use one of the experimental designs in Chapter 7. However, since suitable control groups may be unavailable, a quasi- or preexperimental design might be more practical. Since the major types of these designs are discussed in Chapter 7 we shall discuss a few designs here that are more specifically related to *particular* types of evaluation research: cost-benefit analysis and social audits.

Social Audits

In the social audit, "resource inputs initiated by policy are traced from the point at which they are disbursed to the point at which they are experienced by the ultimate intended recipient of those resources" (Coleman 1972:18). This social audit is then related to research outcomes. Lack of social change can be due to two factors: (1) The resource inputs may have been ineffective or (2) they may never have reached their intended recipients. Thus, this method allows for distinguishing between each source of ineffectiveness, unlike the most traditional research designs that cannot examine possible losses or diversions of resource inputs. While "not a substitute for a study of the effectiveness of the resources . . . it does tell whether the resources are available at point of use, and if they are not, where and how they got lost" (Coleman 1972:19). Hence, social audit designs might effectively be used to *supplement* the more traditional research designs, and social audits are a useful means of getting at *process* and efficiency.

As an example of social audits, consider the tracing of resource inputs from the point of disbursement in voluntary organizations such as the American Red Cross to the point at which those inputs are experienced by the intended recipients. One might analyze, first, which inputs (or portions of inputs) never reach the intended recipient. For example, of voluntary contributions to the American Red Cross, how much actually reaches the intended recipients in some form (sand bags, food and clothing for flood victims)? Of that portion that does not reach the intended recipients, where does this loss of input go—for instance, public relations for more fund raising, organizational salaries?

As a more subtle form of social auditing, consider identical dollar amounts of disbursements by the American Red Cross to two different communities. If the disbursement to one of the communities depreciates more rapidly (through loss or abuse), then the flood victims in that community receive less resource inputs than in the other community. In each of these examples the idea has been to show how a social audit design might yield data of interest to evaluation of some program.

Cost-Benefit Analysis

We noted earlier that the evaluator is often interested in measuring program efficiency. In other words, we often wish to go beyond asking whether a program is effective by asking whether it is effective by comparison to other alternative programs. Cost-benefit analysis makes rational decisions among alternative programs by calculating the probable costs and benefits of alternative programs and then ordering these programs by favorability of cost/benefit ratios. It would be more rational to allocate priority to a mental health program with 60 percent recovery rates as opposed to another program with 65 percent recovery rates if the first program costs only half as much per patient.

There are several problems inherent to cost-benefit analysis. First, it is not always easy to calculate costs and benefits in standard terms. How does one measure "work satisfaction," "marital happiness," or "labor productivity?" Second, since a change in one part of the social system will affect other parts of the same system, it is necessary to make decisions about which effects are the important ones. A program for reducing mental illness may in turn create the need to retrain mental health personnel for other occupations. This points to a problem of how costs and benefits should be aggregated or scaled.

Cost-benefit analysis depends on reliable, valid, and widely available data that may not be obtainable. Rowe and Husby (1973) found divergent models of child care gave extremely divergent cost-benefit ratios. Noble (1977) came to similar conclusions for cost-benefit analyses of rehabilitation programs. Glaser (1973:41) shows that several major problems impede the use of cost-benefit analysis.

> First, the lack of any firm data on the effectiveness of programs; second, the great difficulty in finding control groups with which persons participating in a program can be compared and hence a corresponding inability to estimate the impact effectiveness of programs; third, problems in estimating at a given point in time the benefits that are to accrue in an uncertain future. . . .

Although there are obvious limitations to cost-benefit analysis, it has proven to be a worthwhile method in an increasing number of evaluation studies (such as Rowe and Husby 1974).

The easiest types of *costs* to estimate are "extra expenditures needed to add a particular supplemental service to an ongoing program" (Glaser 1973:25). For instance, cost per client can be determined by adding up the costs of operating the entire supplemental services needed (social workers at a $12,000 yearly salary, a secretary at a $7,500 yearly salary, $5,000 for office space, and $6,000 for supplies) and dividing by the number of clients per year. Then, if the average client stay in the program is for nine months, the yearly cost per client would be divided by 0.75 and so on.

Benefits can be measured by "estimated reductions in social costs" (Glaser 1973:27). If it costs $10,000 a year to keep a convict in prison for an average stay of five years while some new parole-training program costs $2,000 a year per parolee with an average length of eighteen-months rehabilitation, then the program's economic benefits are a savings of $47,000. Of course, recidivistic criminals' costs should also be figured into this analysis. If 30 percent of the parolees in the training program are reinstitutionalized, the researcher must add the costs of their new confinement, court costs, and victim costs.

Glaser (1973:36–39) points out that many social costs are purely speculative. How could one financially express the anguishes of rape, the emotional costs of assault, or murder? Nevertheless, some social costs can be rationally dealt with. The costs of heavy drug usage could be viewed from the point of view of society's loss of the drug user's work power and the loss of the potential tax dollars.

The most objectively supportable costs and benefits are more appropriate than more speculative ones if the researcher is interested in making a strong argument for the validity of the data. Hence, while this practice may understate cases, it is more likely to be acceptable to person's with vested interests in the program being evaluated.

A word on institutional records is in order, given that social audits, cost-benefit analyses, and other more traditional forms of evaluation depend on accurate records of inputs and outputs. Institutional records are notorious for being incomplete, unstandardized, and disordered. Hence, the researcher cannot depend on the quality of records kept by program personnel. While more expensive, it is probably worthwhile developing precoded observational forms like those found in Glaser's (1973) appendices. Rothenberg (1975) has a good nontechnical introduction to cost-benefit analysis that provides useful reading.

A closely related technique is *cost-effectiveness analysis*. Since it is often difficult to construct cost-benefit calculations, some researchers advocate measuring the costs of alternative treatments since cost information is usually easier to find. Levin (1975) gives a good general introduction to this methodology. As an example, Grey and others (1978) examined the relative cost effectiveness of community corrections, probation, and incarceration as alternative means of treating convicted offenders using analytic procedures exemplified in Table 9–3. They found probation to be the most cost effective in the long run although incarceration was more efficient in the short run.

Table 9–3
Concepts Used in Cost-Effectiveness Analysis

	Focus of Analysis		
	How	What	Why
Alternative Conceptualizations			
	Activity, Task, Inputs	Objectives, Subgoals, Intermediate Products, Outputs	Goals, Final Goals, Final Products, Outcomes
Example	Group Counseling, Food and Clothing, Recreation	"Treatment" or "Rehabilitation"	Reduced Recidivism
Cost Measure			
	Input Cost	Output Cost	Outcome Cost
Example	Cost per Day	Cost per Case	Cost per Reduced Arrest

SOURCE: This figure drawn from "Cost effectiveness of residential community corrections: An analytical prototype," by Charles M. Grey, C. Johnston Conover, and Timothy M. Hennessey, published in *Evaluation Quarterly*, 2:3 (August 1978), 375–400, by permission of the publisher, Sage Publications, Inc.

ANALYSIS, RECOMMENDATION,
AND DISSEMINATION

Wholey and associates (1970:46) point out that the real test of evaluation research is its impact on the implementation of policy. Or, as Coleman (1972:6) states, "the ultimate product is not a 'contribution to existing knowledge' in the literature, but a social policy modified by the research results."

Notice how this role differs from the more traditional basic researcher's role where it is more likely that little interest is shown in the utilization of research findings. Of course, some researchers feel data interpretation is the responsibility of the agency whose policy is being evaluated. This is a naive viewpoint because agencies have historically shown a poor track record in policy analysis, recommendation, and dissemination. There are a number of reasons for this. First, one of the major reasons for agency failure to utilize results is ideological. They feel committed to particular ways of doing things despite evidence that the program is ineffective. This is true of the general public too. As Suchman (1967:165) aptly puts it, "the public must be given what it needs, or it will learn to like what it gets." That is, even the public is likely to become so accustomed to policy that it resists changing ineffective programs.

Second (Weiss 1972:114), "revisions in programs may cause changes in relationships to funders, clients, or other community organizations" which produce uneasiness in the organization over called-for program adjustments. Third (Weiss 1972:112), it may not be economically feasible for the organization to change its practices.

It should come as no surprise, then, that organizations tend to resist change unless there is strong reason to do otherwise. Coleman (1972:13) goes so far as to state that unless the research is transmitted back to the organization through *open publication,* the "results will ordinarily not be acted upon nor will they be openly disclosed to others, unless it benefits [the organization's] interest." Coleman points to the Equality of Educational Opportunity study, which criticized existing education policies and was kept inaccessible by HEW until the mass media picked up on its value. Thus, the researcher may find it necessary to insist on public dissemination of project results even *before* committing him- or herself to the evaluation task.

Another reason for the investigator to take the responsibility of reporting findings for dissemination to a larger public is that project decision makers are usually not capable of analyzing data in terms of the sophisticated tools (test factor analysis, regression analysis; see Chapter 14) social scientists have at their disposal. Thus, it is the investigator's responsibility to brief the policy decision makers on the utility of project results.

Other roadblocks to high utilization of evaluations have to do with methodological weakness and design irrelevance (Wholey and others 1970:50). On the one hand, policy makers are more likely to rely on their own experience rather than trust results of poorly done studies. On the other hand, even if the study is well executed, its design may not bear on the "critical issues." Hence, investigators need to design evaluation studies from a knowledge of the effects that the design will have on analysis and recommendations.

On Increasing Utilization of Results

We have stated that the importance of evaluation research will depend on its effectiveness in implementing policy. Williams (1971:55) points to three factors that determine the relevancy of evaluation research: (1) pertinence, (2) soundness, and (3) timeliness of information. Our comments on good research design and measurement cover the first two points. The factor of timely information needs some exposition. Coleman (1972:4) points out that partial information now is better than complete information later in evaluation studies. Most studies have constant time deadlines and demands. If the evaluator fails to supply current information at those deadlines, his or her value to the policy decision process decreases accordingly.

Caro (1972:19) suggests, further, that it is a political mistake for the investigator to judge programs in all-or-none or success-failure terms. As we have seen, ideological resistance can be strong enough to override strong "failure" analysis. Hence, the researcher should focus on the *relative* effectiveness of alternative programs and policies where possible. This may mean that evaluators need to encourage policy makers to build program *variations* into their policies. Likewise, Coleman (1972:5) encourages redundant data collections and multiple methods "to give results relatively independently arrived at which can be compared."

Multiple-method approaches, as we shall see in Chapter 13, may overcome many of the deficiencies of single methods. However, *all* studies have deficiencies that limit their policy applicability. Weiss (1972:120) recommends that the evaluator help decision makers "arrive at responsible choices" by acknowledging the limitations of their design and analysis.

Finally, good, clear writing of projects results is important. Interested parties will be put off by technical jargon. If the researcher cannot write up a nontechnical report he or she should have someone with social science journalistic abilities write up the report for maximum dissemination.

THE FUTURE OF EVALUATION RESEARCH

We live in an age marked by grand scale social changes. Virtually all advanced industrial nations have evolved into some form of a welfare state. The last decade has seen major political changes towards "accountability" of both the public and private sectors, "sunshine laws," and "freedom of information" acts. These signs of the times are part and parcel of a transition towards Campbell's (1972) "Experimenting Society."

Currently, because of this political climate, the act of *doing* evaluation research studies, not their results, provides impact to our complex political mosaic and important policy decisions. It was possible to justify heavy federal participation in "Sesame Street," guaranteed annual wage experiments, and experimental school programs *because* these programs would be subject to evaluation.

Until the late 1960s most evaluation research conducted in the areas of health, social, rehabilitative, and welfare services was done either by university affiliated researchers or private research agencies—usually hired through contract. Since then, public and private service agencies have been hiring their own staff researchers and have been conducting more in-house evaluation research. As a consequence, more well-trained social and behavioral scientists have gravitated towards research jobs in public and private agencies.

Growing interest and faith in evaluation have been unparalleled in history. Requests for technical assistance to establish evaluation systems within local facilities have climbed steeply. The consequence has been the phenomenal growth of Masters and Doctoral degree programs in evaluation research, literature dissemination (600 percent increase in subscribers to *Evaluation* magazine over two years), and summer institute participation and requests (Rossi and Wright 1977). With the establishment of their own professional identity, evaluation researchers have progressed toward creating higher standards of credibility to protect themselves from fly-by-night quackery and client, consumer, and governmental cross-pressures. Much of the excitement to be derived from this growing field lies in working on these developing problems and prospects.

READINGS FOR ADVANCED STUDENTS

SCARVIA ANDERSON AND SAMUEL BALL, *The Profession and Practice of Program Evaluation*, 1978. This book provides much needed information on, and recommendations for, ethics and values in evaluation and evaluator training.

THOMAS COOK AND DONALD CAMPBELL, *Quasi-Experimentation: Design and Analysis Issues for Field Settings*, 1979. Heavy reading if your statistical background is lacking, but it sets the standard for research design and analysis.

DANIEL GLASER, *Routinizing Evaluations: Getting Feedback on Effectiveness of Crime and Delinquency Programs*, 1973. A compact and readable discussion of means by which the researcher can make evaluations with a minimum of stumbling blocks.

MARICA GUTTENTAG AND ELMER STRUENING (eds.), *Handbook of Evaluation Research*, Vols. I and II, 1975. Like most edited books, this one suffers from a wide range of quality. However, chapters by Davis and Salsin (utilization of evaluation) in Vol. I, and Rothenberg (cost-benefit analysis) and Levin (cost effectiveness analysis) in Vol. II are of particularly high quality and readability.

LEONARD RUTMAN, *Evaluation Research Methods: A Basic Guide*, 1977. A good introduction to evaluation research for the neophyte.

PETER SASSONE AND WILLIAM SCHAFFER, *Cost-Benefit Analysis: A Handbook*, 1978. Most of the books on cost-benefit analysis are written for and by economists. This book is addressed to those who wish to understand the workings of cost-benefit analysis at a less technical level.

CAROL WEISS, *Evaluation Research: Methods of Assessing Program Effectiveness*, 1972. Covers a lot of territory in a small space on such topics as the formulation of questions, design of evaluation, and utilization of results.

SUGGESTED RESEARCH PROJECTS

1. Lay out a set of parties and their interests in terms of some proposed social policy change. Using Coleman's criteria on p. 245, anticipate the plausible consequences for each party of policy change such as neighborhood rezoning, lead-poisoning control crackdown, gasoline allocation plans, freeway development, and mass transit development.

2. Search for a local social experiment (new occupancy permit laws, establishment of a high school "without walls," desegregation approaches). Interview someone with expertise in the respective organization, using the questions Suchman suggests on p. 248 and applying the format of Table 9–1 to get at potential input and output measures for evaluation of this project. Write your findings in a report.

3. Become familiar with a local social experiment (as in Project 2) so that you can suggest a specific goal-attainment scale for evaluating project outcomes.

4. Locate several different evaluation studies (in *Evaluation* or *Evaluation Quarterly*) that attempt to evaluate the same or similar treatments. Use Table 9–3 to evaluate the cost effectiveness of these treatments if enough data are given. If the data are not sufficient, discuss the types of data needed for complete analysis.

5. Attempt a social audit of a social service performed by an institution, such as teaching at your university, United Way disbursements, or a state criminal work release program.

6. Attempt a cost-benefit analysis of a social service performed by an institution. Discuss the implications of alternative means of figuring costs and benefits. Discuss the problems involved in obtaining the necessary information.

PART THREE

Improving Data Quality

In science as in love a concentration
on technique is quite likely to lead to
impotence.

Peter Berger,
Invitation to Sociology,
1963:13.

10

Sampling: The Search for Typicality

In chemistry or in physics there is often no problem of finding [the pure case]. When the chemist wants to establish a proposition about sulphur he can use any lump of chemically pure sulphur (provided its crystalline form is irrelevant to the experiment) and treat it as a true and pure representative of sulphur. If a social scientist wants to study the Norwegian voter, it would simplify research enormously if he could find the pure voter, the one person who would be the representative of all Norwegian voters, so that all that was necessary would be to ask him or watch his behavior. At present, the belief in the possibility of finding [the pure case], on the individual or collective level of analysis, seems to have disappeared completely from social research. [1]

[1]Johan Galtung, *Theory and Methods of Social Research* (New York: Columbia University Press, 1967) p. 16. Reprinted by permission of Johan Galtung.

Everyone has had some experience in sampling, whether intentional or not. If you have ever tried out new ways to drive home from school or new methods of studying for exams you've been engaged in a sampling process. *Sampling* is a procedure by which we infer the characteristics of some group of objects (a population) through experience with less than all possible elements of that group of objects (a sample). Since less than all objects are experienced in sampling, the researcher must be concerned that the *numbers* and *kinds* of objects in a sample are sufficiently representative of the total population to enable sound generalizations about that population. In terms familiar from Chapter 7, this means that sampling procedures are a means of developing good external validity. Certainly how we select our data influences the degree to which we may make generalizations from it. This chapter discusses means by which we may objectify and specify sample selection procedures that permit generalizations from our data.

ADVANTAGES OF SAMPLING

Why should we be interested in sampling? Why not take complete counts in our research? In brief, sampling usually permits the researcher to cut costs, reduce work force requirements, gather information more quickly, and obtain more comprehensive data. Take the case of a researcher interested in analyzing the content of the "Peanuts" comic strip for reflections of changing societal norms and values. If every one of the Peanuts strips was analyzed there would be a tremendous amount of material to cover given the fact that the strip appears in the paper 365 days a year. Obviously, if we could devise some means of accurately representing the entire Peanuts strip with a smaller set of the daily output we would save time and money. In addition, it would be advantageous if we could estimate how accurately our sample represented the complete count. Some of the sampling methods we will later note make such estimates possible.

Finally, and this may seem particularly paradoxical on first reflection, some samples actually give *better* estimates of the complete count than would a survey of every possible case. The U.S. Census Bureau has long emphasized that its ten-year population census is in many ways less accurate than its ongoing sample research if only because the population census involves the use of large numbers of relatively inexperienced interviewers. Such a mammoth project normally produces more nonsampling (mechanical and clerical) errors than sampling errors, due to the relatively massive amounts of data being processed. Thus, a carefully designed sample survey may collect more reliable data than an entire population survey simply because certain sources of error can be controlled much more effectively when a relatively small number of cases is examined.

GENERAL UNIVERSES, WORKING UNIVERSES, AND SAMPLES

Given the advantages of sampling, good sampling is still not feasible without some clear conception of *what* the researcher is sampling. As we shall see in later sections of this chapter, there are samples in search of universes and universes in search of samples. Many of these problems can be eliminated through clear conceptualization of the objects that are to be the bases of the researcher's generalizations.

Sjoberg and Nett (1968:130) have contributed to the analysis of this problem through construction of the notions of "general universe" and "working universe." The *general universe* is the abstract, theoretical population to which the researcher wishes to generalize his or her findings. By contrast, the *working universe* is the *concrete* operationalization of that general universe from which he or she will sample. Caplow and McGee (1958) were interested in studying the American academic labor market (general universe). They operationalized this by sampling from *lists* of assistant, associate, and full professors in nine major American universities whose employment terminated between June 30, 1954 and July 1, 1956 (working universe). Operationalization was hampered by diverse factors (Caplow and McGee 1958:24–25).

> In most institutions, records of departed professors are kept very indifferently ... and errors were not uncommon. ... A case was included if it involved an assistant professor replaced by an instructor, but not if it involved an instructor replaced by an assistant professor. If the vacancy occurred between the specified dates, the case would be included even if no replacement had been made at the time of the interview. ·

Notice how Caplow and McGee's operationalization of the academic marketplace is *specified* and *qualified* in the above quotation. They painstakingly point out the means by which they obtained their list of academic vacancies so that the reader may judge the *adequacy* of their generalizations to all "academic vacancies."

It is important to make this working versus general universe distinction since researchers rarely have opportunities to sample from general universes. Suppose a researcher is interested in sampling from all known "small groups." His or her working universe will have to operationalize "small" and "groups." Is the group small if it has seven members? Ten? Twelve? Is a "crowd" considered a group? What is the difference between an "aggregate" and a "group" of four persons? And where do you find representative "small groups"?

Even when a researcher is drawing a sample from a much more concrete phenomenon such as a human population, the general and working universes still do not usually coincide completely. Since 1940 the U.S. Bureau of the Census has measured monthly national "unemployment" rates. "Unemployment" can be (and has been by the Census Bureau) operationalized in many different ways; each way gives a somewhat different picture of unemployment. For instance, is a college sophomore who claims to be looking for a summer job unemployed? What about the high-school football player who says he's looking for a part-time job after school but does not have the time for such a job right now because of football practice? Such questions cannot be taken lightly. In a survey such as the Census Bureau's unemployment survey, each person sampled represents approximately 25,000 others. Thus, slight changes in definition (operationalization) may lead to radically different unemployment rates.

Even if a working universe cannot be empirically demonstrated to represent a general universe, social scientists often are willing to generalize. Reasons for this, as Sjoberg and Nett (1968:132) point out, include the fact that "scientists implicitly or explicitly assume a fundamental invariance in the social phenomena under study. They assume a degree of stability through space and time in the processes being investigated."

Unfortunately, researchers often fail to concern themselves with questions about the working-universe representativeness of their general universes. The number of studies carried out on college sophomores, *as if* they were representative of all homo sapiens, will attest to this fact. The point is that until evidence exists for the typicality of a particular working universe, caution is advised in generalizations drawn from that universe. The increasing use of cross-cultural and longitudinal (time series) studies (see Chapter 13) attests to the caution necessary in such "leaps of faith."

Sjoberg and Nett have keenly pointed out another problem that brings us back to the relation of theory to research, ". . . [the researcher's] particular theoretical and methodological commitment will intervene: the kind of working universe achieved will reflect his own theoretical assumptions" (1968:133). The Census Bureau definition of unemployment states that to be counted as unemployed, a person must have *actively* been looking for work during the week prior to the interview. Yet it is well known that there are many communities (West Virginia coal towns) where there is gross joblessness with no jobs to search out actively. As a consequence, the Census Bureau's operational universe does not adequately include certain types of unemployment phenomena.

SAMPLES IN SEARCH OF UNIVERSES

Perhaps one of the most often committed research errors is sampling without clear conceptions of from what one's sample was drawn and, hence, to what general universe one is actually generalizing. If a professor is describing the assimilation process of white European immigrants into American culture, there always seems to be someone who can point out that his or her second cousin doesn't fit the picture—with the implication that, therefore, the assimilation process is individualistic rather than universalistic. If everyone were exactly alike in every regard, a sample of one person would suffice (the pure case), but since everyone is not alike, good sampling techniques take *heterogeneity* into consideration.

Samples in search of universes usually, but not always, are termed biased samples—that is, they are typically samples that are nonrepresentative because of an unknown universe. It is not uncommon to find neophyte researchers "sampling" without an explicit rationale as to *what* universe it is they are trying to represent. Perhaps the greatest problem in using such samples is that the sample selection is often controlled by unconscious selection procedures. There are studies showing that if subjects are asked to sample "randomly" from a universe of pebbles, they will make *unconsciously* biased selections—some will tend to pick smoother pebbles, others tend to pick larger pebbles, and some will choose particularly colored pebbles. Indeed, this tendency for people to have particular unconscious response biases is so well known to professional sampling experts that most respectable survey research organizations will not allow their interviewers to make *any* sampling decisions. The main problem with nonrandom samples is that they usually have *unmeasurable* biases. Thus, generalizing from them to some universe seems most questionable.

But the problem of samples with questionable generalizations is not limited just to nonrandom samples. We could very easily sample a college student population at random. However, we may still have little idea as to how generalizable that college student working universe is to some more general universe. Are dominance hierarchies, sexual behaviors, and sociometric relationships among college youth generalizable to working-class youth, Eastern Europeans, or Arabs? Just because one has an accessible working universe from which to sample does not settle the question: "Generalizable to what?" The only way this question normally can be settled is through replications of the study across time and cultures. Similarities and differences in several similar samples may be used to show the boundaries of the general universe; replication similarities would show universe inclusions while differences would show universe exclusions.

Earlier we stated that neophytes often make the mistake of drawing samples from working universes without having general universe delimitations clearly drawn. But professional social scientists make this error more often than might be realized simply because many of our general universes are extremely abstract; for instance, bureaucracies, industrialized societies, and groups are intangibles in the sense that one cannot really touch, smell, hear, taste, or see them. Other general universes are hidden from view making them relatively inaccessible to the sociologists' study–such as unwed mothers, marijuana smokers, or homosexuals. There are many classic studies based on one, or just a few, such social structures. Peter Blau's classic *Dynamics of Bureaucracy* (1954) has often been implicitly cited as showing typical bureaucratic processes, and yet it is possible that it typifies a somewhat more narrow general universe such as American federal bureaucracy.

UNIVERSES IN SEARCH OF SAMPLES

One of the ironic twists to social and behavioral research is that, as was stated above, we have a larger number of theoretically interesting general universes that are *relatively* abstract or inaccessible from a sampling viewpoint.

Most of these types of universes are what some researchers call *relational* or *interactive* (Coleman 1959; Denzin 1970:87). Denzin (1970:89–91) distinguishes among five types of interactive samples: encounters, dyadic structures, social groups, social organizations, and communities or entire societies.

An *encounter* is the most transitory of social relationships. As Denzin (1970:90) states, "encounters have no prior or after life. Their existence lasts only as long as persons are in each other's symbolic and physical presence." In encounters mutual influence disappears when the participants are out of each other's symbolic or physical copresence. Thus, examples of encounters cover a broad spectrum of social events such as cocktail-party interaction, conversations with a hitchhiker in a moving automobile, playing bridge, a small-groups laboratory experiment, singles-bar interaction, or behavior in a radar speed-trap. Joint action, interpersonal coordination, and coorientation of behavior are minimal or lacking in an encounter.

Encounters present particularly difficult problems of location of working universe units from which to sample because of their situational nature. Denzin (1970:93) offers a unique solution to the problem which has some merit: "Through empirical examination the potential situations for interaction could be located and enumerated, then a sample of those situations could be drawn at a rate proportionate to the probability that an encounter would occur within them." This is basically the procedure followed by Laud Humphrey (1971) in his studies of homosexual tearoom behavior. Some forms of group sex encounters have been sampled by Bartell (1971), again by isolating bars where such encounters were *likely* to take place and then observing for *prime* periods of interaction. Erving Goffman (1961, 1967) is perhaps the most cited observer of encounters, although it is hard to evaluate whether his methods of selection have been as systematic as, say, Humphrey's or Bartell's.

Dyadic structures, by contrast to encounters, exist outside of the partner's physical copresence. A dyadic structure is a two-person group that shares a common role-set. Such a role-set might include husband-wife, work supervisor–subordinate, colleague-colleague, or friend-friend. James Coleman (1959:29) has suggested a method for studying dyads termed the *snowball technique.* In the *snowball technique,* individuals are asked to list those persons with role relationships of particular interest to the researcher, their addresses, and their specific role relationships to the respondent. This technique is then used on those persons suggested by the researcher's first wave of respondents, second wave of respondents, and so on, until the researcher runs out of new dyads from which to sample.

It is important for the researcher who claims interest in dyadic structures to study the dyad itself and *not* just one of the participants. Often, inferences are made to the whole dyad from one participant such as in studies of Lesbian "dyads" by Bass-Haas (1968). This procedure risks the fallacy of the wrong level of analysis discussed in Chapter 13. Specifically, this procedure potentially confuses prescribed role norms, actual role behavior, and the participants' *perceptions* of each. There is a wealth of information (Sarbin 1968) showing empirical differences between each component. For instance, if the complete marital dyad is interviewed separately it is often found that each partner has different *perceptions* about how often they *actually* have sexual intercourse and different *expectations* as to how often the sex act should take place in their dyad. Of theoretical interest is the fact that dyads with greater differences in such perceptions or expectations have greater divorce rates (Levinger

1968). Without sampling the entire dyad, such findings would have been impossible to uncover.

Social groups are characterized by interaction between three or more individuals. Social groups often are studied in terms of their own characteristics such as cohesion or stratification (Phillips and Conviser 1972), or they may be broken down into dyadic structures or encounter forms. Since social groups may be analyzed by "their focal activity, their places of interaction, and the nature of involvement among participants" (Denzin 1970:91), we can often use these indicators for isolating a working universe from which to sample. For instance, certain types of social groups such as Great Books reading clubs (Davis 1964) have a focal activity (in this case, reading) that naturally fits into some visible organization (such as libraries). Hence, obtaining a working universe list from which to sample may not always be extremely difficult. Other social groups such as parachute jumping clubs (Klausner 1968) are again easily identified because of the more visible organizations that support them.

Social organizations, including bureaucracies, are identified relatively easily. This may partially account for why—relative to studies of encounters, dyads, and social groups—they have drawn more empirical attention from social scientists. Social organizations can be defined as any group composed of large numbers of persons who share specified goals, structured by an internal division of labor, formalized by specified sets of interactions and social controls, and with a legitimated territory for existence.

Some of the more interesting analyses of social organizations have shown how the various social levels within the organization relate to each other. Lipset, Trow, and Coleman's (1956) classic study of union democracy focused on various types of dyadic structures and social groups in addition to formal organization structures. Due to the large size of the International Typographical Union, this study called for a number of different working universes from which samples were then drawn. By contrast, Erickson's (1971) study of a relatively large religious commune obtained a relatively complete picture through sampling of different levels of communal interaction and organization.

Communities present particular problems as concepts. Neighborhoods or communities exist through consensually imposed definitions rather than clearly demarcated geographic realms. Suttles (1972) points out that the neighborhood boundary is an arbitrary street or intersection cognitively differentiated and consensually agreed upon rather than an actual physical, ethnic homogeneity, or economic barrier. He further shows how the rural village prototype of community as a closely interdependent, self-contained entity has never been an appropriate model for urban analysis. Indeed Suttles differentiates three basic levels of urban communities: "face block," "defended neighborhood," and "community of limited liability."

The "face block" is prescribed by the social world of city block face-to-face relations and is often institutionalized in the block association. The "defended neighborhood" is the smallest segment of a city recognized by both residents and outsiders as having some corporate, albeit nonlegal, status or identity. It typically possesses many of the facilities needed to carry out the daily routines of life. The "community of limited liability" has a larger territory and possesses an institutionally secure name and boundary such as "Harlem" or the "East Side." Frequently, some external agent, such as a community newspaper, serves as guardian of the community of limited liabilities' sense of boundaries and purposes. Thus, the single individual typically has multiple claims on his or her involvement in surrounding territories.

Studies of *social organizations, communities,* and *entire societies* share several common problems: (1) access to data, (2) characterizations on several levels or processes of analysis, and (3) relating of different levels of analysis. The problem of access to data always exists, but it presents itself in unique form in any *relational* study. The refusal of an organization to give the researcher access in itself is not much different from an interview refusal by a person. In both instances, it is probably the case that motivations for access refusal are similar. For instance, the general public clearly does not understand what it is that sociologists do (Bode 1972) and, therefore, may refuse the researcher access because of a variety of scientific misconceptions. But at an organizational level of analysis or higher, one has unique access problems created by structural cross-pressures. Peter Blau (1964:34) found that the very fact that management gave him investigative access created suspicion among the rank and file that was likely to cause him loss of their rapport. Even if the researcher lacks problems created by the organizational strata, as in Blau's case, access to particular data may be difficult or impossible because of prior "commitments." Renee Fox (1964) found that by interviewing certain Belgian medical schools first others became suspicious or hostile toward her. Thus, organizational structures may create real problems of sampling bias.

Process analysis and investigation of different levels of analysis also present special sampling problems. There are many different aspects to an organizational (or larger) unit. Lipset, Trow, and Coleman (1956: 474) sampled at least seventeen types of units in their study of a union. McCall and his associates (1970) have delineated a minimal number of social processes one could sample in any organization: recruitment, socialization, interaction, innovation, social control, and logistics. Complicating the picture is the fact that one could study each of these processes at any of the five relational levels of analysis. Clearly, the number of possible samples necessary to get a fairly complete picture of any organization, community, or total society, then, is enormous.

The third problem presented is more a theoretical than a sampling problem: analysis of relations between different levels. The problem, as stated by Lipset, Trow, and Coleman (1956:476), can be visualized in this way:

> Certain properties of one unit (e.g., the total union) are determinants of behavior at another level (e.g., the individual). Yet how is it possible to really bridge the gap between the units? For example, to say that a certain political climate characterizes the union does not mean that this climate is felt by all printers alike. The climate makes itself felt more strongly by some men than others, depending upon their social and political locations.

One must be particularly careful in sampling organizational units so that the fallacy of wrong levels of analysis is avoided (see Chapter 13).

All of the above types of social analysis levels share in common the fate of being underutilized in social and behavioral studies. In practice, this is because of the relative abstractness of each level. Yet if sociology is to avoid becoming just an aggregate psychology (the fallacy of the wrong analytic level once more), it is obvious that sampling practitioners will have to pay more attention to the problems presented by each of these relational levels of analysis.

Furthermore, less attention should be paid to easily accessible populations that are, therefore, overstudied: for instance, college students, lower-class individuals, prisoners, and the mentally ill. Easy access does not insure theoretical relevance; indeed, easy access generally can be expected to cut down on theoretical relevance since such populations are probably more homogeneous than populations including both easily accessible and practically unapproachable subjects. The best test of any theory will generally use samples with great variability or heterogeneity.

We turn now to the various types of samples used by social scientists. We have stated previously that if the researcher wishes his or her samples to *typify* some specified universe, then it should be representative. It will be seen that different types of samples characterize particular universes with different degrees of accuracy. Although it would be nice if we could always depend on using the most accurate sampling techniques available, it will become evident that this is not always possible. The general rule, thus, is to use the sampling technique that best represents our working universe within the monetary means available to the researcher. Accuracy and cost are the key determinants of the type of sample used.

TYPES OF SAMPLING STRATEGIES

The only sampling differentiation made so far has been our distinction between biased and nonbiased samples. A *biased sample* is one in which the working universe is not accurately or fairly represented. At the other extreme are samples which we say are *nonbiased* because they typify the working universe. Actually, biased and unbiased should be taken as *polar types* since it is impossible to draw a *completely* unbiased sample which does not sample the whole universe (making it, by definition, no longer a sample since the sample must always be smaller than the universe from which it is drawn). Some sampling methods are liable to be less biased than others. The danger of a biased sample is that it may give you a representation of your working universe unlike what you would get if you studied the entire population.

"Bias" is not intended to convey value judgments as to how "good" a sample is. Oftentimes bias is introduced into correct sampling procedures. Such distortion requires that the researcher know where the bias is *and* that no part of the working universe be omitted. In other words, *purposely* induced bias is acceptable whenever the researcher corrects for its distortion *in the analysis;* it is for *unwitting* bias that the researcher must be on guard, since then there is no way he or she can know what manner of or degree of distortion is present.

Although we shall discuss some variations, there are two basic types of samples: purposive and probability. The difference between each type revolves around *how* sample units are selected, rather than on *which* elements are selected.

A *probability* sample is defined as any sample where every unit has a chance of being selected that is different from 0 or 100 percent and that chance is a *known* probability. That is, if the researcher has a list of 100 dyads, then every dyad should have a *known chance* of being selected but should not be assured *before* selection of being included (100 percent chance) or excluded (0 percent chance). In order to satisfy both of these conditions, it is necessary to have a complete enumeration of units in the working universe. Unfortunately, this is not always possible. If a researcher was interested in studying homosexual dyads it would be impossible to get anything approaching a complete listing due to the hidden nature of such behavior. In this case some kind of purposive sample would be necessary.

A *purposive* sample lacks one or both of the characteristics of probability samples; a *purposive sample* has a known chance equal to 0 or 100 percent of being selected or, as is more likely, where the chance of being selected is different from 0 or 100 percent, the selection chance is *unknown*. The main problem with purposive samples, then, is that we can rarely tell *how* representative the sample is of some working universe since we cannot estimate sampling bias (which we shall discuss in more detail later).

Purposive Sampling Models

There are several prototypic purposive sampling models: haphazard, homogeneous, rare element, heterogeneous, and structural samples. In this section we shall discuss each type of purposive sample as well as variations or subtypes of each.

Haphazard samples are simply samples that fortuitously present themselves for study. Volunteers form fortuitous sample elements. Samples of items from the past are usually also fortuitous due to selective decay and selective retention. Stone grave markers are more likely to be sampled than those made of wood which decay at faster rates. While some sciences like physics and chemistry can afford to care little about the representativeness of their specimens, archaeology, history, and other social and behavioral sciences are often forced to draw conclusions about the past from whatever items come to hand.

Homogeneous samples depend on a relatively narrow range of some theoretical variable. Homogeneous samples are of two types: (1) *extreme case samples* where only variable values at the extremity of a variable are represented or are overrepresented and (2) *rare element samples* where variable values with low frequencies only are represented or overrepresented. The use of either type of sampling method should be determined by theory. *Extreme case sampling* is particularly appropriate when the researcher is interested in discovering the boundaries of human action or institutions. As such, it acts as a quasi-experimental method of control in that certain variations in the data, which might otherwise obscure the social processes or structures being observed, are by definition excluded. Samuel Klausner (1968) has studied stressful situations and excitement seeking through purposive samples of members of parachute-jumping clubs. Certainly there are other working universes Klausner could have utilized, but the homogeneity of extreme stress and excitement emotions seems such a plausible assumption that a homogeneous sample seems quite reasonable in this case. A more sociological example comes from Richard Emerson's (1966) study of group cohesion and stress under the extremities of climbing Mount Everest. Even though both samples seem to be reasonable approximations of their working universes, it would still be wise, given the limited range of sampling variation, if studies of this nature were replicated with other homogeneous samples which deviated considerably from each sample. Klausner's study would be lent much more scientific weight through cross-cultural replication using samples of the Brazilian natives who dive from hundreds of feet into the Atlantic Ocean (each dive must be timed perfectly so as to catch incoming waves).

There are many types of social variables so rare that it would be extremely inefficient in time and cost to use anything but a *rare elements sample*. The study of the effects of vasectomies on family life presents such problems. Given the fact that few men have had vasectomies, it would be extremely costly to take a large enough probability sample of American males to find enough men with vasectomies to study. One might work around this problem through the selection of subjects from vasectomy clinic files. Vasectomy clinic files do not necessarily completely represent reasons for obtaining a vasectomy since, for one thing, the poor may be overrepresented, but the cost of drawing a more representative sample of vasectomies is virtually incalculable.

Some researchers refer to rare element sampling as deviant case sampling. "Deviant" is an unfortunately value-laden term in that what is "deviant" or "normal" is relative in time and space. Certain types of behavior labeled "psychotic" by Americans are accepted as normal and valued in other cultural contexts. Also, "deviant" behavior is often confused with atypical unapproved behavior; for instance, are the more than 60 percent of Catholic married women who use non-Church approved methods of birth control "deviants"? Obviously, there are good reasons why the terminology "rare elements" sampling is preferred over "deviant case" sampling.

Heterogeneous samples may be divided into (1) representative samples and (2) quota samples. Ouchida (1979), in contrast to Klausner, has been conducting ongoing research into the broadest possible spectrum of excitement seeking and has had to rely on quite heterogeneous purposive samples. She has sought data on excitement-seeking behavior within and outside of groups, among skiers, in the classroom, before and after sexual intercourse, and so on. Ouchida's sample is a *representative sample*. That is, she has attempted to draw a variety of purposive samples that represent all values present in excitement-seeking behavior.

A special case of such representative samples are *quota samples* in which the variable representation is made *proportionate* to the working universe. Quota sampling has been much used in social and behavioral research because it provides some assurances of representativeness with reduced cost since all it involves is decisions before sampling as to the numbers or percentages of units one wishes or needs to sample. If a researcher was interested in effects of sex and race, he or she could have interviewers select the *proportionate* number of subjects needed to insure equivalence to the working universe. Thus, in the case of the United States, approximately 6 percent of the sample would be black males, 6 percent black females, 44 percent white females, and 44 percent white males. Quota sampling tends to insure proportionate heterogeneity of the sample. Nevertheless, it does have several major drawbacks. First, it is difficult to sample on more than three variable dimensions because the number of variables (categories) to be filled is a multiplicative function of the number of values in each variable. If we wished to sample proportionate numbers of persons by sex, social class, and age where there were two sexes, three social classes, and two age divisions, we would have $2 \times 3 \times 2 = 12$ categories of respondents to select. But if we added two levels of religion, we double that number to 24 and so on. Second, the interviewer's freedom to choose which units to fill these quotas insures that nonrandom biases will influence the decision of what to sample. It is well known that quota samplers tend to *over*sample houses on corner lots (which tend to be more expensive); this oversampling insures over-representation of more affluent householders.

Structural samples, unlike the previously defined purposive samples, are those selected because of specific relational properties such as position in a dominance hierarchy, sociometric network, or communication chain. Thus, structural samples use as their units of selection units connected by some specific relationship. Since relational units rarely exist as working universe listings available for sampling, it is usually necessary to draw purposive samples of structural units. Size of free-forming groups has been studied in a rather sophisticated manner by John James and his students (1951, 1953) through multiple replication: Many working universes of free-forming groups were observed (state legislatures, city streets, shopping centers, college campuses). In each case, James found similar patterns of free-forming groups; thus the *diversity* of samples added strength to the findings.

One particularly interesting variant of homogeneous and structural samples is *strategic informant sampling.* Much used by anthropologists, sociologists have started using strategic informant sampling in recent years (see Chapter 4) in order to study certain aspects of social organizations, communities, and total societies in a better way. Strategic informant sampling rests on the assumption that knowledge is unequally distributed. Thus, the researcher often wishes to locate persons who have the most information about a social system or one of its components. Many researchers seek out persons occupying leadership roles to get a picture of the *total* organizational setting. Informants of lower rank would be used to get a fuller comprehension of more *specific* organizational details. Sometimes deviant or marginal (from the organization's point of view) informants are chosen for their distinctive observations of the system's workings.

The major checks on the researcher's data quality in this type of sampling are the repetitiveness and consistency of his or her informants' observations. When inconsistencies are reckoned with and the data form a coherent whole, sampling ceases. In fact, this is a good measure of both data quality and collection termination in any purposive sample. Cuber and Haroff (1968), in their study of upper middle-class family life styles, terminated data collection procedures when their project started collecting repetitious data. Note that they were interested only in data on life style *forms* rather than *distributions.* Purposive sampling usually is strongest in the characterization of social *forms* and weakest in the characterization of actual *distributions* of variable values; the reverse is true for probability sampling. Again, Laud Humphrey's (1970) study of homosexual tearoom behavior followed this pattern of characterizing social types or relationships; then, when data collected became repetitive, Humphrey knew it was no longer productive to collect more data and he ceased sampling.

Two subtypes of strategic informant samples are (1) snowball sampling and (2) expert choice sampling. In *snowball sampling* the researcher builds up a sample of a special population by asking an initial set of informants to supply names of other potential sample members. For instance, members of deaf populations, elites, and foreign expatriots often know about each other while outsiders would tend not to have such information. *Expert choice sampling* asks judgments of an expert(s) to choose "typical" individuals, "representative" cities, or to postulate the parent universe of a sample the researcher has already taken. The problem is that experts often "hold differing views on the best way to choose representative specimens, or to decide which are the most representative" (Kish 1965:19).

PROBABILITY SAMPLING MODELS

There are many purists among the scientific community who refer to probability sampling as the only "true" sampling method. As we have already seen there are numerous cases, however, where it is impossible to employ probability sampling. Nevertheless, where feasible, probability samples should be employed since they are the only sampling procedures by which we can accurately estimate how precisely our sample represents the working universe.

Precision here refers to the degree to which the sample approximates the estimate which would be obtained from a 100 percent count of the working universe if identical data collection methods were used. Thus, precision is a measure of sampling reliability. How much error researchers can tolerate depends on the *use* of their data. If they decide the permissible sampling error can be as much as 5 percent, they could reliably estimate that a city charter amendment will pass if their sample shows 60 percent of the voters favor it since the actual percentage falls between 55 and 65 percent. However, if the amendment is expected to pass by a close margin, they would want to reduce tolerable error to at most 1 or 2 percent by increasing their sample size. If sample size is held constant, the further away from 50 percent the percentage of a universe having a characteristic is, the larger sampling error that can be tolerated.

One of the advantages of probability samples is that the degree of precision desired from the sample estimate can be stipulated *in advance* of sampling. The probability of selection of each unit must be known before probability samples can be drawn. Fortunately, as we shall see, there are many instances where these probabilities can be known in advance.

The number of units in our working universe may be *finite* (limited in number) or *infinite* (indefinitely large). Paradoxically, even a finite universe may be sampled as if it were infinite. If you selected a sample of marbles from a universe of 100 marbles by laying each marble aside, you would be sampling *without* replacement, which is equivalent to sampling from a finite universe. By contrast, if after every draw the marble was replaced, we have the equivalent of sampling from an infinite universe, since each marble drawn has an indefinite number of possible draws. Happily, statistical formulas for calculating sampling error exist for sampling with or without replacement, although they are more complex for sampling without replacement (Kish 1965).

We said that precision can be specified in advance for probability samples. These are called *tolerance limits* since the researcher is assuming a certain *permissible* degree of variation in precision that he or she is willing to tolerate. *Confidence limits*, on the other hand, specify the risks or betting odds for those tolerance limits. For instance, researchers may desire a tolerance of no more than 1 percent error in 99 out of 100 samples drawn. (They do not draw all 100 samples. Rather, they know that if they did draw them, the chances are 99 to 1 that their error would not exceed 1 percent.) Anyone sophisticated in games of chance such as bridge will recognize that one is always limited to such probability statements. If one's bridge hand is void of clubs and hearts it is *almost* assured that someone else is also void in particular suits, but there is always a slim chance that that is not true. One of the paradoxes of sampling is that confidence and tolerance limits do not depend on the size of the *universe* being sampled; rather they depend on the size and type of the probability *samples*, as will be seen in later sections.

In order to take probability samples and to calculate confidence and tolerance limits, one must have an accurate up-to-date *sampling frame*: a list or file of all the units in the working universe. Without such a frame, probability sampling must be bypassed. As will shortly become apparent, for some types of probability samples the frame must be more than just a *simple* list or file. Note that in probability sampling the sampling frame *is* the working universe.

Simple random sampling is the classic form of probability sampling, in that all other forms are variations on its procedures. Simple random sampling is defined as drawing units from the working universe such that every unit has the same chance of selection. (Note that sampling without replacement does not satisfy this requirement in that other units not drawn have more chance of being selected. If you started out with 100 marbles and drew one, the probability on the first draw was 1/100th of selecting that marble, the second draw 1/99th, and so on. However, there are statistical correction formulas for those using simple random sampling without replacement; see Kish 1965.)

Simple random sampling requires statistical independence of the units being sampled—that is, the drawing of each unit must not depend on the drawing of any other unit (as in tossing of a coin where each toss is independent of every other toss). In order to insure independence of draws, some type of mechanical means of sampling should be used, such as a table of random numbers (see Appendix F). Every unit, then, might be assigned a number (1,000 units, for instance, could be assigned numbers 000 to 999), and then numbers could be drawn from a table of random numbers. Assume we wish to draw 10 units from those 1,000. We could go to Appendix F and start at any point on that list—say row 04, column 05—and we could then select units 816, 191, 065, 167, 079, 925, 115, 988, 881, and 502 by reading across row 04. (We could just as well proceed by reading down the 05 column.) If more numbers are needed than exist on a particular row the researcher can continue from left to right on the next row (05 in this case), or the next column to the right from top to bottom if columns are being used. If you have fewer units in your sampling frame than numbers to assign (such as 833 cases in your sampling frame) you ignore those numbers left over (834 to 999 in this example). (Whether or not you ignore the *same* number coming up more than once depends on whether you sample with or without replacement. Without replacement, you will ignore the number on later occasions. With replacement, you will weight that unit double other units if it comes up twice, and so on.) Experience shows the nonrandomness of picking numbers out of one's head or of drawing slips of numbered papers from a bowl. Hence, some mechanical means such as a table of random numbers is preferable to these methods.

Sjoberg and Nett (1968:147) have noted certain implicit sociological premises that occasionally render specious several simple random sampling assumptions.

> It is perhaps of more than passing interest that this notion of equality of units articulates with certain premises underlying democratic industrial orders. Here, theoretically at least, "every man's vote is of equal weight." This pattern explains in part the popularity of random sampling. But it also suggests certain difficulties. All men's opinions do not carry equal weight in a democracy, especially in predicting decisions by governmental leaders.
>
> The premise of equality of units presents a difficulty of another sort, for instance, in cross-cultural research. Here such units as "community" or "family" are difficult to standardize.

There are also statistical reasons why simple random sampling is not used as commonly as might be expected. First, every so often we may select a sample that is more deviant than expected even though the risk of selecting such a poor sample is small. Some other probability sampling procedures have less chance of such lopsided selection and hence may often profitably replace simple random sampling. Second, simple random sampling is difficult when the units in the sampling frame are not numbered or, if numbered, are not arranged in any specified order. In such cases, systematic sampling may be preferable.

Systematic sampling is one of the simplest, most direct, and least expensive sampling methods. It consists of taking every *n*th unit after a randomly chosen starting unit equal or less than *n*. For example, say we have 20 dwelling units on a block of which we wish to sample every fourth one. We would choose randomly a number between 1 and 4 and thereon choose every fourth dwelling unit. If "3" came up as our starting unit, this would be:

$$1 \; 2 \; ③ \; 4 \; 5 \; 6 \; ⑦ \; 8 \; 9 \; 10 \; ⑪ \; 12 \; 13 \; 14 \; ⑮ \; 16 \; 17 \; 18 \; ⑲ \; 20$$

Some statisticians claim this method gives pseudorandom selection since every unit chosen after the first is statistically dependent on its selection. Nevertheless, as Kish (1965:118) notes, if the working universe units are thoroughly mixed or shuffled, systematic sampling would be equivalent to simple random sampling. The danger is in hitting a *cycle*: unusual properties associated with similarly numbered units. For instance, imagine a housing development with 7 houses to each side of every block. With a random start of 2 and a selection interval of 7, corner lots would be undersampled. Unfortunately, many social events such as unemployment and marriage rates are cyclical. Also, many lists have built-in cycles (such as some pupil records that alternately register boys and girls or a list maintained by the Small Business Administration that lists small businesses in order of their employment size). Sometimes, in order to decrease the likelihood of hitting a periodic cycle, a researcher unfamiliar with a particular sampling frame will divide it into equal parts and take *different* random starts *and* selection intervals for each half. Of course, one could also do this according to some stratification principle such as in the previously mentioned Small Business Administration frame where one could draw different systematic samples for differently sized businesses.

Stratified sampling presupposes already existing knowledge of the working universe in order to separate the units into separate types of important categories. A stratified sample involves two stages: (1) The working universe is divided into homogeneous subparts (strata), such as men and women or large cities and small cities and then (2) random samples are taken from each subpart. If you were interested in sampling crime statistics in order to test for the effects of size of city, it would be foolish to treat New York's 11 million population equivalently to Podunk, Iowa's 200. Thus, cities could be stratified according to some criteria such as: populations of more than 1 million; 500,001 to 1 million; 100,001 to 500,000; 25,000 to 100,000; less than 25,000. Within each strata, you then could proceed to take simple random samples of crime statistics. Intuitively one would correctly expect a better estimate from a stratified than a simple random sample since the built-in sampling heterogeneity insures against a lopsided (homogeneous) simple random sample.

The strata should be grounded in theory. In our hypothetical study of the crime rates and size of city, it would be unreasonable to stratify on some variable unrelated directly to size of city such as the city's proportion of research and development firms since variation on the independent and dependent variables are left unaffected. The better the researcher's theoretical judgment in defining the strata, the higher the precision for any given size sample. On the other hand, lists identifying the elements of each stratum are often hard to obtain or information necessary to produce such a list may be lacking.

This type of sampling is a probability sample since every unit's probability of selection is known. In other words, probability sampling does not require that all units have the *same* known probabilities. Only units *within* a particular stratum are required to have the same selection probability.

Sometimes it is theoretically wise to sample disproportionately from different strata. The Bureau of the Census monthly, "Current Population Survey," samples *all* cities over 1 million population and takes proportionately smaller sample fractions of cities of smaller size in order to give proper weight to variables of interest such as unemployment.

In *cluster sampling* one samples from units selected because of close spatial proximity, such as small geographic areas (counties), and then one researches all, or a subsample, of the units within those designated spatial areas. Some examples of kinds of cluster are counties, blocks, or households for the U.S. population; colleges for college students; localities or plants for manufacturing firms; and hospitals for hospital patients. Whenever the sampling frame for a large universe does not list all the elements separately, but only clusters with counts of elements for each cluster (for example, counties), cluster sampling is most appropriate. Sudman (1976:76) points out that in order to use cluster sampling

1. Each cluster has to be well defined with each unit belonging to one and only one cluster.
2. It must be possible to have a reasonable estimate of the number of population elements in each cluster.
3. Clusters should be sufficiently small so that some cost savings are possible.
4. They must be chosen in a way that minimizes the sampling-error increase caused by clustering.

Because different clusters are often unequal in numbers, *stratified cluster sampling* is often utilized where clusters are ordered by some criteria, and then clusters from each strata are sampled. This is particularly appropriate when there are a few clusters with extremely large populations. If a country has two counties with over a million population and the rest are under 100,000 population, it would make more sense sampling separately from two strata based on cluster size rather than chance losing the two largest counties through random selection from all clusters.

In contrast to stratified sampling, the most precise results in cluster samples will be obtained when each cluster is as *heterogeneous* as the population from which the sample is drawn. Unfortunately, this is a rare outcome since social areas tend toward homogeneity—people tend to live with or near people like themselves; similar businesses tend to group together. The criteria for effective stratified sampling are just the reverse —strata should be as internally homogeneous as possible, but strata should differ from each other as much as possible. Stratified samples normally yield more precise estimates than simple random samples of the same size, provided the strata actually turn out to be more internally homogeneous than the population.

We have stated that we could get the same level of precision with a smaller sample if we used stratified rather than simple random sampling. In Table 10–1 we can see the effects of these types of sampling methods on sample size. For the same level of confidence and tolerance levels, we need only approximately 18 percent (175/963) of a simple

Table 10–1
Size of Sample by Type of Sample

Size of Sample for 98% Precision or Better for Airmen Average Base Pay, 99 Samples in 100

Grade	Simple Random Sampling	Stratified Sampling
M/Sgt	—	12
T/Sgt	—	14
S/Sgt	—	26
A/1C	—	33
A/2C	—	44
A/3C	—	36
Airmen Basic	—	10
Total	963	175

SOURCE: Adapted from Slonim (1960:76). Copyright © 1960, by Morris James Slonim. Reprinted by permission of Simon and Schuster, a Division of Gulf & Western Corporation.

random sample's size if we use a stratified sampling technique in this instance. Here the power of stratified sampling compared to simple random sampling is easily seen in that it will cost less than one-fifth as much to gather data at the same levels of tolerance and confidence limits.

By contrast, cluster samples usually give less precise estimates than simple random samples of the same size because of social area tendencies toward homogeneity. Why then should cluster sampling ever be used? Simply because it cuts research costs and time. It would be simpler and cheaper to randomly select some fifty city blocks averaging twenty households each for enumeration rather than randomly select 1,000 households spread over an entire city. Thus, other things being equal, while simple random sampling is more *precise,* cluster sampling is more *efficient* in time and cost.

In actual practice, sampling experts recommend that cluster sampling be used in multistage sampling designs. Imagine a listing of all counties in the United States; these could furthermore be stratified according to size of population. Within each list, stratified clusters (counties) might be sampled as a first stage. In the second stage, clusters (say, city blocks) within those clusters might be sampled (secondary sampling units). Within these secondary sampling units a simple random sample of dwelling units might be drawn at a third stage (technically called *primary sampling units* or p.s.u.'s). Of course, many social elements form *natural* clusters, in which case the utility of cluster sampling is most obvious: for instance, army platoon, school classroom, or industrial department. Cluster sampling is perhaps the most skilled sampling art and demands extremely skilled sampling experts in order to get reliable sampling estimates.

Multistage sampling designs are coming into greater use as sampling experts become more sophisticated. Usually these designs combine various types of sampling methods in order to take advantage of the positive features of each. In studying the American higher education system one could profitably: (1) set up strata (prestige or size of institution) each of which included several clusters (institutional divisions such as schools within universities); (2) select clusters from each stratum; (3) draw a cluster sample (departments) within the first clusters; and, finally, (4) draw a simple random sample of college professors within those subunits.

Time Samples

As we have seen, typical samples involve the selection of elements spread across *space*. However, there are often advantages to sampling elements across time. First, implicit in sampling across space at one point in time is the assumption that time is "typical" of all time periods. However, "the choice of a single time segment is exposed to the risks of seasonal, secular, and catastrophic variations, known or unknown" (Kish 1965:476). Second, it follows that time sampling may yield data about variations between periods, estimates of seasonal and secular trends, and the effects of catastrophes. Third, we can sometimes ingeniously get probability samples of a universe which are otherwise obtainable only through purposive sampling. A researcher interested in crosswalk sign violation behavior might randomly select crosswalk signs for observation as a first stage, then randomly pick times to watch for violations. By weighting for unobserved times he or she can estimate the size of his or her unknown universe.

Size and Precision of Probability Samples

The desired size of any sample depends on the degree of precision desired, the variability of the data to be sampled, and the type of sampling employed. We have already discussed the effects of type of sampling in general. Tables 10–2 and 10–3 specify more clearly these effects in terms of sample size.

Table 10–2 shows the sizes of simple random samples required to estimate the number of sampling units needed with different tolerance

Table 10–2

Size of Universe by Size of Simple Random Sample Needed for Various Confidence and Tolerance Limits

Total Number of A/2C (Size of Universe)	Size of Sample Needed for 99% Precision or Better, 997 Samples in 1,000		Size of Sample Needed for 98% Precision or Better, 99 Samples in 100	
	Number of Units in Sample	Sample Size as % of Universe	Number of Units in Sample	Sample Size as % of Universe
200	171	85.5	105	52.5
500	352	70.4	152	30.4
1,000	543	54.3	179	17.9
2,000	745	37.2	197	9.8
5,000	960	19.2	209	4.2
10,000	1,061	10.6	213	2.1
20,000	1,121	5.6	216	1.1
50,000	1,160	2.3	217	0.4
100,000	1,173	1.2	217	0.2

SOURCE: Adapted from Slonim (1960:74–75). Copyright © 1960, by Morris James Slonim. Reprinted by permission of Simon and Schuster, a Division of Gulf & Western Corporation.

(2 percent and 1 percent) and confidence limits (99 to 1; 997 to 3). It may appear paradoxical, but the table clearly demonstrates that as the working universe increases in size, the sample size remains remarkably constant for 98 percent precision. Note that if we double the size of our working universe from 10,000 to 20,000 units, we need only add 60 sampling units in order to maintain 1 percent tolerance limits in 997 out of 1,000 samples! Note that it is when the universe is very large that we normally expect relatively precise results from relatively small samples. In any universe of over 10,000 population, approximately 1,000 sample subjects are all that are needed for less than 1 percent sampling error in 997 out of 1,000 samples drawn! Hence, we see that once we deal with universes larger than 10,000 we need only have slightly more than 1,000 or 200 sample units in order to gain these levels of precision. This shows, as was stated earlier, that size of universe is largely irrelevant to precision of results, while size of sample is crucial to precision.

Table 10–2 also shows the effects of different levels of precision on sample size. Note that, for example, to increase precision from 98 percent in 99 out of 100 samples to 99 percent precision in 997 out of 1,000 samples, for a universe of 10,000, requires almost five times as large a

Table 10–3
Sample Size by Percentage of Occurrence of Working Universe with 5% Error in 95 out of 100 Samples. (Error not to exceed 5% in 95 out of 100 Samples.)*

Number of Units in Universe	Size of Sample Needed to Yield Error of 5% or Less in 95 out of 100 Samples, if Percentage of Occurrence Is:												
	1%	5%	10%	20%	30%	40%	50%	60%	70%	80%	90%	95%	99%
50	50	50	50	50	50	49	49	48	47	45	39	32	12
100	100	100	100	99	98	96	94	92	87	80	64	45	14
200	200	199	198	194	190	184	178	168	154	132	93	58	15
500	499	492	485	465	440	415	380	337	285	218	128	70	16
1,000	994	967	940	860	790	700	610	507	398	278	146	75	16
2,000	1,975	1,872	1,760	1,520	1,300	1,080	880	678	496	323	158	78	16
5,000	4,841	4,270	3,700	2,800	2,100	1,600	1,200	851	582	357	166	80	16
10,000	9,384	7,449	5,800	3,900	2,700	1,900	1,400	930	618	370	168	81	16

SOURCE: Slonim (1960:78). Copyright © 1960, by Morris James Slonim. Reprinted by permission of Simon and Schuster, a Division of Gulf & Western Corporation.

*It is important to recognize that the 5% error limit specified here refers to a *relative* rather than *absolute* percentage error. For example, if the percentage of occurrence is 20%, a 5% relative error limit would signify that our range of tolerance is 20% ± 5% of 20%, or 20% ± 1%. If we were concerned with a 5% absolute error (20% + 5%) our table of sample sizes would be entirely different from the one above.

sample while the same increase in precision for a universe of 500 would require over twice as large a sample.

Many times the researcher wishes to estimate how large some fraction of the working universe is. Perhaps the researcher is interested in the occurrence of academic tenure decisions in a universe of 5,000 college professors. By making a conservative estimate that 40 percent have been involved in tenure decisions he or she might choose a 30 percent sample occurrence in order to assure a large enough sample. From Table 10–3 it is apparent that he or she would need a total random sample of at least 2,100 professors in order to yield an error of 5 percent or less in 95 out of 100 samples.

Of course, most of the time in social research we are interested in more than one variable since we are interested in variable relationships (see Chapter 3). Thus we will want to insure that we have sampled enough cases for analysis. If we believe we need a minimum of twenty cases per cell and we will be using only two variables (religion, social class) per table with an average of four values per variable (Protestant, Catholic, Jewish, other; upper, middle, working, lower class), we will need *at least* 320 sample cases (see Table 10–4). In some cases Table 10–4 will not insure enough cases for analysis because of highly skewed variable distributions. Nevertheless, these types of questions need to be asked *before* drawing a sample since otherwise we may end up with too few cases. Sometimes the researcher, not having *any* idea about the value distributions of the variables, will select a small presample of units in a rapid, inexpensive manner and use the information from this sample as a basis for determining the size needed for a sample.

See Appendix D in Sudman (1976) for a mathematical formulation for computing sample size.

Table 10-4

Minimum Number of Units of Analysis for an Average of Ten Cases per Cell (Twenty Cases in Parentheses)

		R: Number of Values per Variable		
		2	3	4
n: number of variables	1	20 (40)	30 (60)	40 (80)
per table	2	40 (80)	90 (180)	160 (320)
	3	80 (160)	270 (540)	640 (1,280)
	4	160 (320)	810 (1,620)	2,560 (5,120)

SOURCE: Galtung (1967:60). Reprinted by permission.

SUMMARY

We have discussed a wide variety of sampling techniques in this chapter. Hopefully you have come to understand why the ideal sampling technique is some form of probability sampling. The cardinal rule is to attempt to leave as much to chance as possible so that personal bias does not contaminate the sample selection. Nevertheless, a major consideration in this chapter has been to present alternatives to probability sampling since a multitude of social factors mitigate against the employment of probability samples in many cases. Figure 10–1 summarizes these sampling strategies.

The nature of the working universe and theoretical considerations will largely control the type of sampling finally selected. While one must decide on the type of sampling method, one must also take into consideration more practical matters like time and cost. If one is interested in sampling responses to naturally occurring disasters time factors may mitigate against a completely random sample since there may not be enough time to set up a proper sampling frame. Further, cost is especially important since researchers do have limited resources. Monetary considerations may dictate against or for particular sampling techniques.

Cost and precision are the most important considerations in sampling. Unfortunately, they are directly related—one cannot get higher precision without more cost. Thus, financial resources may well determine whether one's research can just be exploratory or whether it can consist of hypotheses and theory testing.

The social and behavioral researcher can and should, as we have connoted through the term "sampling *unit*," sample many things besides individuals. For example, in addition to the five general relational types (dyads, encounters, social groups, organizations and communities, or total societies), one may also sample *time* periods.

The best sample (Backstrom and Hursh 1963:24) in general

1. Provides ways to determine the number of respondents needed
2. Specifies the chance (probability) that any person will be included in the sample
3. Enables us to estimate how much error results from interviewing a sample of people instead of interviewing all of them
4. Lets us determine the degree of confidence that can be placed in population estimates made from the sample.

Finally, we are bombarded every day with "scientific data" through television, newspapers, and radio. By now you should be able to ask a number of important questions about the quality of sampling of that data.

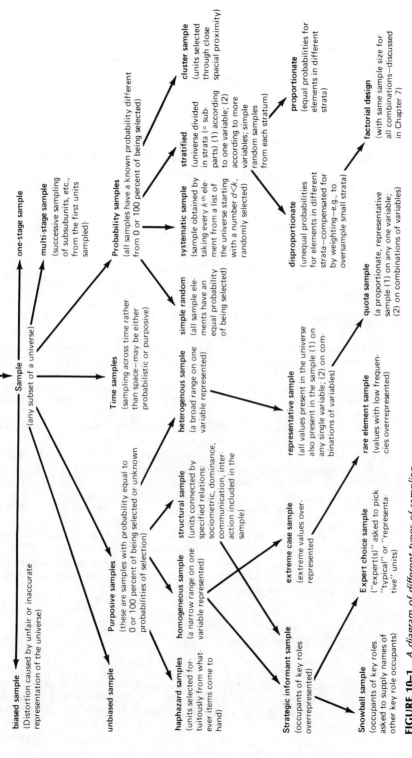

FIGURE 10–1 *A diagram of different types of sampling.*

Source: Extended from Galtung(1967:56).

1. What was the general universe?
2. What was the working universe or sampling frame?
3. How was the sampling carried out and supervised?
4. Was there a probability sampling model? If not, why not? If so, what kind?
5. Did the sampling frame cover the universe?
6. What was the nonresponse rate? (See also Chapter 6.)
7. What was the estimate of sample precision?
8. Was the sample size adequate to provide data to meet the objectives?
9. Are possible biasing effects acknowledged?
10. Did the reported results give only averages or totals, or did they also give some measure of variation of results?

If you cannot find answers to these questions you will find it impossible to evaluate the sampling design. It is wise to be skeptical of any research that does not give you adequate information to evaluate these questions.

READINGS FOR ADVANCED STUDENTS

LINDA BROOKOVER AND KURT W. BACK, "Time Sampling as a Field Technique," *Human Organization* 25 (Spring 1966): 64–70. Time sampling as an alternative to space sampling is discussed.

JAMES S. COLEMAN, "Relational Analysis: The Study of Social Organizations with Survey Methods," *Human Organization* 17 (Summer 1959): 28–36. A discussion of methods of interactive sampling.

BARNEY GLAZER AND ANSELM STRAUSS, *The Discovery of Grounded Theory*, 1967, pp. 62–71. A presentation of some alternatives to probability sampling.

RAYMOND JESSEN, *Statistical Survey Techniques*, 1978. Carefully selected, realistic, and clearly worked through examples make this a highly recommended book for clear comprehensive introduction to statistical sampling.

LESLIE KISH, *Survey Sampling*, 1965. While this is a highly statistical treatment of modern sampling techniques, it is nevertheless the most comprehensive text for an understanding of probability sampling theory.

SEYMOUR M. LIPSET, MARTIN TROW, AND JAMES S. COLEMAN, *Union Democracy*, 1956, Appendix 1, Section A. Discusses problems of sampling in organizational analysis.

SEYMOUR SUDMAN, *Applied Sampling*, 1976. This book has excellent treatments of the topics of when to sample, procedures of simple random sampling, systematic selection, list sampling, stratified sampling, and cluster sampling.

SUGGESTED RESEARCH PROJECTS

1. a. Operationalize working universes for one example of each of the following types of relational units—dyads, encounters, social groups, social organizations, and communities. Discuss the limitations to generalizations to your general universe presented by your choice of working universe.

    b. What types of sampling frame(s), if any, exist that might be used for probability sampling? If one (or more) exists, make a case for some particular type of probability sampling technique.

    c. If no sampling frame exists, what type of purposive sampling technique(s) could you justify using?

2. In the following samples: (a) Is the sample a probability sample—why or why not? (b) If it is not a probability sample, can you justify the purposive technique used? If yes, why? If not, what purposive technique(s) would be better? (c) If it is not a probability sample but random sampling techniques could be used to study the working universe, how would you redesign the sampling techniques? (d) Is the sample (and any redesigned sample) worthwhile in terms of sociological analysis—why or why not?

Sample #1: In order to test for *discrimination* in housing, a researcher sent a white couple to 30 apartments out of 120 listed in a Saturday newspaper as having vacancies by choosing every fourth listing. A white couple was followed by a black couple to make application for each apartment.

Sample #2: A researcher interested in the *homosexual dyad* interviewed 30 homosexual men about their experience in dyads. They were chosen using simple random methods from an underground telephone directory of the Gotham City Mattachine Society.

Sample #3: To test for *police discrimination against auto drivers,* a researcher had 50 of her college students with perfect driving records (30 white, 10 Mexican-American, 10 black) put "Support Socialism" stickers on their cars' rear bumpers. Each student signed a statement promising to abide by all traffic laws during the experiment.

Sample #4: In order to study *cocktail party behavior* two researchers informally let their colleagues and friends know of their research interest in the hope of being asked for this purpose to their up-and-coming cocktail parties.

Sample #5: A researcher interested in *driver behavior at stop signs* spent every Tuesday from 7 to 10 A.M. at several stop sign crossings observing auto violations in stopping.

Sample #6: In order to study *group sex,* two researchers joined the Megopolis Swingers' Association and attended as participant observers various meetings held by this group over a year's period.

3. Your city fathers have asked you as a sampling expert to help them find out what *form(s)* and *distribution(s)* the lead poisoning problem presents for the city.

    a. Design a *purposive* sampling technique for finding these lead poisoning cases. Give your rationale for the operationalizations of your working universe and the sampling strategy you choose.

    b. Design a *probability* sampling technique for studying the city government's *organizational* response to lead poisoning. (Be careful of the fallacy of wrong level of analysis.) Give your rationale for choosing the particular working universe and sampling strategy.

4. In your (3b) probability sample you want to design in enough cases so that you will average 20 cases per table cell for an average of 3 *variables* per table with an average of 4 *values* per table. How large will the sample have to be? (Answer: 1,280)

5. You are willing to tolerate no more than 5 percent error in 95 out of 100 samples. If there were 10,000 units in your universe and lead poisoning cases, you believe, occur about 5 percent of the time you would need a simple random sample at least how large? (Answer: 7,449)

6. If you had a universe of 100,000 lead poisoning cases and you wished to have 98 percent precision in 99 out of 100 samples, you would need at least how many cases in your simple random sample? (Answer: 217)

7. You have decided to replicate a study in a small nation of 100,000. You chose 1,200 persons through simple random sampling. In writing up your research you must give the tolerance and confidence limits for this research. What are they? (Answers: confidence limits of 997 out of 1,000 samples with a tolerance level of 1 percent error)

8. What types of sampling designs might be both possible and useful for studying the following populations or problems? Why?

   a. A rare disease known to affect some segments of the population more than others

   b. A small religious sect

   c. The effects of abortion on family life

   d. Graduates of a major in college who are not employed in an occupation related to that major

   e. Deer hunters who receive doe tags

   f. Extreme cases of anxiety (law school graduates one hour before taking a bar exam; prisoners just prior to execution)

   g. Pool hustlers

   h. The influence of the members of some group of workers (design engineers) on each other

   i. Child abuse

9. Quite often it is impossible to use probability sampling due to lack of sampling frames or prohibitive costs. Give an example for each of the following types of purposive sampling methods:

   a. Quota sampling

   b. Heterogeneous sampling

   c. Homogeneous sampling

   d. Haphazard sampling

   e. Extreme case sampling

   f. Rare element sampling

   g. Structural sampling

   h. Strategic informant sampling

   i. Time sampling

11

On Measurement
and Scaling

*Measurement stands, in fact, as the initial
juncture between theory and . . . experience. . . .* [1]

*The method of analysis then defines
what the information is and may or may
not endow this information with certain
properties. A "strong" method of analysis
endows the data with properties which
permit the information in the data to be
used, for example, to construct a unidimensional scale.* [2]

In Chapter 12 we shall see in Figure 12–1 that there is a direct relationship between the number of items used to measure some variable and

[1]Henry Margenau, "Philosophical problems concerning the meaning of measurements in physics," in C. W. Churchman and P. Ratoosh (eds.), *Measurement: Definitions and
Theories* (New York: John Wiley, 1959), p. 163.
[2]Clyde Coombs, "Theory and methods of social measurement," in L. Festinger and
D. Katz (eds.), *Research Methods in the Behavioral Sciences*, 1953, p. 472.

that variable's operational reliability. Not only is reliability increased by using more than one item, but also validity tends to increase with larger numbers of items used. Let us say we are measuring socioeconomic status (SES) and are using occupation, education, and income with ordinal measures of each (1 = high, 2 = medium, and 3 = low). A Mafia leader might rank high on income but low on education and occupation. Hence, an average of these three indicators for the Mafia leader would yield a score of 2.3, which seems quite a bit more reasonable (valid) than a score of 1 (Income) or scores of 3 (Education and Occupation) as a measure of SES since we would expect his SES to be lower than average (2.0) but not as low as, for instance, an unskilled worker's. In other words, it is better to have more rather than fewer indicators of a variable. When we have some explicit means of combining these indicators into a whole we speak of forming a *scale*. Scaling theory forms one of the most advanced of behavioral and social research methods.

Unfortunately, two myths beset the area. First, many social scientists falsely assume that scaling involves rather vague measurement procedures. Second, scaling has been sometimes falsely relegated to the status of "just" psychological and social psychological research. This chapter will attempt to show that when correct scaling methods are used scaling has a variety of social as well as psychological measurement applications.

Scaling has been most often used at the individual level of analysis. That is, the researcher often desires to categorize persons according to some aspect of their cognitive, affective, or behavioral states. He or she may want to predict individual authoritarianism, self-esteem, or social discrimination. The researcher may often wish to do the same for group characteristics. He or she may wish to measure group cohesiveness, stratification, or communication channeling. Whatever the case, each measurement *element* or indicator of the research variable is called an *indice*. An indice is, thus, a single operationalization of a variable. Income is often used as an indicator of social class. Usually, for reasons of reliability again, the researcher combines several indicators in some manner to represent the variable. For example, the Hollingshead Index of Social Class weights income, education, and occupation according to their relative importance, then sums these weighted components to form social class standing.

Therefore, an *index* is defined as *more than two* indices or indicators which have been combined into a single measurement through some procedural rule or rules. The rest of this chapter will explicate procedural rules currently used by scientists in the study of various social and behavioral phenomena. In the process various assumptions, positive features, and drawbacks of each procedure will be pointed out.

CHARACTERIZING THE VARIABLE'S DOMAIN

In Chapter 3 a number of rules were given for abstracting the various components of one's research variables. To design an index, in other words, we first need to be sure exactly what the domain of our variable is. During the mid-1950s Christie (Christie and Geis 1970) pioneered interest in those persons who are especially adept at the manipulation of others—so-called Machiavellians. A careful search of the literature ranging from Machiavelli's *The Prince* to Eric Hoffer's *The True Believers* led to the following hypothetical role model of a Machiavellian: He or she must have a relative lack of emotional involvement in interpersonal situations, a lack of concern with conventional morality, a lack of gross psychopathology, and low ideological commitment. Each of these characteristics was built upon two assumptions. First, Machiavellians view humans as basically weak, fallible, and gullible. Second, if humankind is weak, rational persons should take advantage of the situation to maximize their own gains. Alternatively, if others cannot be trusted because of their weaknesses, one should take steps to protect oneself from others' follies (Christie and Geis 1970:7).

The next step was to gather statements that might be theoretically consonant with the Machiavellian view. During the first year of the project, seventy-one items were gathered. During the next few years the slow but normal process of administering the scale items to various groups, correlating their responses with expected outcomes, and then reconceptualizing the construct was carried out. The outcome of this rigorous process was the development of two scales (Mach IV and V), each having a satisfactory cluster of initially interrelated items. Notice that good scale indexes are not formed overnight. Scale methodologists want to know what their items are measuring—which may be quite different from what they *think* they measure. Thus, most of their efforts are spent in trying to locate the dimension(s) their scale actually taps. The following sections consider this process further. Then different types of scaling rules and methods used by researchers are introduced.

INFORMAL CRITERIA FOR ATTITUDE STATEMENTS

Christie's Machiavellian scale provides a classic example of attitude scale construction, one we will find ourselves returning to throughout this chapter. It is important that the items making up any such well-constructed attitude scale be carefully selected and edited according to principles that help us evaluate the objectivity of our scale statements. (Note that the researcher forms *statements, not questions,* in making attitude scales.) We want principles that will help us construct statements that are congruent with a major assumption of attitude research: that there will be theoretically important differences in the belief systems of those persons with favorable as opposed to nonfavorable attitudes towards any particular scale item. It is important to note that attitude scales tap *opinion, not fact.* Unlike IQ tests or general knowledge tests, the attitude scale asks for a personal reaction towards some object rather than an answer that is externally verifiable as correct ("The majority of lead poison cases occur in multiple dwelling units."). The following suggestions for constructing such items[3] have been proposed by Edwards (1957:13–14):

1. Avoid statements that refer to the past rather than to the present.
2. Avoid statements that are factual or capable of being interpreted as factual.
3. Avoid statements that may be interpreted in more than one way.
4. Avoid statements that are irrelevant to the psychological object under consideration.
5. Avoid statements that are likely to be endorsed by almost everyone or by almost no one.
6. Select statements that are believed to cover the entire range of the affective scale of interest.
7. Keep the language of the statements simple, clear, and direct.
8. Statements should be short, rarely exceeding twenty words.
9. Each statement should contain only one complete thought.
10. Statements containing universals such as *all, always, none,* and *never* often introduce ambiguity and should be avoided.
11. Words such as *only, just, merely,* and others of a similar nature should be used with care and moderation in writing statements.
12. Whenever possible, statements should be in the form of simple sentences rather than in the form of compound or complex sentences.
13. Avoid the use of words that may not be understood by those who are to be given the completed scale.
14. Avoid the use of double negatives.

Another informal criterion has to do with *direct* questioning. "Only when the social atmosphere is free from felt or actual pressures towards

---

[3]These rules particularly apply to what we shall term "Likert" statements. Some of these rules are not applicable to (or violate) some types of attitude scales. For example, under a later chapter section on "Indirect Scale Measurements" we shall see that rule 2 can be violated. Likewise, rule 5 is inapplicable for Guttman scales.

conformity might we expect to obtain evidence about a person's attitudes by means of direct questioning" (Edwards 1957:3). Christie noted that Machiavellianism denotes rather unfavorable social behavior to many people. If you asked people to express their opinions of Machiavellian behavior they might respond simply in terms of *publicly* approved attitudes because of fear of social disapproval. Thus, Christie attempted to design items that more indirectly measured Machiavellianism. And he laboriously took pains to find out if people could pick out the Machiavellian items in his scales.

Furthermore, simple direct questions are useless in situations where a person is not aware of his or her own attitudes. Many people have relatively unformed feelings toward the word "Machiavellian"—they do not know what it means and, thus, to ask of them their attitude ("Are you Machiavellian?") toward such an object would be meaningless.

Finally, much of human feeling may be both ambiguous and *ambivalent.* One may have extremely positive *and* negative feelings towards an object. Direct questions cannot adequately tap ambivalence. Many people who "hate" violence are often strongly and even unconsciously attracted to violent movies. Attitude measurement techniques cannot now adequately evaluate such opposed feelings.

SYSTEMATIC RESPONSE BIASES

As scientific attitude scale construction has matured it has become increasingly evident that no matter how well constructed the attitudinal index, there will still be extraneous determinants of the participant's responses that undermine the scale's validity. We saw in Chapter 10 that, when left on their own, humans will inevitably choose a biased sample through some sort of systematic, albeit unconscious, bias. Such biased tendencies can also be found in a person's responses to attitude inventories. For instance, most persons have *social desirability* tendencies—they will try to give answers that make themselves appear "well-adjusted, unprejudiced, rational, open-minded, and democratic" (Cook and Selltiz 1964:39). Respondents are often motivated to present an overly favorable picture of themselves. Obviously, in order to present such a favorable self-concept the respondent must know what responses will be favorably regarded. The researcher has several alternative ways of controlling social desirability beyond attempting to disguise questions that might be thought of as socially desirable or undesirable and assuring respondents that their responses will be kept confidential. Christie (1970:26) asked participants to read William Whyte's appendix in *The*

Organization Man (1956) on how to fake a test and then to either "fake low" or "fake high." His rationale was premised on the belief that if neither instruction significantly changes the index scores, then one has evidence that "social desirability" is a relatively implausible explanation. Second, some researchers sprinkle their attitude questionnaires with items keyed to measuring social desirability such as those in Edwards's (1957) or Schuessler and others' (1978) social desirability scale. Then the overall attitude scale score is corrected for these known social desirability responses. An interesting variation on this method is to present several items in combination that are equated for "social desirability" and require that the participant choose the one coming closest to his or her own viewpoint.

Acquiescence tendencies have been found to be widespread in unsophisticated attitude inventories. Some people, Couch and Keniston (1960) point out, tend to accept all or most statements ("yeasayers"); others tend to reject all or most statements ("naysayers"). Often, this problem can be vastly reduced through phrasing statements unambiguously. Another means of reducing acquiescence is through random *reversal* of half of the item content. Christie and Geis (1970:8) randomly reversed half of the Mach IV items. Thus, Machiavelli's belief that "Most men are cowards" was reversed to read "Most men are brave." Agreement with either item gives opposite attitudinal meaning. If a respondent had marked "+3" (strongly agree) towards the statement "Most men are brave," it later will be scored as "–3" by the researcher. This is because agreement (or disagreement) with reversed items, in this case Machiavellianism, implies agreement (or disagreement) with the reverse of that scale. In other words, a Machiavellian should agree that "All men are cowards" while a non-Machiavellian should agree that "All men are brave." The converse should be also true; a person disagreeing that "All men are brave" would be seen as Machiavellian, while a person disagreeing that "All men are cowards" would be non-Machiavellian.

Extremity biases include those tendencies to check (or avoid) the extremes of answer categories—for instance, the tendency to check (or avoid checking) "1's" and "7's" on a seven-point scale. Another form of this bias is the tendency for a respondent to avoid extreme responses by checking "4" (on a scale from "1" to "7") or "don't know." Because of this tendency for some respondents to select neutral scale points, many researchers prefer to "force" the individual to make positive and negative responses by not including such "neutral" categories. While this procedure may encourage *cooperative biases,* since the respondent may not actually have an attitude or feeling towards an object, Ghiselli (1939) found people more willing to respond to a four-step scale than to five-point scales such as shown in Table 11–1. Thus, four-point scales may be more appropriate than five-point scales except when the researcher *expects* less strongly expressed attitudes in which cases a fifth, neutral category should be added. While extreme-response sets have generally been found to influence scale validity only to a small degree, Nunnally (1967:612–613) provides statistical means for determining the extent to which it exists.

Sentence syntax biases also provide a source of response bias. As Micklin and Durbin (1969:205) caution,

> It is time we all recognized that the majority of data collection techniques in sociology and social psychology are rooted in linguistic contexts. . . . We cannot simply assume that linguistic variations result in random rather than systematic error.

Table 11–1
Commonly Used Five-Point Rating Scales

Strongly approve. . . .	Approve	Deadlocked; undecided.	Disapprove . . .	Strongly disapprove
Certainly right.	Probably right	Doubtful	Probably wrong	Certainly wrong
Much greater	Somewhat greater.	Equal.	Somewhat less	Not at all
Very high . .	A little above average	Average	A little below average.	Very low
Practically all	Many	About half	A few	Practically none
Like very much	Like somewhat	Neutral.	Dislike somewhat. . . .	Dislike very much
Everyone. . .	The majority . .	Quite a few	A few	None
Strongly urge	Approve	Neutral.	Slightly disapprove . . .	Strongly disapprove
Favor in all respects. . . .	Favor in most respects	Neutral.	Favor in a few respects . .	Do not favor at all
Absolutely true	Probably or partly true	In doubt; divided; open question	Probably or partly false . . .	Absolutely false

SOURCE: Table from page 192 in *Surveys, Polls, and Samples* by Mildred B. Parten. Copyright © 1950 by Harper & Row, Publishers, Inc. Reprinted by permission of the publisher.

NOTE: The informant may be asked to rate his or her attitudes in numerical terms from 1 to 5, instead of words. The number 5 is used for the strongest reaction. When both positive and negative reactions are to be expressed, the scale numbers may be arranged as follows:

$$+2 \qquad +1 \qquad 0 \qquad -1 \qquad -2$$

Micklin and Durbin isolated the following three types of syntactic sources of biases about items that appear in attitude scales. (1) *Sentence complexity* indicates whether an item is stated as a simple or a complex verbal element. (2) *Voice* indicates whether an item is stated in the active or passive voice. (3) *Direction* indicates whether an item is negative or affirmative. Micklin and Durbin suggest that attitude scales need to be *balanced in terms of* the eight types of syntax derived from these three dichotomies. However, given the fact that we wish to have our respondents presented with clearly understood stimuli, it seems best to use the simple sentences, active voice, and affirmative direction as much as possible. Numerous psychological studies have shown that respondents have much more difficulty understanding statements written in the negative direction, passive voice, and complex form. These forms should be avoided as much as possible.

There are four basic ways of minimizing extraneous response biases: One may "(1) modify the conditions of administration, (2) modify the instrument, (3) detect and discard subjects whose responses are largely affected by irrelevant factors, and (4) correct the scores of all subjects in proportion to the amount of their known contamination" (Scott 1968:238).

Conditions of administration may be more free of response bias contamination if attempts are made to establish rapport with participants prior to the administration. This could include attempts to convince participants of the importance of participation, of the confidentiality of responses, and of the desire to obtain honest opinions.

Instrument construction has been partially discussed in an earlier section. One further point often missed by the novice to scale construction is to provide respondents with a clearly written explanatory preface such as the one in Table 11–2.

We have already discussed counterbalancing statements by using an equal number of randomly placed direct-worded and reverse-worded items. However, sometimes sensible reversal of items is not possible, as many would-be revisers of the Adorno Authoritarianism scale have found. For instance, how would you reverse the following item: "After we finish off the Germans and Japs, we ought to concentrate on other enemies of the human race such as rats, snakes, and germs."

Various indirect measures of attitudes have been used in order to circumvent participant awareness so that his or her biases will not influence the assessments. These will be discussed in more depth in a later section on indirect measurements.

Campbell and Fiske's (1959) multimethod strategy fits in nicely with the argument that since any type of instrument is apt to elicit peculiar

Table 11–2
A Typical Attitude Scale Preface Format

Listed below are a number of statements. Each represents a commonly held opinion and there are no right or wrong answers. You will probably disagree with some items and agree with others. We are interested in the extent to which you agree or disagree with such matters of opinion.

Read each statement carefully. Then indicate the extent to which you agree or disagree by circling the number in front of each statement. The numbers and their meaning are indicated below.

> If you *agree strongly*, circle +3
> If you *agree somewhat*, circle +2
> If you *agree slightly*, circle +1
>
> If you *disagree slightly*, circle –1
> If you *disagree somewhat*, circle –2
> If you *disagree strongly*, circle –3

First impressions are usually best in such matters. Read each statement, decide if you agree or disagree and the strength of your opinion, and then circle the appropriate number in front of the statement. *Give your opinion on every statement.*

---

confounding factors, a variety of procedures should be used in assessing attitudes. Christie and Geis (1970) have almost always used *both* the Mach IV and V scale versions in assessing Machiavellianism.

We have already discussed one method of detecting systematic distortions through Edwards's social desirability scale. Some scales have items built in to measure statements with extremely low probabilities of acceptance. If participants answer a large proportion of such items it is assumed they are being careless or nonserious in their approach to the test, and their scores are thrown out. However, this procedure risks the alternative possibility of throwing out truly deviant persons.

Finally, correction of scores for known response biases may be employed. Assume, for example, that you wish to measure acquiescence response sets. Suppose there are ten directly worded items and ten reversed items. If agreements and disagreements balance out, there is no acquiescence response bias; if they do not balance out, the scale total score might be corrected for the bias.

TYPES OF MEASURING INSTRUMENTS

In Chapter 3 we discussed four types of scales: nominal, ordinal, interval, and ratio. Each of the measurement techniques that will be discussed in this section assumes one of these types of scales properties. Measurement, in its broadest sense, is concerned with the assignment of numerals to objects according to some specified rule. However, numerals are just symbols—one has to determine whether the scale properties are applicable through a determination of the properties of the variable's attributes measured. The permissible rules for the assignment of numerals to objects depend on properties of the object being measured, *not* on properties of the type of scale utilized. Thus, the assignment of numbers like "1" to males and "2" to females is an arbitrary rule since the numbers could have been assigned in reverse manner.

Category Ranks Methods

Often a researcher will present a number of items to a group of subjects with instructions for the participants to rank order the items according to some single criteria. This method has found particular popularity in recent studies in the sociology of science. Roose and Anderson (1970) have asked college professors to rank graduate programs according to quality of graduate faculty and effectiveness of the graduate program; Glenn (1971) has had sociologists rank order the prestige of professional journals; and psychologists have been asked to rank order their most distinguished colleagues. There is no reason, however, why the method has to be limited to one area such as the sociology of science. Holmes and Rahe (1967) asked respondents to rank order events that had caused the most social readjustment in their lives (see Table 11–3). The events then were ranked over all respondents, the highest-ranking event (death of spouse) receiving an *arbitrary* mean value of 100. Lesser-ranked events were given mean values showing how much readjustment was required *by comparison to* death of a spouse.

Several difficulties present themselves in using the ranking method. First, unless less than twenty items are to be ranked, ranking becomes extremely difficult for most participants. With more than twenty items, most researchers use the following modifications. First, a few rank categories will be set up. In Roose and Anderson's (1970) study of graduate-faculty quality seven ranks were set up: (1) Distinguished, (2) Strong, (3) Good, (4) Adequate, (5) Marginal, (6) Not Sufficient for Doctoral Training, and (7) Insufficient Information. Second, every subject then rated every item (departments) according to these categories. Third, a mean or median rank was established for each item. Finally, every item was then reassigned a whole rank number since the differences in mean or median ranks do not indicate interval properties but are only ordinal.

Table 11–3
Social-Readjustment Rating Scale

Rank	Life Event	Mean Value
1	Death of spouse	100
2	Divorce	73
3	Marital separation	65
4	Jail term	63
5	Death of close family member	63
6	Personal injury or illness	53
7	Marriage	50
8	Fired at work	47
9	Marital reconciliation	45
10	Retirement	45
11	Change in health of family member	44
12	Pregnancy	40
13	Sex difficulties	39
14	Gain of new family member	39
15	Business readjustment	39
16	Change in financial state	38
17	Death of close friend	37
18	Change to different line of work	36
19	Change in number of arguments with spouse	35
20	Mortgage over $10,000	31
21	Foreclosure of mortgage or loan	30
22	Change in responsibilities at work	29
23	Son or daughter leaving home	29
24	Trouble with in-laws	29
25	Outstanding personal achievement	28
26	Wife begins or stops work	26
27	Begin or end school	26
28	Change in living conditions	25
29	Revision of personal habits	24
30	Trouble with boss	23
31	Change in work hours or conditions	20
32	Change in residence	20
33	Change in schools	20
34	Change in recreation	19
35	Change in church activities	19
36	Change in social activities	18
37	Mortgage or loan less than $10,000	17
38	Change in sleeping habits	16
39	Change in number of family get-togethers	15
40	Change in eating habits	15
41	Vacation	13
42	Christmas	12
43	Minor violations of the law	11

SOURCE: Holmes and Rahe (1967).

Thurstone Scales

The rank order method is an extremely easy method to use. Many of the methods of scaling to be discussed, in fact, start with (but go beyond) its assumptions. One of those basic assumptions is that attitudes toward various objects may be expressed along a continuum from least to most favorable. Thurstone (Thurstone and Chave 1929) provided three methods that start with this basic assumption: (1) paired comparisons, (2) equal-appearing intervals, and (3) successive intervals. Because an inordinate amount of labor is involved in making a Thurstone scale and because other scaling methods have generally proved to be as good, it is rare to find a Thurstone scale used in recent research. The student who wishes to pursue Thurstone scaling further might profit from reading Chapter 7 in Schuessler's *Analyzing Social Data* (1971) for more specific information on how to form Thurstone scales.

Likert Summated Rating Method

In this method attitudinal statements are constructed that are unfavorable towards the object or issue being investigated. Extremely favorable or unfavorable items are unnecessary since respondents will indicate their *degree* of agreement or disagreement with each item. Generally, only five responses are allowed: (1) strongly agree, (2) agree, (3) uncertain, (4) disagree, and (5) strongly disagree, although sometimes this rule is modified to four, six, or seven responses. The investigator's "a priori" judgment is used at this stage in deciding whether a statement is a direct or reverse measure of the attitude object. Individual scores are then summed up. In Table 11–4 directly worded questions are scored from "strongly agree" (+3) to "strongly disagree" (–3). The researcher sums over all the items to obtain a preliminary total score. Then individuals are ordered from most favorable to least favorable towards the attitudinal object. The most and least favorable 25 percentages (toward the attitudinal object) of subjects are now used for *item analysis.*

Sophisticated researchers do not short-cut item analysis. If a scale has not been item analyzed there is no way of knowing how accurate one's a priori assumptions were, which makes the scale a doubtful measure. In one widely used means of item analysis the responses of the 25 percent most favorable items are compared to the responses of the 25 percent least favorable. If an attitude statement is "good," it will discriminate between the two groups; if not, it should be discarded from the pool of items. Those items found discriminating are summed up for the actual

Table 11–4
Sample of Likert-Type Scale Items

1. Never tell anyone the real reason you did something unless it is useful to do so.						
	+3	+2	+1	−1	−2	−3
2. The best way to handle people is to tell them what they want to hear.						
	+3	+2	+1	−1	−2	−3
3. One should take action only when sure it is morally right.						
	+3	+2	+1	−1	−2	−3
4. Most people are basically good and kind.						
	+3	+2	+1	−1	−2	−3
5. It is safest to assume that all people have a vicious streak and it will come out when they are given a chance.						
	+3	+2	+1	−1	−2	−3
6. Honesty is the best policy in all cases.						
	+3	+2	+1	−1	−2	−3

SOURCE: Christie and Geis (1970).

attitudinal score—low scores indicating unfavorable attitudes, high scores indicating favorable attitudes. The Likert method thus has ordinal scale properties.

Guttman Scalogram Analysis

This analysis is based on the assumptions that (1) a set of items can be ordered along a continuum of difficulty or magnitude and (2) such a set of items measures one unidimensional variable. Assume we know a person can consistently jump a five-foot hurdle. We can predict that he or she can consistently jump a four-, three-, two-, or one-foot hurdle even though we cannot predict, without more information, whether he or she can jump hurdles of more than five feet consistently.

Let us assume now that we have a number of attitude statements spanning the continuum of pro- to antihomosexuality. If these statements can be ordered along a unidimensional continuum such as shown in Table 11–5 then we would have a perfect Guttman scale.

At least 100 individual responses are needed to analyze such a set of attitude statements. The order of both persons and statements is changed by trial and error until a minimum number of inconsistent response patterns is reached. In Table 11–5 an inconsistent response pattern would be "yes-yes-no-yes-no." Response patterns should show inconsistent patterns in no more than 10 percent of the cases. Statements that show more inconsistency are eliminated on the grounds that they do not belong to that particular continuum. In order to assess the reliability of a Guttman scale, the coefficient of reproducibility is used. The researcher needs to know (1) the total number of responses generated by the total sample of respondents and (2) the number of times participants' choices fell outside of the predicted pattern of responses. The following formula is then employed:

$$\text{Reproducibility} = 1 - \frac{\text{total errors}}{\text{total responses}}$$

For example, draw a diagonal line from the lower right (below the "0" in the energy column) of Table 11–6 to the upper left (below the "–" in the political column). You will find that there are no deviations from the expected pattern in the political column, two deviations in the territorial column (the "0" for row C and the "–" for Row D), two deviations for the food column (the "0" in row B and the "+" in row C), and no deviations in the remaining two columns. Since there are 35 total responses (cells) in Table 11–6, our formula will give us

$$\text{Reproducibility} = 1 - \frac{4}{35} = .89$$

Hence, we conclude that the reproducibility coefficient shows slightly more inconsistency than the acceptable 10 percent.

Guttman scaling has been used by a few sociologists to find some type of unidimensional order in social organizations. Otis Dudley Duncan (1964) has ordered types of societies according to their level of com-

Table 11–5
Hypothetical Perfect Guttman Scale for Homosexual Statements

Individuals	A Happenstance Encounter	An Acquaintance	A Friend	A Roommate	A Date
Attitude Statements: "I would not mind having a homosexual for . . . ."					
Very anti-	No	No	No	No	No
Anti-	Yes	No	No	No	No
Somewhat anti-	Yes	Yes	No	No	No
Somewhat pro	Yes	Yes	Yes	No	No
Pro	Yes	Yes	Yes	Yes	No
Very pro	Yes	Yes	Yes	Yes	Yes

plexity on five structural variables. As shown in Table 11–6 there is a remarkable degree of unidimensionality although this Guttman scale gives far-from-perfect unidimensionality. With the vast cross-cultural resources of the Yale Human Relations Area Files (HRAF) it should be possible for sociologists and anthropologists to attempt more usage of scalogram analysis. Ball (1972), in a similar vein, has used Guttman scaling in the study of games and has found evidence for the cumulative summing of skill, strategy, and chance components.

The Guttman scaling technique is limited to the use of dichotomous and trichotomous variables. Thus, one of its strong points is its ability to take *nominal* or qualitative variables and order their relationships in ordinal form. Guttman scaling assumes items to be cumulative. By contrast, in Likert and Thurstone scaling the acceptance of a favorable item is not seen as necessarily inconsistent with the acceptance also of a less favorable item. Cumulative assumptions are often quite unrealistic assumptions. Sherif and Sherif (1967) have demonstrated that pro-civil rights participants will often accept extremely favorable civil rights statements while rejecting milder ones such as "There should be more discussions between white and black leaders."

Table 11–6
Guttman Scale of Societal Complexity

Type of Society	Level	Structural Variable				
		Political	Territorial	Food	Economy	Energy
	Simple	Local	Nomadic	Collection	Self-sufficient	Pre-industrial
A₁		–	–	–	–	–
A₂		0	–	–	–	–
B		+	0	0	–	–
C		+	0	+	–	–
D		+	–	+	0	–
E		+	+	+	+	0
F		+	+	+	+	+
	Complex	Inter-local	Sedentary	Pro-duction	Exchange	Industrial

SOURCE: Duncan (1964:54).

NOTES: – = absence of complex variable, presence of simple variable.
  + = absence of simple variable, presence of complex variable.
  0 = mixed types; both are found in same society *or* different societies of same level have one or the other with no apparent predominance of one of the two variables.

If the Guttman scale is composed of dichotomous responses, at least ten items must be used in the final scale version. Second, scale errors must be random since nonrandom errors are a sign of more than one dimension operating. In fact, most psychological and social psychological theories assume to the contrary that persons normally do *not* respond unidimensionally. Thus, many researchers no longer recommend this method for attitude research.

Forced-Choice Method

An interesting and somewhat new technique requires the participant to choose between several attitudinal statements. Heinemann (1953) used forced-choice formats in which the participant is asked to choose between several equally repulsive statements as to which is most true of him- or herself. Christie and Geis (1970:19) note that many participants understandably object to this procedure, as typified by one who wrote in the scale margin: "This is like asking me whether I would rather rape my mother or take an ax to my father." Steward (1945) has used a more sophisticated variation of this approach. She presented groups of forced-choice items with instructions to choose the one most characteristic and the one least characteristic of the participant. One item was *keyed* to the particular scale of interest. A second item unrelated to the scale of interest was *matched* to the first item in rated social desirability. The third item, the *buffer*, was high in social desirability compared to the other two items. This procedure has several virtues. First, since there is always at least one highly desirable item to choose, participants have little difficulty choosing. Second, the technique makes it difficult for most participants to determine the "socially desirable" answer between the *keyed buffer* scale and *matched* social desirability items. One of Christie and Geis's (1970) Machiavellian Triads in Mach V is

> 12. A. A person shouldn't be punished for breaking a law that he [or she] thinks is unreasonable. (high desirability reversed)
>   B. Too many criminals are not punished for their crimes. (matched social desirability item)
>   C. There is no excuse for lying to someone else. (reversed keyed Mach. [short for Machiavellian] item)

Various methodological administrations of the Mach V scale (Christie and Geis 1970:25) have indicated that when even advanced sociology methods students are given the principle underlying the scoring method and are told that the test is designed to measure Machiavellianism, they cannot identify the keyed items. Thus, unlike Likert type scales (Mach IV), the forced-choice scale appears to reduce social desirability biases significantly.

The scoring of a forced-choice questionnaire is, however, somewhat more complicated than the previously mentioned scales. One scores according to the response pattern for each item before summing across items. In the Mach V triad shown above, 1 point (low Mach) is given for a "most like me (+)" response to 12.C *and* a "most unlike me (–)" response to 12.B; 3 points for either the A+, C– or the B+, A– combinations; and 7 points (high Mach) for the B+, C– combination. This procedure is based on the following rationale (Christie and Geis 1970:30):

> Mach V was developed with two considerations in mind: (a) to have the possible range and theoretical neutral point equivalent to Mach IV, and (b) to take full advantage of the fact that it is probably more Machiavellian to say the Mach item is most like and the matched item least like oneself—a two-step difference—than to say the Mach item is most like and omit the matched item or omit the Mach item and say the matched item is least like oneself—a one-step difference.

It is also important that matched items of this sort be randomized as to order so that participants may not pick up a particular built-in order by which to respond. With the increasing sophistication of participants taking attitudes scales, this type of item will probably come into more usefulness in order to make it more difficult to cheat on attitude scales.

Campbell Bipolar Formats

Donald Campbell has been experimenting at Northwestern University with what he calls bipolar scale formats. The method is sort of a cross between Likert and forced-choice formats. The participant is given sets of two items that are at opposite ends of a continuum (hence, bipolar). The items, however, are scored in Likert style, as shown in Table 11–7. Thus, if it is asterisked, "A" is scored as a "5," "a" as "4," "?" as "3," "b" as "2," and "B" as "1"; this procedure is reversed for items where "B" is asterisked. (Asterisks are not used on actually administered forms.)

The advantages of this method are seen mainly in controls for acquiescence response sets and in a clear definition of the attitude continuum for respondents. Campbell's unpublished works indicate that there is not much manifest difference in Likert and bipolar attitudinal assessments. He feels that attention should be placed on making better scales at the outset rather than on scale format (Campbell 1968:6). Nevertheless, the bipolar scale would appear, by contrast to the forced-choice

Table 11–7
A Bipolar Scale Format Illustration

Various Social Attitude Scales

This is a survey of attitudes and opinions on a variety of topics.

Each item consists of two alternatives, A and B, between which you are asked to choose by circling one of these indicators:

> A = Statement A is entirely preferred to Statement B as an expression of my opinion.
>
> a = Statement A is somewhat preferred over Statement B.
>
> ? = I cannot choose between A and B.
>
> b = Statement B is somewhat preferred to Statement A.
>
> B = Statement B is entirely preferred to Statement A as an expression of my opinion.

Please show your attitude leanings on each item, even though you do not feel strongly on the topic or do not feel well informed. Please choose between alternatives, even though both may seem acceptable to you, or both unacceptable.

Items in the Assessment of Self (*indicates high self-assessment)

A a ? b B 1.   A. My progress toward the goals of success I set for myself has been disappointing.

               *B. I feel that I have made significant progress toward the goals of success I set for myself.

A a ? b B 2. *A. The conception I now have of myself is more complimentary than the conception I have had in the past.

               B. I now have a less complimentary conception of myself than I have had in the past.

A a ? b B 3.   A. In determining how others feel about me, I am not confident in my ability to do so.

               *B. I am confident of my ability to ascertain how others feel about me.

---

triads, to be more easily influenced by social desirability response sets, even though the forced-choice method is admittedly much more difficult to score.

Semantic Differential and Related Techniques

The semantic differential is one of the most adaptable yet, ironically, underutilized scaling methods in behavioral science. In every scaling method so far discussed, a completely new scale must be developed to measure each attitude object. By contrast, the semantic differential, with minor variations, is adaptable to *any* attitude object. The semantic differential (SD) measures participant's responses to stimulus words, concepts, or phrases in terms of bipolar adjective ratings. An example is shown in the accompanying table. Generally speaking, instructions are given that label "0's" as neutral, "1's" as "slightly," "2's" as "moderately," and "3's" as "extremely."

A Communist is:							
good	__;	__;	__;	__;	__;	__;	__;	bad
powerful	__;	__;	__;	__;	__;	__;	__;	powerless
fast	__;	__;	__;	__;	__;	__;	__;	slow
	3	2	1	0	1	2	3	

An impressive variety of studies in a wide sample of cultures has suggested that there are three major dimensions underlying a person's judgments: *Evaluations:* (such as good-bad); *Potency* (powerful-powerless); and *Activity* (fast-slow) (EPA). With a relatively short list of nine to twelve such bipolar adjective scales it is possible to measure the affect experienced by a participant towards any object. Heise (1969) has cogently argued that attitudinal measuring has traditionally been treated too simply (unidimensionally), and that we should be measuring attitudinal affect multidimensionally through techniques such as the SD.

We noted that the SD is an extremely general instrument. EPA ratings have been obtained for thousands of word concepts, for social roles, colors, art works, self-concept, and other diverse stimuli. Furthermore, although the SD is a very general instrument, it has been used quite specifically. Komorita and Bass (1967) used sixteen EPA scales to evaluate the statements "America's foreign policy in Vietnam" and "Draft deferments for married men." They uncovered subtleties such as the fact that many participants who thought of the Vietnam policy as wise, valuable, or beneficial also thought of it as unpleasant, insincere, and dishonest—a more complex attitudinal structure, indeed, than that measured by previously mentioned methods.

Triandis (1964) has developed a behavioral differential (BD), based on the SD concept, to measure behavior intentions of participants towards particular persons or categories of persons. Participants may be asked to evaluate their behavior towards a black ghetto dweller who is a communist (see the accompanying table). The BD can be changed into a normative differential by asking not what one *would* do, but rather what one *should* do or into a role differential (Triandis 1964) where the stimuli are father-son, laborer-foreman, or mother-daughter.

| would | —; | —; | —; | —; | —; | —; | —; | would not |

admire the ideas of the person

| would not | —; | —; | —; | —; | —; | —; | —; | would |

eat with this person

| would | —; | —; | —; | —; | —; | —; | —; | would not |

obey this person

As a final example S. L. Becker in unpublished research has recently tapped respondents feelings toward characteristics of new apartment descriptions as noted in the accompanying table.

				Not Related			
The *sound* at my	free	—;	—;	—;	—;	—;	constrained
new apartment	colorful	—;	—;	—;	—;	—;	plain
should make	good	—;	—;	—;	—;	—;	bad
me feel:	excited	—;	—;	—;	—;	—;	calm
	successful	—;	—;	—;	—;	—;	unsuccessful
	impressive	—;	—;	—;	—;	—;	not impressive
	cheerful	—;	—;	—;	—;	—;	lonely
	wise	—;	—;	—;	—;	—;	foolish
	little	—;	—;	—;	—;	—;	big

The SD has been found to have good predictive validity. Heise (1970) has summarized the positive methodological features of the SD: It is a generalized method, is economical, and has instant readiness for use, cross-cultural comparability, standard metrics, and multidimensionality. Further, the SD has been found to correlate highly with other more traditional attitude scaling techniques.

However, social desirability biases are particularly possible in evaluative dimensions ratings. With especially sensitive topics and respondents it would be well to give special assurance of anonymity of responses. Second, many groups of people, particularly those from lower-class backgrounds, do not feel comfortable with the technique and refuse to participate in its administration (Ballweg 1972). Third, Osgood and his associates (1957) have emphasized that there is significant interaction (nonadditive effects) between the stimulus and participants that should be corrected for by using the techniques they outline. Fourth, the number of issues or objects evaluated must be quite small (less than thirty) when a large number of bipolar scales (more than eight) are used because the tediously large number of responses called for tends to create response biases.

Sociometric and Other Interpersonal Perception Measures

Sociometry is the study and measurement of interpersonal patterns of social choice, communication, and interaction. There are numerous possibilities for measuring sociometric choices. At the simplest level the researcher might ask

1. Which member of this group do you like the least (the most)?
2. Whom would you choose to represent you on a student grievance committee?
3. Whom would you like to sit next to (work with, play with)?

At the other extreme are sociometric questions that *rank order* individuals, choices of minority groups, communication lines, or lines of influence by *degree.* For instance,

1. Rank order each member of your college dorm in terms of preference for a roommate.
2. Indicate your degree of liking for each person in your office from 0 percent (most unliked) to 100 percent (best liked).
3. Indicate the degree, from most influence (100 percent) to least influence (0 percent), each member of your fraternity has.
4. Rank order your preference for friendships from members of the following minority groups, assuming all other factors are equal.

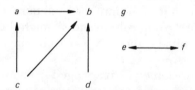

The earliest work with sociometric data dates from the 1930s when J. L. Moreno and his associates used *sociograms* (now often called "directed graphs") to analyze group structure. In the accompanying directed graph there are seven persons (*a* to *g*) connected (or unconnected) by lines of influence, friendship, or whatever. Assuming these lines show dominance, we could say that *a* dominates *b* who is also dominated by *c* and *d.* Members *e* and *f* apparently have reciprocal domination, *g* is isolated from the power structure, and *c* dominates both *a* and *b.* Further, *c* appears to have the most domination and *b* appears to be most dominated.

However, sociograms, while visual aids in sociometric analysis, are virtually impossible to digest when the group analyzed has more than five to twelve members, depending on the complexity of the relational structure being analyzed. Hence, *sociometric* matrices are often used in their place. For the above sociogram, the accompanying matrix could be used (where 1 represents "*i* dominates *j*" and 0 represents "lack of domination of *i* by *j*").

$$
\begin{array}{c}
\\
i
\end{array}
\begin{array}{c}
\\
\begin{array}{c}
a \\ b \\ c \\ d \\ e \\ f \\ g
\end{array}
\end{array}
\begin{array}{ccccccc}
 & & & j & & & \\
a & b & c & d & e & f & g \\
0 & 1 & 0 & 0 & 0 & 0 & 0 \\
0 & 0 & 0 & 0 & 0 & 0 & 0 \\
1 & 1 & 0 & 0 & 0 & 0 & 0 \\
0 & 1 & 0 & 0 & 0 & 0 & 0 \\
0 & 0 & 0 & 0 & 0 & 1 & 0 \\
0 & 0 & 0 & 0 & 1 & 0 & 0 \\
0 & 0 & 0 & 0 & 0 & 0 & 0
\end{array}
$$

Such matrices are easy to read. By reading from left to right for row *f,* for instance, we can see that *f* dominates only *e.* Who chooses whom is analyzed in terms of: (1) one-way choices, (2) mutual choices, and (3) no choice. (Those wanting more complex methods of sociometric matrix analysis might well look at Kemeny, Snell, and Thompson's *Introduction to Finite Mathematics* [1966:217–250, 384–406] for matrix algebra operations that can be used for more sophisticated analyses.)

Summary sociometric indices are often used by behavioral scientists. Moreno (1934) used a ratio of attraction based on dividing the total number of choices and rejections into the total number of choices. Similarly, a useful index of "group cohesiveness" might be made by dividing the total number of mutual choices ($\Sigma\ [i \leftrightarrow j]$) by the number of possible pairs ($n[n - 1]/2$).

Applications of sociometry have ranged from Moreno's (1934) use of the technique's information to restructure groups to more research-oriented studies of ethnic and religious prejudices. While sociometric data have been shown to have high reliability (Mouton, Blake, and Fruchter 1955), their validity can be influenced by lack of respondent privacy and particularistic or situational applicability. For instance, attraction characteristics for dorm roommates may differ from attraction towards work mates.

Sociometry techniques, while useful, basically measure only *perceptions* of attraction and repulsion. Many studies that assess interpersonal perception, by contrast, are interested in assessing *accuracy* of perception. Normally accuracy of perception is assessed in terms of characteristics of the person (or group) being judged, characteristics of the perceiver, and the situational context in which the judgment is made. A classic research example is Allport and Kramer's (1946) study of the relationship between anti-Semitic prejudice and accuracy of identifying Jewish persons from facial photographs. They found prejudiced persons were more accurate than nonprejudiced persons in such assessments. Summers (1970) has a detailed discussion of the methodological problems and procedures in measures of interpersonal perception, which are too vast to detail here.

Direct Observational Indexes

Several of the scaling models discussed have proven useful in attitudinal, behavioral, and social structural research. In this section we mention only a few illustrations of indexes based on direct observation since Chapter 5 gave attention to this issue.

Gage and Shimberg (1949) constructed a measure of Senatorial "Progressivism" by sampling from legislative acts and correlating legislator votes according to the *New Republic*'s designated "progressive" or "antiprogressive" labels. They tested the *New Republic*'s labeling of the bills as a unidimensional Guttman type scale and found that to be the case. Then they assigned each legislator's voting behavior a "progressivism" score. Finally, they correlated "progressivism" with various statuses (age, junior-senior senator, region of country, party affiliation).

Campbell, Kruskal, and Wallace (1966) have pointed out that social science is overdependent upon voluntary verbal self-descriptions. They developed an index of seating aggregation in order to test behavioral aspects of racial attitudes. While too complicated to present here, the index takes into account seating expectations *if random* and compares this to *observed* seating frequencies. On a more macroscopic scale, segregation indexes have been developed by Taeuber and Taeuber (1965) for the study of metropolitan racial segregation.

As another example, Phillips and Conviser (1972) have recently been concerned with quantifying group interdependence and group boundaries. Once again, in past studies, measurement was intuitive rather than quantitative (Homans 1950). Their rationale was to assume that if the parts (roles, individuals) of a system are mutually dependent, then the behavior of each part should be predictable in some degree from the behavior of the others. Parenthetically, Phillips and Conviser (1972:236) note Merton's definition of an *un*organized, anomic situation as one in which people cannot predict the behavior of others. Hence, they discuss a noninterval, information theory statistic of interdependence A_L which measures the improvement in one's ability to predict the behavior of a dependent variable given knowledge of the independent variable. This statistic is also shown to specify the sharpness of group boundaries and the cost in predictability of mislocating group boundaries by statistical decision. One interesting practical problem they propose is the use of the A_L statistic in political sociology such as in measuring the sharpness of group boundaries between Democrat and Republican members of Congress over time.

Most of the scales and indexes discussed up to this section have assumed that participants have self-awareness and a readiness to communicate this self-awareness verbally. However, even if persons can and do communicate their true affective and cognitive states to the researcher, this in no way assumes that those affective or cognitive states correspond to these persons' behavioral or environmental context. Because people perceive their group as cohesive does not insure its cohesiveness. More direct measures of the above sorts are coming into use as alternative indicators of whatever variable is in question.

Also, oftentimes the researcher may wish to short-cut the participant's verbal communications. Galvanic skin responses, pupil dilations, eye-blink rates, heartbeat rates, and so on have increasingly been used to measure various interpersonal responses. Lowenfield (1958) and Woodmansee and Cook (1967) report, however, that physiological measures at the present time can only represent affective *intensity*. In addition, many of these techniques are presently cumbersome to administer.

Most of the measures discussed in this section, unlike most measuring strategies discussed earlier in the chapter, have used single indexes rather than scales. There is no reason, however, why researchers could not sum (as in Likert scaling), cumulate (as in Guttman scaling), or average (as in Thurstone scaling) a number of indexes into a direct observational scale. Consider the following indicators of college formal authority structure:

1. Ratio of administrators to teachers
2. Percentage of junior-level faculty
3. Number of faculty-administration meetings on civil liberties
4. Official strictures on leisure, dress
5. Amount of faculty/student contact
6. Student/faculty ratio
7. Amount of student participation in administration.

We could easily combine these indexes into a single scale by standardizing each index as in Thurstone scaling and then either averaging or summing the indexes. The advantages of this procedure should be intuitively obvious: None of the indexes completely represents the domain of "college formal authority structure," while the total set more accurately represents that domain. Frisbie (1975) creatively operationalized the four dimensions of bureaucracy—hierarchical authority, structured communications, division of labor, and a requirement of thorough and expert training—through a multidimensional construct of measures such as (1) the ratio of administrative, executive, and managerial workers to the total labor force, (2) the ratio of clerical personnel to the total labor force, and (3) the proportion of students at the third organizational level per 100,000 workers.

Indirect Scale Measurements

In many situations the researcher has excellent reason to assume either participant self-awareness, readiness to communicate verbally, or direct method transparency. In other words, if participants are aware of being studied or of what the researcher is studying they may attempt to give a good impression, please the experimenter, and so forth. Thus, some procedures provide disguised appraisals. Various projective tests (Rorschach, Thematic Apperception Test, Blacky Pictures) have been used to measure racial prejudice, authoritarianism, and achievement orientations. Less disguised projective techniques have included sentence completion tests where relevant and neutral items are interspersed (Rotter and Williams 1947).

1. I feel . . .
2. Skin color . . .
3. I hate . . .
4. Maybe . . .
5. Some lynchings . . .
6. Racial intermarriage. . . .

Hammond (cited in Kidder and Campbell 1970:384) attempted to measure attitudes through biased guesses on an "information" test. There were two alternative answers, each wrong by intent but in opposite directions from the correct answer.

Kidder and Campbell (1970) present the most complete discussion of indirect testing of social attitudes. They point out that the measurement of the reliability and validity of most indirect tests are discouragingly low when compared to more direct measures. Campbell has drawn an interesting analogy between individual thresholds in learning and the taking of attitude tests. Campbell (1963:103–104) has shown that tests have progressively lower learning thresholds as follows:

Recall
Recognition
Savings in relearning.

Thus, he hypothesizes that a hierarchy of attitude tests might be

1. Autonomic response—eye-blink rates.
2. Verbal report on perceived character of the stimulus—"The average I.Q. of [blacks] is lower than that of whites."
3. Verbal reports on own response tendency—"I would not let a *black* move onto my block."
4. Overt locomotor response—refusing to serve *black* patrons.

According to this premise, it would be meaningless to say that one test has higher "validity" than another if they come from different levels of this hierarchy since scales with similar thresholds would be expected to correlate more highly than scales from different hierarchies (Kidder and Campbell 1970:371). Kidder and Campbell also discuss the two practical disadvantages of indirect tests. First, indirect tests may be regarded as an invasion of privacy. Again, ethically, it is not enough to say science is neutral since its potential use (or misuse) is certainly not value-free. Second, indirect testing often shows a "deceptive-deprecatory-exploitive" attitude toward participants. Chronic dishonesty of this type has contributed to a general loss of interpersonal trust in research participant relationships (Kidder and Campbell 1970:334).

THE LOGIC OF MULTIDIMENSIONAL APPROACHES

While it is beyond the scope of this book to present details of the many multidimensional approaches that now abound in the social and behavioral sciences, the logic of these approaches will be intuitively presented here. To this point we have been concerned basically with unidimensional measurements. In contrast, much effort has been expended in recent years on the development of techniques for measuring multidimensional social and behavioral structures. Perhaps the simplest way to explain this is to imagine we are interested in mapping out various dimensions of personality and social structure just as a cartographer maps out terrain in terms of dimensions like height, length, and width.

Schneider (reported in Perry 1977) has been using the computer at the University of Michigan in completely innovative ways to make a simple *visual* map of voting behavior, and some social scientists believe it to be the biggest breakthrough in political analysis in years. One of the problems with multidimensional scaling is that there is so much data it becomes incomprehensible; in his quest for simplicity, Schneider took the following approach: First, he knew that earlier in a campaign voters tend to have extremely little specific information about the candidates. Hence, he depended on several sets of questions that are known to be important indicators of voting behavior. Taking voter response to questions that tend to align people on the conservative-liberal dimension (the vertical dimension in Figure 11–1), he measured voter conservatism-liberalism on various social issues such as amnesty, abortion, marijuana, and national defense. These measurements were combined into one single scale score visually graphed in Figure 11–1 with more traditional or conservative at the higher end of the graphs, and more liberal at the lower end.

The next set of questions measured a second dimension: party loyalty or preference. By asking questions on party preference and economic issues that provide traditional separating points for Democrats or Republicans, Schneider was able to scale and map party loyalty on the horizontal axes in Figure 11–1.

Each individual voter in a random sample of 1,500 persons interviewed on June 9, 1976, was mapped on these two dimensions. Distances between pairs of voters are relative to the distances between the other pairs of voters in terms of their conservatism-liberalism and party alignment positions.

Another set of questions measured voter *perceptions* of the candidates in terms of conservatism-liberalism and party loyalty. The average voter perceptions of the candidates were then overlaid on top of the voter's positions in Figure 11–1a. Look at then-President Ford's position.

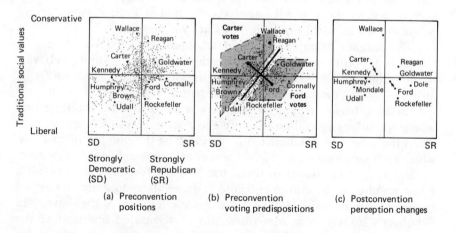

FIGURE 11–1 *Multidimensional mapping of the 1976 presidential campaign voting predispositions.*

He is perceived to be to the right of the vertical line on the horizontal scale where Republicans are perceived to be. But he is way down the vertical scale. Hence, people perceived Ford to be liberal or untraditional on social values. This map showed that Ford could not win at that point in the campaign (preconvention).

Figure 11–1b shows the reasons why the Ford campaign was in trouble. Notice that Schneider ran a line between Carter and Ford and bisected it. The dots close to Carter represent voters predisposed to vote for him, and the dots close to Ford represent his predisposed votes. Notice how few dots were close to Ford. To help the Ford campaign it would have been necessary to (1) run Ford as a Democrat (obviously impossible), (2) change Ford's public image, or (3) change Carter's image. The Ford media team attempted to change Carter's image by touching on vulnerable issues (Carter's record as governor of Georgia, his inexperience in world affairs, his fuzziness on some issues, his postconvention amnesty stand). They also attempted to alter and improve Ford's image through portraying him as a solid, traditional, intelligent American.

Figure 11–1c shows a third map based on interviews conducted on September 9, 1976. This map portrays considerable movement on the parts of both candidates towards the center. Notice that they are farthest apart on the partisan (horizontal) line (as are the two vice-presidential candidates, Mondale and Dole). Also, you can see that Carter's name is surrounded by more predisposed voters than is Ford's name, giving Schneider a successful prediction of Carter's election.

As another example, Schubert analyzed the 1960 U.S. Supreme Court term "on the premise that a justice reacts in his voting behavior to the stimuli presented by cases before the Court, in accordance with his attitudes toward the issues raised for decision" (1962:107). The attitudinal distance between pairs of judges was calculated by counting one whenever judges agreed on the vote and zero in cases of disagreement. Then the total was standardized by dividing by the number of cases on which each judge gave a decision. Factor analysis, a sophisticated, mathematical multidimensional method, which takes correlations between a given number of measurements and reduces them to a smaller set of relatively unidimensional theoretical components, was then used. In Schubert's study two factors (dimensions) accounted for most of the Court decisions: first, civil liberties attitudes; second, economic attitudes on conflicts of interest between private individuals and government (see Figure 11–2).

There are a multitude of multivariate methods that the researcher interested in scaling has at his or her disposal; there are factor analysis, discriminant function analysis, latent structure analysis, Guttman-Lingoes Smallest Space Analysis, and so forth. Students with some math-

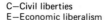

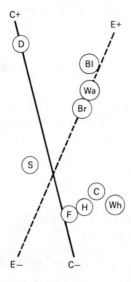

C—Civil liberties
E—Economic liberalism

C+

E+

D

Bl

Wa

Br

S

C

H

Wh

F

E—

C—

Code: Bl Black   D Douglas   S   Stewart
       Br Brennan   F Frankfurter Wa Warren
       C   Clark   H Harlan   Wh Whittaker

FIGURE 11–2 *Map of Supreme Court justices from joint decisions.*

Source: Schubert (1962).

ematical competence may wish to read Cooley and Lohnes's *Multivariate Data Analysis* (1971) or Shephard and his associates' *Multidimensional Scaling* (1972) for an introduction to many of these multivariate methods. While these methods are far from perfected, computer programs are continually being developed that make these complex computational methods accessible to the researcher.

SUMMARY

As summary of the characteristics any attitude measurement should embody, Scott (1968:251) has stated the following characteristics that are herein adapted to the more general case of *any* measurement:

1. The intended property would be reflected with high validity.
2. Irrelevant characteristics of the subject, unit, or measuring situation would not affect the measurement.
3. The property being measured would not be modified in the course of measurement.

4. It would make sufficiently fine distinctions among units to represent grada-
   tions along the dimension(s) as conceived.
5. It would yield results substantially equivalent to those produced by another
   adequate instrument measuring the same property.
6. It would yield equivalent scores on a later retest (assuming the property has
   remained constant).
7. It would be relatively easy to construct, administer, score, and interpret.

With the exceptions of points 5 and 6, these characteristics have been
discussed in some detail for each of the measuring strategies considered.
Points 5 and 6 deal with reliability and will be discussed more generally
in Chapter 12 in terms of test-retest, multiple forms, and split-half techniques of assessing reliability.

READINGS FOR ADVANCED STUDENTS

PAUL LAZARSFELD, ANN PASANELLA, AND MORRIS ROSENBERG (eds.), *Continuities in the Language
   of Social Research,* 1972. Updated version of the classic text of readings on index
   construction.
JOHN P. ROBINSON AND PHILIP R. SHAVER, *Measures of Social Psychological Attitudes,* rev. ed.,
   1973. Over 100 attitude scales are presented with information on their reliability and
   validity.
KARL SCHUESSLER, *Analyzing Social Data,* 1973, Ch. 7. Shows how to use statistics in the
   measurement of attitudes.
ROGER N. SHEPARD, A. KIMBALL ROMNEY, AND SARA B. NERLOVE (eds.), *Multidimensional
   Scaling: Theory and Applications in the Behavioral Sciences,* 1972. In-depth readings on
   methods and assumptions of multidimensional scaling.
GENE F. SUMMERS, *Attitude Measurement,* 1970. Balanced overview of most issues discussed
   in the present chapter.

SUGGESTED RESEARCH PROJECTS

1. The following statements have been selected from various sources. Evaluate each statement in terms of the informal criteria that have been suggested for writing attitude statements.
   Attitudes towards population growth (Barnett 1969)

   a. America does not have to worry about having too large a population
      because science will always find ways to accommodate more people
      easily and comfortably.

   b. Unless America adds to her population, she will be in danger of being
      overpowered by overpopulated and aggressive countries like Red China.

   c. America is rapidly reaching a point where there will be too many people,
      and this coming overpopulation is one of the greatest threats today to
      the future social and economic well-being of the country.

Attitudes towards personal competence (Campbell and others 1960)

a. I have always felt pretty sure my life would work out the way I wanted it to.

b. I never have any trouble making up my mind about important decisions.

c. I have always felt that I have more willpower than most people have.

Attitudes towards self-acceptance (Berger 1952)

a. I can become so absorbed in the work I'm doing that it doesn't bother me not to have any intimate friends.

b. When people say nice things about me, I find it difficult to believe they really mean it. I think maybe they're kidding me or just aren't being sincere.

c. If there is any criticism or anyone says anything about me, I just can't take it.

d. I don't say much at social affairs because I'm afraid that people will criticize me or laugh if I say the wrong thing.

e. I look on most of the feelings and impulses I have toward people as being quite natural and acceptable.

Attitudes towards self-esteem (Coopersmith 1967)

a. I never get scolded.

b. I always do the right thing.

c. I'm never unhappy.

d. Someone always has to tell me what to do.

e. Kids pick on me very often.

Attitudes towards alienation (Middleton 1963)

a. I am not interested in the T.V. programs, movies, or magazines that most people seem to like.

b. I don't really enjoy most of the work that I do, but I feel that I must do it in order to have other things that I need and want.

Attitudes towards teacher evaluation

a. He is sensitive to the response of the class, encourages student participation; welcomes questions and discussion.

b. He is available, helpful, and easily approached by individual students.

c. He appears to enjoy teaching, is enthusiastic about his subject, and makes the course interesting.

2. Evaluate each of the following statements in terms of the informal criteria suggested for writing attitude statements.

Object	*Statements*
a. Alienation	No longer can a young man build his character and hopes on solid ground; civilization is crumbling, the future is dreadfully uncertain, and life hangs by a thread.

b. Authoritarianism	Novels or stories that tell about what people think and feel are more interesting than those that contain mainly action, romance, and adventure.
c. Self-concept	Other people always seem to get the breaks.
d. Self-concept	I am no one. Nothing seems to be me.
e. Ego-strength	I have never had a fainting spell.
f. Ego-strength	I get mad easily and then get over it soon.
g. Political alienation	These days the government is trying to do too many things, including some activities that I don't think it has the right to do.
h. Alienation	We are just so many cogs in the machinery of life.
i. Political alienation	Corning Glass and Ingersole-Rand run the show in this area.

3. a. Design a Likert-type or bipolar-type attitude scale of at least 10 attitudinal statements centering on some common domain (such as prejudice).

   b. Administer these scales to *at least* ten college student friends.

   c. Score each individual's scale by hand, or computer (if available).

   d. Measure the scale's split-half reliability.

   e. Hand in all stages of research with a short paper explaining *to what* working universe, *how*, and *when* you would administer this questionnaire. If any statements are "reversed," note which ones. Define the domain you claim to be tapping.

4. Using Edwards's fourteen criteria for forming attitude statements, make up items that reflect *poorly* designed items. Refer specifically, in parentheses, to what is wrong with each item.

5. Assume the federal government wishes to assess "quality of life" changes in two areas: equality of the sexes and racial discrimination. Rather than use attitudinal measures, they wish to use direct observational indexes such as (a) legal equality, (b) voting and office holding, (c) access to education, (d) access to unemployment, and (e) occupational access and promotion. Discuss ways to operationalize and standardize these indexes. Argue the merits of treating each index as such rather than combining them in some fashion into a single scale. What would be a good means of making a single scale out of these indexes? Why?

6. In the following Guttman scale, find the coefficient of reproducibility

$$
\begin{array}{cccccc}
+ & - & - & - & - & - \\
+ & - & + & - & - & - \\
+ & + & - & - & - & - \\
+ & + & + & + & - & - \\
- & + & + & + & + & + \\
+ & + & + & + & + & + \\
\end{array}
$$

(answer: 0.86)

12

Reliability, Validity, and Operationalization

When a scientist doesn't know the answer to a problem, he is ignorant. When he has a hunch as to what the result is, he is uncertain. And when he is pretty darn sure of what the result is going to be, he is in some doubt. [1]

As far as the laws of mathematics refer to reality they are not certain, and as far as they are not certain, they do not refer to reality. [2]

In its formative years social and behavioral analysis was primarily based on the use of relatively unsystematic data collection methods. Increasingly, social and behavioral analysis has depended on more and more systematic data-collection procedures. In large part this is because certain types of systematic data-collection procedures lead toward higher quality data. And, obviously, the higher the quality of the data, the more confidence the researcher has in those data. Through virtually every chapter

---

[1]Attributed to Lee A. DuBridge.
[2]Attributed to Einstein.

to this point we have been concerned with the quality of our data. Occasionally we have discussed this quality in terms of reliability and validity. This chapter expands on these important principles.

First, science requires *reliable* data. Second, it demands *valid* data. Finally, science demands means or *operations* by which its data may be shown to correspond to whatever it is that those data are meant to represent. Hence, scientists constantly ask themselves: How can we make what we wish to measure more researchable? How reliable is that operation? How valid is that operation? Each question must be dealt with satisfactorily before the scientific community can willingly accept the researcher's work. In this chapter we will consider each of these three criteria in turn.

ON RELIABILITY

The social and behavioral sciences have come to be increasingly concerned with the *reliability* of their methods. Researchers have become increasingly concerned with the question: *Will the same methods used by different researchers and/or at different times produce the same results?* In other words, reliability refers to *consistency* between independent measurements of the same phenomenon. A minimal requirement for any science is that it yield consistent measurements confirmable by independent observers —that it be independently replicable.

Take the case of many participant observation studies. In his study of an organization he once worked for, Melville Dalton (1964) is quite blunt about his inability to specify the particular methods or theoretical assumptions he used. Hence, if some other sociologist were to have independently studied the same organization it is doubtful whether the two studies would have yielded similar results. Another good example of this problem was presented in a replication of Robert Redfield's (1930) classic study of an isolated rural Mexican village by Oscar Lewis (1951). While Redfield found virtually no indication of interpersonal conflict within Tepoztlan, Lewis found the village to be conflict-ridden. There is good reason to believe that the village had not significantly changed in the two decades or so between studies. Rather, the difference in findings probably was due much more to (1) poor reliability of the relatively unsystematic participant observation methods used in conjunction with (2) the different focuses of concern of each researcher. Redfield seemed to be more concerned with describing *ideal* cultural life; Lewis was more concerned with *actual* village interaction and organization. Examples of such conflicting findings in participant observation research are not rare, as pointed out by Pelto (1970:50–53).

It is rare for researchers to obtain perfect reliability between independent measurements; lack of consistency in measurement is a very real problem that the researcher must take into account. At one extreme are simple, highly reliable measurements taken by trained observers of who-speaks-to-whom (Bales 1970) in small groups. In such cases it is possible to get several trained observers to agree up to 97 out of every 100 cases as to who spoke to whom. At the other extreme are measurements of community conflict, such as in the Redfield-Lewis debate mentioned earlier in which reliability was extremely low. Indeed, measurement reliability of a single datum may be complicated by a whole slew of variables. Mouton, Blake, and Fruchter (1955) showed that the reliability of sociometric (friendship) choices differed by age of group members, stability of the group, and intensity of the choice.

Generically, there are four ways to test measurement reliability: test-retest, multiple forms, split-half, and average intercorrelation techniques. In *test-retest reliability*, we take two measurements on the same population with the same instrument used at different times. The higher the agreement between these measurements, the higher the reliability is judged to be. Unfortunately, the first application of the instrument may affect responses on the second administration. This is particularly likely the closer the application of each measurement. Thus, the shorter the period between test and retest, the more chance participants may wish to appear consistent and their memory may cause spuriously high reliability. On the other hand, the longer the test-retest period, the more chance the reliability rate will be spuriously low due to *actual* change in the phenomenon. For this reason, test-retest procedures are said to measure reliability in terms of *stability* of findings.

Second, *multiple (alternate) forms* of the same measuring device may be administered to the same sample. A researcher interested in "group cohesion" might use two measures: first, a measure of the individual's attraction to a group; second, a measure of prestige gains from group membership. Again, a high association between measures is a criteria for high reliability. Multiple-forms measures of reliability are said to provide a measure of equivalence of the forms. Hence, low associations between alternative forms might be due to the forms simply not being equivalent rather than to low reliability.

Third, in the *split-half technique* the measurement (where possible) is randomly split in half. Assume we wish to measure the reliability of a forty-statement attitude scale. We could form two separate scales of twenty items each by random assignment of items to each scale. Each half would be treated as an alternate form of the same scale. The easiest means of finding split-half reliability involves the use of basic statistics. (Any basic statistics book will give the student the formula for computing variances.) It requires the researcher to find the variance of the *difference* between measurements of the two half-tests ($\sigma^2 d$) and the variance of *total* (unsplit) scores ($\sigma^2 x$). Then, the split-half formula (r_{tt}) reads:

$$r_{tt} = 1 - \frac{\sigma^2 d}{\sigma^2 x}$$

Finally, the researcher may correlate (associate) each item in a scale against every other item and obtain the *average* intercorrelation for the entire set of correlations or associations. This procedure provides the most stable index of reliability but requires a great deal of computation with large numbers of scale items. However, Cronbach (1951) has provided an efficient estimate of this average intercorrelation, *coefficient alpha,* which avoids much of the computation drudgery involved in the intercorrelation average. Obviously, it makes sense that items should be highly associated, for if they were not, there would be no grounds for combining them into an overall score. Items with low or negative associations, by contrast, are logical candidates for exclusion from the scale.

One particularly important influence on reliability is scale length. (A scale is *two or more* indicators of the phenomenon being studied *combined* in some fashion to produce a single measure. Socioeconomic status often is formed by combining education, income, and occupation into a single measure.) Longer scales give higher reliability, as evidenced by Figure 12–1 (p. 332) where pxx' stands for the *average* reliability coefficient for an item initially before other scores were added to it to form a scale; $px_n x_n'$ stands for the reliability coefficient for the scale formed from those items; x stands for the first measurement; x' for the second measurement; and n for the number of scale items.

This figure makes several important points visible concerning the relationship of reliability to number of scale items. First, it becomes apparent that the more items (n) added to the scale, the higher the reliability *(pxx')*. Second, the first several items added contribute more heavily to reliability than items added later. Thus, after a point (eight to ten items) any additionally added scale items will contribute almost insignificantly to raising the reliability. The researcher can usually obtain fairly reliable measures with scales of only eight to ten items.

Why does this relationship between scale length and reliability hold in general? *Any* measurement has idosyncratic sources of error. The use of income as a measure of socioeconomic status (SES) has idiosyncratic problems such as including $100,000 salaried Mafia members in the upper class. With every item added to the scale, item-specific errors may be expected to decrease since item-specific errors can normally be expected to cancel each other out. Each measure can be expected to tap factors irrelevant to whatever the researcher is measuring, but since these

BOX 12-1 Finding Split Half Reliability

Assume we have four respondents who took a ten-statement attitude scale and their answers were (1 = strongly agree to 5 = strongly disagree):

Respondent 1: 4, 3, 1, 3, 5, 5, 5, 1, 3, 2
Respondent 2: 1, 4, 3, 2, 1, 5, 5, 3, 2, 5
Respondent 3: 4, 2, 4, 2, 4, 1, 2, 3, 2, 4
Respondent 4: 3, 5, 4, 2, 4, 5, 3, 3, 4, 3

Step 1: Sum the first half and last half of each respondent's items.

Respondent 1	*Respondent 2*	*Respondent 3*	*Respondent 4*
4	1	4	3
3	4	2	5
1	3	4	4
3	2	2	2
5	1	4	4
16	11	16	18
5	5	1	5
5	5	2	3
1	3	3	3
3	2	2	4
2	5	4	3
16	20	12	18
32	31	28	36

Step 2: Subtract second half from first half subtotals to find the differences between halves and find the mean of these differences ($\overline{X}_d$). (Ignore negative signs [treat as absolutes].)

$$\overline{X}_d = \frac{(16 - 16) + (11 - 20) + (16 - 12) + (18 - 18)}{4}$$

$$= \frac{0 + 9 + 4 + 0}{4} = 3.2$$

Step 3: Find the variance of these differences (σd^2).

$$\sigma d^2 = \frac{(0 - 3.2)^2 + (9 - 3.2)^2 + (4 - 3.2)^2 + (0 - 3.2)^2}{4}$$

$$= \frac{10.2 + 33.6 + .6 + 10.2}{4} = 13.7$$

Step 4: Find the means and variance for the *total* scores ($\overline{X}_T$ and σ_T^2).

$$X_T = \frac{32 + 31 + 28 + 36}{4} = 31.7$$

$$\sigma T^2 = \frac{(32-31.7)^2 + (31-31.7)^2 + (31.7-28)^2 + (31.7-36)^2}{4}$$

$$= 8.2$$

BOX 12-1 Continued

Step 5: Substitute your answers for σd^2 and $\sigma_T{}^2$ in the formula

$$r_{tt} = 1 - \frac{\sigma d^2}{\sigma_T{}^2} \text{ and solve.}$$

$$r_{tt} = 1 - \frac{13.7}{8.4} = -.67$$

Step 6: Interpret your answer such that ± 1 equals a perfectly reliable measure and 0 equals total lack of reliability. A −.67 in this example, then, would indicate a moderately reliable measure.

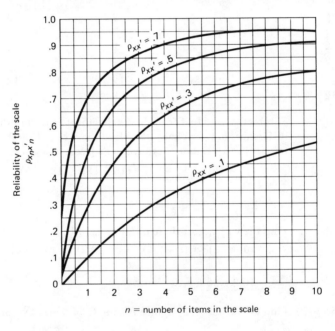

FIGURE 12-1 *Relationship of reliability to number of scale items.*

Source: Adapted from Bohrnstedt (1970:87).

irrelevant components are expected to be *different* across items and since all items share a common focus, the total set of measures should normally provide a purer measure of the phenomenon under study than any single measure. Generally speaking, low reliability is due to *random* errors. If errors are consistently of a particular type we then question the *validity* of our measurements.

It is possible to have very reliable data that has low validity. The undergraduate grade-point average has high reliability: If several researchers jotted down G.P.A.s from university registrar records, we could predict only a few random errors in their work and, hence, high reliability. However, there is a mass of cumulative evidence (Feiring and Korn 1970) showing that undergraduate G.P.A. has extremely poor validity in the prediction of postbaccalaureate income, job prestige, or success in professional school.

ON VALIDITY OF FINDINGS

Validity is defined as the *degree to which the researcher has measured* what he or she set out to measure. Alternatively, validity and invalidity can be thought of as concerning the truth or falsity of the researcher's hypotheses (Cook and Campbell 1979:37). As was true of reliability, researchers are becoming much more critical of the validity of their measurements. We can distinguish two types of validity: validity of findings and validity of measurements. The researcher has an obligation to assess his or her research in terms of both types of validity problems. In the rest of this chapter section we consider assessment of the validity of findings. In the next section we shall consider the validity of measurements.

Campbell and Stanley (1963) and Cook and Campbell (1979) discuss the following major problems in the validity of findings:

A. Internal Validity
    1. History
    2. Maturation
    3. Testing
    4. Instrumentation
    5. Selection
    6. Mortality
    7. Statistical Regression
    8. Selection-Maturation Interaction Effects
B. Statistical Conclusion Validity
    9. Low Statistical Power
   10. Violated Assumptions of Statistical Tests

These sources of invalidity may cause problems of interpretation in any research setting. They offer *plausible, rival interpretations* to the researcher's findings if they are unaccounted for in the study design. Jumping to conclusions makes it easy to overlook evidence that does not fit a preconceived theory. To exclude hypotheses the scientist must use a process of elimination. It is necessary to search for clues that might be used to narrow the field of potentially rival hypotheses or interpretations.

Remembering our comment earlier that poor validity is caused by *biased* or *nonrandom* errors, if these factors are left unaccounted for in the researcher's study design, he or she leaves the data open to potential nonrandom sources of error.

Internal validity concerns the question: Did the methods used make a difference in the specific results? Would different results have been received if different methods had been used? There are at least eight major causes of internal validity problems.

1. *History.* Over the time span of data collection many events occur in addition to the study's independent variable. The history factor refers to the possibility that any one of these events rather than the hypothesized independent variable might have caused observed changes in the dependent variable. A classic example of history confounding research results is provided by a study of the effects of Nazi propaganda materials (Collier 1944) at the same time as France fell. Campbell (1957:298) points out that the resultant attitude change was probably more a result of France falling than of the propaganda to which attitude change was attributed. The effects of history can *only* be ruled out when all stimuli extraneous to the study variables are eliminated or otherwise controlled for experimentally. Another way of stating what history effects are is to view history effects as all those possible independent variables (causes) other than the one(s) that one wishes to study the effects of on some dependent variable(s). The most logical way of ruling out these extraneous variables is to set up the study in such a way that there would be two groups studied that were almost *exactly* alike in every respect except that

into one group (experimental group) you introduced the independent variable and the other group did not have the independent variable introduced (control group). Then, since both groups were similar, particularly in that they passed through the same historical events together, you could rule out history effects since any differences between the two groups could *not* be due to their having experienced similar outside events. (In Chapter 7 we saw that these conditions for ruling out history effects can be created experimentally by *randomly* assigning subjects to experimental and control groups.)

2. *Maturation.* These are any changes in the *internal conditions* of the class of objects being studied (participants, groups, nations) that are *independent* of both the events being analyzed and of history effects, such as growing older, hungrier, more tired, or less interested. Any study involving *lengthy* data-collection time spans (such as child development) is particularly susceptible to maturation effects. However, maturation can be a problem in even one-shot surveys. For example, a person answering questions on "what is most important" to him or her might well respond "food" if he or she were hungry. If interviews with the study population were conducted just before lunch, a significant bias could present itself in this case. Notice that unlike history, maturation effects are *systematic with time passage* and *not* a function of specific historical events. Again, as with the ruling out of history effects, usually the *only* way we can rule out maturation effects is by random assignment of participants to experimental and control group conditions. Then we can be sure that both groups are similar on maturational variables, ruling such variables out as causes of differences found between the groups.

3. *Testing.* Does the prior measurement used affect the participant? If it does, then we speak of testing effects. Methods that affect the participant are called *reactive.* Any time participants *suspect or know* they are being observed, experimented with, or tested there is the chance that their behavior may be modified by the measuring instrument. One of the primary criticisms leveled against the Masters and Johnson sex research has been precisely that the participants' *knowledge* of experimentation *might* have modified or eliminated their normal sexual behaviors during the study. Any measurement *not* a part of the participants' *normal* environment may be considered reactive. Hence, tests, experiments, and observations are *not* reactive per se. If a researcher wished to observe the effects of teaching style on student test scores a test measuring student score changes could be given without fear of reactivity, assuming testing is a *normal* part of that school's environment.

4. *Instrumentation.* Changes in the *measurement* process may be spuriously attributed to the dependent variable. Where interviewers or observers become increasingly sloppy, fatigued, or more competent and experienced, study results may be subtly changed. The U.S. Bureau of the Census finds that new interviewers consistently count slightly more respondents as unemployed than do older interviewers. (Since one respondent represents approximately 30,000 persons in their surveys, high interviewer turnover could lead to grossly overinflated unemployment figures.) Instrumentation changes in researchers or their assistants can be viewed as a special case of *maturation* problems; they are caused by maturation of the *researcher* rather than by maturation of the *participant* as in "maturational effects." Instrumentation changes in the researcher's equipment (electronic eyes, cameras) are often termed *instrument decay.* The fatiguing of a battery-operated tape recorder used to time length of speech would exemplify this problem.

5. *Selection.* A biased or nonrandom selection of participants or units of analysis may also contribute to spurious interpretations of findings. Interviewers (when given the choice) are more likely to select houses on corner lots (which tend to be more expensive) and, hence, relatively richer people tend to be oversampled. Randomization is the key to overcoming differential selection of respondents. Particularly when groups are to be compared it is important to insure that participants are randomly assigned to groups rather than haphazardly selected, differentially recruited, or self-selected. Otherwise, differences between groups on the dependent variable may be due to participant selection procedures rather than to the independent variable. Imagine comparing children who themselves (or whose parents) elect to watch the *Sesame Street* television program series with a group that does not elect to do so. Any differences in achievement scores that appeared could just as easily be attributed to differential participant motivation or participant characteristics as to the effects of *Sesame Street.* Thus, systematic differences that are typically introduced through nonrandom selection may easily confound study results.

6. *Mortality.* Any time nonrandom subsets of units of analysis or participants *drop out* of the study, differences in the dependent variable between groups might be accounted for by these differential "mortality" rates rather than by actual effects of the independent variable. In interviewing persons drawn randomly in their studies of monthly unemployment, the U.S. Bureau of the Census recognizes that unmarried blacks between the ages of eighteen and twenty-five make up a particularly transient and unemployment-prone group. Thus, the loss of significantly

higher numbers of these participants from the final study means that the actual unemployment figure is higher than lack of this knowledge would indicate. Hence, *initial* equivalence between groups is not enough; the equivalence must be *maintained* throughout the study. Often, a researcher may have initially equivalent groups only to find that participants self-select themselves *out* of the study. Imagine a true experiment dealing with the effects of marijuana intoxication. Suppose the participants in the experiment volunteered on the basis of the possibility that they might legally be able to try marijuana. After they had been randomly assigned to research groups (placebo versus actual marijuana), let us assume that somehow the placebos learn they will not receive marijuana, and hence many of them find excuses for discontinuing their experimental participation. This turn of events would mean the two groups had not been exposed to the same selection procedures.

By the same token, the *experimenter* should *not* select participants *out* of any experimental treatment after they have been assigned to a particular condition. Weeding out of participants from the initial pool is permissible only *prior* to random experimental assignment. Weeding out after random treatment assignment presents potential hazards of creating nonequivalent comparison groups.

Differential mortality rates may take other, more subtle, forms. It is not uncommon for trained observers to begin coding various aspects of ongoing interaction only to lose data due to the participant's leaving the field of observation during the coding or due to the participant's turning away from the observer so that particular measures (facial expressions) are no longer observable. Likewise, interviewers often encounter situations where they obtain the interview but lose particular information in patterned, nonrandom ways (income information losses may be greater at higher SES levels).

7. *Statistical regression.* Statistical regression refers to a fact well known among statisticians that quantitative measurements taken at two points in time are subject to misinterpretation if participants were either *initially selected or are compared* on the basis of *extremity* of their scores (extremely overweight, extremely short, upper 10 percent of all IQ scores, low in authoritarianism, or social areas with high crime rates).

Francis Galton (1885) first used the term regression in a study of the relationship between parents and their offspring's heights. He noted that tall parents' children were typically shorter than their parents and short parents' children were taller on the average than their parents. Thus, if one did not know about the regression fallacy, it would be easy to mistakenly conclude that succeeding generations produce children who are closer to the average population height. This is a false conclusion since the conclusion is an artifact of the selection of extreme cases. That is, an examination of cases closer to the mean would show that parents of average height are likely to have children whose height is further away from the mean.

Similarly, unsophisticated analysts often conclude, after looking at data on IQ of the offspring of very bright parents, that we are producing a generation with mediocre IQs. However, if these analysts were to work in reverse and reflect on the IQs of the parents of very bright offspring, they would note that extremely bright children had parents, who, on the average, had IQs closer to the mean! What produces these pseudoeffects?

Regression effects are caused by effects of either "scale reliability," or "natural regression effects," or both in combination. *Natural regression effects* is a phrase used to denote regression stemming from some equilibrating factor(s) found in nature. There are many examples of such equilibrating effects. Bohrnstedt (1969) points out that extremely heavy people tend to weigh less at a second weighing while extremely light people tend to weigh more at a second weighing than they did at the first weighing. Similarly, those persons with initial weight readings near the average tend to have weights more extreme (further from the mean) at a second weighing. This type of regression effect is viewed as an actual, true, or substantive change. The causes of natural regression effects are not well understood. The best we can do is to warn researchers to be wary of using subjects selected on the basis of extreme scores.

By contrast, sometimes regression is viewed as an artifact of poor reliability. That is, the more unreliable the measure—the more pseudo-effects or pseudochange—the more regression will confound results. This was not a problem with weight since the weight scale can be assumed to give essentially true scores. However, when scientists work with social or behavioral scales (attitude scales) where measurement error is likely to be present, regression can be expected as a matter of consequence; the more the measurement error, the greater the regression effects that can be expected. In any case, some persons' scores artificially decrease due to poor reliability. (Previously we spoke of poor reliability as due to unbiased error and poor validity as due to biased error. Hence, regression due to poor reliability is not a validity problem but a reliability problem. It is only when the error is biased—that is, regression *towards* the mean—that the problem is viewed as a validity problem. Regression due strictly to chance occurrence of errors is unbiased and, hence, is a reliability problem.) Further, these errors tend to cancel each other out since they are due to chance factors in the first place.

Sometimes regression effects do not equalize out; thus, Lord (1956) spoke of regression *towards* the mean in the sense that *all* measurements tend towards the mean at time two by comparison to time one. This phenomenon is not clearly understood. In Figure 12–2 assume the measurements represent IQ scores. Extreme IQ scores can be seen to change more than do less extreme scores. Campbell and Stanley (1966:11) explain this phenomenon through the statement that

> ... the more deviant the score, the larger the error of measurement it probably contains. Thus, in a sense, the typical extremely high scorer has had unusually good "luck" (large positive error) and the extremely low scorer bad luck (large negative error). Luck is capricious, however, so on a post test we expect the high scorers to decline somewhat on the average, the low scorers to improve their relative position. (The same logic holds if one begins with the post test scores and works back to the pretest.)

Probably regression towards the mean is an effect of "ceiling" and "floor" effects. If the range of possible scores on an attitude scale is 0 to 100, a person with a score of 100 could only change in one direction, a person with a score of 90 could move up only 10 points but could fall 90, and so on, thus showing regression toward the mean to be an artifact of scale limitations (built-in biases against a score changing equally in either direction).

Parenthetically, regression *away* from the mean may have theoretical importance. For instance, ghetto children bused to superior schools might show regression away from the mean due to the fact that those children with above-average IQ are stimulated by the more challenging

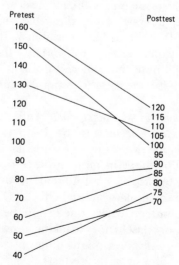

FIGURE 12–2 *Regression scatter of posttest scores from pretest scores and vice versa.*

environment while those with below-normal IQs might find the new competition too stiff and, hence, might give up trying to learn.

It is difficult to control for the effects of regression. Usually, the researcher will control for regression by multiplying the time one measure by that measure's test-retest reliability coefficient (correlation). Or, if a meaningful control group is available for comparison, its regression effects may be subtracted from the experimental group's score changes. Then any score changes left over could be attributed to actual, or time, change. However, this procedure should only be carried out within the framework of a true experimental design (see Chapter 7) where participants are *randomly* assigned to experimental and control groups.

Matching procedures, after-the-fact creation of control groups through some criteria such as similar scores on some variable(s) (age, sex, race, authoritarian scores, IQ) are never recommended. In such cases researchers potentially confound their design with *differential* regression effects. Obviously, there are many research settings where researchers are unable to randomize because of factors beyond their influence (administrative fiat limiting the researcher to the use of particular workgroups, classes, or participants). In such cases researchers must be particularly cautious in comparing change scores for experimental and control groups. Indeed, the more imperfectly matched the groups, the greater the differential regression which is to be expected.

Regression artifacts are one of the most recurrent forms of research self-deception in the analysis of *any* data that are collected over time (Campbell 1969a:414) and that have variability. If you move along the time dimension of any time series graph and pick the "highest (or lowest) point so far," you will note that the *next* point will, on the average, be lower (or higher)—that is, *nearer* the general trend.

8. *Selection-maturation interaction effects.*   Differential sample selection often works *in conjunction with* maturation, history, or testing to produce spurious results. Imagine two groups of students tested for some type of aptitude. If the groups differ in motivation (a maturational effect) the study may be expected to be confounded by differential selection *in conjunction with* differential maturational effects. Or, again, compare two groups of student volunteers where one group, perhaps unbeknownst to the researcher, had more past history in taking aptitude tests. This history–differential selection *combination* might differentially affect each group's answers to attitude scales or aptitude tests.

Campbell (1969a:427) gives some interesting examples of the confounding interaction effects between selection and the independent variable.

... [A]ll careful studies show that most of the effect, and of the superior effect of superior colleges, is explainable in terms of superior talents and family connections rather than in terms of what is learned or even the prestige of the degree ... [thus] there are those treatments that are given to the most promising, treatments like a college education, regularly given to those who need it least ... although, in this setting any comparison [a researcher] might hit upon would be biased in his [or her] favor.

At the other end of the talent continuum are those remedial treatments given to those who need it most. Here the later [effects] of the grounds of selection are poorer success. In the job training corps example, casual comparisons of the later employment rate of those who receive the training with those who did not are in general biased against showing an advantage to the training.

Statistical conclusion validity refers to the possibility of the researcher drawing false conclusions when asking the question: Are the presumed independent and dependent variables related? (Cook and Campbell 1979:37). Researchers are faced with three decisions: (1) Whether the study is statistically sensitive enough to make a reasonable statement about the relationship between variables. (2) If the study is sensitive enough, whether the evidence supports covariation between the presumed cause and effect. (3) If that evidence does exist, measuring the *strength* of covariation between the variables.

Fluctuations in measures, sampling units, or repeated or "equivalent" measures give results different from what would have occurred without those chance fluctuations. Statistical tests of significance are typically used to assess the chance that we can accept, or reject, our data as fluctuating from its true value. There are two possible errors in such tests.

Type I error: Rejecting a decision that is actually true.
Type II error: Accepting a decision that is actually false.

Researchers must continually ask whether there are properly balanced risks of *both* type I and II errors, for, paradoxically, as one decreases, the danger of committing the other error increases. Furthermore, researchers need some means of establishing the probability of each risk occurring if they wish to "exclude the hypothesis of chance," and they wish to do this in "formal, objective, communicable and reproducible procedures rather than by intuition" (Winch and Campbell 1969:143).

The plausibility of the risk can be assessed either by traditional statistical tests of significance or the researcher may use a Monte Carlo type of procedure (Winch and Campbell 1969:140). Whenever researchers adopt a particular level of significance (.05 or 5 out of 100 chances) in any test of significance, in effect they accept a certain risk for *both* type I and II errors. In the .05 case they set a relatively low risk of rejecting a true hypothesis and a relatively high risk of accepting a false hypothesis.

It is always necessary to consider carefully how serious the consequences of each type of error are for a particular circumstance. For instance, in a study of social work practice effectiveness, assume the traditional practice proved to be 50 percent effective, and researchers wish to assess a new social work practice. Clearly the new practice should be better than 50 percent effective since the practical cost of switching over to the new practice would be too high compared to retaining the equally effective old practice. But how much better should the new practice be to protect against an *erroneous* decision that the new practice is superior to the old? If the probability of the new practice working were .52, then its use would lead to the benefit of only two persons among each 50 who would not have benefited without it. By contrast, a probability of .65 for the new practice's effectiveness would lead to the benefit of 30 percent more people than the old practice.

On the surface, the .65 effective study might seem to warrant the adoption of the new practice. However, *no study ever proves a hypothesis—it merely adds plausibility to it.* Hence, if you recommend adoption of the new method, you may actually be recommending a practice as more effective when it actually is not (type I error). On the other hand, you do not want to reject as ineffective a practice that is more effective than the old practice. Thus, you must consider which error is more important. Assuming you consider both errors to be equally serious, then you could set the rejection probability for the practice near that point where it makes no difference whether the new practice is adopted or not (.50 in the social work example). In sum, *statistical conclusion validity,* unlike the other internal validity problems, is *always* present—if you get rid of type I (II) errors, you have then to deal with type II (I) errors.

Campbell (1969a:427) points out that too many social scientists expect single experiments to settle issues once and for all. Replication, however, as he points out, is generic to all science; in fact, it is *more important* to the social sciences where we lack the experimental control found in the physical sciences. Thus, replications are an important component in challenging the potential statistical conclusion validity of study results. Replications as well as tests of significance help answer the question: What *chance* is there that the difference found would be found by chance? There are three important sources of *statistical conclusion validity* we will discuss (see Cook and Campbell 1979:43–44 for other sources).

9. *Low statistical power.* Cohen (1970) gives valuable information on the extent to which particular statistical tests differ in power, or sen-

sitivity, to differences. Other major sources of this problem, besides statistical tests, are sample size and the level of statistical significance accepted. Small sample size and particularly low levels of statistical significance tend to increase type II errors.

10. *Violated assumptions of statistical tests.* Every statistical test is based on known statistical assumptions. Many tests require that groups being compared have similar variances. Robustness of any statistical test has to do with which of these assumptions can be violated without significant losses of sensitivity or power of the test. Cohen (1970) is one of numerous standard statistical references available to the researcher who wishes to check how robust his or her tests are.

11. *Fishing error rate problems.* In Chapter 2 we gave an example of a classic scientific "fishing" expedition. Dunnette (1958) reviewed a study where at least 3,963 hypotheses had been tested. He pointed out that you could expect 160 of those hypotheses to be judged *statistically* significant by chance alone. By chance, we can expect 1 out of 20 hypotheses to be statistically significant at the .05 level without being theoretically significant. These types of considerations must be taken into account so that we do not falsely conclude that covariation exists when it actually does not exist (type I error). Ryan (1959) gives suggestions for adjusting for this error.

External validity concerns a different sort of question than internal validity. It is possible to have high internal validity where the internal rigor of the study argued against the preceding rival causal explanations and yet still have low external validity, or *generalizability,* of a study. Hence, external validity asks: How representative of, or generalizable to, particular populations, settings, independent variables, and dependent variables is the study? There are six additional rival causal explanations we will discuss in terms of external validity.

12. *Reactive effects of measurement.* Methods of measurement, as we saw in discussing testing effects, sometimes modify or otherwise *affect* the participant's behavior or attitudes during the measurement process. Reactive effects of measurement refer *not only* to participant's being *affected by* the measurement. It suggests that the process of measurement also may *change* that which is being measured. In other words, while testing effects refer to participant changes occurring *only* during the measurement process, reactivity refers to the possibility of *relatively permanent* changes caused by the measurement process. One of the classic cases of such change caused by reactive measurement process is the ongoing U.S. National Health Survey that has been found to increase the health

of the sample population compared to the United States population because participants receive a free medical examination that gives many of them knowledge of health problems they were not aware of previously.

Participants made aware of such health problems by the survey are likely to see a physician for correction of the problem—an act they would have been much less likely to have performed if they had not participated in the survey. Likewise, problems relatively remote from the participant's experience or concerns (such as international nuclear proliferation pacts) might be sensitized by a questionnaire on the subject. Those respondents, naive in regards to such questions, might feel propelled to find out more about such remote phenomena. Thus, at a later reinterview the researcher's data could show an increase in sophistication of answers that is not generalizable to the population at large.

13. *Differential selection–independent variable interaction.* This rival causal explanation suggests that samples differentially selected from the group they are to be compared with may give responses unrepresentative of that group. This is particularly common where volunteer participants are depended on since some types of people are more likely to volunteer than others. Halikas and his associates (1971) found that volunteers for marijuana studies were overrepresentative of marijuana smokers who were also into other drugs. The use of such participants in experiments on the effects of marijuana could lead to false conclusions as to the effects of marijuana per se, although they might be somewhat more representative of people who used a variety of drugs.

14. *Reactive effects of data-collection arrangements.* Knowledge of exposure to particular data-collection instruments may lead to a change of study behavior in contrast to normal behavior. Experimental participants in marijuana studies might act differently under conditions of knowing they smoked pot than not knowing, simply because they expect to act and feel particular ways when stoned than when not stoned. Note that these types of reactive effects are *short-lived* in the sense that they apply to changes that are *in effect only during the data collection.* They are thus similar to what we called testing effects, but they refer to a different question since here they refer to the attempt to *generalize* from the participant population to some wider population. Many of these spurious effects are based on participants gearing their responses to match their perceptions of researcher expectations—even though the researcher may not state his or her intentions.

15. *Multiple independent variable interference.* Whenever the independent variable is *repeatedly* introduced into the research setting there is a

likelihood that observed effects will differ from settings with *single* introductions of the independent variable. Assume you had designed an experiment in which one group serves as a control while another group repeatedly smokes cigarettes even-numbered days and does not smoke cigarettes on odd-numbered days. Campbell and Stanley (1963:44) point out that

> The effect of X_1 [treatment variable], in the simplest situation in which it is being compared with X_0 [treatment absent], can be generalized only to conditions of repetitious and spaced presentations of X_1. No sound basis is provided for generalization to possible situations in which X_1 is continually present, or to the condition in which it is introduced once and only once.

A continuous diet of drinking scotch might have different effects from a schedule with days interspersed with other types of liquor. And continuous presentation of scotch drinking would probably differ from alternating days of drinking versus nondrinking. Underwood (1957*a*) found, in agreement with this viewpoint, that many of his findings on participants who had learned dozens of nonsense syllable lists were not generalizable to persons who had learned a single such list.

Multiple treatments interference may also refer to situations in which *combinations* of an independent variable are given to a study group. A researcher interested in the effects of "drugs" might look at the combined effects of marijuana and alcohol. But it would be wise not to generalize from that setting to settings where marijuana and alcohol were used separately.

16. *Irrelevant responsiveness of measures.*   Spurious effects are often noted in research which are actually due to irrelevant components of complex measures. This is the problem of generalizing from an imperfect measure to whatever is ostensibly being measured.

Assume we are studying the effects of marijuana intoxication. Our measuring device (stethoscope) may pick up irrelevant components of faster heart rates such as nonmarijuana-related hyperventilation (which can occur simply by inhaling deeply several times for a few seconds). Or imagine measuring group cohesiveness through asking members to list their preferred associates. A shortcoming of the procedure is that group cohesiveness may be shown to be spuriously low simply because many members have nonmembers as preferred associates. By the same token, work productivity would provide irrelevant responsiveness of cohesiveness in groups that had norms regulating productivity. In a similar vein, Bales (1950) measured group tension *release* through laughter, yet laughter is often a sign of tension *increase.*

All measures have irrelevant components. The point is to reduce these irrelevancies to manageable levels. Later sections (see also Chapters 11 and 13) will consider the use of *multiple* measures as ways of reducing such irrelevant components.

17. *Irrelevant replicability of independent variables.* Just as *measures* are complex (multidimensional) constructs that are subject to irrelevant effects, *variables* of research interest are typically multidimensional. Hence, replications of variables may fail to include that dimension(s) actually responsible for the effects. Turning the question on its head, to what could the original study's independent variable(s) actually be generalized to include if it failed later replication attempts?

Mann and Janis (1968) experimented with the effects of "fear" and "shame" on cigarette smoking habits. However, generalizability may have been sharply limited by the way the independent variables were defined. For instance, would "fear" introduced by visual representations of smoking-caused lung damage have had the same, or similar, effects as verbally induced fear? Would the results have held up if the fear inducer had been a female rather than a male, or black rather than white? To the extent that the effects of the independent variable cannot be replicated under varying circumstances, it has limited generalizability.

The history of the social and behavioral sciences is replete with examples of studies that are lacking in validity because the researcher failed to take these plausible rival causal factors into account. If we had to make a choice between high internal and high external validity, we would probably pick high internal validity since we can make do with low generalizability of findings but cannot ultimately be satisfied with research that is internally open to alternative explanations or interpretations.

As a review of these problems in the validity of interpretation the student may wish to assess critically the article reprinted in Appendix G. The purpose of the exercise is not to criticize the Mazur article as bad research. Indeed, it is good research, having been critically reviewed by one of the leading sociology journals. The exercise is intended to make you more aware of general problems in the validity of scientific interpretations. After a critical reading of the article, you should then return to this section to compare your own assessment of the article with that offered in the remainder of this chapter section.

History definitely presents problems in the Mazur article. Since Mazur has no control over randomizing who in his sample will or will not receive stressful conflict (the independent variable), it is likely that subjects in each condition could have had other differential experiences which explain their reaction to attitudinal balance (the dependent variable). In fact, we can be more sure of history effects for another reason —some of his participants answered at different times (4,870 responded to his questionnaire in September; another 27 percent responded to his second letter later on). Intervening events in the time between each letter might have affected respondents at time two differently from time one.

Maturational effects can be assumed to confound study results since it is plausible to assume that participants who answered the first letter were more highly motivated than those who needed a second request. Since all the participants knew they were part of a scientific study, this knowledge could have changed their "normal" response—an example of potential *testing* effects.

Because interviews were quite long (one-and-a-half hours), interviewer fatigue might have resulted in *instrumentation* changes. The sample is not a random sample of any known population since the researcher haphazardly selected male, Jewish, social science faculty from three Boston-area colleges. Certainly there are problems of *differential selection of participants* as this sample can be assumed to differ somewhat (educationally) from the Jewish population they are expected to represent. *Differential mortality* may present problems also since nonrespondents (25 percent of the total sample) could represent a group of people somewhat different from those interviewed.

Regression effects do not appear to present a problem since the sample does not seem to have been selected on the basis of extreme scores. We have already noted that differential selection of participants and maturation present problems. Hence, there may well be a problem of *interaction* between these effects. For instance, it might well be that Jewish social science faculty who were motivated to respond to the first letter are peculiarly affected by stressful conflict. First, they have gone through a particularly stressful historical event (the Ph.D. comprehensive and defense of thesis) that *might* make them particularly resistant to other stressful situations. Second, as social scientists they recognize the value of research and hence may be more motivated than other Jews to answer this interview.

There is a *type II* problem inherent in this study since the author is willing to accept his initial hypothesis in the face of the risk (however small) that his decision is wrong. (Because statistical conclusion validity depends on statistical knowledge beyond the scope of this text, we shall not specifically analyze the Mazur study using specific indices of statistical conclusion validity here.)

We have seen that the methods used by Mazur could have had an effect on the validity of his study findings. What about the effect of his methods on the generalizability of his findings?

We have suggested that Mazur's study is susceptible to testing effects, but are these effects of a nature that might be long-lasting? We have no way of directly assessing such potential effects in this study; in Chapter 7 we saw that the only way to rule out *reactive effects of testing* completely (other than to employ measurements of which participants are not aware) is to use what will be termed the "Solomon four-group design." Since Mazur used measurements (interviews) of which the participants were aware and since he did not employ a Solomon four-group design, we cannot rule out the possibility that the study had long-term effects on the participants' attitudes or behavior towards the Six Day War. For instance, the participants may have become more pro- or anti-Israel as a result of the measurement process that, if that were true, would then make this sample unrepresentative of Jews in general.

Differential selection–independent variable effects are conceivable given the heretofore discussed differential selection of participants. Jewish professors from the Boston area might give responses inappropriate for generalization to all Jews since, as we have seen, they tend to be unique in their previous experience with the independent variable (stressful conflict).

Reactive effects of data collection arrangement also may pose problems for the study's generalizability. Since the professors may have wished to appear more positive or more indifferent to their ethnicity when faced by the interviewer than they really are, they may be poor representations of Jews in general.

Multiple treatment interference is a problem in this study since the independent variable is measured by war reports and stories. The *constant* bombardment of war reports and stories could have produced different results than if the subject was mentioned only a *few times* or only *once* to participants.

All measurement is suceptible to *irrelevant responsiveness of measures*. In this study, for example, knowledge of the Six Day War events may be a poor means of measuring "stressful conflict" because news coverage from the start of the war indicated that Israel would dominate the war due to their virtually wiping out of Arab air support. Because of this measurement problem it would have been interesting to replicate the Mazur study during the October 1973 Arab-Israel conflict where both sides appeared to be more evenly matched from the start and which therefore provided a much better measurement of Jewish stressful conflict. If such a replication failed, we might say that it was due to *irrelevant replicability of independent variables* since "stressful conflict" in each situation would have been different enough to produce different study results.

OPERATIONALIZATION: A BRIDGE
BETWEEN METHODS AND THEORY

The question of what one *wants* to measure brings up the problem of operationalization. *Operationalization* refers to the concrete and specific means by which observations are to be categorized.

Let us assume that we would like to measure authoritarian behavior. We might start out by using the celebrated Fascism (F) attitude scale developed by Adorno and his co-workers (1950). However, if you had read the empirical and theoretical literature developed in response to the Adorno F-scale you would know that it has many biases, perhaps the worst of which are: (1) It is oriented only toward right-wing authoritarianism; (2) it has response biases (some people tend to answer it in "nonauthoritarian" or "authoritarian" ways simply because they believe some answers are more "socially acceptable" or because they tend to favor certain question wordings); and (3) it only taps certain *attitudes,* not necessarily corresponding *behaviors.* The point is that we should not take operationalizations too literally. The operationalization "may not at all measure the process the researcher wishes to measure; it may measure something quite different" (Underwood 1957*b*:54).

In Chapter 13 we will discuss how, through the use of *multiple operationalization,* we may come to know better how closely our operationalization approaches the theoretical construct it is supposed to measure. Since we cannot do without operationalization of our theoretical construct, we wish to emphasize its limitations and theoretical construction and extensions in the methods chapters to follow.

OPERATIONALIZATION AND VALIDITY
OF MEASUREMENT

Hubert Blalock (1968:11) has most eloquently summarized the dangers of naive operationalism when he states

> Let us admit, with the critics of operationalism, that perhaps it is unwise at this point—when research techniques are quite crude—to become overly rigid by tying down a theoretically defined concept to a particular operation. If we associate the term "prejudice" with a specific paper-and-pencil attitude test, then we run the risk either of adding new concepts to our already vastly overcomplicated theoretical language or of losing the flexibility required of a science in its infancy.

In addition to multiple operationalization as a corrective for naive single methodological operations, researchers have several strategies of investigating and improving the validity of their *measurements* that they should learn to employ: content validity, criterion-related validity, and construct validity.

Content validity refers to the degree that the measurement being used represents the concept about which generalizations are to be made. Bohrnstedt (1970:91–92) recommends the following procedures:

> The researcher needs to search the literature carefully to determine how various authors have used the concept. Moreover, he should rely on his own observations and experiences and ask whether they yield any new facets to the concept under consideration. Whereupon, a series of items can be constructed which measure each of the sub-strata of the domain of content, a procedure referred to as *sampling from a domain of content.*

An excellent case in the use of these procedures came from Melvin Seeman's (1959) research on alienation. Seeman noted, after an exhaustive search of the literature, that alienation had at least five different meanings: powerlessness, meaninglessness, normlessness, isolation, and self-estrangement; he also noted closely related concepts including: apathy, dissension, disenfranchisement, and anomie. Thus, alienation called for a scale that was multidimensional in character so as to capture each of these various meanings.

Bohrnstedt (1970:92) further elaborates on how to insure representativeness of these shades of meaning. First, one should lay out the most important and obvious meanings so as to *exhaust* all meanings of the concept. Second, one may further subdivide those dimensions if any do not appear to represent a single dimension. For example, powerlessness may be subdivided into political, economic, and familial powerlessness. Bohrnstedt notes that the more refined these subareas, the easier item construction will become. Third, *no fewer* than seven to ten items should be used in order to capture the various shades of meaning of each stratum or substratum, in addition to higher reliability. Fourth, quite often items selected do not behave as anticipated and have to be rejected leaving a smaller (and, hence, less reliable) scale. Nevertheless, if items are discovered that appear to tap more than one dimension they should be eliminated, just as should items that appear not to tap the wanted dimension.

Criterion-related validity is evaluated by correlating one's operation with some direct measure of the operation's characteristic. There are two types of criterion-related validity: concurrent and predictive. *Predictive validity* associates the operational instrument with *some variable* of theoretical interest; the higher the association the better the prediction. Thus, if Seeman's alienation attitude scale really measures alienation, we might expect, using predictive validity criteria, that we could predict alienated *behavior* patterns with its use. Again, if we were using predictive validity criteria to assess the validity of organizational formalization, we should predict that measure to correlate highly with certain variables such as organization size.

Another criterion-related validity variation is termed concurrent validity. Here, *known groups or judges are located* (as opposed to variables in predictive validity) who by consensus are defined as high or low on the variable in question in order to demonstrate the predictive ability of the instrument. Let us suppose we had an attitude scale designed to measure religious conservatism. We should predict that if it really measures religious conservativism, Jehovah's Witnesses should score high on the measure while Unitarians should score relatively low. As another example, consider demonstrating the concurrent validity of a measure of bureaucratization where expert judges concurred that the Roman Catholic Church was more bureaucratized than the Southern Baptist Church. In this case, our data should agree with those judgments. Thus, the principle behind this method is that groups known to differ on a particular dimension should show scale discrimination in the appropriate direction.

Construct validity is evaluated through determining the degree to which certain explanatory concepts (constructs) account for performance on the measurement. In other words, studies of construct validity are done to validate the theory underlying the instrument. This is done by investigating whether or not the instrument confirms or denies the hypotheses predicted from a theory based on the constructs. (It should be noted that negative evidence can result from either a lack of construct validity or an incorrect theory.)

Campbell and Fiske (1959) have pointed out that a measurement of some construct should not correlate too highly with measures of different constructs. If there really are five dimensions to alienation, each should *not* be associated too highly with the others. On the other hand, *different* measures of the *same* construct should be associated fairly highly. For example, if we had two different measurements of powerlessness, they should correlate relatively highly. But each of those powerlessness scales should correlate relatively lowly with, say, a normlessness scale. Campbell and Fiske call these construct validation procedures discriminant and convergent validation. *Convergent validation* refers to the idea that when measurements correlate highly with each other, they may be measuring the *same* rather than different constructs. By contrast, with *discriminant validation* we reason that if the measurements correlate lowly, they may be measuring a *different* rather than the same construct.

The various methods of validation should not be treated as mutually exclusive. The good researcher attempts to use as many of them as possible since each provides some unique information. Generally speaking, the more of these strategies used, the better the operationalizations that will be constructed.

THE RELATIONSHIP BETWEEN RELIABILITY AND VALIDITY

In this chapter we have concerned ourselves with problems of reliability and validity. The question often arises as to which of these problems is more important to solve. In considering the worth of a particular measurement, validity is a more important criterion than reliability. As we have seen, we can have high reliability and yet still have low or no validity. If the measurement has no validity, then we have no use for it. It certainly would not make sense to use individual eye-blink rates as measures of tension unless one has some proof of the validity of this assumption (which has been shown to be the case by Weick 1968).

Lord and Novick (1968:72) note that validity and reliability are related. The validity of a measure can *never exceed* the square root of its reliability. Hence, reliability limits validity. If one has a measure with low reliability, a statistical correlation of .49, that measure can never correlate greater than .70 with some other variable. Again, assume you have a split-half test estimate of reliability of .64; then your validity estimate *cannot exceed* .80. Thus, while reliability and validity are related, if one cannot reliably measure a variable, one cannot measure that variable with any assurance of validity.

Do not, however, be misled by this reliability-validity formula. It is *not* true that the validity of a measure can be *determined* by the square root of its reliability coefficient. In the first place, we never know the *actual* reliability of a measure—only its *estimate*. Second, the square root of the reliability is a correlation between the measurement and whatever that measurement is measuring. Whatever is actually being measured may or may not be what one *wants* to measure.

READINGS FOR ADVANCED STUDENTS

Hubert M. Blalock, Jr., "The Measurement Problem: A Gap Between the Language of Theory and Research," in H. M. Blalock, Jr. and A. B. Blalock (eds.), *Methodology in Social Research,* 1968. Discusses operationalization in more social structural terms than the Summers text below.

Edgar F. Borgatta and George W. Bohrnstedt (eds.), *Sociological Methodology 1970,* Part II: Measurement, Reliability, and Validity. An extremely technical but important set of articles on such topics as the effect of reliability and validity on power of statistical tests, coefficients of reliability suitable for observational data, and the multitrait-multimethod technique of validation.

DONALD CAMPBELL AND DONALD FISKE, "Convergent and Discriminant Validation by the Multitrait, Multimethod Matrix," *Psychological Bulletin* 56 (1959). A classic approach to construct validation which deserves wider attention outside of psychologist's circles than it has received.

THOMAS COOK AND DONALD CAMPBELL, *Quasi-Experimentation: Design and Analysis Issues for Field Settings*, 1979. This book gives every indication of joining the earlier Campbell and Stanley (1963) work as a classic sourcebook. (See Chapter 2.)

GENE SUMMERS (ed.), *Attitude Measurement*, 1970. The first part has detailed discussions of reliability, validity, and operationalization. Later sections illustrate these basic considerations in the design of attitude scaling.

SUGGESTED RESEARCH PROJECTS

1. Bielby, Hauser, and Featherman (1977) found persuasive evidence that white males' reports of social background and achievement variables are subject to strictly random errors, while reports by black males appear subject to significant nonrandom error. Using the definitions we have given in this chapter, are these errors ones of reliability or validity? Why?

2. Chirot (1977) has recently suggested that key differences among poor or underdeveloped countries are not their placement on a right-left political continuum but their softness or hardness. He suggests that soft societies are characterized by their openness to the outside world, while hard societies are relatively closed to the outside world.

   a. Suggest at least three different operationalizations of "hardness" to "softness" that might be used, using already available data.

   b. Discuss several different methods of tapping validity of your measurements.

3. Go back over Part 2 chapters on the production of data.

   a. What specific problem(s) of validity of findings tend to present particular problems for particular data production methods? Why?

   b. Which validity of findings problems do not tend to be associated with particular data production methods? Why?

   c. For which validity of findings problems are you unable to find an association with particular data production methods? Why?

4. Which internal and external validity problems discussed must the researcher be careful not to commit in sampling? Why? How can these problems be circumvented or controlled?

5. Take a sociological journal article or professional book (not text) with which you have some knowledge. (If you have no real knowledge, go to *Sociological Abstracts* in order to find an article related to some interest of yours.) Criticize the article (or book) in terms of its implicit paradigmatic assumptions.

6. Criticize a sociological journal article or book in terms of how it measures up to Campbell and Stanley's rival causal (validity) factors. How could the study be improved, using the strategies on validation of measurements?

7. Consider some folk wisdom such as "Absence makes the heart grow fonder." How would you operationalize this in order to gather empirical evidence concerning its truth? Assess the plausible reliability and validity of your measure(s).

8. In a short form of a Likert type scale you found the following raw scores:

   Respondent 1: 6,8,4,5,6,4,7,9
   Respondent 2: 4,2,6,8,9,4,3,1
   Respondent 3: 2,3,1,2,1,6,7,1

   Find the split half reliability for this data. Show all work. Give an interpretation of this reliability coefficient.

   (answer: 0.97)

9. In making up a scale you found that the average item reliability was 0.3. If you had 7 items in your scale your reliability for the total scale should be ...?

   (answer: 0.75)

10. In Project 9 what is the highest that validity can possibly be?

    (answer: 0.86)

Triangulation:
The Necessity for
Multimethod Approaches

We must use all available weapons of attack, face our problems realistically and not retreat to the land of fashionable sterility, learn to sweat over our data with an admixture of judgement and intuitive rumination, and accept the usefulness of particular data even when the level of analysis available for them is markedly below that available for other data in the empirical area. [1]

Each method, tool, or technique presented in previous chapters has been shown to have somewhat unique strengths and weaknesses. Closed-ended questions are most appropriate when a variable's domain or dimensions are clearly understood but inappropriate when the question is likely to be highly reactive or obtrusive. Hidden cameras, by contrast, may be less reactive but may raise ethically sensitive issues and may give distorted or ambiguous data because of camera angle or coverage.

Traditionally most social and behavioral researchers have not given much serious thought to the quality of their research endeavors. Chun

[1] A. Binder, *Statistical Theory,* 1964, p. 294.

and his associates (1972) have shown psychological measures such as attitude scales to be selected almost entirely according to the convenience of their immediate availability rather than by reliability or validity criteria. In addition they note that 63 percent of these measures have been used in research only once and 9 percent only twice while only 3 percent have been used more than ten times. Brown and Gilmartin (1969:288) have shown that 64 percent of research reported in the two most prestigious sociological journals in 1965–1966 were based on verbal reports collected through questionnaires or interviews. They also noted (1969:287) that "three-fourths of today's research has its setting in the United States, and 85 percent refers to one point in time."

Furthermore, the individual person is the most frequent analytic unit in sociology—in 54 percent of the studies surveyed according to Brown and Gilmartin (1969:288). How can sociological theory progress at the macro level with such inordinate attention paid to individuals? Indeed, these figures raise questions about the extent to which the wrong level of analysis mars sociological research—an issue we shall return to in a later chapter section.

These facts paint a rather dismal picture. How can the social sciences progress when they are relatively culture-bound, time-bound, unreplicated, lacking in interest in macroscopic problems, unconcerned with the correspondence between what is done and what is said, and pay only lip service to reliability and validity? Instead, much research has utilized selective methods because of their convenience.

Much research has employed particular methods or techniques out of methodological parochialism or ethnocentrism (Becker 1970; Mack 1969). Methodologists often push particular pet methods either because those are the only ones they have familiarity with or because they believe their method is superior to all others. What are viewed as "problems" or "disadvantages" of a particular method by others are often ignored as "just interesting obstacles" by a method's proponent.

Among the first behavioral scientists to warn of such "method-boundedness" was Boring (1953:172).

> . . . as long as a new construct has only the single operational definition that it received at birth, it is just a construct. When it gets two alternative operational definitions, it is beginning to be validated. When the defining operations, because of proven correlations, are many, then it becomes reified.

Others (Campbell and Fiske 1959) have since reemphasized the need for such *multiple operationisms* as a corrective for irrelevant components of any measurement procedure. That is, logically they assume (p. 82) that

> When a hypothesis can survive the confrontation of a series of complementary methods of testing, it contains a degree of validity unattainable by one tested within the more constricted framework of a single method. . . . Findings from this latter approach must always be subject to the suspicion that they are method-bound: Will the comparison totter when exposed to an equally prudent but different testing method?

Research methods are never atheoretical or neutral in representing the world "out there." They act as filters through which the environment is selectively experienced. By using one's knowledge of how each method may selectively bias or distort the scientist's picture of "reality," combinations of methods may be selected that more accurately represent what is "out there."

Perhaps the logic of the above will become clearer if the reader will consider (1) the original usage of the word triangulation and (2) our earlier discussion of the rationale for scaling (in Chapter 11).

Triangulation has long been used by maritime navigators and military strategists. Consider, first, the navigator's plight in locating the ship's position. If he or she picks up signals from only one known navigational aid the navigator may know he or she is on a certain course but still cannot ascertain the distance from that aid. However, if he or she can locate *two* known navigational aids and knows their distance from each other, then elementary high-school geometry can be used to locate the ship's exact position.

Second, consider the military strategist's concern with knocking out a *known* enemy position. He or she realizes there is more likelihood of achieving this aim if he or she triangulates by catching the enemy in a crossfire from *several* different positions. Now, what these examples have in common is the use of several locational markers aimed at pinpointing a single objective.

Let us consider these triangulatory devices in terms of the researcher's use of scales. Scales can be viewed as primitive triangulatory devices. We have seen that they tend to be more valid and reliable than single indicators of any phenomenon. In terms of our navigational and military *analogies,* scales use a number of locational markers to pinpoint a particular objective.

Why all the fuss about using a number of such locational markers? Because most of our variables are not directly observable—no one has ever seen, smelled, tasted, heard, or felt an attitude or an atom. When we attempt to measure such abstractions we are really like blind people led into an arena and asked to identify an entity (say, an elephant) by touching one part of that entity (say, a leg). Certainly we might make better guesses if we could pool the information of all of the blind people, each of whom has touched a different part of the elephant.

Previously, we said that scales are only primitive triangulatory devices. The reason for this is that most scales, while composed of more than one locational marker, tend to use locational markers with the same biases. For instance, a Likert scale is particularly susceptible to social desirability response. This is like giving the blind in our elephant analogy the use of touch only in identifying the elephant as an elephant. Likewise, we wish to use *complementary* methods in science since each method has advantages and disadvantages that limit its ability to "see," "taste," "feel," "hear," or "smell" abstractions like "social class" and "cohesion." This is why Christie and Geis (1970) used several different types of scales in measuring Machiavellianism. They wished to approach Machiavellianism from several different vantage points in order to use the complementary advantages of each device. Hence, just as we prefer scales to single measures, we prefer the use of several methodological approaches to a single approach.

Denzin (1970:301) has recently extended this view of triangulation as "only the use of multiple methods in the study of the same object" to include several other types of triangulation.

  I. Data Triangulation
     A. Time
     B. Space
     C. Level of triangulation
        1. Aggregate of persons
        2. Interaction persons
        3. Collectivities of persons
 II. Investigator Triangulation (multiple vs. single observers of the same object)
III. Theory Triangulation (multiple vs. single perspectives in relation to the same set of objects)
 IV. Methodological Triangulation
     A. Within-method
     B. Between-method

Time and monetary considerations normally preclude the single scientific investigator from employing all of these triangulatory devices. Nevertheless, researchers who build as many of these devices into their research as their financial and temporal budgets allow help build a more theoretically rigorous science. In the following sections of this chapter each of Denzin's types of triangulatory distinctions will be examined.

THEORETICAL TRIANGULATION

An extensive argument has been presented in Chapter 2 for the interconnection of theory and methods. Researchers tend to be ethnocentric in ways detrimental to the advancement of science. The investigator's ethnocentrism often shows through in adherence to particular theoretical biases as well as methodological biases. The researcher with a social change or dynamics orientation may unwittingly ignore evidence of a social statics nature, and vice versa. Further, particular theoretical biases tend to be supported more by certain methods than others. Thus, cognitive-developmental theorists may end up studying children in only one culture (for example, Piaget) because they *assume* various processes to proceed through set stages regardless of culture. Ironically, the very assumption that should be tested (through cross-cultural studies in this case) is usually implicitly ignored. Kohlberg (1969:357) has shown that the cognitive-developmental assumption of invariant stages through which dreams develop had to be scrapped after cross-cultural testing.

If there is a moral here it is that investigators should be more active in designing research so that competing theories can be tested. Research that tests competing theories will normally call for a wider range of research techniques than has historically been the case; this virtually assures more confidence in the data analysis since it is more oriented towards the testing of rival causal hypotheses.

Indeed, research *designed* with internal and external validity factors (see Chapter 12) explicitly in mind would go a long way towards indirectly bringing alternative theories into the testing process. The investigator should consider other theoretical dimensions possibly responsible for the effects observed. Dream stages might be culturally specific (as is the case) rather than developmentally invariant (as in studies dealing only with Euro-American children's thought processes).

Few published studies go so far as to discuss alternative theories post hoc in light of the methods used, much less consider alternatives prior to the research. Whitt (1979) has outlined the characteristics of three competing models of political power—pluralist, elitist, and class-dialectic as shown in Figure 13–1. He then used systematic case studies of five related political decisions to assess the relative explanatory power of the three models. The Marxian class-dialectic model, he points out, has been neglected by mainstream sociology yet was highly useful in analysis of political power in his study.

But these studies are not typical of social science research. Theoretical *ethnocentrism* can be found in the majority of published research. Until

	Pluralistic	Elite	Class-Dialectic
Basic units of analysis	Interest groups	Institutional elites	Social institutions; social classes
Essential processes	Interest group competition	Hierarchical dominance by elites	Imperatives of social institutions; class domination and conflict
Basis of group power (resources)	Many bases: organizational, governmental, economic, social, personal	Institutional position, common social background, convergent interests	Class position, degree of class consciousness and organization
Distribution of power	Dispersed among competing, heterogenous groups	Concentrated in relatively homogenous elites	Held by dominant class, but potentially available to subordinate classes
Limits and stability of groups' power	Unstable; limited by democratic value consensus, shifting strength among organized interests and by cross-cutting allegiances	Stable, no identifiable limits to elite domination	Historically contingent; generally stable, but limited by class conflict and contradictions within and among social institutions
Conception of role of the state	State is a broker, able to preserve some autonomy by balancing competing interests	State has little, if any, autonomy; captive of elite interests	State serves interests of dominant class, but requires a degree of autonomy from segments of dominant class in order to act to preserve basis of class hegemony

FIGURE 13–1 *Characteristics of models of power*

Source: Whitt (1979:83).

investigators take theories at odds with their own more seriously in the design of their research there will be little progress made towards unified sociological paradigms. Westie (1957:150, 153) recommends the following procedure in theory triangulation:

1. All existing and plausible propositions in a given area are comprehensively listed.
2. For each of these propositions a list of plausible interpretations is constructed.
3. The actual research is conducted to determine which of the presupposed empirical relationships actually exist.
4. Those presupposed relationships and interpretations attached to them that fail to survive the empirical test are thrown out.
5. Subsequent empirical investigation is used to select the best interpretations from the many contradictory propositions initially formulated.

6. A list of those propositions that passed the empirical test are used to reassess the theories from which they were derived.
7. A reformulated theoretical system is stated based at all points on the empirical tests just conducted.

The advantages of this procedure are fourfold: (1) This procedure minimizes the chance of constructing *internally* consistent logical theories that ignore plausible contradictory propositions outside the theoretical system; (2) the procedure builds in means of testing a whole range of plausible theoretical interpretations; (3) the procedure extends confirmation or doubt to a larger number of theoretical propositions than the usual, more particularistic method of testing a particular set of propositions; (4) because alternative explanations are made explicit from the start, they are more likely to survive as alternative explanations after investigation, thus encouraging *research programs* as opposed to *isolated* research projects.

TIME

Sociology, as we have seen earlier, has tended toward temporal provincialism—85 percent of present-day research refers to only one point in time. This indicates a lack of scientific concern with social change and process.

Sometimes a researcher makes an attempt to study change and process through *cross-sectional* data—data collected at one point in time with the intention of making statements concerning time-related processes. Child development is often studied by comparing children of different ages at one point in time. However, such cross-sectional studies are open to more rival alternative explanations than longitudinal, or time-series, data. It is well documented that older persons tend to be more closed minded than younger individuals. With only cross-sectional data one could explain this observation as due to aging processes *or* to other differences such as the lower educational attainment of older persons. If one were to follow a *cohort* (a specific age group) through the life cycle the aging explanation could best be tested; cross-sectional data, by contrast, better tests the educational level thesis. Thus, one must be careful in choosing longitudinal versus cross-sectional methods since each, like every method, has its own weaknesses and strengths.

There are many practical drawbacks to temporal studies. Perhaps the most obvious is the fact that they often require long waiting periods. Few scientists have the job security to play this waiting game. Rarely is a university enlightened enough to sit patiently for a decade or more while one of its scientists "just" collects time-series data. Some researchers bypass this problem through *retrospective* time-series techniques that are more economical and less time consuming. Studies on careers and social mobility use retrospective time-series techniques quite often (by asking subjects what job they had five years ago, ten years ago, and so on). However, memory decay presents severe problems for the analyst of such data.

Second, changes in various conditions may affect the quality of one's time-series data. If an interview question is worded slightly differently at time two, changes in responses may appear to be due *not* to actual social conditions but rather to interview technique or instrumentation change.

Third, changes in one's variables of interest may have to be standardized in terms of other extraneous changes. As an instance of this, consider absolute changes in birth rates. Absolute birth rate changes are meaningless—consider an absolute birth rate of 100 new births in a city of 10,000 compared to the same city 20 years later with a population of 40,000 and 400 yearly births. Absolutely the birth rate has risen fourfold; relative to population size, however, it has not increased. Thus, as Simon (1969:149) notes, "the researcher must separate the change caused by the internal processes of the material, which he is interested in, from the *environmental* change effects."

Fourth, time periods must be appropriately chosen. Some social processes are relatively short-run, such as those found in many attitude-change experiment findings; other changes like developmental changes may take years to work themselves out, such as in Terman's (1925) studies of genius. Thus, repeated observations must correspond with the time of actual change if the process is to be accurately gauged.

Panel analysis is often used to compare the *same* measurements for the *same* sample at several *different* points in time. A special type of panel analysis is termed *cohort analysis*. Cohort analysis uses a sample of relatively narrow ranged ages. A researcher interested in socialization might take a sample of individuals between the ages five to ten and study this *cohort* at several yearly intervals. By contrast, a researcher interested in unemployment might take a sample of all individuals old enough to work full-time legally (fourteen years of age and older) and study this *panel* over several years.

It is important in cohort or panel analysis to analyze the data in unaggregated form since aggregated data can mask actual change. If 20 percent of people change from more positive to less positive attitudes while an equal percent change from less to more positive, separate data in aggregate form could not reveal such changes.

Panel studies also often involve invalidity problems of subject mortality and reactive testing effects. Maslany and MacKay (1974) attempted to locate 320 participants from a large midwestern Canadian city who had served in a study of academic achievement seven years previously. A preliminary search located sixty participants who were sent a list containing the names of persons who could not be located. Participants were given a sum of money for each address they provided from whose residences a properly completed questionnaire was received by the researchers. This procedure resulted in the receipt of over 151 (only 43 percent) follow-up questionnaires of the original study. Kohn and Schooler (1978) were more fortunate in a follow-up study. Of 883 randomly selected men they were able to succeed in locating 820 (93 percent) ten years later. Through the cooperation of the post office, telephone company, past employers, and unions these men were traced even though many had changed residences a great many times.

Sometimes, to avoid problems of reactive effects and participant mortality, the researcher foregoes panel or cohort analysis and takes different samples at different points in time. While this may cut down on costs of finding the same people twice, it is a much less effective approach to the study of change than is panel or cohort analysis. Its disadvantages are that it (1) may introduce invalidity through unequivalent samples (history, maturation, differential selection of participants) and (2) can only be examined in aggregate form since the same participants are not measured at each point in time.

In addition, the panel study is actually a time-series of static "snapshots" or cross-sectional analyses. For this reason some researchers use *trend studies* of selected processes, not at a few isolated points as in a panel study, but continually over time. The major disadvantage of this procedure is that practically one can focus only on relatively few processes in comparison to panel analysis.

Figure 13–2 shows the unmistakably related trend relationship between cigarette smoking and lung cancer. The nature of this relationship is obscure because of the long latent period between the increase in cigarette consumption and the increase in the incidence of lung cancer. In men (top two lines) smoking began to increase at the beginning of the twentieth century, but the corresponding trend in deaths from lung cancer did not begin until after 1920. In women (bottom two lines) smoking began later, and lung cancers are only now appearing.

This comparison of cross-sectional and longitudinal analyses points to the need for combining approaches where structure, structural changes, and intervening processes are to be observed. Kass (1977) compared the longitudinal and the cross-sectional perspectives in

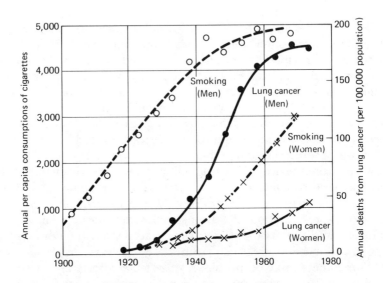

FIGURE 13–2 *Annual per capita cigarette consumption and death rates from lung cancer, England and Wales 1900–1980.*

Source: From "The Cancer Problem" by John Cairns. *Scientific American* (November 1979), p. 72. Copyright © 1975 by Scientific American, Inc. All rights reserved.

examining changes in male income from 1950 to 1970. On a longitudinal basis, as men age to the retirement years their income continues to increase. A cross-sectional analysis leads to the conclusion that there is a decline in income during the later working years. Even after adjusting for change in the cost of living and productivity levels of workers, these conflicting conclusions do not change to any great degree.

SPACE

If the social and behavioral sciences have neglected the time dimension they have been equally negligent of the space dimension. The setting of 75 percent of recently published sociological research was in the United States (Brown and Gilmartin 1969:287). A perusal of the 1972 American Psychological Association *Proceedings* turned up 61 percent of the articles based on college student samples. Not only are the behavioral sciences culture-bound, they are subculture-bound. Yet many such scholarly works are written as if basic principles have been discovered that would hold true as tendencies in any society, anywhere, anytime. As with other methodological decisions, the convenience of available populations is often counterproductive to theory building.

By the use of relatively homogeneous populations we tend to lose potentially large amounts of variance in our variables. LeVine (1966) has cogently developed this thesis. He gives several examples of population variations cross-culturally. For instance, compare Western behavior with the Gussii, an African tribe of southwestern Kenya, where "it is considered appropriate and desirable for females, to resist and cry or moan during sexual intercourse" (LeVine 1966:34). Hong (1978) compared people on Taiwan with Americans and found the Chinese to be more cautious in making solitary and group decisions. Inkeles and Smith (1974) have found significant differences among nations such as Israel, India, and East Pakistan (Bangladesh) in attitudes towards modernity. Caton (reported in *Behavior Today,* February 6, 1979) has found that daily Arabian life is permeated with the use of spoken poetry. Robbins and others (1978) have shown significant differences in the type, number, and rate of nonverbal behaviors used by middle- and working-class speakers in conversational turn-taking.

LeVine (1966) has adopted Campbell and Fiske's (1959) strategy of convergent validation in comparative studies, so that each hypothesized difference between populations is measured by several different instruments designed to capture the same type of choice pattern in different situations.

> I have studied differences in achievement motivation among three Nigerian ethnic groups by the analysis of dream reports, written expressions of values, and public opinion survey data. The convergence of findings from the diverse sets of data (and samples) strengthens my conviction . . . that the differences among the groups are not artifacts produced by measuring instruments. (LeVine 1966:45)

Nevertheless, analysis across space, particularly with comparison of divergent cultures, presents at least six fundamental problems of analysis (Naroll 1968): (1) causal inferences from correlations; (2) societal or subsocietal unit definition; (3) sampling bias; (4) Galton's problem, the problem of interdependence of cases; (5) data quality control, the problem of trustworthiness of data; and (6) categorization, the problem of defining concepts for trait categories that are suitable in any cultural context. Each problem as it presents itself in comparative methods is discussed below.

Causal Inferences from Correlations

A standard cross-cultural project is to show correlations between two variables. Lambert, Triandis, and Wolf (1959) have related beliefs in the malevolence or benevolence of the supernatural world to infant and child-rearing practices of particular cultures. They then went on to assume that there was a *causal* relationship accounting for the correlation. This temptation to assume that correlation means causation is often great even though any introductory statistics student realizes correlation is only a necessary, not sufficient, condition for causation. The problem is more critical in cross-cultural than in more traditional research since the observed correlation may well be an *artifact* of one or more of the five other cross-cultural problems (Naroll 1968:244). Stated somewhat differently, cross-culturally generated correlations generally have more plausible rival explanations than more traditional research.

Societal and Subsocietal Unit Definitions

Naroll (1968:248) lists six criteria that have been used to define societal or subsocietal units of comparison.

1. Distribution of particular traits being studied
2. Territorial contiguity
3. Political organization
4. Language
5. Ecological adjustment
6. Local community structure.

(For a more extensive view of the different definitions of "societies" compare the following contributions to the *International Encyclopedia of the Social Sciences:* "Chinese Society," "Anglo-American Society," "Asian Society: South Asia," "Near Eastern Society: Israel," "African Society: North Africa," and "Oceanian Society.")

Defining units of analysis by such means becomes complex and somewhat arbitrary when one encounters situations such as political states with mutually unintelligible dialects (Zulus). Thus, unique problems concerning operationalization of comparative units of analysis occur in cross-cultural research.

Vallier (1971b:208–227) believes cross-cultural researchers have an overconcern with society as the unit of selection and observation. While he admits that societies are of special theoretical interest because of problems of "integration, legitimacy, continuity, and order, that are not exhibited in other types of collectivities," he points out that there is a chief drawback in characterizing societies in terms of cultural terms such as "dominant values," "modal personality," "overriding beliefs," and "typical patterns" since such explanations tend to "close off other explanatory levels." Vallier believes more attention should be placed on selection of the *structural components* (role systems, status hierarchies) of societies so that cultural explanations may be balanced by possible structural interpretations. As Vallier (1971*b*:210) puts it, "the 'cultural' fallacy in certain kinds of macro-structural studies is as prevalent, and perhaps as misleading, as the ecological fallacy in studies of behavior." Paige (1975) neatly side-stepped this old problem by concentrating on "agricultural export sectors" rather than nations in his study of the agrarian revolution in underdeveloped countries. He used the Brazilian coffee area as one unit and the Brazilian sugar area as another.

In addition to the theoretical problems of sampling societies, there are several practical problems. First, it is extremely difficult to observe a total primitive society much less a total contemporary, complex society. Thus, the use of total societies as the unit of analysis puts the researcher "under pressure to search for distinct 'essences' and comprehensive summations of typicality." These procedures have the unfortunate consequence of tending to represent societies as more homogeneous and harmonious than may actually be the case. As Vallier (1971*b*:215 notes,

> . . . very important intra-societal variations in structure . . . exist and constitute very important sources of the society's dynamic, including types of cleavages, forms of competition and conflict, and the strains that accrue from sectorial lags and imbalances. Intra-societal variations in structure are undoubtedly the frontier for future studies of cross-national scope.

Second, using the total society as the unit of analysis "the number of cases that can be studied tends to be limited and consequently the range of variation considered is limited" (Linz and Miguel 1966:268). While there are an estimated 5,000 distinct societies, ethnographic data exist on only about 2,000. The most assessable and complete documentation—Murdock's World Ethnographic Sample—contains data on only 500 societies.

Sampling Bias

It has been pointed out (Naroll 1968:253) that published cross-cultural surveys to date have depended on *purposive* sampling to choose the societies studied, and then sampling judgments have been made "without much care or precision." Ideally, stratified probability sampling, based on geographical area, is particularly desirable since neighboring societies are more likely than nonneighboring societies to share similar cultural traits and artifacts. Such similarities between neighboring societies create problems for correlational analysis since cultural diffusion will tend to inflate correlations spuriously.

Galton's Problem

The major weakness of cross-cultural methodology is Galton's problem: using cultural units as *independent* tests of correlations between variables when each cultural unit may not actually represent independent trials. Both the Hopi and Navajo Indians use a rain dance. But the researcher should not assume these dances exist independently of each other just because these neighboring tribes have different cultural origins. Cultural diffusion of the rain dance from one culture to the other is a distinct possibility; independence of cases may be a false assumption in this example. Indeed, Naroll (1965) presents evidence that variables are often highly correlated cross-culturally because of geographical diffusion of traits between neighboring cultures. Thus, he suggests measuring the possible effects of geographical propinquity (closeness) and diffusion in cross-cultural studies as a means of checking whether the correlation holds up independently of geographical propinquity and diffusion.

Data Quality Controls

In the chapter on field work we considered several means of checking data quality control. The same reliability and validity problems occur in cross-cultural research but are usually more suspect due to the greater possibilities of ethnocentrism, unawareness of the complexities of non-Western societies, and translation difficulties. Naroll (1968:266–276) suggests six means of assessing quality of cross-cultural field data.

1. Field time in terms of months in field and number of field workers
2. Degree of participation in daily life of the natives
3. Native language familiarity
4. Field report lengths
5. Publication date of field report
6. Number of native helpers and informants.

It should be recognized that these means of assessment will not always work nor always be necessary. One of the greatest anthropologists —Evans-Pritchard—worked alone. And Edmund Leach lost his field books yet wrote a highly regarded work on a Burmese tribe.

Verba (1971:320) suggests a partial solution. Cross-cultural researchers should use multiple measures, since they "allow one to test whether the alternative items cluster together and can be assumed to be indeed measuring the same thing." Since some measures may be culturally specific it may be possible to test whether these items measure the same dimension cross-culturally through measuring the degree to which these cultural-specific items cluster with items that are "identical" across cultures. Verba provides an example of this from his own research on types of cultural participation. He studied participation in voting, campaigning beyond the vote, cooperative group activity, and contacting officials in India and the United States. Some of the indicators of each type of participation were identical while others were different "since each nation provides citizens with a different repertory of participatory acts." Nevertheless, analysis supported the assumption that most of the country-specific participatory acts clustered together under the expected type of participatory act.

Cross-Cultural Categorization

If operationalization of noncomparative research presents problems, then cross-cultural operationalism is even more difficult. In addition to typical operational problems of finding reliable and valid indicators or classifications, one is faced with maximizing equivalence of stimuli cross-culturally. While the concept "mother" may be compared cross-culturally, the terms "uncle," "aunt," and "cousin" are too ambiguous to be used loosely in comparative studies. Thus: How can one faithfully translate or reproduce the *ambiguity* and *complexity* of one culture into another culture's terminology? Or, more simply: What is equivalent? Clearly, the more complex (multidimensional) or ambiguous a stimuli, the more difficult comparison becomes. For instance, Anderson (1967) points out that

> A non-verbal personality test, such as the TAT or Rorschach, appears to avoid the problem of translation except with respect to instructions given during administration. Lindzey rightly observes that differences in response language in cross-cultural testing by these techniques result in a shift of the location of the translation problem rather than its elimination. The Welsh Figure Preference Test minimizes these problems of response translation by asking the respondent to indicate whether or not he likes each stimulus—rather than asking for complex responses as with other "projective" tests.
>
> Even with the Welsh test where the problems of comparing verbal responses in different languages have been effectively eliminated by reducing the content of the responses to a binary choice situation, translation difficulties remain. Consider, for example, Figure 13–3a taken from this instrument. A biology student in any Western European society could clearly and unambiguously interpret this stimulus—and his [or her] liking or disliking of it would probably be influenced by his [or her] interpretation. Figure 13–3b, on the other hand, has no clearly understood meaning to a

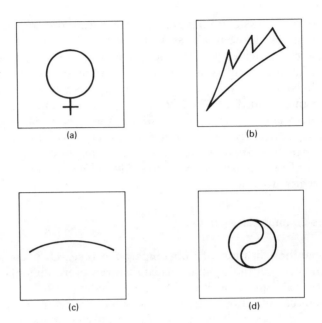

(a)

(b)

(c)

(d)

FIGURE 13–3 *Pictures adapted from the Welsh Figure Preference Test.*

Source: Published by Consulting Psychologists Press, Inc., Palo Alto, California. Research edition, Copyright 1949 by George S. Welsh, released for research use, 1959, by the publishers.

Western European—yet an American Indian might well interpret it in terms of the pictographic symbol for "mountain" as can be seen by comparison with Figure 13–4a. It would be naive to assume that these and similar differences in interpretation which might obtain across societies would not influence responses differentially.

Verba (1971:327–331), in addition to his already suggested use of a multiple measures approach, argues for "contextual comparisons" cross-culturally.

What is compared is not the absolute frequency of, say, voting between two systems, nor even the absolute frequencies of voting within comparable subgroups in two systems. Rather, one compares systems in terms of the ways in which voting rates *differ* among subgroups within the several systems. Does voting turnout increase as one moves up the status hierarchy in all systems under study? ... Thus, the comparative question one asks is not whether Americans participate more actively than Frenchmen ... but how workers in each nation differ from other occupational groups. (Verba 1971:327–328)

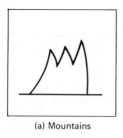

(a) Mountains

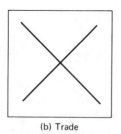

(b) Trade

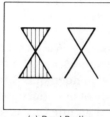

(c) Dead Bodies

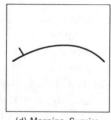

(d) Morning, Sunrise

FIGURE 13–4 *Pictures adapted from "Pictography and Ideography of the Sioux and Ojibway Tribes of North American Indians" by William Tomkins.*

Source: In *Universal Indian Sign Language of the Plains Indians of North America* by William Tomkins. Published at San Diego, California, in 1929 by the author. The section from which these pictures are adapted is pp. 70–78 in this volume.

Contextual comparisons achieve at least two positive results. First, they *control* for many possible differences in the cultural systems (education level, social class). Second (Verba 1971:329), while it is difficult to

> ... find equivalent absolute measures of social class or education in different political contexts, it is quite easy to find ordinal measures such that we can be sure that within each individual system we have people who are arrayed on similar hierarchies.

Lincoln and others (1978) found that Western versus Japanese work and authority relations were dependent on the proportion of Japanese nationals and Japanese-Americans who were employees in Japanese business organizations in the southern California region.

Furthermore, the researcher need not look for items that are equivalent in all respects. Rather, he or she may use "functional equivalents." That is, the researcher may make use of the fact that the same function or basic dimension may be performed by alternative institutions or in alternative ways. It may be better to begin comparative research by searching for fairly *general* variables before searching for equivalent measures. As an example, status may be best measured by wealth in one nation, ownership of cattle in another, and multidimensionally by an index of wealth, occupation, and education in still another. Thus, the cross-cultural researcher need not be concerned with total equivalence of measures. What is important is that his or her measures be equivalent in terms of the dimensions they tap or functions they serve.

In contrast, items that appear on the surface to be equivalent (political positions, occupational rankings) may not be equivalent cross-culturally. Rather, individuals in different cultures may *interpret,* or otherwise give subjective meanings, dissimilarly. Acts of prostitution are subjectively viewed negatively in most contemporary Western countries, yet they may be viewed by some cultures as religious acts of a most positive nature. Verba (1971:321) suggests that open-ended question design will typically provide "the researcher with a body of material out of which one can more easily locate lack of equivalence than one can in response to a fixed choice question" design. Fixed response categories are too rigid to pick up richly and subtly textured differences between cultures.

Given the unique pitfalls and problems of the cross-cultural method, what are its advantages? First, it acts as a check on the culture-boundedness versus generality of our findings. Second, "it increases the range of variation of many variables" (Whiting 1968:694). Figure 13–5 beautifully shows the culture-boundedness of much American child-rearing and mental illness data. Without the cross-cultural cases (dotted line), we could easily be misled into thinking that later child-weaning is directly related to incidence of emotional disturbance. However, the cross-cultural cases show that the relationship between age of weaning and emotional disturbance may be curvilinear (an inverted U), so that weaning after eighteen months shows an inverse relationship.

Third, Whiting (1968:696) further points out that

> The cross-cultural method, by studying cultural norms, holds individual variation constant. Psychological studies of individuals in a single society do just the opposite, in that cultural norms are held constant and individual variations are studied.

Of course, the logic of Whiting's comments holds for sociological studies in single societies since there, too, cultural norms are held constant while social variations are studied. Three other advantages to cross-cultural research are pointed to by Marsh (1961): Fourth, comparative analysis may be used to replicate studies done in similar societies; fifth, it may be used to generalize propositions from one type of society to

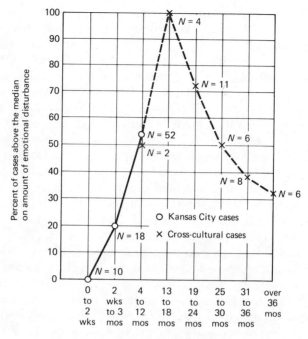

FIGURE 13–5 *Relation between age at onset of weaning and amount of emotional disturbance shown by child. Comparable data from 80 individual children from Kansas City (Sears and Wise 1950) and from 37 societies (Whiting and Child 1953) are presented.*

Source: Lindzey and Aronson, *Handbook of Social Psychology,*© 1968, Addison-Wesley Publishing Company, Inc., from "Methods and problems in cross-cultural research" by Whiting. Pages 693–728. Reprinted with permission.

other types; sixth, it may lead to apparently discrepant findings over different societies that may then lead to the development of a more encompassing theory to account for those discrepancies.

DIMENSIONS OF ANALYSIS

Although there are a multitude of levels at which one can collect sociological data (voter precinct, individual, top-level management, census tract), there are quite basic differences among, and uses of, seven prototype levels or dimensions of data collection and analysis: (1) aggregative (individual), (2) interactive (or group or relational), (3) organizational, (4) ecological, (5) institutional, (6) cultural, and (7) societal units.

Aggregative analysis fails "to establish social links between those observed" (Denzin 1970:302). Most demographic studies (birth and death rates statistics) and survey sampling are aggregative by nature. Indeed, one must be particularly wary of the fallacy of the wrong level of analysis in the use of such aggregative data for sociological purposes. Many studies that *appear* to focus on the marital dyads actually sample one member of the dyad and use that person's data *as if* it represented the entire dyad.

Most sociological research has utilized aggregative data as either its primary or sole source of characterization. Aggregative variables derive from accumulations of individual characteristics. For instance, per capita income is an average income standardized on individuals which is often used to characterize the wealth of geographic regions; homogeneity of groups is often measured through some measure of dispersion or distribution (standard deviation) of individuals on a particular variable.

By contrast to aggregative analysis, the other six levels of analysis are more global in that they characterize the collective as a whole and do not derive from an accumulation of individual characteristics.

Relational (group) analysis is concerned with interactional network patterns between individuals and groups. Kendall (1963) has used relational variables such as workload ratios of patients to hospital staff and degree of intern-resident affiliation. Coleman (1959) points to homogeneity indices within friendship cliques and sociometric pair analysis as further techniques for analyzing relations between individuals. Barton (1961:240) has referred to relational studies using amount of communication, referrals, joint activities, and transfer of resources between different types of organizations. Notice in each of these cases that a *group* characteristic is analyzed without reference to individual properties. The recently established journal *Network Analysis* specializes in reporting these types of studies.

While organizations may be viewed as being made up of individual members, organizations usually can additionally be seen as having qualities unattributable to those individuals. This can be inferred from the simple observation that organizations tend to persist with membership change. Thus, many organizational properties simply cannot be inferred from cumulations of individual properties. Some examples of *organizational units of analysis* that have consistently proven worthwhile to examine are: bureaucratization, criteria (universalistic versus particularistic) of promotion and recruitment, fineness of hierarchical discrimination, rigidity of rules, and type of organizational control (public versus private, sectarian versus nonsectarian, decentralized versus centralized).

Institutional analysis compares relationships within and across the legal, political, economic, and/or familial institutions of society. On the one hand, elements may be compared within institutions. Many researchers interested in familial patterns examine the relationships between variables like familial authoritarian structures and familial division of labor. On the other hand, comparisons across institutions might also prove interesting. What similarities and differences, for example, exist in the relationship between authority structure and division of labor in familial as compared to religious organizations? Rosenberg (1968:24) points out that classical sociology was strongly associated with institutional analysis. Marx analyzed the political, scientific, legal, artistic, and religious institutional "superstructures" partially in terms of the economic "substructure." Similarly, Durkheim discussed changes in the economy as a function of changes in the legal system.

Ecological analysis is concerned with spatial explanations. The field of crime and delinquency has used ecological data quite often for analytic purposes. Studies abound using variables such as proportion of broken homes, average voting rate, mean rental rates, or average income rates for particular *areas* (census tracts) to explain crime rates, delinquency rates, or patterns of social disorganization. Some of the classic studies of cities used ecological analysis as a primary descriptive-explanatory device. Land-use patterns have been studied as a function of transportation networks in a large number of ecological studies. At a more micro level of analysis, recent interest has sprung up concerning face-to-face spatial patterns (Hall 1959, 1963).

Cultural analysis, as we stated earlier in the chapter, refers to the association of norms, values, practices, traditions, ideologies, technological objects, and other artifacts of culture. Since we have already discussed this in detail under the chapter section on "space" triangulation, no further discussion is needed here.

Societal analysis typically uses gross indicators such as degree of urbanization, industrialization, education, gross national product, and distribution of political power and wealth. Lipset (1963) has shown the political stability of democratic nations to be a function of high wealth, industrialization, education, and urbanization.

The distinctions between these seven types of analysis are blurred by the fact that properties of one type of characteristic sometimes may be constructed from properties of another type. For example, "being a worker in a *big shop*" uses a group characteristic context while "being a worker *in a shop with high consensus*" is a property that could be constructed from aggregative data (the percentage of individuals having agreement on some normative matter).

Since individuals may be influenced by, or as part of, many different levels of an organization at any particular time, it is often useful to design a study that analyzes more than one level simultaneously, much as one might analyze the human body through plastic overlays of skin, muscular materials, and skeletal and organ fabrics. Thus, inhabitants, precincts, and cities might all be elements of the same study. More specifically, as in Lipset, Trow, and Coleman's (1956) study of union democracy, one could analyze union shops simultaneously as aggregates of individual workers, members of local shops, and collectives.

Kanter's (1977) well-received *Men and Women of the Corporation* likewise has received its acclaim in large part because in it she explores three crucial organizational structures and processes salient in determining the behavior of employees: vertical mobility opportunity structures, power structures, and the relative numbers of socially diverse people as an effect on fates of individuals by using a blend of types of data (interviews, observations, content analysis of corporation documents). As Denzin (1970:302) has aptly pointed out, those sociological studies that have commonly come to be regarded as classic usually have *combined* several levels of analysis.

FALLACY OF THE WRONG LEVEL OF ANALYSIS

In the last section we saw that disciplinary problems are often defined by a particular *level* of analysis. Occasionally, researchers working at a particular level of analysis uncritically assume that their findings can be generalized to some other level of analysis without additional empirical verification. The Parsons (1966) sociological school of thought has treated small, informal groups as microcosms of the larger society. On the other hand, other social scientists (Homans) believe that society is more than its constituent groups and that societal processes involve complex ties not exhibited by small, informal groups. Clearly, we have here an instance of different paradigms concerning the legitimate *scope* of our empirical generalizations.

Galtung (1967:45) terms this problem of scope the *fallacy of the wrong level of analysis*. It is committed by researchers who make inferences, *without empirical justification,* to a theoretical unit that is smaller or larger than the unit of observation. One must be particularly cautious in interpreting data that shares this problem. As Coleman (1964a:84) notes,

> One important measurement problem in sociology concerns the two levels on which the sociologist must work: the level of the individual and that of the group. We have observations at two levels, and relationships at two levels. Furthermore, it is often necessary to shift back and forth: measuring group-level concepts from individual data; or inferring individual relationships from group-level relations.

Changing levels of analysis would not be a problem if researchers would make an effort to *test empirically* changes in theoretical level of analysis, rather than *assume* that their theory generalizes to different levels of analysis.

As a matter of practicality, the researcher is limited by his or her data in the attempt to deal empirically with this problem. For instance, research based on census data deals with pooled data on individuals as a matter of protection of individual privacy. Nevertheless, researchers often feel no hesitancy about making generalizations to individuals from this aggregated data. Generalizing aggregated data to individuals is most susceptible to the fallacy of the wrong level of analysis. One basic reason for this is that individuals are not normally *randomly* spaced. Individuals tend to be *clustered* in relatively small, homogeneous groupings that are reflected in statistical analysis. Yule and Kendall (1950) present a classic example of aggregation effects. They calculated the degree of association between wheat and potato yields for 48 English counties. The association was quite low (it was only +0.219 on a scale from 0.0 to 1.0). However, when they *pooled* data on contiguous counties they were able to get a reasonable high association (+0.765) between wheat and potato yields.

As a general rule measures of association tend to increase with increasing aggregation. As another example, Gehlke and Biehel (1943) progressively grouped Cleveland census tracts into larger units. They found as they analyzed larger units that the association between male juvenile deliquency rates and monthly rental rates increased. It would obviously be fallacious to take such aggregated data to mean that higher rental rates caused more delinquency, or vice versa. But the researcher unaware of this problem is likely to take such data seriously.

A common occurrence of this fallacy (Robinson 1950) is the *ecological correlation*. Robinson demonstrated that it was *fallacious* to assume that properties found to be correlated (associated) at the group level (for example, mental illness incidence and census tracts nearer the central city) are also correlated at the individual level. Thus, in designing research involving different levels of analysis, it is wise not to assume that associations computed for variables at one level of analysis (census tracts) will hold for variables computed at another level (individuals living in those same tracts). This is always an *empirical* question and quite often the fallacy is recommitted. The Bureau of Federal Narcotics based its original fallacious claim that marijuana smoking leads to heroin usage on a weak association between marijuana and heroin usage among lower-class blacks. They were arguing from a relatively small group of users to the total society. (A second additional fallacy was the assumption that an association implies causality. It does not, as evidenced by the positive association between being bottle-fed as a baby and later marijuana smoking.)

The fallacy of the wrong level of analysis keeps popping up in disguised or partially disguised form. A recent example can be seen in a work by Polsby (1969:118) where it is assumed that one can deduce a special stratification theory of *community* power from a general theory of social stratification at the *societal* level. Again, this should be a matter of *empirical* research and not an unquestioned theoretical assumption. For instance, it is well known that some state governmental social structures differ from the national governmental from (that is, unicameral legislatures); why, therefore, should community and national power *necessarily* be stratified in the same way?

Firebaugh (1978) has given us a rule for knowing when aggregate level data provide unbiased estimates of individual-level relationships: Bias is absent when, and only when, the group mean of the independent variable has no effect on the dependent variable, with the independent variable controlled. Hence, cross-level inferences from higher to lower levels of analysis can be made without bias when, and only when, effects of the mean of the independent variable are absent. (Inferences from individual to group or higher levels are no problem since the researcher can group the data as desired.)

INVESTIGATOR TRIANGULATION

"Investigator triangulation simply means that multiple as opposed to single observers are employed" (Denzin 1970:303). The use of multiple observers, if properly handled, may lead to more reliable and valid data quality controls. We have shown in Chapter 4 that participant observers tend to have quite different observation patterns—some being more "empirical," others more "holistic," and still others more "social anthropological" ethnographers.

Further, there are variations in how some people identify odors, tastes, and emotional states, and there are differences in observational frames of reference. If multiple observers are used, their data can be compared in order to check for such potentially biased reporting. Investigator bias is always a potential problem regardless of method.

Even though more highly structured methods have less need for investigator triangulation, the need is always there for reliability and validity quality controls. Interinvestigator reliability correlations can tell much about the consistency of our methods. Strauss and his colleagues (1964:36) illustrate this in an observational study of mental hospital interaction.

> There were three fieldworkers subjected for the most part to the same raw data. Search for pinpointing and negative evidence was abetted by the

collective nature of our inquiry. If the colleague reported the same kind of observation as another without prior consultation, confidence grew. If after hearing the report of an observation, a colleague was himself able unquestionably to duplicate it, it indicated that our observational techniques had some degree of reliability. If no colleague did corroborate an observation —which did happen—if it seemed important then, or later, further inquiry was initiated. Something like a built-in reliability check was thus obtained because several fieldworkers were exposed directly to similar or identical data.

Perhaps the greatest use of investigator triangulation centers around validity rather than reliability checks. More to the point, investigators with differing perspective or paradigmatic biases may be used to check out the extent of divergence in the data each collects. Under such conditions if data divergence is minimal then one may feel more confidence in the data's validity. On the other hand, if their data are significantly different, then one has an idea as to possible sources of biased measurement that should be further investigated.

METHODOLOGICAL TRIANGULATION

Triangulation of methods takes two forms: within methods and between methods. Each type will be discussed in turn in this section.

Within Methods

Triangulation within methods usually involves *replication* for purposes of reliability and theory confirmation. That is, within-methods triangulation can be used as a test-retest reliability check on data quality and as a means of confirming the validity of earlier findings through checks on the stability of earlier findings.

Ironically, while replication is a basic tenet of scientific advancement, there have been few published replications in the social and behavioral sciences. Indeed, some social science journals have traditionally rejected replications, particularly those showing evidence contrary to originally published materials.

Even more dismaying from this standpoint is the fact that much of published research produces ex post facto theory. Ex post facto theory is particularly in need of confirmation by replication since unanticipated results are conceivably due to chance factors. (By chance alone, five out of 100 results should be statistically significant at the .05 level.)

Between Methods

Triangulation, through the use of different methods, finds its main value in *dis*confirming the tenability of arguments that findings are artifacts of particular methods. Conversely, it may show findings to be simple artifacts of particular methods. A classic paper by Hovland (1959:13) on attitude change studies shows very clearly some of the limitations of experiments and survey methods.

> What seems to me quite apparent is that a genuine understanding of the effects of communications on attitudes requires both the survey and the experimental methodologies. At the same time, there appear to be certain inherent limitations of each method which must be understood by the researcher if he is not to be blinded by his preoccupation with one of the other types of design. Integration of the two methodologies will require on the part of the experimentalist an awareness of the narrowness of the laboratory in interpreting the larger and more comprehensive effects of communication. It will require on the part of the survey researcher a greater awareness of the limitations of the correlational method as a basis for establishing relationships.

In Table 13–1 some inadequacies and deficiencies of five different data-gathering devices are visually displayed. This table shows how much better it would be to combine our methods, so that we could take advantage of the strong points of each type of data, cross-check data collected by each method, and collect information that is available only through particular techniques.

Sieber (1973) has given the most exhaustive rationale to date for integrating particular methods. He shows how field work may contribute to survey data design, collection, and analysis, and vice versa. He points out (1973:1343) that field work may often valuably precede surveys by providing "information about the receptivity, frames of reference and span of attention of respondents." On the other hand, surveys may contribute to field work through (1973:1354) "(1) correction of the holistic fallacy [tendency of the field observer to perceive all aspects of a social situation as congruent], (2) demonstration of the generality of a single observation, (3) verification of field interpretations, and (4) the casting of new light on field observations."

One of the more glaring needs is for triangulation for verbal data on behavior. As we have seen from the argument in Chapter 6, survey data often correlates very poorly with observational data, yet survey results that ask people what they did or do are generally accepted at face value. Wilson and Nisbet (1978) present evidence that people's introspective reports are highly inaccurate. Their findings indicate that re-

Table 13–1

Comparison of Five Methods for Researching Informal Communication in Organizations

Method	Operational Approach	Principal Data Secured	Main Strength(s)	Main Weakness(es)
Participant-observer	Long-run operational contact	Examples and judgments	Provides insights into ongoing communication	Time consuming; often nonquantitative; may influence data
Continuous observation	Observation of one person or job	Information flow through one person or job	Portrays communication role of one job; quantitative	Does not reveal broad patterns of communication; may influence data
Communication sampling	Statistical sample of communication	Variety of communication events	Sample is more economical than 100 percent observation	Interrupts work
General communication surveys	Questionnaire and/or interview	Unlimited quantitative and qualitative information	Secures more data for less cost	Responses based mainly on memory and judgments
Networks surveys (ECCO surveys)	Timely survey of a communication episode	Information on communication flow and networks	Relates networks to communication and organizational variables	Effective only in smaller groups up to 500 persons

SOURCE: Keith Davis, "Methods for Studying Informal Communication," *Journal of Communication* (Winter 1978).

search that relies on people's introspective reports about the causes of their behavior may have little value as a guide to the true causal influences.

Community power studies have afforded an interesting debate in recent years over the possible theoretical biases particular research methods may have (Walton 1966; Clark and others 1968; Polsby 1969; Kerbo and Fave 1979). There are two controversial methodological orientations in this debate. The first is the *reputational* method in which the researcher asks panels of "judges" to identify community leaders. The second, in contrast, is the *decisional* method or, in other words, some combination of methods in which relatively eclectic methods are used, generally case studies collected in an anthropological or journalistic manner. Walton (1966) and Clark and others (1968) found that researchers who used the reputational method exclusively tend to find more centralized decision-making structures than researchers using other methods. That is, the reputational method appears to channel descriptions of community power structure toward "elitists" interpretations and *away from* "pluralistics" state of affairs. As described by Polsby (1969:118), pluralistic power structures tend to have

> ... dispersion of power among many rather than a few participants in decision making; competition or conflict among political leaders; specialization of leaders to relatively restricted sets of issue areas; bargaining rather than hierarchical decision making; elections in which suffrage is relatively wide-spread as a major determinant of participation in key decisions; bases of influence over decisions relatively dispersed rather than closely held; and so on.

Of course, there are alternative explanations for this method-theory correspondence. For example, as Clark and associates (1968:215) state, it is possible that researchers who use particular methods tend to select (consciously or not) particular types of communities.

Studies of theories of crime afford another assessment of the effects of method on theory testing. Hindelang (1978) has indicated that black overrepresentation in arrestees for common personal crimes can be attributed to at least two causes: (1) disproportionate involvement in criminal offenses and (2) criminal justice system selection biases. Studies relying on official data have generally supported the differential involvement hypothesis, while studies relying on self-report techniques generally have supported the differential selection hypothesis.

While there are several other plausible explanations for method-theory correspondence in community power and crime studies, it can nevertheless be stated that *particular types of methods are usually interpretable only through particular types of theory and will generally produce only selective theoretical explanations.* Thus, our plea is for a social research norm that gives lowest degrees of confirmation to propositions confirmed by only one method and higher degrees of confirmation when multiple methods are used.

Indeed, Campbell and Fiske's (1959) rationale for convergent and discriminant validation of research operations gives a final rationale for multimethod approaches since measures should correlate more highly with other measures of the same concept using different methods (convergent validation) than with a measure of a different concept using the same method (discriminant validation).

READINGS FOR ADVANCED STUDENTS

RICHARD W. BRISLIN, WALTER J. LONNER, AND ROBERT M. THORNDIKE, *Cross-Cultural Research Methods*, 1973. The chapter on wording and translation is particularly good in this book. The book is psychologically oriented but has good advice on surveys, experiments, and psychological testing.

DONALD T. CAMPBELL AND DONALD W. FISKE, "Convergent and Discriminant Validation by the Multitrait-Multimethod Matrix," *Psychological Bulletin* 56 (1959):81–105. Sophisticated argument for multiple operationalism.

PAUL F. LAZARSFELD, ANN K. PASANELLA, AND MORRIS ROSENBERG (eds.), *Continuities in the Language of Social Research,* 1972, Sections III and IV. Excellent selection of articles and annotated bibliographies on the study of change using panels and relational and collectivity measures of analysis.

W. D. WALL AND H. L. WILLIAMS, *Longitudinal Studies and the Social Sciences,* 1970. The Social Science Research Council commissioned this important review of longitudinal collection methods, and the reader will find many practical suggestions, particularly in Chapter 3.

DONALD P. WARWICK AND S. OSHERSON, *Comparative Research Methods,* 1973. The discussion of important topics such as conceptual equivalence, cultural bias, measurement equivalence, and translation.

SUGGESTED RESEARCH PROJECTS

1. Design a sociological study in which you use as many of the means of triangulation found in this chapter as possible.
2. Criticize some sociological journal article or monograph from the standpoint of its need for specific types of triangulations. Show how specific triangulatory devices might increase its validity.
3. Use Westie's seven recommendations (pp. 360–361) to construct or reformulate a better theory in an area of interest to you (such as racial discrimination, sex roles, socialization effects).

PART FOUR

Analysis and Presentation of Data

Facts discipline reason; but reason is the advanced guard in any field of learning.

C. Wright Mills,
The Sociological Imagination
(New York: Oxford University
Press, 1959), p. 205.

14

Strategies
and Logic
of Data Analysis

Seek simplicity and distrust it. [1]

Data analysis decisions in well-constructed research are rarely made solely after data have been collected. As has been repeatedly emphasized, data analysis should be anticipated in earlier phases of the research. When researchers fail to anticipate analysis in earlier sequences, they normally end up with insufficient or inappropriate data. It is not uncommon for researchers who have failed to anticipate data analysis to fail in their ability to analyze the data they have collected, even though they may have ended up with a massive repository of data. In fact, ironically, it is often these massive data stockpiles that go unanalyzed, perhaps due to the fatalistic what-do-I-do-with-all-this-data dilemmas they may create.

One solution, offered repeatedly in this text, is to collect only data that has some direct linkage to theory. Indeed, Chapter 2 stressed the utility of gathering data only in the service of theory. This procedure not

[1]Alfred North Whitehead.

only reduces the amount of data to be collected to a relatively manageable size, but it also focuses researchers' collection efforts on data that
are most relevant to their hypotheses. Blau and Duncan (1967:18–19) in
their analysis of the American occupational structure note that

> the general plan of the analysis had, therefore, to be laid out a year or more
> before the analysis actually began, although there turned out to be "seren-
> dipitous" elements in the tabulation specifications we drew up; some tabu-
> lations proved to be amenable to analytical procedures not initially
> contemplated . . . there are many combinations we might have desired but
> could not afford, and many others we would later have liked to see but that
> we simply had not thought of when dummy tables were drawn up. We were
> conscious of the very real hazard that our initial plans would overlook
> relations of great interest. However, some months of work were devoted
> to making rough estimates from various sources to anticipate as closely as
> possible how tables might look. This time was well spent, for, on the whole,
> the tabulations have proved satisfactory.

Herein lies the core of successful research: letting one's theory
guide the analysis. It should be evident from Blau and Duncan's statement that this procedure does not necessarily stifle or suppress the serendipitous as some researchers might claim. Not only does theoretically
directed research often lead to unexpected findings, it also guards against
data-collection overkill. Put somewhat differently, research that is directly
tied to theory helps focus analysis on the most plausible variable(s) of
interest while ignoring those of least importance.

Undergirding this general solution to data analysis are a number of
particular strategies of data analysis. Many of these strategies concern the
logic of relationships between variables. Hence, this chapter takes as its
point of departure the testing of variable relationship models.

BASIC ASSUMPTIONS

Science depends on hypothesis testing as a basic tenet. A basic rationale
for hypothesis testing is that *ex post facto* (after-the-fact) interpretations
are not based on external confirmation.

Rosenberg (1968:232–234) points to nonnullifiability (lack of theoretical underpinning) and excessive flexibility (freedom to choose or
change one's interpretation at will) of ex post facto explanations as limitations of their usefulness. Thus, hypothesis testing normally is preferred
to ex post facto interpretation. There are times, however, when researchers have no choice but to interpret data ex post facto—for instance,
serendipitous findings or lack of theory. Then one should test inferences
drawn from the interpretation, as Rosenberg (1968:234) clarifies.

The [ex post facto] interpretation is made *conditional* upon the presence of other evidence to support it. One reason is that *if* the interpretation one has assigned to a relationship were correct, *then* certain empirical consequences would follow. If these empirical consequences do in fact appear, then the relationship is strengthened. If they do not appear, then a new interpretation is required, which is also subject to further empirical test.

Rosenberg (1965:86), during data analysis, found unexpectedly that children of divorce tend to have lower self-esteem than children from intact families. He interpreted this to be due to stigmatization of divorce and relatively discordant family life. He then reasoned that *if* his interpretation were true, *then* groups in which divorce is strongly condemned (Catholics, Jews) should lead to greater social stigma and, thus, lower self-esteem than among groups where divorce is not as great a social stigma (Protestants). Further data analysis supported this interpretation.

Second, a major assumption in social science is that unicausal explanations (*A* causes *B*) should be distrusted. The social and behavioral sciences appear to lack the simplicity of explanation found in many other sciences. Generally speaking, it is rare to find correlation higher than ± .40 in the social sciences. (Perfect explanation would require correlations of ±1.00.) Thus, social and behavioral research that deals with simple two-variable distributions (zero-order correlations, two-variable cross-tabulations) is to be suspected of being too simplistic. (While parsimony is a scientific ideal, it must be remembered that explanations may be too parsimonious.) This chapter, thus, will emphasize variable relationships where more than two variables are involved.

Third, the effects of particular independent variables may be interactive rather than additive: The effects of each variable may not add up. Additiveness is often a valid assumption. Smith (1972c) recently found the effects of secularization and urbanization to be additive in explaining certain aspects of ministers' and dentists' wives roles. All too often, however, independent variables are assumed to be additive without data analysis verification. Thus, much of this chapter will center around interaction effects in variable relationships.

Fourth, univariate distributions, as we saw in Chapter 3, are of no intrinsic value to scientific analysis. Thus, we shall pursue two or more variable analyses throughout this chapter.

UNIVARIATE ANALYSIS

Univariate analysis refers to the examination of only one variable at a time. While of no intrinsic explanatory worth, we often need to use univariate analysis for *descriptive* purposes. We may wish to describe the ages of a sample of respondents in order to show how similar (or dissimilar) this sample is to some general universe. We can describe this variable in several ways. First, we might give the *raw frequency distribution*—for example, the number of persons aged 18, 19, 20, and so on. Second, we might *group data*—that is, we might give the number of persons between the ages 18 to 20, 21 to 24, and so on. While somewhat easier to read than raw frequency distributions when there are a large number of variable categories, this tactic has the disadvantages of losing some information (the numbers of persons age 18) and arbitrary groupings or "cutting points."

Third, we can express the variable distribution in terms of *percentages:* the percentage of 18-year-olds, 18 to 20-year-olds, or whatever else.

Fourth, we may use a statistical summary *average* to present our data: the *mode* (most frequently reported raw grouped category), the *median* (the category with half of the responses on either side of it), or the arithmetic *mean* (the sum of all responses divided by the number of responses).

Since averages reduce the raw data to single scores, we often find it useful to summarize the distribution through some measure of *dispersion* such as the *range* (the lowest and highest categories for which we have data or more sophisticated measures such as the *standard deviation*).

Whatever type of univariate analysis chosen, we must attempt to present our data in a manageable, readable, and understandable form.

TWO-VARIABLE RELATIONSHIPS

Since we are primarily interested in variable analysis, as opposed to description, univariate analysis offers little informational value. Rather, the first analytic step normally will be to examine bivariate relationships. Blalock (1961) notes three possible *bivariate* relationship meanings: (1) *symmetrical,* where *neither* variable influences the other variable; (2) *reciprocal,* where *both* variables influence one another; and (3) *asymmetrical,* where *one* variable influences the other variable. After considering each of these relational meanings we shall consider the problems of asymmetry that present the key problems of scientific explanation.

Symmetrical relationships generally take one of four forms (Rosenberg 1968:4–6): (1) alternative indicators of the same concept, (2) effects of a common cause, (3) functional interdependence, or (4) parts of a common "system" or "complex."

Alternative indicators of the same concept are often highly associated due to the fact that they are components of the same phenomenon. High correlation between income and occupation is most likely due to each factor being a component of socioeconomic status. By contrast, effects of a common cause means that the same conditions independently promote the development of other variables. The number of newspapers read per 1,000 population is positively correlated with the Gross National Product not through one variable causing the other but rather as effects of industrialization.

In any organism, all the parts are dependent on one another. This functional interdependence of the elements insures a positive correlation between presence or absence of the various component elements. Thus, the facts that all known societies have incest taboos and stratification systems may mean only that these units perform distinctive functions for social systems. While functional interdependence implies indispensability of units to the system, some system elements are dispensable and are arbitrarily associated; in other words, they occur together as part of some nonfunctional complex. In the United States burning the flag is assumed to imply antipatriotism even though in many countries such behavior would not be associated with antipatriotism; the two traits hang together in American society because of "style of life," not because of functional necessity.

From the preceding examples it should by now be apparent why variable correlation and association do not necessarily imply causation. Indeed, since the preceding examples present interesting scientific problems in and of themselves, it should also be realized that causal analysis is not the only phenomenon of interest to the scientist.

Borgatta and Evans (1969:x) give a light-hearted example of lay conceptions of causality that is quoted here as a contrast to our scientific conceptions of causation

> This case arose when the car in which a seventeen year old girl was riding struck a steel bridge abutment. Although there was evidence that the boy driving the car had been negligent in hitting the bridge, the trial court directed a verdict in his favor at the end of plaintiff's case since, as a matter of law, the girl's negligence proximately contributed to the accident.
>
> This court (Tennessee Court of Appeals) agreed that the girl was contributorily negligent as a matter of law not only in distracting the driver with her amorous activities but also in failing to protest that the driver was not taking proper precautions for her safety. The boy and girl had been "petting" on the return trip from the Smoky Mountains. She had removed some of her underclothes and was lying on the front seat of the car with her head on the driver's lap and her body, naked above the waist, exposed to his sight and touch. During the twenty miles the couple had travelled with the girl in this position and the driver's hand on her body, the boy had become so aroused that his mind was centered on her rather than his driving and he was so distracted that he was hardly aware of what he was doing.

The court rejected the argument that since the driver had removed his hand from the girl one minute before the impact and lit a cigarette, her conduct could not have been the proximate cause of the accident. That argument erroneously assumed that in such a short interval of time the driver with the girl's body still exposed could have regained his composure and again devoted his attention to driving. Moreover, the girl was also contributorily negligent in reaching for the cigarette which he attempted to hand her underneath the steering wheel when he saw another car containing people who knew his father. The boy was concerned since his father did not know that he smoked.

More seriously, when our interest does center on assignment of causality we can make our decision on direction of influence through four criteria: (1) statistical association, (2) time sequence, (3) variable permanence, and (4) tests for spurious association. Temporally prior variables and fixed or unchangeable variables (race, sex) are viewed as logical candidates for influence over later-occurring and alterable variables (friendship cliques).

Statistical association implies that we show that the variables covary. Tests for *spuriousness* mean that the association between the variables should not disappear when the effects of other variables causally prior to the original variables are removed (Hyman 1955).

A problem is that it is not always possible to specify causality. Homans's classic propositions that liking leads to more interaction that, in turn, leads to more liking is a reciprocal relationship. Blalock (1961:56–57) proposes that reciprocal relations are actually *alternating* causal forces since it is unlikely that two variables can simultaneously cause each other. In Homans's propositions it would be assumed that liking promotes more interaction at a later time that generates more liking at a still later time. Thus, reciprocal relationships may be viewed as special cases of asymmetrical (unidirectional) relationships.

The most basic variable relationship is bivariate; thus, analysis normally begins with two-variable tables or correlations.

Percentage Tables

Table 14–1 has been adapted from Adam's *Kinship in an Urban Setting* (1968) to illustrate the basic principles of tabular analysis using percentages. The researcher does not normally want to compare absolute cell frequenceis (numbers in parentheses) since "*N's*" or "marginals" (336, 361) are usually unequal, as in Table 14–1. Thus, these inequalities are controlled through percentaging. Where there is an explicit independent

Table 14-1

Expression of Closeness to the Age-Near Sibling in Relation to Enjoyment of and Obligation to the Sibling, as Important Reasons for Keeping in Touch

Closeness to Sibling		Enjoyment Only	Enjoyment and Obligation	Obligation Only	Neither Very Important	Totals (Marginals) (N's)
			Important Reasons for Keeping in Touch			
Close	No.	(207)	(90)	(13)	(26)	(336)
	%	61.6	26.8	3.9	7.7	100.0
Not close	No.	(112)	(79)	(49)	(121)	(361)
	%	31.0	21.9	13.6	33.5	100.0

SOURCE: Adapted from Adams (1968:115).

variable the total number of cases for each of that variable's categories is used as the base for percentaging. Comparisons are then made opposite to computation of percentages. In Table 14–1, since percentaging was done *across* rows, the researcher would compare percentages *down* columns. Thus, one usually compares different proportions in the independent variable categories for particular categories of the dependent variable. In Table 14–1 we *compare* the proportion of persons feeling close to their age-near sibling who keep in touch for enjoyment only *with* the corresponding proportion among those who do not feel close to their age-near sibling (61.6 to 31.0 percent).

How one percentages can grossly affect results. Cole (1979) challenged the long-standing belief that age is negatively associated with scientific productivity and creativity by showing that earlier methods of percentaging were incorrect. If one examines the percentage of scientists making important discoveries by dividing total scientists into the number of scientists making important discoveries at ages under 30, 30–39, 40–49, 50–59, and 60 and over, the percentages of scientists making important discoveries would drop from 40 percent at age 30 and under to 4 percent at age 60 and over. The problem with this type of percentaging is that it ignores the fact that there are many more younger scientists than older scientists, due to mortality rates and increasing graduate school enrollments over time. Hence, when Cole percentaged the number of scientists making important discoveries based on the total number of scientists *of each age group,* he found a slight curvilinear relationship between age and productivity with increases in productivity through the thirties and forties.

Tables Where Percentaging Is Impossible

Percentage tables are possible means of analysis only when researchers are cross-tabulating complete raw or group frequency counts for two variables. Some of the time, however, they wish to cross-tabulate some other type of data such as averages, dispersion measures, correlations, or incomplete frequency counts (where the percentages do not total 100 percent).

Nonpercentaged tables are set up similarly to percentage tables in that they must have headings for variables and variable categories and rows and columns with cells. But these cells, unlike percentage tables, do not contain (or are not based on) frequency counts, but rather are based on some summary statistic. For instance, in Table 14–2, the cells contain the arithmetic means. It is important for the table heading to contain information identifying the statistic in the cell. In cases where the statistic summarizes arbitrary scoring systems (nominal or ordinal), it also is necessary to identify the meaning of the scoring system. If one of the table variables was Machiavellianism scored from 1 to 7, then it would be necessary to identify whether 1 represents high or low Machiavellianism if the table reader is to understand what cell figures mean. In Table 14–2 this presents no problem because the table cells have a ratio base.

Correlation and Regression

Many researchers do not analyze their data in tabular form but instead use correlational analysis or linear regression analysis. The logic of these approaches is the same as that employed in tabular analysis, but it requires somewhat more of an understanding of statistics on the reader's part.

Unlike looking at percentages (or other summary statistic differences) as in tabular analysis, the researcher using correlational analysis

Table 14–2
Mean Number of Children Considered Ideal by Non-Catholic Women over Twenty-one of Differing Education Levels, 1968

Education Level		
College	High School	Grade School
3.2	3.3	3.7

SOURCE: Judith Blake, "Population Policy for Americans: Is the Government Being Misled?" *Science*, Vol. 164 (May 1969) p. 524, Table 2. Copyright 1969 by the American Association for the Advancement of Science.

expresses the relationship between two variables through the correlation coefficient, r.

In order to get an intuitive feel for what a correlation coefficient summarizes, consider the scattergram in Figure 14–1. (A *scattergram* is a two-dimensional graph similar to our two-variable tables in that we plot one variable on the vertical axis and the other on the horizontal axis just like in tabular analysis where we put one variable along the rows and the other along the columns. Again, each of the dots in Figure 14–1 represents a person's scores for occupation and education just as we could cross-tabulate those scores in a bivariate cell.)

The scattergram is a visual means of examining the question: If we know a person's score on one variable, how well can we predict his or her score on another variable? By examining the scattergram we can see that education and occupation are pretty closely related. (If they were perfectly related, all of the points would fall along the straight line, r would equal $+1.0$, and we could perfectly predict x from y and y from x.)

The correlation coefficient ranges from -1.0 (perfect negative association) to 0 (no association) to $+1.0$ (perfect positive association). Hence, the closer to ± 1.0, the better the prediction of y from x, and vice versa.

The straight lines that best predict x from y and y from x are called *regression lines,* and they can be seen to serve several important functions: Since they offer a graphic picture of the relationship between x and y, they summarize that relationship and can be used to infer one set of variable values from another set of variable values.

The regression line is the line of best prediction for x from y or y from x. That is, if you took all of the actual scores and the predicted scores (those along the regression line) in Figure 14.1 and squared the differences between actual and predicted scores, the sum of these squared deviations around the regression line would be smaller than for any other straight line. Hence, this regression line gives the best prediction of x from y. There is also a regression line that gives the best prediction of y from x.

Just as means and standard deviations are used as summary statistics for univariate distributions, researchers rarely use scattergrams to report their data but instead rely on correlation coefficients and regression coefficients. From your high school mathematics you may recall that any linear equation of the form $y = bx + a$ is composed of several important pieces of information. First, the b, or beta, is the *slope* of the straight line that is predicted by the linear equation. Hence, it gives us information that as x increases by some amount, y will increase by some other amount. If in Figure 14–1, the regression line was represented by $y = 1.5x$ we would know that as x increases one unit, y increases 1.5 units. Second,

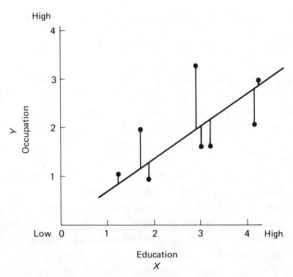

FIGURE 14–1 *Scattergram for education and occupation.*

the *a*, or *y*-intercept, tells us where on the *y*-axis (vertical axis) the line crossed. Hence, in our example, since *a* = 0, it crosses the vertical axis at 0. In a later section of this chapter we shall briefly discuss regression analysis and path analysis. These techniques now dominate quantitative sociological analysis and depend on summary statistics such as the correlation coefficient, partial correlation coefficient, and regression coefficient.

THREE-VARIABLE RELATIONSHIPS

The simplest means of control, just seen in the last chapter section, is to use relative frequencies (percentages) rather than absolute frequencies (raw cell scores). In this section we shall see that two-variable relationships can often be viewed profitably through "controlling for" some third variable—that is, by holding constant the third "test" factor. (It is called a "test" factor since it is introduced to test properties of the original bivariate relationship.)

Basic Ideas

We have a means of examining the relationship of independent and dependent variables through use of a third variable—the *test factor*. The logic is the same for correlational analysis where the researcher often uses test-factor analysis under a different name—*partial* correlation analysis. Partial correlations control for the effects of third (and even other) variables in the same way that test-factor analysis does here. For instance, when we say that a tabular relationship disappears when controlled on a test factor, using correlational analysis we would say that the correlation between x and y disappears (becomes equal to 0) when partialled on a third variable. Table 14–3 adds a test factor, location of sibling, to Table 14–1. The three-variable table allows for the examination of the indepen-dent-dependent variable relationship under each *condition* of the test factor. Note that a three-variable table is actually a set of two-variable subtables—that is, there is a two-variable table for each partial relation-ship, or condition, of the test factor. We wish to examine whether or not the test factor has changed the original independent-dependent variable relationship. If we compare the Greensboro subtable and the Elsewhere subtable of Table 14–3 we find essentially the same relationship between sibling closeness and reasons for keeping in touch. For example, for both the Greensboro and Elsewhere age-near siblings, close siblings keep in touch (54 versus 65 percent) primarily out of enjoyment while many fewer (31 versus 31 percent) of the nonclose siblings keep in touch out of enjoyment only.

If our theoretical perspective is important in analyzing three-way tables, as will be more fully explained in the next chapter section, Rosen-berg (1968:40) emphasizes that we should not introduce test factors into

Table 14–3

Expression of Closeness to the Age-Near Sibling in Relation to Enjoyment of and Obligation to the Sibling, as Important Reasons for Keeping in Touch, According to Whether the Sibling Lives in Greensboro or Elsewhere

		Important Reasons for Keeping in Touch				
Location of Sibling	Closeness to Sibling	Enjoy-ment Only	Enjoy-ment and Obli-gation	Obliga-tion Only	Neither Very Im-portant	Totals (Marginals) (N's)
Greensboro	Close no.	(55)	(34)	(4)	(9)	(102)
	%	54	33	4	9	100
	Not close no.	(32)	(28)	(10)	(33)	(103)
	%	31	27	10	32	100
Elsewhere	Close no.	(152)	(56)	(9)	(17)	(234)
	%	65	24	4	7	100
	Not close no.	(80)	(51)	(39)	(88)	(258)
	%	31	20	15	34	100

SOURCE: Adapted from Adams (1968:115).

the table unless "(1) there is a theoretical reason or empirically based reason for assuming that it accounts for the relationship, and (2) there is no evidence indicating that it is not related both to the independent and dependent variable."

Controls Through Elaboration

This section will consider six prototype test factors: extraneous, component, intervening, suppressor, antecedent, and conditional variables. This process is called *elaboration* since we are interested in obtaining greater information about the two-variable relationship or stating and developing that relationship in more detail.

Extraneous variables. One theoretical reason for introducing a test factor involves the testing of hypothesized extraneous variables. The more particular variables that can be introduced *without substantially* changing the original bivariate relationship, the more confidence that the original relationship is real and meaningful rather than spurious or accidental. Unfortunately, it is impossible to control all extraneous factors, which means there can be no complete proof that some extraneous factor yet uncovered is not actually responsible for the relationship. (You may see now why multivariate analysis does not have the power of controls found in a true experiment since multivariate analysis cannot control for all possible extraneous variables.) The causal form of the extraneous *relation* would actually be

$$T \underset{Y}{\overset{X}{\diagup\diagdown}}$$

which is a logical, theoretical, and empirical issue. Note that the XY relationship here is spurious and symmetrical rather than causal and asymmetrical. The original relationship *disappears* when controlled on the test factor simply because X and Y are related because of the dependence of both on a common antecedent variable. Cole (1972:104) gives some simple examples of extraneous variable relationships. He shows that the relationship between number of fire engines at the scene of a fire and the amount of fire damage disappears when size of fire is taken into account (controlled for). (See Figure 14–2.) Notice in Figure 14–2 that while the *interpretation* of the original relationship may be said to be spurious, this interpretation is due to some *extraneous* variable.

Component variables. In science a great deal of time is spent trying to specify which component or element of a *global* independent variable is responsible for effects on some dependent variable. A biochemist may try to isolate which component of all the chemical compounds in marijuana produces the drug's "high." The social scientist may introduce various components of an independent variable into a bivariate table to specify each component's effect on the relationship. Thus, we often wish to specify which dimension(s) of a multidimensional independent variable is responsible for some particular relationship. For example, which element in alienation (powerlessness, normlessness) is responsible for voter registration apathy? Which element of status inconsistency (education-occupation inconsistency, income-ethnicity inconsistency, visible versus nonvisible lower statuses) produces political liberalism? Which element of social class (respondent's occupation, father's education) is responsible for attitudes held towards work?

Indeed, social class is one of the more complex variables we deal with and consequently one which often needs componential specification. Schuman (1971:46) has specified the social class components of respondent's occupation and education and father's education as affecting the importance attached to working.

Lipsitz (1965) specified a number of components of "working class life" that influence individual authoritarianism that had not been isolated by Lipset's earlier work on the same subject (see Table 14–4). Lipsitz hypothesized that education was the most important component of the social class concept in accounting for authoritarianism. As expected by Lipsitz, total figures for the middle and working class give radically different authoritarian percentages when education is controlled as in

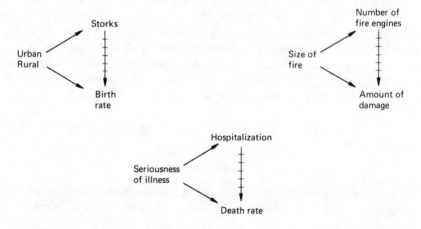

FIGURE 14–2 *Spurious causal interpretations.*

Source: Stephan Cole, *The Sociological Method,* © 1976 by Markham Publishing Company, Chicago, p. 49. Reprinted by permission of Rand McNally College Publishing Company.

Table 14–4
Social Class and Agreement with "Strict Leader" Statement, by Educational Level (Men Only)

	0–8 Education		9–11 Education		12 or More Years Education	
	Middle Class	Working Class	Middle Class	Working Class	Middle Class	Working Class
Proportion agreeing with "Strict Leader" statement Number	83% (88)	67% (121)	58% (121)	56% (129)	44% (126)	62% (13)

SOURCE: Lewis Lipsitz, "Working-Class Authoritarianism: A Re-Evaluation," *American Sociological Review* 30 (Feb. 1965): 106–108, Table 1 (abridged and adapted).

Table 14–4. Thus, we say that education level largely explains authoritarianism, although it is evident that education does not completely wash out the remaining effects of social class. (Note that Table 14–4 gives only an *abridged* version of the complete table since the proportion of persons disagreeing with the "Strict Leader" statement is not given. Since this abridged portion of the original table is not necessary for this particular analysis, it has been left out. It is a good idea, particularly when first starting out analyzing multivariate tables, to treat them in this less complex, subtable manner for ease of analysis.)

Rosenberg (1968:47) aptly points out that this type of analysis *"suggests that the 'same' variables are not always the same."* That is, different components of a more global variable may produce different effects on different dependent variables. A large number of studies have shown the effects of alienation. However, componential analysis by type of alienation might show normlessness to be the crucial component in one variable relationship, powerlessness in another, and other components crucial to still different relationships.

Intervening and antecedent variables. *Intervening* variable relationships take the form

$$X \rightarrow T \rightarrow Y$$

That is, the original $X \rightarrow Y$ relationship is assumed to be mediated by a third. The *antecedent* variable relationship, likewise, takes a causal chain form

$$T \rightarrow X \rightarrow Y$$

Once again, as was true of other test factors, these test variable decisions are basically theoretical, logical, and empirical issues since causal order determines whether the test factor is antecedent, intervening, or consequent. Then, once one has found theoretical grounds for introducing one of these as a test factor, there are statistical means of specifying whether the theory is plausibly correct. For instance, "if the test factor is intervening, the relationship between the independent and dependent variable should vanish" (Rosenberg 1968:74). By contrast, if the test factor is *antecedent*,

1. All three bivariate relationships (*XY*, *XT*, and *YT*) must show statistical association.
2. When the antecedent variable (*T*) is controlled, the independent-dependent relationship should *not* vanish.
3. When the independent variable (*X*) is controlled, the antecedent-dependent relationship *should* disappear.

Thus a number of tables must be generated to show antecedent characteristics: three bivariate tables and two three-variable tables with the independent variable controlled.

Causal chain analysis of one of the above two types can have great bearing on the development of theory since many of our propositions are linked in chains. Nye, White, and Frideres (1968) have proposed that greater marital partner role and value congruence leads to more positive affectual balance which in turn leads to greater marital stability. Hopkins (1964), likewise, has proposed chain propositions such as: A person's rank in the group affects his or her centrality in the group, which in turn affects his or her influence over the group, which in turn affects his or her rank.

Suppressor and distorter variables. A *suppressor* variable is called such because it acts "to suppress the 'true' strength of some variable relationship which only becomes apparent when *T* has been controlled" (Davis 1971:82). Thus, the *XY* relationship actually *increases* when *T* is controlled. Notice that the suppressor variable increases the original *XY* relationship by contrast to an extraneous, component, or intervening variable where the original relationship decreases or vanishes. How can this happen? McNemar (1955, cited in Pasanella 1972:383) gives a good example (see Table 14–5). He pointed out that during World War II a test of mechanical aptitude correlated fairly well with pilot performance in a training program. A test of verbal ability did not correlate with pilot performance. However, the verbal and spatial tests were statistically related. McNemar reasoned that since some verbal ability is needed to read and understand items on this test of mechanical ability, verbal ability should thus be "subtracted from" the mechanical ability test since that portion is actually irrelevant to pilot performance.

Table 14–5
Relationship Between Mechanical Aptitude, Pilot Performance, and Verbal Ability

		A. Original Relationship Pilot Performance for Total Group		B. Elaboration Relationship by Verbal Ability			
				+ Pilot Performance		− Pilot Performance	
		+	−	+	−	+	−
Mechanical Aptitude for Total Group	+	60	40	40	35	20	5
	−	50	50	15	10	35	40
Totals		110	90	55	45	55	45

SOURCE: Pasanella (1972:383). In P. Lazarsfeld, A. Pasanella, and M. Rosenberg (eds.), *Continuities in the Language of Social Research*. Copyright 1972, The Free Press.

One way of doing the "subtracting" is shown in the tabular elaboration of the original mechanical aptitude–pilot performance relationship. Notice in Table 14–5 that a potential pilot with low verbal aptitude and high mechanical ability had greater chance of success (20 out of 25) than if he had both high verbal and mechanical aptitude (40 out of 75). Pasanella (1972:382) explains the logic of the suppressor variable in this way: "It might be equally appropriate to call it a *releasor* variable, since it frees the [independent variable] from encumbering elements and allows it to function effectively as a forecaster." Davis (1971:95–96) notes that sex is often a suppressor variable in sociological research and gives an example from 1960 census data to show how sex suppresses the relationship between occupation and earnings.

Rosenberg (1968:94*ff*) has coined the term *distorter* variable for test factors that actually reverse the original *XY* relationship. He notes that Schnore once found suburban dwellers to have higher incomes than city dwellers. Paradoxically, when this relation was controlled by race it was found that the relation was *reversed* with both higher white and black median incomes in the city than suburb. As Schnore (1962:255) states, "the higher average income of the more numerous suburban whites raises the overall suburban average above that of the city, despite the fact that city incomes are *higher* for each of the two constituent color groups taken separately." Thus a test factor sometimes can be shown to distort the actual relationship just as it can suppress it.

Rosenberg (1968:99–100), in comparing types of test factors, notes that the consideration of extraneous variables enables us to avoid the danger that we will accept as true a false hypothesis while a suppressor variable enables us to avert rejecting a true hypothesis. Further, distorter variables may help avoid both the acceptance of false hypotheses and the rejection of a true one. Other test-factor comparisons can be seen in Table 14–6.

Conditional relationships. Davis (1970:22) points out that to say "the relationship between X and Y is due to T" is *not* the same as "the relationship between X and Y depends on the *level* of T." Thus, when one introduces a test factor it is possible to find a partial association that is strong at one level of T, weak at another level of T, or even to find reversed associations—one positive, another negative. Thus, a conditional relationship may *specify, clarify,* or *modify* some XY relationship.

If you turn back to Table 14–4 you will note that years of education specifies the relation between social class and authoritarianism since almost twice as many men are regarded as authoritarian with eight years or less education as with over eight years of formal education.

Income maintenance experiments carried out in Denver and Seattle (Tuma, Hannan, and Groeneveld 1979) afford another example of condi-

Table 14–6
Properties of Test Factors

	Extraneous Component Intervening	Antecedent	Suppressor	Distorter
1. Original association between independent and dependent variables is	Positive	Positive	Zero	Positive
2. Relationships in contingent associations are	Zero	Positive	Positive	Negative
3. Compared to the original relationship, the relationships in the contingent associations	Vanish (reduce)	Remain unchanged	Emerge	Reverse
4. Test factor related to independent and dependent variables with	Same signs	Same signs	Opposite signs	Opposite signs
5. Independent, test factor, and dependent all related	Yes	Yes	No	Yes
6. Steps involved in procedure	1	2	1	1

SOURCE: Chart 4-1, from *The Logic of Survey Analysis,* by Morris Rosenberg. Copyright 1968, Basic Books, Inc., Publishers, New York, p. 101.

tional effects. They found that the effects of income-maintenance support on white women's marital dissolution rates were conditional on the level of income maintenance. Women receiving $5,600 in annual support differed significantly from women receiving $3,800 and $4,800 in annual income support.

The condition where an original *XY* relationship with an apparent lack of association is shown to be due to partial associations—one negative, the other positive—canceling each other out is particularly interesting since it shows the danger of "spurious *non* correlations." The previously cited article by Lipsitz has an interesting example of this (see Table 14–7). Lipsitz (1965) found that roughly the same percentages of working- and middle-class men agreed that "any good leader should be strict with people under him in order to gain their respect." But as Table 14–7 shows, when he controlled for education, the discrepancy in education and social class shows that the upwardly mobile (high class with low education) show less authoritarianism while the downwardly mobile (low class with high education) show more authoritarianism. Such findings challenge us to try to find a single, as opposed to separate, interpretation for the contradiction in findings. Turner and Martinez (1977) offer a classic example of this type of finding. For men with above-average education, they found that Machiavellianism was associated with higher occupational prestige and larger incomes. Men with below-average education, by contrast, had an inverse relationship between occupational attainment and Machiavellianism and no relationship between income attainment and Mach-V scores.

Table 14–7
Social Class, Education, and Response to Authoritarianism Questions in Three Surveys (Men Only)

	Percent Giving Authoritarianism Response							
	0–8 Years Education		9–11 Years Education		12 or More Years Education		Total	
	Middle class	*Working class*	*Middle class*	*Working class*	*Middle class*	*Working class*	*Middle class*	*Working class*
High on A-scale score	82.9	89.2	59.5	72.1	38.2	50.0	35.9	59.5
Percentage difference	6.3		12.6		11.8		23.6	

SOURCE: Lewis Lipsitz, "Working-Class Authoritarianism: A Re-Evaluation," *American Sociological Review* 30 (Feb. 1965): 106–108, Table 1 (abridged and adapted).

Davis (1970:101) appropriately warns that conditional specifications are delicate and complex operations since it is often hard to tell whether differences in the conditions (levels of T) are minor statistically or worthy of consideration. Nevertheless, because conditional relationships demonstrate the effects of statistical interaction, they tremendously increase the amount of information concerning a variable relationship.

BEYOND THREE-VARIABLE RELATIONSHIPS

Although four (and even five) variable tables can be found in the literature if we search hard enough, as pointed out in the last chapter section the number of partial associations we have to look at grows geometrically with each added test factor. Thus, we typically come to depend on other, more summary, ways of looking at multivariate relationships involving four or more variables. Normally these more summary procedures involve some type of correlation (or derivatives of correlations) between variables.

Two of the more useful multivariate techniques of analysis based on correlation and regression are *multiple regression* and *path analysis.*

Multiple regression analysis is based on several assumptions that must be met before it can be used properly. First, the independent-dependent variable relationships must be related in a *linear* fashion as seen earlier in our discussion of linear regression lines. Hence, it is useful to check the scattergrams for violations of this assumption. (Sometimes simple algebraic transformations, for example, logarithms, may be used to transform nonlinear regression lines to linear form.) Second, the effects of all independent variables must *add up* (they must be additive) to form a prediction of the dependent variable. Third, the correlation between independent variables should not be extremely high, so that the effects of each independent variable on the dependent variable can be reliably computed.

Multiple regression, when these assumptions are met, provides us with a basis for comparing the *relative* contribution of each independent variable in predicting the dependent variable.

Multiple regression shares some characteristics of the logic of test-factor and partial correlation analysis since each reflects the effect of an independent variable on a dependent variable when the effects of other independent variables are controlled statistically.

Path analysis uses multiple regression to examine theoretical models like the Sewell Model of Occupational Aspiration in Figure 3–2 (Chapter

3). The objective is to examine the fit of the model to the data. If the fit is close, the model is retained; if not close, it is modified to fit the data better and then subjected to further tests on the new data.

In order to use path analysis, several assumptions, in addition to those already specified for multiple regression, must be made. First, the causal ordering of the independent and dependent variables should be known so that independent variables change first and dependent variables later. Second, the model must be treated as a closed system—all relationships in the system should remain unchanged by controlling for any variables omitted. Finally, it must be assumed that the influence of one variable on another is asymmetrical (path analysts use the term "recursive"). In other words, there can be no reciprocal (nonrecursive) variable relationships where both variables influence one another causally.

Multiple regression analysis and path analysis (see Heise 1969) increasingly compete with the more traditional multivariate strategies of elaboration. This is because multiple regression analysis has solved the problem of measuring the relative (controlled) effects of a large number of independent variables, while path analysis likewise has extended multiple regression analysis in the realm of causal analysis.

THE USE OF FORMAL MODELS

To this point we have been concerned with analysis that examines associations (or correlations) between variables as observed in our data. Since we have consistently argued throughout this text (and particularly in Chapter 2) for data collection in the service of particular theories, we should likewise wish to analyze our data in light of its "fit" to our conceptual models or theories. Thus, we wish to *systematize* relationships between variables through theory and then examine the data to see if the empirical relationships observed correspond to our postulated models. In this section several illustrations will be given to show how the logic of models may aid the researcher in the analysis of the correspondence between observed data and his or her conceptual model.

Let us start by assuming we wish to test Becker's (1953) hypothesis that marijuana effects are learned in positive reference groups. To date no one has isolated the specific components of this alleged learning process. One alternative model to Becker's is the physiological model. According to proponents of this model we should expect experimental participants randomly and blindly given either active marijuana (THC present) or placebo marijuana (THC extracted) to have effects shown in Table 14–8A. Thus, if participants are administered THC or the placebo without knowing which it is that they are receiving, according to the physiological model, we should expect that only those receiving the THC would claim to experience a "high" while those experiencing the placebo would be the only ones claiming to have experienced no effects. If we control for type of reference group (positive or negative), we would expect as a null hypothesis to Becker's reference group hypothesis that the effects are clearly physiological (Table 14–8B). By contrast, the strongest fit of the data to the reference group model would predict Table 14–8C outcomes where the only participants experiencing "highs" would be those smoking within positive reference groups, *regardless* of whether they had smoked THC or the placebo. Then, again, all other participants would be expected to experience "no effects."

Finally (Table 14–8D), the "no association" hypothesis would predict equal numbers of subjects experiencing "highs" or "no effects" regardless of reference group experience. Obviously the test for the reference group, physiological, and independence models would be between which is the *better* predictor of observed outcomes. Consider the fact that nonaddicts given single shots of heroin and placebos, without their knowing which, report greater pleasure from the placebos than the heroin!

Similarly, Coleman, Katz, and Menzel (1957) have collected data on the diffusion (increased usage) of innovative drugs by physicians. Figure 14–3 shows three models of this diffusion process based (1) on "individual innovation" where the number of doctors introducing the drug each

Table 14–8
Some Simple Mathematical Models of Plausible Determinants of Getting "High" on THC

(A) Physiological hypothesis

	No Effect	"High"
THC	0	X
Placebo	X	0

(B) Null hypothesis for reference group

	Pos. Ref. Group		Neg. Ref. Group	
	No Effect	"High"	No Effect	"High"
THC	0	X	0	X
Placebo	X	0	X	0

(C) Reference group hypothesis

	Pos. Ref. Group		Neg. Ref. Group	
	No Effect	"High"	No Effect	"High"
THC	0	X	X	0
Placebo	0	X	X	0

(D) No association hypothesis

	No Effect	"High"
THC	X	X
Placebo	X	X

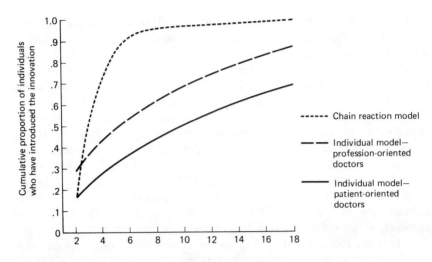

FIGURE 14–3 *Three models of innovation diffusion.*

Source: Adapted from Coleman, Katz, and Menzel (1957).

month remains a constant percentage of those who have not already adopted it, and (2), secondarily, on whether the doctors are primarily patient or colleague-oriented versus (3) "chain reaction" innovation where physicians who have used the drug introduce it to their colleagues so that the number of doctors introducing the new drug each month would increase in proportion to those who have already been converted.

DYNAMIC STUDY ANALYSIS

The methods of analysis discussed to this point have presented means of interpreting cross-sectional data. However, in addition to static cross-sectional analyses, we saw in Chapter 13 that the researcher is often interested in analyzing trends or panels over time.

Trend Study Analysis

In the trend study, you may remember from the discussion in Chapter 13, we usually study a small number of variables at a large number of points in time. The main problem in such studies is to control for all variables extraneous to the variables of interest since we wish to study the "pure" effects of the variables of interest, not the confounding effects of extraneous variables. One means of controlling for extraneous variables is to *standardize*. We can standardize marriage rates for any particular year by multiplying the rate in each age category by the number of persons in that category in the standard year and then totaling over all age categories. This method gives a weighted (standardized) marriage rate based on population distributions, which change from year to year. Obviously this weighting is important for comparing marriage rates over time since relatively younger populations would be expected to have lower marriage rates, and vice versa. In this manner we may study changes over time *as if* the variables of interest were equal on the standardized variables at each time period. Notice how, in Table 14–9 the change in marriage rate is less pronounced when standardized on population distribution than when compared as a crude percentage rate. Thus, much of the original trend toward higher marriage rates can be seen as largely spurious, that is, attributable to a shifting age distribution.

In addition to standardization, *identification of which parts,* or properties, of a system are contributing to the trend is important to many trend studies. Similar to component variable analysis, trend studies often map out particular wholistic trends and then break these down into their *main components* for comparative purposes.

A good example of the identification of key components in trend analysis comes from the heretofore mentioned Coleman, Katz, and Menzel (1957) study of drug innovation. They broke down the trends by (1) profession-oriented doctors, (2) patient-oriented doctors, and (3) integration of doctors into physician friendship cliques. The actual trends, shown in Figure 14–4, were compared to each other as well as the mathematically hypothesized trends shown in Figure 14–3.

Table 14–9

Changes in Marital Status with Age (Distribution Standardized)

	Selected Figures for Males	
Year	Crude Percentage Married	Percentage Married Based on 1950 Age Distribution as Standard
1890	52.1	61.2
1930	58.4	62.1
1950	68.0	68.0

SOURCE: Matilda White Riley, Table 10-A, "Changes in marital status with age distribution standardized," from *Sociological Research I: A Case Approach* (New York: Harcourt Brace Jovanovich, Inc., 1963), p. 553.

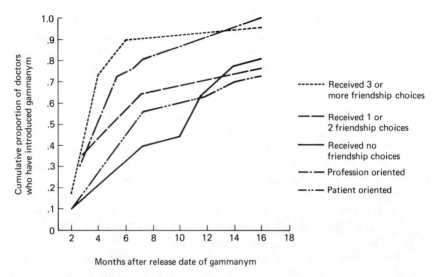

FIGURE 14–4 *Cumulative proportion of doctors introducing gammanym by selective characteristics.*

Source: Adapted from Coleman, Katz, and Menzel (1957).

Panel Study Analysis

Panel studies, in contrast to trend studies, usually involve a larger number of variables on a *single* sample followed over a smaller number of times. Kendall (1972) gives an example of a simple panel analysis, as shown in Table 14–10.

In trend analysis our concern is with what is termed *net shifts* in totals over time periods. Compare that with panel analysis where the characteristic we are interested in is what is termed *turnover,* or shifts over time. For this reason, researchers doing panel studies often refer to tables such as Table 14–10 as turnover tables. Note that Table 14–10 shows 217 (114 + 103) turnovers in mood between times 1 and 2 and 297 *static associations* between the two moods over both time periods. Obviously, it is possible to do more elaborate analysis by further subdividing categories (in this case, perhaps, by *strength* of mood), adding and analyzing more time periods, or studying more than two variables over time. Also, Coleman (1964) has shown how to use mathematical models in conjunction with simple dichotomous tables such as Table 14–10. For instance, we could study the percentages of shifts, or turnovers, from mood state to mood state over time in terms of particular models of mood state change just as Coleman, Katz, and Menzel (1957) studied drug diffusion in terms of particular models.

Table 14–10
Evaluation of Mood at Two Different Times

| | Interview I | | |
	Good Mood	Bad Mood	Total
Good Mood	171	103	274
Bad Mood	114	126	240
Total	285	229	514

SOURCE: Kendall (1972:344).

The major advantage of a panel study is that it gives information on *what* changed, how much, and in what direction. Maccoby and Hyman (1959) nevertheless point out a number of problems inherent in panel studies. First, there are "ceiling effects," or limitations, in comparing change over time; for instance, individuals at the top of a scale (high socioeconomic class) have little chance to improve relative to someone at the lower end of the scale. Second, unreliability in the measurement instrument may create pseudochanges rather than show *real* change. In particular this means the panel researcher should be on the look-out for statistical regression effects (see Chapter 12).

Lazarsfeld (1972:358) points out, in stating a position sympathetic to this view that theory and research should go hand in hand, that "turnover measures should be related to substantive ideas about the nature of change." He himself followed this rule in the same paper by studying an "oscillation model" in which it was assumed that people (in his study) had a basic position from which they stray occasionally but to which they are continuously "pulled back again," and then he linked this model to observed data over time.

THE FLOW OF ANALYSIS

Rosenberg (1968:207) has aptly characterized the close interplay of theory and research in data analysis by pointing out that "the data suggest, stimulate, and generate the theory, and the theory is restrained, controlled, and disciplined by the data." If you follow the logic and strategies of elaboration and other multivariate analysis suggested in this chapter, you cannot go far off the track in interpretation of your data since your assaying of the evidence will be controlled and, at the same time, unpredictable enough so that it is open to new theory.

READINGS FOR ADVANCED STUDENTS

FRANK ANDREWS AND OTHERS, *A Guide for Selecting Statistical Techniques for Analyzing Social Science Data,* 1974. A concise decision-tree source of questions and answers on appropriate statistics in analysis.

OTIS DUDLEY DUNCAN, *Introduction to Structural Equation Models,* 1975. If you have had a good college algebra and statistics course, this is one of the most useful introductions to regression and path analyses, which now dominate analysis in sociology.

STEPHEN E. FIENBERG, *The Analysis of Cross-Classified Categorical Data,* 1977. This is written for the nonstatistician with familiarity with two-variable table analysis, regression analysis, and analysis of variance. As Duncan has pointed out in his review of this book, once you have learned these new techniques of tabular analysis, you can accomplish with ease a great deal more than was ever possible under the test factor approach used in this text.

CHARLES LAVE AND JAMES MARCH, *An Introduction to Models in the Social Sciences,* 1975. A delightful, self-programmed book for thinking analytically about human behavior. Its pleasure derives from showing how the power, beauty, and pleasure of models come from inventing and elaborating them.

GRAHAM UPTON, *The Analysis of Cross-Tabulated Data,* 1978. The enormous strides in the development of the analysis of cross-tabulated data since 1970 is introduced to the reader familiar with basic statistics. This may be a better introduction than the Fienberg book for those who wish chapters on reminders of basic statistical techniques and "traditional" methods of analysis.

SUGGESTED RESEARCH PROJECTS

1. Use each of the types of test factors introduced in this chapter to write an analysis of possible alternative explanations of each of the following findings:

   a. The finding of no relationship between teaching and research quality

   b. Higher insurance rate premiums for younger drivers because younger drivers have more accidents and more expensive accidents

   c. The finding that college GPA successfully predicts graduate school success

   d. The finding that GPA has no relationship to job performance.

2. Use each of the following findings in analysis of the *type* of test factor relationship implied by the results:

   a. The positive correlation between years of schooling and Republican Party preference disappeared when Weiner and Eckland (1979) controlled for inherited partisan loyalties, class origins, and SES attainment.

   b. Weiner and Eckland (1979) found a stronger correlation between educational attainment and Republican Party preference for females (.12) than for males (.03).

   c. Alston and McIntosh (1979) point out that higher socioeconomic status generally leads to higher rates of participation in religious services for whites, but that no relationship exists for blacks.

   d. In this same article, black Protestants and white Catholics had concerns in the clergy enough to affect their church attendance, but not white Protestants nor black Catholics.

e. Gove, Hughes, and Galle (1979) found that physical health differences between men and women disappeared when they controlled for marital status, living arrangements, psychiatric symptoms, and nurturant role obligations.

f. Black (1976) indicates that the greater the difference in wealth between a rich victim and a poor offender, the greater the amount of law invoked against the offender. For the rich offender and poor victim, the lesser the amount of law invoked against the offender.

g. Previous research indicated that stable working-class communities had the highest levels of institutional integration, the largest number of local institutions, and the largest number of gathering places. Yancey and Ericksen (1979) controlled on race and found a relative absence of such facilities and services.

h. In the above article, they also found that when they controlled on other factors assumed to account for differences in the institutional completeness of black and white communities, this racial difference remained.

i. Studies of female labor force participation and fertility have established a negative relationship between the two. By controlling background factors such as education and marital duration, this negative relationship can be reduced but still remains according to Smith-Lovin and Tickamyer (1978).

j. Reskin (1977) found that early scientific productivity and collegial recognition contributed to chemists' productivity over a decade, but that early productivity was more important for those employed in universities, whereas collegial recognition was particularly important for chemists in work contexts that do not stress scholarly publications.

k. Vanneman and Pampel (1977) found evidence that occupational prestige is more a middle-class concern than a manual worker concern for status perceptions.

l. Extra-legal variables (sex, race, home situation) were shown to affect juvenile court case dispositions when offense seriousness and prior records of delinquency were held constant in a study by Thomas and Cage (1977).

m. Glenn and Gotard (1977) found that marriages of frequent church attenders were more stable than those of infrequent attenders. This was found to be true to a greater extent for white Catholics than for white Protestants. However, no beneficial effects of attendance was observed for black Protestants.

3. Try to get from one of your professors some data you can use to experiment with elaboration. Argue for the introduction of appropriate test factor(s), introduce the factor(s), and interpret the results.

4. Scan the professional literature for examples of two-variable relation analysis. Theorize the types of test factors that might, if introduced, help elaborate the study's results.

5. Work out a logical but simple predictive mathematical model of plausible outcomes for a panel or trend study based on some professionally published research. Show how the model outcomes are related to theory.

15

Reporting Research

Simple English is no one's mother tongue. It has to be worked for. [1]

I feel lucky if I write two pages of double spaced typed shit each day. [2]

Writing well cannot be learned from a book. The most you can expect from any book is help in considering how to express your thoughts, because truly effective communication is learned through practice. This chapter is provided to give you direction based on others' experiences, and it will focus on some essentially basic areas: how to get ideas, choice of words, the shape of thought-building, developing ideas, and the relationship between writers and their audiences.

THE SHAPE OF IDEAS

In Chapter 2 it was suggested that you start doing research by choosing a topic of interest to you. If a topic bores you, you probably will not be

[1] Attributed to Jacques Barzun.
[2] Attributed to Ernest Hemingway.

able to motivate yourself to follow through to completion. If you do endure the frustration and follow a boring task through to completion, you will undoubtedly reveal your lack of interest through a sloppy and (for your reader) uninteresting presentation. Generally, a topic that interests you will make the routine of shaping ideas much less painful. Readable and sensible shaping of those ideas may be made easier by the following suggestions from Mills (1959:212–216).

First you should be keeping a research file as suggested and outlined in Chapter 2. Play "fifty-two pickup" with your file. That is, mix up your file folders, index cards, and any other file material. Many of a writer's best ideas evolve through the unforeseen linkages that one finds between ideas.

Second, play with synonyms of your key terms and phrases. Break down higher concepts into several components. This helps you clarify and make your research problem more precise. Also, play around with making your statements more abstract. The idea is to track every possible nuance by working back and forth between levels of abstraction.

Third, develop habits of searching for new classifications of your ideas. Do not be content with existing classifications. Make your classifications as systematic and explicit as possible. Mills said that charts, tables, and diagrams are to the working sociologist "what diagramming a sentence is for the diligent grammarian" (1959:213). They help clear thinking and writing. This is what Hage (1972:27) did to generate the idea of normative equality. He noticed when he cross-classified four dimensions with social structure (see p. 59) that the dimension of rights lacked a variable conception.

Fourth, think in terms of opposites and extremes. If you are interested in revolution, then you should also study periods of political stability. The process of contrast and comparison helps focus ideas.

Fifth, "deliberately invert your sense of proportion. If something seems very minute, imagine it to be simply enormous . . ." (p.215). Incongruity often helps focus ideas. Try to imagine the effects of increased literacy on political stability, or the effects of starvation on literacy.

Sixth, a comparative analysis also tends to aid the contrast and comparison of ideas. Do bureaucracies have the same effects in Japan as in Western Europe? Do they have the same effects today as forty years ago? Once again, this principle helps us to release our imaginations and aids us in making sense of our ideas.

Developing one's ideas presents one set of problems; narrowing one's ideas presents another. If a topic interests you, you will at some point find it necessary to limit it in order to keep it to a manageable size. At long last conciseness is becoming a virtue in the social sciences. Federal grant guidelines now often have fifteen- to twenty-page limits. Many journals have similar page limits. One of my own interests is in the

Citizens' Band, or CB, radio phenomenon of the last ten years. I could well have spent considerable time collecting information on the history of CBs, the relationship of the Federal Communication Commission's (FCC) control over CB broadcasting, and the flagrant abuse of FCC rules by CBers. But in order to make my study manageable I chose to narrow my interests to the CB handle as a reflection of CBers' presentation of self.

DEVELOPING IDEAS INTO A REPORT

Once you have developed your ideas, limited your topic, collected and analyzed data, you will be ready to shape it into a report. Schopenhauer once said that we should write the way an architect builds—"who first drafts his plan and designs every detail." Hence, an outline is a good point of departure from which you may fill in the details.

Most scientific reporting includes the following details:

1. TITLE: The subject of the research. A subtitle is sometimes appropriate.
2. STATEMENT OF THE PROBLEM AND A BRIEF DESCRIPTION OF IT: What is the purpose of this study? Why is it necessary or advisable? Describe it briefly and succinctly.
3. REVIEW OF THE LITERATURE: Summarize briefly the work already done, emphasizing any significant contributions. Refer freely here to your bibliography.
4. THE QUESTION AT ISSUE: State the hypothesis or hypotheses to be tested or the information expected from the study. What are you trying to discover that is not already known?
5. METHOD AND PROCEDURE: What subjects are to be or were used, how many, and with what characteristics? What was done with the sample? Make a list of the steps involved of the procedures and methods in direct, simple, easily understood language including:

   a. Specification of the sample

   b. Means of evaluating the hypotheses or concepts

   c. Tests or procedures used

   d. Other methods.
6. FINDINGS: Present the analysis of data collected. Your evidence is presented here with statistical or other means of evaluation.
7. DISCUSSION: Usually research reports evaluate what was found and discuss explanations and implications of the findings in a discussion section.
8. SUMMARY AND CONCLUSIONS: The statement of your problem and this section are extremely important. First and last impressions of research reports are somewhat like first and last impressions of people; they tend to be remembered longer and more deeply. Remember that it has been said that everything written is meant to please or to instruct and that it is difficult to achieve the second objective without attending to the first.

Outlines help you get your pencil moving or your fingers typing. Remember Hemingway's quote at the start of the chapter. Hemingway's polished style did not emerge at first stroke. He made rough outlines of ideas at the start, filled in gaps, and then polished them off. I like to take a yellow pad and note ideas I want to include in my work, then play with means of organizing those ideas into conceptually similar patterns and logical flows of ideas. Then I attempt to make a rough draft, crossing out ideas as I cover them. If you try for perfection on the first go-round, you'll probably never lift your pencil off the pad.

POLISHING YOUR IDEAS

Writing requires some arrogance on the part of the writer because writing presupposes an assertion that one has something to say and it is worthy of the attention of the reader. Hence, after you have put on paper what you want to say it is worthwhile pondering whether you have said everything you meant and meant everything you said—to paraphrase an old adage. The list of do's and don't's is probably infinite, but one can focus on a few major common problems.

Audiences

The basic problem in writing is that there is no direct feedback from your audience. Feedback means that behavior is scanned for its results, and that the success or failure of this result modifies future behavior. Writing well requires us to "see" our invisible audience as we write. We must imagine how they will behave, what they like and dislike, whether they need more or less information on some topic. Goethe once said that "everyone hears but what he understands." No word means exactly the same thing to different people. The basic problem with most novice writers is that they have not learned that many of those who read their writing will read them wrong. The art of interesting and understandable writing is predicting what your reader needs to hear.

One useful technique is to form a reciprocal relationship with a friend on the understanding that each of you read the other's writing with an eye to what it is and is not communicating. Most successful writers have "friendly critics," people they trust to tell them what is wrong with their writing *before* it goes to a publisher. If your friends aren't being critical of your writing, they're not your friends. Once you get a poor grade for a paper because it did not communicate what you intended, it is too late. Much better that you find a friendly critic to tell you what needs improving before the paper is turned in.

Generalities

Science strives for generalities. Clearly, generalities may add order and understanding. But generalities need to be translated into concrete, specific facts and illustrations. Flesch (1954:100) said that "concreteness isn't something you sprinkle on your words like Parmesan cheese. It's internal." There's nothing wrong per se with statements like "Propinquity continues to foster solidarity, resisting the centrifugal effects of urbanization." Certainly that may indicate what some people take to be sociologese or socspeak. But such statements cry for the basic rule of "Specify!" The task of communication reminds us of the necessity to be concrete. It stimulates us to mention names, dates, places; to be exact; to spell out details; to use images, cases, illustrations.

Readability

Scientists are often accused of being unreadable. In this section some common causes and solutions to the problem will be discussed.

Active versus the passive voice. Scientists are often accused of using the passive voice, whereas the active voice is preferable. One of my best courses was in eighth grade English. My teacher would do crazy things like throw chalk at one of us and saying "I am throwing chalk at you!" This type of exercise was intended to show the *liveliness* of the active voice. By contrast the passive voice is not only deadening, it is inefficient and irritating. Compare the following sentence starts:

Passive: It was stated by him that . . .
Active: He stated that . . .
Passive: It was found that . . .
Active: I found that . . .
Passive: The respondents were observed objecting to . . .
Active: Respondents objected to . . .

Sentence length and complexity. In several chapters we have argued that survey question (Chapter 6) and attitude statement length (Chapter 11) should not run over twenty words if at all possible. Gustave Flaubert is reputed to have said, "Whenever you can shorten a sentence, do. And one always can. The best sentence? The shortest." Reading comprehension is clearly related to sentence length. Sentence lengths of twenty-one to twenty-four words are *fairly difficult* to comprehend for the average reader. Those of twenty-five to twenty-eight words are, generally speaking, *difficult* to read. Those over twenty-eight words are *very difficult* for the average reader to understand.

Furthermore, sentence length is associated with sentence complexity. Most complex sentences can be broken down into several distinct thoughts. Compound sentences (those with *ands* and *buts*) do not usually cause too much trouble for writer and reader. Complex sentences that use words like *if, because,* and *as* are the ones that often need to be split up.

Vocabulary and jargon. Words exist for reasons. One of the strengths of the English language is precisely its adaptability to the expression of new ideas. Hence, it is foolish to think that difficult, many-syllable words are necessarily pretentious and jargonish. Why say "a first year college student" when that may be simply stated as "freshman"?

The problem occurs when our writing and speaking becomes affected. Perhaps the best measure of affectation in communication is a paraphrase of Rousseau. He felt it unfortunate that we should have more words than ideas; that we should be able to say more than we think. Unaffected communication, then, for me occurs when we have more ideas than words; when we think more than we communicate; when we do not thoroughly grasp our ideas. If you do not let your words outstrip your ideas you will find it much easier to communicate your ideas.

Negation. Much has been written about the double negative; so much so that little more need be said about it. Less has been written about the use of the simple negation. It is difficult for someone to understand a thought communicated through negation. Consider the following examples:

Negation: I don't really enjoy my work.
Positive: I dislike my work.

While both sentences are understandable, psychological research shows it takes much longer for negatively expressed ideas to be understood and comprehended.

Furthermore, the first sentence is much weaker than the second one. For example, just because I don't enjoy my work doesn't mean I dislike it—I might feel neutral towards it. It is better practice to state your thoughts forthrightly than to leave them ambiguously hidden behind a negation.

Detail and preciseness. In the same manner that you want to rely on active constructions to make your writing more effective, you will find that detail and precision help your style.

General/Vague: Lawson found men and women perceive unusual names differently from usual names.

Detailed/Precise: Lawson found men and women perceive unusual names as less desirable, weaker, and more passive than usual names.

General/Vague: CB handles were coded independently.

Detailed/Precise: Two coders independently content analyzed and coded handles.

Revision. Good writers are constantly searching for more effective ways to state their case. Wordiness is a sin in our pressure-cooker world. Two general rules of thumb may help you. First, run a pen through every other word you have written. Second, underline words you think are essential to a complex sentence, arrange these in a sensible way, and then add whatever words you need to make a decent sentence (see Box 15–1).

Copy editors spend much of their time doing exactly these things. They delete words from manuscripts and shift those that are left. Become your own editor. The volume of words you like so well probably can be cut in half and rearranged to make your point clearer. At least a dozen great writers have been said to have written: "I apologize for this long letter; I didn't have enough time to shorten it."

Special reporting styles. Advice given to this juncture has been applicable to writing in general. However, scientific writing often has special requirements. Some professional societies have published guidelines on writing: the American Psychological Association's *Publication Manual,* Modern Language Association's *MLA Guide,* and the University of Chicago's *Handbook of English.*

BOX 15–1   Example of Revising a Wordy Paragraph

~~There is some evidence that observational accuracy is related to age~~. A research summary
                                                                           showed
of over 130 sample groups ~~has shown~~ that younger American subjects seem less sensitive to

nonverbal messages than older subjects. For very young subjects, this research indicates

particularly poor observational accuracy ~~in the reading~~ of facial cues. ~~It has been assumed~~
    Perhaps
~~that~~ younger subjects simply have less developed verbal, nonverbal and test-taking skills,
 ^
                                          Since
~~than adults. However, the fact that~~ differences in observational accuracy are observable
                                                                                        is
through the college age years would indicate that this assumption ~~may be~~ weak. ~~Consequently,~~
                                                                                    '*s age*
~~T~~he present paper seeks to further specify the relationship between ~~age of~~ observer ^ and ob-

servational recall accuracy.

Unfortunately, although there has been much talk about standardizing research-reporting conventions and style in sociology, the American Sociological Association has not yet published a guide. However at least once a year both of the two major journals in the field, the *American Sociological Review* and the *American Journal of Sociology* publish a short guide for contributors with information on margins, quotations, references, headings, and abbreviations. You may find these style guides of help in writing research reports.

SUMMARY

Good communication is essential to the scientific research report. First this requires that you have an ear for the audience with whom you are communicating. The audience should dictate what you say and how you say it. Effective writing reads painlessly. (That's an excellent sign that it was a pain to write.) Expect to struggle with the shaping and polishing of your ideas. This usually means paying closer attention to (1) checking for the active voice, (2) breaking up complex and lengthy thoughts, (3) not taking vocabulary and jargon for granted, (4) avoiding negations, (5) striving for detail and precision, and (6) assuming that what you have written can be better stated through revision.

If you work at these basic principles, the more special conventions of reporting and research style will simply be ornaments on a diamond. Once you have proven you have something to say, the battle is largely won. This is not to discredit standardized reporting conventions, because they are important. But they can easily be checked against the style sheets of various professions and journals. You can memorize or refer to them. But again, there are no ten rules for effective communication. That comes only from honest sweat.

READINGS FOR ADVANCED STUDENTS

LEONARD BECKER, JR. AND CLAIR GUSTAFSON, *Encounter with Sociology: The Term Paper*, 1976. Much valuable advice is offered to the undergraduate student on paper format, library research, tables, and choosing, narrowing, and developing a topic.

J. B. SYKES (ed), *The Concise Oxford Dictionary of Current English*, 1976. While British in orientation, and thus in need of supplementation by an American-usage text such as Horwill's *A Dictionary of Modern American Usage*, this is the standard for all English-language dictionaries.

C. WRIGHT MILLS, *The Sociological Imagination*, Chapter 2, 1959. This chapter is a classic example of the promise of good sociological writing. In some twenty-five pages, Mills reduces the late Talcott Parsons's *The Social System* for human consumption.

CAROLYN J. MULLINS, *A Guide to Writing and Publishing in the Social and Behavioral Sciences*, 1977. While much of the valuable information in this reference work is intended for the graduate student and professional, any student may profit from its advice—particularly from the first chapter.

WILLIAM STRUNK, JR. AND E. B. WHITE, *The Elements of Style*, 1972. And yet another oldie but goodie. This one dates back forty-five years. The amount of excellent advice on elementary rules of usage, composition, and style is astounding for this slender volume.

KATE L. TURABIAN, *A Manual for Writers of Term Papers, Theses and Dissertations*, 1973. Twenty-five years in print and four editions attest to the indispensability of this short reference work.

SUGGESTED RESEARCH PROJECTS

1. Write up the research from one of your earlier projects using the special stylistic conventions of a major sociological journal.

   a. Rewrite a section of that article limiting your sentences to seventeen words.

   b. Rewrite a section using as many different punctuation marks as you can.

   c. Rewrite a section with a minimum of punctuation.

   d. Write a section expressing your ideas as much as possible by quoting what other authors have said on the subject.

   e. Rewrite that section paraphrasing their ideas in your own words.

   f. Write a section of that exercise in the first person as much as possible.

   g. Rewrite that section using the second person as much as possible.

   h. Rewrite that section using the third person as much as possible.

   i. Rewrite a passage using entirely different words.

   j. Use Box 15–1 as an example for rewriting a passage by crossing out unnecessary words and reordering the important remaining words into a meaningful whole again.

   k. Discuss the effectiveness of these writing and revision exercises for communication of your thoughts.

APPENDIX A

Sample Fieldnotes[1]

The fieldnotes presented below are in the raw form of a transcription. No attempt was made to edit them for presentation purposes.

The reader can better see the steps we used by beginning with this raw form. The set of notes selected are not particularly thorough, for they were written at the time when the research(er) seemed to stagnate. But they illustrate a variety of points. Ordinarily a transcription for a Sunday morning would run twice the length of this set. Finally, as has been the case in the thesis, names are pseudonymns, but not necessarily those employed in the text itself.

FIELD NOTES: DATE XX SUNDAY MORNING WORSHIP

Leadership   We arrived shortly after 9:30 A.M., the service was already in progress. George was the song leader. It soon became obvious by

[1]Adapted from Erickson (1971:196–201).

the introductory and transitional comments he made to each song, that Sunday's music portion anyway was being devoted to the

Peace Movement — memory of Martin Luther King, Jr. We sang a lot of spirituals, and various songs associated with the peace movement and ended up with "We Shall Overcome." Most of these songs have simple lyrics. No songbooks were used

Socialization Products — and everybody seemed to have great familiarity with them.

At the end of the singing George began to dismiss the younger children and Theo-

Familial Rituals — dore jumped up and said he wanted the little children to remain because his family had something special they wanted to do. He then asked his wife to bring up their infant daughter. (Later while having dinner with the Johnsons, it was mentioned that she is an adopted infant of mixed race.) Theodore then proceeded to go through a christening or dedication service for the child, functionally equivalent to infant baptism. He and his wife both spoke about the child as a gift and a responsibility and mentioned that she was part of the community and that others had done a tremendous amount of sharing of the

Quasi-Kindred Activities — burden of having an infant in their home and mentioned specifically that the Joneses had been quite helpful and that a lot of children in the apartment house had pitched in folding diapers, etc.

Leadership — They then asked that Robert Jones would say a prayer which he apparently had been forewarned about because he seemed to be prepared to speak a prayer emphasizing the induction of the child into the community and membership in that sense.

Leadership — After this ceremony then, Theodore dismissed the younger children and then he was the leader for the concerns and thanksgiving section. He asked first for thanksgivings and

Communication Information — there were very few; a long, long silence followed his initial invitation. Elaine, an inten-

Personal (Cl_{ps})   tional neighbor, said something about a thanksgiving that Suzanne is able to walk and Theodore looked at Suzanne rather surprised and asked if there was some reason to be surprised that she could walk. Suzanne indicated that she had hurt her foot yesterday or some-

Cl_{shalom} thing, that a lot of people had come to her aid. Apparently she didn't see it as much of a big deal. As she spoke and talked about other people helping her, this generated somebody else to pipe in about thanksgiving for the way in which they share with one another. It was at

Cl_s this point that Theodore himself elaborated on help that fellow Shalomites had given him and his wife relative to the baby and said this was the way it always is, that people are willing to help one another and pitch in when something needs to be done.

Communication   After that, there was another silence and the oldest Smith daughter said she was thank-
Petitional   ful that Friday night she had the opportunity to attend a Bas Mitsvah for one of her girl-
Supra-Kindred   friends in College City. Again silence. Finally Theodore said, "Well we should turn up to concerns." Basically it amounted to things coming up. Samuel said that they should remember Tom Doe from Koinonia who will be a speaker at Koiné College the upcoming week, that he had expressed concern about his
Supra Kindred   speaking there, that he would say the right thing, etc. Samuel said that he had answered Tom's letter by saying he didn't know what to tell him what to say but that the Shalom people would remember him in their prayers and this apparently is meaningful to him and certainly the Shalom people see this as meaningful when they say they remember somebody in their prayers, they clearly conceptualize this as doing something for that person.

Mary raised the question of the country home, saying "we should remember that in our prayers," and at the same time she made
Cl_s the announcement that a busload would go

Rural Move out to look at the property on Wolf River this afternoon for a little trip and that anybody that wanted to go should indicate so after the service. They were leaving at noon.

Culture Robert announced that some man associated with radical Quakers was going to be on Shalom site on Friday and Saturday of next week and that people should try to get an

Cl_s opportunity to engage him in conversation. He elaborated on the many things that this person is purported to have done relative to radical Christianity in small foreign aid projects, etc.

Potential Steven said it was perhaps not too soon
Supra Kindred to remember in prayer the conference coming up in the Midwest, in a couple weeks where a number of people from communes were get-

CP_s ting together.

Allen then closed the concerns and thanksgivings and rather than praying, suggested that we sing a song that is known to the community. The basic gist of the song, as I can best recall, was something about God's providence and turning concerns over to Him.

The next portion was in the hands of Peter; it was a film about the counter-reformation and it showed the Calvinists in a pretty poor light as it did the Jesuit counter-reformation. The discussion afterward was quite varied. A number of people remarked that it showed the reformation in a pretty poor light, that the warring and inquisitory things that took place are things that they don't care to identify with. A fair amount of the discussion was related to a number of theses analogous to Weber's *Protestant Ethic and Spirit of Capitalism;* in fact Walter specifically mentioned a revision of the Weberian interpretation although he didn't refer to it that way.

Theoretical The relationship between the ideology
Note (*TN*) of predestination and possible latent implications for capitalism seemed to be newsy for a lot of people. (It persistently interests me that

Shalom members have little apparent awareness of a number of philosophical argumenta-
tions that historically have been used to
eventuate in their position. For example, their
unawareness of basic Marxian concepts, again
the unawareness of the Weberian ideas of capitalism and protestantism. They talked about
things like protestant ethic and protestant
work ethic on occasion but I've found that
they are quite novitiant in this literature. All of
their tenets are directly related to Christian
literature. This seems to underscore that they
are clearly a religious commune, not a social
commune.

Leadership
Authority

The discussion group this morning was
fairly large (15–18) and perhaps because of
that, the discussion of fairly (sic) didactic with
Peter and Samuel taking over particularly
Samuel speaking at great length on various
historical topics related to the film. One thing
that was rather interesting was the way in
which he interprets church history in a way
that selection and interpretation process is
controlled by first of all, anabaptist settings
and secondly, communitarian ideals. An example was the way in which today he por-
trayed the definition of the church given by
Martin Luther. His quotations were accurate
and the characteristics of the church were accurately quoted having to do with preaching
and sacraments but his interpretation was that
Luther's definition was the same as the Roman
Catholic and was clearly misreading the original context. While it's not surprising it's illustrative of the way in which historical details
are somewhat glossed over and opposing

TN

camps can be made into one camp depending
on the way in which one wants to interpret
these things. That of course, is the nature of
historical interpretation anyway.

Observational
Note (*ON*)

(I think I ought to spend the next couple,
three weeks trying to do some informant interviews, particularly with outsiders. I'm really

going stale. Then maybe come back fresh to some informant interviews.)

I arrived over at the Johnson house about 11:25 A.M. We had been invited to dinner. Barb and the kids had walked over and were already there when I arrived. Stewart wasn't there and I sat down out in the kitchen to talk with Barb and Sally as she was preparing dinner. Among other things I asked her about the Coffee House. I said that I knew that she and Stewart were responsible for it—it was their project and I was wondering if that involved the money too, if they paid for all the popcorn, pop, etc. She said no, the fellowship provides a budget for it, $60 a month but that actually doesn't cover the expenses and they're going to ask for some more. She indicated that there would be no problem in seeking more funds. She said that besides the money that they spent for pop, coffee, tea, popcorn, a fair amount goes for candles, even though she gets them cheap and makes many of them by melting down old ones, it amounts to a lot of money.

Actually I'm surprised that they get by for so little money, $15 a night considering the number of people involved and the quantities that seemed to be consumed.

Intentional Neighbor

While we were exchanging small talk, Elaine, an intentional neighbor, came in. It was obvious that she had been invited to dinner also. She seemed to be quite at home

Logistics

there, participating as if she had spent some time, seemed to be well integrated in the Johnson routine and setting.

Youth

Sally had mentioned before that Stewart was off somewhere picking up his class, class of seven- and eight-year old boys, and that they were off sledding and tobogganing. She also offered the information that her class had gone off shoveling sidewalks this morning. I asked her about that. Ordinarily they sing and take guitar lessons. She has a class of girls and they were tired of singing and doing the same thing and that they wanted to go out in the neighborhood and shovel people's walks for them. I got the impression that they were doing it for free.

Youth

I asked her if there was some sort of educational goal involved in these classes or if they were more oriented to having group activities. She said it was the latter. I asked her how she happens to have girls and he has boys, if there was an effort to separate the classes or what explained that. She explained that basically that's just the way it worked out age wise and that there were only a couple girls that were in the age group of Stewart's class. They try to keep them down to a small size, 8–10 people, and there were enough boys to make up that class and the girls wanted to go off and do something else so that's the stated explanation for the sex differentiation. As far as I know, none of the other classes are sex segregated.

I asked Sally how she thought Wednesday night's meeting would come out relative to the country place. She said she really didn't

Rural Move

know; we figured that they would decide to get some country place but she wasn't going to get up her hopes; actually I had begun this by saying I halfway expected them to go on the trip to the country and she said she didn't want to go, she had been on a lot of those trips before and then after asking her what she felt Wednesday night would bring, she made this comment about not letting her hopes get up. She said she had been on a lot of the trips in the past and had gone out to look at the land and built up her hopes. When she looked at a piece of property, she sees that this ought to be changed and that ought to be changed and she starts going wild about getting all sorts of good ideas for using the property and now is tired of building up her hopes.

Rural Move

I asked Stewart, when he came back, a similar question about what he felt would happen on Wednesday night. Again I started by

Interaction and Decision Process

Former Members

saying that I halfway thought he would be going on this trip this afternoon. He said that as I knew, he had been there already and that they were more interested in getting more people out there to give a variety of descriptions. He said you never know how biased your own description is. Shortly after he came in, Jerry, the fellow that I'd been talking to Friday night at the Coffee House who claimed to have been written out of the fellowship, came in to get instructions for finding the place. He was going on the trip and had been raised near the area so presumably he had some familiarity with it. It was interesting that Stewart, when he mentioned that Jerry was coming over to get the instructions, asked me if I knew him and referred to him as one of the single people and didn't refer to him as a former member.

The kids ate first in the kitchen and then the 5 of us adults ate in the dining room. One of the first things after food had been passed around, etc., Stewart asked for a capsule of the program this morning, namely the film. It was pointed out that he and Sally never get to participate in that portion of the program since they both have classes and their classes are not the kind where the instructor or whatever you want to call him, rotates, because they feel it's important to have continuity, particularly with their particular groups. We gave him a capsule summary of the thing and he didn't pick up on anything, just seemed to want straight shots and not too anxious to discuss anything.

Vocation

As we were talking about their classes again, I asked Stewart if he had always wanted to be a teacher when he went to college or how this had developed. He said that when they were first married, his father had given them a farm and that he farmed it for a while and then decided against that type of life. In his words, "it's too much work for what you get out of it and just too total a commitment, no opportunity for anything except taking care of animals."

After a couple of years of farming, he returned to college. He had had some college before that and this time went to Goshen and at Goshen in his senior year, decided to be a teacher and that year or the following year was when he and Sally got involved in the discussion that eventually became Shalom.

TN

Vocation

Design

I may want to pursue this aspect a bit in looking through the patterns of careers for other people, the fact that he was vocationally up in the air and then went to college to resolve vocational unrest and then eventually ended up in the Shalom experiment. It was quite obvious, at least on an impressionistic basis, a good number of the people at Shalom have had vocational unrest as well as any other thing that goes into their selection of or recruitment to Shalom and communitarianism.

At 1:15 P.M., which came rather soon, as we were finishing the meal I announced that we would have to go. Last night when Stewart called to invite us, I told him that we'd have to leave at 1:15 because of Barb's schedule so we rather hurriedly got the children together with their things and departed.

APPENDIX B

The Revised
IPS Categories[1]

Category 1 (*1a*). *Common social acknowledgement:* This category is composed primarily of greetings and social acknowledgments, including approaching and "breaking the ice" in initial participation. In this category should go the common friendly gestures, the routine acknowledgments such as the offer of a cigarette or the routine thanks in accepting one.

Category 2 (*1b*). *Shows solidarity through raising the status of others:* This category includes the deliberate or effective raising or enhancing the status of others. This may be done collectively or through individual praise or enthusiastic acceptance of the other. Characteristic expressions would be: "We've done well." "That's a good way to put it." "I think you summarized that beautifully." Included here also are the "buttering up" approaches such as "John, you always do such a good job in this kind of business. (Why don't you outline what we should do?)" Included also are statements of direct identification such as: "I certainly can see your point here." "I sympathize with your position." "I wish I could phrase it as well as you have." This category also is scored in behavior that is directed

---

[1]Source: Borgatta and Crowther (1965:26–30). Reprinted by permission. References to the Bales system indicating where the current category would belong in the original system are given in italics in parentheses.

432

toward the creation of "togetherness," as in the offers of assistance and of working closer together in a collaborative way. In general, actions are scored in this category that are directed toward the building of the solidarity of the group, whether these are through directly raising the status of an individual by coordinating the activities of members to assist one or another, or to alleviate conflict that may exist. The contrast between 1 and 2 is directed toward routine actions implicit in all social procedures, whereas 2 is defined more actively in terms of response meant to intensify the relationship in a direction of cohesiveness.

In the original publication by Bales joking was scored in Category 2, but subsequently it has been scored in Category *1* or Category *12*. If joking is directed toward the amusement of the group rather than as aggression toward some individual member of the group it should go into Category 1. If the aggression is directed to a member of the group and is stronger than the showing of solidarity in its consequences, it should be in Category 17.

Category 3 (2). *Shows tension release, laughs:* The most common response for this category is that of laughter subsequent to some event or joke. It should be distinguished, however, from the nervous laughter, smiles, grins, and other responses that often occur as an indication of tension rather than tension release. Habitual smiling or laughing to responses that is apparently a defensive action and does not indicate good feelings, should be scored in Category 15. Each wave of laughter should be scored as a separate response, and if the laughter should see-saw from one subgroup to another or from one person to another, each such movement of the laughter should be scored. Other indications of being pleased should be scored in Category 3. However, if the pleasure indicated is so obvious as to give the other pleasure, it should be scored as Category 2.

Category 4 (*3a*). *Acknowledges, understands, recognizes:* This category includes all passive indications of having understood or recognized the communication directed toward the recipient. The most common score for this category is a nod or saying: "Uhuh," "Yes," "O.K.," "Mum," "Right," "Check," "I see," "That may be, but . . ." In general, items are scored into this category if they indicate the acceptance of an item of communication, but this does not require agreement with the communication, the presence of which would place the response in Category 5.

Category 5 (*3b*). *Shows agreement, concurrence, compliance:* This category includes all items that indicate agreement with the speaker or with a conclusion that has been presented to the group. The respondent may vote to accept a decision or may indicate that it is correct, or that he will comply with the decision or suggestion that is made. This may constitute the suggestion that the action is agreed upon, that the individual is willing to cooperate, that the individual sees it in the indicated way, that the speaker is correct in his assertion, that the assertion is correct. Typical expressions might be: "That sounds right to me," "I agree with that," "I agree with John's point," "I think that John is correct in his assertion," "I think we ought to do that also," "Yes, that's right," "I feel the same way you all do." It should be noted that if the agreement is entirely passive, i.e., essentially nonresistance, it should go into Category 4. If the agreement is complete and overwhelming and obviously raises the status of the speaker or the group, then it should be scored in 2.

Category 6 (*4a*). *Gives a procedural suggestion:* This category includes actions that are directed toward organization for attaining a given goal, commonly by dividing responsibility or by dividing the task. Sample statements of this sort are: "Possibly we ought to organize to do this." "Suppose that you act as recorder." "I think we ought to organize what we are going to do so that we'll know how we are working." "I can handle this kind of problem if some of you can take care of the others." "Why don't you take this kind of role, and then I'll take this and John can take that." In this category are also included procedural suggestions of a normative nature when they are directed to some immediate action such as: "You should do this," "Why don't you do this?" "Please try to do this." When such normative suggestions are future oriented they should be scored as giving opinion below. When the statements are of such strength that they do not imply autonomy, but are a demand, then they should be scored in Category 17. If the demands are normal expectations for the situation, however, and conformance would naturally be expected in the situation, the procedural suggestion would be scored in Category 6.

Category 7 (*4b*). *Suggests solution:* In this category are placed statements that attempt to resolve the problem accepted by the group or defined for the group directly. Included here are such statements as: "I think that the point of the whole discussion that we're supposed to hold is to come out with the answer that the democratic way is the best." "I think the answer is there are 80 dots." "Colonel Blimp should go for a long ride and never come back." "Do you think the answer to your problem is that it is caused by some emotional disturbance?" "I believe that if we make one more move in this direction we will have the answer." "Don't you feel that if the Colonel took the lady the whole problem would be resolved in time?"

Category 8 (*5a*). *Gives opinion, evaluation, analysis, expresses feeling or wish:* This category includes the general evaluative or opinion expressing comments of the actor, generally in the form of drawing a conclusion or expressing an opinion about a future action. Typical expressions would be: "I think Colonel Blimp was probably a little confused at this point."

"I sort of like to relax when I work." "I want to find the solution to this problem." "I wish this problem had been defined better for us." "We should come up with a good solution." "They shouldn't step on each other's toes." "It's possible that the weather had some effect on his behavior."

Category 9 (*5b*). *Self-analysis and self-questioning behavior:* In this category goes behavior of a relatively objective self-evaluative sort. If it is self-questioning in an anxiety sense it is scored in Category 15. Scores placed in this category would include the following types: "The reason I probably did this was that I wasn't paying attention to what he was saying." "I just wasn't aware of what I was doing." "It makes me wonder why I took this kind of self-attitude." "Sometimes I am lonely and I don't know why." "I wish I could do that but I'm not good enough." "If I could only do that I would probably feel much better."

Category 10 (*5c*). *Reference to the external situation as redirected aggression:* In this category go all actions of aggression, hostility, nastiness, etc., that are directed out of field. There are the negative opinions that are expressed about a third person outside the group, about the administration that organized the group, about superiors, about others who are not present. Comments may include: "Well, you know how he always behaves, he's just a louse about these things." "She sounds like an old prude to me." "I don't know why these people don't give us more attention when we need it." "Well, this is a lousy outfit anyway, the way it's organized." Such statements may become group status raising, as when the third party is the subject of hostility for the organization of the group morale, such as the making of the third party the butt of a joke. If it is an effective joke it is scored in Category 2; if it tends to be more hostile than funny, the joke is scored in Category 10.

Category 11 (*6a*). *Gives orientation, information, passes communication:* In this category go the actions that are directed toward passing objective information, so far as can be defined in a situation. "It seems that that night it was raining." "On top of the hill there was a great fire." "I believe there are eight wheels to a problem." "Colonel Blimp had seven secretaries. One was a short one, one was a tall one, one was in between, and the four other were nondescript." "I am 18 years old." "My son's name is John." "My mother died of cancer." "The therapist has gray hair."

Category 12 (*6b*). *Draws attention, repeats, clarifies:* In this category are placed items that are designed to draw attention to a problem or a situation or a statement (or the person about to make same). For example: "Listen, John, . . ." "This is the issue I'd like to consider." "If I may take up that question, . . ." "I believe that what you said was that the cow was brown." "In review of our previous comments, it would seem that what we said is that he ate olives." Clarifications of meaning in a monologue are scored here. Elaboration and expansion are scored in the category of the original statement.

[Category 7. *Asks for orientation information, clarification:* In this revision of the category systems this is a void cell. The category has not appeared important in data analyses, and these responses appear better handled in other categories. For example, when one is listening to a conversation and misses a piece of information and asks: "What?" or "What was that?" the meaning may be interpreted as *suggesting* another repeat or clarify (6), or possibly even as drawing attention (12). On the other hand, if the respondent is answering with some embarrassment or disorientation, the response may be scored in Category 15. If the implication is that the speaker has not made the statement clear and is therefore inadequate, then it may be scored in Category 17, and similarly if the question implies incredulity. Questions that are phrased in terms of "Where are we?" or "How do we stand?" essentially suggest: "Let's review our activities." Therefore they should be scored as procedural suggestions (6), as should be such implicit questions. Questions that are of information or orientation that serve the purpose of ice-breakers should be entered into Category 2, unless they are more obvious expressions of anxiety or insecurity, in which case they get scored in Category 15. For example: "What time is it?" Category 1 (rather than 6) receives responses that are directed toward continuity, including some of the extremely routine, emotionally neutral suggestions such as: "Please pass the ashtray." "Please repeat what you said so that we can understand it better." "Do you mean that Colonel Blimp was a fuddy-duddy?" (Assuming he has been so described.)]

Category 13 (*8*). *Asks for opinion, evaluation, analysis, expression of feeling:* While the implicit eliciting response is scored in Category 1, the more direct one in regard to expression of opinion, evaluation, analysis, or feeling is scored in 13. Examples may be as follows: "What do you think about this?" "Tell me how you feel about this." "Go ahead, say what you like." "I'd appreciate your reaction to this." "Do we have any other opinions on this?" "I wish you would indicate your feelings [thoughts, conclusions, cogitations, insights, etc.] on this matter." "Do you think we can finish in time?" "Do you think Colonel Blimp was that kind of a person?" "What do you believe?"

[Category 9. *Asks for suggestion, direction, possible ways of action:* This is also a void category. In particular, the question: "What do you suggest?" may be interpreted as the direction on the part of the speaker to another to proceed in a given way. Thus, requests for suggestions are to be scored as suggestions themselves. The exception in this case is where a person requests suggestion from an apparent inadequacy or anxiety. In this case the question is scored in Category 15. Broader questions asking for suggestions may fall into Category 1, that is, of breaking the ice. Typical of these would be: "What shall we talk about today?" "Does anyone have suggestions about how to start?"]

Category 14 (*10*). *Disagrees, maintains a contrary position:* This category includes primarily those responses that are indications of disagreement with the contents of the statement or position of another. It may be a simple statement such as: "I don't agree with this." "I would have thought it had been otherwise." It may also be expressed by direct resistance such as refusing to be convinced or acquiescent. The negativistic response is thus scored in this category provided it is not directly hostile and antagonistic, in which case it would be scored in Category 17. Negativism in this sense includes resistance to suggestions, opinions, and other approaches of the other members. Emotional rejection in a more direct sense should be scored in Category 17.

Note: The objective response of "No" sometimes is a mere acknowledgment of the statement that has been made. Thus, the simple incidence of the word "no" does not mean disagreement any more than "yes" means agreement, and both of these may be acknowledgments that something has been understood and are to be scored in Category 4. In the discussion of a debated point, statements that are persistent and in contradiction to positions held by others, are scored as disagreements. In general, however, actions that are directed to essentially annihilate the other in a social or psychological sense are to be scored in Category 17. The hostile, impersonal, unapproachable, and forbidding responses should be scored to Category 17 when they occur in this sense, unless they are more prominent as assertions of the self than the annihilation of the other, in which case they are scored as 18.

Category 15 (*11a*). *Shows tension, asks for help by virtue of personal inadequacy:* In this category are scored the general characteristics of nervousness, including the tapping of fingers, squirming, toying with pencils, cigarettes, cigarette lighters, etc. Where the behavior appears to be entirely habitual on the part of the respondent, it should be scored only each time that he or she apparently draws attention of the observer or of the members of the group through such behavior. While this is an arbitrary method of scoring such behavior, it is not less arbitrary than doing so on a time basis and may be much more meaningful since the observer is constantly scanning the group and should be aware of the fluctuations of responses of the individual. Included in this category also are the startle or anxiety responses of the individual, the displays of obvious fluster and disorganization, including stammering, flushing, rocking, obvious perspiration, or other similar signs. False starts in speaking, indicating that the person is nervous, should be scored in this category. Obvious withdrawal behavior of any type, such as moving out of field by leaning back in a chair when all others are moving forward, etc., should be scored here. In general, all direct indications of social and psychological inadequacy are to be scored in this category, including the responses that indicate being out of step, such as being the focus of attention because of inappropriate comment, so-called hollow laughing, etc. Any indication of response in this direction indicating guilt, shame, or other inadequacy should also be scored. However, being self-critical or questioning in the more detached manner of merely examining one's self should be scored in Category 9 indicated above. That is, detached self-criticism, whether positive or negative, should be scored as Category 9. Requests for assistance, when they carry the connotation of inadequacy of a personal sort, should be scored in this Category 15. Requests for assistance may have a cohesiveness function also and in these cases should be scored in Category 2.

In general, thus, this category receives behavior that is associated with the inadequacy of the individual as expressed either through nervous behavior or other signs of anxiety, or withdrawal. Requests for help, however, need not fall into this category and may belong in other categories above. Similarly, withdrawal may be an indication of negativism as scored in Category 14, or rejection of the other as scored in Category 17. Displays of inattentiveness or boredom and other forms of rudeness are scored in Category 17.

Category 16 (*11b*). *Shows tension increase:* In this category are scored the periods of tenseness that grow largely out of impasses or bankruptcy of conversation. Most of the scores that fall into this category are the awkward pauses that occur for a group as a whole. These should be scored in terms of the apparent cycles of these pauses, which are usually punctuated by clearing of throats, looking around by one person or another, etc. For the whole group, however, it is sometimes noted that the level of participation grows more tense because of the general personal involvement of the group. When this is noticed for the group as a whole, a group score should be given also. In general, Category 16 is a score that is applied to the group as a whole only.

Category 17 (*12a*). *Shows antagonism, hostility, is demanding:* In this category are all actions that are directed to be either socially or psychologically destructive of the other or his position. This includes the use of the ad hominem argument, the calling of names or indicating that one's motives are questionable, of directly and emotionally contradicting the other, or suggesting that he has no reasonable grounds on which to stand. Negativism that is personal and flouting of authority is scored in this category, as are other actions of wilfulness and deliberate nonconformity. Harassing and taking advantage of the other through aggressive personal attack, even when directed to humor, is scored in this category.

This includes techniques of confrontation, of ignoring the other's position as though he did not exist, ridiculing, being sarcastic, etc.

Category 18 (*12b*). *Ego defensiveness:* In this category are placed all actions that are direct expressions of assertive ego defensiveness. Denials of others that are stated in the first person, asserting one's own authority, are scored here. For example "I am *too* right." "I don't see how you can possibly criticize my position." "*I* wouldn't say that!" Also included in this category are direct attempts to attract attention through being associated with self-approval, including actions of braggadocio, etc. In actions of rivalry, if the attempt is the destruction of the other, it is scored in 17; if it is the defense and assertion of the self, it goes into Category 18. In Category 18 also go the scores that may be classed as self-righteous and indicating the superiority of the self over others. Similarly, paranoid type responses, unless they are more obviously indications of inadequacy, should be scored in Category 18.

APPENDIX C

An Example
of an Interview Guide[1]

GENERAL INSTRUCTIONS:

1. Be sure to keep your cards in a safe place. If they become illegible, check with the corresponding McBee-card (they are arranged numerically), and/or with the three directories: *City Directory, Telephone Book,* and *University Directory.*
2. The quota is 5 pr. day, preferably more, but 5 is OK. Rather quality than quantity when you are sure you make 5 (the days of arrival and departure count as 1 day together). Generally it is wise to make as many telephone-calls as possible well in advance and have fixed dates with the respondents. All respondents have been "warned" by mail, so there is no obligation to call them before you visit them—and telephone-calling may be unwise as it is easier to refuse over the telephone.
3. Be sure to write on your white card whether the respondent was
   completely   partly   unwilling   impossible   absent, ill,
   interviewed   interviewed   to locate   vacation, etc.
4. Be sure to put on the schedule, upper right hand corner on the first page, the number of the respondent (the number of his card). This is our only means of identifying him; however, the schedules will be treated confidentially as promised. Put the number on *immediately after the interview,* so as not to make the respondent 'feel like a number.' Never put his name on the

[1]Source: Galtung (1967:161–163). Reprinted by permission.

schedule anywhere.

5. When the interview is completed, fill in the questions about the interview, the last with your own initials; and put your initials on the white card. Keep all cards and schedules until all is over.

6. Do not tell the respondent that he probably will be reinterviewed.

GENERAL INSTRUCTIONS
FOR THE INTERVIEWING:

1. Please remember that these people are under the strain of conflict, that the whole issue is very painful for them, so be as tactful as possible. Further, methodological ends do not warrant ethically dubious means. As a general attitude, be maximally *open-minded,* curious, receptive, without committing yourself to either camp. When asked what you mean and think, tell them you are here to learn, not to pass any judgment, that the situation is very complex, that the Northern and foreign press are biased, and that we are more interested in studying a community under *conflict* (but be careful with this word) than the race-issue.

2. *Introduce yourself something like this:* How do you do, my name is—, I am one of a team of interviewers under the direction of Professor N. N.—I think you got a letter from him some days ago—Do you think I may have an interview with you? It does not last long, it is completely confidential, and not for any magazine or newspaper.

3. *Why do you do it then?* Well, this is a social science study, and we are interested in learning something about a community in the kind of situation X-ville is in right now.
Why me? We picked some 300 people at random, and you happened to be one of them. You would do us a great favor—
I don't know anything! Very few people know anything for certain in this situation, but we would very much like to hear your opinions. *Do you get any money for this? I never heard of anybody who did anything for nothing!* I just get my expenses covered (and barely that!)—but you are right insofar as I do not do it for nothing. I am very interested in the situation myself, and it is very good training for me as a student.
And what is going to happen to this schedule? Well, it will all be put on small cards and analyzed to find out something about who thinks what.

4. As far as possible, know the questions by heart so you can have eye-contact with the respondent. Remember that each page is a unit in itself. Keep the schedule so the respondent does not see what you write, but not so that it looks like you try to hide it (difficult, training in front of a mirror is advisable). Do not turn pages too often. Check the correct category in a discrete way. Remember to write down something verbatim even though it is covered by the precoding just once in a while, otherwise the respondent feels badly about it. However, do not write too much, it takes time, and the respondent feels awkward, the flow of conversation stops.

5. As a rule, let the respondent lead, do not argue, but cut him short on some places if the 'story' becomes unnecessarily involved. However, some of these stories may be extremely valuable. Be sure you know where the

questions are placed, so you can easily check as the respondent tosses around.

6. Make use of the background questions as a quick cooling-off. They should give both parties a feeling of being through, which is important.

7. If the respondent wants to see the schedule, tell him to wait till the interview is over. If he insists, give him a few questions as a sample. When the interview is completed, give him a blank schedule to look at, but tell him you must have it back as 'they are scarce.'

8. If a husband or wife is to be interviewed, the situation will often be problematic. Ideally, they should be interviewed alone, with nobody, especially not the wife or the husband, listening. To achieve this, two obvious techniques may be used:

   a. Get the husband on the job, e.g., during the lunch-break, or in connection with the lunch-break so as not to ruin it for him.

   b. Get the wife at home when the husband is working (but she may be afraid to let you in).

   If you meet the couple at home, proceed as follows:
   Talk to both of them if you meet them, just to introduce yourself, let the husband inspect you, and then say something like: 'Well, we drew a random sample, and it happened to be *Mr.* Smith (*Mrs.* Smith) in this family—', but say it with tact so that the implication is not too obvious. If this has no effect, say: 'So, do you think I may interview Mr. Smith alone?' If this has no effect, or if the mate explicitly asks for permission to stay, try for the third and last time: 'According to my instructions, I should try to interview the person we selected alone—', but do not say it if the situation is already tense. If you have to take 'both or none' (and in addition you may get one dog, two children, the laundry, and some in-laws who just dropped in) then make yourself comfortable and go ahead, addressing yourself to the respondent only. This may work all right. If it does not, you may have to decide whether what you are doing is.

   a. Conducting two interviews at the same time, with two schedules (then take up another schedule, and say, 'if you do not object, I find that what you say is so interesting that I would like to put that down too').

   b. Conducting one interview with two persons at the same time, where they arrive at a common answer after some decision-making. This is the least preferable situation.

9. Do not forget to make compliments about X-ville if you feel they are justified (do not be a hypocrite, you are not a salesman). Further, it is very important to mention the good reception we have been given (and which we expect we shall get this time too)—this can mean quite a lot in establishing rapport.

10. When the interview is completed, and you have left the house and can no longer be seen, look the schedule over, add comments that are still fresh in your memory, make sure that your coding has been correct, etc. This will save all of us an enormous amount of work later on.

11. You will undoubtedly be told stories, some of them extremely interesting. Put them down on the back of a sheet in the schedule, and type it out as soon as possible so that you can get some of the flavor. Put the respondent's number on it, and append it to the schedule (preferably, take a copy of the story or whatever you find interesting).

APPENDIX D

Sample
Interview Schedule

CONFIDENTIAL

NATIONAL OPINION RESEARCH CENTER
University of Chicago
Survey 4139
Feb., 1972

BEGIN DECK 01

TIME		
INTERVIEW		AM
BEGAN:	_____	PM

07–08/ 09

First, I have a few factual questions about yourself.

1. Which of the categories on this card come closest to the type of place you were living in when you were 16 years old?

HAND CARD A	In open country but not on a farm 1	10/9

In open country but not on a farm	1
On a farm	2
In a small city or town (under 50,000)	3
In a medium-size city (50,000–250,000)	4
In a suburb near a large city	5
In a large city (over 250,000)	6
Don't know	8

2. In what state or foreign country were you living when you were 16 years old?

    REFER TO STATE CODES BELOW AND
       ENTER CODE NUMBER IN BOX ...... ☐☐   11–12/

IF STATE NAMED IS SAME STATE R LIVES IN NOW, ASK A:

A. When you were 16 years old, were you living in this same (city/town/county)?

                    yes 1
                    no 2   13/9

                                                    DECK 01

STATE CODES

Alabama	01	Maine	19	Oregon	37
Alaska	02	Maryland	20	Pennsylvania	38
Arizona	03	Massachusetts	21	Rhode Island	39
Arkansas	04	Michigan	22	South Carolina	40
California	05	Minnesota	23	South Dakota	41
Colorado	06	Mississippi	24	Tennessee	42
Connecticut	07	Missouri	25	Texas	43
Delaware	08	Montana	26	Utah	44
Florida	09	Nebraska	27	Vermont	45
Georgia	10	Nevada	28	Virginia	46
Hawaii	11	New Hampshire	29	Washington	47
Idaho	12	New Jersey	30	West Virginia	48
Illinois	13	New Mexico	31	Wisconsin	49
Indiana	14	New York	32	Wyoming	50
Iowa	15	North Carolina	33	Foreign country	51
Kansas	16	North Dakota	34	Don't know	52
Kentucky	17	Ohio	35		
Louisiana	18	Oklahoma	36		

3. Were you living with both your own mother and father around the time you were 16? (*IF NO:* With whom were you living around that time?)

            Both own mother and father 1
            Father and stepmother 2   14/9
            Mother and stepfather 3

Father only 4
Mother only 5
Some other male relative (SPECIFY) 6

Some other female relative (SPECIFY) 7

Other arrangement (SPECIFY) 8

IF NOT LIVING WITH OWN FATHER—ASK LATER QUESTIONS ABOUT "FATHER" (Q. 4 AND SECOND COLUMN OF Q. 91) IN TERMS OF STEPFATHER OR OTHER MALE RESPONDENT WAS LIVING WITH AS CODED ABOVE. IF NO STEPFATHER OR OTHER MALE, SKIP Q. 4 AND SECOND COLUMN OF Q. 91.	SAME APPLIES TO "MOTHER" (FROM THIRD COLUMN OF Q. 91).

DECK 01

4. A. What kind of work did your father (FATHER SUBSTI-
   TUTE) normally do? That is, what was his job called?
   OCCUPATION: _____

   B. *IF NOT ALREADY ANSWERED, ASK:*
   What did he actually do in that job? Tell me, what were some
   of his main duties?

   C. What kind of place did he work for?
   INDUSTRY: _____

   D. *IF NOT ALREADY ANSWERED, ASK:*
   What did they (make/do)?

   E. Was he self-employed, or did he work for someone else?
   Self-employed 1
   Someone else 2
   Don't know 8

15–17/
18–19/

5. Thinking about the time when you were 16 years old, compared with American families in general then, would you say your family income was—far below average, below average, average, above average, or far above average? (PROBE: Just your best guess.)

Far below average	 1	20/9
Below average	 2	
Average	 3	
Above average	 4	
Far above average	 5	
Don't know	 6	

---

6. From what countries or part of the world did your ancestors come?

IF *SINGLE COUNTRY* IS NAMED, REFER TO NATIONAL CODES BELOW, AND ENTER CODE NUMBER IN BOXES 21–22/

IF *MORE THAN ONE COUNTRY* IS NAMED, ENTER CODE 88 AND ASK A.

DECK 01

A. *IF MORE THAN ONE COUNTRY NAMED:* Which one of these countries do you feel closer to?
IF ONE COUNTRY NAMED, REFER TO
CODES BELOW, AND ENTER NUMBER HERE: _____ 23–24/
IF CAN'T DECIDE ON ONE COUNTRY,
ENTER CODE 88

NATIONAL CODES

Africa	01	Mexico	17	
Austria	02	Netherlands (Dutch/Holland)	18	
Canada (French)	03	Norway	19	
Canada (Other)	04	Philippines	20	
China	05	Poland	21	
Czechoslovakia	06	Puerto Rico	22	
Denmark	07	Russia (USSR)	23	
England and Wales	08	Scotland	24	
Finland	09	Spain	25	
France	10	Sweden	26	
Germany	11	Switzerland	27	
Greece	12	West Indies	28	
Hungary	13	Other (SPECIFY)	29	
Ireland	14			
Italy	15			
Japan	16	More than one country/can't decide on one	88	
		Don't know	98	

7. How many brothers and sisters did you have? (Count those born alive, but no longer living, as well as those alive now. Also include stepbrothers and stepsisters, and children adopted by your parents.)

None 0   25/9

One 1

Two 2

Three 3

Four 4

Five 5

Six 6

Seven or more 7

Don't know 8

8. Are you currently—married, widowed, divorced, separated, or have you never been married?

Currently married (ASK A & B) 1   26/9

Widowed .... (ASK A & B) 2

Divorced .... (ASK A) 3

Separated ...... (ASK A) 4

Never married .. (GO TO Q. 9) 5

                                            DECK 01

IF EVER MARRIED:

A. How old were you when you
first married? ENTER EXACT AGE: ☐☐   27–28/

B. *IF CURRENTLY MARRIED OR WIDOWED:*
Have you ever been divorced or legally separated?   29/9

Yes 1

No 2

9. Last week were you working full time, part time, going to school, keeping house, or what?

IF MORE THAN ONE RESPONSE, GIVE PREFERENCE TO CODES IN NUMERICAL ORDER—FROM LEAST TO HIGHEST NUMBERS. CIRCLE ONE CODE ONLY.

Working full time (35 hours or more) 1   30/9

Working part time (1 to 34 hours) 2

With a job, but not at work because of temporary illness, vacation, strike 3

Unemployed, laid off, looking for work 4

Retired .... (ASK A) 5

In school ...... (ASK A) 6

Keeping house .. (ASK A) 7

Other (SPECIFY AND ASK A) 8

A. *IF RETIRED, IN SCHOOL, KEEPING HOUSE, OR OTHER:* Did you ever work for as long as one year?

Yes .... (ASK Q. 10) 1
No .... (SKIP TO Q. 13) ... 2

31/9

10. A. What kind of work do you (did you normally) do? That is, what (is/was) your job called?

OCCUPATION: _____

B. *IF NOT ALREADY ANSWERED, ASK:* What (do/did) you actually do in that job? Tell me, what (are/were) some of your main duties?

C. What kind of place (do/did) you work for?

INDUSTRY: _____

D. *IF NOT ALREADY ANSWERED, ASK:* What (do/did) they (make/do)?

E. (Are/Were) you self-employed or (do/did) you work for someone else?

Self-employed 1
Someone else 2

32–34/
35–36/

DECK 01

IF CURRENTLY WORKING FULL TIME, ASK Q'S. 11 AND 12.

11. What days of the week do you normally work? CODE ALL THAT APPLY.

Monday	1	37/9
Tuesday	2	38/9
Wednesday	3	39/9
Thursday	4	40/9
Friday	5	41/9
Saturday	6	42/9
Sunday	7	43/9
No set schedule, varies	8	44/9

12. What hours do you usually work—days, evenings, or nights? CIRCLE ONE CODE.

Days (Between 8 A.M. and 6 P.M.) 1
Evenings (Between 6 P.M. and midnight 2
Nights (Between midnight and 8 A.M.) 3
No set schedule, varies 4
Other (SPECIFY) _____ 5

45/9

IF R. IS MARRIED, ASK Q. 13.
OTHERS SKIP TO INSTRUCTIONS BEFORE Q. 17.

13. Last week was your (wife/husband) working full time, part time, going to school, keeping house, or what?

> IF MORE THAN ONE RESPONSE, GIVE PREFERENCE TO CODES IN NUMERICAL ORDER—FROM LEAST TO HIGHEST NUMBERS. CIRCLE ONE CODE ONLY.
>
> Working full time (35 hours or more) 1   46/9
> Working part time (1 to 34 hours) 2
> With a job, but not at work because of temporary
>   illness, vacation, strike 3
> Unemployed, laid off, looking for work 4
> Retired .... (ASK A) 5
> In school .... (ASK A) 6
> Keeping house ..... (ASK A) 7
> Other (SPECIFY AND ASK A) 8

A. *IF RETIRED, IN SCHOOL, KEEPING HOUSE, OR OTHER:* Did (he/she) ever work for as long as one year?
> Yes .....(ASK Q. 14) 1
> No ... (SKIP TO Q. 17) .. 2   47/9

Note to reader of this appendix: Q. 14–16 are the same as Q. 10–12 except they refer to the spouse.

DECK 01

IF R. IS CURRENTLY WORKING (FULL OR PART TIME)—
ASK Q'S 17 AND 18 ABOUT R.
IF R. IS MARRIED PERSON WHO IS NOT WORKING—ASK
ABOUT SPOUSE IF SPOUSE IS WORKING.
ALL OTHERS, SKIP TO Q. 19.

17. Do you (does your [SPOUSE]) have a supervisor on your (his/her) job to whom you are (he/she is) directly responsible?
> Yes ..... (ASK A) 1
> No 2   64/9

A. *IF YES:* Do any of *those* persons supervise anyone else?
> Yes 3
> No 4   65/9

BEGIN DECK 02

ASK EVERYONE:

19. Now a few questions about this household.
> A. First, how many persons *altogether* live here, related to you or not? Please include any persons who usually live here but are away temporarily—on business, on vacation, or in a gen-

eral hospital—and all babies and small children. Do *not* include—college students who are living away at college, persons stationed away from here in the Armed Forces, or persons away in institutions. (Don't forget to include *yourself* in the total.)

> IF TOTAL IS ONE PERSON,
> ENTER 01 AND
> SKIP TO Q. 21

TOTAL PERSONS [|] 07–08/

B. How many of these persons are babies
   or children *under* 6 years old   UNDER 6 YEARS: [|] 09–10/

C. How many are children age 6 thru 12?   6–12 YEARS: [|] 11–12/

D. How many are teenagers 13 thru 17   13–17 YEARS: [|] 13–14/

E. And how many are persons 18 and over?   18+ YEARS: [|] 15–16/

B-E SHOULD TOTAL TO A: IF NOT,
CHECK ANSWERS WITH RESPONDENT

---

20. Is everyone in the household related to you in some way?
    Yes 1
    No .. (ASK A) .. 2   17/9

A. *IF NO*: How many persons in the household are
   not related to you in any way?   [|] 18–19/

DECK 02

21. (Just thinking about your family now—those people in
    the household who *are* related to you . . .) How many
    persons in the family (including yourself) earned any
    money last year—1971—from any job or employment?   [|] 20–21/

---

22. In which of these groups did your total *family* income, from *all*
    sources, fall last year—1971—before taxes, that is?

> HAND
> CARD
> B

A. Under $2,000 01   22–23/99
B. $2000 to 3999 02
C. $4000 to 5999 03
D. $6000 to 7999 04
E. $8000 to 9999 05
F. $10,000 to 12,499 06

                G. $12,500 to 14,999 07
                H. $15,000 to 17,499 08
                I. $17,500 to 19,999 09
                J. $20,000 to 24,999 10
                K. $25,000 to 29,999 11
                L. $30,000 or over 12

                Refused 13
                Don't know 98

---

23. If you were asked to use one of four names for your social class,
    which would you say you belong in: the lower class, the working
    class, the middle class, or the upper class?
                Lower class 1   24/9
                Working class 2
                Middle class 3
                Upper class 4

---

24. How many children have you ever had? Please count all that
    were born alive at any time (including any you had from a
    previous marriage).
                None 0   25/9
                One 1
                Two 2
                Three 3
                Four 4
                Five 5
                Six 6
                Seven 7
                Eight or more . 8

---

25. *ASK EVERYONE, UNLESS TOTALLY INAPPROPRIATE.*
    IF INAPPROPRIATE, CIRCLE CODE 4.
    Do you expect to have any (more) children?
                Yes   26/9
                (ASK A & B) . 1
                No 2
                Uncertain 3
                Not asked, in-
                   appropriate .. 4

                                                        DECK 02

IF YES:
A. How many (more)? .... _____   27/
                                                            28/
B. How many (more) in the next five years? .... _____   29/
                                                            30/

26. What do you think is the ideal number of children for a family
    to have?

None	00
One	01
Two	03
Three	03
Four	04
Five	05
Six	06
Seven or more	07
As many as you want	08
Don't know	98

31–32/99

27. Do you approve or disapprove of a married woman earning
    money in business or industry if she has a husband capable
    of supporting her?

Approve	1
Disapprove	2
Don't know	8

33/9

28. If your party nominated a woman for President, would you vote
    for her if she were qualified for the job?

Yes	1
No	2
Don't know	8

34/9

29. Are you in favor of the death penalty for persons convicted
    of murder?

Yes	1
No	2
Don't know	8

35/9

30. Would you favor or oppose a law which would require a person
    to obtain a police permit before he or she could buy a gun?

Favor	1
Oppose	2
Don't know	8

36/9

31. In general, do you think the courts in this area deal too harshly
    or not harshly enough with criminals?

Too harshly	1
Not harshly enough	2
About right	3
Don't know	8

37/9

32. There's been a lot of discussion about the way morals and attitudes about sex are changing in this country. If a man and
a woman have sex relations before marriage, do you think
it is always wrong, almost always wrong, wrong only sometimes,
or not wrong at all?

        Always wrong 1   38/9

        Almost always wrong ... 2

        Wrong only sometimes . 3

        Not wrong at all 4

        Don't know 8

---

33. There are always some people whose ideas are considered bad
or dangerous by other people. For instance, somebody who is
against all churches and religion. . . .

A. If such a person wanted to make a speech in your city (town, community) against churches and religion, should he be allowed to speak, or not?

    Yes, allowed to speak .. 1   39/9

    Not allowed 2

    Don't know 8

B. Should such a person be allowed to teach in a college or university, or not?

    Yes, allowed to teach .. 1   40/9

    Don't know 8

    Not Allowed 2

C. If some people in your community suggested that a book he wrote against churches and religion should be taken out of your public library, would you favor removing this book, or not?

    Favor 1   41/9

    Not favor 2

    Don't know 8

Note to reader of this appendix: Since question 34–50 are similar in format to
Q. 33, they have been deleted.

---

51. Have you heard or read about fluoridating public water supplies?

        Yes (ASK A & B) 1   07/9

        No (SKIP TO Q. 55) .. 2

IF YES:

A. As you understand it, what is the purpose of water fluoridation? FIELD CODE: RECORD VERBATIM: THEN CODE
AS MANY AS APPLY.

Helps prevent tooth decay, it is
   good for teeth 1   08/9
Purifies water 2   09/9
Other 3   10/9
Don't know, vague answer 4   11/9

                                      12/   13/   14/

DECK 04

B. What is your opinion on fluoridating public water supplies?
Do you feel it is very desirable, desirable, undesirable, or very
undesirable?
       Very desirable 1   15/9
       Desirable 2
       Undesirable 3
       Very undesirable 4
       Doesn't make any difference to me 5
       Don't know 6

---

52. Do you think the decision about whether or not to fluoridate
the water supply should be made at the federal level, at the
state level, or do you think it should be left to each local community?
       Federal 1   16/9
       State 2
       Local 3
       Don't know 4

---

53. Who should decide to fluoridate—elected officials, a health
authority such as the health department, or do you think the
people themselves should decide by a special vote?
       Elected officials 1   17/9
       Health authority/department .. 2
       Special vote 3
       Don't know 4

Note to reader of this appendix: Since Q's 54 to 90 add no new principles of
interview schedule construction, they have been deleted.

DECK 03

Now just a few more background questions.

91. ASK ALL PARTS OF QUESTION ABOUT RESPONDENT BEFORE GOING ON TO ASK ABOUT R'S FATHER: AND THEN R'S MOTHER: THEN R'S SPOUSE IF R IS CURRENTLY MARRIED.

A. What is the highest grade in elementary school that (you/your father/your mother, your husband/wife) finished and got credit for? CODE EXACT GRADE.

	RESPONDENT	R'S FATHER (FATHER SUBSTITUTE)	R'S MOTHER (MOTHER SUBSTITUTE)	R'S SPOUSE
	23–24/99	28–29/99	34–35/99	40–41/99
No formal schooling	.00	.00	.00	.00
1st grade	.01	.01	.01	.01
2nd grade	.02	.02	.02	.02
3rd grade	.03 GO	.03 GO	.03 GO	.03 GO
4th grade	.04 TO	.04 TO	.04 TO	.04 TO
5th grade	.05 Q'S	.05 Q'S	.05 Q'S	.05 Q. 92
6th grade	.06 FOR	.06 FOR	.06 FOR	.06
7th grade	.07 FATHER	.07 MOTHER	.07 SPOUSE	.07
8th grade	.08	.08	.08	.08
9th grade	.09	.09	.09	.09
10th grade	.10	.10	.10	.10
11th grade	.11	.11	.11	.11
12th grade	.12 GO TO B	.12 GO TO B	.12 GO TO B	.12 GO TO B
Don't know	–	98	98	98

	RESPONDENT	R'S FATHER	R'S MOTHER	R'S SPOUSE
B. Did (you/he/she) ever get a high school diploma?	25/9	30/9	36/9	42/9
Yes	1	1	1	1
No	2	2	2	2
DK		8	8	8

	RESPONDENT	R'S FATHER	R'S MOTHER	R'S SPOUSE
C. Did (you/he/she) complete one or more years of college for credit?	26/9	31–32/99	37–38/99	43–44/99
No	0 GO TO NEXT PERSON	00 GO TO NEXT PERSON	00 GO TO NEXT PERSON	00 GO TO Q. 92
DK		88 GO TO NEXT PERSON	88 GO TO NEXT PERSON	88 GO TO Q. 92
(*IF YES:* How many years did (you/he/she) complete?) 1 yr.	1	01	01	01
2 yrs.	2	02	02	02
3 yrs.	3	03	03	03
4 yrs.	4	04	04	04
5 yrs.	5	05	05	05
6 yrs.	6	06	06	06
7 yrs.	7	07	07	07
8+ yrs.	8	08	08	08
DK		98	98	98

	RESPONDENT	R'S FATHER	R'S MOTHER	R'S SPOUSE
D. Do you (Does [he/she]) have any college degrees? (*IF YES:* What degree?)	27/9	33/9	39/9	45/9
No	1	1	1	1
Jr. College	2	2	2	2
Bachelor's	3	3	3	3
Graduate	4	4	4	4
DK		8	8	8

92. In what year were you born?

46–47/60

---

93. CODE RESPONDENT'S SEX:
           Male 1   48/
           Female 2

---

94. CODE WITHOUT ASKING *ONLY* IF THERE IS NO DOUBT
     IN YOUR MIND.
     What race do you consider
     yourself?
     RECORD VERBATIM
     AND CODE.
           White 1
           Black 2
           Other (SPECIFY) . . . 3   49/

           NOTE: IF YOU ASKED R'S RACE, CHECK BOX   50

---

95. Thank you very much for your time and help.
     May I have your name and telephone number just in case my
     office wants to verify this interview?
                                                   TELEPHONE
     RESPONDENT'S NAME   NUMBER
           No phone 1   51/9
           Refused phone # . . 2
     IF TELEPHONE NUMBER IS GIVEN,
     ASK A:
     A. Is this phone located in
         your own home?
               Yes . . (ASK [1]) 3
               No (SPECIFY WHERE
               PHONE IS
               LOCATED) 4
           (1) IF PHONE IN HOME: Is the number for this phone
               listed in the phone book?
               Yes 5
               No 6

Thank you.

TIME INTERVIEW ENDED:	AM PM
52–53/	54/

FILL IN THE FOLLOWING ITEMS IMMEDIATELY AFTER LEAVING RESPONDENT

A. Total length of interview: _____ minutes   55–57/999

B. Date of interview: _____ / _____
                        (Month)   (Day)
                        58–59/   60–61/

C. Code day of week of interview: 62/9
                        Monday 1
                        Tuesday 2
                        Wednesday 3
                        Thursday 4
                        Friday 5
                        Saturday 6
                        Sunday 7

D. In general, what was the respondent's attitude toward the interview?
                        Friendly and eager 1   63/9
                        Cooperative but not
                          particularly eager 2
                        Indifferent and bored 3
                        Hostile 4

E. Was respondent's understanding of the questions (CODE ONE).
                        Good 1   64/9
                        Fair 2
                        Poor 3

F. RECORD FROM SURS:

PSU # . . . .

⌷⌷⌷ 65–67/

SU # . . . .

⌷⌷⌷⌷ 68–71/

SURS LINE #: _____

SURS PAGE #: _____

G. Interviewer's I.D. # . . . .

⌷⌷⌷⌷⌷ 72–76/

H. Interviewer's signature: _____

Note to reader of this appendix: Since some of the terms and figures used in the above appendix may appear confusing to you the following notations are explained below:

1. "DECK" refers to the number of the IBM card on which particular information is keypunched.
2. Numbers with slashes (i.e., 62/9) in the right-hand margins refer to the IBM card column in which data appears (to the left of the slash) and the code for missing data (to the right of the slash).
3. DK symbolizes "Don't know."
4. R symbolizes "Respondent."
5. Q symbolizes "Question."
6. Sentences which are completely done in upper case type (capitalized) are notes to the interviewer, *not* statements to be read to the respondent.

APPENDIX E

Questionnaire for OCG Survey

OFFICE OF
THE DIRECTOR
FORM CPS-516
(12-15-61)

U.S. DEPARTMENT OF COMMERCE
BUREAU OF THE CENSUS
WASHINGTON 25, D.C.

March 19, 1962

Dear Mr. _____ :

We appreciate your cooperation in connection with our regular Current Population Survey program. Now we would like to ask you to answer a few additional questions about your earlier background and on the occupation of your father. If you are married, there are also a few questions about your wife and her father's occupation. This information is needed to help in forecasting the kinds of changes that are likely to occur in the future and to help develop programs to meet changing conditions.

Please complete this form and mail it within the next three days in the enclosed envelope, which requires no postage. All information provided will be held in strict confidence and only statistical totals will ever be published.

Sincerely yours,

Richard M. Scammon
Director
Bureau of the Census

Control and line number		BUDGET BUREAU NO. 41-6155
		APPROVAL EXPIRES JUNE 30, 1962

QUESTIONNAIRE FOR OCCUPATIONAL CHANGES IN A GENERATION

1. Where were you born? *(Name of State, foreign country, U.S. possession, etc.)*

2. In what country was your father born?

   United States ☐   or

   (Name of foreign country; or Puerto Rico, Guam, etc.)

3. In what country was your mother born?

   United States ☐   or

   (Name of foreign country; or Puerto Rico, Guam, etc.)

4. Number of brothers and sisters
   (Count those born alive but no longer living, as well as those alive now. Also include stepbrothers and sisters and children adopted by your parents.)

   a. How many sisters did you have? .... _____
      or ☐ None

   b. How many of these sisters were older than you (born earlier)? ...... _____

   c. How many brothers did you have? .. _____
      or ☐ None

   d. How many of these brothers were older than you (born earlier)? ...... _____

   e. Did any of your older brothers live to age 25?
      ☐ Yes   ☐ No
     (Answer Question 5)   *(Skip to Question 6)*

5. If "Yes" in 4e, please indicate the highest grade of school the oldest brother completed.

   (Check one box; if you are not sure, please make a guess.)

   Never attended school ..... ☐

   | 1 | 2 | 3 | 4 | 5 | 6 |
   Grades 1 to 12 .... ☐ ☐ ☐ ☐ ☐ ☐
   | 7 | 8 | 9 | 10 | 11 | 12 |
   ☐ ☐ ☐ ☐ ☐ ☐

   | 1 | 2 | 3 | 4 | 5 or more |
   College (Academic years) ... ☐ ☐ ☐ ☐ ☐

6. Where were you living when you were 16 years old?

   a. The same community (city, town, or rural area) as at the present time? .... ☐ 1

   b. Different community
                         (Check one):
   In a large city (100,000) population or more)? .... ☐ 2
   In a suburb near a large city? .... ☐ 3
   In a middle-sized city or small town (under 100,000 population) but not in a suburb of a large city? .... ☐ 4
   Open country (but not on a farm)? ...... ☐ 5
   On a farm? .... ☐ 6

7. Which of the following types of school did you attend before you were 16 years old?

   (If you attended more than one kind, please check all that you did attend.)

   Public .... ☐ 1

   Parochial .... ☐ 2

   Other private .... ☐ 3

8. Please think about the first full-time job you had after you left school. (Do not count part-time jobs or jobs during school vacation. Do not count military service.)

   a. How old were you when you began this job? _____

   b. What kind of work were you doing?

   _____

   (For example: Elementary school teacher, paint sprayer, repaired radio sets, grocery checker, civil engineer, farmer, farm hand)

   c. What kind of business or industry was this?

   _____

   (For example: County junior high school, auto assembly plant, radio service, retail supermarket, road construction, farm)

   d. Were you—
                         (Check one)
   an employee of a PRIVATE company, business, or individual for wages, salary, or commissions? .... ☐ 1

   a GOVERNMENT employee (Federal, State, County, or local government)? .... ☐ 2

   self-employed in OWN business, professional practice, or farm? .... ☐ 3

   working WITHOUT PAY in a family business or farm? .... ☐ 4

   working FOR PAY in a family business or farm? .... ☐ 5

9. Were you living with both your parents most of the time up to age 16?
       ☐ Yes   ☐ No
    (Skip to Question 10)   *(Answer Question 9a)*

   a. If "No" above, who was the head of your family?   *(Check one)*
   Father .... ☐ 1
   Mother .... ☐ 2
   Other male .... ☐ 3
   Other female .... ☐ 4

10. Now we would like to find out what kind of work your father did when you were about 16 years old. If you were not living with your father, please answer for person checked in Question 9a.

    a. What kind of work was he doing?

    _____

    (For example: Elementary school teacher, paint sprayer, repaired radio sets, grocery checker, civil engineer, farmer, farm hand)

    b. What kind of business or industry was this?

    _____

    (For example: County junior high school, auto assembly plant, radio service, retail supermarket, road construction, farm)

    c. Was he— *(Check one)*

    an employee of a PRIVATE company, business, or individual for wages, salary, or commissions? .... ☐ 1

    a GOVERNMENT employee (Federal, State, County or local government)? ...... ☐ 2

    self-employed in his OWN business, professional practice, or farm? .... ☐ 3

    working WITHOUT PAY in his family's business or farm? .... ☐ 4

11. What is the highest grade of school your father (or person checked in Question 9a) completed? *(Check one box. If you are not sure, please make a guess)*

    Never attended school .... ☐

    Grades 1 to 12 ....
    1 2 3 4 5 6
    ☐ ☐ ☐ ☐ ☐ ☐
    7 8 9 10 11 12
    ☐ ☐ ☐ ☐ ☐ ☐

    College (Academic years) ....
    1 2 3 4 5 or more
    ☐ ☐ ☐ ☐ ☐

12. Are you now married?

    ☐ Yes— *(If "Yes," please answer Questions 13 and 14 below concerning your wife. If you are not sure of the answer, please ask her for the information.)*

    ☐ No — *(Omit the next two questions)*

13. a. How many brothers did your wife have?

    or ☐ None _____

    b. How many sisters did your wife have?

    or ☐ None _____

14. Now we would like to find out what kind of work your wife's father did when she was about 16 years old. If she was not living with her father, please check here ☐ and answer for the person who was the head of her family at that time.

    a. What kind of work was he doing?

    _____

    (For example: Elementary school teacher, paint sprayer, repaired radio sets, grocery checker, civil engineer, farmer, farm hand)

    b. What kind of business or industry was this?

    _____

    (For example: County junior high school, auto assembly plant, radio service, retail supermarket, road construction, farm)

    c. Was he— *(Check one)*

    an employee of a PRIVATE company, business, or individual for wages, salary, or commissions? .... ☐ 1

    a GOVERNMENT employee (Federal, State, County, or local government)?..... ☐ 2

    self-employed in his OWN business, professional practice, or farm? .... ☐ 3

    working WITHOUT PAY in his family's business or farm? .... ☐ 4

Please use this space to clarify any problems the questions caused.

_____

_____

_____

_____

_____

_____

APPENDIX F

Five Thousand
Random Digits

	00–04	05–09	10–14	15–19	20–24	25–29	30–34	35–39	40–44	45–49
00	54463	22662	65905	70639	79365	67382	29085	69831	47058	08186
01	15389	85205	18850	39226	42249	90669	96325	23248	60933	26927
02	85941	40756	82414	02015	13858	78030	16269	65978	01385	15345
03	61149	69440	11286	88218	58925	03638	52862	62733	33454	77455
04	05219	81619	10651	67079	92511	59888	84502	72095	83463	75577
05	41417	98326	87719	92294	46614	50948	64886	20002	97365	30976
06	28357	94070	20652	35774	16249	75019	21145	05217	47286	76305
07	17783	00015	10806	83091	94530	36466	39981	62481	49177	75779
08	40950	84820	29881	85966	62800	70326	84740	62660	77379	90279
09	82995	64157	66164	41180	10089	41757	78258	96488	88629	37231
10	96754	17676	55659	44105	47361	34833	86679	23930	53249	27083
11	34357	88040	53364	71726	45690	66334	60332	22554	90600	71113
12	06318	37403	49927	57715	50423	67372	63116	48888	21505	80182
13	62111	52820	07243	79931	89292	84767	85693	73947	22278	11551
14	47534	09243	67879	00544	23410	12740	02540	54440	32949	13491
15	98614	75993	84460	62846	59844	14922	48730	73443	48167	34770
16	24856	03648	44898	09351	98795	18644	39765	71058	90368	44104
17	96887	12479	80621	66223	86085	78285	02432	53342	42846	94771
18	90801	21472	42815	77408	37390	76766	52615	32141	30268	18106
19	55165	77312	83666	36028	28420	70219	81369	41943	47366	41067
20	75884	12952	84318	95108	72305	64620	91318	89872	45375	85436
21	16777	37116	58550	42958	21460	43910	01175	87894	81378	10620
22	46230	43877	80207	88877	89380	32992	91380	03164	98656	59337
23	42902	66892	46134	01432	94710	23474	20423	60137	60609	13119
24	81007	00333	39693	28039	10154	95425	39220	19774	31782	49037
25	68089	01122	51111	72373	06902	74373	96199	97017	41273	21546
26	20411	67081	89950	16944	93054	87687	96693	87236	77054	33848
27	58212	13160	06468	15718	82627	76999	05999	58680	96739	63700
28	70577	42866	24969	61210	76046	67699	42054	12696	93758	03283
29	94522	74358	71659	62038	79643	79169	44741	05437	39038	13163
30	42626	86819	85651	88678	17401	03252	99547	32404	17918	62880
31	16051	33763	57194	16752	54450	19031	58580	47629	54132	60631
32	08244	27647	33851	44705	94211	46716	11738	55784	95374	72655
33	59497	04392	09419	89964	51211	04894	72882	17805	21896	83864
34	97155	13428	40293	09985	58434	01412	69124	82171	59058	82859
35	98409	66162	95763	47420	20792	61527	20441	39435	11859	41567
36	45476	84882	65109	96597	25930	66790	65706	61203	53634	22557
37	89300	69700	50741	30329	11658	23166	05400	66669	48708	03887
38	50051	95137	91631	66315	91428	12275	24816	68091	71710	33258
39	31753	85178	31310	89642	98364	02306	24617	09609	83942	22716
40	79152	53829	77250	20190	56535	18760	69942	77448	33278	48805
41	44560	38750	83635	56540	64900	42912	13953	79149	18710	68618
42	68328	83378	63369	71381	39564	05615	42451	64559	97501	65747
43	46939	38689	58625	08342	30459	85863	20781	09284	26333	91777
44	83544	86141	15707	96256	23068	13782	08467	89469	93842	55349
45	91621	00881	04900	54224	46177	55309	47852	27491	89415	23166
46	91896	67426	04151	03795	59077	11848	12630	98375	52068	60112
47	55751	62515	21108	80830	02263	29303	37204	96926	30506	09808
48	85156	87689	95493	88842	00664	55017	55539	17771	69118	87530
49	07521	56898	12236	60277	39102	62315	12239	07105	11844	01117

Reproduced from Geroge W. Snedecor, *Statistical Methods*, 5th ed. (The Iowa State University Press, Ames, Iowa, 1956).

	50-54	55-59	60-64	65-69	70-74	75-79	80-84	85-89	90-94	95-99
00	59391	58030	52098	82718	87024	82848	04190	96574	90464	29065
01	99567	76364	77204	04615	27062	96621	43918	01896	83991	51141
02	10363	97518	51400	25670	98342	61891	27101	37855	06235	33316
03	86859	19558	64432	16706	99612	59798	32803	67708	15297	28612
04	11258	24591	36863	55368	31721	94335	34936	02566	80972	08188
05	95068	88628	35911	14530	33020	80428	39936	31855	34334	64865
06	54163	47237	73800	91017	36239	71824	83671	39892	60518	37092
07	16874	62677	57412	13215	31389	62233	80827	73917	82802	84420
08	92494	63157	76593	91316	03505	72389	96363	52887	01087	66091
09	15669	56689	35682	40844	53256	81872	35213	09840	34471	74441
10	99116	75486	84989	23476	52967	67104	39495	39100	17217	74073
11	15696	10703	65178	90637	63110	17622	53988	71087	84148	11670
12	97720	15369	51269	69620	03388	13699	33423	67453	43269	56720
13	11666	13841	71681	98000	35979	39749	81899	07449	47985	46967
14	71628	73130	78783	75691	41632	09847	61547	18707	85489	69944
15	40501	51089	99943	91843	41995	88931	73631	69361	05375	15417
16	22518	55576	98215	82068	10798	86211	36584	67466	69373	40054
17	75112	30485	62173	02132	14878	92879	22281	16783	86352	00077
18	80327	02671	98191	84342	90813	49268	95441	15496	20168	09271
19	60251	45548	02146	05597	48228	81366	34598	72856	66762	17002
20	57430	82270	10421	05540	43648	75888	66049	21511	47676	33444
21	73528	39559	34434	88596	54076	71693	43132	14414	79949	85193
22	25991	65959	70769	64721	86413	33475	42740	06175	82758	66248
23	78388	16638	09134	59880	63806	48472	39318	35434	24057	74739
24	12477	09965	96657	57994	59439	76330	24596	77515	09577	91871
25	83266	32883	42451	15579	38155	29793	40914	65990	16255	17777
26	76970	80876	10237	39515	79152	74798	39357	09054	73579	92359
27	37074	65198	44785	68624	98336	84481	97610	78735	46703	98265
28	83712	06514	30101	78295	54656	85417	43189	60048	72781	72606
29	20287	56862	69727	94443	64936	08366	27227	05158	50326	59566
30	74261	32592	86538	27041	65172	85532	07571	80609	39285	65340
31	64081	49863	08478	96001	18888	14810	70545	89755	59064	07210
32	05617	75818	47750	67814	29575	10526	66192	44464	27058	40467
33	26793	74951	95466	74307	13330	42664	85515	20632	05497	33625
34	65988	72850	48737	54719	52056	01596	03845	35067	03134	70322
35	27366	42271	44300	73399	21105	03280	73457	43093	05192	48657
36	56760	10909	98147	34736	33863	95256	12731	66598	50771	83665
37	72880	43338	93643	58904	59543	23943	11231	83268	65938	81581
38	77888	38100	03062	58103	47961	83841	25878	23746	55903	44115
39	28440	07819	21580	51459	47971	29882	13990	29226	23608	15873
40	63525	94441	77033	12147	51054	49955	58312	76923	96071	05813
41	47606	93410	16359	89033	89696	47231	64498	31776	05383	39902
42	52669	45030	96279	14709	52372	87832	02735	50803	72744	88208
43	16738	60159	07425	62369	07515	82721	37875	71153	21315	00132
44	59348	11695	45751	15865	74739	05572	32688	20271	65128	14551
45	12900	71775	29845	60774	94924	21810	38636	33717	67598	82521
46	75086	23537	49939	33595	13484	97588	28617	17979	70749	35234
47	99495	51434	29181	09993	38190	42553	68922	52125	91077	40197
48	26075	31671	45386	36583	93459	48599	52022	41330	60651	91321
49	13636	93596	23377	51133	95126	61496	42474	45141	46660	42338

	00–04	05–09	10–14	15–19	20–24	25–29	30–34	35–39	40–44	45–49
50	64249	63664	39652	40646	97306	31741	07294	84149	46797	82487
51	26538	44249	04050	48174	65570	44072	40192	51153	11397	58212
52	05845	00512	78630	55328	18116	69296	91705	86224	29503	57071
53	74897	68373	67359	51014	33510	83048	17056	72506	82949	54600
54	20872	54570	35017	88132	25730	22626	86723	91691	13191	77212
55	31432	96156	89177	75541	81355	24480	77243	76690	42507	84362
56	66890	61505	01240	00660	05873	13568	76082	79172	57913	93448
57	48194	57790	79970	33106	86904	48119	52503	24130	72824	21627
58	11303	87118	81471	52936	08555	28420	49416	44448	04269	27029
59	54374	57325	16947	54356	78371	10563	97191	53798	12693	27928
60	64852	34421	61046	90849	13966	39810	42699	21753	76192	10508
61	16309	20384	09491	91588	97720	89846	30376	76970	23063	35894
62	42587	37065	24526	72602	57589	98131	37292	05967	26002	51945
63	40177	98590	97161	41682	84533	67588	62036	49967	01990	72308
64	82309	76128	93965	26743	24141	04838	40254	26065	07938	76236
65	79788	68243	59732	04257	27084	14743	17520	95401	55811	76099
66	40538	79000	89559	25026	42274	23489	34502	75508	06059	86682
67	64016	73598	18609	73150	62463	33102	45205	87440	96767	67042
68	49767	12691	17903	93871	99721	79109	09425	26904	07419	76913
69	76974	55108	29795	08404	82684	00497	51126	79935	57450	55671
70	23854	08480	85983	96025	50117	64610	99425	62291	86943	21541
71	68973	70551	25098	78033	98573	79848	31778	29555	61446	23037
72	36444	93600	65350	14971	25325	00427	52073	64280	18847	24768
73	03003	87800	07391	11594	21196	00781	32550	57158	58887	73041
74	17540	26188	36647	78386	04558	61463	57842	90382	77019	24210
75	38916	55809	47982	41968	69760	79422	80154	91486	19180	15100
76	64288	19843	69122	42502	48508	28820	59933	72998	99942	10515
77	86809	51564	38040	39418	49915	19000	58050	16899	79952	57849
78	99800	99566	14742	05028	30033	94889	53381	23656	75787	59223
79	92345	31890	95712	08279	91794	94068	49337	88674	35355	12267
80	90363	65162	32245	82279	79256	80834	06088	99462	56705	06118
81	64437	32242	48431	04835	39070	59702	31508	60935	22390	52246
82	91714	53662	28373	34333	55791	74758	51144	18827	10704	76803
83	20902	17646	31391	31459	33315	03444	55743	74701	58851	27427
84	12217	86007	70371	52281	14510	76094	96579	54853	78339	20839
85	45177	02863	42307	53571	22532	74921	17735	42201	80540	54721
86	28325	90814	08804	52746	47913	54577	47525	77705	95330	21866
87	29019	28776	36116	54791	64604	08815	46049	71186	34650	14994
88	84979	81353	56219	67062	26146	82567	33122	14124	46240	92973
89	50371	26347	48513	63915	11158	25563	91915	18431	92978	11591
90	53422	06825	69711	67950	64716	18003	49581	45378	99878	61130
91	67453	35651	89316	41620	32048	70225	47597	33137	31443	51445
92	07294	85353	74819	23445	68237	07202	99515	62282	53809	26685
93	79544	00302	45338	16015	66613	88968	14595	63836	77716	79596
94	64144	85442	82060	46471	24162	39500	87351	36637	42833	71875
95	90919	11883	58318	00042	52402	28210	34075	33272	00840	73268
96	06670	57353	86275	92276	77591	46924	60839	55437	03183	13191
97	36634	93976	52062	83678	41256	60948	18685	48992	19462	96062
98	75101	72891	85745	67106	26010	62107	60885	37503	55461	71213
99	05112	71222	72654	51583	05228	62056	57390	42746	39272	96659

	50-54	55-59	60-64	65-69	70-74	75-79	80-84	85-89	90-94	95-99
50	32847	31282	03345	89593	69214	70381	78285	20054	91018	16742
51	16916	00041	30236	55023	14253	76582	12092	86533	92426	37655
52	66176	34047	21005	27137	03191	48970	64625	22394	39622	79085
53	46299	13335	12180	16861	38043	59292	62675	63631	37020	78195
54	22847	47839	45385	23289	47526	54098	45683	55849	51575	64689
55	41851	54160	92320	69936	34803	92479	33399	71160	64777	83378
56	28444	59497	91586	95917	68553	28639	96455	34174	11130	91994
57	47520	62378	98855	83174	13088	16561	68559	26679	06238	51254
58	34978	63271	13142	82681	05271	08822	06490	44984	49307	62717
59	37404	80416	69035	92980	49486	74378	75610	74976	70056	15478
60	32400	65482	52099	53676	74648	94148	65095	69597	52771	71551
61	89262	86332	51718	70663	11623	29834	79820	73002	84886	03591
62	86866	09127	98021	03871	27789	58444	44832	36505	40672	30180
63	90814	14833	08759	74645	05046	94056	99094	65091	32663	73040
64	19192	82756	20553	58446	55376	88914	75096	26119	83898	43816
65	77585	52593	56612	95766	10019	29531	73064	20953	53523	58136
66	23757	16364	05096	03192	62386	45389	85332	18877	55710	96459
67	45989	96257	23850	26216	23309	21526	07425	50254	19455	29315
68	92970	94243	07316	41467	64837	52406	25225	51553	31220	14032
69	74346	59596	40088	98176	17896	86900	20249	77753	19099	48885
70	87646	41309	27636	45153	29988	94770	07255	70908	05340	99751
71	50099	71038	45146	06146	55211	99429	43169	66259	97786	59180
72	10127	46900	64984	75348	04115	33624	68774	60013	35515	62556
73	67995	81977	18984	64091	02785	27762	42529	97144	80407	64524
74	26304	80217	84934	82657	69291	35397	98714	35104	08187	48109
75	81994	41070	56642	64091	31229	02595	13513	45148	78722	30144
76	59537	34662	79631	89403	65212	09975	06118	86197	58208	16162
77	51228	10937	62396	81460	47331	91403	95007	06047	16846	64809
78	31089	37995	29577	07828	42272	54016	21950	86192	99046	84864
79	38207	97938	93459	75174	79460	55436	57206	87644	21296	43395
80	88666	31142	09474	89712	63153	62233	42212	06140	42594	43671
81	53365	56134	67582	92557	89520	33452	05134	70628	27612	33738
82	89807	74530	38004	90102	11693	90257	05500	79920	62700	43325
83	18682	81038	85662	90915	91631	22223	91588	80774	07716	12548
84	63571	32579	63942	25371	09234	94592	98475	76884	37635	33608
85	68927	56492	67799	95398	77642	54913	91853	08424	81450	76229
86	56401	63186	39389	88798	31356	89235	97036	32341	33292	73757
87	24333	95603	02359	72942	46287	95382	08452	62862	97869	71775
88	17025	84202	95199	62272	06366	16175	97577	99304	41587	03686
89	02804	08253	52133	20224	68034	50865	57868	22343	55111	03607
90	08298	03879	20995	19850	73090	13191	18963	82244	78479	99121
91	59883	01785	82403	96062	03785	03488	12970	64896	38336	30030
92	46982	06682	62864	91837	74021	89094	39952	64158	79614	78235
93	31121	47266	07661	02051	67599	24471	69843	83696	71402	76287
94	97867	56641	63416	17577	30161	87320	37752	73276	48969	41915
95	57364	86746	08415	14621	49430	22311	15836	72492	49372	44103
96	09559	26263	69511	28064	75999	44540	13337	10918	79846	54809
97	53873	55571	00608	42661	91332	63956	74087	59008	47493	99581
98	35531	19162	86406	05299	77511	24311	57257	22826	77555	05941
99	28229	88629	25695	94932	30721	16197	78742	34974	97528	45447

APPENDIX G

Article for Review
of Reliability, Validity,
Operationalization,
and Research Design

INCREASED TENDENCY TOWARD BALANCE
DURING STRESSFUL CONFLICT[1]

Allan Mazur
Syracuse University

Empirical tests of Heider's (1958) notion of structural balance have been equivocal. Here it is hypothesized that *the tendency toward balance increases when ego becomes involved in a stressful conflict.* This would explain why many of the empirical studies of balance have not been supportive, i.e., because they were carried out in low-stress situations. The Six Day War between Israel and the Arab nations provided a unique natural experimental test which supports the hypothesis.

Heider's (1958) notion of structural balance has spawned a great deal of theoretical and empirical research which was recently reviewed and organized by Taylor (1970). Empirical tests have been equivocal, and most of the positive findings may be explained by assumptions that are simpler than balance, e.g., "friends tend to agree with each other" (Taylor, 1970; Davis, 1970; Mazur, 1971).

[1]From *Sociometry*, vol. 36, no. 2 (1973):279–283. This research was partially funded by the Memorial Foundation for Jewish Culture and the American Jewish Congress.

In attempting to apply the balance assumption to a problem of coalition formation (Mazur, 1968), it was hypothesized that *the tendency toward balance increases when ego becomes involved in a stressful conflict.* If this hypothesis is correct, it could explain why many of the empirical studies of balance have not been strongly supportive of Heider's position because they were carried out in low-stress situations.

The hypothesis is difficult to test in the laboratory because of practical and moral problems of placing subjects into a stressful conflict. This paper reports a unique natural experiment (which arose by chance) that allows a test of balance behavior in stressful conflict.

A number of Jewish academicians were interviewed in early 1967 for a study of ethnic self-concept (Mazur, 1969; forthcoming). A few months after these interviews had been completed, in June 1967, the Six Day War broke out between Israel and the Arab nations. The concern of the American Jewish community during this crisis had an unexpected intensity, and this concern extended into the academic community. Many Jewish academics participated in pro-Israel activities and showed very high emotional involvement during the period of the War. A comparison of subjects' prewar attitudes with their reactions to the War allows a test of the hypothesis that balance tendency increases under stressful conflict.

METHOD

The original sample was obtained by requesting the participation of all male Jewish faculty members in the social science departments (mainly sociology, anthropology, psychology, and political science) at Harvard, Brandeis, and Boston universities. There were seventy-five men in all. Excluding seven, who were out of the Boston area at the time of the study, 93% participated. Subjects were fairly equally distributed among the three schools.

Interviews averaged about one and one-half hours in duration and were tape recorded. Two questions are of particular concern here:

1. "How strong an interest or feeling would you say you have for Israel?" Responses were coded as *high, slight or qualified, none,* and *negative* feelings toward Israel.
2. "Roughly 15% of the Nobel Prize Laureates since 1907 have been Jewish. Also several of the major intellects of the last 100 years were Jewish. Do you feel any sort of pride in this intellectual achievement of Jews?" Responses were coded as *yes, slight or qualified,* and *no.*

In September 1967, a letter was sent to each subject asking his reactions to the War. One question is of concern here: "Some respondents have mentioned to me that they were surprised at the extent of their own emotional involvement, or lack of involvement, in the fighting. Did you experience any similar sort of 'surprise'?" No respondent indicated surprise at his *lack* of involvement. Responses were coded as *surprised* and *no indication of surprise.*

Forty-eight percent of the original interviewees responded to the letter. A second letter brought the total response rate up to 75% (47 respondents), and these are the subjects of the present analysis. Several checks indicate that the mail respondents are not a biased sample of the subjects who had been interviewed prior to the War (Mazur, 1969:192–193).

RESULTS

Table 1 shows a preliminary result based on prewar interview data. Interest in Israel is cross-tabulated against pride in Jewish intellectual achievements. I am assuming that the main diagonal cells (upper left to lower right) represent balanced states.[2] Subjects on this diagonal are consistent, i.e., they are either highly ethnocentric, slightly ethnocentric, or not ethnocentric on both attitudes; off-diagonal subjects are not balanced in this manner.

If balance tendency increased during stressful conflict, the unbalanced subjects (in the off-diagonal cells) should experience a relatively high tendency toward balance during the crisis. Thus, subjects with pride in Jewish intellect but little interest in Israel should feel an unusual increase of concern for Israel (or a drop of pride in Jewish intellect). This

Table 1

Frequency Distribution of Subjects as a Function of Pride in Jewish Intellect and Interest in Israel*

	Pride in Jewish Intellect			
Interest in Israel	Yes	Slight or Qualified	No	Total
High	9	4	0	13
Slight or qualified	16	2	6	24
None or negative**	1	2	7	10
Total	26	8	13	47

*Balanced states are the cells in the main diagonal.
**Two subjects who had only negative feelings about Israel were combined with the "Nones."

[2]Actually two separate assumptions are necessary here: (1) There is a "positive" relationship (in the balance sense) between Jewish intellectual achievement and Israel. (2) Responses to each question form comparable scales.

means, in operational terms, that the off-diagonal subjects should be most "surprised" at their emotional shift during the War.[3]

Eleven subjects (23%) reported that they were surprised at the extent of their own involvement in the fighting.[4] Table 2 shows the percentage of subjects in each cell who reported surprise. Ten of the eleven surprised subjects (91%) appear in the off-diagonal cells at the lower left.

Table 2
Percentage of Subjects Who Were Surprised at the Extent of Their Emotional Involvement in the Fighting, as a Function of Pride in Jewish Intellect and Interest in Israel*

	Pride in Jewish Intellect			
Interest in Israel	Yes	Slight or Qualified	No	Total
High	11%	0%	. . .	
	($n = 9$)	(4)	(0)	(13)
Slight or qualified	50%	0%	0%	
	(16)	(2)	(6)	(24)
None or negative	100%	50%	0%	
	(1)	(2)	(7)	(10)
Total	(26)	(8)	(13)	(47)

*Balanced states are the cells in the main diagonal.

Table 3 shows those same data in another format. Surprise at involvement is cross-tabulated against prewar state of balance. Yule's Q for

Table 3
Surprise at Involvement Versus Prewar State of Balance

Surprise at Involvement	Prewar State of Balance		Total
	Balanced	Not Balanced	
Surprised	1	10	11
Not surprised	17	19	36
	18	29	47

[3]An alternate (and more direct) test of the hypothesis could have been made if respondents had been asked their attitudes toward Israel, and Jewish intellectual achievement, during the fighting. The hypothesis predicts that these two variables would be more strongly associated during the War than in the prewar interview. Data for this direct test were not obtained however.

[4]Eighty-nine percent of the mail responses were clearly pro-Israel. The remainder indicated either mixed feelings, detachment from the crisis, or an ambiguous response. No respondent expressed a wholly anti-Israel position.

this table is –.80. This is an association of relatively high magnitude, and is in the appropriate direction.

DISCUSSION

This evidence supports the hypothesis that the tendency toward balance increases when ego becomes involved in a stressful conflict.

The absence of surprised subjects in the off-diagonal cells to the upper right has a reasonable explanation. Since these subjects already had stronger positive feelings toward Israel than toward Jewish intellectual achievement, they would be most likely to achieve balance by increasing their positive feelings toward intellectual achievement. The postwar questionnaire asked specifically about surprising feelings toward Israel and therefore would not detect sharp changes in feelings about Jewish intellect.

There are several alternatives to balance. Davis (1970) prefers a "clustering" assumption which differs from balance on the liklihood that three negative relations will occur in a triad. The data presented here do not differentiate between balance and the clustering, so one could interpret these results to say that clustering tendency increases during stressful conflict.

It is possible that some factor other than stressful conflict caused the ratings of "surprise." The War made Israel a focus of attention and perhaps this saliency, rather than stressful conflict per se, brought about an emotional shift in the previously unbalanced subjects.

REFERENCES

DAVIS, J. 1970 Clustering and hierarchy in interpersonal relations: Testing two graph theoretical models on 742 sociomatrices. *American Sociological Review* 35 (October):843–851.

HEIDER, F. 1958 *The Psychology of Interpersonal Relations.* New York: Wiley.

MAZUR, A. 1968 A nonrational approach to theories of conflict and coalitions. *Journal of Conflict Resolution* 12 (June):196–205.

1969   Resocialized Ethnicity: A Study of Jewish Social Scientists. Unpublished Ph.D. thesis, Baltimore: Johns Hopkins University.

1971   Comment on Davis's graph models. *American Sociological Review* 26 (April):308–309.

Forthcoming. Jewish social scientists: Apathy: The Six Day War. *Jewish Social Studies.*

TAYLOR, H. 1970 *Balance in Small Groups.* New York: Van Nostrand Reinhold.

Bibliography

ABELSON R. P. 1968 "Simulation of social behavior." Pp. 274–356 in G. Lindzey and E. Aronson (eds.), *Handbook of Social Psychology,* vol. II. Reading, Mass.: Addison-Wesley.

ADAMS, B. N. 1968 *Kinship in an Urban Setting.* Chicago: Markham.

ADORNO, T. W., E. FRENKEL-BRUNSWIK, D. H. LEVINSON, AND R. N. SANFORD. 1950 *The Authoritarian Personality.* New York: Harper & Row, Pub.

ALLEN, H. 1972 "Bystander intervention and helping on the subway." Pp. 22–33 in L. Bickman and T. Henachy (eds.), *Beyond the Laboratory: Field Studies in Social Psychology.* New York: McGraw-Hill.

ALLPORT, G. W. 1942 *The Use of Personal Documents in Psychological Research.* New York: Social Science Research Council.

ALLPORT, G. W., AND B. M. KRAMER. 1946 "Some roots of prejudice." *Journal of Psychology* 22:9–39.

ALSTON, J. P. AND W. A. McINTOSH 1979 "An assessment of the determinants of religious participation." *Sociological Quarterly* 20:49–62.

American Psychological Association 1977 *A Guideline for Nonsexist Language in APA Journals.* Washington, D.C.: American Psychological Association.

ANDERSON, R. B. W. 1967 "On the comparability of meaningful stimuli in cross-cultural research." *Sociometry* 30:124–136.

ANDERSON, S. B., AND S. BALL 1978 *The Profession and Practice of Program Evaluation.* San Francisco: Jossey-Bass.

ANDREWS, F. M., L. KLEM, T. N. DAVIDSON, P. M. O'MALLEY, AND W. L. RODGERS. 1974 *A Guide for Selecting Statistical Techniques for Analyzing Social Science Data.* Ann Arbor Mich.: Survey Research Center.

472

ARONSON, E., AND J. M. CARLSMITH. 1968 "Experimentation in social psychology." Pp. 1–79 in G. Lindzey and E. Aronson (eds.), *Handbook of Social Psychology*, vol. II. Reading, Mass.: Addison-Wesley.

ARONSON, E., AND J. MILLS. 1959 "The effect of severity of initiation on liking for a group." *Journal of Abnormal and Social Psychology* 59:177–181.

ASCH, S. E. 1956 "Studies of independence and conformity: A minority of one against a unanimous majority." *Psychological Monographs* 70 (no. 9).

ASTIN, A. W., AND R. F. BORUCH. 1970 "A 'Link' system for assuring confidentiality of research data in longitudinal studies." *American Educational Research Journal* 7:615–624.

AUMANN, R. J., AND M. MASCHLER. 1964 "The bargaining set for cooperative games." Pp. 443–476 in M. Dresher, L. S. Shapley, and A. W. Tucker (eds.), *Advances in Game Theory. Annals of Mathematical Study, 52*. Princeton: Princeton University Press.

BACK, K. W. 1950 "Influence through social communication." *Journal of Social Issues* 4:61–65.

BACKSTROM, C. H., AND G. D. HURSH. 1963 *Survey Research*. Chicago: Northwestern University Press.

BAILAR, B. A. 1979 "The evaluation of sample survey data." Paper read at American Association for the Advancement of Science, annual meeting, Houston, Texas.

BAILAR, J. C. 1978 *Imputation and Editing of Faulty or Missing Survey Data*. U.S. Department of Commerce, Bureau of the Census, October.

BAKER, C. M., AND M. H. FOX. 1972 *Classified Files: The Yellowing Pages*. New York: The Twentieth Century Fund.

BALES, R. F. 1950. *Interaction Process Analysis*. Cambridge, Mass.: Addison-Wesley.

———1970 *Personality and Interpersonal Behavior*. New York: Holt, Rinehart & Winston.

BALL, D. W. 1972 "The scaling of games: skill, strategy and chance." *Pacific Sociological Review* 15:277–294.

BALLWEG, J. A. 1972 "Use of semantic differential as an interview technique." Paper read at Midwestern Sociological Society, annual meeting, Kansas City, Mo.

BANAKA, W. 1971 *Training in Depth Interviewing*. New York: Harper & Row, Pub.

BANCROFT, G., AND E. H. WELCH. 1946 "Recent experience with problems of labor force measurement." *Journal of the American Statistical Association* 41:303–312.

BARKER, R. G. 1968 *Ecological Psychology*. Stanford: Stanford University Press.

BARKER, R. G., AND H. E. WRIGHT. 1955 *Midwest and Its Children*. Evanston, Ill.: Row, Peterson.

BARNES, S. D. 1972 "On the reception of scientific beliefs." Pp. 269–291 in B. Barnes (ed.), *Sociology of Science*. Baltimore: Penguin.

BARNETT, L. D. 1969 "Women's attitudes toward family life and U.S. population growth." *Pacific Sociological Review* 12:95–100.

BARTELL, G. D. 1971 *Group Sex*. New York: Peter H. Wyden.

BARTON, A. H. 1961 *Organizational Measurement and Its Bearing on the Study of College Environments*. Princeton: College Entrance Examination Board.

BARTON, A. H., AND P. F. LAZARSFELD. 1955 "Some functions of qualitative analysis in social research." *Frankfurter Beiträge zur Soziologie* 1:321–361.

BASS-HASS, R. 1968 "The lesbian dyad: basic issues and value systems." *Journal of Sex Research* 4:108–126.

BECKER, H. S. 1953 "Becoming a marihuana user." *American Journal of Sociology* 59:235–242.

———1958 "Problems of inference and proof in participant observation." *American Sociological Review* 23:652–660.

———1963 *Outsiders*. London: Free Press.

_____1964 "Problems in the publication of field studies." Pp. 267–284. in A. J. Vidich, J. Bensman, and M. R. Stein (eds.), *Reflections on Community Studies.* New York: John Wiley.

_____1967 "History, culture and subjective experience: An exploration of the social bases of drug-induced experiences." *Journal of Health and Social Behavior* 8:163–176.

_____1968 "———" Pp. 414–415 in A. J. Vidich and J. Bensman, (eds.), *Small Town in Mass Society.* Princeton: Princeton University Press.

_____1970 *Sociological Work: Methods and Substance.* Chicago: Aldine.

BECKER, H. S., B. GEER, E. C. HUGHES, AND A. L. STRAUSS. 1961 *Boys in White: Student Culture in a Medical School.* Chicago: University of Chicago Press.

BECKER, L., JR., AND C. GUSTAFSON. 1976 *Encounter with Sociology: The Term Paper.* San Francisco: Boyd and Fraser.

BEEZER, R. H. 1956 *Research on Methods of Interviewing Foreign Informants.* George Washington University, Human Technology Reports, No. 30.

Behavior Today. October 11, 1971 "Goldzieher case raises ethical storm."

_____October 7, 1974 "Nursery stereotypes."

_____October 10, 1977 "Nonverbal lie detectors."

_____December 12, 1978 "Hemispheres on the brain."

_____February 5, 1979 "Studies of oral poetry challenge: Social and political assumptions."

_____May 14, 1979 "News roundup."

BELL, D. C. 1975 "Simulation games: Three research paradigms." *Simulation and Games* 6:271–287.

BELLMAN, B. L., AND B. JULES-ROSETTE 1977 *A Paradigm for Looking.* Norwood, N.J.: Ablex.

BENNETT, J. M. 1960 "Individual perspective in field work: An experimental training course." Pp. 431–442 in R. N. Adams and J. J. Preiss (eds.), *Human Organization Research.* Homewood, Ill.: Dorsey.

BERGER, E. M. 1952 "The relation between expressed acceptance of self and expressed acceptance of others." *Journal of Abnormal and Social Psychology* 47:778–782.

BERGER, P. L. 1963 *Invitation to Sociology.* Garden City, N.Y.: Anchor.

BERKUM, M., H. M. BIALEK, R. P. KERN, AND K. YAGI. 1962 "Experimental studies of psychological stress in man." *Psychological Monographs 76,* No. 15 (Whole No. 534).

BERMAN, G., H. C. KELMAN, AND D. P. WARWICK (eds.). 1976 *The Ethics of Social Intervention.* New York: Halsted.

BERNHARDT, R. G. 1978 "Four way decision making." *Simulation and Games* 9:227–233.

BERSTEIN, I. N., AND H. E. FREEMAN. 1975 *Academic and Entrepreneurial Research: The Consequences of Diversity in Federal Evaluation Studies.* New York: Russell Sage Foundation.

BICKMAN, L., AND T. HENACHY. (eds.). 1972 *Beyond the Laboratory: Field Research in Social Psychology.* New York: McGraw-Hill.

BIELBY, W. T., R. M. HAUSER, AND D. L. FEATHERMAN. 1977 "Response errors of black and nonblack males in models of the intergenerational transmission of socioeconomic status." *American Journal of Sociology* 82:1242–1288.

BINDER, A. 1964 "Statistical Theory." Pp. 277–310 in P. R. Farnsworth, O. McNemar, and Q. McNemar (eds.). *Annual Review of Psychology*, Vol. 15.

BINDER, A., D. McCONNELL, AND N. SJOHOLM. 1957 "Verbal conditioning as a function of experimental characteristics." *Journal of Abnormal and Social Psychology* 55:309–314.

BIRDWHISTELL, R. 1970 *Kinetics and Context.* Philadelphia: University of Pennsylvania Press.

BLACK, D. 1976 *The Behavior of Law.* New York: Academic Press.

BLAKE, J. 1969 "Population policy for Americans: Is the government being misled?" *Science* 164:522–529.

BLALOCK, H. M., JR. 1961 *Causal Inference in Nonexperimental Research.* Chapel Hill: University of North Carolina Press.

———1968 "The measurement problem: A gap between the language of theory and research." Pp. 5–27 in H. M. Blalock, Jr. and A. B. Blalock (eds.), *Methodology in Social Research.* New York: McGraw-Hill.

———1969 *Theory Construction.* Englewood Cliffs, N.J.: Prentice-Hall.

BLAU, P. M. 1960 "A theory of social integration." *American Journal of Sociology* 65:545–556.

———1964 "The research process in the study of *The Dynamics of Bureaucracy.*" Pp. 18–57 in P. E. Hammond (ed.), *Sociologists at Work.* Garden City, N.Y.: Doubleday.

———1977 *Inequality and Heterogeneity: A Primitive Theory of Social Structure.* New York: Free Press.

BLAU, P. M., AND O. W. DUNCAN. 1967 *The American Occupational Structure.* New York: John Wiley.

BODE, J. G. 1972. "The silent science." *American Sociologist* 7:3–6.

BOGDAN, R., AND S. J. TAYLOR. 1975 *An Introduction to Qualitative Research Methods: A Phenomenological Approach to the Social Sciences.* New York: John Wiley-Interscience.

BOHRNSTEDT, G. W. 1970 "Reliability and validity assessment in attitude measurement." Pp. 80–99 in G. F. Summers (ed.), *Attitude Measurement.* Chicago: Rand McNally.

BORGATTA, E. F. 1961. "Toward a methodological codification: The shotgun and the salt-shaker." *Sociometry* 24:432–435.

———1962 "A systematic study of interaction process scores, peer and self-assessments, personality and other variables." *Genetic Psychology Monographs* 65:269–290.

BORGATTA, E. F., AND G. W. BOHRNSTEDT (eds.). 1970 *Sociological Methodology 1970.* San Francisco: Jossey-Bass.

BORGATTA, E. F., AND B. CROWTHER. 1965 *A Workbook for the Study of Social Interaction Process.* Chicago: Rand McNally.

BORGATTA, E. F., AND R. R. EVANS. 1969 *Smoking, Health and Behavior.* Chicago: Aldine.

BORING, E. G. 1953 "The role of theory in experimental psychology." *American Journal of Psychology* 66:169–184.

BORUCH, R. F., A. J. McSWEENY, AND E. J. SODERSTROM. 1978 "Randomized field experiments for program planning, development, and evaluation: An illustrative bibliography." *Evaluation Quarterly* 2:655–695.

BOTT, H. M. 1934 "Method in social studies of young children." Toronto University Studies in Child Development Series, No. 1. Toronto: University of Toronto Press.

BRADBURN, N. M. 1969 *The Structure of Psychological Well-Being.* Chicago: Aldine.

BRADBURN, N. M., S. SUDMAN, AND Associates. 1979 *Improving Interview Method and Questionnaire Design.* San Francisco: Jossey-Bass.

BRAZELTON, T. V., B. KOSLOWSKI, AND M. MAIN. 1974 "The origins of reciprocity: The early mother-infant interaction." Pp. 49–76 in M. Lewis and L. A. Rosenblum (eds.), *The Effect of the Infant on Its Caregiver.* New York: John Wiley.

BRISLIN, R. W., W. J. LONNER, AND R. M. THORNDIKE. 1973 *Cross-Cultural Research Methods.* New York: John Wiley.

BROOKOVER, L., AND K. W. BACK. 1966 "Time sampling as a field technique." *Human Organization* 25:64–70.

BROOKS, M. P. 1965 "The community action program as a setting for applied research." *Journal of Social Issues* 21:29–40.

BROOM, L., AND F. L. JONES. 1969 "Career mobility in three societies: Australia, Italy and the United States." *American Sociological Review* 34:650–658.

BROWN, J. S., AND B. G. GILMARTIN. 1969 "Sociology today: Lacunae, emphasis and surfeits." *American Sociologist* 4:283–291.

BRYAN, J. H., AND M. A. TEST. 1972 "Models and helping: Naturalistic studies in aiding behavior." *Archives of Genetic Psychiatry* 9:280–294.

BURSTEIN, P., AND W. FREUDENBURG. 1978 "Changing public policy: The impact of public opinion, anti-war demonstrations, and war costs on senate voting on Vietnam war motions." *American Journal of Sociology* 84:99–122.

BYRNE, D. 1964 "Assessing personality variables and their alteration." Pp. 38–68 in P. Worchel and D. Byrne (eds.), *Personality Change*. New York: John Wiley.

CAIRNS, J. 1975 "The cancer problem." *Scientific American* (November):64–79.

CAMPBELL, A., P. E. CONVERSE, W. E. MILLER, AND D. E. STOKES. 1960 *The American Voter*. New York: John Wiley.

CAMPBELL, D. T. 1957 "Factors relevant to the validity of experiments in social settings." *Psychological Bulletin* 54:297–312.

———1958a "Common fate, similarity and other indices of the status of aggregates of persons as social entities." *Behavioral Science* 3:14–25.

———1958b "Systematic error on the part of human links in communication system." *Information and Control* 1:334–369.

———1961 "The mutual methodological relevance of anthropology and psychology." Pp. 333–352 in F. L. K. Hsu (ed.), *Psychological Anthropology*. Homewood, Ill.: Dorsey.

———1963 "Social attitudes and other acquired behavioral dispositions." Pp. 84–176 in S. Koch (ed.), *Psychology: A Study of a Science*. New York: McGraw-Hill.

———1968 "Likert versus bipolar formats: A comparison of strengths and weaknesses." Unpublished paper, Northwestern University.

———1969a "Reforms as experiments." *American Psychologist* 24:409–429.

———1969b "Ethnocentrism and the fish-scale model of omniscience." Pp. 328–348 in M. Sherif and C. W. Sherif (eds.), *Interdisciplinary Relationships in the Social Sciences*. Chicago: Aldine.

———1972 "Methods for the experimenting society." *American Psychologist*. 27:810–818.

CAMPBELL, D. T., R. F. BORUCH, R. D. SCHWARTZ, AND J. STEINBERG. 1977 "Confidentiality —preserving modes of access to files and to interfile exchange for useful statistical analysis." *Evaluation Quarterly* 1:269–300.

CAMPBELL, D. T., AND K. N. CLAYTON. 1961 "Avoiding regression effects in panel studies of communication impact." *Studies in Public Communication* 3:99–118.

CAMPBELL, D. T., AND D. W. FISKE. 1959 "Convergent and discriminant validation by the multitrait-multimethod matrix." *Psychological Bulletin* 56:81–105.

CAMPBELL, D. T., W. KRUSKAL, AND W. WALLACE. 1966 "Seating aggregation as an index of attitude." *Sociometry* 29:1–15.

CAMPBELL, D. T., AND H. L. ROSS. 1968 "The Connecticut crackdown on speeding: Time series data in quasi-experimental analysis." *Law and Society Review* 3:33–53.

CAMPBELL, D. T., AND J. C. STANLEY. 1963. *Experimental and Quasi-Experimental Designs for Research*. Chicago: Rand McNally.

CANNELL, C. F. 1977 *Experiments in Interviewing Techniques*. Washington, D.C.: National Center for Health Service Research.

CANNELL, C. F., AND R. L. KAHN. 1968 "Interviewing." Pp. 526–595 in G. Lindzey and E. Aronson (eds.), *Handbook of Social Psychology*, vol. II. Reading, Mass.: Addison-Wesley.

CAPLOW, T. 1968 *Two Against One: Coalitions in Triads*. Englewood Cliffs, N.J.: Prentice-Hall.

CAPLOW, T., AND R. J. MCGEE. 1958. *The Academic Marketplace*. New York: Basic Books.

CARNEY, T. F. 1972. *Content Analysis.* Winnipeg: University of Manitoba.

CARO, F. G. 1972 "Evaluation research: an overview." Pp. 1–36 in F. G. Caro (ed.), *Readings in Evaluation Research.* New York: Russell Sage Foundation.

CASSOTTA, L., J. JAFFE, S. FELDSTEIN, AND R. MOSES. 1964 *Operating Manual: Automatic Vocal Transaction Analyzer.* New York: William Alanson White Institute, Research Bulletin No. 1.

CASTANEDA, C. 1971 *Separate Reality.* New York: Simon and Schuster.

———1973 *The Teachings of Don Juan: A Yaqui Way of Knowledge.* New York: Simon and Schuster

———1974a *Journey to Ixtlan.* New York: Simon and Schuster.

———1974b *Tales of Power.* New York: Simon and Schuster.

———1978 *The Second Ring of Power.* New York: Simon and Schuster.

CHAFETZ, J. S. 1978 *A Primer on the Construction and Testing of Theories in Sociology.* Itasca, Ill.: Peacock.

CHAPPLE, E. D. 1949 "The interaction chronograph: Its evaluation and present application." *Personnel* 25:295–307.

CHERLIN, A. 1978 "Remarriage as an incomplete institution." *American Journal of Sociology* 84:634–650.

CHERRY, C. 1978 *On Human Communication: A Review, A Survey and A Criticism.* Cambridge, Mass.: MIT Press.

CHIROT, D. 1977 *Social Change in the Twentieth Century.* Chicago: Harcourt Brace Jovanovich.

CHRISTENSEN, H. T. 1960 "Cultural relativism and premarital sex norms." *American Sociological Review* 25:31–39.

CHRISTIE, R., AND F. L. GEIS. (eds.) 1970 *Studies in Machiavellianism.* New York: Academic Press.

CHUN, K., J. T. BARNOWE, K. WYKOWSKI, S. COBB, AND J. R. FRENCH. 1972 "Selection of psychological measures: Quality or convenience?" *American Psychological Association Proceedings,* 1972 (vol. 1): 15–16.

CICOUREL, A. 1964 *Method and Measurement in Sociology.* New York: Free Press.

CLARK, B. R., AND M. A. TROW. 1960 "Determinants of college student culture." Unpublished manuscript, Center for the Study of Higher Education, University of California, Berkeley.

CLARK, T. N., W. KORNBLUM, H. BLOOM, AND S. TOBIAS. 1968 "Discipline, method, community structure, and decision-making: The role and limitations of the sociology of knowledge." *American Sociologist* 3:214–217.

CLYNES, M. 1973 "Sentics: Biocybernetics of emotion communication." *Annals of the New York Academy of Science* 220:Article 3.

COHEN, J. 1970 *Statistical Power Analysis for the Behavioral Sciences.* New York: Academic Press.

COLE, S. 1972 *The Sociological Method.* Chicago: Rand McNally.

———1979 "Age and scientific performance." *American Journal of Sociology* 84:958–977.

COLEMAN, J. S. 1959 "Relational analysis: The study of social organizations with survey methods." *Human Organization* 17:28–36.

———1964a *Introduction to Mathematical Sociology.* London: Free Press.

———1964b "Mathematical models and computer simulation." Pp. 1027–1062 in R. E. L. Faris (ed.), *Handbook of Modern Sociology.* Chicago: Rand McNally.

———1966 "In defense of games." *American Behavioral Scientist* 10:3–4.

———1972 *Policy Research in Social Science.* Morristown, N.J.: General Learning Press.

COLEMAN, J. S., E. KATZ, AND H. MENZEL. 1957 "The diffusion of an innovation among physicians." *Sociometry* 20:253–270.

COLLIER, R. M. 1944 "The effect of propaganda upon attitude following a critical examination of the propaganda itself." *Journal of Social Psychology* 20:3–17.

CONNOR, R. F. 1977 "Selecting a control group: An analysis of the randomization process in twelve social reform programs." *Evaluation Quarterly* 1:195–244.

CONRAD, B. 1958 *The Death of Manolete.* Cambridge: Houghton-Mifflin.

COOK, S. W., AND C. SELLTIZ. 1964 "A multiple-indicator approach to attitude measurement." *Psychological Bulletin* 62:36–55.

COOK, T. D., AND D. T. Campbell. 1979 *Quasi-Experimentation: Design and Analysis Issues for Field Settings.* Chicago: Rand McNally.

COOLEY, W. W., AND P. R. LOHNES. 1971 *Multivariate Data Analysis.* New York: John Wiley.

COOMBS, C. 1953 "Theory and methods of social measurement." Pp. 471–535 in L. Festinger and D. Katz (eds.), *Research Methods in the Behavioral Sciences.* New York: Dryden. Dryden.

COOPERSMITH, S. 1967 *The Antecedents of Self-Esteem.* San Francisco: W. H. Freeman & Company Publishers.

COSPER, R. 1972 "Interviewer effect in a survey of drinking practices." *Sociological Quarterly* 13:228–236.

COUCH, A., AND K. KENISTON. 1960 "Yeasayers and naysayers: Agreeing response set as a personality variable." *Journal of Abnormal and Social Psychology* 60:151–174.

CRANE, D. M. 1972. *Invisible Colleges: Diffusion of Knowledge in Scientific Communities.* Chicago: University of Chicago Press.

CRONBACH, L. J. 1951 "Coefficient alpha and the internal structure of tests." *Psychometrika* 16:197–334.

CUBER, J. F., AND P. HAROFF. 1968 *Sex and the Significant Americans.* Baltimore: Penguin.

CYTRYNBAUM, S., Y. GINATH, J. BIRDWELL, AND L. BRANDT. 1979 "Goal attainment scaling: A critical review." *Evaluation Quarterly* 3:5–40.

DALE, E., AND J. S. CHALL. 1948 "A formula for predicting readability." *Educational Research Bulletin* (Ohio State University) 27:11–54.

DALTON, M. 1964 "Preconceptions and methods in *men who manage.*" Pp. 58–110 in P. E. Hammond (ed.), *Sociologists at Work.* Garden City, N.Y.: Doubleday.

DARLEY, J. M., AND C. D. BATSON. 1973 "From Jerusalem to Jericho: A study of situational and dispositional variables in helping behavior." *Journal of Personality and Social Psychology* 27:100–108.

DAVIS, J. A. 1964 "Great books and small groups: An informal history of a national survey." Pp. 244–269 in P. E. Hammond (ed.), *Sociologists at Work.* Garden City, N.Y.: Doubleday.
_____1970 *Elementary Survey Analysis.* Englewood Cliffs, N.J.: Prentice-Hall.

DAVIS, K. 1978 "Methods for studying informal communication." *Journal of Communications* 90:112–116.

DAVIS, K., AND J. BLAKE. 1956 "Social structure and fertility: An analytic framework." *Economic Development and Cultural Change* 5:211–235.

DAVIS, M. D. 1970 *Game Theory: A Nontechnical Introduction.* New York: Basic Books.

DEAN, J. P., R. L. EICHHORN, AND L. P. DEAN. 1967 "Observations and interviewing." Pp. 274–304 in J. P. Doby (ed.), *An Introduction to Social Research* (2nd ed.). New York: Appleton-Century-Crofts.

DENZIN, N. K. 1970 *The Research Act.* Chicago: Aldine.

DIENER, E., AND R. CRANDALL. 1978 *Ethics in Social and Behavioral Research.* Chicago: University of Chicago Press.

DIESING, P. 1971 *Patterns of Discovery in the Social Sciences.* Chicago: Aldine.

DILLMAN, D. 1978 *Mail and Telephone Surveys.* New York: John Wiley.

DODGE, D. 1971 "A computer model for prediction of voting in the United Nations." *Simulation and Games.* 2:455–471.

DORFMAN, D. D. 1974 "The Cyril Burt question: New findings." *Science* 201:1177–1186.

DOUGLAS, J. D. 1967 *The Social Meanings of Suicide.* Princeton, N.J.: Princeton University Press.

DOWNS, A. 1965. "Some thoughts on giving people economic advice." *American Behavioral Scientist* 9:30–32.

DRABEK, T., AND J. HASS. 1965 "Realism in laboratory simulation: Myth or method?" Paper presented at the American Sociological Association, annual meeting, Chicago.

DREHER, M., L. S. SHAPELY, AND A. W. TUCKER (eds.). 1964 *Advances in Game Theory.* Pp. 343–376 in Annals of Mathematical Study, 52. Princeton: Princeton University Press.

DUKE, R. D. 1974 "Toward a general theory of gaming." *Simulation and Games* 5:131–146.

DUNCAN, O. D. 1964 "Social organization and the ecosystem." Pp. 37–82 in R. E. Faris (ed.), *Handbook of Modern Sociology.* Chicago: Rand McNally.

———1972 "Changing times." Reported in *Behavior Today,* vol. 3, no. 32 (August 7): 2.

———1975 *Introduction to Structural Equation Models.* New York: Academic Press.

———1979 "How destination depends on origin in the occupational mobility table." *American Journal of Sociology* 84:793–803.

DUNCAN, O. D., AND B. DUNCAN. 1955 "A methodological analysis of segregation indexes." *American Sociological Review* 20:210–217.

DUNNETTE, M. D. 1958 "Leadership: Many stones and one monument." *Contemporary Psychology* 3:362–363

DURKHEIM, E. 1951 *Suicide.* J. A. Spaulding and G. Simpson (trans.). New York: Free Press.

DUTTON, J. M., AND W. H. STARBUCK (eds.). 1971 *Computer Simulation of Human Behavior.* New York: John Wiley.

EDWARDS, A. L. 1957 *Techniques of Attitude Scale Construction.* New York: Appleton-Century-Crofts.

EKMAN, P. 1965 "Communication through nonverbal behavior: A source of information about an interpersonal relationship." Pp. 390–442 in S. S. Tomkins and C. E. Izard (eds.), *Affect, Cognition and Personality.* New York: Springer-Verlag.

EKMAN, P., AND W. V. FRIESEN. 1965 "System for the classification and analysis of non-verbal behavior." Unpublished manuscript, Langley Porter Institute.

EL-HAKIM, S. AND J. MARKOFF. 1974 "Solid waste accumulation in residential neighborhoods as a socio-political process." Pp. 212–231 in J. Aschenbrener and L. Collins (eds.), *The Process of Urbanism.* The Hague: Mouton.

EMERSON, R. M. 1966 "A case study in communicative feedback and sustained group goal-striving." *Sociometry* 29:213–227.

ERICKSON, K. T. 1967 "A comment on disguised observation in sociology." *Social Problems* 14:366–73.

ERICKSON, W. L. 1971 "An urban commune as a quasi-kindred." Unpublished Ph.D. dissertation, University of Illinois-Chicago Circle.

———1972a "Quasi-kindreds: A key structure in the transformation of kinship functions?" Paper read at American Sociological Association, annual meeting, New Orleans.

———1972b "Social psychological factors in vasectomy decisions." Unpublished manuscript, University of Missouri.

———1973 "Some observations on self-observation in observational research." University of Missouri, Social Observation Center, Research Report No. 1.

EXLINE, R. V. 1963 "Explorations in the process of person perception: Visual interaction in relation to competition, sex, and need for affiliation." *Journal of Personality* 31: 1–20.

FARBER, B. 1968 *Comparative Kinship Systems.* New York: John Wiley.

FEIRING, C., AND J. H. KORN. 1970 "A base for predicting success." *Science* 170:491–492.

FELDMAN, A., AND C. HURN. 1966 "The experience of modernization." *Sociometry* 29:378–395.

FIENBERG, S. E. 1977 *The Analysis of Cross-Classified Categorical Data.* Cambridge, Mass: The MIT Press.

FIREBAUGH, G. 1978. "A rule for inferring individual-level relationships from aggregate data." *American Sociological Review* 43:557–572.

FISHER, R. A. 1935 *The Design of Experiments.* London: Oliver and Boyd.

FLANDERS, N. A. 1960. "Teacher influence, pupil attitudes and achievement." Minneapolis: University of Minnesota Press (mimeo).

FLESCH, R. 1954. *How to Make Sense.* New York: Harper & Row, Pub.

FORRESTER, J. W. 1971 "Counter-intuitive behavior of social systems." *Technology Review* 73:52–68.

FOX, R. C. 1964 "An American sociologist in the land of Belgium medical research." Pp. 399–452 in P. E. Hammond (ed.), *Sociologists at Work.* Garden City, N.Y.: Doubleday.

FRIEDMAN, N. 1967 *The Social Nature of Psychological Research.* New York: Basic Books.

FRIEDRICHS, R. W. 1970 *A Sociology of Sociology.* New York: Free Press.

FRISBIE, P. 1975 "Measuring the degree of bureaucratization at the societal level." *Social Forces* 53:563–572.

FRYER, M. J. 1978 *An Introduction to Linear Programming and Matrix Game Theory.* New York: Halsted.

GAGE, N. L., AND B. SHIMBERG. 1949 "Measuring senatorial 'progressivism.' " *Journal of Abnormal and Social Psychology* 44:112–117.

GALENTER, E. (ed.). 1957 *Automatic Teaching: The State of the Art.* New York: John Wiley.

GALLE, O. M., W. R. GOVE, AND J. M. MCPHERSON. 1972 "Population density and pathology: What are the relations for man?" *Science* 176:23–30.

GALLIHER, J. F. 1973 "The protection of human subjects: A reexamination of the professional code of ethics." *American Sociologist* 8:93–100.

GALLUP, G. 1947 "The quintamensional plan of question design." *Public Opinion Quarterly* 11:385–393.

GALTON, F. 1885 "Regression towards mediocrity in hereditary stature." *Journal of the Anthropological Institute* 15:246–263.

GALTUNG, J. 1967 *Theory and Methods of Social Research.* New York: Columbia University Press.

GAMSON, W. A. 1978 *SIMSOC: A Participant's Manual and Related Readings,* 2nd ed. New York: Free Press.

GEARING, F., AND W. HUGHES. 1975 *On Observing Well: Self-Instruction in Ethnographic Observation for Teachers, Principals, and Supervisors.* Buffalo, N.Y.: Center for Studies of Cultural Transmission.

GEHLKE, C., AND R. BIEHEL. 1934 "Certain effects of grouping upon the size of the correlation coefficient in census tract material." *Journal of the American Statistical Association Supplement* 29:159–170.

GELLERT, E. 1955 "Systematic observation: A method in child study." *Harvard Educational Review* 25:179–195.

GERBNER, G., L. GROSS, M. JACKSON-BEECK, S. JEFFRIES-FOX, AND N. SIGNORIELLI. 1978 "Cultural indicators: Violence profile no. 9." *Journal of Communication* 28, no. 3:176–207.

GHISELLI, E. E. 1939 "All or none versus graded response questionnaires." *Journal of Applied Psychology* 23:405–413.

GLASER, D. 1973 *Routinizing Evaluations: Getting Feedback on Effectiveness of Crime and Delinquency Programs.* Washington, D.C.: U.S. Government Printing Office.

GLAZER, B. G. 1965 "The constant comparative method of qualitative analysis." *Social Problems* 12:436–445.

GLAZER, B. G., AND A. L. STRAUSS. 1967 *The Discovery of Grounded Theory.* Chicago: Aldine.

GLENN, N. D. 1971. "American sociologists' evaluations of sixty-three journals." *American Sociologist* 6:298–303.

GLENN, N. D., AND E. GOTARD. 1977. "The religion of blacks in the United States: Some recent trends and current characteristics." *American Journal of Sociology* 83:443–452.

GOFFMAN, E. 1961 *Encounters.* Indianapolis: Bobbs-Merrill.
_____1967 *Interaction Ritual.* New York: Doubleday.
_____1971 *Relations in Public.* New York: Basic Books.
_____1976 "Gender advertisements." *Studies in the Anthropology of Visual Communication* 3:55–154.

GOLD, R. L. 1958 "Roles in sociological field observations." *Social Forces* 36:217–223.

GOODE, W. J., AND P. K. HATT. 1962 *Methods in Social Research.* New York: McGraw-Hill.

GOODMAN, L. A. 1978 *Analyzing Qualitative/Categorical Data: Log-Linear Models and Latent Structure Analysis.* Cambridge, Mass.: Abt Books.
_____1979 "Multiplicative models for the analysis of occupational mobility tables and other kinds of cross-classification tables." *American Journal of Sociology* 84:804–821.

GORDEN, R. L. 1954 "An Interaction Analysis of the Depth Interview." Doctoral dissertation, University of Chicago.

GOTTSCHALK, L., C. KLUCKHOHM, AND R. ANGELL, 1945 *The Use of Personal Documents in History, Anthropology and Sociology.* New York: Social Science Research Council.

GOVE, W. R., M. HUGHES, AND O. GALLE. 1979 "Possible causes of the apparent sex differences in physical health: An empirical investigation." *American Sociological Review* 44:126–146.

GRANBERG, D., J. S. STEVENS, AND S. KATZ, 1975 "Effects of communication on cooperation in expanded prisoner's dilemma and chicken games." *Simulation and Games* 6:166–187.

GRAY, D. 1968 "Ode to behavioral science." *Sociological Quarterly* 9:176.

GREEN, L. W. 1969 "East Pakistan: Knowledge and the use of contraceptives." *Studies in Family Planning* 39:9–14.

GREENBERG, B. G. 1972 "Evaluation of social programs." Pp. 155–174 in F. G. Caro (ed.), *Readings in Evaluation Research.* New York: Russell Sage Foundation.

GREENBLAT, C. S., AND R. D. DUKE. 1975 *Gaming-Simulation: Rationale, Design, and Applications.* New York: John Wiley.

GREY, C. M., C. J. CONOVER, AND T. M. HENNESSEY. 1978 "Cost effectiveness of residential community corrections: An analytical prototype." *Evaluation Quarterly* 2:375–400.

GUEST, L. L. 1947 "A study of interviewer competence." *International Journal of Opinion and Attitude Research* 1:17–30.

GUETZKOW, H., C. F. ALGER, R. A. BRADY, R. C. NOEL, AND K. C. SNYDER. 1963 *Simulation in International Relations.* Englewood Cliffs, N.J.: Prentice-Hall.

GUTTENTAG, M., AND E. STRUENING. (eds.). 1975 *Handbook of Evaluation Research,* vols. I and II. Beverly Hills: Sage Publications, Inc.

HABENSTEIN, R. W. (ed.) 1970 *Pathways to Data; Field Methods for Studying Ongoing Social Organizations.* Chicago: Aldine.

HAGE, G. 1972 *Techniques and Problems of Theory Construction in Sociology.* New York: John Wiley.

HALIKAS, J. A., D. W. GOODWIN, AND S. B. GUZE. 1971 "Patterns of marihuana use: A survey of one hundred regular users." *Comprehensive Psychiatry* 13:161–163.

HALL, E. T. 1959 *The Silent Language.* Garden City, N.Y.: Doubleday.
_____1963 "A system for the notation of proxemic behavior." *American Anthropologist* 65:1003–1026.
_____1966 *The Hidden Dimension.* Garden City, N.Y.: Doubleday.
_____1976 *Beyond Culture.* Garden City, N.Y.: Anchor/Doubleday.

HAMBLIN, R., D. BUCKHOLDT, D. FERRITOR, M. KOZLOFF, AND L. BLACKWELL. 1971 *The Humanization Process: A Social Behaviorist Analysis of Children's Problems.* New York: John Wiley.

HAMBURGER, H. 1979 *Games as Models of Social Phenomena.* San Francisco: W. H. Freeman & Company Publishers

HARDYCK, C., AND L. F. PETRINOVICH. 1977 "Lefthandedness." *Psychological Bulletin* 84:385–404.

HARGREAVES, W. A., AND J. A. STARKWEATHER. 1963 "Recognition of speaker identity." *Language and Speech* 6:63–67.

HARPER, R. G., A. N. WIENS, AND J. D. MATARAZZO. 1978 *Nonverbal Communication: The State of the Art.* New York: John Wiley.

HARRIS, B. 1968 "Quantitative models of urban development: Their role in metropolitan policy-making." Pp. 363–412 in H. S. Perloff and L. Wingo, Jr. (eds.), *Issues in Urban Economics.* Baltimore: Johns Hopkins Press.

HARRISON, A. A., M. HWALEK, D. F. RANEY, AND J. G. FRITZ. 1978 "Cues to deception in an interview situation." *Social psychology* 41:156–161.

HAWKINS, D. F. 1977 *Nonresponse in Detroit Area Study Surveys: A Ten-Year Analysis.* Chapel Hill, N.C.: Institute for Research in Social Science, Working Paper Number 8.

HAYNER, N. S. 1964 "Hotel life: proximity and social distance." Pp. 314–324 in E. S. Burgess and D. J. Bogue (eds.), *Contributions to Urban Sociology.* Chicago: University of Chicago Press.

HEINEMANN, C. E. 1953 "A forced-choice form of the Taylor anxiety scale." *Journal of Consulting Psychology* 17:447–454.

HEISE, D. R. 1969 "Problems in path analysis and causal inference." Pp. 38–73 in B. F. Borgatta (ed.), *Sociological Methodology, 1969.* San Francisco: Jossey-Bass.
_____1970 "The semantic differential and attitude research." Pp. 235–253 in G. F. Summers (ed.), *Attitude Measurement.* Chicago: Rand McNally.

HESHKA, S., AND Y. NELSON. 1972 "Interpersonal speaking distance as a function of age, sex, and relationship." *Sociometry* 35:491–498.

HEYNS, R. W., AND A. F. ZANDER. 1953 "Observation of group behavior." Pp. 381–417 in L. Festinger and D. Katz (eds.), *Research Methods in the Behavioral Sciences.* New York: Dryden.

HINDELANG, M. J. 1978 "Race and involvement in common law personal crimes." *American Sociological Review* 43:93–109.

HILDUM, D., AND R. W. BROWN. 1956 "Verbal reinforcement and interviewer bias." *Journal of Abnormal and Social Psychology* 53:108–111.

HOLMES, T. H., AND R. H. RAHE. 1967 "The social readjustment rating scale." *Journal of Psychosomatic Research* 11:213–218.

HOLSTI, O. E. 1969 *Content Analysis for the Social Sciences and Humanities.* Reading, Mass.: Addison-Wesley.

HOMANS, G. C. 1950 *The Human Group.* New York: Harcourt Brace Jovanovich, Inc.

———1961 *Social Behavior: Its Elementary Forms.* New York: Harcourt Brace Jovanovich, Inc.

HONG, L. K. 1978 "Risky shift and cautious shift: Some direct evidence on the culture-value theory." *Social Psychology* 41:342–345.

HOPKINS, T. K. 1964 *The Exercise of Influence in Small Groups.* Totowa, N.J.: Bedminster Press.

HOROWITZ, I. L. 1965 "The life and death of Project Camelot." *Transaction* 3:44–48.

———1972 "On entering the tenth year of transaction: The relationship of social science and critical journalism." *Transaction* 10:49–79.

HOVDE, H. T. 1936 "Recent trends in the development of market research." *American Marketing Journal* 3:3

HOVLAND, C. I. 1959 "Reconciling conflicting results derived from experimental and survey studies of attitude change." *American Psychologist* 14:8–17.

HUMPHERYS, L. 1970 *Tearoom Trade: Impersonal Sex in Public Places.* Chicago: Aldine.

HYMAN, H. H. 1955 *Survey Design and Analysis.* New York: Free Press.

INBAR, M., AND C. S. STOLL (eds.). 1972 *Simulation and Gaming in Social Science.* New York: Free Press.

INGELFINGER, F. J. 1975 "Ethics and high bloodpressure." *New England Journal of Medicine* 292:43–44.

INKELES, A., AND D. H. SMITH. 1974 *Becoming Modern: Individual Change in Six Developing Countries.* Cambridge, Mass.: Harvard.

Institute for Survey Research. 1975 "Americans enjoy participating in surveys, ISR study shows." *ISR Newsletter* 3:7.

———1976 "SRC researchers compare effectiveness of personal vs. telephone interviews" *ISR Newsletter* (Fall) 4:2.

———1977 "Refined survey techniques greatly improve quality of data; require increased effort for researchers." *ISR Newsletter* (Summer) 5:4–5.

ISEN, A. M., AND S. SIMMONDS. 1978 "The effect of feeling good on a helping task that is incompatible with good mood." *Social Psychology* 41:346–349.

JACOBS, J. 1967 "A phenomenological study of suicide notes." *Social Problems* 15:60–72.

JACOBS, S., AND S. CYTRYNBAUM. 1977 "The goal attainment scale: A test of its use on an in-patient crisis intervention unit." *Goal Attainment Review* 3:77–98.

JAMES, J. 1951 "A Preliminary study in the size determinant in small group interaction." *American Sociological Review* 16:474–477.

———1953 "The distribution of free-forming small group size." *American Sociological Review* 18:569–570.

JANES, R. W. 1961. "A note on phases of the community role of the participant observer." *American Sociological Review* 26:446–450.

JANOWITZ, M. 1956 "Some consequences of social mobility in the United States." *Transactions of the Third World Congress of Sociology* 3:191–201.

———1958 "Inferences about propaganda impact from textual and documentary analysis." Pp. 732–735 in W. E. Daugherty and M. Janowitz (eds.), *A Psychological Warfare Casebook.* Baltimore: John Hopkins Press.

JASSO, G. 1978 "On the justice of earnings: A new specification of the justice evaluation function." *American Journal of Sociology* 83:1398–1419.

JENNINGS, C. 1978 "Have the Samaritans lowered the suicide rate? A controlled study." *Psychological Medicine* 8:413–422.

JESSEN, R. J. 1978 *Statistical Survey Techniques*. New York: John Wiley.

JONES, N. B. (ed.). 1972 *Ethological Studies of Child Behavior*. New York: Cambridge University Press.

KAHN, R. L., AND C. F. CANNELL. 1957 *The Dynamics of Interviewing*. New York: John Wiley.

KAHN, R. L., AND F. MANN. 1952 "Developing research partnerships." *Journal of Social Issues* 8:4–10.

KAMIN, L. 1976 *The Science and Politics of IQ*. Potomac, Md.: Eribaum.

KANTER, R. M. 1977 *Men and Women of the Corporation*. New York: Basic Books

KASS, R. 1977 "Recent changes in male income." *Sociological Quarterly* 18:367–377.

KELMAN, H. C. 1967 "Human use of human subjects: The problem of deception in social psychological experiments." *Psychological Bulletin* 67:1–11.

KEMENY. J., J. SNELL, AND G. THOMPSON. 1966 *Introduction to Finite Mathematics* (2nd ed.). Englewood Cliffs, N.J.: Prentice-Hall.

KENDALL, P. 1963 "The learning environments of hospitals." Pp. 110–131 in E. Friedson (ed.), *The Hospital in Modern Society*. New York: Free Press.
_____1972 "The nature and determinants of turnover." Pp. 342–349 in P. Lazarsfeld, A. Pasanella, and M. Rosenberg (eds.), *Continuities in the Language of Social Research*. New York: Free Press

KERBO, H. R., AND L. R. D. FAVE. 1979 "The empirical side of the power elite debate: An assessment and critique of recent research." *Sociological Quarterly* 20:5–22.

KEY, W. M. 1974 *Subliminal Seduction*. New York: Signet.
_____1976 *Media Sexploitation*. Englewood Cliffs, N.J.: Prentice-Hall.

KIDDER, L. H., AND D. T. CAMPBELL. 1970 "The indirect testing of social attitudes." Pp. 333–385 in G. F. Summers (ed.), *Attitude Measurement*. Chicago: Rand McRally.

KIM, J., AND J. CURRY. 1977 "The treatment of missing data in multivariate analysis." *Sociological Methods and Research* 6:215–240.

KINSEY, A. C., W. B. POMEROY, AND C. E. MARTIN. 1948 *Sexual Behavior in the Human Male*. Philadelphia: Saunders.

KIRK, J., AND J. S. COLEMAN. 1963 *The Use of Computers in the Study of Social Structure: Interaction in a 3-person Group*. Baltimore: Johns Hopkins University (mimeo.).

KISH, L. 1965 *Survey Sampling*. New York: John Wiley.

KLAUSNER, S. Z. (ed.). 1968 *Why Man Takes Chances: Studies in Stress-Seeking*. New York: Doubleday.

KNOX, J. B. 1961 "Absenteeism and turnover in an Argentine factory." *American Sociological Review* 26:424–428.

KOESTLER, A. 1971 *The Case of the Midwife Toad*. New York: Random House.

KOHLBERG, L. 1969 "Stage and sequence: The cognitive-developmental approach to socialization." Pp. 347–480 in D. A. Goslin (ed.), *Handbook of Socialization Theory and Research*. Chicago: Rand McNally.

KOHN, M. L., AND C. SCHOOLER. 1978 "The reciprocal effects of the substantive complexity of work and intellectual flexibility: A longitudinal assessment." *American Journal of Sociology* 84:24–52.

KOMORITA. S. S., AND A. R. BASS. 1967 "Attitude differentiation and evaluation scales on the semantic differential." *Journal of Personality and Social Psychology* 6:241–244.

KRASNER, L. 1958 "Studies of the conditioning of verbal behavior." *Psychological Bulletin* 55:148–170.

KUHN, H. W., AND A. W. TUCKER. 1953 *Contributions to the Theory of Games*. Princeton: Princeton University Press, 1:97–103.

KUHN, T. S. 1970 *The Structure of Scientific Revolutions*. Chicago: University of Chicago Press.

LABOV, W. 1964 "Stages in the acquisition of standard English." Pp. 77–103 in R. W. Shuy (ed.), *Social Dialects and Language Learning*. Champaign, Ill.: National Council of Teachers of English.

LAMB, M. E. 1979 "The effects of the social context on dyadic social interaction." Pp. 253–268 in M. E. Lamb, S. J. Suomi, and G. R. Stephenson (eds.), *Social Interaction Analysis: Methodological Issues*. Madison: University of Wisconsin Press.

LAMB, M. E., S. J. SUOMI, AND G. R. STEPHENSON (eds.). 1979 *Social Interaction Analysis: Methodological Issues*. Madison: University of Wisconsin Press.

LAMBERT, W. W., L. M. TRIANDIS, AND M. WOLF. 1959 "Some correlates of beliefs in the malevolence and benevolence of supernatural beings." *Journal of Abnormal and Social Psychology* 58:162–169.

LANSING, J. B., AND J. N. MORGAN. 1971 *Economic Survey Methods*. Ann Arbor: Survey Research Center.

LASHUTKA, S. 1977 "A cross-cultural simulation as a predictor of cross-cultural adjustment." *Simulation and Games* 8:481–492.

LAVE, C. A., AND J. G. MARCH. 1975 *An Introduction to Models in the Social Sciences*. New York: Harper and Row, Pub.

LAZARSFELD, P. F. 1972 "The problem of measuring turnover." Pp. 358–362 in P. F. Lazarsfeld, A. Pasanella, and M. Rosenberg (eds.), *Continuities in the Language of Social Research*. New York: Free Press

LAZARSFELD, P. F., A. K. PASANELLA, AND M. ROSENBERG (eds.). 1972 *Continuities in the Language of Social Research*. New York: Free Press.

LEHMANN, R. S. 1977 *Computer Simulation and Modeling: An Introduction*. Hillsdale, N.J.: Erlbaum.

LENSKI, G. E., AND J. C. LEGGETT. 1960 "Caste, class and deference in the research interview." *American Journal of Sociology* 65:463–467.

LEVENTHAL, H., AND E. SHARP. 1956 "Facial expressions as indicators of distress." Pp. 296–318 in S. S. Tomkins and C. E. Izard (eds.), *Affect, Cognition, and Personality*. New York: Springer-Verlag, N.Y.

LEVER, J. 1978 "Sex differences in the complexity of children's play and games." *American Sociological Review* 43:471–482.

LEVIN, H. M. 1975 "Cost-effectiveness analysis in evaluation research." Pp. 89–124 in M. Guttentag and E. L. Struening (eds.), *Handbook of Evaluation Research*. Beverly Hills: Sage Publications, Inc.

LEVINE, R. A. 1966 "Towards a psychology of populations; the cross-cultural study of personality." *Human Development* 9:30–46.

LEVINGER, G. 1968 "Systematic distortion in spouses' reports of preferred and actual sexual behavior." *Sociometry* 29:291–299.

LEWIS, M., AND L. A. ROSENBLUM. 1974 *The Effects of the Infant on its Care-giver*. New York: John Wiley.

LEWIS, O. 1951 *Life in a Mexican Village: Tepoztlan Revisited*. Urbana, Ill.: University of Illinois Press.

LEWIS-BECK, M. S. 1979 "Some economic effects of revolution: Models, measurement, and the Cuban evidence." *American Journal of Sociology* 84:1127–1149.

LEY, D., AND R. CYBRIWSKY. 1974 "Urban graffiti as territorial markers." *Annals of the Association of American Geographers* 64:491–507.

LIEBOW, E. 1967 *Tally's Corner*. Boston: Little, Brown.

LIGHT, D., JR. 1975 "The sociological calendar: An analytic tool for fieldwork applied to medical and psychiatric training." *American Journal of Sociology* 80:1145–1164.

LINCOLN, J. R., J. OLSON, AND M. HANADA. 1978 "Cultural effects on organizational structure: The case of Japanese firms in the United States." *American Sociological Review* 43:829–847.

LINZ, J. J., AND A. DE MIGUEL. 1966 "Within-nation differences and comparisons: The eight Spains." Pp. 267–319 in R. L. Merritt and S. Rokkan (eds.), *Comparing Nations: The Use of Quantitative Data in Cross-National Research.* New Haven: Yale University Press.

LIPSET, S. M. 1963 *Political Man.* Garden City, N.Y.: Doubleday.

LIPSET, S. M., M. TROW, AND J. S. COLEMAN. 1956 *Union Democracy.* Glencoe, Ill.: Free Press.

LIPSITZ, L. 1965 "Working-class authoritarianism: A re-evaluation." *American Sociological Review* 30:106–108.

LOFLAND, J. 1966 *Doomsday Cult: A Study of Conversion, Proselytization and Maintenance of Faith.* Englewood Cliffs, N. J.: Prentice-Hall.

LORD, F. M. 1956 "The measurement of growth." *Educational and Psychological Measurement* 18:437–451.

LORD, F. M., AND M. R. NOVICK. 1968 *Statistical Theories of Mental Test Scores.* Reading, Mass.: Addison-Wesley.

LOWENFIELD, I. E. 1958 "Mechanisms of reflex dilation of the pupil: Historical review and experimental analysis." *Documenta Ophthalmologica* 12:185–448.

LYNCH, F. R. 1977 "Field research and future history: Problems posed for ethnographic sociologists by the 'Doomsday Cult' making good." *The American Sociologist* 12:80–88.

McCALL, G. J. 1969a "Data quality control in participant observation. Pp. 126–141 in G. J. McCall and J. L. Simmons (eds.), *Issues in Participant Observation: A Text and Reader.* London: Addison-Wesley.

———1969b "The problem of indicators in participant observation research." Pp. 230–238 in G. J. McCall and J. L. Simmons (eds.), *Issues in Participant Observation: A Text and Reader.* London: Addison-Wesley.

———1972 "Proposal for a systematic observation center at the University of Missouri-St. Louis." Department of Sociology, University of Missouri-St. Louis (mimeo.)

McCALL, G. J., AND J. L. SIMMONS (eds.). 1969 *Issues in Participant Observation: A Text and Reader.* London: Addison-Wesley.

McCALL, G. J., M. M. McCALL, N. K. DENZIN, G. D. SUTTLES, AND S. B. KURTH, 1970 *Social Relationships.* Chicago: Aldine.

McCALL, G. J., N. MAZANEC, W. L. ERICKSON, AND H. W. SMITH. 1974 "Same-sex recall effects in tests of observational accuracy." *Perceptual and Motor Skills* 38:830.

MACCOBY, E. E., AND R. HYMAN. 1959 "Measurement problems in panel studies." Pp. 67–79 in E. Burdick and A. Brodbeck (eds.), *American Voting Behavior.* New York: Free Press.

MACCOBY, E., AND N. MACCOBY. 1954 "The interview: A tool of social science." Pp. 449–487 in G. Lindzey (ed.), *Handbook of Social Psychology,* vol. I. Cambridge, Mass.: Addison-Wesley.

MACCOBY, N., J. JECKER, H. BREITROSE, AND E. ROSS. 1964 "Sound film recordings in improving classroom communications: Experimental studies in non-verbal communication." Institute for Communication Research, Stanford University. Stanford, Calif.: Stanford University Press.

McGUIRE, W. J. 1967 "Some impending reorientations in social psychology: Some thoughts provoked by Kenneth Ring." *Journal of Experimental Social Psychology* 3:124–139.

MACK, R. W. 1969 "Theoretical and substantive biases in sociological research." Pp. 52–64 in M. Sherif and C. Sherif (eds.), *Interdisciplinary Relationships in the Social Sciences.* Chicago: Aldine.

McKeachie, W. J. 1972 "Academician." *Psychology Today* 6:63–67.

McKillip, J. 1979 "Impact evaluation of service programs: Three flexible designs." *Evaluation Quarterly* 3:97–104.

McNemar, Q. 1955 *Psychological Statistics.* New York: John Wiley.

Mahl, G. F. 1956 "Disturbances and silences in the patient's speech in psychotherapy." *Journal of Abnormal Psychology* 53:1–15.
———1957 "Speech disturbances and emotional verbal content in initial interviews." Paper presented at Eastern Psychological Association, annual meeting.
———1959 "Exploring emotional states by content analyses." Pp. 89–130 in E. Pool (ed.), *Trends in Content Analysis.* Urbana: University of Illinois Press.

Mahl, G. F., and G. Schulze. 1964 "Psychological research in the extra-linguistic area." Pp. 51–124 in T. A. Sebeok, A. S. Hayes, and M. C. Bateson (eds.), *Approaches to Semiotics.* London: Mouton and Co.

Mandler, G., and W. K. Kaplan. 1956 "Subjective evaluation and reinforcing effect of a verbal stimulus." *Science* 124:582–583.

Mann, R. D. 1967 *Interpersonal Styles and Group Development.* New York: John Wiley.

Mann, L., and I. Janis. 1968 "A follow-up on the long term effects of emotional role playing." *Journal of Personality and Social Psychology* 8:339–342.

Margenau, H. 1959 "Philosophical problems concerning the meaning of measurement in physics" in C. W. Churchman and P. Ratoosh (eds.), *Measurement: Definitions and Theories.* New York: John Wiley.

Marks, C. 1972 "Encounter group observation methods." Paper read at American Psychological Association, annual meeting, Honolulu.

Marsh, R. 1961 "The bearing of comparative analysis on sociological theory." *Social Forces* 43:188–196.

Maslany, G. W., and J. McKay. 1974 "A method of minimizing attrition in longitudinal studies." *JSAS Catalog of Selected Documents in Psychology* 4:69.

Mazur, A. 1973 "Increased tendency toward balance during stressful conflict." *Sociometry* 36:279–283.

Mead, G. H. 1934 *Mind, Self and Society.* Chicago: University of Chicago.

Mehrabian, A. 1972. *Nonverbal Communication.* Chicago: Aldine.

Melbin, M. 1978 "Night as frontier." *American Sociological Review* 43:3–22.

Menzel, E. W., Jr. 1979 "General discussion of the methodological problems involved in the study of social interaction." Pp. 291–310 in M. E. Lamb, S. J. Suomi, and G. R. Stephenson (eds.), *Social Interaction Analysis: Methodological Issues.* Madison: University of Wisconsin Press.

Merton, R. K. 1949 *Social Theory and Social Structure.* Glencoe, Ill.: Free Press
———1967 *On Theoretical Sociology.* New York: Free Press.

Micklin, M., and M. Durbin. 1969 "Syntactic dimensions of attitude scaling techniques: Sources of variation and bias." *Sociometry* 32:194–205.
———1963 "Alienation, race and education." *American Sociological Review* 28:973–977.

Middleton, R. 1960 "Fertility values in American magazine fiction: 1916–1956." *Public Opinion Quarterly* 24:139–143.

Milgram, S. 1963 "Behavioral study of obedience." *Journal of Abnormal and Social Psychology* 67:371–378.

Mills, C. Wright 1959 *The Sociological Imagination.* New York: Oxford Press.

Mindak, W. A., A. Neibergs, and A. Anderson. 1963 "Economic effects of the Minneapolis newspaper strike." *Journalism Quarterly* 40:213–218.

Monroe, M. W. 1968 "Games as teaching tools: An examination of the community land use game." M. S. thesis, Cornell University

MOORE, J. H. 1973 "Creationism and evolution," Letters to the Editor, *Science* 179:953.

MORENO, J. L. 1934 *Who Shall Survive?* Washington: Nervous and Mental Disease Monograph No. 58

Mosaic. 1979 "Archaelogy reconstructs the present." 10:30–37.

MOSKOS, C. C., JR. 1976 *Peace Soldiers: The Sociology of a United Nations Military Force.* Chicago: University of Chicago.

MOSTELLER, F. 1955 "Use as evidenced by an examination of wear and tear on selected sets of ESS." Pp. 167–174 in K. Davis et al., *A Study of the Need for a New Encyclopedic Treatment of the Social Sciences.* Unpublished manuscript.

MOUTON, J. S., R. R. BLAKE, AND B. FRUCHTER. 1955 "The reliability of sociometric measures." *Sociometry* 18:7–48.

MULLINS, C. J. 1977. *A Guide to Writing and Publishing in the Social and Behavioral Sciences.* New York: John Wiley

MURRAY, S. O. 1978 "The scientific reception of Castaneda." *Contemporary Sociology* 8:189–192.

NAGEL, E. 1961 *The Structure of Science.* Princeton: Princeton University Press.

NAROLL, R. 1965 "Galton's problem: The logic of cross-cultural research." *Social Research* 32:428–451.

_____1968 "Some thoughts on comparative methods in cultural anthropology." Pp. 236–277 in H. M. Blalock and A. B. Blalock (eds.), *Methodology in Social Research.* New York: McGraw-Hill.

NOBLE, J. H., JR. 1977 "The limits of cost-benefit analysis as a guide to priority-setting in rehabilitation." *Evaluation Quarterly* 1:347–380.

NORTH, C. C., AND P. K. HATT. 1947 "Jobs and occupations: A popular evaluation." *Opinion News* (Sept. 1):3–13.

NUNNALLY, J. C. 1967 *Psychometric Theory.* New York: McGraw-Hill.

NYE, F. I., L. WHITE, AND J. FRIDERES. 1968 "A preliminary theory of marital stability." Paper read at American Sociological Association, annual meeting, Boston.

Office of Federal Statistical Policy and Standards. 1978 Statistical Policy Working Paper 2: Report on Statistical Disclosure and Disclosure-Avoidance Techniques. Washington, D.C.: Department of Commerce.

ORBACK, E. 1979 "Simulation games and motivation for learning." *Simulation and Games* 10:3–14.

OSGOOD, C. E. 1960 "Some effects of motivation on style of encoding." Pp. 293–306 in T. A. Sebeok (ed.), *Style in Language.* Cambridge, Mass.: M.I.T. Press.

OSGOOD, C. E., G. J. SUCI, AND P. H. TANNEBAUM. 1957 *The Measurement of Meaning.* Urbana: University of Illinois Press.

OUCHIDA, M. 1979 "Human excitement seeking." Unpublished dissertation, University of Wisconsin.

PAIGE, J. M. 1975 *Agrarian Revolution: Social Movements and Export Agriculture in the Underdeveloped World.* New York: Free Press.

PAPPWORTH, M. H. 1968 *Human Guinea Pigs: Experimentation on Man.* Boston: Beacon.

PARKE, R. D. 1978 "Parent-infant interaction: Progress, paradigms, and problems." Pp. 69–94 in G. P. Sackett (ed.), *Observing Behavior Volume 1: Theory and Applications in Mental Retardation.* Baltimore: University Park Press.

PARSONS, T. 1963 "On the concept of influence." *Public Opinion Quarterly* 27:37–62.

_____1966 *Societies: Evolutionary and Comparative Perspectives.* Englewood Cliffs, N.J.: Prentice-Hall.

PARTEN, M. 1950 *Surveys, Polls and Samples.* New York: Harper & Row, Pub.

PASANELLA, A. K. 1972 "Moderators, suppressors and other stratifying devices." Pp. 376–387 in P. F. Lazarsfeld, A. K. Pasanella, and M. Rosenberg (eds.), *Continuities in the Language of Social Research.* New York: Free Press.

PATTERSON, G. R., AND D. MOORE. 1979 "Interactive patterns as units of behavior." Pp. 77–96 in M. E. Lamb, S. J. Suomi, and G. R. Stephenson (eds.), *Social Interaction Analysis.: Methodological Issues.* Madison: University of Wisconsin Press.

PAYNE, D. E. 1978 "Cross-national diffusion: Effects of Canadian TV on rural Minnesota viewers." *American Sociological Review* 43:740–756.

PAYNE, D. E., AND C. A. PEAKE. 1977 "Cultural diffusion: The role of U.S. TV in Iceland." *Journalism Quarterly* 54:523–531.

PAYNE, S. L. 1951 *The Art of Asking Questions.* Princeton: Princeton University Press.

PELTO, P. 1970 *Anthropological Research: The Structure of Inquiry.* New York: Harper & Row, Pub.

PELZ, D. C., AND F. M. ANDREWS. 1964 "Detecting causal priorities in panel study data." *American Sociological Review* 29:836–848.

PERRY, J. M. 1977 "AMDAHL speaks: Carter really won the election." *The National Observer* (February 12): 5.

PHILLIPS, D. L. 1971 *Knowledge from What? Theories and Methods in Social Research.* Chicago: Rand McNally.

PHILLIPS, D. P., AND R. H. CONVISER. 1972 "Measuring the structure and boundaries of groups: Some uses of information theory." *Sociometry* 35:235–254.

PITTENGER, R. E., C. F. HOCKETT, AND J. J. DANEHY. 1960 *The First Five Minutes: A Sample of Microscopic Interview Analysis.* Ithaca, N.Y.: Paul Martineau.

PLATTNER, S. 1975 "PEDLAR: A computer game in economic anthropology." *Formal Methods in Economic Anthropology.* Washington, D.C.: American Anthropological Association.

POGGIE, J. J., JR. 1972 "Toward quality control in key informant data." *Human Organization* 31:23–30.

POINCARÉ, H. 1921 *Science and Method* (G. E. Halsted trans.) Garrison, N.Y.: The Science Press.

POLSBY, N. W. 1969 " 'Pluralism' in the study of community power, or, *Erkläring* before *Verkläring* in *Wissenssoziologie.* " *American Sociologist* 4:118–122.

PONDER, E., AND W. P. KENNEDY. 1927 "On the act of blinking." *Quarterly Journal of Experimental Physiology* 18:89–110.

POPPER, K. R. 1961 *The Logic of Scientific Discovery.* New York: Science Editions.

PORTER, J. N. 1977 Untitled letter. *The American Sociologist* 12:203.

POWERS, D. E., AND D. L. ALDERMAN. 1979 "Practical techniques for implementing true experimental designs." *Evaluation Quarterly* 3:89–96.

PRICE, J. L. 1972 *Handbook of Organizational Measurement.* Toronto: D. C. Heath.

QUAY, H. 1958 "The effect of verbal reinforcement on the recall of early memories." *Journal of Abnormal and Social Psychology* 59:254–257.

RAPOPORT, A. 1968 "Forward." Pp. xii–xxii in W. Buckley (ed.), *Modern Systems Research for the Behavioral Scientist.* Chicago: Aldine.

RASER, J. R. 1969 *Simulation and Society: An Exploration of Scientific Gaming.* Boston: Allyn & Bacon.

RAUSH, H. L. 1965 "Interaction sequences." *Journal of Personality and Social Psychology* 2:487–499.

REDFIELD, R. 1930 *Tepoztlan: A Mexican Village.* Chicago: University of Chicago Press.

REISS, A. J., JR. 1967 *Studies in Crime and Law Enforcement in Major Metropolitan Areas.* Field Studies III, Vol. II, Section I. Washington, D.C.: Government Printing Office.

———1968 "Police brutality—answer to key questions." *Transaction* 5:10–19.

———1971 "Systematic observation of natural social phenomena." Pp. 3–33 in H. L. Costner (ed.), *Sociological Methodology, 1971.* San Francisco: Jossey-Bass.

RESKIN, B. F. 1977 "Scientific productivity and the reward structure of science." *American Sociological Review* 42:491–504.

RICHARDSON, S. A. 1953 "A framework for reporting field relations experiences." *Human Organization* 12:31–37.

RICHARDSON, S. A., B. S. DOHRENWEND, AND D. KLEIN. 1965 *Interviewing.* New York: Basic Books.

RICHARDSON, S. A., A. H. HASTORE, AND S. A. DORNBUSCH. 1964 "Effects of physical disability on a child's description of himself." *Child Development* 35:893–907.

RIESMAN, D., AND J. WATSON. 1964 "The sociability projects: A chronical of frustration and achievement." Pp. 235–321 in P. E. Hammond (ed.), *Sociologists at Work.* New York: Basic Books.

RILEY, M. W. 1963 *Sociological Research I: A Case Approach.* New York: Harcourt Brace Jovanovich, Inc.

RING, K. 1967 "Experimental social psychology: Some sober questions about some frivolous values." *Journal of Experimental Social Psychology* 3:113–123.

RING, K., WALLSTON, K., AND M. COREY. 1970 "Mode of debriefing as a factor affecting subjective reaction to a Milgram-type obedience experiment: An ethical inquiry." *Representative Research in Social Psychology* 1:67–88.

RITZER, G. 1975 *Sociology: A Multiple Paradigm Science.* Boston: Allyn & Bacon.

RIVLIN, R. M., AND P. M. TIMPANE. 1975 *Ethical and Legal Issues of Social Experimentation.* Washington, D.C.: The Brookings Institution.

ROBBINS, O., S. DEVOE, AND M. WIENER. 1978 "Social patterns of turn-taking: Nonverbal regulators." *Journal of Communication* 90:38–46.

ROBERTSON, C. N. 1972 *Oneida Community: The Breakup, 1876–1881.* Syracuse: Syracuse University Press.

ROBINSON, J. P., AND P. R. SHAVER. 1973, Rev. ed. *Measures of Social Psychological Attitudes.* Ann Arbor, Mich.: Survey Research Center.

ROBINSON, W. S. 1950 "Ecological correlations and the behavior of individuals." *American Sociological Review* 15:351–357.

———1951 "The logical structure of analytic induction." *American Sociological Review* 16:812–818.

RODMAN, H., AND R. KOLODNY. 1972 "Organizational strains in the researcher-practitioner relationship." Pp. 117–135 in F. Caro (ed.), *Readings in Evaluation Research.* New York: Russell Sage Foundation.

ROGERS, C. K. 1942 *Counseling and Psychotherapy.* Boston: Houghton Mifflin.

———1951 *Client-Centered Therapy.* Boston: Houghton Mifflin.

ROKEACH, M., AND R. COCHRANE. 1972 "Self-confrontation and confrontation with another as determinants of long-term value change." *Journal of Applied Social Psychology* 2:283–293.

ROOSE, K. D., AND C. J. ANDERSON. 1970 *A Rating of Graduate Programs.* Washington, D.C.: American Council of Education.

ROSENBERG, M.

———1965 *Society and the Adolescent Self Image.* Princeton: Princeton University Press.

———1968 *The Logic of Survey Analysis.* New York: Basic Books.

ROSENBERG, M., AND L. I. PEARLIN. 1978 "Social class and self-esteem among children and adults." *American Journal of Sociology* 84:53–77.

ROSENBERG, M. J. 1960 "Cognitive reorganization in response to the hypnotic reversal of attitudinal affect." *Journal of Personality* 28:39–63.

ROSENTHAL, R. 1966 *Experimenter Effects in Behavioral Research.* New York: Appleton-Century-Crofts.

ROSSI, P. H., AND S. R. WRIGHT. 1977 "Evaluation research: An assessment of theory, practice, and politics." *Evaluation Quarterly* 1:5–52.

ROTHENBERG, J. 1975 "Cost-benefit analysis: A methodological exposition." Pp. 55–88 in M. Guttentag and E. L. Struening (eds.), *Handbook of Evaluation Research,* vol. 2. Beverly Hills: Sage Publications, Inc.

ROTTER, J. B., AND B. WILLIAMS. 1947 "The incomplete sentences tests as a method of studying personality." *Journal of Consulting Psychology* 11:43–48.

ROWE, M. P., AND R. D. HUSBY. 1973 "Economics of child care: Costs, needs and issues." Pp. 98–122 in P. Roby (ed.), *Child Care—Who Cares?* New York: Basic Books.

RUTMAN, L. 1977 *Evaluation Research Methods: A Basic Guide.* Beverly Hills: Sage Publications, Inc.

RYAN, T. A. 1959 "Multiple comparisons in psychological research." *Psychological Bulletin* 56:26–47.

RYNKIEWICK, M. A., AND J. P. SPRADLEY. 1976 *Ethics and Anthropology: Dilemmas in Field Work.* New York: John Wiley.

SACKETT, G. P. 1974 "A nonparametric lag sequential analysis for studying dependency among responses in observational scoring systems." Unpublished manuscript, University of Washington.

―――(ed.). 1978a *Observing Behavior Volume 1: Theory and Applications in Mental Retardation.* Baltimore: University Press.

―――(ed). 1978b *Observing Behavior Volume 2: Data Collection and Analysis Methods.* Baltimore: University Press.

SAKODA, J. M. 1971 "The checkerboard model of social interaction." *Journal of Mathematical Sociology* 1:119–132.

SALZINGER, K., AND S. PISON. 1960 "Reinforcement of verbal affect responses of normal subjects during an interview." *Journal of Abnormal and Social Psychology* 60:127–130.

SALZINGER, S. 1956 "Rate of affect response in schizophrenics as a function of three types of interviewer verbal behavior." Paper read at Eastern Psychological Association meeting, Atlantic City.

The Sampler from Response Analysis. 1975 "James W. Gourthro on the partnership concept." 4:3.

―――1979a "Paul A. Scipeone on random-digit sampling." 12:3.

―――1978b "Sponsor identification raises response rates." 12:1.

SAPOLSKY, A. 1960 "Effect of interpersonal relationships upon verbal conditions." *Journal of Abnormal and Social Psychology* 60:241–246.

SARASON, I., AND J. MINARD. 1963 "Test anxiety and experimental conditions." *Journal of Personality and Social Psychology* 1:87–91.

SARBIN, T. R. 1968 "Role: Psychological aspects." In *International Encyclopedia of the Social Sciences,* vol. 13. New York: Free Press.

SASLOW, G., J. D. MATARAZZO, J. S. PHILLIPS, AND R. G. MATARRAZZO. 1957 "Test-retest stability of interaction patterns during interviews conducted one week apart." *Journal of Abnormal and Social Psychology* 54:295–302.

SASSONE, P., AND W. SCHAFFER. 1978 *Cost-Benefit Analysis: A Handbook.* New York: Academic Press.

SAWYER, H. G. 1961 "The meaning of numbers." Speech before the American Association of Advertising Agencies.

SAWYER, J. AND H. SCHECHTER. 1968 "Computers, privacy, and the national data center: The responsibility of social scientists." *American Psychologist* 23:810–818.

SCHATZMAN, L., AND A. L. STRAUSS. 1973 *Field Research: Strategies for a Natural Sociology.* Englewood Cliffs, N.J.: Prentice-Hall.

SCHEFLEN, A. E. 1964 "The significance of posture in communicative systems." *Psychiatry* 27:316–331.

SCHEIRER, M. A. 1978 "Program participants' positive perceptions: Psychological conflict of interest in social program evaluation." *Evaluation Quarterly* 2:53–70.

SCHNORE, L. F. 1962 "City-suburban income differential in metropolitan areas." *American Sociological Review* 27:254–255.

SCHUBERT, G. 1962 "The 1960 term: A psychological analysis." *American Political Science Review* 56:90–107.

SCHUESSLER, K. 1971 *Analyzing Social Data.* Boston: Houghton Mifflin.

SCHUESSLER, K., D. HITTLE, AND J. CARDASCIA. 1978 "Measuring responding desirably with attitude-opinion items." *Social Psychology* 41:224–234.

SCHULMAN, J. C., AND J. M. REISMAN. 1959 "An objective measure of hyperactivity." *American Journal of Mental Deficiency* 64:455–456.

SCHUMAN, H. 1971 "The religious factor in Detroit: Review, replication and reanalysis." *American Sociological Review* 36:30–46.

SCHWARTZ, H., AND J. JACOBS. 1979 *Qualitative Sociology: A Method to the Madness.* New York: Free Press.

SCHWARTZ, M. S., AND C. G. SCHWARTZ. 1956 "Problems in participant observation." *American Journal of Sociology* 60:343–354.

Science News. 1972. "Suing over the antiproton." 102 (no.2):17–32.

SCOTT, W. A. 1968 "Attitude measurement." Pp. 204–273 in G. Lindzey and E. Aronson (eds.), *Handbook of Social Psychology,* vol. II. Reading, Mass.: Addison-Wesley.

SEEMAN, M. 1959 "On the meaning of alienation." *American Sociological Review* 24:783–791.

SELLTIZ, C., M. JAHODA, M. DEUTSCH, AND S. W. COOK. 1959 *Research Methods in Social Relations.* New York: Holt.

SEWELL, W. H., A. O. HALLER, AND A. PORTES. 1969 "The educational and early occupational process." *American Sociological Review* 34:82–92.

SHAPIRO, S., AND J. C. EBERHART. 1947 "Interviewer differences in an intensive interview survey." *International Journal of Opinion and Attitude Research* 1:1–17.

SHAW, M. E., AND P. R. COSTANZO. 1972 *Theories of Social Psychology.* New York: McGraw-Hill.

SHEPARD, R. N., A. K., ROMNEY, AND S. NERLOVE. (eds.). 1972 *Multidimensional Scaling: Theory and Applications in the Behavioral Sciences.* New York: Academic Press, New York.

SHERIF, M., AND C. W. SHERIF. 1967 "Attitude as the individual's own categories: the social judgmental approach to attitude and attitude change." Pp. 105–139 in C. W. Sherif and M. Sherif (eds.), *Attitude, Ego-Involvement and Change.* New York: John Wiley.

SHIRTS, R. G. 1974 *BAFA' BAFA': A Cross-Cultural Simulation.* Del Mar, Calif: SIMILE II.

SIEBER, S. D. 1973 "The integration of fieldwork and survey methods." *American Journal of Sociology* 78:1335–1359.

SIMON, A., AND E. G. BOYER. 1974 *Mirrors for Behavior III: An Anthology of Observation Instruments.* Wyncote, Pa.: Communication Materials Center.

SINGER, E. 1971 "Adult orientation of first and later children." *Sociometry* 34:328–345.

_____1978 "Informed consent: Consequences for response rate and response quality in social surveys." *American Sociological Review,* 43:144–161.

Siu, R. C. P. 1964 "The isolation of Chinese laundrymen." Pp. 429–442 in E. W. Burgess and D. J. Bogue (eds.), *Contributions to Urban Sociology.* Chicago: University of Chicago Press.

Sjoberg, G., and R. Nett. 1968 *A Methodology for Social Research.* New York: Harper & Row, Pub.

Skipper, J. K., Jr., and C. H. McCaghy. 1972 "Respondent's intrusion upon the situation: The problem of interviewing subjects with special qualities." *Sociological Quarterly* 13:237–243.

Slonim, M. J. 1960 *Sampling in a Nutshell.* New York: Simon & Schuster.

Smith, H. W. 1970 "Some developmental antecedents of adult interpersonal behavior." Unpublished Ph.D dissertation, Northwestern University.

_____1972a "Child Egocentrism and simultaneous group behavior." *Proceedings of the American Psychological Association, 1972.* 7:103–104.

_____1972b "Marijuana intoxication and dyadic interaction." Unpublished manuscript, Department of Sociology-Anthropology, University of Missouri-St. Louis.

_____1972c "Urbanization, secularization and roles of the professional's wife." *Review of Religious Research* 13:134–138.

_____1973 "Some developmental interpersonal dynamics through childhood." *American Sociological Review* 38:543–552.

_____1977 "Small group interaction at various ages: Simultaneous talking and interruptions of others." *Small Group Behavior* 8:65–74.

_____1978 "Effects of set on subject's interpretation of placebo marijuana effects." *Social Science and Medicine* 12:107–109.

Smith-Lovin, L., and A. R. Tickamyer. 1978 "Nonrecursive models of labor force participation, fertility behavior, and sex role attitudes." *American Sociological Review* 43:541–557.

Soskin, W. F., and P. E. Kauffman. 1961 "Judgment of emotion in word-free voice samples." *Journal of Communication* 11:73–80.

Stephans, J. 1978 "The other side of the looking glass: Problems encountered in fieldwork." *Mid-American Journal of Sociology* 3:95–104.

Steward, N. 1945 "Methodological investigation of the forced-choice technique, utilizing the officer description and the officer evaluation blanks." AGO, Personnel Research Section, Report No. 701.

Stinchcombe, A. 1968 *Constructing Social Theories.* New York: Harcourt Brace Jovanovich, Inc.

Strauss, A., L. Schatzman, L. Bucher, D. Ehrlick, and M. Sabshin. 1964 *Psychiatric Ideologies and Institutions.* New York: Free Press.

Strodtbeck, F. L., R. M. James, and C. Hawkins. 1955 "Social status in jury deliberations." *American Sociological Review* 22:713–719.

Strunk, W., Jr., and E. B. White. 1972 *The Elements of Style.* New York: Macmillan.

Stuart, I. R. 1963 "Minorities as minorities: Cognitive, affective and conative components of Puerto Rican and Negro acceptance and rejection." *Journal of Social Psychology* 59:93–99.

Suchman, E. A. 1969 *Evaluative Research: Principles and Practice in Public Service and Social Action Programs.* New York: Russell Sage Foundation.

Sudman, S. 1967 *Reducing the Cost of Surveys.* Chicago: Aldine.

Sudman, S. 1976 *Applied Sampling.* New York: Academic Press, New York.

Sudman, S., and N. M. Bradburn. 1974 *Response Effects in Surveys.* Chicago: Aldine.

SULLIVAN, D. G. 1972 "Inter-nation simulation: A review of its premises." Pp. 111–124 in M. Inbar and C. S. Stoll (eds.), *Simulation and Gaming in Social Science.* New York: Free Press.

SUMMERS, G. F., (ed.). 1970 *Attitude Measurement.* Chicago: Rand McNally.

Survey Research Center. 1974 *Interviewer's Manual.* Ann Arbor: Survey Research Center, University of Michigan.

SUTTLES, G. D. 1972 *The Social Construction of Communities.* Chicago: University of Chicago Press.

SYKES, J. B. 1976 *The Concise Oxford Dictionary of Current English.* New York: Oxford University Press.

SZASZ, T. S. 1961 *The Myth of Mental Illness.* New York: Hoeber.

SZENT-GYORGYI, A. 1972 "Dionysians and Apollonians." *Science* 176:966.

TAEUBER, K. E., AND A. F. TAUBER. 1965 *Negroes in Cities: Residential Segregation and Neighborhood Change.* Chicago: Aldine.

TART, C. T. 1972 "States of consciousness and state-specific sciences." *Science* 173:1203–1210.

TERMAN, L. M. 1925 *Genetic Studies of Genius.* Stanford, Calif.: Stanford University Press.

THARP, R. G., AND R. GALLIMORE. 1976 "What a coach can teach a teacher." *Psychology Today* (January):75–77.

THOMAS, C. W., AND R. J. CAGE. 1977 "The effect of social characteristics on Juvenile Court dispositions." *Sociological Quarterly* 18:237–252.

THOMAS, W. L., AND F. ZNANIECK. 1927 *The Polish Peasant in America.* New York: Knopf.

THORNDIKE, E. L., AND I. LORGE. 1944 *The Teacher's Word Book of 20,000 Words.* New York: Columbia University Press.

THURSTONE, L., AND E. CHAVE. 1929 *The Measurement of Attitude.* Chicago: University of Chicago Press.

TRIANDIS, H. C. 1964 "Exploratory factor analysis of the behavioral component of social attitudes." *Journal of Abnormal and Social Psychology* 68:420–430.

TRUZZI, M. 1977 "Review of Castaneda's journey." *The Zetetic* 87–7.

TUMA, N. B., M. T. HANNAN, AND L. P. GROENEVELD. 1979 "Dynamic analysis of event histories." *American Journal of Sociology* 84:820–854.

TURABIAN, K. L. 1973 *A Manual for Writers of Term Papers, Theses and Dissertations.* Chicago: University of Chicago.

TURNER, C. F., AND D. C. MARTINEZ. 1977 "Socioeconomic achievement and the Machiavellian personality." *Sociometry* 40:325–336.

TURNER, J. H. 1974 *The Structure of Sociological Theory.* Homewood, Ill.: Dorsey.

———1978 "A theory of social structure: An assessment of Blau's strategy." *Contemporary Sociology: A Journal of Reviews* 7:698–704.

TUMA, N. B., M. T. HANNAN, AND L. P. GROENEVELD. 1979 "Dynamic analysis of event histories." *American Journal of Sociology* 84:820–854.

UNDERWOOD, B. J. 1957a "Interference and forgetting." *Psychological Review* 64:49–60.

———1957b *Psychological Research.* New York: Appleton-Century-Crofts.

U.S. Department of Health, Education and Welfare. 1971 *The Institutional Guide to DHEW Policy on Protection of Human Subjects.* Washington, D.C.: U.S. Government Printing Office.

UPTON, G. J. G. 1978 *The Analysis of Cross-Tabulated Data.* New York: John Wiley.

VALLIER, I. (ed.). 1971a *Comparative Methods in Sociology.* Berkeley: University of California Press.

————1971*b* "Empirical comparisons of social structure: Leads and lags." Pp. 203–266 in I. Vallier (ed.), *Comparative Methods in Sociology*. Berkeley: University of California Press.

VANNEMAN, R., AND F. C. PAMPEL. 1977 "The American perception of class and status." *American Sociological Review* 42:422–437.

VERBA, S. 1971 "Cross-national survey research: The problem of credibility." Pp. 309–356 in I. Vallier (ed.), *Comparative Methods in Sociology*. Berkeley: University of California Press.

VIDICH, A. J., AND J. BENSMAN. 1968 *Small Town in Mass Society*. Princeton: Prrinceton University Press.

VIETZE, P. E., S. R. ABERNATHY, M. L. ASHE, AND G. FAULSTICH. 1978 "Contingency interaction between mothers and their developmentally delayed infants." Pp. 115–134 in G. P. Sackett (ed.), *Observing Behavior Volume 1: Theory and Applications in Mental Retardation*. Baltimore: University Press.

WALL, W. D., AND H. L. WILLIAMS. 1970 *Longitudinal Studies and the Social Sciences*. London: Heinemann.

WALLACE, W. (ed.). 1969 *Sociological Theory*. Chicago: Aldine.

————1971 *The Logic of Science in Sociology*. Chicago: Aldine.

WALTON, J. 1966 "Discipline method and community power: A note on the sociology of knowledge." *American Sociological Review* 31:684–699.

WARD, L. 1906 *Applied Sociology*. Boston: Ginn.

WARWICK, D. P., AND S. OSHERSON (eds.). 1973 *Comparative Research Methods*. Englewood Cliffs, N.J.: Prentice-Hall.

WATTS, H. W., AND A. REES (eds.). 1977 *The New Jersey Income Maintenance Experiments, Vol. 2: Labor-Supply Responses*. New York: Academic Press.

WEBB, E. J., D. F. CAMPBELL, R. D. SCHWARTZ, AND L. SECHREST. 1966 *Unobtrusive Measures: Nonreactive Research in the Social Sciences*. Chicago: Rand McNally.

WEICK, K. 1968 "Systematic observation." Pp. 357–451 in G. Lindzey and E. Aronson (eds.), *Handbook of Social Psychology*, vol. II. Reading, Mass.: Addison-Wesley.

WEINER, T. S., AND B. K. ECKLAND. 1979 "Education and political party: The effects of college or social class?" *American Journal of Sociology* 84:820–854.

WEISS, C. 1972 *Evaluation Research: Methods of Assessing Program Effectiveness*. Englewood Cliffs, N.J.: Prentice-Hall.

WESTIE, F. R. 1957 "Towards closer relations between theory and research: A procedure and an example." *American Sociological Review* 22:149–154.

WHITING, J. W. M. 1968 "Methods and problems in cross-cultural research." Pp. 693–728 in G. Lindzey and E. Aronson (eds.), *Handbook of Social Psychology*, vol. II. London: Addison-Wesley.

WHITT, J. A. 1979 "Toward a class-dialectic model of power: An empirical assessment of three competing models of political power." *American Sociological Review* 44:81–99.

WHOLEY, J. S., J. W. SCANLON, H. G. DUFFY, J. S. FUKUMOTO, AND L. M. VOGT. 1970 *Federal Evaluation Policy: Analyzing the Effects of Public Programs*. Washington, D.C.: The Urban Institute.

WHYTE, W. F. 1956 *The Organization Man*. Garden City, N.J.: Doubleday Anchor Co.

WIGGINS, J. A. 1968 "Hypothesis validity and experimental laboratory methods." Pp. 390–427 in H. M. Blalock, Jr. and A. B. Blalock (eds.), *Methodology in Social Research*. New York: McGraw-Hill.

WILLARD, D., AND F. L. STRODTBECK. 1972 "Latency of verbal response and participation in small groups." *Sociometry* 35:161–175.

WILLER, D., AND M. WEBSTER, JR. 1970 "Theoretical concepts and observables." *American Sociological Review* 35:748–757.

WILLIAMS, W. 1971 *Social Policy Research and Analysis. The Experience in the Federal Agencies.* New York: American Elsevier.

WILSON, T. D., AND R. E. NISBETT. 1978 "The accuracy of verbal reports about the effects of stimuli on evaluations and behavior." *Social Psychology* 41:118–130.

WINCH, R. F., AND D. T. CAMPBELL. 1969 "Proof? No. Evidence? Yes. The significance of tests of significance." *The American Sociologist* 4:140–143.

WINCH, R. F., S. GREER, AND R. BLUMBERG. 1967 "Ethnicity and extended familism in an upper middle class suburb." *American Sociological Review* 32:265–272.

WISH, M., AND S. J. KAPLAN. 1977 "Toward an implicit theory of interpersonal communication." *Sociometry* 40:234–246.

WOHLSTEIN, R. T., AND C. MCPHAIL. 1979 "Judging the presence and extent of collective behavior from film records." *Social Psychology Quarterly* 42:76–81.

WON, G., AND G. YAMAMOTO. 1968 "Social structure and deviant behavior: A study of shoplifting." *Sociology and Social Research* 53:44–53.

WOODMANSEE, J. J., AND S. W. COOK. 1967 "Dimensions of verbal racial attitudes: Their identification and measurement." *Journal of Personality and Social Psychology* 7:240–250.

World Medical Association. 1964 "Declaration of Helsinki." *Medical Journal of Australia* (August 22).

YANCEY, W. L., AND E. P. ERICKSEN. 1979 "The antecedents of community: The economic and institutional structure of urban neighborhoods." *American Sociological Review* 44:253–261.

YARROW, M. R., J. D. CAMPBELL, AND R. G. BURTON. 1964 "Reliability of maternal retrospection: A preliminary report." *Family Process* 3:207–218.

YULE, G. U., AND M. G. KENDALL. 1950 *An Introduction to the Theory of Statistics.* London: Charles Griffin.

ZALTMAN, G. 1972 "Simulations for learning: A case in consumer economics." Pp. 125–146 in M. Inbar and C. S. Stoll (eds.), *Simulation and Gaming in Social Science.* New York: Free Press.

ZELDITCH, M., JR. 1962 "Some methodological problems of field studies." *American Journal of Sociology* 67:566–576.

ZERMOLO, E. 1912 "Uber eine Aniverdung der Mengenlehre und der Theorie des Schacspiels." *Proceedings of the Fifth International Congress of Mathematicians* (Cambridge) 2: 501–504.

ZETTERBERG, H. L. 1963 *On Theory and Verification in Sociology.* Totowa, N.J.: Bedminster Press.

Author Index

Subject Index